STUDY GUIDE

for use with

COST ACCOUNTING
USING A COST MANAGEMENT APPROACH

Fifth Edition

Letricia Gayle Rayburn
Memphis State University

IRWIN
Homewood, IL 60430
Boston, MA 02116

©Richard D. Irwin, Inc., 1983, 1986, 1989, and 1993

Printed in the United States of America.

ISBN 0-256-08651-6

1 2 3 4 5 6 7 8 9 0 VK 0 9 8 7 6 5 4 3

CONTENTS

Chapter

1 Cost Accounting in the New Automated Manufacturing Environment-- Today and Tomorrow

Chapter Outline

What is Cost Accounting?
Cost Management Systems
Comparison of Cost Accounting with Financial Accounting
Cost Defined
Role of Controller and Cost Accountant
Planning and Control Activities
CIM's Impact on Cost Accounting Tasks
What Cost Accountants Do
Standards of Ethical Conduct
Automation and Cost Management Concepts
Flexible Manufacturing Systems
Zero Defect Program
Nonvalue-Added Time
Just-in-Time Concept
Pull Rather than Push System
Activity-Based Management
Life-Cycle Costing
Target Costing
Change in Performance Evaluation
Professional Organizations
Professional Certifications
Governmental Agencies

Chapter Objectives

After studying this chapter, you should be able to:

1. Contrast cost accounting and financial accounting.

2. Discuss the role of cost accountants and their interaction with various players in the new automated environment of manufacturing.

3. Recognize the changes cost management concepts are making to traditional accounting systems.

4. Identify the professional certifications available for cost accountants.

5. Define and apply the new terms introduced.

Chapter Review

What Is Cost Accounting?

1. Cost accounting identifies, defines, measures, reports, and analyzes the various elements of direct and indirect costs associated with manufacturing and marketing a good and/or service.

   a. Cost accounting also measures product quality, productivity, product innovation, employee morale, and customer satisfaction.
   b. The traditional uses of manufacturing cost accounting systems include measuring performance, justifying investment, calculating product costs, and valuing inventories.
   c. Valuing inventories is largely dictated by government reporting requirements.
   d. Because cost accounting supplies information used by managers for guiding their decisions to make more informed decisions, modern cost accounting is often called management accounting.

Cost Management Systems

2. Cost management information helps managers judge whether opportunities for economic exchange within their own enterprise are as profitable as opportunities in another enterprise or in the market.

   a. Because resources are limited, managers must rely on cost data in deciding which actions provide optimal returns to the company.
   b. Cost accounting information is used in directing day-to-day operations and supplying feedback to evaluate and control performance.

Comparison of Cost Accounting with Financial Accounting

3. Financial accounting results in reports to *external* parties on the status of assets, liabilities, and equity; results of operations; changes in owners' equity; and cash flow for an accounting period.

   a. Creditors, present owners, potential owners, employees, and the public at large use financial accounting reports in decision making.
   b. Income determination is a primary concern of financial accounting, and cost data are developed for inventory valuation.

4. Cost information needed promptly for managerial control differs from cost data needed periodically for summary financial statements.

   a. Cost accounting accumulates data for both external financial accounting and internal management purposes.
   b. Cost accounting uses quantitative methods to accumulate, classify, and interpret information concerning the cost of materials, labor, and other costs of manufacturing and marketing.

Cost Defined

5. Cost is a term used to measure the efforts associated with manufacturing a good or providing a service.

   a. For a good, cost represents the monetary measurement of material, labor, and overhead used.
   b. For a service, cost is the monetary sacrifice made to provide the service.

6. Different costs may be used for different purposes.

    a. Whether the cost system is designed for product costing, inventory valuation, or operational control, performance measurements influence the collecting, summarizing, and reporting process.
    b. The type, purpose, and nature of a cost outline its usage.
    c. Cost accountants use professional judgment in choosing the most appropriate cost concept for specific situations.

Roles of Controller and Cost Accountant

7. Controllers play a significant role in planning and controlling activities by helping managers in the decision-making process.

    a. The controller is the chief accounting officer and manager of the accounting department in a company.
    b. Designing systems to prepare internal reports for management and external reports for the public and government is the controller's function.
    c. Analyzing profitability and establishing budgets is another function of controllers.
    d. The controller's duties differ significantly from those of the treasurer, who is concerned primarily with managing cash.

Planning and Control Activities

8. The cost accountant plays an important role in coordinating external and internal data so that management can formulate better plans.

    a. Cost accounting data concerned with production and the pricing of goods or services is important when managers are formulating plans.
    b. Cost accounting assists management by providing budgets reflecting cost estimates of material, labor, technology and robotics, and other activities involved in manufacturing and marketing a product or providing a service.
    c. Control activities involve monitoring production processes and reporting variations from budgets and plans.
    d. Feedback is information about current performance reported in such a way that future performance may be changed.

9. Under the cost-benefit approach, cost analysis and control techniques should not be used unless the anticipated benefits in helping achieve management goals exceed the cost.

CIM's Impact on Cost Accounting Tasks

10. Digital control links the entire factory together from design to production in computer-integrated manufacturing (CIM).

    a. CIM removes the barrier between accounting, engineering, and manufacturing.
    b. Rather than separating these functions, a new networking form of organization brings together all functions to promote team-based management.
    c. Such a firm recognizes cross-functional processes that cut across many organizational areas.

What Cost Accountants Do

11. The cost accountant frequently works with the following departments:

    a. Manufacturing--Cost accounting measures the efficiency with which the production department has scheduled and transformed material into finished units.

b. Engineering--Cost accountants prepare cost estimates for a proposed product so management can decide whether manufacturing is profitable.

c. Systems design--Cost accountants are becoming more involved in designing computer-integrated manufacturing (CIM) systems and data bases which correspond to cost accounting needs.

d. Treasurer--Budgets and related accounting reports developed by cost accountants are used by the treasurer to forecast cash and working capital requirements.

e. Financial accounting--Cost information is used for inventory valuation in external reporting and income determination.

f. Marketing--Cost estimates supplied to marketing are used to establish selling prices and sales policies.

g. Personnel--Cost accounting uses the wage rates and pay methods supplied by personnel to cost products and services.

Standards of Ethical Conduct

12. To be successful, accountants equip themselves to meet changing cost accounting needs while also meeting the standards of ethical conduct.

Automation and Cost Management Concepts

13. Mass production of a mature product with known characteristics and a stable technology was the basis of traditional cost accounting models.

a. With automation, the labor content in manufacturing processes diminishes while other costs increase.

b. Automated manufacturing usually requires large investments in engineering design and in new processes.

c. The cost management concept developed in response to deficiencies in traditional cost accounting.

d. Cost management combines familiar costing techniques with new methods of monitoring economic performance against plans.

Flexible Manufacturing Systems

14. The use of computer-controlled production processes, including CAD/CAM, programmable machine tools, and robots results in flexible manufacturing.

a. A product life cycle is the time between designing and introducing a new product and removing it from the market because of insufficient demand.

b. Flexible manufacturing systems shift the emphasis from large-scale manufacturing processes of standard products to highly automated job shop environments.

Zero Defect Program

15. The performance standard of the zero defects concept is to *do it right the first time.*

a. Operators, not the inspector, become responsible for zero defects.

b. Operators stop the manufacturing process to take immediate corrective action on discovery of an error or defect.

Nonvalue-Added Time

16. Nonvalue-added time represents the time a part is delayed, moved, or inspected. It is *waste time* because no value is created for a customer when the product is not being processed.

a. Throughput time is value-added time plus nonvalue-added time.

b.   Throughput time represents the interval between starting a part in manufacturing and shipping it in a finished state to a customer.

Just-In-Time Concept (JIT)

17.   The Just-In-Time (JIT) management philosophy minimizes throughput time by emphasizing continuous improvements.

a.   JIT reduces inventories by achieving a continuous production process.
b.   Only the inventory needed in production until the next order arrives is kept on hand in a JIT setting.

Pull Rather than Push System

18.   Using a pull system, managers realize that it is better not to produce than to manufacture unnecessary parts resulting in excessive inventories.

Activity-Based Management

19.   The activity-based management system links resource consumption to the activities a company performs and costs the activities to products or customers.

a.   Activity-based management uses activity-based costing (also called transaction-based costing) to measure and control these relationships.
b.   Activity-based costing (ABC) results from the belief that products consume activities; an activity is a process or procedure causing work.
c.   ABC encourages an identification of value- and nonvalue-added activities so nonvalue-added activities are eliminated.

Life-cycle Costing

20.   Life-cycle costing tracks and collects the costs attributable to each product or service from its initial research and development to final marketing to customers.

Target Costing

21.   Target costing compares costs to date with target costs, beginning from the design stage to the completion of a product.

a.   This approach classifies functional areas of a new product by use and value.
b.   A target cost should be established for all activities of a new product's life cycle.

Change in Performance Evaluation

22.   Traditional labor productivity measures become irrelevant with the adoption of JIT, life-cycle costing, and other innovative management techniques.

Goal Congruence

23.   The cost accounting system should encourage goal congruence in which managers aspire to achieve overall organizational goals while also fulfilling their personal goals.

24.   By breaking company goals down into subgoals for individual employees, the chance of achieving goal congruence is improved.

a.   These subgoals must be consistent with the company's overall goals.

b. Goal congruence is difficult to achieve but the possibility of achievement is improved if managers explain to employees the company goals so employees better understand their responsibility in achieving these goals.

Professional Organizations

25. Several private organizations have professional certifying examinations for cost accountants.

Professional Certifications

26. The Institute of Management Accountants (formerly the National Association of Accountants) established the Institute of Certified Management Accountants which administers the Certificate in Management Accounting (CMA) program.

27. The American Institute of Certified Public Accountants (AICPA) prepares, administers, and grades the CPA examination.

28. The Institute of Internal Auditors (IIA) was organized to develop the professional status of internal auditing; the IIA also established the Certified Internal Auditing (CIA) program.

29. Society of Cost Estimating and Analysis is a nonprofit professional organization whose purpose is to bring together all persons who are interested in cost analysis or the pricing decision. The Certified Cost Analyst (CCA) designation is granted to members who qualify through a combination of documented evidence and examination.

Government Agencies

30. Numerous government organizations have influenced the development of cost accounting theory including the following:

a. Cost Accounting Standards Board (CASB) was created by the U.S. Congress to promulgate cost accounting standards designed to achieve uniformity and consistency for government agencies in connection with cost-type negotiated contract.
b. Internal Revenue Service (IRS) has issued a number of regulations regarding which costs must be included in inventory because of the impact of cost accounting practices on taxes.

Demonstration Problem

Goal Congruence

Four people who wish to cross a river—each for a different reason—combine their efforts in rowing the only available boat. How does this illustrate the concept of goal congruence? What actions could the individuals in the boat take that would destroy goal congruence?

_____

_____

_____

_____

_____

_____

_____

_____

_____

_____

_____

_____

_____

_____

_____

_____

_____

_____

_____

_____

_____

_____

_____

_____

Solution to Demonstration Problem

Goal Congruence

The four people in the boat can be viewed as employees with different needs, wants, and individual goals in an organization. The boat is viewed as the organization. The four people wanted to cross the river and there was goal congruency by the four of them working together.

All corporate personnel bring different personal objectives to the organization, such as the need for power or security. A need exists for an all-encompassing goal to which employees can see their actions contributing while at the same time meeting their individual needs and objectives. The four people in the boat joined together in order to achieve their separate aspirations. By rowing together they chose a means to accomplish their personal objectives. Individuals in an organization retain those aspirations which they bring to the organization. Management tries to motivate employees to work toward the organization's goals while at the same time recognizing that individuals have their own goals which may or may not be consistent with the organization's goals. The desired state for both organizational goals and individual goals is goal congruence.

Individuals in the boat could row against one another, face each other, or choose other seating positions in the boat that would prevent them crossing the river. In this manner, they would destroy goal congruence. Suboptimization occurs when individuals place their own individual goals in such priority over organization's goals, that the organization fails to achieve its goals.

Matching

Referring to the terms listed in the left column, place the appropriate letter next to the corresponding description. A term may not be used or may be used more than once.

a. Controller

b. Cost

c. Cost Accounting Standards Board

d. Cost-benefit approach

e. Feedback Reports

f. Flexible manufacturing systems

g. Goal congruence

h. Networking form of organization

i. Pull system

j. Push system

k. Treasurer

l. Zero defects

_____1. Ideal situation where individual employees' goals are consistent with the company's overall goals.

_____2. A performance standard whose theme is to do it right the first time.

_____3. A manufacturing system designed to produce goods only for stock.

_____4. Chief accounting executive that is responsible for designing a cost accounting system including establishing budgets and standard cost variance analysis.

_____5. Provided for control activities which compare actual results with planned goals.

_____6. Concerned with cash management and maintaining investor relationships.

_____7. Term used for the measure of the efforts associated with manufacturing a good or providing a service.

_____8. Production systems which shift the emphasis from large scale manufacturing processes of standard products to a highly automated job shop environment featuring the manufacture of items in small batches for specific customers.

_____9. A manufacturing system designed to produce goods only when a sales order is received.

_____10. Involves a trade-off between the advantages acquired and the resources required.

Completion and Exercises

1. The Institute of Management Accountants established the _____,
_____ _____ _____ which
administers the Certificate in Management Accounting (CMA) program. The CMA examination
consists of the following four parts:

a. _____

b. _____

c. _____

d. _____

2. Cost is defined as _____

_____

_____

3. Discuss whether you think the rule that all purchases must be given to the lowest bidder has inherent
weaknesses.

_____

_____

_____

_____

4. Indicate the organization involved:

a. The_____
issues regulations regarding what costs can be capitalized to inventory for tax purposes.

b. The_____
_____ promulgates cost accounting standards used in
pricing, administration, and settlement of negotiated defense contracts and subcontracts with
relevant federal agencies. This organization was created by Congress to achieve uniformity and
consistency for government agencies in cost-type negotiated contracts.

5. List four departments which cost accountants frequently work with and discuss the type of
interaction between these departments.

a._____

_____

b._____

_____

c._____

_____

d._____

_____

6. The _____ prepares, administers, and grades the Certified Public Accountant (CPA) examination which consists of the following four parts beginning in May 1994: (a)_____ _____ , (b)_____ (c)_____ and (d) _____ .

7. Is Smaller Better?

Large manufacturers often say the way their companies operate cuts sales volume and profitability. For example, by the time salespersons discuss details of the potential order with their regional sales manager, who then confers with the division sales manager, who then goes to manufacturing to schedule the order, some "mom-and-pop" competitor had made the product and delivered it to the customer. Thus, big companies are trying to find efficiency by emulating smaller ones, finding that "small is beautiful now." One technique they are using is dividing large-scale operations into smaller divisions.

Required:

List five advantages that you think large corporations hope to gain by splitting their operations into more manageable sizes.

_____
_____
_____
_____
_____
_____
_____
_____
_____
_____
_____
_____
_____
_____
_____
_____
_____
_____
_____
_____
_____

8. Evaluating Purchasing System

You have been hired as a consultant by the Miller Company to study their purchasing system. Last week at a dinner party you overheard the wife of one of the purchasing agents talking about the amount of liquor, hams, and tickets to sports events that her husband receives. The wife didn't know that you were a business consultant and remarked to you "Why, you wouldn't believe the number of hams I had to throw away last Christmas."

With her comments still fresh in you mind, you visit the company's Purchasing Department. In your analysis of the purchasing system you ask about the availability of purchase discounts. The purchasing agents inform you that this is not their problem and send you to the Accounting Department. Upon entering the Accounting Department you find that they are having a farewell party for one of their clerks who is transferring to the Purchasing Department. You overhear one of the accountants remark, "Now, Joe, next Christmas remember to bring a truck to work in order to haul away all the goodies you get."

Being hardworking accountants, they soon end the party to answer your questions. You do find that cash discounts are available from some suppliers if the invoice is a large amount. However, they are quick to point out that they have had to miss taking some discounts because of lack of funds. They emphasize that just last week there were three invoices totaling $10,000 with credit terms of 2/10, n/30 which they could not pay because of a shortage of cash.

This problem concerns you, so you visit the treasurer. He is not aware that all purchase discounts are not being taken. After asking about what financing arrangements he has with the local bank, you find the company has an open agreement to borrow funds up to $200,000 for a 30-day period at prime + 1 percent. Currently the prime interest rate is 9 percent.

Required:

a. What suggestions can you make in regard to the company's purchasing system?

b. How much money could be saved if the company borrowed money to pay for the three invoices with credit terms?

a._____

_____

_____

_____

_____

_____

_____

b._____

_____

_____

_____

_____

_____

_____

_____

_____

_____

_____

9. Centralized versus Decentralized Accounting Functions

Fain Company is highly diversified with branches scattered throughout the United States. Each branch manufactures different products for specific markets. Presently, each branch has its own production vice president, and only minimum accounting is performed on site. Nearly all accounting data is forwarded to the home office where skilled cost and financial accountants are employed to process the information. In fact, only cost clerks and bookkeepers are hired for each branch, and they also perform secretarial duties.

   The company asks your advice regarding decentralizing its accounting functions and employing either a CPA or CMA to head each branch's accounting department, and who would report directly to the branch's production vice president. The president is not in support of this proposal even though it is recognized that there could be less communication problems, and that an accountant would be readily available when the branch manufacturing management needed advice regarding cost control and record-keeping.

Required:

Evaluate this situation and list advantages and disadvantages of centralizing accounting functions for diversified operations. Suggest an optimum solution for Fain Company.

_____

_____

_____

_____

_____

_____

_____

_____

_____

10. Accounting and Behavioral Problems Expected

Assume you have recently acquired an electrical contracting and supply company owned by Harold Douglas who is retiring. Douglas has owned and operated the company 30 years and can reflect back with pride on the rate of growth he has achieved. He is further pleased that he was able to run the affairs in a highly personal way while at the same time being responsible for all production, financial, and personnel problems.

Required:

What problems from a behavioral viewpoint and accounting system perspective do you expect to encounter?

_____

_____

_____

_____

_____

_____

_____

_____

_____

11. Analyzing Division of Duties

As controller for Saliba Company, you and the treasurer report directly to the vice president of finance. You have just finished negotiating with a local bank for a short-term loan. Since credits and collections are handled by the treasurer's department, you had to request this information from these personnel.

However, you did not hesitate to go directly to the employees in the treasurer's department and ask for this assistance because last week one of your employees spent many hours supplying cost data to assist the treasurer in implementing budgetary procedures. The vice president of finance has given both you and the treasurer permission to use each other's personnel in projects and analysis if this assistance is needed. The vice president feels that since both of you have functional authority it isn't necessary to inform each other before you enlist the assistance of each other's personnel. Functional authority is a defined right of authority to direct certain activities of another department because of specialized knowledge.

Lately this has created some problems, however, as so many of your employees are busy working on tax data requested by the treasurer. While you recognize that the treasurer has a tax return deadline to meet, you also must prepare an analysis and recommendations to be presented to the board of directors next month. In addition, monthly cost analysis for each department is due on the president's desk in three days. You hesitate to ask employees in your department to work overtime, but it appears necessary.

Required:

Discuss the factors that have led to this situation.

12. Information Obtained from Accounting System

Several years ago Bob Overbey purchased a small pharmaceutical company which manufactures "over-the-counter" medicines such as aspirin, cough syrup, and cold pills. The company had been family owned and had not experienced a rapid growth primarily because the family wanted to keep it small. Since all family members participated in the management, they felt that the sole purpose of accounting records was to fulfill income tax requirements. Their bookkeeper was responsible for making all cash disbursements, including payroll. At year-end a local public accounting firm prepared annual financial statements and income tax returns. When Bob assumed ownership, he inherited the accounting system and has made no changes. Bob has been warned by friends in other businesses that a more elaborate accounting system would be very costly and not worthwhile.

Bob has devoted his attention to the increasing pressure he is receiving from competitors, and he has continued to manufacture the same product lines as his predecessor. In addition, each year he has raised the sales price of each product line 4 percent.

Last year Bob began experiencing cash problems. He was forced to float short-term loans to meet several payrolls. He realized that part of his problem was the rise in the cost of certain ingredients used in manufacturing aspirin and cough medicine.

Required:

a.   What kinds of information is Bob obtaining now from his accounting system? _____
     _____
     _____
     _____

b.   What other accounting information should Bob be receiving? How could he use this information?
     _____
     _____
     _____
     _____
     _____

c.   Would you recommend making any changes to the cost accounting system? Comment on Bob's concern for a costly, elaborate accounting system.

     _____
     _____
     _____
     _____
     _____
     _____
     _____
     _____
     _____

True-False Questions

Indicate whether the following statements are true or false by inserting in the blank space a capital "T" for true or "F" for false.

_____ 1. Cost management can help executives plan how the future will change and what future operating cost scenarios will be.

_____ 2. A cost can be either an asset or an expense.

_____ 3. Inventory costs increase when a company undertakes investment projects to reduce setup costs or to schedule deliveries and production so that there is less overall uncertainty in the production system.

_____ 4. Short-term profits always represent a good index of the ability of top management to turn a company around.

_____ 5. The need for a detailed tracking of goods a company is working on in manufacturing operations is reduced as JIT inventory policies become more prevalent.

_____ 6. Cost accounting is accumulated only for internal management purposes while financial accounting is used for external purposes.

_____ 7. Even though goal congruence is difficult to achieve, there are such things as breaking down company goals into subgoals which are helpful.

_____ 8. When robots make errors, they are random, rather than deterministic, and this explains the reason automation produces higher quality products.

_____ 9. The true cost can more likely be determined if there is only one product or one service.

_____ 10. The American Institute of Certified Public Accountants differs from the Cost Accounting Standards Board because the AICPA was established by the U. S. Congress to achieve uniformity and consistency in defense contracts while the CASB was established by the accounting profession to regulate itself.

SOLUTIONS

Matching

1.	g	6.	k
2.	l	7.	b
3.	j	8	f
4	a	9.	i
5.	e	10.	d

Completion and Exercises

1. Institute of Certified Management Accountants;(a) economics, finance, and management; (b) financial accounting and reporting; (c) management reporting, analysis, and behavioral issues; and (d) decision analysis and information systems.

2. Cost represents the monetary measurement of material, labor, and overhead used in manufacturing a product or rendering a service.

3. The rule that all purchases must be given to the lowest bidder <u>has</u> inherent weaknesses. It encourages the policy of trying to drive down the price of anything purchased, with no regard to quality and service. Such policy can drive good vendors and good services out of business. Enforcing such a rule ignores whether the vendor has had any experience in the line of work sought or has any employee capable of directing it.

4. a.   Internal Revenue Service
   b.   Cost Accounting Standards Board

5. There is interaction between the cost accountant and the following departments:

   a.   Personnel -- Cost accounting uses the wage rates and pay methods supplied by the personnel department; in addition, adequate labor records are used in cost analysis.
   b.   Treasurer -- Cost accounting supplies information used for budgets and forecasts of cash and working capital. Cost accounting information is also useful when the treasurer is making decisions regarding the investment of temporary excess funds.
   c.   Engineering -- Cost accounting works closely with engineers in setting standards regarding the quality and quantity of material and labor required to produce a product.
   d.   Production -- Cost accounting works closely with production personnel measuring the efficiency of operating departments.
   e.   Financial accounting -- Because cost accounting data is integrated within financial reports, there is a close relationship. Cost accounting data is input for income determination and inventory valuation.
   f.   Marketing -- Cost estimates are used in establishing selling prices and policies even though factors such as supply, demand, and competition also affect the sale price determination.

6. American Institute of Certified Public Accountants (AICPA); auditing; business law & professional responsibility; accounting and reporting (taxation, managerial-cost, and governmental and not-for-profit organizations); and financial accounting and reporting.

7. *Is Smaller Better?*

   The advantages some large corporations hope to gain by splitting their operations into more manageable size include:

   1.   The excessive levels of staff and other forms of bureaucracy are eliminated.

   2.   There is better, closer relations with employees, resulting from workers' greater sense of having an impact on results, which are more apparent at a small plant.

3. Workers are more likely to have the opportunity to participate in management.

4. Risk through theft is minimized.

5. There is closer control; shorter lines of communication, resulting in faster distribution of information.

6. Easier, faster retooling in keeping up with technological change.

7. Greater utilization of plant capacity.

8. There is greater specialization possible within individual units.

8. *Miller Company*

a. The organization needs to have a publicized policy that no purchasing agent can accept gifts from suppliers over a specified dollar amount. Otherwise, the suppliers may attempt to receive orders by giving the purchasing agents large gifts. As a result the price charged the company may not be competitive.

b. Communications should be encouraged between the treasurer and the accounting staff as the company could have saved $145.56 by borrowing money to pay for the three invoices with credit terms.

Purchase Discount	$200.00
Interest on paying $9,800 for	
20 days at 10%	54.44
Savings	$145.56

In order to further ensure that competitive prices are received, written bids should be obtained from suppliers based on Miller Co. specifications. The grade and quality of the item should be specified so that factors other than price can be properly considered.

9. *Fain Company*

Advantages of centralizing accounting functions include:

a. More effective use of computer facilities may be obtained.

b. By concentrating accounting skills in one place, there will more likely be a consistency in reporting accounting data and following accounting policies.

c. Accountants need to operate independently of the people they are evaluating. Placing the branch accountant under the production vice president on whose operations the accountant is reporting, will lead to a breakdown in independence.

d. External reporting is facilitated because data concerning all branches is located in one common place.

e. Short-run cost efficiencies may result from reduced personnel needs.

Disadvantages of centralizing accounting functions include:

a. There may be a lack of accounting skill on site, which may be needed by the branch engineers and manufacturing personnel.

b. More rapid detecting and reporting of areas needing corrections may be achieved under a decentralized system rather than a centralized accounting system.

c. With the diversity of operations, an on-site accountant would be more likely to understand the unique problems of each branch better than a centralized accountant.

The optimum solution may be to employ division controllers for each branch who report to a centralized vice president of finance. Each division controller would be responsible for maintaining each branch's records, with the centralized vice president of finance having the authority to evaluate each division and the responsibility for the internal audit function.

10. *Harold Douglas*

From a behavioral viewpoint, the following factors will likely result:

1. Harold Douglas has probably been the father image for the employees and this role may be difficult to follow.

2. While Douglas was familiar with all aspects of operation, a new owner would not be and would require time to become knowledgeable.

3. Lack of management depth.

4. Not enough training of present employees to assume management successor.

5. All decision making probably assumed by Douglas so there is likely no real organizational structure as all employees can be assumed to go directly to Douglas.

From an accounting system perspective, the following factors will likely result:

1. Expertise in the area of accounting probably has been lacking.

2. Lack of adequate cost control.

3. Financial person probably no more skilled than a bookkeeper.

11. *Saliba Company*

The functions of the controller and treasurer have not been defined correctly. Short-term financing and investment responsibilities should be assigned to the treasurer while the controller should handle budgeting functions and tax administration. This incorrect assignment of duties causes the treasurer and controller to request the assistance of personnel in each other's department because an area of information is not centralized in one department.

Giving permission to the treasurer and controller to request the assistance of each other's personnel has only compounded the problem. Employees in these two departments don't really know who they should be reporting to. The vice president is incorrect in his definition of functional authority. The controller and treasurer have line authority over the individuals in each of their departments. In turn they have functional authority in relation to other departments because of their specialized knowledge.

Until the duties of the controller and treasurer are better assigned, conditions of increased workloads and overtime can be expected.

12. *Bob Overbey*

Note: Even though limited information is given, you are encouraged to think what the cost information suggested should be used for and whether cost accounting is worthwhile.

a.   Limited information is obtained now from the system primarily to fulfill income tax requirements. Bob Overbey receives the balance of cash disbursements and receipts, limited payroll data, and annual external financial reports. Almost no information for planning and decision making is obtained, however.

b.   Bob should be receiving more internal reports. For example, he should be receiving detailed cost analysis so that his pricing system could possibly be changed and tighter controls on inventory made. Costs by product lines, including a breakdown by component parts, are needed so that profitability analysis by product lines can be made. Actual expenses incurred should be periodically compared against the budget as this data would help in cash planning.

c.   Definite changes should be made in the cost accounting system so that additional internal reports can be prepared. Costs will have to be obtained for each product line. Bob is correct in guarding against a more elaborate accounting system than he can afford, as the benefit of the data should be matched against the cost involved in obtaining the data. However, an adequate cost accounting system does not have to be extremely costly or elaborate to be effective.

True - False

1. T

2. T

3. F Large savings in inventory costs occur under these manufacturing conditions.

4. F Managers can increase profits by deferring maintenance, cutting out research, or by acquiring another company. A better indicator than short-term profit is the effect of company operations on long-run productivity.

5. T

6. F Cost accounting is used both for external and internal accounting purposes.

7. T

8. F Robots make deterministic errors.

9. T

10. F The descriptions of the AICPA and the CASB are reversed.

2

Production, Marketing, and Administrative Cost Flows

Chapter Outline

Manufacturing Inventory Accounts
Production, Marketing, and Administrative Costs
    Direct Material
    Direct Labor
    Factory Overhead
    Prime and Conversion Costs
Application of Factory Overhead
    Entry to Apply Overhead
    Disposition of Under- or Overapplied Overhead
Manufacturing Inventory Flows
    Cost of Goods Manufactured Statement Using Applied Overhead
    Manufacturer's Statement of Income
    Retailer's Statement of Income
    Cost of Goods Manufactured Statement Using Actual Overhead
    Inventory Physical Flow
Volume-Related Cost Drivers
    Machine-Hours
    Direct Materials Cost
    Units of Production
    Direct Labor Cost
    Direct Labor-Hours
Impact of Computer-Integrated Manufacturing
    Cost Mix
    Labor-Based Application Rates
    Quality Control
Appendix: Inventory Costing Methods

Chapter Objectives

After studying this chapter, you should be able to:

1. Identify the components of production, marketing, and administration costs.

2. Demonstrate the flow of manufacturing costs through the inventory account which is reflected on a cost of goods manufactured statement.

3.   Understand the effect of automation on volume-based overhead application rates.

4. Cost material inventory using FIFO, LIFO, or average costing methods.

5. Define and apply the new terms introduced.

Chapter Review

Manufacturing Inventory Accounts

1. There is a significant difference in the inventory account titles used by a merchandising company, a manufacturing company, and a service company.

    a. Retailers and other merchandisers sell their product in substantially the same form as they purchased it.
    b. Manufacturers convert material into finished goods and this requires these additional inventory accounts: Direct Materials Inventory, Factory Supplies Inventory, Work in Process Inventory, and Finished Goods Inventory.
    c. A service organization furnishes intangible services rather than tangible goods and may have a Direct Materials Inventory.

2. A manufacturer generally has four inventory accounts:

    a. Direct Materials Inventory--raw material on hand which will become a part of the finished product.
    b. Factory Supplies Inventory--materials and supplies which will be used in factory maintenance, repair, and cleaning.
    c. Work in Process Inventory--products that are semifinished.
    d. Finished Goods Inventory--products which are ready for sale to outsiders.

Production, Marketing, and Administrative Costs

3. Production, marketing, and administrative are the three general classifications in which all costs fall.

    a. Production costs include direct materials, direct labor, and factory overhead incurred to make a good or service.
    b. Marketing costs are those costs that are incurred in promoting and distributing the product or service.
    c. Administrative costs are incurred in directing and controlling the company and for general activities such as personnel and legal functions.

Direct Material

4. Direct material is the raw material which is processed to become the finished product.

    a. Direct material may be purchased in various forms as some companies may buy finished parts and merely assemble them while other companies change the form of direct material.
    b. When material is received, Direct Materials Inventory is debited and the offsetting credit is to Accounts Payable (if on credit) and to Cash (if a cash disbursement is made.)

Direct Labor

5. The amount of wages earned by workers who are actually engaged in transforming the material from its raw state to a finished product is referred to as direct labor costs.

Factory Overhead

6. Factory overhead comprises all production costs other than direct material and direct labor.

    a. Marketing and administrative costs are excluded from factory overhead.
    b. Indirect materials which are small, insignificant items of material become part of factory overhead; factory supplies are indirect materials.
    c. Salaries of production workers that are not actually engaged in manufacturing the product become part of factory overhead.

d. Rent, taxes, insurance, repairs, and depreciation on production facilities are also classified as factory overhead.

Prime and Conversion Costs

7. Prime cost is comprised of direct material and direct labor; usually these two cost elements can be measured easily and accurately.

8. Direct labor and factory overhead are classified as conversion costs or processing costs.

Application of Factory Overhead

9. When a product is finished, its actual direct material, actual direct labor, and applied factory overhead are debited to Finished Goods Inventory and Work in Process is credited.

    a. Actual factory overhead cannot be distributed until after the month or period ends; thus, actual factory overhead is not practical to use. Instead, factory overhead is estimated and applied on some basis such as machine hours.

    b. By applying factory overhead, a job that is finished during the month can be transferred into Finished Goods Inventory with an estimate of factory overhead.

    c. The application rate is determined by the following formula:

$$\frac{\$XXX \text{ budgeted factory overhead cost}}{\$XXX \text{ budgeted direct labor dollars or XXX budgeted machine-hours}}$$

    d. At the end of the accounting period, overhead is applied to any job that is remaining unfinished.

Entry to Apply Overhead

10. The entry to apply overhead is to debit Work in Process Inventory and to credit Factory Overhead Control.

    a. The Factory Overhead Control follows this pattern:

Factory Overhead Control	
Actual	Applied

    b. A separate Factory Overhead Applied account to accumulate applied overhead may be used.

    c. If a separate Factory Overhead Applied account is used, Factory Overhead Applied is credited and Work in Process Inventory is debited for the applied amounts.

    d. Factory Overhead Applied must be closed out at the end of the accounting period as it is a suspense account like Factory Overhead Control.

Disposition of Under- or Overapplied Overhead

11. If the overhead applied to production is greater than total actual factory overhead incurred, the credit balance in the Factory Overhead Control represents overapplied overhead.

12. If instead, the overhead applied to production is less than total actual factory overhead incurred, the debit balance in the Factory Overhead Control represents underapplied overhead.

13. The under- or overapplied overhead should be closed into Cost of Goods Sold if the amount is small.

14. If the amount is significant, the over- or underapplied overhead should be allocated between inventory and cost of sales based on the relative proportion of units sold and remaining in inventory.

Manufacturing Inventory Flows

15. Accountants trace the flow of costs through these four inventory accounts: Factory Supplies, Direct Materials, Work in Process, and Finished Goods.

   a. Actual direct material, actual direct labor, and applied factory overhead are debited to Work in Process Inventory.

   b. The Factory Overhead Control account is supported by a subsidiary ledger listing the separate cost items comprising the total overhead.

Cost of Goods Manufactured Statement Using Applied Overhead

16. The purpose of the Cost of Goods Manufactured Statement is to summarize all production costs for a cost accounting period.

   a. This statement is also known as the Statement of Manufacturing Costs or the Manufacturing Statement.
   b. The production costs consist of direct material, direct labor, and factory overhead.

17. Exhibit 2-1 shows the Cost of Goods Manufactured Statement if applied factory overhead is included. Assume actual factory overhead is $39,500.

Exhibit 2-1

Bell Manufacturing Company
Cost of Goods Manufactured Statement
For the Year Ended December 31, 19X1

Direct materials inventory, January 1, 19X1	$26,000	
Add: Purchases (net of discount)	33,000	
Direct materials available for use	59,000	
Less: Direct materials inventory, December 31,19X1.	40,000	
Direct materials used		$ 19,000
Direct labor		63,000
Factory overhead applied		40,100
Total manufacturing costs for the period		$122,100
Add: Work in process inventory, January 1, 19X1		51,000
Manufacturing costs to account for		173,100
Less: Work in process inventory, December 31, 19X1		40,000
Cost of goods manufactured		$133,100

Note the following:

   a. The third line of the heading is for the accounting period covered.
   b. Both actual and applied factory overhead are not shown. If applied overhead is as shown in Exhibit 2-1, the over- or underapplied overhead must also be shown either by including it with the balance of cost of goods sold as in Exhibit 2-2 or prorating it between inventory and cost of sales.

c. Beginning work in process inventory is added to total manufacturing costs to give manufacturing costs to account for.

d. Ending work in process inventory is deducted from manufacturing costs to account for to give cost of goods manufactured.

Manufacturer's Statement of Income

18. The manufacturer's income statement illustrated in Exhibit 2-2 picks up the cost of goods manufactured shown in the Cost of Goods Manufactured statement.

   a. The cost of goods manufactured shown Exhibit 2-1 is added to the beginning balance in finished goods inventory to arrive at the cost of goods available for sale.

   b. Overapplied overhead is deducted from Cost of Goods Sold as illustrated for the $600 overapplied factory overhead in Exhibit 2-1.

   c. If instead there was underapplied overhead, it would be added to Cost of Goods Sold.

Exhibit 2-2

Bell Manufacturing Company
Statement of Income
For the Year Ended December 31, 19X1

Sales		$400,000
Less cost of goods sold:		
Finished goods inventory, January 1, 19X1	$ 9,000	
Cost of goods manufactured	133,100	
Cost of goods available for sale	$142,100	
Less: Finished goods inventory, December 31, 19X1	8,000	
Cost of goods sold	134,100	
Less: Overapplied factory overhead	600	133,500
Gross margin		$266,500
Expenses: Marketing costs	$ 50,000	
Administrative costs	100,000	150,000
Income before taxes		$116,500

19. The manufacturer's Statement of Income could be combined with the Cost of Goods Manufactured.

   a. The cost of goods manufactured is shown on the statement of income.
   b. Finished goods inventory is shown on the statement of income while materials inventory and work in process inventory are shown on the cost of goods manufactured statement.

Retailer's Statement of Income

20. The terminology used in a manufacturer's income statement and a retailer's income statement varies.

   a. Retailers buy goods that are already finished and their inventory account is called Merchandise Inventory.
   b. The goods that a merchandiser buys is classified as Purchases.

Cost of Goods Manufactured Statement Using Actual Overhead

21. Exhibit 2-3 illustrates a cost of goods manufactured statement using actual factory overhead instead of applied factory overhead.

   a. Exhibit 2-3 shows $11,000 factory supplies were available for use, but only $6,000 indirect materials were used.

b. Accountants do not adjust cost of goods sold for over- or underapplied overhead on the Income Statement when using actual factory overhead only.

Exhibit 2-3   Bell Manufacturing Company
                         Cost of Goods Manufactured Statement
                          For the Year Ended December 31, 19X1

Direct materials inventory, January 1, 19X1	$26,000	
Add: Purchases (net of discount)............................	33,000	
Direct materials available for use.............................	59,000	
Less: Direct materials inventory, December 31,19X1.	40,000	
Direct materials used...		$19,000
Direct labor...		63,000
Factory overhead costs:		
Factory supplies, January 1, 19X1...........................	4,000	
Add: Purchases..	7,000	
Supplies available for use	11,000	
Less: Factory supplies, December 31, 19X1.............	5,000	
Indirect materials used..	6,000	
Indirect labor...	10,000	
Depreciation..	15,000	
Rent	5,000	
Taxes...	2,500	
Miscellaneous	1,000	
Total factory overhead costs		39,500
Total manufacturing costs for the period.........................		$121,500
Add: Work in process inventory, January 1, 19X1............		51,000
Manufacturing costs to account for.................................		172,500
Less: Work in process inventory, December 31, 19X1.....		40,000
Cost of goods manufactured		$132,500

Inventory Physical Flow

22. The flow of costs through merchandise inventory is similar to the flow through a manufacturer's inventory accounts, as in Exhibit 2-4.

Exhibit 2-4   **Inventory Cost Flow**

Retail Accounting

Merchandise inventory:
      Beginning inventory
Plus: Net purchases
Equals: Available for sale
Minus: Ending inventory
Equals: Cost of goods sold

Manufacturing Accounting

Raw material inventory:
      Beginning inventory
Plus: Net material purchases
Equals: Available for use
Minus: Ending inventory
Equals: Raw material used.

Manufacturing Accounting

Work in process inventory:
      Beginning Inventory
Plus: Cost of direct material,
         direct labor, and overhead
Equals: Manufacturing costs to
         account for
Minus: Ending Inventory
Equals: Cost of goods manufactured

Manufacturing Accounting

Finished goods:
      Beginning inventory
Plus: Cost of goods
         manufactured
Equals Available for sale
Minus: Ending inventory
Equals: Cost of goods sold

Volume-Related Cost Drivers

23. A cost driver is the factor that causes an activity to occur.

    a. Accountants ensure they properly apply costs by analyzing the components of factory overhead to determine appropriate cost drivers.
    b. Accountants must apply overhead costs to products and other objects based on the causes of costs or the benefits received rather than some arbitrary basis.
    c. They expect nonvolume-related (also known as nonunit-related) activities such as numbers of inspections, setups, or scheduling transactions to become increasingly the factors that drive overhead cost.

24. Typical volume-related (unit-related) application bases accountants use are:
    a. Machine-hours.
    b. Direct material costs.
    c. Units of production.
    d. Direct labor cost.
    e. Direct labor-hours.

Machine-Hours

25. Machine-hours may be the most accurate overhead allocation basis if the factory is highly automated.

    a. Use of machine-hours may require additional clerical effort in calculating machine-hours by jobs or by departments.
    b. If there is a fixed relationship between direct labor-hours and machine-hours (as one direct labor worker is stationed at each machine), use of direct labor-hours as a base may be more feasible.

    c. The formula is: $\dfrac{\$XXX \text{ estimated factory overhead}}{XXX \text{ estimated machine-hours}} = \$XXX \text{ per machine-hour}$

Direct Materials Cost

26. Direct materials costs is an appropriate base if a logical relationship between direct materials usage and overhead costs exists.

    a. A logical relationship between direct materials usage and overhead costs exists if the same amount of material is applied hourly or if each product involves about the same material costs.

    b. The formula is: $\dfrac{\$XXXX \text{ estimated factory overhead cost}}{\$XXX \text{ estimated material cost}} = XX \text{ percent of material cost}$

Unit of Production Base

27. Units of production base may be appropriate if only one product is manufactured or a simple production process is involved.

    a. The formula is: $\dfrac{\$XXX \text{ estimated factory overhead}}{XXX \text{ estimated number of units}} = \$XX \text{ per unit}$

    b. Nonmanufacturing organizations use variations; for example, a healthcare institution uses the number of beds.

Direct Labor Cost

28. Direct labor cost as a basis assumes that higher paid workers are incurring a larger share of factory overhead than are lower paid workers.

a. This may be true if the more highly paid workers are better trained and operate the expensive and more sophisticated machinery and plant facilities.
b. Direct labor costs may not be appropriate if a majority of the factory overhead items are related to resources consumed over a period of time.
c. Under a system using direct labor costs as a basis for applying factory overhead, an inefficient use of direct labor will in turn cause an excessive amount of factory overhead to be applied.
d. The formula is: $\dfrac{\$XXX \text{ estimated factory overhead}}{\$XXX \text{ estimated direct labor costs}}$ = XX percent of direct labor costs

Direct Labor-Hours

29. Use of direct labor hours basis assumes that factory overhead costs are related to the use of labor hours.

a. An inherent weakness is that in using actual direct labor hours, this is a measure of input and a better basis for applying factory overhead is some measure of output.

b. The formula is: $\dfrac{\$XXX \text{ estimated factory overhead}}{\$XXX \text{ estimated direct labor-hour}}$ = $XX per direct labor-hour

Impact of Computer-Integrated Manufacturing

30. Labor is no longer the focus of cost control in an automated factory.

Cost Mix

31. The traditional cost mix is changing as highly automated companies report labor costs as low as 10 percent, compared with the traditional labor cost of a much higher percent.

a. Overhead is often 500 percent of direct labor costs in CIM factories.
b. New overhead cost categories are emerging.

Labor-Based Application Rates

32. Managers as well as accountants are questioning whether direct labor hours and direct labor costs are good predictors of the value added to a product because of changes in cost mix.

Quality Control

33. Material utilization will increase with an emphasis on reducing or eliminating scrap and rework costs.

Appendix: Inventory Costing Methods

34. FIFO Inventory Method

a. The first-in-first-out (FIFO) method assumes that the first costs incurred are the first costs selected, regardless of the physical flow. Inventory issues are costed at the unit cost of the oldest supply on hand.
b. A disadvantage of using the FIFO inventory costing method is that a rise in material price matched by a corresponding increase in sales price tends to inflate income.
c. In a period of rising cost and sale prices, the FIFO costs charged against revenue come from the older, lower priced inventory on hand.
d. Ending inventory under FIFO is made up of the new, higher priced stock.
e. An advantage of FIFO is that it produces an ending inventory valuation which approximates current replacement costs.

35. **LIFO Inventory Method**

    a. Using the last-in-first-out (LIFO) method of inventory valuation, the cost of the latest items purchased or produced is assumed to be the first to be assigned to units issued or sold.

    b. Ending inventory under LIFO is costed at prices existing at a much earlier date since they represent the cost of the oldest stock on hand.

    c. LIFO has the advantage of matching current inventory costs with current revenues.

    d. In a period of rising prices, the cost of goods sold or used is priced out with the higher inventory costs which results in a tax savings.

36. **Average Costing Methods**

    a. A number of variations of the average costing method are available; some are appropriate for perpetual inventory systems while others are appropriate only for periodic inventory systems.

    b. Average costing methods assume that the cost of inventory on hand at the end of the accounting period is the average of the cost of the inventory on hand at the beginning of the period and the cost of the inventory purchased during the period.

    c. The average inventory methods tend to "even out" the effect of net increases or decreases in costs.

    d. The moving-average method allows the issues to be costed out currently at the average unit cost of goods on hand as of the withdrawal date.

Demonstration Problem

Cost of Goods Manufactured and Income Statement

Data from the records of Downs Company show the following:

Accounts receivable	$14,700
Administrative expense control.......................................	10,015
Cash...	800
Depreciation on factory building.....................................	1,600
Direct labor...	7,500
Factory insurance	5,070
Factory miscellaneous expense......................................	850
Indirect labor...	1,210
Indirect material used	860
Marketing expense control..	15,600
Purchase discount on direct materials	670
Purchases of direct materials	18,800
Direct materials inventory, December 31, 19X1	12,260
Direct materials inventory, January 1, 19X1	25,000
Sales	98,000
Work in process, December 31, 19X1	12,080
Work in process, January 1, 19X1	7,800

There were 2,100 units completed and transferred to the finished goods storeroom during the year. Finished goods inventory on January 1 contained 500 units at a value of $10,250. Sales during the year totaled 2,500 units. Inventory is costed out on a last-in, first-out basis.

Required: From the above data, prepare a Cost of Goods Manufactured Statement and an Income Statement for the year 19X1.

Paper for working Demonstration Problem

Solution to Demonstration Problem

Downs Company
Cost of Goods Manufactured
For the Year Ended December 31, 19X1

Direct material inventory, 1-1, 19X1.......................		$25,000	
Purchases...	$18,800		
Less Purchase discount..............................	670	18,130	
Direct materials available for use............................		$43,130	
Less: Direct materials inventory 12-31, 19X1........		12,260	
Direct material used..			$30,870
Direct Labor...			7,500
Factory Overhead:			
Depreciation..		$1,600	
Insurance..		5,070	
Indirect material..		860	
Indirect labor..		1,210	
Miscellaneous expense		850	9,590
Total manufacturing costs for the period			$47,960
Add: Work in process January 1, 19X1			7,800
Manufacturing costs to account for			$55,760
Less: Work in Process, December 31, 19X1			12,080
Cost of Goods Manufactured.......................			$43,680

Downs Company
Income Statement
For the Year Ended December 31, 19X1

Sales		$98,000
Beginning finished goods, 500 units $\left(\dfrac{\$10,250}{500} = \$20.50\right)$	$10,250	
Cost of goods manufactured $\left(\dfrac{\$43,680}{2,100} = \$20.80\right)$	43,680	
Cost of goods available for sale...	$53,930	
Less: Ending finished goods (100 x $20.50)	2,050	
Cost of goods sold..		51,880
Gross margin		$46,120
Administrative expense..	$10,015	
Marketing expense	15,600	25,615
Income Before Income Tax..		$20,505

Matching

Referring to the terms listed in the left column, place the appropriate letter next to the corresponding description. A term may not be used or may be used more than once.

a. Conversion costs

b. Cost of Goods Manufactured Statement

c. Direct labor cost

d. Direct material

e. Factory overhead

f. Income statement

g. Indirect labor cost

h. Indirect material

i. Overapplied overhead

j. Prime cost

k. Subsidiary factory overhead accounts

l. Underapplied overhead

_____ 1. Wages earned by the factory supervisor.

_____ 2. Direct material and direct labor.

_____ 3. Represents the total of factory overhead and direct labor.

_____ 4. Production costs other than direct material and direct labor.

_____ 5. This statement contains Finished Goods Inventory.

_____ 6. This statement contains Direct Materials Inventory and Work in Process Inventory.

_____ 7. Wages paid to a machine operator on an assembly line.

_____ 8. Credit balance in Factory Overhead Control after all applications of overhead and actual overhead have been recorded.

_____ 9. Accounts which detail actual factory overhead costs.

_____ 10. Inexpensive thread and glue used in manufacturing, repair supplies, and maintenance supplies are examples of this type of factory overhead.

Completion and Exercises

1. Define the three general classifications of cost:

   a._____

   b._____

   c._____

2. Labor and material which are directly attachable to the unit are referred to as _____ cost.

3. The main distinction between a manufacturer's balance sheet and a retailer's balance sheet lies in the _____ accounts.

4. Give the ledger account classification of the following:

Account	Classification
a. Work in Process	_____
b. Factory Overhead Control	_____
c. Finished Goods	_____
d. Cost of Goods Sold	_____
e. Accumulated Depreciation	_____
f. Payroll Payable	_____

5. Conversion costs consist of both _____ and _____.

6. **Cost of Goods Manufactured Statement with Unknowns**

   A simple cost system is used by Sexton Company to account for costs incurred in the manufacture of its single product. A review of the cost of goods manufactured statement for the fiscal year ended December 31, 19X1, discloses the following information and relationships:

   1. Total manufacturing costs were $1,034,000 based on actual direct material used, actual direct labor, and applied factory overhead as a percentage of actual direct labor dollars.
   2. Cost of goods manufactured was $974,000, also based on actual direct material, actual direct labor, and factory overhead.
   3. Factory overhead was applied to work in process at 55 percent of direct labor dollars. Applied factory overhead for the year was 25 percent of the total manufacturing costs.
   4. Beginning work in process inventory was 40 percent of ending work in process inventory.

   Required:

   Reconstruct the cost of goods manufactured statement for the year ended December 31, 19X1, in good form. Show supporting computations.

   _____

   _____

   _____

   _____

   _____

   _____

_____

_____

_____

_____

_____

_____

_____

_____

_____

_____

_____

_____

_____

_____

_____

_____

_____

_____

7. Preparing Cost of Goods Manufactured Statement and Income Statement

Glenrock, Inc., provides the following data for its year ended June 30, 19X2:

Sales	$8,300,000
Gross margin	1,970,000
Administrative expenses	411,000
Marketing expenses	965,000
Direct labor costs (385,000 hours)	1,380,000

Factory overhead is applied at the rate of $3.75 per direct labor-hour. Selected inventory accounts have the following beginning and ending balances:

	July 1, 19X1	June 30, 19X2
Work in process	$190,000	$320,000
Finished goods	$570,000	$400,000

Required:

Prepare a cost of goods manufactured statement and an income statement.

7. Paper for working

8. **Determining Costs Put Into Process and Goods Manufactured and Sold**

Inventories on the books of the McDowell Company on June 1 and June 30 were as follows:

	June 1	June 30
Direct material inventory	$30,000	$45,000
Work in process inventory	60,000	67,000
Finished goods inventory	90,000	85,000

Direct material costing $43,000 was put into process during the month. Timecards for direct labor workers showed a total of 40,000 hours in the Mixing Department and a total of 35,000 hours for direct labor workers in the Finishing Department. The labor rate is $4 for the Mixing Department and $5 for the Finishing Department. Factory overhead is applied at 80 percent of direct labor cost in the Mixing Department and at $2.30 per hour in the Finishing Department.

Required:

Without preparing a formal income statement, determine--
a. Total manufacturing costs for the period.
b. Cost of goods manufactured.
c. Cost of goods sold.

True-False Questions

Indicate whether the following statements are true or false by inserting in the blank space a capital "T" for true or "F" for false.

_____ 1. Administrative costs are incurred to assist production and are incurred in promoting sales, retaining customers, and providing proper warehousing.

_____ 2. The three types of factory costs incurred in manufacturing an item are direct material, indirect labor, and factory overhead.

_____ 3. Prime cost is the total of direct materials and direct labor.

_____ 4. Direct labor is determined by multiplying the worker's basic wage rate by the hours indicated on the clock cards or other time record.

_____ 5. Production costs, marketing costs and factory overhead are the three types of costs incurred in operating a company.

_____ 6. Application of indirect factory costs to the units of product manufactured is recorded by debiting Work in Process Inventory and crediting Factory Overhead Control.

_____ 7. Costs are transferred from one asset account to another asset when the journal entry debiting finished goods and crediting work in process is recorded.

_____ 8. The purpose of the manufacturing statement is to summarize all production costs and changes in the balance of finished goods inventory.

_____ 9. The major difference in a balance sheet prepared for a retail company and a manufacturing company is the number and types of inventory accounts.

_____ 10. One of the considerations in classifying a raw material into direct or indirect material is the ease of attaching the material cost to the finished product.

_____ 11. The cost mix of material, labor, and overhead will remain essentially the same with the introduction of new manufacturing technology.

_____ 12. There is a danger in applying factory overhead on the basis of actual direct labor costs because an excessive amount of direct labor can cause factory overhead to be overapplied.

SOLUTIONS

Matching

1.	g	6.	b
2.	j	7.	c
3.	a	8.	i
4	e	9.	k
5.	f	10.	h

Completion and Exercises

1. a. Production costs include direct materials, direct labor, and factory overhead incurred to produce a good or service; product engineering and design are also included in this classification.
    b. Marketing costs are incurred in selling and delivering products and include those costs involved in promoting sales and retaining customers.
    c. Administrative costs are incurred in directing and controlling the company and for general activities such as personnel and legal functions.

2. prime

3. inventory

4. a. asset
    b. suspense
    c. asset
    d. expense
    e. contra asset
    f. liability

5. factory overhead, direct labor

6.
Sexton Company
Statement of Cost of Goods Manufactured
For the Year Ended December 31, 19X1

Direct material used	$ 305,500
Direct labor	470,000
Factory overhead applied	258,500
Total manufacturing costs for the period	$1,034,000
Add beginning work in process inventory	40,000
Manufacturing costs to account for	$1,074,000
Less ending work in process inventory	- 100,000
Cost of Goods Manufactured	$ 974,000

Supporting Computations
Factory overhead applied: 25% x total manufacturing costs = 25% x $1,034,000 = $258,500
Direct labor:
55% of direct labor equals $258,500 so direct labor was $470,000 [($258,500 ÷ 55%) = $470,000]
Work in process inventories:
Let X = ending work in process inventory.......................... $1,034,000 + .40X-X = $974,000
$$- .60X = - 60,000$$
$$X = \$100,000$$
$$.40X = \$ 40,000$$

Direct material used equals total manufacturing costs less direct labor and factory overhead applied
[$1,034,000 - ($470,000 + $258,500)] = $305,500

7.

Glenrock, Inc.
Income Statement
For Year Ended June 30, 19X2

Sales		$8,300,000
Finished goods, July 1, 19X1	$ 570,000	
Cost of goods manufactured	6.160.000	
Cost of goods available for sale	6,730,000	
Less finished goods June 30, 19X2	400.000	
*Cost of goods sold		6.330.000
Gross margin		$1,970,000
Marketing expenses	$ 965,000	
Administrative expenses	411.000	1.376.000
Income before tax		$ 594,000

*This is the starting point since gross margin is given.

Glenrock, Inc.
Cost of Goods Manufactured Statement
For Year Ended June 30, 19X2

Direct materials used (must work backwards to find)	$3,466,250
Direct labor	1,380,000
Factory overhead ($3.75 x 385,000 hours)	1.443.750
Total manufacturing costs for the period	$6,290,000
Work in process, July 1, 19X1	+ 190.000
Manufacturing costs to account for	$6,480,000
Work in process, June 30, 19X2	- 320.000
Cost of goods manufactured (from Income Statement)	$6,160,000

8. **McDowell Company**

Direct Material Inventory

6-1	Balance	30,000	To production	43,000
	Purchases	58,000	6-30 Balance	45,000

Work in Process Inventory

6-1	Balance	60,000	To finished goods	579,500
	Material	43,000	6-30 Balance	67,000
	Labor (Mixing)	160,000		
	(Finishing)	175,000		
	Overhead (Mixing)	128,000		
	(Finishing)	80.500		
		646,500		

Finished Goods Inventory

6-1	Balance	90,000	To cost of goods sold	584,500
	From work in process	579.500	6-30 Balance	85.000
		669,500		669,500

a.	Material	$ 43,000
	Labor (Mixing)...	160,000
	Labor (Finishing)..	175,000
	Overhead (Mixing)	128,000
	Overhead (Finishing)	80,500
	Total manufacturing costs for the period	$586,500
	+ Work in process inventory, 6-1	60,000
	Manufacturing costs to account for	$646,500
	- Work in process, 6-30..	67,000
b.	Cost of goods manufactured	$579,500
	+ Finished goods inventory, 6-1	90,000
	Cost of goods available for sale...............................	$669,500
	- Finished goods inventory, 6-30..............................	85,000
c.	Cost of goods sold..	$584,500

True-False

1.   F   Marketing costs are incurred to promote sales, retain customers, and provide sufficient warehousing.

2.   F   The three types are direct material, direct labor, (not indirect labor--this is part of factory overhead), and factory overhead.

3.   T

4.   T

5.   F   Production costs, marketing costs and administrative costs are the three types of costs incurred in operating a company. Factory overhead is part of production costs.

6.   T

7.   T

8.   F   A manufacturing statement does not reflect changes in the finished goods inventory balance as this is shown on the income statement. A manufacturing statement does summarize all production costs.

9.   T

10.   T

11.   F   Labor significantly diminishes to less than 10 percent of the cost of sales from at least a 30-40% in a traditional manufacturing environment.

12.   T

3 Cost Behavior and Cost Estimation

Chapter Outline

Cost Behavior Patterns
Fixed and Variable Costs
Relevant Range
Nonlinear Relationships
Unit versus Total Costs
Semivariable (Mixed) Costs
Importance of Cost Behavior to Nonmanufacturing Organizations
Impact of Automated Manufacturing
Economies of Scale and Scope
Cost Behavior
Cost Estimation
Cost Functions and Linearity
Cost Estimation Methods
Industrial Engineering Approach
Account Analysis
Scattergraph
High-Low Method
Regression Analysis
Criteria for Regression Analysis
Budgeted Allowance Using Cost Estimating Function
Appendix: Learning Curve Theory

Chapter Objectives

After studying this chapter, you should be able to:

1. Understand cost behavior patterns and the impact of automated manufacturing on these patterns.

2. Identify the important role of cost accountants in advising management about predicted cost behavior.

3. Use cost estimation methods, including regression analysis, to separate costs into their fixed and variable components.

4. Prepare cost estimating functions for determining budgeted costs to compare with actual costs.

5. Calculate the learning rate and account for deferred learning curve costs.

6. Define and apply the new terms introduced.

Chapter Review

Cost Behavior Patterns

1. Cost behavior refers to the relationship of expenses to activity level or volume.

Fixed and Variable Costs

2. Cost accountants analyze cost behavior and break costs down into either fixed, variable, or semivariable.

   a. Variable costs vary directly with changes in volume of output; direct material is an example.
   b. Fixed costs remain the same in total for a given time period and production level; insurance and rent are examples.
   c. Semivariable (or mixed) costs vary with volume but less than proportionately; indirect material, indirect labor, and utilities are examples.

3. Some fixed costs result from prior commitments to provide a certain capacity of operations and these are referred to as committed costs.

   a. Committed cost are the result of previous managerial actions such as depreciation and property taxes.

4. Discretionary costs result when management uses its professional judgment each period to decide the amount of such costs.

Relevant Range

5. Relevant range helps define the specific period of time and range of production for which costs are classified as either fixed or variable.

Nonlinear Relationship

6. Even if a cost is not linear over the entire range of volume, there may be a range which permits a linearity assumption within specified output limits. Economies and diseconomies of scale can cause nonlinear cost behavior.

Unit versus Total Costs

7. Exhibit 3-1 illustrates the unit versus total costs of both fixed and variable costs.

   a. Note that the total fixed cost is $100, but when this lump-sum fixed cost is divided by volume, unit fixed costs result. For example, if two units are produced, unit fixed cost is $50 ($100 fixed costs divided by 2 units). If 10 units are produced, the unit fixed cost is $10 ($100 total fixed costs divided by 10 units.)
   b. Total variable costs increase in proportion to volume increases, but unit variable costs remain constant. For example, Exhibit 3-1 takes $2 per unit of variable costs: if one unit is produced, total variable cost is $2, but if 10 units are produced, the total variable cost is $20.
   c. Total cost per unit and total cost are plotted by adding the fixed and variable cost. Total cost increases with volume because of variable costs. Average unit costs decrease with volume because the $100 fixed cost is spread over more units.

Exhibit 3-1

Cost Behavior Patterns

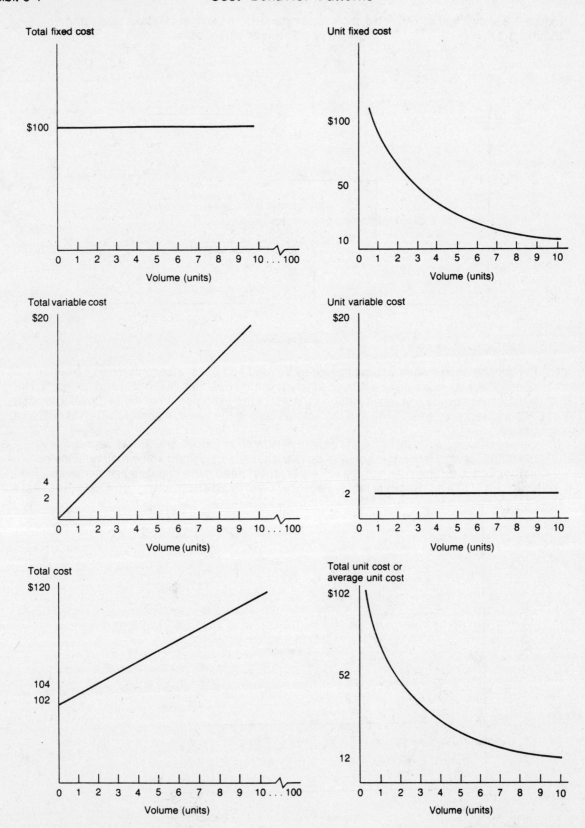

Semivariable (Mixed) Costs

8. Exhibit 3-2 shows that semivariable costs (also referred to as step costs) take many forms.

Exhibit 3-2   **Step-Type Semivariable Costs**

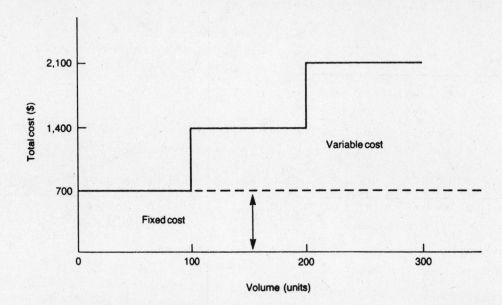

a. Exhibit 3-2, shows when volume increases beyond 100 units, a second repair person is needed; a third repair person is needed when volume reaches 300 units, and so forth. The $700 earned by the first repair person represents the fixed portion of the semivariable costs. The difference between $700 and the amount paid is the variable portion, which is related to usage.

b. Other semivariable costs follow the pattern illustrated in Exhibit 3-3. Costs such as maintenance may follow this behavior as management may keep some maintenance personnel at the plant at all times. As volume increases, they need more supplies and personnel.

Exhibit 3-3   **Total Semivariable Factory Overhead-Increasing at Constant Rate**

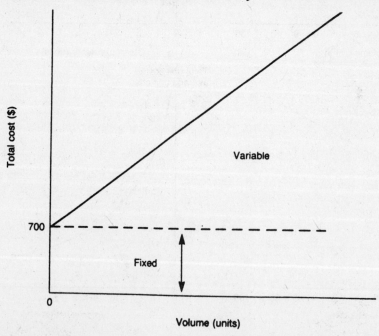

c. Heat, light, and power as well as other semivariable costs may increase either at a decreasing or increasing rate.
d. There are many varied cost behavior patterns in practice and many are not linear.
e. Even though direct material and direct labor are usually called variable costs, their behavior is often semivariable. Direct material is variable more often than direct labor because direct material does not have to be used if there is no production.

   1. Direct labor often results in a cost even if there is no production in the short run because it will take longer to lay off employees, and direct labor cost is not as flexible as direct material.
   2. Despite the fixed portion in direct labor costs, usually direct labor costs tend to be variable when measured over a longer period than one day in a labor-paced environment.

Importance of Cost Behavior to Nonmanufacturing Organizations

9. Cost behavior is important to all organizations, including not-for-profit and service industries.

   a. Understanding these organizations' unique cost mix is essential to their effective management.

Impact of Automated Manufacturing

10. The cost impact of idle capacity concerns managers because at this low volume, total product costs may not be recoverable at competitive prices.

Economies of Scale and Scope

11. Economies of scale assume that costs of changing from the manufacture of one product to another on the same machine are high.

12. Long production runs of standard products avoid these costs with lower per unit manufacturing costs.

   a. In a fully automated factory, the firm can make the first copy of a product for little more than the cost of the thousandth item.
   b. More managers are realizing that it is better not to produce than to manufacture an unnecessary part or product which results in excessive inventory.
   c. Large inventories stored for future use may become obsolete before they can be sold.

13. As accountants recognize that sales generate profits, not production, they are rethinking the variable-fixed cost relationships.

Cost Behavior

14. Direct material and direct labor are usually variable costs in a labor-paced environment.

   a. In the new automated factory, direct labor has essentially become a fixed cost, not a variable cost.
   b. The labor cost that remains in a computer-integrated manufacturing (CIM) system represents the cost of individuals performing the initial machine and material loading, but only for a single shift of a three-shift operation.
   c. In an automated factory, factory workers are highly trained.

      1. These trained factory workers are more likely to be paid on a fixed salary basis, rather than on a per hour basis.
      2. Materials, operating supplies, and energy are often the only significant component of variable manufacturing costs in the new automated factory environment.
   d. Fixed costs cannot be eliminated easily in the short run because it will take some time for management to sublease or sell their plant facilities.

Cost Estimation

15. Cost estimation studies involve an attempt to find predictable relationships between a cost driver or activity component and costs.

    a. An attempt is made to identify some independent variable and functional relationships that will permit computation of the corresponding value of the dependent variable.
    b. Finding the relation between costs and one important variable that affects costs-cost drivers- is essential.
    c. Cost drivers include machine hours, transactions, units of sales, work cells, order size, direct labor hours, value of materials, and quality requirements.

16. The cost estimating function is this cost equation: $y = a + bx$.

    a. y represents total cost, a equals the fixed component that does not change with activity levels, b refers to variable costs, and x represents the activity volume.
    b. The cost to be predicted (the dependent variable) is y in the above formula.
    c. The independent variable is represented by x in the above formula.
    d. The independent variable is called the *explanatory variable* and is usually a measure of activity controllable by a decision maker.

Cost Functions and Linearity

17. Assumptions are made when using linear cost functions to estimate the relationships of total costs to a specific range of output or input.

    a. One assumption is that the cost of securing each input must be a linear function of the quantity bought.
    b. Another assumption is that each finished product contains the same amount of direct labor or direct material.
    c. All input acquired is assumed to be fully utilized.
    d. Another assumption is that variations in the total cost level can be explained by variations in a single variable such as machine hours.

18. After making these assumptions, the cost function or underlying cost behavior pattern of each cost is found.

Cost Estimation Methods

19. The following five cost estimation techniques are used to measure the variability of costs when volume changes.

    a. Industrial engineering estimates
    b. Account analysis
    c. Scattergraph (visual fit)
    d. High-low method
    e. Regression analysis

Industrial Engineering Approach

20. With an industrial engineering approach, the focus is on what the cost should be to produce a finished product using the company's facilities.

    a. Time and motion studies are needed.
    b. An engineering approach analyzes the relationships between inputs and outputs by carefully studying each phase of the manufacturing process together with the kinds of work performed and the costs involved.

21. The engineering approach is used widely by companies with standard cost systems.

   a. Cost standards are scientifically predetermined costs of production used as a basis for measurement and comparison.
   b. Engineering estimates often help reveal areas where slack and inefficiencies exist.

Account Analysis

22. Using the account method, accountants examine and classify each ledger account into whether variable, fixed, or mixed.

   a. Mixed accounts are broken down into their variable and fixed component.
   b. These classifications may be based on past experience, on inspection of cost behavior for several past periods, or on managers' intuitive feelings.
   c. Total cost curves are developed from prior operations' cost data in using a historical cost approach.
   d. Experienced people, relying on their knowledge of existing cost behavior, can analyze each cost component to arrive at initial cost estimates.

Scattergraph

23. The scattergraph is a simple analysis that employs only two variables, such as cost and machine-hours.

   a. Each point on a scattergraph represents a cost observation.
   b. A trend line may be fitted mathematically or visually. It should be fitted so that there is an equal distance between the plotted points above and below the trend line.
   c. If the plotted points of the two variables on the scattergraph follow a generally straight line, a linear relationship between the two variables is assumed to exist.
   d. If the two variables show a linear relationship, they are correlated with each other.

High-Low Method

24. The high-low method is an inexpensive method for separating semivariable costs into their fixed and variable components.

   a. Two periods are chosen at different levels of activity; both levels should be within a relevant range.
   b. The difference in the volume between these two periods is divided into the difference in the costs at these two levels to give the variable rate.
   c. Either volume level can then be used to determine the total variable costs which is subtracted from the total costs to give the fixed costs.
   d. The high-low cost estimates can be diagrammed.

25. The high-low method allows the determination of a cost estimating function which expresses the variable cost per unit plus total fixed costs.

Regression Analysis

26. Regression analysis or the least squares method is another means of separating fixed and variable costs which is more sophisticated than the high-low method or the scattergraph.

   a. The method of least squares is the most widely used regression analysis which can be performed using standardized computer programs.
   b. Regression analysis can be used to measure the average amount of change in a dependent variable that is associated with unit increases in the amounts of one or more independent variables.

c. The least squares method is a mathematical approach based on the straight-line equation ($y = a + bx$) with y representing the costs; a, the fixed component; b, the variable element; and x, the volume.
   d. The least squares method is more objective than the scattergraph because personal bias does not enter into fitting the trend line.
   e. The data should first be plotted on a scattergraph before attempting to use the least squares method to ascertain that there is a reasonable degree of correlation.
   f. The correlation coefficient (r) is the most commonly used statistic to measure the relationship between the independent and dependent variable because r^2 expresses the extent to which the variation in the dependent variable is explained by changes in the independent variable.
   g. The closer the correlation coefficient is to either +1 or -1, the stronger the statistical relationship between the two variables.

Criteria for Regression Analysis

27.   There are certain criteria that must be met for regression analysis to be of benefit. These are given below:

   a. Reasonableness of relationship as a degree of correlation must exist that meets economic and professional judgment.

      1. A spurious correlation, which is a high correlation between two variables that do not seem related at all, should be guarded against.

   b. Examination of r^2 or other tests of goodness of fit help in interpreting the extent to which the independent variable accounts for the variability in the dependent variable.
   c. The following assumptions of regression analysis must be met:

      1. Representative observation
      2. Linearity in the relevant range
      3. Constant variance
      4. Independence
      5. Normality
      6. Absence of multicolinearity, which applies only to multiple regression

Representative Observations

28.   It is assumed in applying regression analysis that observations come from a uniform population.

   a. Unusual observations, referred to as outliers, may be thrown out in the analysis.

Linearity and Relevant Range

29.   Linearity must exist between x and y using the equation $y = a + bx$; the presence of linearity can be checked by plotting the data on a scattergram if there is one independent variable.

Constant Variance

30.   Homoscedasticity or constant variance is indicated when the spread of observations around the regression line is constant throughout the entire range of observations.

31.   Heteroscedasticity, or nonconstant variance, is often found in cost data because it is reasonable to expect a higher degree of variability of costs at high levels of volume than at low levels.

Independence

32. According to the independence assumption, the sequence of observations makes no difference in the level of costs because costs may follow one pattern when volume increases but a different pattern when volume decreases.

    a. Autocorrelation exists when this assumption of observations is not met.

Normality

33. The normality assumption, which assumes that the points around the regression line are normally distributed, is needed to make probability statements using the standard error of the estimate.

Absence of Multicolinearity

34. The absence of multicolinearity is applicable only to multiple regression in which there are two or more independent variables.

Budgeted Allowance Using Cost Estimating Function

35. Accountants separate costs into their fixed and variable components using high-low or least squares to better budget costs.

Appendix: Learning Curve Theory

36. The learning curve theory is based on the proposition that as workers gain experience in a task, less time is needed to complete the job and productivity increases. Learning curves are also called *progress functions* and *experience curves.*

    a. Experience has shown that the time needed to complete an operation becomes progressively smaller at a constant percentage.
    b. The slope of the curve for routine, repetitive operations will not be as steep as that for complex operations.
    c. Improvement curve theory, which is another name for learning curve theory, provides insight into the ability of workers to learn new skills.
    d. Bonus pay should not be established until the learning stage has leveled off; at this point when the skill has been learned, standards may be properly established so employees can earn a bonus if they complete a task in less time than standard.

Learning Rate

37. The reduction in time varies depending upon the repetitiveness of labor operations.

    a. The learning rate is defined as:

    $$\frac{\text{Average input quantity (cost) for the first 2X units}}{\text{Average input quantity (cost) for the first X units}}$$

    b. The time varies between 10 and 40 percent depending upon the repetitiveness of labor operations, with 20 percent being a common reduction.

Deferred Learning Curve Costs

38. In competitive bidding, the effect of learning on costs is important if repeat orders are expected because labor decreases with increases in orders up to the point where the learning stage levels off.

a. For financial accounting purposes, the units are usually charged to cost of goods sold at the average cost expected to be incurred for all units in the production run.
b. The deferred cost is placed in a suspense account titled Deferred Learning Curve Costs.
c. In the beginning of a project, actual labor costs for the units manufactured will exceed average production cost, but later in the run, the reverse occurs with actual cost being less than average.

39. Use of the Deferred Learning Curve Costs account causes a smoothing effect on reported company earnings; however, the disclosure of deferred learning curve costs on a company's balance sheet is at variance with generally accepted accounting principles.

40. Learning curves bring the behavioral and the quantitative aspects of labor management together as well as introduce more predictive ability in cost estimates for labor.

Impact of Automation on Learning Curve Theory

41. Learning curve theory has limited usefulness at the machine level in a flexible manufacturing system or computer-integrated manufacturing setting.

a. The whole concept of learning curve costs is altered because after the system has learned the operation method, it will repeat the task identically each time.
b. Reduction in labor hours of workers ceases to be an important issue because direct labor comprises such a small percent of total production costs in a machine-paced environment.

Demonstration Problem

Cost Estimating Formula and Budget Preparation

Phoenix, Inc. plans to produce 10,000 motors each month. Time and motion studies reveal it takes 5 machine hours per motor. The established monthly manufacturing overhead budget is:

Maintenance & repairs	$130,000
Utilities	157,500
Factory supplies	67,500
Rent	30,000
Insurance	18,000
	$403,000

Maintenance and repairs, utilities, and factory supplies vary directly with production.

Assume a rental contract with a specified monthly payment and monthly insurance payments. At the end of the month, it was determined that 45,600 actual machine hours were incurred in making 9,120 motors and actual manufacturing costs were:

Maintenance and repairs	$118,000
Utilities	144,100
Factory supplies	63,400
Rent	32,000
Insurance	16,500
	$374,000

Required:

a. What is the cost estimating formula for each fixed and variable costs? Express the total cost estimating formula on the basis of machine hours.

b. Prepare a budget for the actual production level and determine variances from budget for each detailed expense.

c. List some factors that could cause the variances you determined in Requirement *b*.

Paper for working Demonstration Problem

a.

b.

c.

Solution to Demonstration Problem

Phoenix, Inc.

a.

	Budget at Normal Capacity (50,000 Hours)	Variable Cost per Machine Hour	Fixed Cost
Maintenance and repairs	$130,000	$2.60	
Utilities	157,500	3.15	
Factory supplies	67,500	1.35	
Rent	30,000		$30,000
Insurance	18,000		18,000
	$403,000	$7.10	$48,000

Cost Estimating Formula = $7.10 variable cost per machine hour + $48,000 fixed overhead.

b.

	Actual Cost	Budget for 45,600 actual machine hours		Variance	
Maintenance & repairs	$118,000	$118,560	($2.60 X 45,600 hrs.)	$ 560	Favorable
Utilities	144,100	143,640	($3.15 X 45,600 hrs.)	460	Unfavorable
Factory supplies	63,400	61,560	($1.35 X 45,600 hrs.)	1,840	Unfavorable
Rent	32,000	30,000		2,000	Unfavorable
Insurance	16,500	18,000		1,500	Favorable
	$374,000	$371,760		$2,240	Unfavorable

c. The following factors could have caused the variances determined in Requirement *b* above:

1. More careful use of equipment and facilities so that less repairs were needed.

2. Inefficient use of utilities by Phoenix, Inc.

3. Utility rates increased.

4. Inefficient use of factory supplies, change in production process so that more maintenance or inspection supplies are needed.

5. Change in rental contract with higher rent.

6. Change to insurance agencies with lower rates, decrease in rates with present company, coverage of less assets.

Matching

Referring to the terms listed in the left column, place the appropriate letter next to the corresponding description. A term may not be used or may be used more than once.

a. Coefficient of correlation

b. Coefficient of determination

c. Cost estimating function

d. High-low method

e. Learning curve theory

f. Least squares method

g. Line of best fit

h. Linear programming

i. Regression analysis

j. Relevant range

k. Scattergraph

l. Semivariable costs

m. Unit fixed costs

n. Unit variable costs

_____ 1. Based on the proposition that as workers gain experience in a task, less time is needed to complete the job and productivity increases.

_____ 2. Cost will not change within a relevant range.

_____ 3. Determined by squaring r.

_____ 4. Is fitted so that there is an equal distance between the points plotted above and below.

_____ 5. $8.00 per direct labor hour and $3,600 per month is an example.

_____ 6. Technique used to measure the average amount of change in a dependent variable that is associated with unit increases in the amount of one or more independent variable(s).

_____ 7. A measure of the extent to which two variables are related linearly.

_____ 8. Another name for a trend line which may be fitted mathematically or visually.

_____ 9. Costs which vary in relation to production, but not proportionally.

_____ 10. Method that will give the most precise measure of the fixed and variable components of a semivariable cost.

_____ 11. Simple analysis method that employs only two variables for use in dividing a semivariable cost into its fixed and variable cost components.

_____ 12. The specified time period and designated production volume range used in cost behavior.

Completion and Exercises

1. Into which of the three behavior patterns, variable, fixed, or semivariable, does each of the following costs usually fall:

   a. Direct material_____

   _____

   _____

   b. Direct labor_____

   _____

   _____

   c. Factory overhead costs_____

   _____

   _____

2. Describe each of the following and give an appropriate example.

   a. Variable indirect factory overhead_____

   _____

   b. Fixed indirect factory overhead_____

   _____

   c. Semivariable indirect factory overhead_____

   _____

   d. Indirect labor_____

   _____

   e. Indirect materials_____

   _____

3. When relating total costs to output, the following assumptions provide adequate conditions for linearity to exist.

   a. _____

   _____

   _____

   b. _____

   _____

   c. _____

   _____

4. Total _____ costs remain the same regardless of output while total variable costs

   change directly with volume changes.   Direct material and direct labor are _____ (variable or fixed) costs because they are expected to increase or decrease proportionately with corresponding changes in volume.

5. _____costs vary with volume changes, but the proportional relationship found in variable costs is missing. Fixed costs such as depreciation, rent, and insurance generally remain the _____ (same or change) within a relevant volume range.

6. The _____ , _____ , and _____ _____ are three methods of dividing semivariable costs into their fixed and variable components.

7. Assume the cost estimating function is $.50 per machine-hour + $800 per month. In this situation, $.50 represents _____ (fixed or variable) costs, and $800 represents _____ _____ (total fixed or total variable) costs.

8. How is a trend line fitted? _____
_____

9. **High-Low Method**

   Power cost is budgeted at the following amount for Lisa, Inc.

Machine hours	Amount
300	$4,000
1,000	$6,100

   Required:

   Determine the fixed and variable components.

10. **Learning Curve Theory and Deferred Learning Cost**

    In 19X1, Leggett, Inc. built 2 units of a complex fan for a major airline manufacturer. The first unit required 2,200 direct labor hours to construct. In 19X2, the firm constructed 2 additional units and in 19X3, 4 more units were built. Materials costs have remained constant at $6,000 per unit, but labor has followed a 90% learning curve. Labor is paid $10 per hour and variable overhead is charged to production at the rate of $2 per direct labor hour.

    Required:

    a. Calculate the anticipated costs that Leggett should expect to incur in 19X3.
    b. Assume instead that management expects learning to continue through the manufacture of 32 units and that total demand Leggett will experience for this product will be 64 units. If the company makes 8 more units in 19X4 and charges to cost of goods sold for the total 16 units made are based on the average cost for the entire production run for which learning will occur, what will be the balance in the Deferred Learning Cost account at the end of 19X4 for labor and overhead?

a.

b.

11. Developing Cost Estimating Function Using High-Low Method

The following actual cost of Midtown, Inc., are arranged in alphabetical order for use in determining the cost estimating formula:

	Twelve months ago	Three months ago	Last month
Direct labor-hours	300,000	350,000	310,000
Direct labor	$ 335,000	$ 422,500	$ 308,500
Direct material	450,000	525,000	465,000
Factory supplies	130,000	135,000	131,000
Factory utilities	60,000	63,000	60,600
Indirect material	66,000	77,000	68,200
Plant maintenance	133,000	145,500	135,500
Plant repair salaries	80,000	80,000	80,000
President and vice president's salaries	110,000	110,000	110,000
Rent on plant	60,000	60,000	60,000
Salesperson's salaries	120,000	125,000	125,000
Sales promotion	9,300	11,300	9,610
	$1,553,300	$1,754,300	$1,553,410

Required:

Determine an overall variable factory overhead rate per direct labor-hour and total fixed factory overhead for the cost estimating formula using the high-low method assuming management believe there are no other major factors that affect cost behavior.

12. Use of Learning Curve Theory in Bidding

Miller Manufacturers has just completed the production and sale of a complex electronic unit. Management believes an opportunity exists to apply a 70 percent learning curve. In determining the cost of the first unit manufactured, the following data were obtained:

Material (60 pounds @ $4 per pound)	$ 240
Direct labor (80 hours @ $10 per hour)...........................	800
Factory overhead ($2 per direct labor-hour)	160
Total	$1,200

A potential customer approaches management wanting to buy three units for a total price of $2,500.

Required:

a. Provide supporting data indicating the estimated profit or loss if the bid is accepted. Assume no quantity discount exists for materials.
b. How would your approach be different in determining whether the bid should be accepted if the potential customer brought specifications for the electronic unit? i.e., Miller Manufacturers had never made a unit like the one requested.

13.

High-Low and Least Squares Methods

Doe Company provides the following overhead costs for the past year:

Month	Volume of Production (Machine-Hours)	Overhead Costs
January	18,500	$32,070
February	16,100	31,900
March	13,890	29,850
April	10,780	27,500
May	10,000	26,000
June	12,700	28,600
July	13,900	29,300
August	15,000	29,900
September	17,100	31,000
October	19,000	33,000
November	21,500	34,500
December	22,000	35,000

Required:

a. Compute the budget formula for the fixed and variable amounts using the high-low method of determining the fixed and variable costs.
b. Prepare monthly budgets of fixed and variable overhead for the first quarter using the following capacity volumes:

Estimated Machine-Hours

January	19,700
February	16,890
March	14,700

c. Use the least squares method to determine the fixed and variable cost elements.
d. Account for any difference between the answers determined in Requirement *a* and those determined in Requirement *c*.

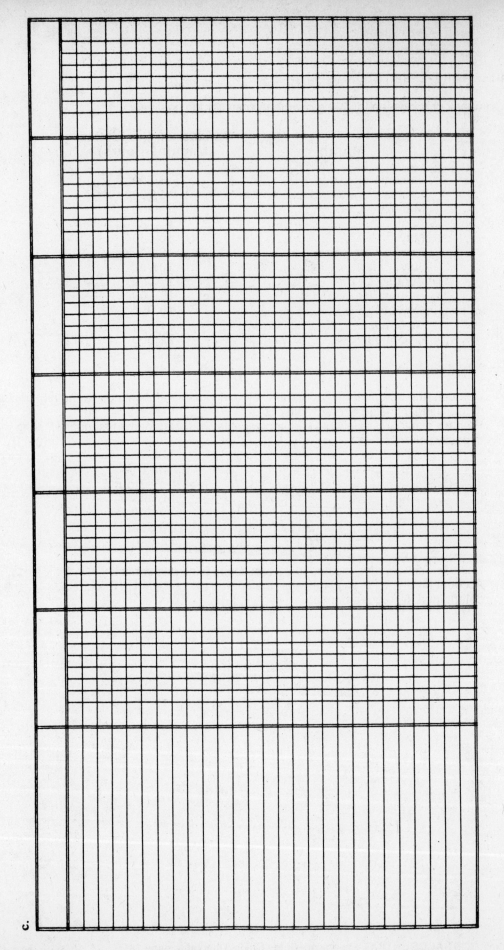

True-False Questions

Indicate whether the following statements are true or false by inserting in the blank space a capital "T" for true or "F" for false.

_____ 1. Fixed costs do not change in total with changes in the rate of output within a relevant range.

_____ 2. Straight-line depreciation is classified as a variable factory expense.

_____ 3. The unit cost of variable manufacturing overhead is the same for all volumes of production within the same relevant range.

_____ 4. Unit fixed costs vary inversely with the volume of production.

_____ 5. A semivariable expense is variable some months and is fixed in other months during the year.

_____ 6. Fixed, variable, and semivariable are the three behavior patterns.

_____ 7. According to the learning curve theory, the reduction in time will be greater for routine repetitive operations and the slope of the curve will be less than for complex operations requiring much technical skill.

_____ 8. Simple regression analysis, also known as least squares method, produces measures of probable error.

_____ 9. Learning curve theory can be more appropriately applied to jobs which are dissimilar and require creative efforts.

_____ 10. The learning rate is 90% for a project whose first lot of 4 units required 8,000 total labor hours and whose second lot of four more units required an additional 6,400 labor hours.

_____ 11. A linear relationship between two variables is assumed to exist if the plotted points of the two variables on the scattergraph follow a generally straight line.

_____ 12. The straight-line equation ($y = a + bx$) forms the basis for the least squares method with y representing the costs; a, the fixed component; b, the variable element, and x, the volume.

_____ 13. A trend line on a scattergraph should be fitted so that there is equal distance between the plotted points above and below the trend line.

_____ 14. Assuming a 70 percent learning curve, the predicted total hours to perform the task of producing 4 units would be 4.2 hours if it took 3 hours to make the first unit.

SOLUTIONS

Matching

1.	e	7.	a
2.	n	8.	g
3.	b	9.	l
4.	g	10.	f or i
5.	c	11.	d or k
6.	f or i	12.	j

Completion and Exercises

1. a. Direct material --- Variable costs
   b. Direct labor -- Variable in a labor-paced environment except for the effect of improvement curves. Also there is a fixed component because workers must be given notice by law before they are laid off. Thus, they are not completely variable even in a nonautomated environment.
   -- Somewhat fixed in a flexible, automated factory. The highly trained workers remaining after machines replace the wage-per-hour laborers receive a salary and this represents a fixed cost.
   c. Factory overhead -- Semivariable costs

2. a. Variable indirect factory overhead changes in proportion to changes in volume: such costs cannot be traceable to the segment or unit in question. Examples include unit of production depreciation on the factory-wide facilities and the segment being studied in a specific department, wages paid per hour to a repairer who is not assigned to a specific department, and hourly wages paid a factory-wide maintenance worker.
   b. Fixed indirect factory overhead remains unchanged over a given range of activity and cannot be traced to the segment or unit in question. Examples include salaries paid to supervisors, repairers, and maintenance workers who are not assigned to the segment being studied, but instead rotate their services throughout the plant.
   c. Semivariable indirect factory overhead contains both fixed and variable elements; these indirect costs cannot be traced to the segment being studied. Examples include electricity and water costs for an entire factory where each department does not have its own meter. Conditions in which a repairer or maintenance worker is employed regardless of the level of operations with additional repair and maintenance workers hired as volume increases also incur semivariable indirect factory overhead.
   d. Indirect labor is labor expended that does not affect the construction or the composition of the finished product. Examples include the cost of factory custodians and plant supervisors.
   e. Indirect materials are those materials needed for the completion of the product but whose consumption is either so small or so complex that their treatment as direct materials would not be feasible. Examples include factory repair and maintenance supplies, and nails and thread used to make the product.

3. Any of the following assumptions are made when relating total costs to output:
   a. The cost of securing each input must be a linear function of the quantity acquired.
   b. Each finished product contains the same amount of direct labor or direct material.
   c. All input acquired is fully utilized.
   d. Variations in the total cost level can be explained by variations in a single variable such as machine hours.

4. fixed; variable

5. Semivariable (mixed); same

6. High-low; scattergram; least squares (regression) analysis

7. $.50 represents *variable* ; $800 represents *total fixed*

8. A trend line can be fitted mathematically or visually. It should be fitted so that there is an equal distance between the plotted points above and below the trend line.

9. *Lisa, Inc.*

	Hours
$6,100	1,000
4,000	300
$2,100	÷ 700 = $3 variable rate

$6,100	total cost		or	$4,000	total costs
- 3,000	($3 x 1,000) variable			- 900	($3 x 300) variable
$3,100	fixed portion			$3,100	fixed portion

10. *Leggett, Inc.*

a.

	Total Number of Units Produced	Average Hours per Unit		Total Hours
19X1	1	2,200		2,200
19X1	2	1,980	(90% X 2,200)	3,960
19X2	4	1,782	(90% X 1,980)	7,128
19X3	8	1,603.8	(90% X 1,782)	12,830.4

Units 5 through 8 were built in 19X3. The hours required by these units should be:

12,830.4
-7,128.0
5,702.4 hours

The costs for these four units are expected to be:

Materials	4 X $6,000	$24,000.00
Labor	$10 x 5,702.4	57,024.00
Overhead	$2 x 5,702.4	11,404.80
Anticipated cost for 19X3		$92,428.80

b. Learning curve theory is applicable through 32 units as follows:

Total Number of Units Produced	Average Hours per Unit	Total Hours
1	2,200	2,200
2	1,980 (90% x 2,200)	3,960
4	1,782 (90% x 1,980)	7,128
8	1,603.8 (90% x 1,782)	12,830.4
16	1,443.42 (90% x 1,603.8)	23,094.72
32	1,299.078 (90% x 1,443.42)	41,570.496

The average time for all the units in the production run is 1,299.078. The hours represented in the deferred cost account would be:

16 x 1,443.42	23,094.72
16 x 1,299.078	20,785.25
Hours deferred	2,309.47

The deferred costs would be:

Labor ($10 x 2,309.47)	$23,094.70
Overhead ($2 x 2,309.47)	4,618.94
Total deferred cost at end of 19X4	$27,713.64

11. *Midtown Inc.*

Note to Instructor:

It is helpful to emphasize that direct material, direct labor, president and vice president's salaries, salespersons' salaries, and sales promotion are not factory overhead, and that direct labor often is semivariable (as in this situation) and may even be fixed.

Semivariable Overhead	*Highest Activity (350,000 hours)*	*Lowest Activity (300,000 hours)*
Factory supplies	$135,000	$130,000
Factory utilities	63,000	60,000
Plant maintenance	145,500	133,000
	$343,500	$323,000

$\dfrac{\$20,500 \text{ Difference in total overhead}}{50,000 \text{ Hours difference in volume}}$ = $.41 Variable overhead rate included in semivariable
for highest and lowest activity

$343,500	Total Semivariable overhead for 350,000 hours
143,500	Variable portion for 350,000 hours (350,000 hours X $.41)
$200,000	Fixed portion of semivariable

$.41	Variable overhead rate included in semivariable overhead
.22	Variable rate for indirect material ($77,000 ÷ 350,000 hours)
$.63	Total variable rate

$200,000	Fixed portion of semivariable overhead
80,000	Plant repair salaries
60,000	Rent on plant
$340,000	Total fixed overhead

Cost estimating formula: $.63X + $340,000

12. *Miller Manufacturers*

a.

Cumulative Units	Cumulative Average Worker Hours per Unit		Total Hours
1..................................	80		80.0
2..................................	56	(80 x 70%)	112.0
4..................................	39.2	(56 x 70%)	156.8

Hours for first four units	156.8
Hours for first unit..	80.0
Hours for three units	76.8

Bid Price		$2,500.00
Cost of Three Units:		
Material (3 x $240)...................................	$720.00	
Direct Labor (76.8 x $10).........................	768.00	
Overhead applied (76.8 x $2).	153.60	1,641.60
Estimated Income..		$ 858.40

b. Application of the learning curve theory would begin with making the first unit. Instead of subtracting out the 80 hours associated with making the first unit, the cost of the 80 hours must be included in the calculations. Note that in doubling production, cumulative units are used.

Doe Company

13.

a.

$35,000 - $26,000 = $9,000 = $.75 Variable overhead rate
22,000 - 10,000   12,000

$35,000 Total overhead costs
 16,500 Variable overhead costs ($.75 x 22,000)
$18,500 Fixed overhead costs
$.75 variable overhead rate and $18,500 fixed overhead cost

b.

	January		February		March	
Variable	$14,775	($.75 x 19,700)	$12,667.50	($.75 x 16,890)	$11,025	($.75 x 14,700)
Fixed	18,500		18,500.00		18,500	
	$33,275		$31,167.50		$29,525	

c.

Month	Column 1 Machine-Hours (x)	Column 2 Difference From Average of 15,872.5 Hours (X)	Column 3 Total Costs (y)	Column 4 Difference From Average of $30,718.3333 (Y)	Column 5 Column 2 Squared (X²)	Column 6 Column 2 x Column 4 XY
Jan.	18,500	+2,627.50	$ 32,070	$+1,351.6667	6,903,756	3,551,504
Feb.	16,100	+227.50	31,900	+1,181.6667	51,756	268,829
March	13,890	-1,982.50	29,850	- 868.3333	3,930,306	1,721,471
April	10,780	-5,092.50	27,500	-3,218.3333	25,933,556	16,389,362
May	10,000	-5,872.50	26,000	-4,718.3333	34,486,256	27,708,412
June	12,700	-3,172.50	28,600	-2,118.3333	10,064,756	6,720,412
July	13,900	-1,972.50	29,300	-1,418.3333	3,890,756	2,797,662
Aug.	15,000	-872.50	29,900	-818.3333	761,256	713,995
Sept.	17,100	+1,227.50	31,000	+281.6666	1,506,756	345,745
Oct.	19,000	+3,127.50	33,000	+2,281.6666	9,781,256	7,135,912
Nov.	21,500	+5,627.50	34,500	+3,781.6666	31,668,756	21,281,329
Dec.	22,000	+6,127.50	35,000	+4,281.6666	37,546,256	26,235,912
Total:	190,470	-0-	$368,620	-0-	166,525,422	114,870,545
Average	15,872.5		$30,718.3333			

13.

Doe Company (concluded)

Using the straight line equation the computation is:

$y = a + bx$

where $b = \dfrac{\Sigma XY}{\Sigma X2} = \dfrac{\$114,870,545}{166,525,422} = \$.68981$ variable rate

$\$30,718.3333 = a + (\$.68981 \times 15,872.50)$
$\$30,718.3333 = a + \$10,949.0092$
$\$30,718.3333 - \$10,949.0092 = a$
$a = \underline{\$19,769}$ (fixed overhead costs)

d. The least squares method is more exact, but it is time consuming to apply manually. A computer significantly reduces the time required to make the computations. The high-low method is easy to apply but lacks the sophistication found in the least squares method.

True-False

1. T

2. F   Straight-line depreciation is a fixed factory expense; units-of-production depreciation is, however, a variable expense.

3. T   However, total variable costs change with production volume directly.

4. T

5. F   A semivariable expense is comprised of both fixed and variable costs; this is why it is referred to also as a mixed cost. However, in any month, it is both fixed and variable, not fixed one month entirely and variable entirely in other months.

6. T

7. T

8. T

9. F   Learning curve theory can be more appropriately applied to repetitive jobs which are similar in nature.

10. T $$\frac{(8,000 + 6,400)/8}{8,000/4} = \frac{1,800 \text{ avg. hours}}{2,000 \text{ avg. hours}} = 90\%$$

11. T

12. T

13. T

14. F   It should take 5.88 hours to make 4 units assuming a 70 percent learning curve as follows:

Cumulative Quantity	Cumulative Average Worker-Hours per Week		Predicted Total Hours	
1	3.0		3.0	
2	2.1	(70% x 3.0 hours)	4.2	(2 x 2.1 hours)
4	1.47	(70% x 2.1 hours)	5.88	(4 x 1.47 hours)

4 Activity-Based Costing and Volume-Based Cost Assignments

Chapter Outline

Plant Capacity Concepts
    Comparison of Capacity Levels
Allocating Service Department Costs to Production (Operating) Departments
    Direct and Indirect Costs
    Allocating Indirect Costs versus Allocating Service Department Costs
    Direct Method
    Step Method
    Linear Algebra or Reciprocal Method
    Behavioral Aspects of Allocating Service Department Cost
    Multiple Rates versus a Single Plant-wide Rate
Applied and Actual Factory Overhead
    Allocating Actual Overhead to Producing Departments
    Spending and Volume Variances
    Disposition of Over- or Underapplied Overhead
Activity-Based Costing
    Volume-Related and Nonvolume-Related Cost Drivers
    Activities/Transactions as Cost Drivers
    Product Diversity and Volume Diversity
    Two-Stage Allocation Process Compared
    Activity-Based Management
ABC for Materials Acquisition and Handling
    Application of Materials Acquisition and Handling Costs Illustrated

Chapter Objectives

After studying this chapter, you should be able to:

1. Understand the concepts of traceability that distinguish direct costs from indirect costs.

2. Allocate service department overhead to producing departments to determine overhead application rates.

3. Prepare overhead variances for a normal costing system, recognizing they represent over- or underapplied overhead.

4. Assign costs using activity-based costing with volume- and nonvolume-related cost drivers.

5. Apply materials acquisition and handling costs.

6. Define and apply the new terms introduced.

Chapter Review

1. Overhead differs from material and labor because the total costs may not be known until the end of the cost accounting period; because of this, accountants apply overhead.

2. Overhead also varies considerably from one month to another such that if actual overhead was used to assign to inventory, the value assigned could fluctuate significantly.

3. To minimize fluctuations in overhead costs assigned to inventory and to provide timely product costing data, overhead costs can be estimated based on some attainable volume to arrive at a factory overhead application rate.

Plant Capacity Concepts

4. The first step in applying factory overhead is to choose the capacity concept to apply.

Idle Capacity versus Excess Capacity

5. There is a difference between idle capacity and excess capacity.

   a. Idle capacity is the temporary nonuse of facilities resulting from a decrease in demand for the company's services or products.
   b. Excess capacity refers to facilities that are not necessary; for example, management may have acquired plant facilities that are larger than are presently needed because this was the less expensive approach in the long-range.

6. The approach chosen depends upon whether a short- or long-run viewpoint is adopted and how much allowance management wants to make for possible volume interruptions.

7. Four capacity approaches are available; theoretical, practical, normal, and expected actual capacity.

Theoretical Capacity

8. Theoretical capacity assumes all personnel and equipment will operate at peak efficiency and that the company will use 100 percent of its plant capacity.

9. Theoretical capacity does not allow for unavoidable or normal interruptions and this makes it a questionable basis for determining cost allocation rates.

Practical Capacity

10. Practical capacity is more realistic than theoretical capacity since it allows for unavoidable delays due to holidays, vacations, and machine breakdowns.

    a. Practical capacity does not consider the idle time due to inadequate sales demand; it assumes that sales demand is high enough for the company's product to allow the plant to operate continuously at some hypothetical level determined by the engineering staff.
    b. Practical capacity offers the advantage of representing the level of activity at which a plant can operate realistically if it does not lack production orders.
    c. Anticipated losses due to weekends and holidays and unavoidable repairs are deducted from theoretical capacity to arrive at practical capacity.
    d. Practical capacity represents higher level of operations than does normal capacity.

Normal Capacity

11. Normal capacity includes considerations of both idle time due to limited sales and also due to human and equipment inefficiencies.

12. Normal capacity is generally less than practical capacity and reflects a long-range approach.

13. Normal capacity is determined by deducting hours lost because there are not enough production orders from practical capacity.

   a. Normal capacity represents an average sales demand which is expected to exist over a long enough period that peak demand and slack demand are leveled out.
   b. Normal capacity usually is the basis for long-range planning, standards, and the allocation of overhead costs.

Expected Actual Capacity

14. Expected actual capacity is the volume that is necessary to meet short-range sales demand.

   a. Expected actual capacity concept is a short-range approach that does not attempt to level out the highs and lows in volume.
   b. For a company experiencing seasonal or cyclical operations, expected actual capacity presents weaknesses as a basis for applying overhead if product costs strongly influence pricing policies and for government contracting.

Comparison of Capacity Levels

15. A company should estimate total fixed costs for a period after the capacity level is chosen which will serve as the budgeted volume.

   a. Normal or practical capacity is usually chosen as the basis for applying factory overhead.
   b. One level, called the denominator capacity, is chosen for recording purposes.

Effect on Unit Fixed Costs

16. The capacity concept chosen affects unit fixed costs; thus, the capacity chosen is a major decision that should be made by top management.

17. The feasibility of attaining a capacity level should be considered; otherwise if an unrealistic level is chosen, a large unfavorable volume variance will result that will have limited meaning and usefulness.

Allocating Service Department Costs to Production (Operating) Departments

18. After choosing whether to use theoretical, practical, normal, or expected actual capacity, accountants accumulate costs for production and service departments.

Production and Service Departments

19. Production departments are directly involved in processing materials into finished goods.

20. Service departments provide support to production departments and are only indirectly involved in manufacturing items.

21. Service departments' activities facilitate other departments' operations and contribute to their efficiency.

23. Often service departments perform specialized activities and their personnel and equipment are centralized for economy and control.

Direct and Indirect Costs

24. The distinction between direct and indirect costs depend on the attachability or traceability of the cost element.

25. Direct costs do not have to be allocated to the costing center because they arise within the department or job and can be clearly traced to the cost center.

26. Indirect costs are also referred to as common costs because they serve two or more costing centers.

27. The object of costing must first be defined before a cost can be classified as direct or indirect.

28. The plant supervisor's salary is an indirect cost for all service and production departments because it cannot be traced to any one department, but when the overall company becomes the costing object, the plant supervisor's salary is a direct cost of production.

Allocating Indirect Costs versus Allocating Service Department Costs

29. All service department costs must be allocated to production departments; the direct, step, or linear algebra methods are available for this allocation.

    a. Before proceeding with the allocation of service departments, the total costs of each service department must be determined.
    b. Total service department costs includes those direct costs which can be attached without allocation to the service department as well as those indirect costs which require an allocation such as plant insurance allocated on square footage.

Direct Method

30. Under the direct method of allocating service department costs, overhead of service departments is allocated to only production departments.

Step Method

31. Under the step method or step-down method, service department costs are allocated to other service departments and to production departments which have received their services.

Linear Algebra or Reciprocal Method

32. Under the linear algebra, reciprocal, or matrix method, simultaneous equations are used to take into account that service departments render reciprocal services.

Behavioral Aspects of Allocating Service Department Cost

33. Having service department rates available may cause cost center managers to refrain from using services even though needed.

    a. Cost center managers avoid service department expense by failing to take advantage of their services.
    b. To encourage the use of services by producing departments, management may not allocate service department cost to the user.
    c. Conversely if management expects excessive use of some service, service department charges should be known in advance and allocated to user departments.

Multiple Rates versus a Single Plantwide Rate

34. A consideration in selecting a plantwide rate or departmental rate is whether all departments use similar operating processes, direct labor, and machines.

    a. A single plantwide rate may be appropriate in a small plant with production moving through all departments.
    b. Multiple overhead rates are considered desirable when plants manufacture various products that do not go through the same departments or use the same technology.

1. Products are subject to different cost drivers, such as man-hours, machine hours, throughput, order size, value of material or quality requirements under these manufacturing circumstances.
2. Multiple rates should also be used if an organization has extensive machine-paced operations.

35. A factory should be broken down into various processes or production centers so that different overhead rates can be developed on the basis of the level of technology and the types of machines, services, and support used in each of these processes.

   a. Organizations that use only direct labor as the measure of activity assign the same average overhead rate to all direct labor.

      1. Under this method, a significant portion of overhead costs is allocated to wrong product units just because they use longer labor hours.
      2. Labor hours have very little impact on how overhead costs are driven up in the new technological environment.

36. Reliance on a single allocation basis often leads to miscosting and mispricing of products.

   a. Single cost allocations make a dangerous assumption that the costs are driven by a single variable.
   b. Use of a single rate usually does not yield product cost information useful for managerial decision making.

Applied and Actual Factory Overhead

37. A normal costing system applies overhead on actual cost drivers.

Allocating Actual Overhead to Producing Departments

38. Accountants debit actual overhead to each service and producing department's Factory Overhead Control account.

39. Accountants allocate actual indirect cost to each service and producing department on an appropriate basis such as square footage or kilowatt-hours.

Spending and Volume Variances

40. Variance analysis can be used in both cost systems employing standards as well as actual cost systems if overhead application rates are used.

41. Spending and volume variances which equal the over-or underapplied overhead can be computed in an actual cost system employing overhead application rates.

   a. The spending variance is also called the budget variance and is due to incurring higher or lower costs on overhead items than originally estimated.
   b. When actual overhead is less than budgeted overhead adjusted to actual capacity, the spending variance is favorable.
   c. Unfavorable spending variances result when actual overhead exceeds the budgeted overhead for the actual capacity attained.

42. The volume variance is called the idle capacity variance and is due to activity or volume factors.

   a. If actual production-hours exceed the planned or budgeted hours or units, the volume variance is favorable.
   b. If there are idle hours, less volume was used than planned and an unfavorable volume variance is the result.

43. The spending and volume variances may be established in ledger accounts or the over- or underapplied factory overhead may remain in Factory Overhead Control.

Disposition of Over- or Underapplied Overhead

44. The over- or underapplied overhead amount must be disposed of at the end of the accounting period; it may be remaining in Factory Overhead Control if spending and volume variances were not journalized. If these variances were entered in ledger accounts, the spending and volume variance accounts must be closed out. The following two alternatives are available for this disposition. The over- or underapplied overhead may be:

    a. Treated as a period cost and charged to Cost of Goods Sold or directly to Income Summary.
    b. Prorated to Work in Process, Finished Goods Inventory, and Cost of Goods Sold.

Activity-Based Costing

45. Volume-based or unit-based drivers are allocation measures based on product attributes, such as labor hours, machine hours, and materials cost.

Cost Drivers

46. After choosing whether to use theoretical, practical, normal, or expected actual capacity, the activity volume for this capacity level is expressed in such terms as machine-hours, direct-labor costs, or work cells.

    a. In choosing the activity basis, accountants should study the components of factory overhead.
    b. If many of the factory overhead costs are related to labor, the most accurate allocation basis is either direct labor-hours or direct labor-dollars.
    c. Machine-hours is often the cost driver in automated factories.

Activities/Transactions as Cost Drivers

47. Traditionally, cost accountants have used only volume-related allocation bases (e.g., labor hours, machine hours, and material dollars) to allocate overhead from cost pools to products.

    a. Under this approach, costs are assumed to vary only with the changes in the volume of production.
    b. This assumption is correct for such volume-related activities as production supplies and parts.

48. Many costs in the plants are non-volume related costs and do not vary with the volume of production but with transactions.

    a. Non-volume-related costs vary with transactions such as the number of inspections performed, the number of setups, and the quantity of scheduling.
    b. Allocating a non-volume-related cost requires the selection of an allocation base that is itself non-volume-related.

49. The overriding principle is to allocate overhead costs to products and other objects based on the causes of costs or the benefits received rather than some arbitrary basis.

50. Activity-based costing (ABC) recognizes that performance of activities triggers the consumption of resources that are recorded as costs. Transaction-based costing is another name for ABC.

    a. Activity is a process or procedure that causes work. ABC traces costs to the activities identified.
    b. Companies engage in batch-level activities and product-level activities.
    c. If costs add value to the product, those costs should be accumulated at the work cell level and distributed to products according to the cell time a product takes within each cell.

1. Inventory velocity (how fast the inventory moves through the cell) is appropriately used as the basis for assigning overhead to products in this situation.

2. Whatever base is chosen, the data should be broken down by departments or jobs.

Product Diversity and Volume Diversity

51. Product diversity occurs when products consume activities and inputs in different proportions.

52. Volume diversity or batch-size diversity occurs when there is a difference in the number of units manufactured by product lines.

53. Products having materials that take longer to machine may consume a disproportionate share of unit-level inputs; this is called material diversity.

Two-Stage Allocation Process Compared

54. Both traditional and activity-based costing use a two-stage allocation process.

55. Accountants express the volume for the capacity level selected (i.e., theoretical, practical, normal, or expected actual capacity) in either volume-related (i.e., machine-hours, direct labor costs) or nonvolume-related cost drivers (i.e., setups or work cells).

   a. In the first stage, we assign costs to cost centers either through direct charges or some appropriate allocation basis such as floor space for rent.
   b. In the second stage of a traditional volume-based system, we allocate costs to products using machine-hours or other bases that vary directly with the volume of products manufactured. In the second stage of an ABC system, we trace costs from activities to products based on the product's demand for these activities.

Activity-Based Management

56. Activity-based costing yields much information about activities and the resources required to perform these activities. Thus, ABC is much more than a cost assignment process.

57. ABC supplies the information and activity-based management (ABM) uses this information in various analyses designed to result in ongoing improvement.

ABC for Materials Acquisition and Handling

58. Application rates can be developed for material acquisition and handling.

   a. If extra handling costs are incurred because of the nature of the order, application rates are appropriate and worth the extra effort involved.
   b. The application rate for material handling can be developed using the following formula:

$$\frac{\text{Estimated cost such as purchasing, receiving, warehousing}}{\begin{array}{c}\text{Estimated basis for applying overhead such as square feet}\\ \text{or dollar value of purchases received}\end{array}}$$

   c. Similar treatment is used for applying material handling costs that is used for factory overhead. The control account appears below: (Receiving Department Expense Control is illustrated.)

Receiving Department Expense Control	
Actual expenses	Applied expenses based on dollar value of purchases received or some other appropriate basis.

Demonstration Problem

Determining Application Rates Using Linear Algebra (Reciprocal)

The controller for Keaton Company estimates that direct and indirect departmental factory overhead will be as follows for its two producing departments and three service departments:

Cafeteria	$ 25,000
Storeroom	42,000
Factory Repair	58,000
Fabricating	250,000
Finishing	310,000

The controller also provides the following tabulation of the interdependence of departments:

	Services provided to				
Department rendering service	Cafeteria	Storeroom	Factory Repair	Fabricating	Finishing
Cafeteria	---	10%	5%	55%	30%
Storeroom	10%	---	20	40	30
Factory Repair	---	---	---	60	40

Required:

a. Determine the total estimated overhead for each of the three service departments after reciprocal transfer costs have been calculated algebraically.
b. Determine the total overhead of each producing department.
c. Determine factory overhead rates for the production departments assuming that budgeted labor dollars are $108,427 for Fabricating and machine-hours for Finishing are 79,930.

a.

b.

Solution to Demonstration Problem

Keaton Company

a. Cafeteria total overhead: $C = \$25{,}000 + .10S$
    Storeroom total overhead: $S = \$42{,}000 + .10C$
    Factory repair total overhead: $R = \$58{,}000 + .05C + .20S$

Substituting Equation S into Equation C:

$$C = \$25{,}000 + .10\,(\$42{,}000 + .10C)$$
$$C = \$25{,}000 + \$4{,}200 + .01C$$
$$.99C = \$29{,}200$$
$$\underline{C = \$29{,}495}$$

Substituting Equation C into Equation S:

$$S = \$42{,}000 + .10\,(\$29{,}495)$$
$$S = \$42{,}000 + \$2{,}950$$
$$S = \underline{\$44{,}950}$$

Substituting Equation C and S into Equation R:
$$R = \$58{,}000 + .05\,(\$29{,}495) + .20\,(\$44{,}950)$$
$$R = \$58{,}000 + \$1{,}475 + \$8{,}990$$
$$R = \underline{\$68{,}465}$$

b.

	Cafeteria	Storeroom	Factory Repair	Fabricating	Finishing
Direct and Indirect Departmental Expense	$25,000	$42,000	$58,000	$250,000	$310,000
Distribution of Cafeteria Department	(29,495)	2,950	1,475	16,222	8,848
Distribution of Storeroom Department	4,495	(44,950)	8,990	17,980	13,485
Distribution of Factory Repair			(68,465)	41,079	27,386
Total	-0-	-0-	-0-	$325,281	$359,719

c. Factory Overhead Application Rates

	Fabricating	Finishing
	300% DL$ ($325,281/ $108,427)	$4.50 per hour ($359,719/ 79,930 hours)

Matching

Referring to the terms listed in the left column, place the appropriate letter next to the corresponding description. A term may not be used or may be used more than once.

a. Application rates

b. Direct labor-hours

c. Direct method

d. Expected actual capacity

e. Linear algebra method

f. Machine-hours

g. Materials cost

h. Normal capacity

i. Production department

j. Service department

k. Step or sequential method

l. Theoretical capacity

_____ 1. This capacity concept considers idle time due to both limited sales order and human and equipment inefficiencies.

_____ 2. Administrative support departments in non-profit organization are of this type.

_____ 3. Department for which overhead rates are established so that products can be costed as they travel through operations.

_____ 4. This capacity concept assumes all personnel and equipment will operate at peak efficiency and that 100 percent of plant capacity will be used.

_____ 5. This activity volume is an appropriate basis for applying overhead if the same amount of material is applied per hour.

_____ 6. An appropriate basis for applying factory overhead if the plant operations are highly automated.

_____ 7. This method of allocation recognized that service departments render reciprocal services.

_____ 8. Service department costs are allocated to other service departments and to production departments under this method, but without the use of simultaneous equations.

_____ 9. This allocation method uses simultaneous equations to recognize the interaction of service departments with each other.

_____ 10. Overhead and other service department costs are allocated only to production departments when this method is used.

_____ 11. A department which is directly involved in processing materials into finished goods.

_____ 12. Another name for ancillary departments.

_____ 13. A short-range approach to capacity which does not even out the cyclical changes in sales demand.

_____ 14. Can be developed for purchasing and receiving of materials when certain types of material require extra handling.

Completion and Exercises

1. A _____ department is directly involved in processing raw material into finished products or in rendering service to patients or clients. Examples of this type of department include (a) _____, (b) _____,

    (c)_____and (d) _____.

2. The cost associated when facilities are shared by many revenue-producing activities is referred to as _____ costs.

3. _____ capacity and _____

    _____ capacity represent the two extremes of volume for applying factory overhead.

4. _____ capacity and

    _____ capacity are the two most common bases for applying factory overhead.

5. List four bases which are appropriate for expressing capacity level to be used in applying factory overhead.

    a._____

    b._____

    c._____

    d._____

6. The three methods available for allocating service department costs to production departments are

    _____ , _____ , and _____ _____ .

    Of these three methods, the _____ _____ method has the

    strongest theoretical basis while the _____ method has the weakest theoretical basis.

7. Over- or underapplied overhead can be analyzed by breaking this amount down into _____ and _____ variances.

8. A(n) _____ (favorable or unfavorable) _____ variance results when actual overhead is less than budgeted overhead adjusted to actual capacity achieved.

9. A(n) _____ (favorable or unfavorable) _____ variance results when less volume was used than planned.

10. A _____ department usually engages in specialized activities requiring unique skills and equipment. Examples of this type of department include

    (a)_____, (b) _____, (c) _____ and

    (d) _____.

11. Nut Company budgeted overhead for the mixing department at $825,000 for the period based on a budgeted volume of 500,000 machine-hours. At the end of the period the factory overhead control account for the Mixing Department had total debits of $843,750; actual machine-hours were

510,000. The overapplied (underapplied) overhead for the period was _____ .

12. **Comparison of Allocations using Traditional and ABC Costing Methods**

Strength Company provides the following information concerning its two product lines.

	Product A	Product B
Number of units produced	250	250
Number of production runs scheduled	22	4
Machine hours per unit	3	5

Total budgeted production scheduling cost - $13,000

Required:

a. How much production scheduling cost is allocated each to Product A and B lines if Strength Co. uses activity-based costing, how much machine setup-related cost is allocated to each Product A and B lines? What is the cost per unit for Product A and B?

b. If instead, Strength Co. uses a traditional cost allocation system based on machine hours? What is the production scheduling cost per unit for Product A and B?

c. Is overhead allocation to Product A and B lines evidence of product diversity or volume diversity?

a.

b.

c. _____

Journal Entries to Record Spending and Volume Variances

13. Hutson Manufacturing Company provides you with the following data concerning their operations for the year ended December 31, 19-.

Predetermined variable overhead rate per machine-hour	$3.00	
Predetermined total overhead rate per machine-hour	$5.10	
Budgeted capacity	20,000	machine-hours
Actual capacity during year	19,650	machine-hours
Actual factory overhead costs	$99,700	

Required:

a. Compute the amount of overhead applied during the year and prepare a summary journal entry to record this.
b. Determine the amount of over- or underapplied overhead.
c. Compute the factory overhead spending and volume variance.
d. Prepare the journal entries required to record the variances and to close the Factory Overhead Control account; close variances to the Cost of Goods Sold account.

13. Paper for working

14. From an analysis of the records of Hicks Production Company, the following data is determined:

Budgeted machine-hours......................................	800,000
Budgeted fixed factory overhead cost......................	$280,000
Budgeted variable factory overhead cost.................	$400,000
Actual machine-hours...	750,000
Actual fixed factory overhead costs.........................	$283,000
Actual variable factory overhead costs.....................	$390,000

a. The total estimated factory overhead rate is $_____ per hour.

b. The applied factory overhead cost is $_____.

c. The amount of under-or overapplied (circle one) factory overhead cost is

   $_____.

d. The spending and volume variances are: (indicate whether favorable or unfavorable).

15. Factory overhead for the Douglass Company has been estimated as follows:

	Unit Cost per Machine-hour	Total Cost
Variable factory overhead...........	$3	$36,000
Fixed factory overhead..............	4	48,000

Production for the month reached 90 percent of the budget, and actual factory overhead totaled $76,100.

Required:

a. The over- or underapplied factory overhead is _____ Over-

   Underapplied (circle one).

b. Calculate the spending and volume variances.

16. Step and Direct Allocation Methods

Carrol Company's annual budget is presented below for its three service departments (buildings, administration, and maintenance) and its two production departments (machining and assembly). The buildings department is responsible for providing heat and lighting for all departments. Administration includes factory scheduling, storage, and all accounting functions. The annual budgets of the direct charges and the budgeted operating data for the departments follow:

	Building	Adminis- tration	Mainte- nance	Machining	Assembly	Total
Indirect labor	$500	$ 800	$200	$1,600	$1,900	$5,000
Indirect materials.....	50	80	90	150	200	570
Depreciation	125	60	50	180	160	575
Insurance...............	80	70	90	125	80	445
Miscellaneous........	20	30	10	20	30	110
	$775	$1,040	$440	$2,075	$2,370	$6,700
Floor Space (square feet)......	200	500	250	600	200	1,750
Number of employees	20	30	0	200	210	480
Service-hours	10	20	15	75	50	170

Required:

a. Prepare a cost distribution sheet allocating service department costs in the following sequence and on the following basis: (1) buildings---floor space; (2) administration---number of employees; and (3) maintenance---service hours. Calculate factory overhead allocation rates under the step method using 1,675 estimated machine-hours for the machining department and 670 estimated direct labor-hours for the assembly department.

b. Compute an overhead allocation rate per service unit using the direct method in which no service department is charged for services provided by other service departments. Calculate factory overhead allocation rates using the same direct labor-hours and machine-hours estimated for the step method.

17. Journal Entries Recording Applied and Actual Material Costs

Diamond Company uses the following estimates for applying material acquisition costs:

Annual estimated Purchasing Department costs................	$ 45,000,000
Annual estimated Inspection Department costs	$ 28,125,000
Annual estimated Receiving Department costs.................	$ 2,500,000
Annual estimated direct materials purchases	$562,500,000
Estimated number of items to be received.........................	500,000

Required:

a.   Develop application rates for the material handling costs applying Purchasing and Inspection Department costs on the basis of the dollar value of materials purchased and Receiving Department costs on the basis of items received. Freight on incoming material is available for each invoice.

b.   Prepare the journal entry(s) to record the actual cost of a purchase including the application of material acquisition costs if 600 items are bought on account at a cost of $67,500 with freight of $1,280.

c.   Using the following actual data for the period, which has been recorded, prepare journal entries to close the balances of the material acquisition ledger accounts to Cost of Goods Sold.

Direct materials purchases	
(includes $67,500 purchased in Requirement *b*)	$560,000,000
Purchasing department cost	$ 44,850,000
Inspection department cost	$ 28,010,000
Receiving department cost	$ 2,400,100
Number of items received	487,500

Date		Description	Post Ref.	Debit	Credit	

18. Responsibility for Costs of Idle Capacity

Management of Horn Corporation decides to expand its current operation by purchasing a new automated machine because the current machinery in their production plant is operating at almost full capacity and parts of orders received need to be sub-contracted out. If all of the manufacturing is performed in its own plants, management believes that it can achieve a better quality product than in the past. Based on its estimation, the new machine will be used at 70 percent capacity during the peak season and 40 percent capacity during the remaining months. As demand grows for Horn's products, management believes all machines will be used at full capacity. This capacity level is expected to be achieved within five years.

Cost of the new machine differs considerably from old machinery because it is several times greater than the cost when the old machines were purchased. Since the old plant was built at a much lower cost and a substantial portion of the equipment is fully depreciated, the cost per unit processed is much lower on the old machines. Because of these conditions, when full capacity is not required on all machines, old machines are used to capacity with the new machine absorbing any excess.

The company is decentralized with a superintendent responsible for each machine. Rather than apply factory overhead, actual factory overhead costing rates are determined by dividing actual costs for each factory by the units processed. Superintendents are responsible for the volume variances on their new machines.

Management set budgeted costs on the basis that the new machine will be operated at 50% capacity. All relevant costs related to the new machine are not included in its overhead.

Horn Corporation's cost accountants developed a new budgeted costs for products manufactured on the new machine.

Required:

a. Evaluate any potential problem and make suggestions for improving the situation.
b. What effect (if any) would the above assumption for the new machine have on the product cost?
c. What impact do you think improved quality should have on the company's use of machinery?

True-False Questions

Indicate whether the following statements are true or false by inserting in the blank space a capital "T" for true or "F" for false.

_____ 1. When actual service department cost is allocated to production departments, cost inefficiencies of the service department are passed on to user departments.

_____ 2. The costs of idle capacity result more from fixed costs behavior rather than from variable cost influences.

_____ 3. Practical capacity represents the level of activity at which a plant can operate realistically if it does not lack production orders.

_____ 4. Overhead rates based on expected actual capacity represent an attempt to apply fixed overhead by using a long-run average expected activity.

_____ 5. The direct method of allocating service departments is generally preferred over the step method.

_____ 6. After the costs of service departments are allocated using such techniques as the linear algebra method, the next step is distributing the indirect costs to each department using such basis as square footage for indirect costs such as insurance and rent.

_____ 7. Few companies would ever use the theoretical capacity as a basis for developing overhead application rates because this basis is not practical.

_____ 8. If an unrealistically high level of capacity is chosen as a basis for applying overhead, a favorable volume variance will likely result.

_____ 9. Assume Service Department A's share of direct and indirect costs totals $10,000 and it receives 8% of Service Department B's services. If Service Department A renders 20% of its services to B and B's share of direct and indirect costs totals $18,000, using the linear algebra method the following formula represents Service Department A's costs:

Service Department A = $10,000 X .08 ($18,000 + .20B)

_____ 10. Difference in labor rate per hour will be ignored if factory overhead is applied on the direct labor dollar basis.

_____ 11. Accountants should use the term service department when referring to a mixing department which is processing materials into finished goods.

_____ 12. Such departments as cost accounting, repairs and maintenance, and factory personnel are typical service departments in a manufacturing company.

SOLUTIONS

Matching

1.	h	6.	f	11.	i
2.	j	7.	e	12.	j
3.	i	8.	k	13.	d
4.	l	9.	e	14.	a
5.	g	10.	c		

Completion and Exercises

1. production: Examples of production departments include: (a) mixing; (b) spinning; (c) finishing; (d) fabricating; (e) surgery in hospitals; (f) assembly.

2. (indirect or common)

3. Theoretical; expected actual

4. Practical; normal

5. The following are bases on which the capacity level may be expressed:
   a. units of production
   b. direct labor dollars or cost
   c. direct labor-hours.
   d. machine-hours
   e. materials cost

6. direct; step; linear algebra.
   linear algebra; direct

7. spending; volume

8. favorable spending

9. unfavorable volume

10. service; Examples of service departments include: (a) repairs and maintenance; (b) accounting; (c) engineering; (d) patient accounting in a hospital; (e) pharmacy in a hospital; (f) purchasing; (g) payroll.

11.

$$\frac{\$825,000 \text{ budgeted overhead}}{500,000 \text{ budgeted machine hours}} = \$1.65 \text{ overhead}$$

$843,750	Actual overhead	
- 841,500	Applied overhead ($1.65 X 510,000 actual hours)	
$ 2,250	Underapplied overhead	

12. *Strength Company*

a. If ABC is used, costs are traced consistent to each product's characteristics which in turn drive production scheduling cost:

$$\frac{\$13,000 \text{ budgeted production scheduling cost}}{26 \text{ production runs}} = \$500 \text{ application rate per production run}$$

	Product A	**Product B**
Total production scheduling cost applied to each product line.....	$11,000	$2,000
	($500 X 22 prod. runs)	($500 X 4 prod. runs)
Production scheduling cost per product unit......................	$44	$8
	($11,000 ÷ 250 units)	($2,000 ÷ 250 units)

b. Total machine hours are budgeted as follows: (3 X 250 Product A units) + (5 X 250 Product B units) = 2,000 machine hours. This yields the following application rate:

$$\frac{\$13,000 \text{ budgeted production scheduling cost}}{2,000 \text{ budgeted machine hours}} = \$6.50 \text{ application rate per machine hour}$$

	Product A	**Product B**
Total production scheduling cost applied to each product line	$4,875	$8,125
	($6.50 X 750 hrs.)	($6.50 X 1,250 hrs.)
Production scheduling cost per product unit...................	$19.50	$32.50
	($4,875 ÷ 250 units)	($8,125 ÷ 250 units)

c. Product diversity for Products A and B

13. *Hutson Manufacturing Company*

a. 19,650 hours x $5.10 = $100,215 overhead applied

Work in Process Inventory.. 100,215
    Factory Overhead Control...   100,215

b. $ 99,700   Actual Factory Overhead
        100,215   Applied Factory Overhead
     $ 515   Overapplied Factory Overhead

c. $5.10   Total Overhead Rate
      3.00   Variable Overhead Rate
     $2.10   Fixed Overhead Rate

$2.10 x 20,000 hrs. = $42,000 Budgeted Fixed Overhead

Total Factory Overhead Spending Variance:
     Actual Factory Overhead................................. $ 99,700
     Budget Based on Actual Capacity:
         Budgeted fixed overhead........................... $42,000
         Variable ($3.00 x 19,650 hours)   58,950   100,950
             actual capacity $ 1,250   favorable

Factory Overhead Volume Variance:
(20,000 Budgeted hours - 19,650 Actual hours) x $2.10 = $735 unfavorable

d. Factory Overhead Volume Variance......................... 735
     Factory Overhead Control...................................... 515
         Total Factory Overhead Spending Variance   1,250

Total Factory Overhead Spending Variance 1,250
         Factory Overhead Volume Variance...................   735
         Cost of Goods Sold   515

14. *Hicks Production Company*

a.

$$\frac{\$400,000 \ + \ \$280,000 \ = \$680,000}{800,000 \ \text{hours}} = \$.85 \ \text{per hour}$$

b. $.85 x 750,000 = $637,500 applied overhead

c. $673,000   Actual overhead ($390,000 + $283,000)
  637,500   Applied overhead
$ 35,500   Underapplied overhead

d. *Spending Variance*
$673,000   Actual Factory Overhead
 655,000   [($.50 variable overhead rate x 750,000) + $280,000]
$ 18,000   Unfavorable

Volume Variance

(800,000 budgeted hours - 750,000 actual hours) x $.35 = $17,500 Unfavorable

Proof: $17,500 + $18,000 = $35,500 underapplied overhead

15. *Douglass Company*

$$\frac{\$48,000 \ \text{fixed overhead}}{\$4 \ \text{unit fixed overhead}} = 12,000 \ \text{budgeted hours}$$

a. Actual factory overhead $76,100
  Applied factory overhead
    90% x $84,000 total budgeted overhead   75,600
  Underapplied factory overhead .... $ 500

b. *Spending Variance*
  Actual factory overhead $76,100
  Budget allowance:
    Budgeted fixed overhead... $48,000
    Variable factory overhead
    (90% x 12,000 hours x $3)......................................   32,400   80,400
  Favorable spending variance... $ 4,300

  Volume Variance
  (12,000 budgeted hours - 10,800 actual hours) X $4 fixed rate = $4,800
  unfavorable or
  Applied factory overhead... $75,600
  Budget allowance...   80,400
  Unfavorable volume variance... $ 4,800

16.

Carrol Company

a.

| | *Service Departments* | | | *Producing Departments* | | |
Overhead Costs:	Building	Administration	Maintenance	Machining	Assembly	Total
Indirect labor	$500	$ 800	$200	$1,600	$1,900	$5,000
Indirect materials	50	80	90	150	200	570
Depreciation	125	60	50	180	160	575
Insurance	80	70	90	125	80	445
Miscellaneous	20	30	10	20	30	110
Total Departmental Costs	$775	$1,040	$440	$2,075	$2,370	$6,700
$775/1,550 fl. sp. = $.50	(775)	250	125	300	100	
	-0-	1,290				
$1,290/430 emp. = $3		(1,290)	60	600	630	
		-0-	625			
$ 625/125 Hrs. = $5			(625)	375	250	
			-0-	$3,350	$3,350	$6,700

Rates:

Machining--Based on the machine-hours $\frac{\$3,350}{1,675 \text{ hrs.}}$ = $2 per machine hour

Assembly--Based on direct labor-hours $\frac{\$3,350}{670 \text{ hrs.}}$ = $5 per direct labor hour

b. **Carrol Company (concluded)**

Building

$$\frac{\$775}{800 \text{ sq. feet}} = \$.96875 \text{ per square foot}$$

Administration

$$\frac{\$1,040}{410 \text{ employees}} = \$2.5366 \text{ per employee}$$

Maintenance

$$\frac{\$440}{125 \text{ service hours}} = \$3.52 \text{ per service hour}$$

	Building	Administration	Maintenance	Machining	Assembly	Total
Total Departmental Cost from above	$775.00	$1,040.00	$440.00	$2,075.00	$2,370.00	$6,700.00
	(775.00)			581.25	193.75	
	-0-	(1,040.00)		507.32	532.68	
		-0-	(440.00)	264.00	176.00	
Total			-0-	$3,427.57	$3,272.43	$6,700.00

Rates:

Machining--Based on the machine-hours $\frac{\$3,427.57}{1,675 \text{ hrs.}} = \$2.0463$ per machine hour

Assembly--Based on direct labor-hours $\frac{\$3,272.43}{670 \text{ hrs.}} = \$4.8842$ per direct labor hour

17.

Diamond Company

a.

Purchasing Department: $\dfrac{\$45,000,000}{\$562,500,000}$ = 8% Rate per Purchase Dollar for Purchasing Department

Inspection Department: $\dfrac{\$28,125,000}{\$562,500,000}$ = 5% Rate per Purchase Dollar for Inspection Department

Receiving Department: $\dfrac{\$2,500,000}{500,000 \text{ items}}$ = $5 Rate per Item Received for Receiving Department

b. Direct Materials Inventory 67,500
    Freight-In 1,280
        Accounts Payable..   68,780

    Direct Materials Inventory 11,775
        Purchasing Department Expense Control (8% x $67,500)   5,400
        Inspection Department Expense Control (5% X $67,500)   3,375
        Receiving Department Expense Control ($5 x 600)   3,000

c. Cost of Goods Sold 22,600
    Receiving Department Expense Control [$2,437,500* - $2,400,100)................37,400
        Purchasing Department Expense Control [$44,850,000 - $44,800,000**)...   50,000
        Inspection Department Expense Control [$28,010,000 - $28,000,000***)....   10,000

_____

   *Applied Receiving Department cost = $5 x 487,500 = $2,437,500
  **Applied Purchasing Department cost = 8% x $560,000,000 = $44,800,000
 ***Applied Inspection Department cost = 5% x $560,000,000 = $28,000,000

18. *Horn Corporation*

a. If the estimation of future production is correct, misleading volume variance for individual machines will result. As company volume drops, old machinery is run at capacity allowing the new machine to suffer all reductions in volume. The result is that the cost per unit increases on the new machine as volume decreases because all fixed costs of operation are absorbed by fewer units of output. Thus, performance of the new machine shows up less favorably than the old machines when operations are below capacity. In addition, the 50 percent capacity assumption will suggest a favorable volume variance during the peak season and an unfavorable variance for the remaining year. Then the volume variance will not provide any valuable information to the management because of the fallacious assumption.

Since it appears that the full capacity of the new machine is not needed now, even in peak seasons, Horn managers should study the feasibility of expanding product lines or increasing demand.

Superintendents should not be held accountable for volume variances over which they have no control. Superintendents appear not to have the authority to determine which machine produces units. A responsibility accounting system should be installed in which each superintendent is held accountable for controllable costs.

Management should consider adopting a standard cost system using variable costing to illustrate clearly each machine's performance in relation to its controllable costs.

b. If actual rates are continued, overhead should be broken down into its variable and fixed components. Each machine should bear all of its variable costs and its fixed costs in proportion to the amount of capacity used. The remaining fixed costs of the new machines would be split among all machines based on the quantity of units produced by each. This would relieve the superintendent of the new machine of part of his/her volume variance.

The cost of the idle space and equipment would be reflected in increased overhead cost which would increase the cost of the products manufactured. By computing idle capacity cost as part of overhead, cost per unit would come closer to the average cost per unit for the company as a whole.

If idle capacity is reduced, the cost per product would be decreased since the fixed cost would be spread over more units.

c. The choice of machinery should be considered in relation to the cruciality of the quality problem. If much consumer goodwill is being lost due to poor product quality, returns, and defects, then it may be less expensive overall to manufacture on the newer machine.

True-False

1. T   In addition, the service department rate is not known in advance and is not subject to control by the requesting department. A better approach is to allocate budgeted costs rather than actual costs.

2. T

3. T

4. F   It is normal capacity that represents an attempt to level out the highs and lows in capacity and represents a long-run average expected activity.

5. F   Normally the step method is preferable to the direct method because it takes into account the benefits rendered by one service department to other service departments.

6. F   The procedures described are in reverse as the indirect costs must first be allocated and added with each service department's direct costs before the service departments' costs are distributed to producing departments.

7. T

8. F   Instead, an unfavorable volume variance would be expected under these circumstances.

9. F   The formula should read A = $10,000 + .08 ($18,000 + .20A)

10. F   Difference in labor rate is recognized when direct labor dollars are used as a basis because cost centers using higher paid workers will be allocated more factory overhead.

11. F   A department engaged in processing materials into finished goods can only be correctly referred to as a production department. A service department provides support to production departments.

12. T

5 JOB ORDER COSTING

Chapter Outline

Job Order, Process, and Operation Costing
    Job Order Costing
    Process Costing
    Operation Costing
Accounting for Materials in Job Order Systems
    Material Requisitions and Issues
Labor Accounting
    Timekeeping Records
Factory Overhead Application
Job Order Sheet
Basic Journal Entries in Job Order Costing
    Subsidiary Factory Ledgers
Appendix: Reciprocal Accounts

Chapter Objectives

After studying this chapter, you should be able to:

1. Identify the manufacturing characteristics that help determine whether a job order, process, or operation costing assignment is most appropriate.

2. Understand the source documents for the job order cost sheet which accountants use to determine product costs.

3. Prepare basic journal entries associated with job order cost accounting systems.

4. Use reciprocal factory and home office ledger accounts.

5. Define and apply the new terms introduced.

Chapter Review

Job Order, Process, and Operation Costing

1. After costs are accumulated by departments, they are assigned to products or orders through either job order costing, process costing, or operation costing.

    a. Job order and process costing are the two polar extremes.
    b. Operation costing represents a hybrid-costing system.
    c. The nature of manufacturing activities determines which cost application system is used.

Job Order Costing

2. Under a job order costing system, costs are assigned to and accumulated for each job which may be an order, a contract, or a unit of production.

    a. Job order costing should be used if the service or production is being performed to customer specification or if a company makes different components for inventory.
    b. The direct material and direct labor associated with each job are identified and accumulated and overhead will be applied on some rational basis.

Process Costing

3. Under process costing, costs are accumulated for each department for a time period and allocated among all the products manufactured during that period.

Operation Costing

4. An operation costing system is used in the manufacture of goods that have some common characteristics plus some individual characteristics.

    a. An operation is a routine production method, techniques, or step which is repetitively performed.
    b. Distinctions are made between batches of product.
    c. Direct materials are specifically allocated to the batches.
    d. Direct labor and overhead are absorbed in the same manner as under process costing.
    e. Operation costing best meets the needs of a batch manufacturer whose products have variations of a single design and require a varying sequence of standardized operations.

Accounting for Materials in Job Order Systems

5. A key internal control procedure is having a material requisition form which informs the cost accounting department that material has been issued to a specific department.

Material Requisitions and Issues

6. Material requisition form is a basic source document which informs the cost accounting department that material has been issued.

    a. The entry to record the issuance of direct material is:
    Work in Process Inventory--Job No. XXX...................................... $XXX
       Direct Materials Inventory.. $XXX
    b. No material should be issued from the storeroom if a material requisition is not processed.

7. Material credit slips are issued when a department returns material to the storeroom.

    a. The entry is the reverse of the entry to record the issuance of material. It is:

    Direct Materials Inventory.. $XXX
       Work in Process Inventory- -Job No. XXX.............................. $XXX
    b. Material credit slips can also be used to correct errors in material issuance.

Labor Accounting

8. Companies use a variety of labor systems to best meet their needs.

   a. Wages designates hourly or piece rate payments which represents a variable cost.
   b. Salaries describe a fixed periodic payment, such as a weekly or monthly payment.

9. Payroll taxes, bonuses, holiday and vacation pay are among the many labor-related costs.

Timekeeping Records

10. Well-documented time records are important for employees morale; in addition, management is interested in not overpaying employees.

    a. A clock card or time card provides evidence of when the employee was on the work site.
    b. A job time ticket shows the time each employee spent on individual jobs during the day.
    c. Daily job time tickets eliminate having more than one ticket per employee each day.

Factory Overhead Application

11. The source documents for some factory overhead are generated internally while other factory overhead arise from external source documents.

Job Order Sheet

12. Job order sheets indicate the amount of direct material, direct labor, and factory overhead applied to each job.

Basic Journal Entries in Job Order Costing

13. The following outline in debit and credit format shows the general ledger accounts used in a typical job order costing system.

    a. *Direct and indirect materials purchased on account:*

    Direct Materials Inventory
    Factory Supplies Inventory (for indirect materials)
       Accounts Payable

    b. *Direct and indirect materials issued:*

    Work in Process Inventory (for direct material)
    Factory Overhead Control-Indirect Material
       Direct Materials Inventory
       Factory Supplies Inventory

    c. *Factory labor incurred:*

    Work in Process Inventory (for direct labor)
    Factory Overhead Control-Indirect labor
       Payroll Payable

    d. *Marketing and administrative salaries:*

    Marketing Expense Control-Salaries
    Administrative Expense Control-Salaries
       Payroll Payable

    e. *Factory depreciation:*

    Factory Overhead Control-Depreciation Expense
       Accumulated Depreciation

f.   *Marketing and administrative depreciation:*

Marketing Expense Control-Depreciation Expense
Administrative Expense Control-Depreciation Expense
   Accumulated Depreciation

g.   *Factory insurance:*

Factory Overhead Control-Insurance Expense
   Prepaid Insurance

h.   *Property taxes recorded on credit:*

Factory Overhead Control--Property Tax Expense
   Taxes Payable

i.   *Factory miscellaneous costs paid in cash:*

Factory Overhead Control--Miscellaneous Expense
   Cash

j.   *Factory overhead applied:*

Work in Process Inventory
   Factory Overhead Control

k.   *Transfer to finished goods:*

Finished Goods Inventory
   Work in Process Inventory

l.   *Sale is made:*

Accounts Receivable
   Sale
Cost of Goods Sold
   Finished Goods Inventory

Subsidiary Factory Overhead Accounts

14.   Subsidiary factory overhead accounts detail the actual overhead incurred.

a. The total of the subsidiary factory overhead accounts should equal the balance of the Factory Overhead Control account in the general ledger.
b. Factory overhead accounts should be closed out at the end of the accounting period using the following format.

1.   If factory overhead is underapplied, the entry needed is:

Cost of Goods Sold
   Factory Overhead Control

NOTE THAT IF FACTORY OVERHEAD IS UNDERAPPLIED, THERE IS A DEBIT BALANCE IN FACTORY OVERHEAD CONTROL AND THIS MUST BE CLOSED OUT.

2.   If factory overhead is overapplied, the entry needed is:
Factory Overhead Control
   Cost of Goods Sold

NOTE THAT IF FACTORY OVERHEAD IS OVERAPPLIED, THERE IS A CREDIT BALANCE IN FACTORY OVERHEAD CONTROL AND THIS MUST BE CLOSED OUT.

15. If a company has branch production plants, each branch may keep only a limited number of ledger accounts that apply directly to production rather than a complete set of books.

   a. At a minimum the factory would keep a factory journal and factory ledger with subsidiary ledgers for materials inventory, work in process, and factory overhead control.
   b. Two reciprocal accounts used are a home office ledger account on the branch books and a factory ledger on home office books.
   c. When the factory ledger account is credited by the general office, the home office ledger account is debited by the factory and vice versa.
   d. The number of accounts designated to the branch varies depending upon the skill of the accounting personnel employed at the factory and on the size of the production plant.

Demonstration Problem

Forecasted Income Statement Based on Projections Given

The following information regarding one unit of product has been abstracted from the records for the year ending March 31, 19X2, of Donnell Manufacturing Company.

	Per Unit	
Sales Price	$120	
Direct Material	30	
Direct Labor	20	
Variable Factory Overhead	15	
Fixed Factory Overhead	20	
Marketing Expense	8	(35% is variable)
Administrative Expense	6	(10% is variable)

Management is formulating a strategy to increase company sales over the 5,000 units sold last year. The alternative that is presently being considered is a sales price reduction to stimulate sales. It has been determined that a 10 percent reduction in unit sales price will result in a 20 percent increase in the number of units sold. The existing plant facilities are adequate for producing the increased volume. Because the company will be able to take advantage of quantity discounts, direct material cost will decrease by $1.50 per unit. There will be, however, a 5 percent increase in the labor cost per unit. No other changes are projected. Provide for no change in the level of inventories maintained.

Required:

a. Prepare a pro forma statement of income for the next year using the projections presented. No cost of goods manufactured statement is required; instead, detail the cost of sales on the statement of income.

b. Prepare a statement of income for 19X2. Compare the income before taxes on this statement to that on the pro forma and advise management regarding the proposed price reduction and sales increase. Support your conclusions.

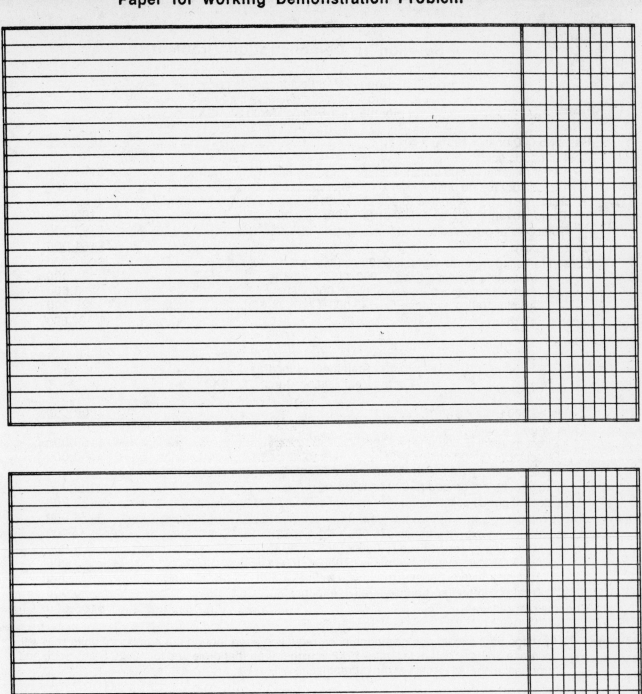

Solution to Demonstration Problem

Donnell Manufacturing Company
Pro Forma Statement of Income
For the Year Ending March 31, 19X3

a.

Sales [(5,000 units x 120%) x $108]	$648,000
Cost of goods sold:	
Direct material (6,000 units x $28.50)	$171,000
Direct labor [6,000 units x ($20 x 105%)]	126,000
Factory overhead-variable (6,000 units x $15)	90,000
Factory overhead-fixed (5,000 units x $20)	100,000
Total cost of goods sold	$487,000
Gross margin	$161,000
Less: Marketing expense-variable [6,000 x (35% x $8)]	$ 16,800
Marketing expense-fixed [5,000 x (65% x $8)]	26,000
Administrative expense-variable [6,000 x (10% x $6)]	3,600
Administrative expense-fixed [5,000 x (90% x $6)]	27,000
Income before taxes	$ 87,600

Donnell Manufacturing Company
Statement of Income
For the Year Ending March 31, 19X2

b.

Sales (5,000 units x $120)	$600,000
Cost of goods sold:	
Direct material (5,000 units x $30)	$150,000
Direct labor (5,000 units x $20)	100,000
Variable factory overhead (5,000 units x $15)	75,000
Fixed factory overhead (5,000 units x $20)	100,000
Total cost of goods sold	$425,000
Gross margin	$175,000
Less: Marketing expense-variable [5,000 x (35% x $8)]	$ 14,000
Marketing expense-fixed [5,000 x (65% x $8)]	26,000
Administrative expense-variable [5,000 x (10% x $6)]	3,000
Administrative expense-fixed [5,000 x (90% x $6)]	27,000
Total marketing and administrative expenses	70,000
Income before taxes	$105,000

Note: Management should not initiate the price reduction even though the number of units sold will increase. Income before taxes for 19X2 is higher than that projected for 19X3. Sales price and production should remain at the current levels.

Matching

Referring to the terms listed in the left column, place the appropriate letter next to the corresponding description. A term may not be used or may be used more than once.

a. Factory Overhead Control account

b. Job order costing

c. Job order cost sheet

d. Job time ticket

e. Material credit slips

f. Material requisition form

g. Operation costing

h. Process costing

i. Reciprocal account

j. Salaries

k. Time card

l. Wages

_____ 1. Source documents used by the accounting department to recognize the return of materials by departments.

_____ 2. A form showing the direct material, direct labor incurred and factory overhead applied on each job.

_____ 3. A home office ledger and a factory ledger are examples of this.

_____ 4. Source document informing the cost accounting department that material has been issued.

_____ 5. In this system, costs are assigned to and accumulated by batches.

_____ 6. In this system, costs are assigned to departments for a time period.

_____ 7. A hybrid-costing system having characteristics of both process and job order costing

_____ 8. Direct payroll benefits that represent a fixed periodic payment.

_____ 9. Direct payroll benefits designating hourly or piece rate payment.

_____ 10. Shows the time each employee spends on individual jobs during the day.

Completion and Exercises

1. The entry applying factory overhead requires a debit to the _____ _____ _____ account and a credit to the _____ _____ _____ account.

2. Wages earned by the factory cost accountant would be classified as _____ _____ and the cost would be debited to the _____ _____ _____ account; wages earned by an employee molding the product would be classified as _____ _____ and debited to the _____ _____ _____ account.

4. Assume the factory overhead application rate was $5 per machine-hour, actual machine hours were 2,000 and actual factory overhead was $10,800; factory overhead would be _____ _____ (indicate in the blank over- or underapplied) by $_____ resulting in a _____ (debit or credit) balance in the Factory Overhead Control account.

5. Materials which are issued from the _____ _____ _____ account are charged to Factory Overhead Control while materials issued from the _____ _____ _____ account are charged to Work in Process Inventory.

6. **Cost of Goods Manufactured Statement with Separate Factory Overhead Schedule**

LACO Management Company records provide the following data:

Direct material, January 1, 19X1	$25,000
Direct material, December 31, 19X1	34,000
Direct material purchased	60,000
Work in process, January 1, 19X1	45,800
Work in process, December 31, 19X1	55,400
Finished goods, January 1, 19X1	75,000
Finished goods, December 31, 19X1	88,000
Repair supplies, January 1, 19X1	15,000
Repair supplies, December 31, 19X1	20,000
Repair supplies purchased	18,000
Direct labor (20,000 hours)	92,000
Indirect labor	34,000
Factory Utilities (10,000 machine-hours)	15,500
Factory Depreciation	18,000
Factory Insurance	6,500
Factory Property taxes	3,800

Factory overhead is applied at $9 per machine-hour.

Required:

A cost of goods manufactured and sold statement for the year ended December 31, 19X1, showing actual factory overhead costs on the manufacturing statement. Also prepare a separate schedule for factory overhead and a calculation of over- or underapplied factory overhead.

6. Paper for working

7. Preparing Journal Entries and Using a Subsidiary Ledger for Work in Process

Before operations begin for the year 19X2, the management of the Dollar Company predicts factory overhead to be $51,200 while estimated machine hours will be 6,400.

At the beginning of 19X2, the Work in Process account and the job order ledger appear as follows:

Work in Process Inventory			Job No. 1	
Balance	4,025		Direct material	500
			Direct labor	1,000
			Applied factory	
			overhead	875
				2,375

Job No. 2			Job No. 3	
Direct material	250		Direct material	200
Direct labor	375		Direct labor	300
Applied factory			*Applied* factory	
overhead	300		overhead	225
	925			725

Required:

a. Record the following journal entries using general ledger accounts; in addition, use subsidiary ledger accounts for work in process assuming that a perpetual inventory system is employed.

Jan. 2 Purchased direct material of $2,000 and repair supplies of $1,000 for cash.
  4 Issued materials as follows:

> Job No. 1 .... $125
> Job No. 2 175
> Job No. 3 600
> Repair supplies......................... 825

10 Job No. 1 was finished and transferred to the storeroom. It was determined that during the month of January direct labor cost on this job was $250 while machine-hours totaled 150 for January.

16 The following factory items were paid in cash:

> Rent $400
> Utilities..................................... 300
> Miscellaneous expense 150

19 Additional material was issued from the storeroom:

> To Job No. 2............................ $154
> To Job No. 3............................. 62
> Repair supplies......................... 60

20 Job No. 1 was sold for $4,750 on account.
24 Job No. 2 was finished and transferred to the storeroom. It was determined that, during the month of January, direct labor cost on this job was $173 while machine-hours totaled 100.

31 Analysis of the time sheets showed the following unrecorded factory labor:

Job No. 3, $112; Factory supervision, $100; and Maintenance employees, $75.

Dollar Co (concluded)

31 Overhead was applied to the remaining jobs in process. Machine-hours on Job No. 3 during January amounted to 35 hours.

31 Depreciation of $338 on the factory building was recorded.

31 Close the over- or underapplied overhead to cost of goods sold.

b. Prove your balance in a work in process inventory.

a.

Date	Description	Post. Ref.	Debit	Credit

Date	Description	Post. Ref.	Debit	Credit

b.

8. **Journal Entries and Cost of Goods Manufactured Statement**

Neil Company had the following inventories on February 1, 19X1:

Work in Process Inventory	$ 6,910
Finished Goods Inventory	5,680
Direct Materials Inventory	12,215
Indirect Materials Inventory	700

The following transactions were completed during the month of February:

1. Direct material purchases of $6,090 and indirect materials of $2,000 were made on account.
2. Paid factory rent, $1,675.

3. Issued direct materials costing $7,870 and indirect materials costing $2,570 into production.

4. Recorded expired factory insurance, $380.

5. Distributed labor costs for the month as follows:

Direct	$7,680
Indirect	4,900

    A payroll summary account has been used at each pay period.

6. Applied manufacturing expenses at $40 per machine hour; actual machine hours total 288.

7. Paid cash of $830 for miscellaneous factory expense.

8. Goods completed during the month, $31,404.

9.   Recorded depreciation of factory machinery, $1,500.

10. Closed the under- or overapplied factory overhead to Cost of Goods Sold.

11. Shipped goods costing $26,900 at a selling price of $42,700. The sale was made on account.

Required:

a. Journal entries to record the transactions. Use a subsidiary ledger for factory overhead control.
b. Prepare a cost of goods manufactured and sold statement for February using applied factory overhead. Include a separate schedule of factory overhead showing the amount incurred and the difference. General and subsidiary ledger accounts will be of aid in preparing the statements.

Date	Description	Post. Ref.	Debit	Credit

8. Paper for working

a.

Date	Description	Post. Ref.	Debit	Credit

b.

	Debit	Credit

9. Home Office-Factory Ledger Journal Entries

M.R.S. Company uses a home office ledger and a factory ledger. All asset accounts except the Direct Materials Inventory, Factory Supplies Inventory, Work in Process Inventory, and Finished Goods Inventory are maintained at the home office. All liabilities are also kept on the home office books. The following transactions occurred:

Jan. 5 Cash was paid for factory overhead of $9,340.

Jan. 6 Direct material costing $18,000 and factory supplies costing $7,500 were purchased on account for the factory.

Jan. 8 Requisitions of $6,380 of direct materials and $1,600 for factory supplies were filled from the storeroom.

Jan. 9 A weekly factory payroll of $17,400 was paid by the home office consisting of $13,000 for factory direct labor and $4,400 for maintenance personnel. F.I.C.A. taxes of $1,226 and income taxes of $1,390 were withheld. (Ignore the recording of employer's payroll taxes at this time.)

31 Depreciation on factory building and equipment was recorded in the amount of $3,850.

31 Factory overhead was applied at $2.10 per machine-hour. Machine-hours for the month totaled 15,700.

31 Goods costing $19,800 were completed and transferred to the finished goods storeroom.

31 Goods costing $14,150 were sold on account for $19,500.

Required:

Prepare journal entries on the factory books and the home office books.

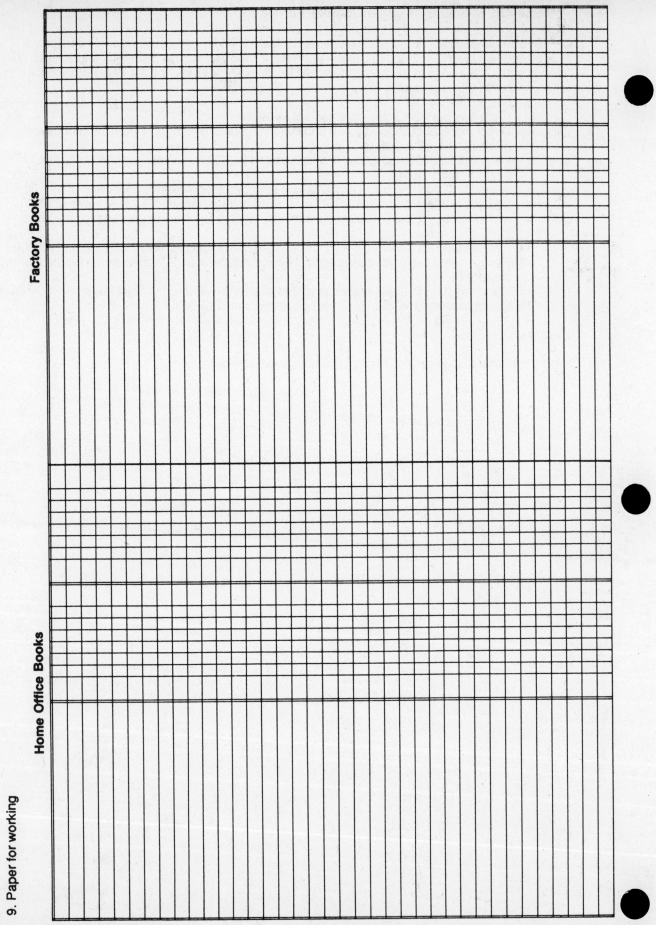

9. Paper for working

Home Office Books

Factory Books

True-False Questions

Indicate whether the following statements are true or false by inserting in the blank space a capital "T" for true or "F" for false.

_____ 1. A process costing system is used in continuous subsequent operations and emphasizes the accumulation of costs for a given time.

_____ 2. A credit balance in the Factory Overhead Control account indicates the company has underapplied overhead.

_____ 3. A company provides the following data pertaining to Job 14: direct materials used--$1,000; direct labor hours worked--150; direct labor hourly rate--$10; machine hours used--60; applied factory overhead rate per machine hour--$30. Based on this data, the conversion costs for Job 14 are $4,300.

_____ 4. Salaries paid to the tax accountant and factory cost accountant are both part of factory overhead.

_____ 5. If a company uses $200,000 direct materials during the month and its beginning balance of direct materials is $50,000 while the ending direct materials balance is $30,000 for the period, its direct material purchases for the period total $220,000.

_____ 6. The debits to Work in Process Inventory typically include actual direct material, actual direct labor, and actual factory overhead costs.

_____ 7 The Factory Overhead Control account reflects as debits the amount of overhead applied during the period and as credits, the actual overhead incurred during the same period.

_____ 8. If management budgets $36,000 in direct material, $50,000 in direct labor, and $75,000 for factory overhead for an expected volume of 25,000 machine hours, the application rate is $3 per machine hour.

_____ 9. The Factory Overhead Control account is an asset account whose balance accumulates and reflects the difference between actual and applied overhead over several years' operations.

_____ 10. Process costing is most appropriate for organizations that have a continuous flow of goods employing a mass-production, assembly-line operation.

SOLUTIONS

Matching

1.	e		6.	h
2.	c		7.	g
3.	i		8.	j
4.	f		9.	l
5.	b		10.	d

Completion and Exercises

1. Work in Process; Factory Overhead Control

2. indirect labor; Factory Overhead Control; direct labor; Work in Process

4. Underapplied; $800; debit

5. Factory Supplies Inventory; Direct Materials Inventory

6.
LACO Management Company
Statement of Cost of Goods Manufactured and Sold
For Year Ended December 31, 19X1

Direct material, January 19X1	$ 25,000
Purchases..	60,000
Direct materials available for use	$ 85,000
Less Direct Material, December 31, 19X1	34,000
Direct material used..	$ 51,000
Direct labor...	92,000
Actual factory overhead (Schedule A)	90,800
Total manufacturing costs..	$233,800
Add work in process, January 1, 19X1...................................	45,800
	$279,600
Less work in process, December 31, 19X1	55,400
Cost of goods manufactured	$224,200
Add finished goods inventory January 1...............................	75,000
	$299,200
Less finished goods, December 31, 19X1............................	88,000
Cost of Goods Sold	$211,200

Schedule A
LACO Management Company
Factory Overhead
For Year Ended December 31, 19X1

Repair supplies, January 19X1..	$15,000
Repair supplies purchased...	18,000
Repair supplies available for use	$33,000
Less repair supplies, December 31, 19X1	20,000
Repair supplies used	$13,000
Indirect labor...	34,000
Factory utilities...	15,500
Factory depreciation	18,000
Factory insurance	6,500
Factory property taxes..	3,800
Total actual factory overhead	$90,800
Applied factory overhead (10,000 x $9).................................	90,000
Underapplied Factory Overhead..	$ 800

7.

Dollar Company

a.

$$\frac{\$51,200}{6,400 \text{ hours}} = \$8.00 \text{ estimated factory overhead per machine hour.}$$

			Subsidiary Ledger			
Jan. 2	Direct Materials Inventory				2,000	
	Repair Supplies Inventory				1,000	
	Cash					3,000
Jan. 4	Work in Process Inventory	Job #1	125		900	
		Job #2	175			
		Job #3	600			
	Factory Overhead Control				825	
	Direct Materials Inventory					900
	Repair Supplies Inventory					825
Jan. 10	Work in Process Inventory	Job #1	250		250	
	Payroll Payable					250
	Work in Process Inventory	Job #1	1,200		1,200	
	Factory Overhead Control (150 hrs. x $8.00)					1,200
	Finished Goods Inventory				3,950	
	Work in Process Inventory	Job #1	3,950			3,950
Jan. 16	Factory Overhead Control				850	
	Cash					850
Jan. 19	Work in Process Inventory	Job #2	154		216	
		Job #3	62			
	Factory Overhead Control				60	
	Direct Materials Inventory					216
	Repair Supplies Inventory					60
Jan. 20	Cost of Goods Sold				3,950	
	Finished Goods Inventory					3,950
	Accounts Receivable				4,750	
	Sales					4,750
Jan. 24	Work in Process Inventory	Job #2	173		173	
	Payroll Payable					173
	Work in Process Inventory	Job #2	800		800	
	Factory Overhead Control (100 hrs. x $8)					800
	Finished Goods Inventory				2,227	
	Work in Process Inventory	Job #2	2,227			2,227
Jan. 31	Work in Process Inventory	Job #3	112		112	
	Factory Overhead Control				175	
	Payroll Payable					287
Jan. 31	Work in Process Inventory	Job #3	280		280	
	Factory Overhead Control (35 hrs. x $8)					280
Jan. 31	Factory Overhead Control				338	
	Accumulated Depreciation					338
Jan. 31	Factory Overhead Control				32	
	Cost of Goods Sold					32

Dollar Company (concluded)

a.

Subsidiary Ledger

Job #1

Balance	$2,375	January 10	$3,950
January 4	125		
10	250		
10	1,200		
	$3,950		

Subsidiary Ledger

Job #2

Balance	$925	January 24	$2,227
January 4	175		
19	154		
24	173		
24	800		
	$2,227		

Subsidiary Ledger

Job #3

Balance	$725
January 4	600
19	62
31	112
31	280
	$1,779

General Ledger

Factory Overhead Control

January 4	$825	January 10	$1,200
16	850	24	800
19	60	31	280
31	175		$2,280
31	338		
	$2,248		

b.   General Ledger

Work In Process Inventory

Balance		$4,025	January 10	$3,950
January 4		900	24	2,227
10		250		
10		1,200		
19		216		
24		173		
24		800		
31		112		
31		280		
		$7,956		
Balance		$1,779		

Balance of $1,779 in Work in Process Inventory equals the only balance in the Job ledger for Job #3.

8.

Neil Company

a.

(1) Direct Materials Inventory.. 6,090
    Indirect Materials Inventory 2,000
        Accounts Payable.. 8,090

(2) Factory Overhead Control - Factory Rent 1,675   1,675
        Cash... 1,675

(3) Work in Process Inventory...................................... 7,870
    Factory Overhead Control - Indirect Materials 2,570   2,570
        Direct Materials Inventory.......................... 7,870
        Indirect Materials Inventory 2,570

(4) Factory Overhead Control - Factory Insurance........ 380   380
        Prepaid Insurance................................... 380

(5) Work in Process Inventory..................................... 7,680
    Factory Overhead Control-Indirect Labor.............. 4,900   4,900
        Payroll... 12,580

(6) Work in Process Inventory..................................... 11,520
        Factory Overhead Control - Applied Overhead (11,520)   11,520

(7) Factory Overhead Control - Miscellaneous
        Factory Expense 830   830
        Cash... 830

(8) Finished Goods Inventory 31,404
        Work in Process Inventory....................... 31,404

(9) Factory Overhead Control - Depreciation of
        Factory Machinery... 1,500   1,500
        Accumulated Depreciation of Factory
            Machinery 1,500

(10) Cost of Goods Sold.. 335
        Factory Overhead Control 335

(11) Accounts Receivable... 42,700
     Cost of Goods Sold.. 26,900
        Finished Goods Inventory 26,900
        Sales 42,700

b.

Neil Company
Costs of Goods Manufactured and Sold
For the Month Ended February 28, 19X1

Cost of Goods Sold:

Direct materials inventory, 2-1-19X1	$12,215	
Purchases of direct materials	6,090	
Direct materials available for use	$18,305	
Less direct materials inventory, 2-28-19X1	10,435	
Direct material used		$ 7,870
Direct labor		7,680
Factory overhead applied	$11,520	
Add underapplied overhead	335	11,855*
Total manufacturing costs for the period		$27,405
Add work in process, 2-1-19X1		6,910
Manufacturing costs to account for		$34,315
Less work in process, 2-28-19X1		2,576
Cost of goods manufactured		$31,739
Add finished goods, 2-1-19X1		5,680
Cost of goods available for sale		$37,419
Less finished goods, 2-28-19X1		10,184
Cost of Goods Sold		$27,235

---

*An alternative procedure is to include $335 underapplied overhead as an additional cost of goods sold item.

Neil Company
Schedule of Factory Overhead Costs
For the Month Ended February 28, 19X1

Factory overhead applied		$11,520
Actual factory overhead:		
Depreciation of machinery	$1,500	
Factory rent	1,675	
Indirect materials	2,570	
Factory insurance	380	
Indirect labor	4,900	
Miscellaneous factory expense	830	11,855
Underapplied Factory Overhead Costs		$ 335

b.

General Ledger		Factory Overhead Ledger

Work in Process Inventory

balance	6,910	(8)	31,404
(3)	7,870		
(5)	7,680		
(6)	11,520		
balance	2,576		

Finished Goods Inventory

balance	5,680	(10)	26,900
(8)	31,404		
balance	10,184		

Direct Materials Inventory

Balance	2,215	(3)	7,870
(10)	6,090		
balance	435		

Indirect Materials Inventory

Balance	700	(3)	2,570
(1)	2,000		
Balance	130		

Factory Overhead Control

		(6)	11,520
(2)	1,675	(9)	335
(3)	2,570		11,855
(4)	380		
(5)	4,900		
(7)	830		
(9)	1,500		
	11,855		

Depreciation of Machinery

(1)	1,500

Factory Rent

(1)	1,675

Indirect Materials

(3)	2,570

Factory Insurance

(4)	380

Indirect Labor

(5)	4,900

Miscellaneous Factory Expense

(7)	830

Applied Overhead

(6)	11,520

9. *M.R.S. Company*

	Home Office Books				Factory Books		
Jan.5	Factory Ledger	9,340			Factory Overhead Control	9,340	
	Cash		9,340		Home Office Ledger		9,340
Jan.6	Factory Ledger	25,500			Direct Materials Inventory	18,000	
	Accounts Payable		25,500		Factory Supplies Inventory	7,500	
					Home Office Ledger		25,500
Jan.8	No entry				Work in Process Inventory	6,380	
					Factory Overhead Control	1,600	
					Direct Materials Inventory		6,380
					Factory Supplies Inventory		1,600
Jan.9	Factory Ledger	17,400			Work in Process Inventory	13,000	
	FICA Tax Payable		1,226		Factory Overhead Control	4,400	
	Federal Income				Home Office Ledger		17,400
	Tax Payable		1,390				
	Accrued Payroll		14,784				
	Accrued payroll	14,784					
	Cash		14,784				
Jan.31	Factory ledger	3,850			Factory Overhead Control	3,850	
	Accumulated				Home Office Ledger		3,850
	Depreciation		3,850				
Jan.31	No entry				Work in Process Inventory		
					($2.10 x 15,700)	32,970	
					Factory Overhead Control		32,970
					Finished Goods Inventory	19,800	
					Work in Process Inventory		19,800
Jan.31	Cost of Goods Sold	14,150			Home Office Ledger	14,150	
	Factory Ledger		14,150		Finished Goods Inventory		14,150
	Accounts Receivable	19,500					
	Sales		19,500				

True-False

1. T

2. F Because actual overhead is recorded as a debit in the Factory Overhead Control account, and applied overhead as a credit, a credit balance indicates overapplied overhead.

3. F Conversion costs consist only of direct labor and factory overhead. The conversion costs for Job 14 are $1,500 plus $1,800; the total manufacturing costs for Job 14 would be $4,300 which includes direct materials.

4. F The salary paid to the tax accountant is correctly classified as an administrative expense and the factory cost accountant's salary is factory overhead.

5. F The net direct material purchases are $180,000 computed as follows:

   $50,000 + X = $200,000 + $30,000

   X = $180,000

6. F The debit to work in process for factory overhead is for applied overhead, not actual overhead. Actual direct material and actual direct labor can be recorded because these costs can be determined when the job is completed unlike factory overhead.

7. F The debits and credits are reversed as actual overhead is debited and applied overhead is credited.

8. T

9. F The Factory Overhead Control account is a suspense account and the balance is closed out at the end of each period's operations.

10. T

6 Process Costing - Weighted-Average and FIFO

Chapter Outline

Contrast between Job Order, Process, and Operation Costing
> Departmentalization of Work in Process Inventory
> Equivalent units

Weighted-Average and FIFO Costing
> Sources of Units Transferred
> Cost of Production Report
> Four Steps to Preparing a Cost of Production Report
> Steps Illustrated using Weighted-Average Costing
> FIFO Costing Illustrated
> Subsequent Month Using Weighted Average
> Subsequent Month Using FIFO
> Materials Issued at Various Stages
> Journal Entries using Process Costing

Impact of Flexible Manufacturing & JIT on Process Costing
> Less Costing of Inventory Flow
> Ignore EU Calculations in JIT

Appendix: Completed and Not Transferred Inventory

Chapter Objectives

After studying this chapter, you should be able to:

1. Contrast the difference between process, job order, and operation costing in assigning costs to products.
2. Discuss what characteristics of manufacturing procedures make process costing appropriate.
3. Prepare departmental cost of production reports using weighted-average and FIFO costing.
4. Understand the change an automated manufacturing environment has on process costing and equivalent unit calculations.
5. Define and apply the new terms introduced.

Chapter Review

Contrast between Job Order, Process, and Operation Costing

1. Under a job order costing system, costs are assigned to and accumulated for each job which may be an order, a contract, or a unit of production.

   a. Job order costing should be used if the service or production is being performed to customer specification or if a company makes different components for inventory.
   b. The direct material and direct labor associated with each job are identified and accumulated and overhead is applied on some rational basis.

2. Process costing is most appropriate for companies mass producing goods using an assembly line in which there is a continuous flow of goods.

3. An operation costing system represents a hybrid method having some of the characteristics each of process and job order costing.

   a. An operation is a routine production method, techniques, or step which is repetitively performed.
   b. Operation costing is used in the manufacture of goods that have some common characteristics plus some individual characteristics.
   c. Operation costing best meets the needs of a batch manufacturer whose products have variations of a single design and require a varying sequence of standardized operations.

Departmentalization of Work in Process Inventory

4. Under process costing, costs are accumulated for each department for a time period and allocated among all the products manufactured during the period.

Equivalent Units

5. Units partially completed are converted into equivalent whole units for costing purposes.

   a. The stage of completion of work in process is used in computing equivalent units.
   b. When a unit is referred to as finished, it has completed the entire operating cycle of that department--it still may not have completed the entire manufacturing operating cycle.

6. Unit cost is determined through use of equivalent units and is used in assigning cost to units transferred and to units in ending inventory.

Weighted Average and FIFO Costing

7. FIFO and weighted-average costing are the two methods used to account for opening inventory costs.

8. Accountants calculate equivalent units using the following formulas, either for weighted-average or FIFO costing: (Note this includes units completed and on hand in ending inventory that are introduced in Chapter 6 appendix.)

EU, weighted-average =	Units completed and transferred X 100%	+	Units completed and on hand in ending inventory X 100%	+	Partially completed ending inventory X stage of completion

$$\text{EU, FIFO} = \begin{array}{c} \text{Units} \\ \text{completed} \\ \text{and} \\ \text{transferred} \\ \text{X 100\%} \end{array} + \begin{array}{c} \text{Units} \\ \text{completed} \\ \text{and on} \\ \text{hand in} \\ \text{ending} \\ \text{inventory} \\ \text{X 100\%} \end{array} + \begin{array}{c} \text{Partially} \\ \text{completed} \\ \text{ending} \\ \text{inventory} \\ \text{X stage of} \\ \text{completion} \end{array} - \begin{array}{c} \text{Beginning} \\ \text{inventory} \\ \text{X stage of} \\ \text{completion} \end{array}$$

Sources of Units Transferred

9. The total units transferred to the next department come from the following two sources regardless of whether a company uses FIFO or weighted-average costing:

   a. Beginning inventory
   b. Current production--units started and finished during the period.

Cost of Production Report

10. Each cost center's total and unit costs are summarized on one cost of production report.

    a. Several department's cost data may be summarized on one cost of production report.
    b. Regardless of the approach or format used, an orderly approach to the analysis is imperative.

Four Steps to Preparing a Cost of Production Report

11. There are four steps to preparing a cost of production report. They are:

    a. Quantity schedule showing that all units are accounted for and what their disposition is-- whether transferred out, lost, or remaining in ending inventory.
    b. Calculating equivalent units and unit costs for each cost element. The FIFO and weighted-average method of process costing will result in different figures.
    c. Determining the costs to account for; costs may come from beginning inventory, current costs, or transferred from a previous department.
    d. Accounting for the disposition of all costs that the department is responsible for.

Subsequent Month Using Weighted Average and FIFO

12. Additional complexities arrive in determining unit cost for a department subsequent to the first because accountants must determine preceding department(s) unit cost.

Materials Issued at Various Stages

13. Material enters the various production operations at different stages of processing; no assumptions should be made regarding this as production personnel must provide accountants this data.

Journal Entries Using Process Costing

14. The material journal entry using process costing is as follows:

        Work in Process---Department 1 XX
        Work in Process---Department 2 XX
            Direct Materials Inventory XX

    Note that now the work in process accounts have department indications.

15. The journal entry for labor using process costing is as follows:

    Work in Process---Department 1 XX
    Work in Process---Department 2 XX
          Payroll XX

16. If production is stable from one period to another, application rates based on estimated factory overhead may not be needed in process costing; actual cost may be appropriate.

Impact of Flexible Manufacturing and JIT on Process Costing

17. In a flexible manufacturing environment, workers and even materials are frequently transferred between job orders to insure a smooth flow of process.

    a. Job orders become less useful in an automated setting because companies are less likely to be mass producing inventory for stock.
    b. Lot sizes become too small to have a unique job order attached to each lot.
    c. Accounting reports are based on time periods rather than the closing of work orders.

Less Costing of Inventory Flow

18. In JIT environments there is no significant difference between units completed and amount of work performed in the current period only.

    a. This results because ending and beginning work in process and finished goods inventory are insignificant.
    b. Accountants could forgo the calculation of equivalent units entirely under these circumstances.
    c. Rather than allocating direct labor and factory overhead costs to ending work in process and finished goods inventories, conversion costs are charged to the cost of goods sold directly.

Ignore EU Calculations In JIT

19. Equivalent unit calculations may be ignored without materially misstating product costs under the newer manufacturing approaches.

    a. Just-in-Time (JIT) is a recent concept whose basic principle is receiving production components as they are required, rather than stockpiling inventory to have when needed.
    b. The JIT approach depends on orders arriving regularly and on time.
    c. JIT is based on short, rapidly changing production runs operating in a timely and efficient manner, rather than long, inflexible runs.
    d. The composition of inventory changes in a JIT setting.

Appendix: Completed and Not Transferred Inventory

20. Some units will become finished near the end of the period and there will not be enough time to transfer these to the next department; such units are referred to as completed and on-hand inventory.

    a. Completed units are included in the inventory along with the partially completed units with separate costing for each type of inventory.
    b. These completed units then become the beginning inventory for the next period and their cost is averaged in with the cost of partially completed units in computing unit cost under weighted-average costing.

Demonstration Problem

Process Costing: FIFO and Weighted-Average Costing, Second Department

The following information is given for Department 2 of the Tennyson Company, for the month of June, 19X1, The company uses a process cost system.

Beginning inventory..............................	600	units (1/3 material, 1/6 conversion costs)
Prior department costs.....................	$925	
Material..	$280	
Conversion costs	$270	
Received from previous department......	5,000	units
Current costs:		
Material..	$ 7,245	
Conversion costs	$13,832	
Costs received from prior department	$ 7,750	
Transferred...	5,300	units
Ending inventory.................................	300	units (1/4 material, 2/5 conversion costs)

Required:

   a.   Prepare a production cost report using FIFO.
   b.   Prepare a production cost report using the weighted-average method.

Paper for working Demonstration Problem

a.

Rayburn, COST ACCOUNTING, 5th edition, Study Guide, Chapter 6, page 6

Paper for working Demonstration Problem

b.

Solution to Demonstration Problem

NOTE: It should be pointed out that due to the limited dollars used, results from the FIFO and weighted-average costing are similar. However, this difference is often significant in practice.

a.

Tennyson Company
Cost of Production Report--Department 2--FIFO
For the month of June, 19X1

Beginning Inventory.................................	600	(1/3 material, 1/6 conversion costs)
Received from Preceding Department......	5,000	
	5,600	
Transferred..	5,300	
Ending Inventory....................................	300	(1/4 material, 2/5 conversion costs)
	5,600	

	Total Costs	Unit Costs
Value of Beginning Inventory:		
Prior Department Costs	$ 925	
Material	280	
Conversion Costs	270	
Value of Beginning Inventory..................................	$ 1,475	
Prior Department Costs	7,750	$1.55
Material..	7,245	1.40
Conversion Costs	13,832	2.60
Total Costs to Account For....................................	$30,302	$5.55
Costs Transferred:		
From Beginning Inventory......................................		$1,475
Materials added (2/3 x 600 x $1.40).............................		560
Conversion costs added (5/6 x 600 x $2.60)...............		1,300 $ 3,335
From current production (4,700 x $5.55)........................		26,085
Total Costs Transferred..		$29,420
Value of Ending Inventory		
Prior Department Costs (300 x $1.55)......................		$ 465
Material (300 x 1/4 x $1.40)................................		105
Conversion Costs (300 x 2/5 x $2.60).....................		312 882
		$30,302

Additional Computations

$$\text{EU, Prior Department Costs} = 5,300 + 300 - 600 = 5,000 \quad \frac{\$7,750}{5,000} = \$1.55$$

$$\text{EU, Material} = 5,300 + 75 - 200 = 5,175 \quad \frac{\$7,245}{5,175} = \$1.40$$

$$\text{EU, Conversion Costs} = 5,300 + 120 - 100 = 5,320 \quad \frac{\$13,832}{5,320} = \$2.60$$

Solution to Demonstration Problem

b.

Tennyson Company
Cost of Production Report--Department 2--Weighted Average
For the month of June, 19X1

Beginning Inventory	600	(1/3 material, 1/6 conversion costs)
Received from Preceding Department	5,000	
	5,600	
Transferred	5,300	
Ending Inventory	300	(1/4 material, 2/5 conversion costs)
	5,600	

	Total Costs	Unit Costs
Value of Beginning Inventory:		
Prior Department Costs	$ 925.00	
Material	280.00	
Conversion Costs	270.00	
Value of Beginning Inventory	$ 1,475.00	
Prior Department Costs	7,750.00	$1.54910
Material	7,245.00	1.40000
Conversion Costs	13,832.00	2.60185
Total Costs to Account For	$30,302.00	$5.55095

Costs Transferred (5,300 x $5.55095)		$29,420.04
Ending Inventory		
Prior Department Costs (300 x $1.54910)	$464.73	
Material (300 x 1/4 x $1.40)	105.00	
Conversion Costs (300 x 2/5 x $2.60185)	312.23	881.96
		$30,302.00

Additional Computations

EU, Prior Department Costs = 5,300 + 300 = 5,600

$$\frac{\$925 + \$7,750}{5,600} = \frac{\$8,675}{5,600} = \$1.54910$$

EU, Material = 5,300 + 75 = 5,375

$$\frac{\$280 + \$7,245}{5,375} = \frac{\$7,525}{5,375} = \$1.40$$

EU, Conversion Costs = 5,300 + 120 = 5,420

$$\frac{\$270 + \$13,832}{5,420} = \frac{\$14,102}{5,420} = \$2.60185$$

Matching

Referring to the terms listed in the left column, place the appropriate letter next to the corresponding description. A term may not be used or may be used more than once.

a. Cost of production report

b. Conversion costs

c. Direct materials inventory

d. Equivalent units

e. Equivalent unit section

f. FIFO process costing

g. Job order costing

h. Prime costs

i. Process costing

j. Quantity schedule

k. Total units transferred

l. Units started and finished

m. Weighted-average costing

_____ 1. Used to convert partially finished units into finished units for costing purposes.

_____ 2. Costing procedure for use in a standardized, assembly line operation where products are produced for stock.

_____ 3. Contains quantity schedule and accounting for costs charged to a department.

_____ 4. Costing procedure for use in an operation where products are produced to customer's specifications.

_____ 5. Section on the cost of production report which accounts for whole units assigned to departments.

_____ 6. Process costing procedure in which all units are transferred at the same unit cost.

_____ 7. All units sent to the next department regardless of their source.

_____ 8. Process costing procedure in which the cost of the beginning inventory transferred is kept separate within the department from other units transferred.

_____ 9. Units transferred that were not in the department's beginning inventory.

_____ 10. Direct labor and factory overhead costs.

Completion and Exercises

1. Equivalent units, FIFO =
   + _____

   + _____

   -- _____

2. Equivalent units, weighted average =
   + _____

   + _____

3. Do all departments have prior department cost? Why or why not? _____

   _____

   _____

4. Where is the proof on a cost of production report? _____

   _____

5. Would a job order or process costing system be more appropriate for a production operation in
   which a continuous assembly-line procedure is used? _____

6. What detailed cost information concerning beginning inventory is needed for weighted-average
   costing that is not needed for FIFO costing? _____

   _____

7. What is another name for units started and finished? _____

8. Assuming there is beginning inventory, will all units transferred using FIFO costing leave at the
   same unit cost? Why or why not? _____

   _____

   _____

9. **EU and Costs Distribution for FIFO & Weighted Average**

   Data for Scarlet Company are supplied as follows: Beginning inventory 3,500 units, one-fifth complete
   for material, three-fourths complete for conversion costs; started in process 6,100 units; ending
   inventory in process, 2,400 units, one-sixth complete for material, two-thirds complete for conversion
   costs. The remaining units were transferred. Beginning inventory was comprised of $1,200 material
   and $5,800 conversion costs. Current cost totaled $13,800 materials, and $18,525 conversion costs.

   Required:
   a. Compute equivalent units assuming FIFO costing for materials and conversion costs.
   b. Compute equivalent units assuming weighted-average costing for materials and conversion costs.
   c. Unit cost for material and conversion costs using FIFO costing.
   d. Unit cost for material and conversion costs using weighted-average costing.
   e. Total cost transferred using FIFO costing.
   f. Total cost transferred using weighted-average costing.
   g. The value of ending work in process using FIFO costing.
   h. The value of ending work in process using weighted-average costing.

9. Paper for working

10. Analysis of the records of the Burnett Company revealed the following:

    Beginning inventory .... 3,000 units
        1/5 of inventory is 1/3 complete
        4/5 of inventory is 1/4 complete
            Transferred .... 30,000 units
            Started .... 32,000 units

    Ending inventory
        1/5 of inventory is 1/10 complete
        4/5 of inventory is 3/4 complete

    Required:

    a. Calculate equivalent units for FIFO costing.

    b. Calculate equivalent units for weighted-average costing.

11. FIFO Process Costing: Cost Accounted for Section

Hastings Company places material in production at the beginning of operations. In September, material costs totaled $6,240; direct labor, $10,500; and factory overhead, $5,724. On September 1, there were 600 units in process, one-third completed as to direct labor and one-fourth completed as to factory overhead; these had a total cost of $1,310. There were 4,600 units completed and transferred during the month. Ending inventory consisted of 800 units, three-fourths completed as to direct labor and two-fifths completed as to factory overhead. The company uses the FIFO method of costing.

Required:

a. Determine the costs to be assigned to the units in ending inventory.
b. Determine the costs to be assigned to the units transferred.

a.

b.

12. FIFO Costing; Determining Costs

You are able to obtain only limited data from Steele Company before having to prepare cost sections of the production report. The ending balance in Work in Process for the previous month shows 500 units having three fifths of their material at a cost of $324 and one fifth of their conversion costs, which are $68. After calculating material equivalent units of 3,800, management is glad to find that current material unit cost has decreased $0.02. However, management is not pleased with the $0.05 increase in current unit conversion cost with conversion cost equivalent units of 3,200. A total of 3,100 units were transferred to the next department.

Required:

Prepare the "costs to account for" and the "costs accounted for" sections of a production report using FIFO costing.

13. Three Departments, No Beginning Inventory

Gill Manufacturing Company has the following three departments in which units are produced. After units are finished in Department A, they are transferred to Department B, and finally to Department C. Since this is the first month of operation, there is no beginning inventory.

	Departments		
	A	B	C
Units started	30,000	28,000	23,000
Units in ending inventory	2,000	5,000	3,000
Units transferred	28,000	23,000	20,000
Direct material used	$34,500	$19,320	$42,000
Direct labor	25,650	49,200	12,180
Factory overhead	21,660	25,920	9,135

The material in Department A and B is issued at the beginning of the process; in Department C, at the end of the process. Ending inventory is assumed to have one-fourth of its conversion cost for Department A, one fifth for Department B, and one-tenth for Department C.

Required:

Prepare a production cost report for the three departments.

13. Paper for working

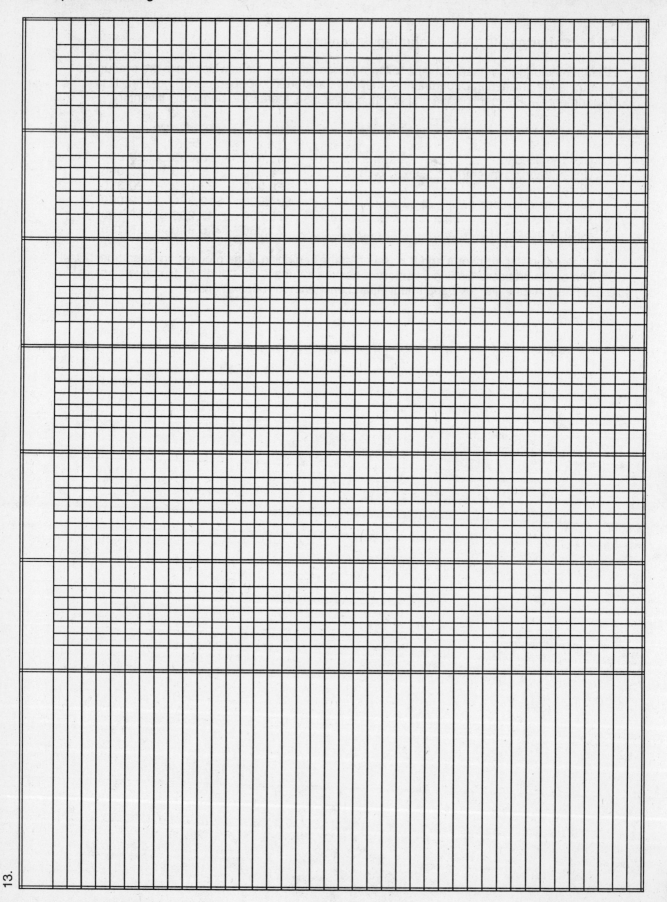

True-False Questions

Indicate whether the following statements are true or false by inserting in the blank space a capital "T" for true or "F" for false.

_____ 1. At the end of the preceding period, a company had no ending inventory. This period the accountant decides to switch from FIFO to weighted-average costing because there will be no effect due to this change.

_____ 2. Using FIFO, the accountant does not need the detailed cost components of beginning inventory to complete the cost of production report as only the total cost is needed.

_____ 3. Units transferred and units started and finished are always synonymous terms.

_____ 4. In the computation of manufacturing cost per equivalent unit, the weighted-average method of process costing considers current costs plus cost of ending work in process inventory.

_____ 5. Units received by a second department from a preceding department should be included in the computation of the equivalent units for the second department for only the weighted-average process costing method.

_____ 6. Assume a company transferred 10,000 units, had 100 units completed and on hand, and 400 units that were 1/8 complete at the end of the period. Beginning inventory for the company consisted of 300 units that were 1/5 complete. Under FIFO costing the equivalent units would be 10,090 and under weighted average, equivalent units would be 10,150.

_____ 7. If on the quantity schedule for a department, 1,000 units are indicated as finished and transferred, this always means that 1,000 units are in a finished stage ready for sale to a customer.

_____ 8. If beginning inventory cost was $100, current cost was $500, and equivalent units were 400, the equivalent unit cost would be $1.50 under FIFO.

_____ 9. If materials costing $1,000 and $2,000 were charged to Departments 1 and 2 respectively, and the cost of the goods transferred from Department 1 to Department 2 totaled $10,000, the entry to record the issuance of materials and the transfer of goods between departments would require a credit to Direct Materials Inventory of $13,000.

_____ 10. In the computation of materials cost per equivalent unit under FIFO process cost system, only current costs are considered.

SOLUTIONS

Matching

1. d   6.   m
2. i   7.   k
3. a   8.   f
4. g   9.   l
5. j   10.   b

Completion and Exercises

1. EU, FIFO* = Units completed and transferred x 100% + Partially completed ending inventory x stage of completion − Beginning inventory x stage of completion

2. EU, weighted* = average Units completed and transferred x 100% + Partially completed ending inventory x stage of completion

    *Order of additions is not important

3. No, only departments subsequent to the first department have prior department cost. The first department in an operation would not have prior department cost.

4. The Total Cost to Account For should equal Total Cost Accounted For

5. process

6. Only the total cost incurred for beginning inventory is needed for FIFO costing; however, a detailed breakdown as to how much material, labor, and overhead was incurred for beginning inventory is needed for weighted-average costing.

7. current production

8. No, using FIFO costing, the beginning inventory is first costed which is composed of costs from preceding periods and current costs. The units started and finished are then transferred at total current unit cost.

9. *Scarlet Company*

Beginning inventory (1/5 M, 3/4 CC)........................... 3,500
Started. 6,100   9,600

Ending inventory (1/6 M, 2/3 CC).............................. 2,400
Transferred... 7,200   9,600

a. EU, FIFO, Material = 7,200 transferred + 400 ending inventory - 700 beginning inventory = 6,900
                              (2,400 X 1/6)   (3,500 X 1/5)

  EU, FIFO, Conversion costs = 7,200 transferred + 1,600 - 2,625 beginning inventory = 6,175
                                   (2,400 X 2/3)   (3,500 X 3/4)

b. EU, Weighted-average costing, Material = 7,200 transferred + 400 ending inventory = 7,600

  EU, Weighted-average costing, Conversion costs = 7,200 transferred + 1,600 = 8,800

c.   FIFO, Material

$$\frac{\$13,800}{6,900 \text{ units}} = \$2$$

    FIFO, Conversion costs

$$\frac{\$18,525}{6,175 \text{ units}} = \$3$$

d.   Weighted-Average, Material

$$\frac{\$13,800 + \$1,200}{7,600 \text{ units}} = \$1.9737$$

    Weighted-Average, Conversion Cost

$$\frac{\$18,525 + \$5,800}{8,800 \text{ units}} = \frac{\$24,325}{8,800 \text{ units}} = \$2.7642$$

e. Cost transferred using FIFO:
    Value of beginning inventory....................................... $7,000
    Material added (3,500 x 4/5 x $2) 5,600
    Conversion costs added (3,500 x 1/4 x $3).................... 2,625 $15,225

    Costs transferred from current production (3,700 x $5) ...   18,500
    Total cost transferred.. $ 33,725

f.   Costs transferred using weighted-average costing: 7,200 x $4.7379 = $34,112.88

g.   Ending inventory, FIFO:
    Material (2,400 x 1/6 x $2) $ 800
    Conversion Costs (2,400 x 2/3 x $3)   4,800
                                                          $5,600

h.   Ending inventory, Weighted-average costing:
    Material (2,400 x 1/6 x $1.9737) $ 789.48
    Conversion costs (2,400 x 2/3 x $2.7642)   4,422.72
                                                          $ 5,212.20

handwritten annotation:
transf 7200
- B I 3500
      3700

10. *Burnett Company*

    a.   FIFO =   30,000 transferred + 100 ending inventory + 3,000 ending inventory
                                (1/10 x 1,000)   (3/4 x 4,000)

                    -    200 beginning   -   600 beginning =   32,300
                           inventory   inventory
                          (1/3 x 600)   (1/4 x 2,400)

    b.   Weighted Average = 30,000 transferred + 100 ending inventory +

        3,000 ending inventory = 33,100

11. *Hastings Company*

	Transferred	+	Ending Inventory	–	Beginning Inventory		
EU, Material	4,600	+	800	–	600	=	4,800

$$\frac{\$6,240}{4,800} = \$1.30$$

	Transferred	+	Ending Inventory	–	Beginning Inventory		
EU, Labor =	4,600	+	600 (3/4 X 800)	–	200 (1/3 X 600)	=	5,000

$$\frac{\$10,500}{5,000} = \$2.10$$

	Transferred	+	Ending Inventory	–	Beginning Inventory		
EU, Overhead =	4,600	+	320 (2/5 X 800)	–	150 (1/4 X 600)	=	4,770

$$\frac{\$5,724}{4,770} = \$1.20$$

    a.   800 units X $1.30   = $1,040
        600 units X $2.10   =   1,260
        320 units X $1.20   =   384

        Value of ending inventory $ 2,684

    b.   Costs transferred:
        From Beginning Inventory $ 1,310
        Labor added (600 X 2/3 X $2.10)   840
        Overhead added (600 X 3/4 X $1.20)   540
        Costs transferred from beginning inventory $ 2,690
        Costs transferred from current production (4,000 X $4.60) 18,400
        Total Costs Transferred   21,090
         Total Costs Accounted for..................................... $23,774

12. *Steele Company*

Costs to account for:
Beginning inventory
    Material ($324/300 = $1.08 unit cost) .... $ 324
    Conversion costs ($68/100 units = $.68 unit cost) 68
Total beginning inventory .... $ 392
Current costs
    Material (3,800 X $1.06) 4,028
    Conversion costs (3,200 X $.73) 2,336
Total costs to account for $6,756

Costs accounted for as follows:
Costs transferred:
    Value of beginning inventory .... $ 392
    Material added (500 X 2/5 X $1.06) 212
    Conversion costs added (500 X 4/5 X $.73) .... 292 $ 896
    From current production (2,600 X $1.79)   4,654
    Costs transferred $5,550

Costs of ending inventory:
    Material (1,000* X $1.06) $1,060
    Conversion costs (200* X $.73) 146   1,206
    Total costs accounted for $6,756

---

   * Transferred - Beginning   +   Ending
               Inventory   Inventory
     3,100   - 300   +   1,000** = 3,800 EU material
            (500 X 3/5)
     3,100   - 100   +   200** = 3,200 EU CC
            (500 X 1/5)
** Represents the difference

Note: It should be emphasized that the 1,000 EU of material and 200 EU of conversion cost in ending inventory are equivalent units only, not whole units. There is nothing in the problem which indicates how many whole units are in ending inventory.

13.

Gill Manufacturing Company
Cost of Production Report
For the Month Ending---

	A		B		C	
	30,000	(all material, 1/4 CC)	28,000	(all material, 1/5 CC)	23,000	(no material, 1/10 CC)
	Total Costs	**Per Unit**	**Total Costs**	**Per Unit**	**Total Costs**	**Per Unit**
Physical flow						
Units started						
Units in ending inventory	2,000		5,000		3,000	
Units transferred	28,000		23,000		20,000	
Units accounted for	30,000		28,000		23,000	
Costs to Account For:						
Costs received from prior department	-0-	-0-	$ 78,680	$2.81	$152,490	$6.63
Material	$34,500	$1.15	19,320	.69	42,000	2.10
Labor	25,650	.90	49,200	2.05	12,180	.60
Factory overhead	21,660	.76	25,920	1.08	9,135	.45
Total cost to account for	$81,810	$2.81	$173,120	$6.63	$215,805	$9.78
Costs transferred	$78,680 (23,000 x $6.63)	(28,000 x $2.81)	$152,490	(20,000 x $9.78)	$195,600	
Ending inventory:						
Prior department costs	-0-		14,050	(5,000 x $2.81)	19,890	(3,000 x $6.63)
Material (2,000 x $1.15)	2,300	(5,000 x $.69)	3,450		-0-	
Labor (500 x $.90)	450	(1,000 x $2.05)	2,050		180	(300 x $.60)
Overhead (500 x $.76)	380	(1,000 x $1.08)	1,080		135	(300 x $.45)
Total costs accounted for	$81,810		$173,120		$215,805	

Additional Computation:

	A	B	C
EU, Material	28,000 + 2,000 = 30,000	23,000 + 5,000 = 28,000	20,000
EU, Labor and Overhead (CC)	28,000 + 500 = 28,500	23,000 + 1,000 = 24,000	20,000 + 300 = 20,300
EU, Prior Department		23,000 + 5,000 = 28,000	20,000 + 3,000 = 23,000

	A	B	C
Material:	$34,500 + 30,000 = $1.15	$19,320 + 28,000 = $ .69	$42,000 + 20,000 = $2.10
Labor:	$25,650 + 28,500 = $ .90	$49,200 + 24,000 = $2.05	$12,180 + 20,300 = $ .60
Factory Overhead:	$21,660 + 28,500 = $ .76	$25,920 + 24,000 = $1.08	$9,135 + 20,300 = $ .45
Prior Department:		$78,680 + 28,000 = $2.81	$152,490 + 23,000 = $6.63

True-False

1.   T   The difference between FIFO and weighted-average costing lies in the treatment of beginning inventory; thus, if there is no beginning inventory, the results would be the same.

2.   T   Under FIFO, equivalent unit cost is determined by dividing equivalent units into only current cost.

3.   F   Units transferred includes all units sent to the next department regardless of whether they come from current production (units started and finished) or from beginning inventory which has been finished.

4.   F   Under weighted-average process cost method, current costs plus the cost of beginning inventory are taken into account in the numerator of the cost per equivalent unit computation.

5.   F   Units transferred into the second department should be taken into account in the equivalent units computation for the second department under both FIFO and weighted average.

6.   T   EU, FIFO = 10,000 + 100 completed and on hand + $\underset{(400 \times 1/8)}{50}$ $\underset{(300 \times 1/5)}{60}$ = 10,090

              EU, Weighted average = 10,000 + 100 + 50 = 10,150

7.   F   Units that are classified as "Finished" refer to being complete as far as the individual department is concerned.

8.   F   Under FIFO, only current costs are used in the computation of equivalent unit cost yielding a cost per unit of $1.25 ($500/400 units).

9.   F   The entries involved would be:

	Dr.	Cr.
Work in Process---Department 1	1,000	
Work in Process---Department 2	2,000	
Direct Materials Inventory		3,000
Work in Process---Department 2	10,000	
Work in Process---Department 1		10,000

10.   T

7 Process Costing - Addition of Materials and Lost Units

Chapter Outline

Addition of Materials
> Effect of Addition of Materials on Total Units to Account for Using Weighted Average
> Effect of Addition of Materials on Unit Costs Using Weighted Average
> Effect of Addition of Materials on Total Units to Account for Using FIFO
> Effect of Addition of Materials on Unit Costs Using FIFO

Loss of Units
> Normal versus Abnormal Loss
> Normal Tolerance Limits

Quality Control Concepts and Zero Defect Programs
> Produce-and-Rework-if-Defective Program
> On-the-Spot Correction
> Future Spoilage Minimized

Timing of Inspections
> Inspection at End of Operations
> Inspection at the Intermediate Point of Operations

Allocation of Normal Loss

Chapter Objectives

After studying this chapter, you should be able to:

1. Show the effect on product costs of additional materials.

2. Illustrate the costing procedure when the addition of material results in an increase in units to account for.

3. Prepare cost of production reports using FIFO and weighted-average costing when normal and abnormal losses occur.

4. Understand the impact of quality control concepts and zero defects programs on abnormal and normal losses.

5. Define and apply the new terms introduced.

Chapter Review

Addition of Materials

1. Material additions can have the following two effects:

    a. The number of units that must be accounted for can be increased; for example, diluting a mixture.
    b. The unit costs of the product can be increased; for example, adding buttons to a shirt does not increase the number of shirts to be accounted for.

Effect of Addition of Materials on Total Units to Account for Using Weighted Average

2. When a mixture is diluted by other materials, the mixture cannot be distinguished so the cost from the preceding department must be spread over the entire mixture.

Effect of Addition of Materials on Unit Costs Using Weighted Average

3. All units transferred under weighted-average costing will continue to leave at the same unit cost.

4. The same equivalent unit formula can be used that was introduced in the previous chapter; the only difference is that the units to account for have increased due to the addition of material.

    a. The preceding department cost is spread over the entire mixture which results in a decrease in unit cost.
    b. The material cost causing the increase in units should not be included in the preceding department cost; a separate unit cost calculation is required for material.

Effect of Addition of Materials on Total Units to Account for Using FIFO

5. Under FIFO, the larger base of units is assumed to relate only to new production, not to units in beginning inventory when operations began for the period.

    a. Beginning inventory multiplied by its stage of completion is subtracted in the equivalent unit calculation as illustrated previously when there was no increase in units to account for.

Effect of Addition of Materials on Unit Costs Using FIFO

6. The value of beginning inventory is not averaged in with current cost to arrive at the unit cost per cost component.

Loss of Units

7. Some loss through spoilage and evaporation may be inherent in the production process even though losses are to be avoided if possible.

Normal versus Abnormal Loss

8. Losses are classified as abnormal or normal depending upon whether they fall within the normal tolerance limits for such losses.

Normal Tolerance Limits

9. Normal tolerance limits can be expressed as a percentage of the good units that pass the inspection point of the operations.

Quality Control Concepts and Zero Defect Programs

10. Accounting for normal and abnormal losses may change as more companies successfully adopt quality control concepts and zero defects programs.

a. Zero defects is a performance standard whose theme is to do work right the first time.
b. The zero defects philosophy is not limited to production efforts.

Produce-and-Rework-if-Defective Program

11. Most errors which result in product losses arise because employees lack attention to their jobs.

    a. Employees operate to the tolerance level of authority---they make errors at work that they never make in their personal lives.
    b. When managers accept a level of performance containing a loss allowance, no future improvement is likely to occur.
    c. Instead, if managers set the performance standard at zero, workers will come closer to operating with no defects.

On-the-Spot Correction

12. After adopting quality control concepts, employees pledge to make a constant conscious effort to do their job correct the first time.

    a. Employees recognize that their individual contribution is a vital part of the organization-wide effort.
    b. Controlling quality in early manufacturing stages is emphasized under a zero defect program.
    c. When a mistake does occur, employees try to determine what caused the error and then consider what might be done to prevent similar mistakes in the future.
    d. The number of full-time inspectors at the end of the production line can be reduced with increased reliance on workers' self inspection.

13. Errors are likely to still occur under conventional inspection systems, regardless of the number of inspectors in a plant operations.

    a. Errors occur because each inspector depends on the others to find the error.
    b. Errors are not reported because inspectors are confident the other inspectors will not observe errors, and they do not wish to discredit their colleagues.

14. Total commitment from top management down to factory employees is needed when changing from the conventional produce-and-rework-if-defective routine to a zero defects concept.

    a. The attitude of defect prevention must be treated with seriousness and attention by management.

Future Spoilage Minimized

15. Defects detected at the end of the line are studied and used as feedback information using the traditional produce-and-rework-if-defective routine.

    a. On-the-spot correction is preferred because the time lag between the detection and correction of the defect is reduced sharply.
    b. On-the-spot correction generally produces less defective units because of the immediate feedback workers receive.

Timing of Inspections

16. The loss of units may occur at the beginning, during, or at the end of operations within a department.

    a. Lost units are discovered when inspection is made.
    b. Rather than inspect at the end of the department's process, frequent on-the-spot inspection and correction is often less costly than running the risk of applying cost to a unit that has already been spoiled.
    c. A trade-off between the expense of additional inspections and the risk of incurring material and conversion costs for a unit that unknowingly has become spoiled usually occurs.

Inspection at End of Operations

17. While the loss may occur at any time, it is discovered at the inspection points.

18. When inspection is at the end of operations, none of the lost units come from the ending inventory composed of partially finished units; thus, no spoilage cost is allocated to ending inventory.

19. There is an alternative method of handling lost units which adjusts the costs from preceding departments for the lost units by excluding the lost units from the equivalent unit calculation.

20. Accountants assign the cost of the normal loss of units to the good units while they treat the cost of abnormal loss as a period cost as shown below:

    Cost of Lost Units ....
            Work in Process---Processing Department in which Loss Occurred ....

    a. If the spoiled goods have some value, accountants make the following entry, establishing this value and crediting the department in which the loss occurred.

    Spoiled Goods or Scrap Material Inventory..
            Work in Process---Processing Department in which Loss Occurred ....

    b. When a company sells the units lost through normal conditions, accountants make the following entry which removes the asset balance from the accounting records.

    Cash or Accounts Receivable...
            Spoiled Goods or Scrap Material Inventory..

Inspection at the Intermediate Point of Operations

21. Inspection may also occur at various stages of completion; units lost receive only their conversion cost up to the point of inspection. The stage at which material enters the process determines whether they have received the current department's material.

    a. If there has been a preceding department, all spoiled units would have gone through this department and should receive the preceding department cost.
    b. A change in the per unit cost will occur when units are lost because the good units finished will have to bear this spoilage.

22. When inspection occurs at the beginning of operations, lost units have only the preceding department(s) costs and are not assigned any of the current department's costs.

23. It is assumed with inspection at the beginning of operations, that the units lost were never put into process.

Allocation of Normal Loss

24. If the normal loss is allocated to units transferred and to ending inventory as opposed to all the cost being assigned to the good units transferred, the following is used to arrive at the allocation.

    a. The allocation to the cost of units transferred is:

    $$\frac{\text{Costs transferred before loss allocation or units transferred}}{\text{Total costs or total units}} \times \text{Cost of normal loss} = \text{Cost assigned to units transferred}$$

b. The allocation to the cost of ending inventory is:

$$\frac{\text{Ending inventory costs before loss allocation or units in ending inventory}}{\text{Total costs or total units}} \times \text{Cost of normal loss} = \text{Cost assigned to ending inventory}$$

Demonstration Problem

Normal Loss, Weighted-Average and FIFO

Spiller Company has the following data for the month of March. Any units that are not accounted for are to be considered lost through the normal process. Inspection occurs at the end of the process.

Department 1

Beginning inventory	4,000	(100% material, 40% labor, overhead)
Units entered into process this month	17,000	
Units transferred	16,000	
Ending inventory	4,500	(100% material, 30% labor, overhead)

Beginning inventory cost:
Prior department costs	-0-
Materials	$2,000
Labor and overhead	3,500

Current cost:
Material	10,600
Labor and overhead	33,985

Required:

a. Prepare a production cost report using the weighted-average method.
b. Prepare a production cost report using the first-in, first-out method.

a.

Paper for working Demonstration Problem

b.

Solution to Demonstration Problem

a.

Spiller Company-- Department 1
Cost of Production Report-Weighted Average
For the Month Ended March 31, 19XX

Beginning inventory	4,000	(100% material, 40% labor, overhead)
Started in process	17,000	
	21,000	
Units transferred	16,000	
Ending inventory	4,500	(100% material; 30% L, OH)
Normal loss of units	500	
	21,000	

	Total Costs	Unit Costs
Costs to be Accounted For:		
Beginning inventory:		
Material	$ 2,000	
Labor & overhead	3,500	
Current costs:		
Material	10,600	$ .60
Labor & overhead	33,985	2.10
Total costs to account for	$50,085	$ 2.70

Costs Accounted for as Follows:		
Costs transferred before loss ($2.70 x 16,000)	$43,200	
Cost of lost units ($2.70 x 500)	1,350	
Total costs transferred		$44,550
Ending inventory		
Material ($.60 x 4,500)	2,700	
Labor and overhead ($2.10 x 1,350)	2,835	5,535
Total Costs Accounted for		$50,085

Additional Computations

EU, Material = 16,000 + 4,500 + 500 = 21,000; $2,000 + $10,600 = $12,600 ÷ 21,000 units = $.60

EU, Labor and Overhead = 16,000 + 1,350 + 500 = 17,850;

    $3,500 + $33,985 = $37,485 ÷ 17,850 units = $2.10

Solution to Demonstration Problem

b.
Spiller Company--Department 1
Cost of Production Report--FIFO
For the Month Ended Month 31, 19XX

Beginning inventory	4,000	(100% material; 40% L, OH)
Started in process	17,000	
	21,000	
Units transferred	16,000	
Ending inventory	4,500	(100% material; 30% L, OH)
Normal loss of units	500	
	21,000	

	Total Costs	Unit Costs
Costs to be Accounted For:		
Beginning inventory:		
Material	$ 2,000.00	
Labor & overhead	3,500.00	
	$ 5,500.00	
Current costs:		
Material	10,600.00	$ .62353
Labor & overhead	33,985.00	2.09138
Total costs to account for	$50,085.00	$2.71491
Costs Accounted For as Follows:		
Transferred:		
From beginning inventory	$ 5,500.00	
Costs added (60% x 4,000 x $2.09138)	5,019.31	
Total costs beginning inventory:		
Before spoilage	$10,519.31	
Costs of units started and completed:		
Before spoilage (12,000 x $2.71491)	32,578.98*	
Costs of lost units (500 x $2.71491)	1,357.46	
Total costs transferred out		$44,455.75
Ending inventory:		
Material (4,500 x $.62353)	$2,805.89	
Labor and overhead (1,350 X $2.09138)	2,823.36	5,629.25
Total costs accounted for		$50,085.00

*Rounded by $.06 so totals will balance.

Additional Computations

EU, Material = 16,000 + 4,500 + 500 - 4,000 = 17,000;
$$\frac{\$10,600}{17,000} = \$.62353$$

EU, Labor, Overhead = 16,000 + 1,350 + 500 - 1,600 = 16,250;
$$\frac{\$33,985}{16,250} = \$2.09138$$

Matching

Referring to the terms listed in the left column, place the appropriate letter next to the corresponding description. A term may not be used or may be used more than once.

a. Abnormal loss

b. Addition of material where a larger base unit count occurs

c. Addition of material where only unit cost is increased

d. Allocation of normal loss cost to units transferred and ending inventory

e. Assignment of normal loss cost to units transferred only

f. Cost of Production Report

g. Equivalent units

h. Income statement

i. Inspection

j. Normal loss

_____ 1. An evaporation or spoilage which falls within the tolerance limits established by management.

_____ 2. Through this calculation, lost units are multiplied by their stage of completion at inspection to affect unit cost.

_____ 3. The appropriate treatment for normal loss cost if ending inventory has not passed the stage of inspection.

_____ 4. A loss which falls outside the normal tolerance limits.

_____ 5. The type of material addition which occurs when a display decal is sewed to each shirt being processed.

_____ 6. The type of loss which occurs frequently when on-the-job training is used.

_____ 7. On this statement, cost is assigned to the normal loss of units which in turn increases the cost of the good units.

_____ 8. This phase of operations usually affects the equivalent units to add for lost units.

_____ 9. A spoilage resulting from a supplier sending the incorrect grade of material would be classified as this type of loss.

_____ 10. The appropriate treatment for the cost resulting from the normal loss of units if ending inventory has passed the inspection stage.

Completion and Exercises

1. How are the costs assigned to normal loss and abnormal loss accounted for differently?

   _____

   _____

   _____

2. If an incorrect grade of material was received and this caused spoilage, is this a normal or abnormal loss cost?

   _____

3. Give two reasons why the total unit cost from the prior department may not be the same as the computed prior department unit cost in the subsequent department.

   a. _____

   _____

   _____

   b. _____

   _____

   _____

4. How does the accounting treatment of the addition of material which does not increase the units to account for differ from the treatment of material which increases the units to be accounted for?

   _____

   _____

   _____

   _____

5. What is the criteria that is usually used for determining whether to classify a spoilage as normal or abnormal?

   _____

   _____

6. The _____   _____
   determines the stage of completion for units that are lost assuming the cost element is added continuously throughout the processing.

7. The cost element which is affected mostly by the addition of material which increases the

   units to account for is _____ _____

   _____.

8. The Mixing Department of McAlprin Company had 900 pounds of minerals that were two-fifths complete in beginning inventory. When the 8,500 pounds received from the preceding department entered mixing operations, 2,000 pounds of thinner were added to dilute the solution. At the end of operations, 144 pounds of mixture were in ending inventory, one-fourth complete.

   a. The equivalent unit calculation for the prior department costs using--

      1. FIFO costing is _____.

      2. Weighted-average costing is _____.

   b. The equivalent unit calculation for Mixing Department material and conversion costs using--

      1. FIFO costing is _____.

      2. Weighted-average costing is _____.

9. Given for a process costing operation of the Fain Company:

Beginning work in process (1/4 completed) .... 500 units
Received from preceding department .... 2,500 units
Good units transferred out .... 1,800 units
Ending work in process (2/5 completed) .... 600 units
Labor costs in beginning inventory .... $ 320
Current labor costs $5,881

One third of the units lost were due to abnormal conditions. Inspection is at the midpoint of operations.

Required:

Find by the weighted-average method:

a. The units lost due to normal conditions _____ .

b. Equivalent units for labor costs are _____

_____

c. The unit labor costs are _____

_____

d. Total labor costs transferred out to the next process are _____

e. Total labor costs of units lost due to abnormal conditions are _____

f. Total labor costs in ending inventory are _____

10. Tolerance Limits: FIFO and Weighted-Average

Borto Company uses a process costing system for its processing and assembling departments. Due to the nature of the product, evaporation occurs. In the processing department for the month of May 19X1, there were 200 units lost; management considers four fifths of this due to normal causes. A normal tolerance limit of 10 percent of the good units finished and transferred has been established for the assembling department; any units lost over this limit is considered due to abnormal causes. Inspection is at the end of the operations in both departments.

The following data are obtained from each department's records:

	Processing Department	Assembling Department
Beginning inventory	1,700 units	2,540 units
Stage of completion	(1/4 material, 3/5 conversion cost)	(All material, 4/5 conversion cost)
Ending inventory	2,340 units	3,030 units
Stage of completion	(2/9 material, 2/3 conversion cost)	(All material, 2/3 conversion cost)
Started in process	6,300 units	5,460 units
Transferred to next department	?	4,500 units
Costs of beginning inventory:		
Prior department costs		$8,490
Material	$ 489	3,048
Conversion Cost	2,040	1,717
Current costs:		
Materials	6,927	6,712
Conversion cost	14,566	4,574

Required:

Prepare a cost of production report using:

a. FIFO costing.
b. Weighted-average costing.

10. Paper for working

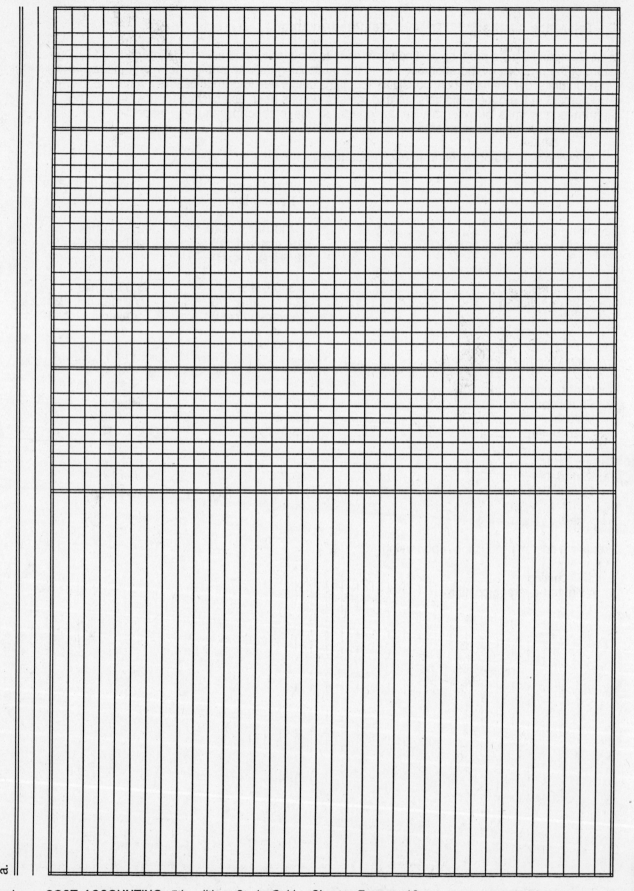

a.

10. Paper for working

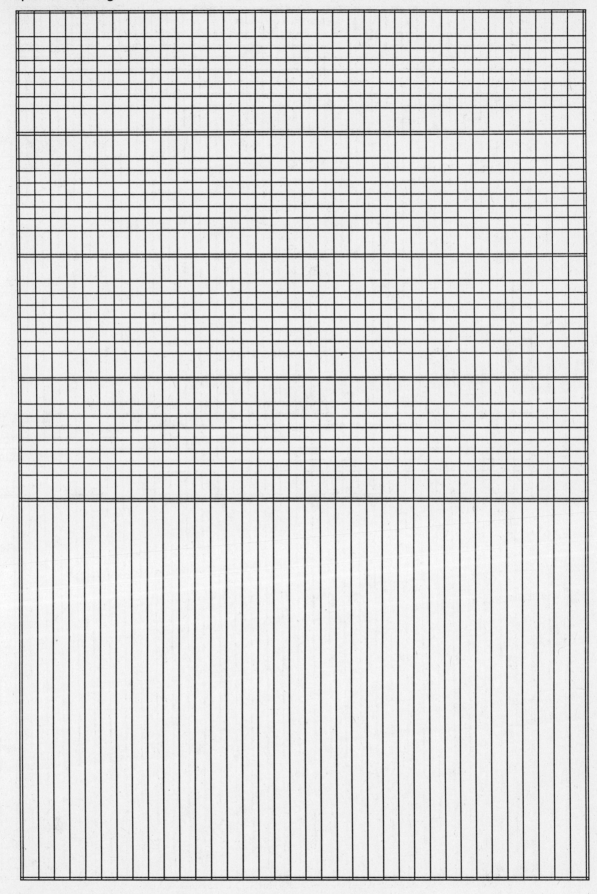

10. Paper for working

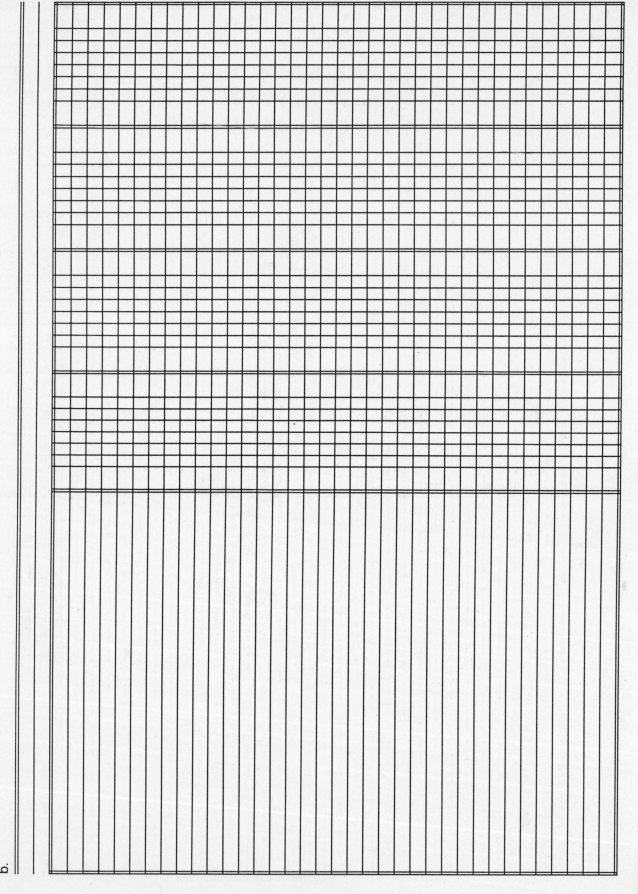

b.

10. Paper for working

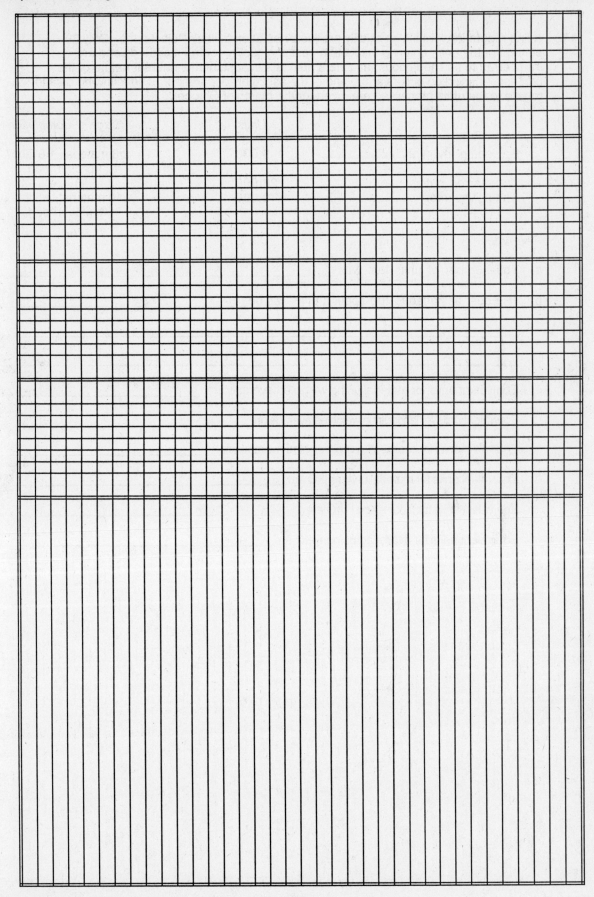

11. A fine reputation for its high-quality products has been built by Rejects, Inc. Only 80 percent of the units entering inspection pass the quality control standards and are transferred to finished goods; all others are lost because of the inherent nature of the process. Inspection occurs at the end of the assembly department. The following data in regard to the units processed are given for the month of October:

	Units	Stage of Completion
Beginning inventory	3,000	2/3 material, 1/6 labor, 1/5 overhead
Transferred out............................	28,800	
Ending inventory	2,000	1/10 material, 4/5 labor, 1/4 overhead

Required:

a. The number of units lost was_____.

b. The cost assigned to the spoiled units will be:_____

_____

_____

c. Equivalent units for material using weighted average are _____.

Equivalent units for labor using weighted average are_____.

Equivalent units for overhead using weighted average are_____.

d. Equivalent units for material using FIFO are_____.

Equivalent units for labor using FIFO are_____.

Equivalent units for overhead using FIFO are_____.

12. Specific FIFO and Weighted-Average Cost Questions

Molt Company has three processing department, L, M, N. Department M reveals the following information:

Work in process, April 1: 1,500 pounds

Department L: Cost (100%)	$4,710
Department M: Material (80%)	1,710
Department M: Conversion costs (70%).........................	1,365
	$7,785

During April, 6,000 pounds from Department L plus 3,000 pounds in Department M, were put into process:

Department L: Cost added in April.................................	$28,125
Department M: Material cost added in April.....................	13,320
Department M: Conversion costs added in April	9,990
Total costs to account for..	$59,220

Completed in April and transferred to Department N........	7,500	pounds
Lost in April*..	750	pounds
Work in process, April 30...	2,250	pounds
Department L: Cost...		100%
Department M: Material..		60%
Department M: Conversion costs		40%

*525 pounds is considered a normal loss.

Losses are discovered when the process reaches the 90 percent stage of completion for Department M material and Department M conversion costs.

Required:

a. Assume that Molt Company uses the weighted-average method of determining cost. Calculate each of the following, rounded to five decimal places.

    (1)   Total cost of the 7,500 good pounds completed and transferred to Department N.
    (2)   The total cost of the 225 pounds of abnormal loss.
    (3)   The total cost of the 2,250 pounds in the ending inventory.

b. Instead, assume the Molt Company uses the FIFO method of determining cost. Make the same three calculations as in Requirement *a.*

a.

12. Paper for working

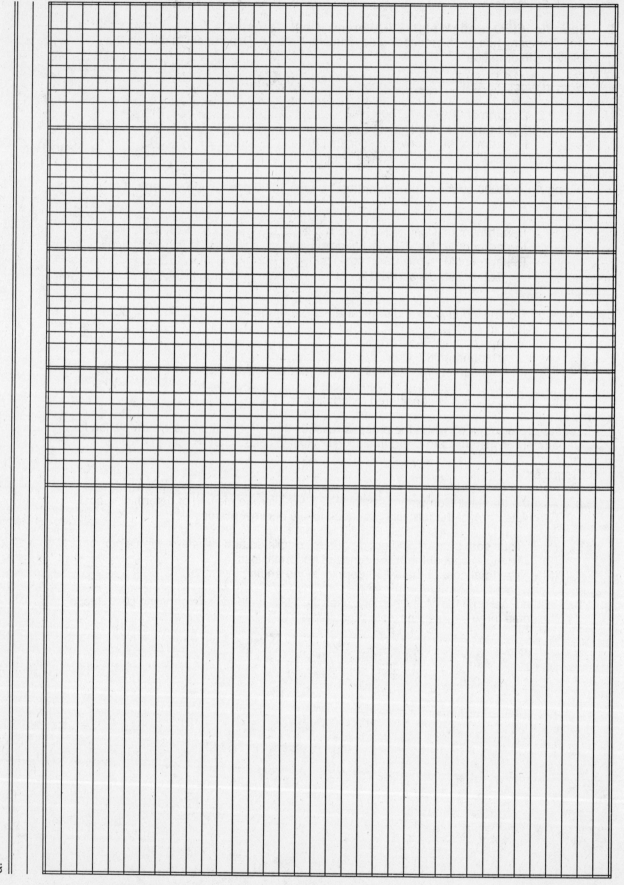

12. Paper for working

b.

1.

2.

3.

13. Weighted Average; Addition of Material Which Increases Base Unit Count

Fitzpatrick Manufacturing Company produces paint in the mixing department and assembly departments. For the month ending January 31, 19--, they had 600 gallons having one half of their material and one third of their conversion cost in beginning inventory in the mixing department, and 200 gallons in the assembly department having one fourth of their material and one fifth of their conversion cost. Forty-five hundred gallons of pigment were entered into production in the mixing department and 3,700 gallons of pigment mixture were transferred to the assembly department. Upon its arrival in the assembly department, 500 gallons of oil were added to the pigment mixture; 3,650 gallons of paint were transferred to finished goods. The ending inventory in the mixing department had one fifth of its material and two sevenths of its conversion cost; the ending inventory in the assembly department had one third of its material and three fifths of its conversion cost. There were no units lost in either department.

Cost data for the month is as follows:

	Mixing Department	Assembly Department
Work in process, January 1, 19---:		
Costs from preceding department		$ 615.00
Material	$ 195.10	45.00
Conversion cost	445.50	16.50
Current costs:		
Material	2,431.70	3,582.00
Conversion cost	8,697.50	1,459.50

Required:

Prepare a cost of production report for both departments using the weighted-average method of process costing.

13. Paper for working

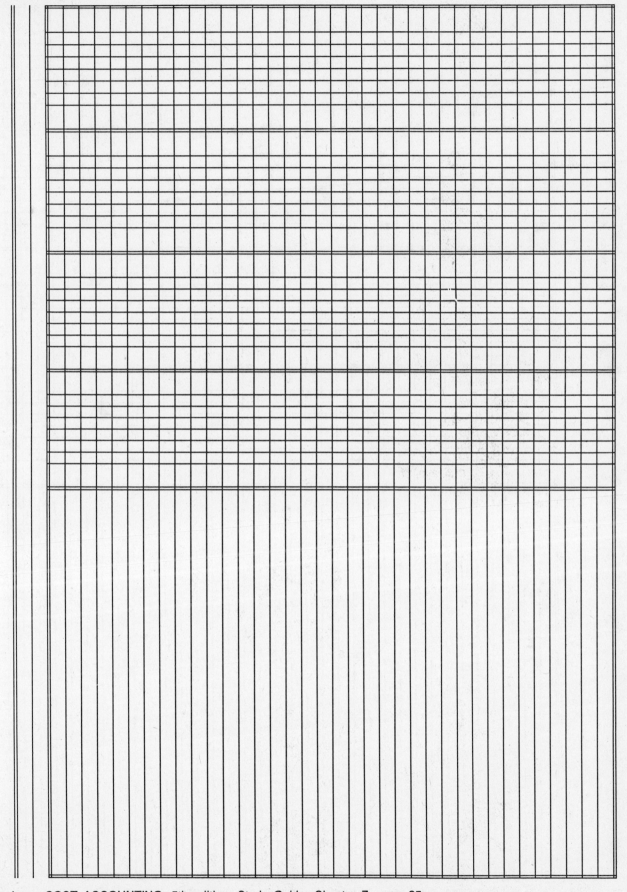

13. Paper for working

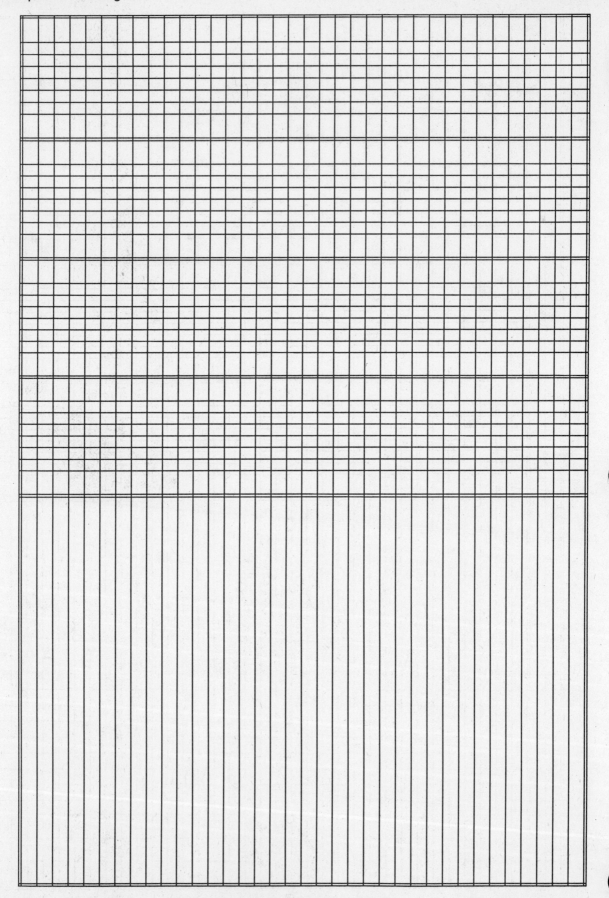

14. Abnormal and Normal Loss and FIFO

JTT Company has adopted the FIFO method of process cost accounting. After units leave Department 1, they are transferred to Department 2, then to finished goods. Inspection for rejects occurs when the units are at a two-thirds stage of completion within each department. The company is quite concerned this month because there has been heavy spoilage. In Department 2, all materials are added only to the units that pass inspection just as the units leave the accept-reject point. The company does not allocate any spoilage to ending inventory. Assume that material, labor, and overhead are at the same stage of completion at Department 1's inspection point while labor and overhead are two-thirds complete at Department 2's inspection point.

The following data are gathered from the company's records:

	Department 1	Department 2
Beginning inventory	100 units (1/5 material, 1/10 labor, 1/4 overhead)	60 (1/3 labor, 1/4 overhead)
Started in process	2,000 units	(?)
Abnormal spoilage	300 units	150 units
Normal spoilage	600 units	90 units
Ending inventory	200 units	300 units
Stage of completion	1/4 material, 1/5 labor, 1/10 overhead	5/6 labor, 4/5 overhead

	Department 1	Department 2
Cost of beginning inventory:		
Prior department cost		$ 480
Material	$ 45	-0-
Labor	20	55
Factory overhead	75	63
Current costs:		
Material	4,075	2,624
Labor	3,260	2,275
Factory overhead	4,785	2,534

Required:

a. Prepare a cost of production report. (Use next two pages for working Requirement a.)
b. Make the journal entries recording the transfer of goods out of Departments 1 and 2 and the cost of abnormal spoilage in both departments.
c. What detailed cost information is given to you that is not needed for FIFO process cost?

b.

Date	Description	Post Ref.	Debit	Credit

c. _____

_____

_____

14. Paper for working

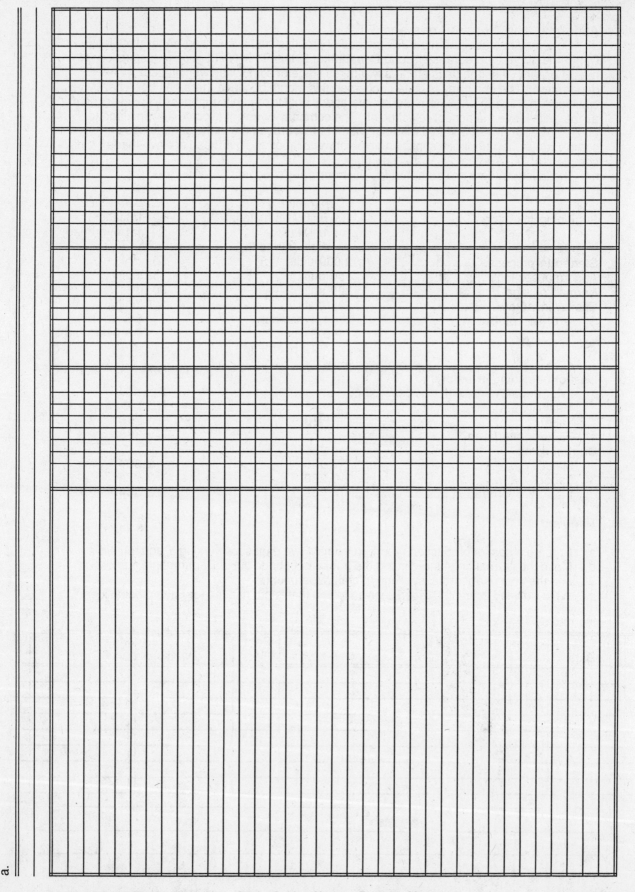

a.

14. Paper for working

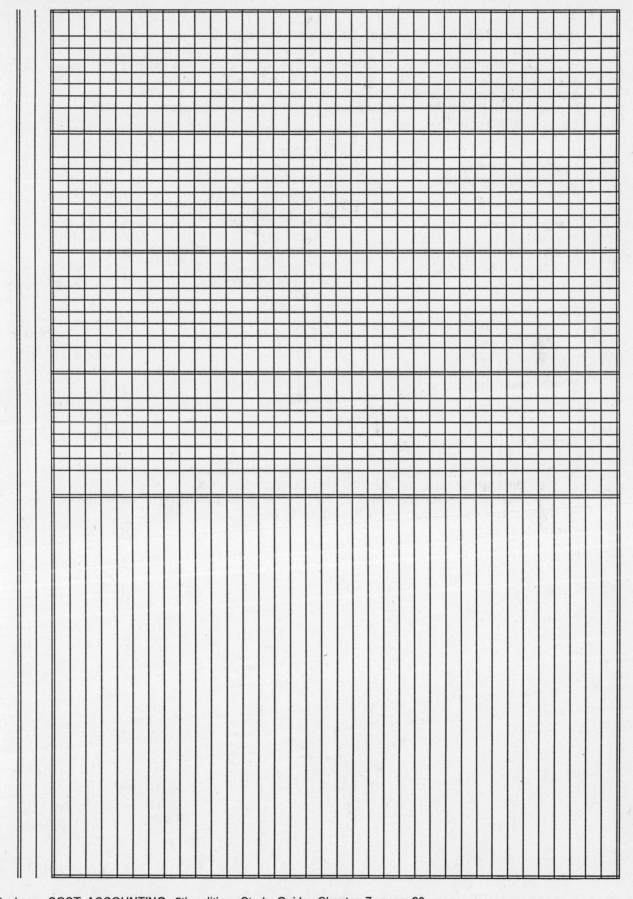

15. Normal and Abnormal Spoilage, Weighted-Average Costing, and FIFO

Friday Company manufactures clocks with production completed in two departments: processing and assembling. The company normally experiences spoilage; however, for the month of May abnormal spoilage has accounted for one fourth of the total spoiled units. Spoilage is detected at the end of the processing. The following data is accumulated for the month of May 19X1.

	Processing	Assembling
Beginning inventory	120 units	50 units
Stage of completion	1/3 materials	1/5 material,
	1/6 conversion cost	1/10 conversion cost
Started in process	580 units	?
Transferred	500 units	502 units
Ending inventory	100 units	48 units
Stage of completion	1/5 material,	1/6 material,
	1/4 conversion cost	1/8 conversion cost

Beginning inventory:		
Costs from preceding department	$ -0-	$ 250.00
Material	80.50	39.50
Conversion cost	66.00	30.16

Current cost:		
Material	1,020.10	2,070.00
Conversion cost	1,643.00	2,545.18

Required:

a. Prepare a cost of production report for the processing and assembling departments for the month of May using the weighted-average costing method.
b. Prepare a cost of production report for the processing and assembling departments for the month of May using the FIFO costing method.

15. Paper for working

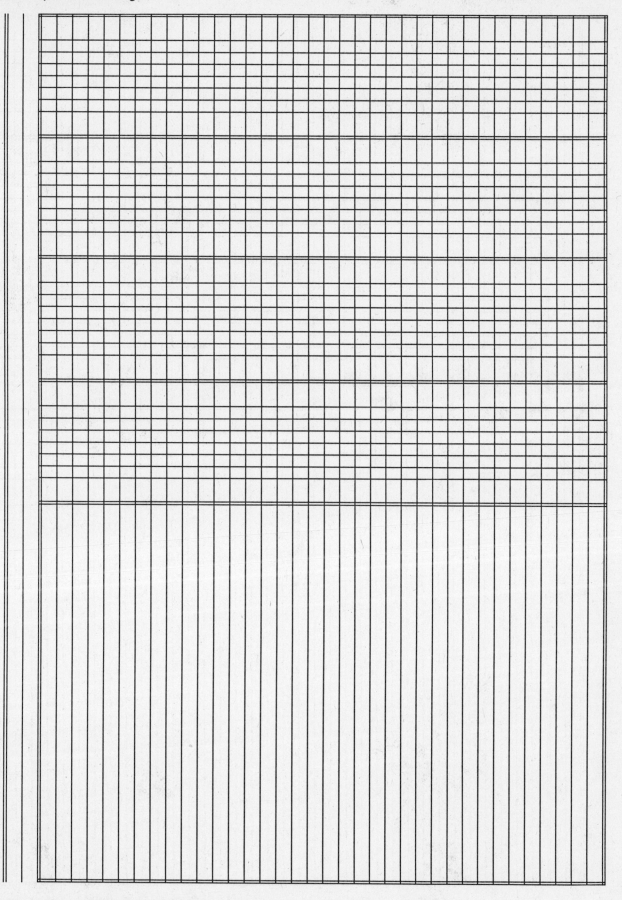

a.

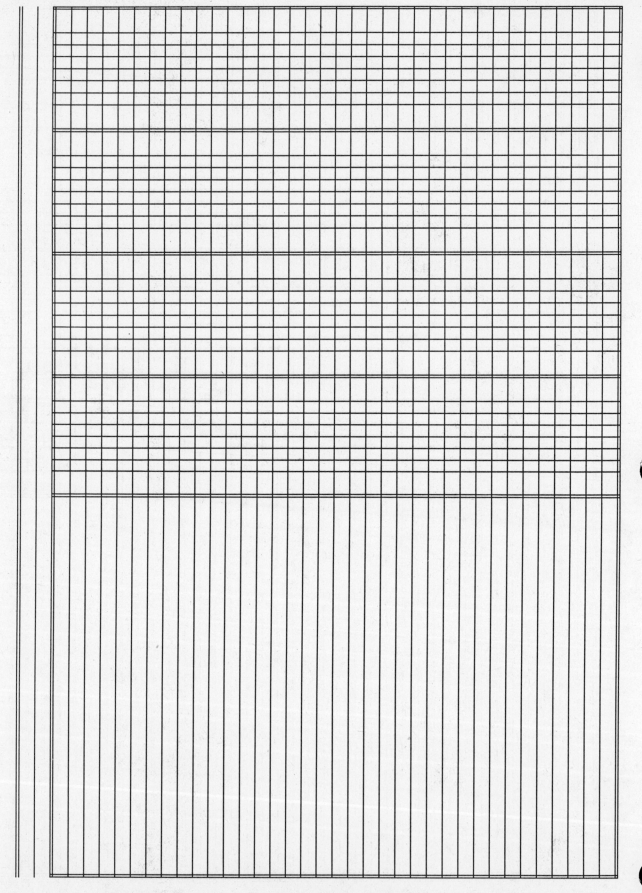

15. Paper for working

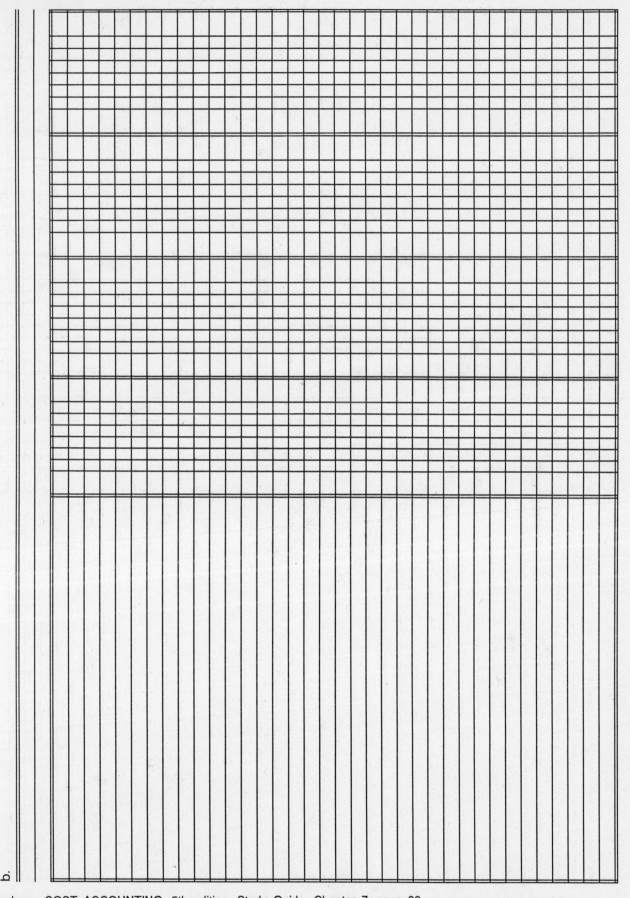

b.

15. Paper for working

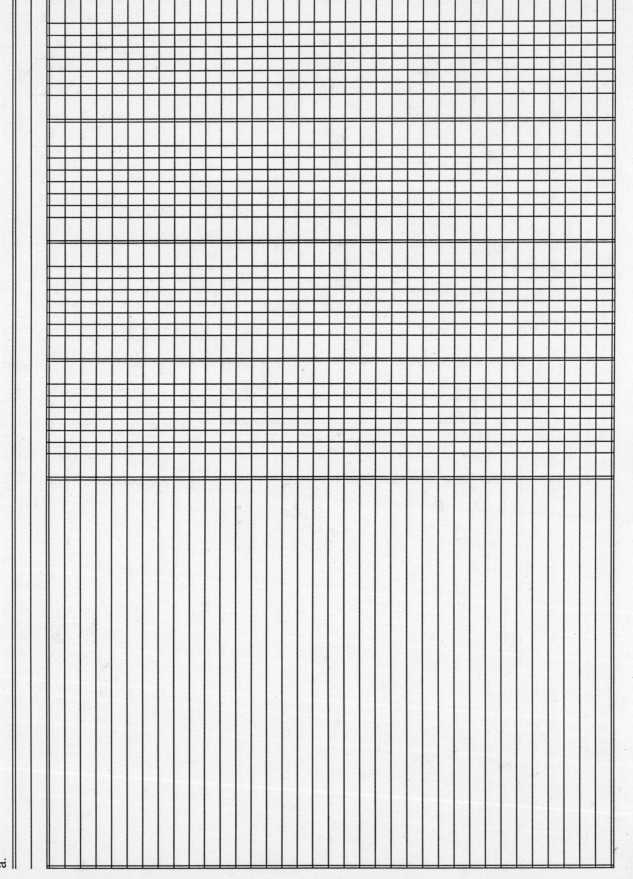

a.

16. **Inspection at One-Fourth Stage, FIFO, Weighted-Average, and Allocation of Normal Loss**

Operations of the Murray Manufacturing Company take place in the Mixing and Finishing departments. Management allocates the normal loss to the finished goods transferred and ending work in process. Inspection is at the point where the units reach a stage of one-fourth completion of operations in the department. Assume that at the inspection point material and conversion cost are at the same stage of completion. The following data is obtained from the records for June 19---:

	Mixing	Finishing
Beginning work in process	2,100 units	600 units
Preceding department costs		$ 832
Material	$ 284 (1/4 stage)	2,252 (1/5 stage)
Conversion cost	1,050 (1/3 stage)	1,904 (1/4 stage)
Units started in production.................	6,700 units	5,400 units
Abnormal loss....................................	300 units	200 units
Normal loss......................................	1,600 units	1,000 units
Ending work in process (2/5 material, 1/3 conversion cost stage of completion)	1,500 units	2,300 units (3/4 material, 2/5 conversion cost stage of completion)

Current costs:

	Mixing	Finishing
Material	$ 3,570	$23,548
Conversion cost	10,215	15,953

Required: (Allocate normal loss on number of units.)

a. Prepare a cost of production report using FIFO costing.

b. Prepare a cost of production report using weighted-average costing.

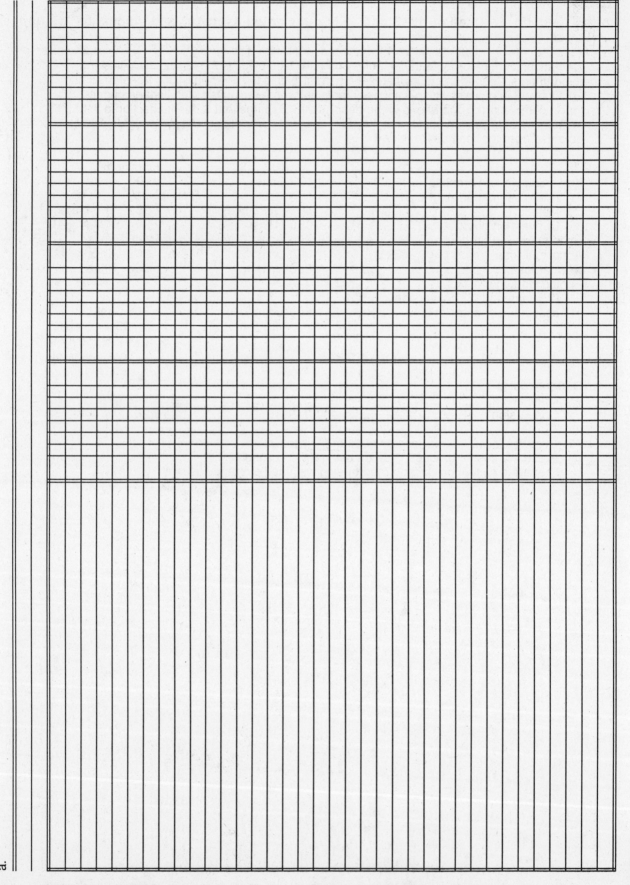

a.

16. Paper for working

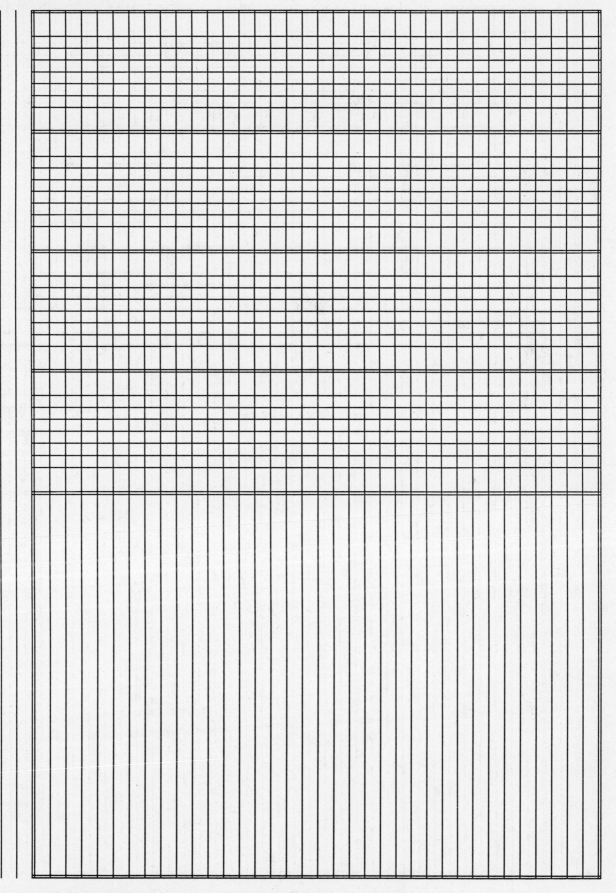

16. Paper for working

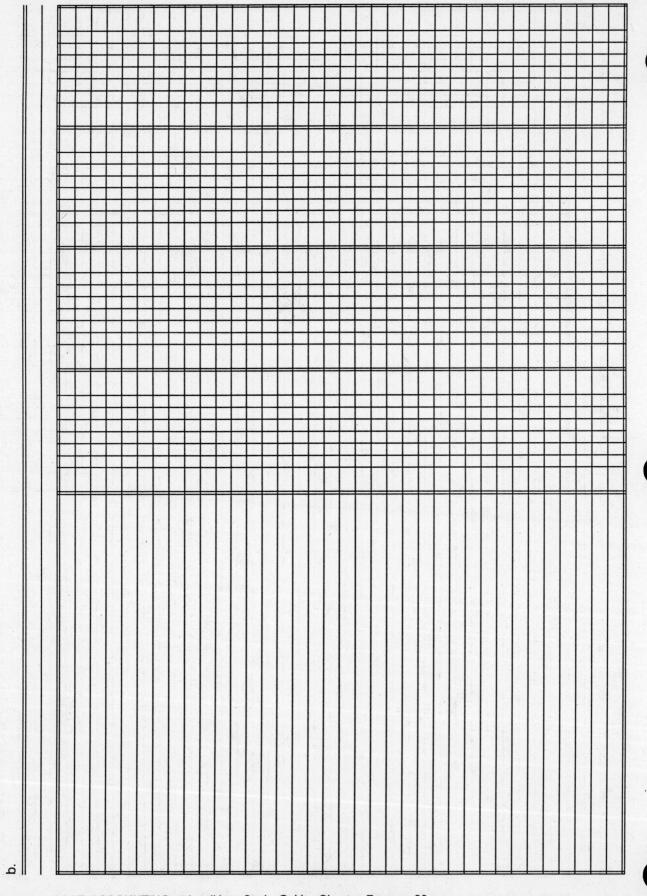

b.

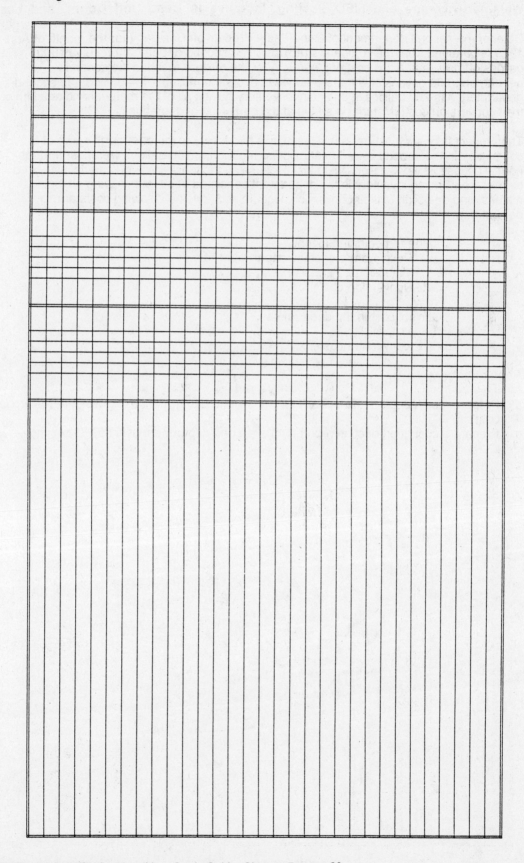

17. **Weighted-Average and FIFO Costing, Increase In Base Unit Count, and Lost Units**

Data for the second department of Gene Peery Production Company for the month of April 19X1 is obtained from the company's records. The second department receives 500 gallons of mixture at a unit cost of $2.968. After the mixture reaches the second department, 200 gallons of water are added to dilute the mixture. In addition, the second department has 200 gallons in beginning inventory having all of the material and one fifth of their conversion cost. Material is added at the beginning of operations.

The product is of such nature that inspection is necessary at the one-fourth stage of completion in the second department. During the month, 100 gallons were lost through normal causes while 40 gallons were lost because an incorrect grade of material was used by mistake. Ending inventory in the department consisted of 60 units having all their material and one sixth of their conversion cost. In addition, the following costs are determined:

Value of beginning inventory:	
Costs from preceding department	$400
Material	500
Conversion costs	30

Current cost in the department:	
Material	770
Conversion costs	564

Required:

a. Prepare a cost of production report for the second department using weighted-average costing.
b. Prepare a cost of production report for the second department using FIFO costing.

17. Paper for working

a.

b. 17. Paper for working

True-False Questions

Indicate whether the following statements are true or false by inserting in the blank space a capital "T" for true or "F" for false.

_____ 1. Equivalent units for preceding department costs always equal the total units to account for.

_____ 2. Since abnormal loss and normal loss are generally discovered at the same inspection point, they can be added together for costing purposes.

_____ 3. Assume the total costs to account for in Department 1 is $50,000 and the unit cost is $2; this always means that equivalent units were 25,000.

_____ 4. Information concerning Department 1 of a company is as follows: Beginning inventory -- $12,800 (17,000 units); started during the month--82,000; units transferred--85,000; ending work in process--20,000 units (70 percent complete). The cost per equivalent unit for this cost is $0.83 if the current cost is $69,700 and weighted-average costing is used.

_____ 5. Materials that dilute the mixture and increase the number of units to account for are handled the same way if this occurs in Department 1 or subsequent departments.

_____ 6. Assume the cost from preceding departments has an equivalent unit cost of $5 and that ending inventory consists of 1,000 units, 50 percent complete in Department 3. The preceding department cost assigned to the ending inventory would be $5,000.

_____ 7. If inspection occurs at the midpoint of operations, the cost from preceding operations that is assigned to the lost units is the equivalent unit cost determined for preceding departments multiplied by 1/2 of the units lost.

_____ 8. If the inspection point is at the midpoint of operations and ending inventory is 2/3 complete, normal loss cost is assigned to both the units completed and transferred and the ending inventory either on a unit basis or a cost basis.

_____ 9. Assume FIFO costing is used and material is added at the beginning of operations in a process costing system. If 100 units were in beginning inventory, 1/4 complete and the equivalent unit cost for materials is $1, material cost assigned this period to finish beginning inventory would amount to $75.

_____ 10. If inspection is at the midpoint of operations and ending inventory is 1/4 complete, the cost of the abnormal loss is assigned only to the good units completed and transferred.

Solutions

Matching

1.	j	6.	a
2.	g	7.	f
3.	e	8.	i
4.	a	9.	a
5.	c	10.	d

Completion and Exercises

1. The cost assigned to normal loss is assigned to the good units transferred and this total cost is sent to the subsequent department. An alternative way of treating normal loss cost is to distribute it between ending work in process and the good units finished. However, the cost of abnormal loss is treated as a separate item of Factory Overhead and is not assigned to any specific finished units. The application rate for overhead may reflect this abnormal loss.

2. Abnormal

3. The total unit cost from the prior department may differ from the computed preceding department cost because:

   a. There is strict FIFO costing within each department, but modified FIFO costing between departments. The batches from beginning inventory finished and the units started and finished are not separated when they enter a new department. When costs vary between accounting periods, the averaged cost would cause this difference.
   b. If additional units are added in the subsequent department, the preceding department cost is spread over more units, causing the prior department cost to be less than computed earlier.
   c. If there is normal loss in the preceding department, a portion or an allocated amount will be assigned to the good units transferred which causes the preceding department cost to be higher in the subsequent department.

4. Material additions which do not increase the number of units to account for are much simpler to handle because this cost represents only an additional cost component. Material additions which increase the number of units to account for require the spreading of preceding department cost over the increased mixture. When the material dilutes the mixture, the resulting preceding department cost is less than previously computed.

5. If the spoilage falls within the normal tolerance limits established, it is classified as a normal loss; otherwise, it is an abnormal loss.

6. inspection point

7. preceding department cost

8. *McAlprin Company*

Beginning inventory.	900 (2/5)
Pounds Received from Preceding Department.	8,500
Increase in Pounds.	2,000
Pounds to Account For.	11,400
Transferred.	11,256
Ending Inventory.	144 (1/4)
	11,400

8.

	Transferred	+	Ending Inventory	--	Beginning Inventory		
a. 1. EU, Preceding Department Costs, FIFO	= 11,256	+	144	-	900	=	10,500
2. EU, Preceding Department Costs, Weighted Average	= 11,256	+	144			=	11,400
b. 1. EU, Material and Conversion Costs, FIFO	= 11,256	+	36	-	360	=	10,932
			(1/4 x 144)		(2/5 x 900)		
2. EU, Material and Conversion Costs, Weighted Average	= 11,256	+	36			=	11,292

9. Fain Company

a.
Beginning inventory	500	
Received from preceding department	2,500	3,000
Ending inventory (2/5)	600	
Good units transferred out	1,800	2,400
Total units lost		600
Less abnormal loss (1/3 x 600)		200
Normal loss (2/3 x 600)		400

b. $1,800 + 240 + 100 + 200 = 2,340$
       (2/5 x 600)   (1/2 x 200)   (1/2 x 400)

c.

$$\frac{\$5,881 + \$320}{2,340} = \frac{\$6,201}{2,340} = \$2.65$$

d. Good units transferred (1,800 x $2.65) $4,770
    Normal loss (400 x 1/2 x $2.65)   530
                                                $5,300

e. Abnormal loss (200 x 1/2 x $2.65) $ 265

f. Ending inventory (600 x 2/5 x $2.65) $ 636

10.
a.

Borto Company
Cost of Production Report--FIFO
For the Month of May, 19X1

Quantity Schedule	Processing		Assembling	
Beginning Inventory	1,700	(1/4 Material, 3/5 Conversion Costs)	2,540	(All Material, 4/5 Conversion Costs)
Started in Process	6,300		5,460	
Units to Account For	8,000		8,000	
Ending Inventory	2,340	(2/9 Material, 2/3 Conversion Costs)	3,030	(All Material, 2/3 Conversion Costs)
Transferred to Next Dept.	5,460		4,500	
Abnormal Spoilage	40	(1/5 x 200)	20	
Normal Spoilage	160	(4/5 x 200)	450	(10% x 4,500)
Units Accounted For	8,000		8,000	

	Total Costs	Unit Costs	Total Costs	Unit Costs
Costs Received from Preceding Department	-0-		$19,589	$3.58773
Value of Beginning Inventory	$ 2,529		13,255	
Materials	6,927	$1.20365	6,712	1.22930
Conversion Cost	14,566	2.34935	4,574	.92255
Total Costs to Account For	$24,022	$3.55300	$44,130	$5.73958

Processing:

Costs Transferred from		
Beginning Inventory		$ 2,529
Material Added:		
(3/4 x 1,700 x $1.20365)		1,535
Conversion Costs		
(2/5 x 1,700 x $2.34935)		1,598
Total Costs Transferred from Beginning Inventory		$ 5,662
Normal Loss (160 x $3.553)		568
Costs Transferred from		
Current Production (3,760 x $3.553)		13,359
Total Costs Transferred		$19,589
Abnormal Loss (40 x $3.553)		142

Assembling:

Costs Transferred from		
Beginning Inventory		$13,255
(2,540 x 1/5 x $.92255)		469
Total Costs Transferred from Beginning Inventory		$13,724
Normal Loss (450 x $5.73958)		2,583
Costs Transferred from		
Current Production (1,960 x $5.73958)		11,250
Total Costs Transferred		$27,557
Abnormal Loss (20 x $5.73958)		115

10. (continued)
Borto Company - FIFO (concluded)

Ending Inventory
Prior Department Costs .... $ 626
Material (2/9 x 2,340 x $1.20365) 3,665
Conversion Cost (2/3 x 2,340 x $2.34935) ... 4,291

(3,030 x $3.58773) ... $10,870*
(3,030 x $1.2293) 3,725
(2,020 x $.92255) 1,863*
                       16,458
Value of Ending Inventory $24,022
Total Costs Accounted For $44,130

*Didn't round to nearest dollar because of decimal discrepancy.

Additional Computations

	Transferred	+	Ending Inventory	+	Abnormal Spoilage	+	Normal Spoilage	-	Beginning Inventory	=	
EU, Processing, Material =	5,460	+	520 (2,340 x 2/9)	+	40	+	160	-	425 (1,700 x 1/4)	=	5,755
EU, Processing, Conversion Costs =	5,460	+	1,560 (2,340 x 2/3)	+	40	+	160	-	1,020 (1,700 x 3/5)	=	6,200
EU, Assembling, Preceding Department Costs =	4,500	+	3,030 (3,030 x 100%)	+	20	+	450	-	2,540	=	5,460
EU, Assembling, Material =	4,500	+	3,030	+	20	+	450	-	2,540	=	5,460
EU, Assembling, Conversion Costs =	4,500	+	2,020 (2/3 x 3,030)	+	20	+	450	-	2,032 (2,540 x 4/5)	=	4,958

$\dfrac{\$6,927}{5,755} = \$1.20365$

$\dfrac{\$14,566}{6,200} = \$2.34935$

$\dfrac{\$19,589}{5,460} = \$3.58773$

$\dfrac{\$6,712}{5,460} = \$1.22930$

$\dfrac{\$4,574}{4,958} = \$.92255$

10. (continued)
b.

Borto Company
Cost of Production Report--Weighted Average
For the Month of May, 19X1

Quantity Schedule	Processing		Assembling	
Beginning Inventory	1,700	(1/4 Material, 3/5 Conversion Costs)	2,540	(All Material, 4/5 Conversion Costs)
Started in Process	6,300		5,460	
Units to Account For	8,000		8,000	
Ending Inventory	2,340	(2/9 Material, 2/3 Conversion Costs)	3,030	(All Material, 2/3 Conversion Costs)
Transferred to Next Dept.	5,460		4,500	
Abnormal Spoilage	40	(1/5 x 200)	20	
Normal Spoilage	160	(4/5 x 200)	450	(10% x 4,500)
Units Accounted For	8,000		8,000	

	Processing Total Costs	Processing Unit Costs	Assembling Total Costs	Assembling Unit Costs
Beginning Inventory:				
Prior Department Costs	-0-		$ 8,490	
Materials	$ 489		3,048	
Conversion Costs	2,040		1,717	
Value of Beginning Inventory	$ 2,529		$13,255	
Costs Received from Preceding Department	-0-		19,670	$3.52
Current Costs:				
Materials	6,927	$1.20	6,712	1.22
Conversion Cost	14,566	2.30	4,574	.90
Total Costs to Account For	$24,022	$3.50	$44,211	$5.64
Costs Transferred before Spoilage (5,460 X $3.50)	$ 19,110			
Costs Transferred before Spoilage (4,500 X $5.64)			$25,380	
Normal Spoilage (160 X $3.553)	560			
Normal Spoilage (450 X $5.64)			2,538	
Total Costs Transferred	$19,670		$27,918	
Abnormal Spoilage (40 X $3.50)	140			
Abnormal Spoilage (20 X $5.64)			113	
Ending Inventory:				
Prior Department Costs (3,030 X $3.52)			10,665	
Material (2/9 x 2,340 X $1.20)	624			
Material (3,030 X $1.22)			3,697	
Conversion Costs (2/3 X 2,340 X $2.30)	3,588			
Conversion Costs (3,030 x 2/3 X $.90)			1,818	
Value of Ending Inventory	4,212		16,180	
Total Costs Accounted For	$24,022		$44,211	

10. (concluded)

Borto Company - Weighted Average (concluded)

Additional Computations

	Transferred	+	Ending Inventory	+	Abnormal Spoilage	+	Normal Spoilage	=	
EU, Processing, Material =	5,460	+	520 (2,340 x 2/9)	+	40	+	160	=	6,180
EU, Processing, Conversion Costs =	5,460	+	1,560 (2,340 x 2/3)	+	40	+	160	=	7,220
EU, Assembling, Prior Department Costs =	4,500	+	3,030 (3,030 x 100%)	+	20	+	450	=	8,000
EU, Assembling, Material =	4,500	+	3,030	+	20	+	450	=	8,000
EU, Assembling, Conversion Costs =	4,500	+	2,020 (2/3 x 3,030)	+	20	+	450	=	6,990

EU, Processing, Material =

$$\frac{\$489 + \$6,927}{6,180} = \frac{\$7,416}{6,180} = \$1.20$$

EU, Processing, Conversion Costs =

$$\frac{\$2,040 + \$14,566}{7,220} = \frac{\$16,606}{7,220} = \$2.30$$

EU, Assembling, Prior Department Costs =

$$\frac{\$8,490 + \$19,670}{8,000} = \frac{\$28,160}{8,000} = \$3.52$$

EU, Assembling, Material =

$$\frac{\$3,048 + \$6,712}{8,000} = \frac{\$9,760}{8,000} = \$1.22$$

EU, Assembling, Conversion Costs =

$$\frac{\$1,717 + \$4,574}{6,990} = \frac{\$6,291}{6,990} = \$.90$$

11. Rejects, Inc.
a.

$$\frac{28,800 \text{ units transferred}}{.80} = 36,000 \text{ units finished that were inspected}$$

    36,000 finished
- 28,800 goods units transferred
     7,200 units lost due to normal spoilage

b. The cost of the 7,200 units lost due to normal spoilage will be assigned to the 28,800 good units transferred to finished goods.

c. EU, Weighted average, material = 28,800 + 7,200 + 200 = 36,200
EU, Weighted average, labor = 28,800 + 7,200 + 1,600 = 37,600
EU, Weighted average, overhead = 28,800 + 7,200 + 500 = 36,500

d. EU FIFO, material = 28,800 + 7,200 + 200 - 2,000 = 34,200
EU FIFO, labor = 28,800 + 7,200 + 1,600 - 500 = 37,100
EU FIFO, overhead = 28,800 + 7,200 + 500 - 600 = 35,900

12.
Molt Company
Quantity Schedule

Beginning inventory	1,500	
Received from preceding dept.	6,000	
Pounds added in dept	3,000	10,500
Transferred	7,500	
Ending inventory	2,250	
Abnormal loss	225	
Normal Loss	525	10,500

a.

Department L Cost: $\dfrac{\$4,710 + \$28,125}{7,500 + 750 + 2,250} = \dfrac{\$32,835}{10,500} = \$3.12714$

Department M Material: $\dfrac{\$1,710 + \$13,320}{7,500 + (750 \times .90) + (2,250 \times .60)} = \dfrac{\$15,030}{9,525} = 1.57795$

Department M Conversion Costs: $\dfrac{\$1,365 + \$9,990}{7,500 + (750 \times .90) + (2,250 \times .40)} = \dfrac{\$11,355}{9,075} = \underline{1.25124}$

Total cost per equivalent unit .... $\underline{\$5.95633}$

1. 7,500 Good Pounds x $5.95633 .... $44,672.52*
   525 Pounds Normal Loss:
   525 x $3.12714 .... $1,641.75
   525 x .90 x $1.57795 .... 745.58
   525 x .90 x $1.25124 .... 591.21
   Total Cost of 7,500 Good Pounds $47,651.06

2. 225 Pounds Abnormal Loss:
   225 x $3.12714 .... $703.61
   225 x .90 x $1.57795 .... 319.53
   225 x .90 x $1.25124 .... 253.38
   Total Cost of 225 pounds of Abnormal Loss 1,276.52

*Rounded up $.04 due to decimal discrepancy

3. 2,250 Pounds Ending Inventory:
   2,250 x $3.12714... $7,036.07
   2,250 x .60 x $1.57795....................................... 2,130.23
   2,250 x .40 x $1.25124....................................... 1,126.12
   Total Cost of 2,250 Pounds Ending Inventory 10,292.42
   Total Cost Accounted for.. $59,220.00

   Summary
a. 1. = $47,651.06
    2. = $ 1,276.52
    3. = $10,292.42

b.

Department L Cost: $$\frac{\$28,125}{7,500 + 750 + 2,250 - 1,500} = \frac{\$28,125}{9,000} = \$3.12500$$

Department M Material: $$\frac{\$13,320}{7,500 + (750 \times .90) + (2,250 \times .60) - (1,500 \times .80)} = \frac{\$13,320}{8,325} = 1.60000$$

Department M Conversion Costs: $$\frac{\$9,990}{7,500 + (750 \times .90) + (2,250 \times .40) - (1,500 \times .70)} = \frac{\$9,990}{8,025} = \underline{1.24486}$$

Total cost for equivalent unit $5.96986

1. Completion of 1,500 Pounds in Beginning Inventory:
   Beginning Inventory Cost.. $7,785.00
   Department M Material Added (1,500 x .20 x $1.60)....................... 480.00
   Department M Conversion Added (1,500 x .30 x $1.24486).............. 560.18
   Cost of 1,500 Pounds.. $ 8,825.18
   Cost of 6,000 Pounds (7,500 - 1,500) started and completed
   in April (6,000 x $5.96986).. 35,819.16

   525 Pounds Normal Loss:
   525 x $3.125.. $1,640.63
   525 x .90 x $1.60... 756.00
   525 x .90 x $1.24486.. 588.20
                                                                   2,984.83
   Total cost of 7,500 Good Pounds $47,629.17

2. 225 Pounds Abnormal Loss:
   225 x $3.125.. $ 703.13
   225 x .90 x $1.60... 324.00
   225 x .90 x $1.24486... 252.08
   Total cost of 225 Pounds of Abnormal Loss 1,279.21

3. 2,250 Pounds Ending Inventory:
   2,250 x $3.125.. $7,031.25
   2,250 x .60 x $1.60... 2,160.00
   2,250 x .40 x $1.24486... 1,120.37
   Total Cost of 2,250 Pounds Ending Inventory 10,311.62
   Total Cost accounted for $59,220.00

Summary
b. 1. = $47,629.17
    2. = $ 1,279.21
    3. = $10,311.62

13.

Fitzpatrick Manufacturing Company
Cost of Production Report--Weighted-Average Costing--Addition of Material
For the Month Ending January 31, 19XX

Quantity Schedule

	Mixing Department	Assembly Department
Beginning Inventory (Mixing 1/2 M, 1/3 CC) (Assembly 1/4 M, 1/5 CC)	600	200
Received from Preceding Department	-0-	3,700
Increase in Units Put in Process	-0-	500
Started in Process	4,500	
	5,100	4,400
Transferred to Next Department	3,700	3,650
Ending Inventory (Mixing 1/5 M, 2/7 CC) (Assembly 1/3 M, 3/5 CC)	1,400	750
	5,100	4,400

Costs Charged to Department:

	Mixing Total Costs	Mixing Unit Costs	Assembly Total Costs	Assembly Unit Costs
Work in Process: Beginning Inventory				
Costs from Preceding Department			$ 615.00	
Material	$ 195.10		45.00	
Conversion Costs	445.50		16.50	
	$ 640.60		$ 676.50	
Costs from Preceding Department			10,693.00	
Current Cost in Department				
Material	2,431.70	$ .66	3,582.00	.93
Conversion Costs	8,697.50	2.23	1,459.50	.36
Total Costs to Account for	$11,769.80	$2.89	$16,411.00	$3.86

Costs Accounted for as Follows:

	Mixing Total Costs	Assembly Total Costs
Costs Transferred to Next Department (Mixing 3,700 x $2.89) (Assembly 3,650 x $3.86)	$10,693.00	$14,089.00
Work in Process: Ending Inventory		
Cost from Preceding Department (750 x $2.57)		$ 1,927.50
Material (Mixing 1,400 x 1/5 x $.66) (Assembly 750 x 1/3 x $.93)	$184.80	232.50
Conversion Costs (Mixing 1,400 x 2/7 x $2.23) (Assembly 750 x 3/5 x $.36)	892.00	162.00
	1,076.80	2,322.00
Total Costs Accounted for	$11,769.80	$16,411.00

13. Fitzpatrick Manufacturing Company (concluded)

EU, Mixing Department, Material = Transferred + Ending Inventory

$$3,700 + \begin{matrix} 280 \\ (1,400 \times 1/5) \end{matrix} = 3,980$$

$$\frac{\$195.10 + \$2,431.70}{3,980} = \frac{\$2,626.80}{3,980} = \$.66$$

EU, Mixing Department, Conversion Cost =

$$3,700 + \begin{matrix} 400 \\ (1,400 \times 2/7) \end{matrix} = 4,100$$

$$\frac{\$445.50 + \$8,697.50}{4,100} = \frac{\$9,143.00}{4,100} = \$2.23$$

EU, Preceding Department Cost =

$$3,650 + \begin{matrix} 750 \\ (750 \times 100\%) \end{matrix} = 4,400$$

$$\frac{\$615.00 + \$10,693.00}{4,400} = \frac{\$11,308.00}{4,400} = \$2.57$$

EU, Assembly Department, Material =

$$3,650 + \begin{matrix} 250 \\ (750 \times 1/3) \end{matrix} = 3,900$$

$$\frac{\$45.00 + \$3,582.00}{3,900} = \frac{\$3,627.00}{3,900} = \$.93$$

EU, Assembly Department, Conversion Cost =

$$3,650 + \begin{matrix} 450 \\ (750 \times 3/5) \end{matrix} = 4,100$$

$$\frac{\$16.50 + \$1,459.50}{4,100} = \frac{\$1,476.00}{4,100} = \$.36$$

JTT Company

Department 1

Physical flow:		
Beginning inventory	100	(1/5 Material, 1/10 Labor, 1/4 Overhead)
Started in process	2,000	
Units to account for	2,100	
Abnormal loss of units	300	(2/3)
Normal Loss of units	600	(2/3)
Ending inventory	200	(1/4 Material, 1/5 Labor, 1/10 Overhead)
Transferred	1,000	
	2,100	

	Total Costs	Unit Costs
Prior department costs	--0--	
Beginning inventory	$ 140.00	
Current costs		
Material	4,075.00	$2.50
Labor	3,260.00	2.00
Overhead	4,785.00	3.00
Costs to account for	$12,260.00	$7.50

Costs transferred		
From beginning inventory	$140.00	
Material added (4/5 x 100 x $2.50)	200.00	
Labor added (9/10 x 100 x $2.00)	180.00	
Overhead added (3/4 x 100 x $3.00)	225.00	$ 745.00
From current production (900 x $ 7.50)		6,750.00
Costs of normal loss (600 x 2/3 x $7.50)		3,000.00
Total costs transferred		$10,495.00
Costs of abnormal loss (300 x 2/3 x $7.50)		1,500.00
Ending inventory		
Prior department costs		
Material (200 x 1/4 x $2.50)	$125.00	
Labor (200 x 1/5 x $2.00)	80.00	
Overhead (200 x 1/10 x $3.00)	60.00	265.00
Total ending inventory		
Total costs accounted for		$12,260.00

Department 2

Physical flow:		
Beginning inventory	60	(1/3 Labor, 1/4 Overhead)
Started in process	1,000	
Units to account for	1,060	
Abnormal loss of units	150	
Normal Loss of units	90	
Ending inventory	300	(5/6 Labor, 4/5 Overhead)
Transferred	520	
	1,060	

	Total Costs	Unit Costs
Prior department costs	$10,495.00	$10.495
Beginning inventory	598.00	-0-
Current costs		
Material	2,624.00	3.200
Labor	2,275.00	2.500
Overhead	2,534.00	2.800
Costs to account for	$18,526.00	$18.995

Costs transferred		
From beginning inventory	$598.00	
(60 x $3.20)	192.00	
(60 x 2/3 x $2.50)	100.00	
(60 x 3/4 x $2.80)	126.00	$ 1,016.00
From current production (460 x $18.995) See (1)		8,737.70
Costs of normal loss See (2)		1,262.55
Total costs transferred		$11,016.25
Costs of abnormal loss		2,104.25
Ending inventory		
Prior department costs (300 x $10.495)	$3,148.50	
Material (300 x $3.20)	960.00	
Labor (300 x 5/6 x $2.50)	625.00	
Overhead (300 x 4/5 x $2.80)	672.00	5,405.50
Total ending inventory		
Total costs accounted for		$18,526.00

14. JTT Company (concluded)

	Transferred	Ending Inventory	Abnormal Spoilage	Normal Spoilage	Beginning Inventory	EU		
EU, material, Dept. 1	1,000	+ 50	+ 200	+ 400	- 20	= 1,630	=	$\dfrac{\$4,075}{1,630} = \$2.50$
EU, labor, Dept. 1	1,000	+ 40	+ 200	+ 400	- 10	= 1,630	=	$\dfrac{\$3,260}{1,630} = \$2.00$
EU, overhead, Dept. 1	1,000	+ 20	+ 200	+ 400	- 25	= 1,595	=	$\dfrac{\$4,785}{1,595} = \$3.00$
EU, prior dept. cost	520	+ 300	+ 150	+ 90	- 60	= 1,000	=	$\dfrac{\$10,495}{1,000} = \$10.495$
EU, material, Dept. 2	520	+ 300	+ 0	+ 0	- 0	= 820	=	$\dfrac{\$2,624}{820} = \$3.200$
EU, labor, Dept. 2	520	+ 250	+ 100 (150 X 2/3)	+ 60 (90 X 2/3)	- 20	= 910	=	$\dfrac{\$2,275}{910} = \$2.500$
EU, overhead, Dept. 2	520	+ 240	+ 100	+ 60	- 15	= 905	=	$\dfrac{\$2,534}{905} = \$2.800$

FOOTNOTES

(1) Normal Spoilage
Prior Dept. Cost (90 x $10.495)........ $ 944.55
Labor (90 x 2/3 x $2.50)............... 150.00
Overhead (90 x 2/3 x $2.80)........... 168.00 $1,262.55

(2) Abnormal Spoilage
Prior Dept. Cost (150 x $10.495)...... $1,574.25
Labor (150 x 2/3 x $2.50)............. 250.00
Overhead (150 x 2/3 x $2.80).......... 280.00 $2,104.25

b. Cost of Lost Units......... 3,604.25
   Work in Process--Department 1........... 1,500.00
   Work in Process--Department 2........... 2,104.25
   Work in Process--Department 2........... 10,495.00
   Work in Process--Department 1........... 10,495.00
   Finished Goods 11,016.25
   Work in Process--Department 2........... 11,016.25

c. With the FIFO method of process costing, the details of beginning inventory are not needed; only the total cost incurred is needed. In addition the stage of completion of each cost component of beginning inventory is also needed.

15.

Friday Company
Cost of Production Report--Weighted-Average Costing
For the Month of May, 19X1

a.

	Processing		Assembling	
Quantity Schedule:				
Beginning Inventory	120	(1/3 material, 1/6 conversion costs)	50	(1/5 material, 1/10 conversion costs)
Started in Process	580		500	
Units to Account For	700		550	
Ending Inventory	100	(1/5 material, 1/4 conversion costs)	48	(1/6 material 1/8 conversion cost)
Transferred to Next Department	500		502	
Abnormal Spoilage (1/4 X 100)	25		-0-	
Normal Spoilage (3/4 X 100)	75		-0-	
Units Accounted For	700		550	

	Total Costs	Unit Costs	Total Costs	Unit Costs
Beginning Inventory:				
Prior Department Cost			$ 250.00	
Materials	$ 80.50		39.50	
Conversion Costs	66.00		30.16	
Value of Beginning Inventory	$ 146.50		$ 319.66	
Cost Received from Preceding Department			2,593.00	$ 5.16909
Current Costs:				
Material	1,020.10	$1.77516	2,070.00	4.13627
Conversion Costs	1,643.00	2.73440	2,545.18	5.06957
Total Cost to Account For	$2,809.60	$4.50956	$7,527.84	$14.37493

15. Friday Company-Weighted-Average (concluded)

Costs Transferred (500 x $4.50956)	$2,254.79	(502 x $14.37493)	$7,216.21
Normal Loss (75 x $4.50956)...............	338.21		-0-
Total Costs Transferred........................	$2,593.00		$7,216.21
Ending Inventory:			
Prior Department Cost........................	$-0-	(48 x $5.16909) 248.12	
Material (1/5 x 100 x $1.77516)...........	35.50	(48 x 1/6 x $4.13627) 33.09	
Conversion Cost (1/4 x 100 x $2.73440)	68.36	(48 x 1/8 x $5.06957) 30.42	
Value of Ending Inventory..................	103.86		311.63
Abnormal Spoilage (25 x $4.50956).......	112.74		
Total Cost Accounted For.....................	$2,809.60		$7,527.84

EU Processing Materials = 500 transferred + 75 Normal Loss + 25 Abnormal Loss
+ 20 ending inventory = 620
(1/5 X 100)

$$\text{Processing Material Unit Cost} = \frac{\$80.50 + \$1,020.10}{620} = \$1.77516$$

EU Processing Conversion Cost = 500 transferred + 75 Normal Loss + 25 Abnormal Loss + 25 = 625
(1/4 x 100)

$$\text{Processing Conversion Unit Cost} = \frac{\$66.00 + \$1,643.00}{625} = \$2.73440$$

EU Prior Dept. Cost = 48 ending inventory + 502 transferred = 550

$$\text{Prior Dept. Unit Cost} = \frac{\$2,593.00 + \$250.00}{550} = \$5.16909$$

EU Assembling Material = 502 + 8 ending inventory = 510
(48 x 1/6)

$$\text{Assembling Material Unit Cost} = \frac{\$2,070.00 + \$39.50}{510} = \$4.13627$$

EU Assembling Conversion Cost = 502 + 6 ending inventory = 508
(48 x 1/8)

$$\text{Assembling Conversion Unit Cost} = \frac{\$2,545.18 + \$30.16}{508} = \$5.06957$$

b. 15 (continued)

Friday Company
Cost of Production Report--FIFO
For the Month of May, 19X1

	Processing		Assembling	
Quantity Schedule:				
Beginning Inventory	120	(1/3 material, 1/6 conversion costs)	50	(1/5 material, 1/10 CC)
Started in Process	580		500	
Units to Account For	700		550	
Ending inventory	100	(1/5 material, 1/4 conversion costs)	48	(1/6 material 1/8 CC)
Transferred to Next Department	500		502	
Abnormal Spoilage (1/4 x 100)	25		-0-	
Normal Spoilage (3/4 x 100)	75		-0-	
Units Accounted For	700		550	

	Total Costs	Unit Costs	Total Costs	Unit Costs
Costs Received from Preceding Department	-0-		$2,594.67	$5.1893
Value of Beginning Inventory	$ 146.50		319.66	
Material	1,020.10	$1.75879	2,070.00	4.1400
Conversion Costs	1,643.00	2.71570	2,545.18	5.0600
Total Cost to Account For	$2,809.60	$4.47449	$7,529.51	$14.3893

Costs Transferred				
From Beginning Inventory	$ 146.50		$ 319.66	
Material Added: (2/3 x 120 x $1.75879)	140.70	(4/5 X 50 X $4.14)	165.60	
Conversion Costs (5/6 x 120 x $2.71570)	271.57	(9/10 X 50 X $5.06)	227.70	
Total Costs Transferred from				
Beginning Inventory	$ 558.77		$ 712.96	
Costs Transferred from Current				
Production ($4.47449 x 380)	1,700.31	($14.3893 X 452)	6,503.98*	
Normal Loss (75 x $4.47449)	335.59		-0-	
Total Costs Transferred		$2,594.67		$7,216.94
Ending Inventory:				
Prior Department Costs	$ -0-	(48 X $5.1893) $249.09		
Material (1/5 x 100 x $1.75879)	35.18	(48 x 1/6 x $4.14) 33.12		
Conversion Cost (1/4 x 100 x $2.71570)	67.89	(48 x 1/8 x $5.06) 30.36		
Value of Ending Inventory		103.07		312.57
Abnormal Loss (25 x $4.47449)		111.86		-0-
Total Costs Accounted For		$2,809.60		$7,529.51

*Rounded by $.02

15. Friday Company--FIFO (concluded)

EU Processing Materials = 500 transferred + 75 Normal + 25 Abnormal + 20 end. inv. - 40 begin. inv. = 580
$\qquad\qquad\qquad\qquad\qquad\qquad\qquad$ Loss $\qquad\qquad$ Loss $\qquad$ (1/5 X 100) $\quad$ (120 x 1/3)

Processing Material Unit Cost = $\dfrac{\$1,020.10}{580}$ = \$1.75879

EU Processing CC = 500 transferred + 75 Normal + 25 Abnormal + 25 end. inven. - 20 begin. inv. = 605
$\qquad\qquad\qquad\qquad\qquad\qquad$ Loss $\qquad\qquad$ Loss $\qquad$ (1/4 X 100) $\qquad$ (120 x 1/6)

Processing Conversion Costs Unit Cost = $\dfrac{\$1,643.00}{605}$ = \$2.71570

EU Prior Dept. Cost = 502 transferred + 48 ending inventory - 50 beginning inventory = 500

Prior Dept. Unit Cost = $\dfrac{\$2,594.67}{500}$ = \$5.1893

EU Assembling Material = 502 + 8 ending inventory - 10 beginning inventory = 500
$\qquad\qquad\qquad\qquad\qquad\quad$ (48 x 1/6) $\qquad\quad$ (50 X 1/5)

Assembling Material Unit Cost = $\dfrac{\$2,070.00}{500}$ = \$4.14

EU Assembling Conversion Costs = 502 + 6 ending inventory - 5 beginning inventory = 503
$\qquad\qquad\qquad\qquad\qquad\qquad\quad$ (48 x 1/8) $\qquad\quad$ (50 X 1/10)

Assembling Conversion Costs Unit Cost = $\dfrac{\$2,545.18}{503}$ = \$5.06

Murray Manufacturing Company
Cost of Production Report--FIFO
For the Month Ending June, 19XX

16. a.

	Mixing		Finishing	
Quantity Schedule:				
Beginning inventory (1/4 M, 1/3 CC)	2,100		(1/5 M, 1/4 CC) 600	
Started in production	6,700 → 8,800		5,400 → 6,000	
Transferred	5,400		2,500	
Abnormal loss	300		200	
Normal loss	1,600		1,000	
Ending inventory (2/5 M, 1/3 CC)	1,500 → 8,800		(3/4 M, 2/5 CC) 2,300 → 6,000	

	Total Costs	Unit Costs	Total Costs	Unit Costs
Costs charged to department:				
Beginning inventory:				
Costs from preceding department			$ 832	
Material	$ 284		2,252	
Conversion costs	1,050		1,904	
Costs of beginning inventory	$1,334		$4,988	
Current costs:				
Costs received from preceding department			13,470	$ 2.4944
Material	3,570	$ .60	23,548	5.3457
Conversion costs	10,215	1.80	15,953	4.4686
Total costs to account for	$15,119	$2.40	$57,959	$12.3087

Costs accounted for as follows:

	Mixing	Finishing
Transferred from beginning inventory		
Costs of beginning inventory	$1,334	$ 4,988
Material added (2,100 x 3/4 x $.60)	945	
Material added (600 x 4/5 x $5.3457)		2,566
Conversion costs (2,100 x 2/3 x $1.80)	2,520	
Conversion costs (600 x 3/4 x $4.4686)		2,011
Total costs of beginning inventory finished before loss allocation	$4,799	$9,565
Transferred from current production (3,300 x $2.40)	7,920	
Transferred from current production (1,900 x $12.3087)		23,387
Costs transferred before loss allocation	$12,719	$32,952
Loss allocation (5,400/6,900 x $960)	751	
Loss allocation (2,500/4,800 x $4,947)		2,577
Total costs transferred	$13,470	$35,529

16. a.   Murray Manufacturing (continued)

Ending Inventory			
Costs from preceding department...................	(2,300 x $2.4944)	$ 5,737	$ 360
Materials (1,500 x 2/5 x $.60)...................	(2,300 x 3/4 x $5.3457)	9,221	900
Conversion costs (1,500 x 1/3 x $1.80)........	(2,300 x 2/5 x $4.4686)	4,111	$1,260
Costs of Ending Inventory Before Loss Allocation....		$19,069	
Loss Allocation (1,500/6,900 x $960)............	(2,300/4,800 x $4,947)	2,370	209
Total Costs of Ending Inventory..................		21,439	1,469
Abnormal loss			
Prior Department Costs...........	(200 x $2.4944)	501*	
Materials (300 x 1/4 x $.60).....	(200 x 1/4 x $5.3457)	267	45
Conversion Costs (300 x 1/4 x $1.80)....	(200 x 1/4 x $4.4686)	223	135
Total Costs of Abnormal Loss................		991	180
Total Costs Accounted For.............		$57,959	$15,119
Loss Allocation:			
Costs of Normal Loss:			
Prior Department Costs.........	(1,000 x $2.4944)	$2,494	
Current:			
Material (1,600 x 1/4 x $.60).....	(1,000 x 1/4 x $5.3457)	1,336	240
Conversion Costs (1,600 x 1/4 x $1.80)...	(1,000 x 1/4 x $4.4686)	1,117	720
Total Costs of Normal Loss...........		$4,947	$ 960

16. Murray Manufacturing a. concluded)
Additional Computations:

	Transferred		Ending Inventory		Abnormal Spoilage		Normal Spoilage		Beginning Inventory	
EU, Mixing, Material	5,400	+	600 (1,500 × 2/5)	+	75 (300 × 1/4)	+	400 (1,600 × 1/4)	−	525 (2,100 × 1/4)	= 5,950
EU, Mixing, Conversion Costs	5,400	+	500 (1,500 × 1/3)	+	75 (300 × 1/4)	+	400 (1,600 × 1/4)	−	700 (2,100 × 1/3)	= 5,675
EU, Finishing, Prior Department Costs	2,500	+	2,300 (2,300 × 100%)	+	200 (200 × 100%)	+	1,000 (1,000 × 100%)	−	600 (600 × 100%)	= 5,400
EU, Finishing, Material	2,500	+	1,725 (2,300 × 3/4)	+	50 (200 × 1/4)	+	250 (1,000 × 1/4)	−	120 (600 × 1/5)	= 4,405
EU, Finishing, Conversion Costs	2,500	+	920 (2,300 × 2/5)	+	50 (200 × 1/4)	+	250 (1,000 × 1/4)	−	150 (600 × 1/4)	= 3,570

EU, Mixing, Material
$$\frac{\$3,570}{5,950} = \$.60$$

EU, Mixing, Conversion Costs
$$\frac{\$10,215}{5,675} = \$1.80$$

EU, Finishing, Prior Department Costs
$$\frac{\$13,470}{5,400} = \$2.4944$$

EU, Finishing, Material
$$\frac{\$23,548}{4,405} = \$5.3457$$

EU, Finishing, Conversion Costs
$$\frac{\$15,953}{3,570} = \$4.4686$$

*Rounded up by $2

16. b.

Murray Manufacturing Company
Cost of Production Report--Weighted Average
For the Month Ending June, 19XX

	Mixing		Finishing	
	Total Costs	Unit Costs	Total Costs	Unit Costs
Quantity Schedule:				
Beginning inventory (1/4 M, 1/3 CC)	2,100		600 (1/5 M, 1/4 CC)	
Started in production	6,700		5,400	
	8,800		6,000	
Transferred	5,400		2,500	
Abnormal loss	300		200	
Normal loss	1,600		1,000	
Ending inventory (2/5 M, 1/3 CC)	1,500		2,300 (3/4 M, 2/5 CC)	
	8,800		6,000	
Costs charged to department:				
Beginning Inventory:				
Costs from preceding department			$ 832	
Material	$ 284		2,252	
Conversion costs	1,050		1,904	
Costs of Beginning Inventory	$1,334		$ 4,988	
Current costs:				
Costs received from preceding dept.			13,496	$ 2.3880
Material	3,570	$ .5952	23,548	5.7017
Conversion costs	10,215	1.7671	15,953	4.8003
Total Costs to Account For	$15,119	$2.3623	$57,985	$12.8900
Costs Accounted For As Follows:				
Costs Transferred before Loss				
Allocation (5,400 x $2.3623)	$12,756		(2,500 x $12.8900) $32,226*	
Loss Allocation (5,400/6,900 x $945)	737		(2,500/4,800 x $5,013) 2,607	
Total Costs Transferred	13,493		$34,833	
Ending Inventory:				
Costs from preceding dept.			(2,300 x $2.3880) 5,492	
Materials (1,500 x 2/5 x $.5952)	357		(2,300 x 3/4 x $5.7017) 9,835	
Conversion Costs (1,500 x 1/3 x $1.7671)	884		(2,300 x 2/5 x $4.8003) 4,416	
Costs of Ending Inventory Before Loss Allocation	$1,241		$19,743	
Loss allocation (1,500/6,900 x $945)	208		(2,300/4,800 x $5,013) 2,406	
Total Costs of Ending Inventory	1,449		22,149	

* Rounded up by $1

16.
b.

Abnormal loss

Prior Department Costs...........		(200 x $2.3880) $ 478
Material (300 x 1/4 x $.5952)......	$ 44	(200 x 1/4 x $5.7017) 285
Conversion Costs (300 x 1/4 x $1.7671)......	133	(200 x 1/4 x $4.8003) 240
Total Costs of Abnormal Loss......	$ 177	1,003
Total Costs Accounted For......	$15,119	$57,985

Loss Allocation:

Costs of Normal Loss:		
Prior Department Costs......		(1,000 x $2.388) $ 2,388
Current Department Costs:		
Material (1,600 x 1/4 x $.5952)......	$ 238	(1,000 x 1/4 x $5.7017) 1,425
Conversion Costs (1,600 x 1/4 x $1.7671)......	707	(1,000 x 1/4 x $4.8003) 1,200
Total Cost of Normal Loss......	$ 945	$ 5,013

Additional Computations:

	Transferred	+	Ending Inventory	+	Abnormal Spoilage	+	Normal Spoilage	=

EU, Mixing, Material = $\dfrac{\$284 + \$3,570}{6,475} = \$.5952$

	Transferred	+	Ending Inventory	+	Abnormal Spoilage	+	Normal Spoilage	=	
6,475	5,400	+	600	+	75	+	400	=	6,475
			(1,500 X 2/5)		(300 x 1/4)		(1,600 x 1/4)		

EU, Mixing, Conversion Costs $\dfrac{\$1,050 + \$10,215}{6,375} = \$1.7671$

	5,400	+	500	+	75	+	400	=	6,375
			(1,500 X 1/3)		(300 x 1/4)		(1,600 x 1/4)		

EU, Mixing, Prior Department Costs $\dfrac{\$832 + \$13,496}{6,000} = \$2.3880$

	2,500	+	2,300	+	200	+	1,000	=	6,000
			(2,300 x 100%)		(200 x 100%)		(1,000 x 100%)		

EU, Finishing, Material $\dfrac{\$2,252 + \$23,548}{4,525} = \$5.7017$

	2,500	+	1,725	+	50	+	250	=	4,525
			(2,300 x 3/4)		(200 x1/4)		(1,000 x 1/4)		

EU, Finishing, Conversion Costs $\dfrac{\$1,904 + \$15,953}{3,720} = \$4.8003$

	2,500	+	920	+	50	+	250	=	3,720
			(2,300 x 2/5)		(200 x 1/4)		(1,000 x 1/4)		

17.
a.
Gene Peery Production Company
Cost of Production Report--Weighted Average
For the Month of April 30, 19X1

Quantity schedule:

Units in beginning inventory (All Mat., 1/5 CC)...	200	
Units received from preceding department...	500	
Increase in units put into process...	200	900
Units transferred...	700	
Units in ending inventory (All Mat., 1/6 CC)	60	
Normal loss of units..	100	
Abnormal loss of units...	40	900

	Total Costs	Unit Costs

Costs to be accounted for:
Work in Process: Beginning Inventory

Costs from preceding department..	$ 400.00	
Material	500.00	
Conversion costs..	30.00	
Total value of beginning inventory	$ 930.00	

Current Costs:

Cost from preceding department (500 x $2.968).............................	$1,484.00	$2.0933333
Material	770.00	1.4111111
Conversion costs...	564.00	.7973154
Total current costs	$2,818.00	
Total costs to account for..	$3,748.00	$4.3017598

Costs accounted for:
Abnormal loss:

Cost from preceding department (40 x $2.0933333)................................	$ 83.73	
Material (40 x $1.4111111)..	56.44	
Conversion cost (40 x 1/4 x $.7973154)...	7.97	
Total value of abnormal loss...		$148.14
Costs transferred (700 x $4.3017598)	$3,011.25*	

Normal loss:

Cost from preceding department (100 x $2.0933333).............. $209.33		
Material (100 x $1.4111111)........................... 141.11		
Conversion costs (100 x 1/4 x $.7973154)........................ 19.93		
Total value of normal loss...	370.37	
Total costs transferred..		3,381.62

Ending inventory

Costs from preceding department (60 x $2.0933333)................................	125.60	
Material (60 x $1.4111111)..	84.67	
Conversion costs (60 x 1/6 x $.7973154)...	7.97	218.24
Total costs accounted for		$3,748.00

*Rounded up by $.02 to account for decimal discrepancy

EU, Preceding Department = 700 + 40 + 100 + 60 = 900

$$\frac{\$400 + \$1,484}{900} = \$2.0933333$$

EU, Material = 700 + 40 + 100 + 60 = 900

$$\frac{\$500 + \$770}{900} = \$1.411111$$

17. Gene Peery Production Company - a. weighted average (concluded)

EU, Conversion Cost = 700 + 25 + 10 + 10 = 745
(100 x 1/4) (40 x 1/4) (60 x 1/6)

$$\frac{\$30 + \$564}{745} = \$.7973154$$

b.

Gene Peery Production Company
Cost of Production Report--FIFO Cost
For the Month of April, 19X1

Quantity schedule:

Units in beginning inventory (All Mat., 1/5 CC)	200	
Units received from preceding department	500	
Increase in units put into process	200	900
Units transferred	700	
Units in ending inventory (All Mat., 1/6 CC)	60	
Normal loss of units	100	
Abnormal loss of units	40	900

	Total Costs	Unit Costs
Costs to be accounted for:		
Work in Process: Beginning Inventory		
Costs from preceding department	$ 400.00	
Material	500.00	
Conversion Costs	30.00	
Total value of beginning inventory	$ 930.00	
Current costs:		
Cost from preceding department (500 x $2.968)	$1,484.00	$2.12
Material	770.00	1.10
Conversion Cost	564.00	.80
Total current costs	$2,818.00	
Total costs to account for	$3,748.00	$4.02

Costs accounted for:			
Costs Transferred to Next Department			
From Beginning Inventory			
Value of Beginning Inventory		$930.00	
Conversion Costs Added (200 x 4/5 x $.80)		128.00	$1,058.00
From Current Production (500 x $4.02)			2,010.00
Total Costs Transferred Before Normal Loss			$3,068.00
Costs of Normal Loss:			
Cost from Preceding Department (100 x $2.12)		$212.00	
Material (100 x $1.10)		110.00	
Conversion costs (100 x 1/4 x $.80)		20.00	
Total value of normal loss			342.00
Total Costs Transferred			$3,410.00
Costs of Abnormal Loss:			
Cost from preceding department (40 x $2.12)		$ 84.80	
Material (40 x $1.10)		44.00	
Conversion cost (40 x 1/4 x $.80)		8.00	
Total value of abnormal loss			136.80
Work in Process: Ending Inventory			
Costs from preceding department (60 x $2.12)		$127.20	
Material (60 x $1.10)		66.00	
Conversion costs (60 x 1/6 x $.80)		8.00	201.20
Total costs accounted for			$3,748.00

17.
b. Gene Peery Production Company   (concluded)

Additional Computations:	Transferred	+	Ending Inventory	+	Normal Loss	+	Abnormal Loss	-	Beginning Inventory	
EU, Preceding Department =	700	+	60	+	100	+	40	-	200	= 700
			(60 x 100%)		(100 x 100%)		(40 x 100%)		(200 x 100%)	

$$\frac{\$2.968 \times 500 = \$1,484.00}{700} = \$2.12$$

EU, Department Two, Material	=	700	+	60	+	100	+	40	-	200	= 700
				(60 x 100%)	(100 x 100%)	(40 x 100%)				

$$\frac{\$770}{700} = \$1.10$$

EU, Department Two, Conversion Costs	=	700	+	10	+	25	+	10	-	40	= 705
				(60 x 1/6)	(100 x 1/4)	(40 x 1/4)		(200 x 1/5)		

$$\frac{\$564}{705} = \$.80$$

True-False

1.   F   This is true under weighted average but not under FIFO because beginning inventory is deducted under FIFO.

2.   F   Normal loss is attached to the good units transferred or if ending inventory has passed inspection, the cost of the normal loss is allocated to ending inventory and the good units transferred. The cost of the abnormal loss is transferred into Cost of Lost Units as a period cost.

3.   F   This statement is false for several reasons. Material, labor, and overhead may be at different stages of completion and require separate calculations of equivalent units which will not result in the same answer. Also if FIFO costing is used, total costs to account for include the value of beginning inventory, but this cost is not used in the equivalent unit cost calculation.

4.   T   The equivalent units are: 85,000 transferred + 14,000 = 99,000
                                                        (20,000 x 70%)

     The cost per equivalent unit is: $12,800 + $69,700 current cost = $82,500
     $82,500/99,000 = $.83

5.   F   In Department 1 there is no cost from the preceding department to adjust for the increase in units; this adjustment is made in subsequent departments.

6.   T

7.   F   All units lost in this department have been through preceding departments and they must all be assigned equivalent unit costs for preceding departments even though they are discovered lost at the midpoint in operations. Costs from the current department in which the loss is discovered would reflect the midpoint inspection.

8.   T   If ending inventory is past the inspection point, normal loss cost is assigned to both ending inventory and units transferred.

9.   F   No material cost would be assigned to finish the beginning inventory because it would have received all of its material costs when it was begun last period since material is added at the beginning of operations.

10. F   Abnormal loss cost is never assigned to good units; it is accounted for separately as a period cost. The statement would have been true if it had said cost of normal loss.

8 Joint Product and By-Product Costing

Chapter Outline

Joint Products, By-Products, and Scrap
    Joint Costs and Common Costs
    Why Allocate Joint Costs?
    Split-off point and Separable Costs
Accounting for By-Products
    Costing By-Products Illustrated
    Journal Entries for By-Products
Assignment of Costs to Joint Products
    Physical Measures
    Market or Sales Value
    Multiple Split-offs
    Are Allocation Methods Arbitrary?
Process Further Decision Making
    Irrelevance of Joint Costs
    Erroneous Results Using Joint Costs

Chapter Objectives

After studying this chapter, you should be able to:

1. Distinguish between joint products, by-products, and scrap.

2. Determine what value, if any, companies should assign to by-products before selling them.

3. Identify the uses of allocating joint costs.

4. Recognize the limitation of joint cost allocations for future planning and control.

5. Choose the most appropriate method for distributing joint costs to by-products and joint products for inventory valuation.

6. Apply differential analysis in deciding whether to further process products.

7. Define and apply the new terms introduced.

Chapter Review

Joint Costs and Common Costs

1. Joint products result in manufacturing processes in which two or more products of significant sales value are produced simultaneously.

2. By-products are incidental products which result when joint products are manufactured.

   a. The market value of the products involved determine whether they are classified as by-products or joint products.
   b. By-products have small market values in relation to joint products.
   c. The dividing line between joint products and by-products is not firm and can change; professional judgment is needed often in the classification.

3. The distinction between scrap and by-products is not clear; the correct accounting treatment is to deduct their value, if any, from the cost of the main products.

Joint Costs and Common Cost

4. Joint costs are more restrictive than the term common costs which refer to the sharing of facilities in which products may or may not actually be manufactured.

   a. The common cost product or service could have been obtained separately rather than produced simultaneously.
   b. Common costs include such service department costs as repair and maintenance.

Why Allocate Joint Costs

5. Joint costs are allocated for the following reasons.

   a. Valuing inventory and computing cost of goods sold for external financial reporting according to accounting standards and for reporting to taxing authorities.
   b. Valuing inventory for insurance purposes when casualty losses occur.
   c. Valuing inventory and computing cost of goods sold for internal financial reporting.

      1. Examples include cost allocations for pricing the cost of goods sold and calculating executive compensation on the basis of each executive's segment earnings.
      2. If two or more segments sell a joint product, the cost of material and processing must be allocated to the products involved.

   d. Determining cost reimbursement under contracts where only part of the jointly produced services and products is sold or delivered to one customer.
   e. Determining the regulated rate where only a subset of the jointly manufactured product or services is subject to price regulation.

Split-Off Point and Separable Costs

6. The point at which joint products and by-products are separately identifiable is referred to as the split-off point or point of separation.

   a. The split-off point can occur at different stages of operations.
   b. Costs are accumulated up to the split-off point and treated as joint costs and then allocated to the products involved.

7. Separable costs are those costs of material, labor, and overhead which are used in the later processing of the distinguishable products.

a. The total inventory valuation of each joint product is its allocation of joint cost plus the separable costs necessary for sale.

Accounting for By-Products

8. There are two basic approaches to accounting for by-products; they are:
   a. By-products are assigned an inventory cost equal to their net market (realizable) value at the time they are produced, and this amount is deducted from the cost of production.

   1. The maximum amount that should be assigned to by-products is their net market (realizable) value which is the market value of the by-products produced less (a) cost of material, labor, and overhead used in further processing; (b) marketing costs; and (c) administrative cost.

   b. By-products are assigned no inventory value. At the time of sale, the net market (realizable) value is shown as other income.

Costing By-Products

9. An advantage of assigning a value to by-products before they are sold is that this method most nearly resembles those employed in joint product costing.

   a. If any value is assigned, the cost of further processing, marketing, and administration must be estimated.
   b. There are no additional processing costs if the by-products can be sold in their original form at the split-off point.

10. A memorandum entry is made to record only the physical amount of by-products manufactured if income is not recorded until the by-products are sold.

Journal Entries for By-Products

11. The estimated net market value is charged to the By-products Inventory account as follows:

       By-Products Inventory
           Work in Process Inventory

12. As additional processing is done, actual costs are charged to the By-products Inventory account:

       By-Products Inventory
           Material
           Payroll
           Factory Overhead Costs

13. The application of marketing and administrative costs would be as follows:

       By-Products Inventory
           Marketing Expense Control
           Administrative Expense Control

Assignment of Costs to Joint Products

14. The physical measure and the market or sales value methods are the two basic costing procedures for joint products. Variations of these two methods are:

Physical measures.	**Market sales value.**
a. Quantity method.	a. Gross market value.
b. Average unit cost.	b. Net market (realizable) value.
c. Weighted factor.	

Diagram Processing Operations

15. If multiple split-off points are utilized, it will be helpful to diagram the processing operations.

Physical Measures

16. Using the quantity method, all products receive a share of the joint costs based on a physical measure.

    a. The market value of the products involved is ignored.
    b. The inventory valuation is the allocated share of joint product cost and separable costs incurred after the split-off point.

17. A variation of the physical measure is to assign joint production costs on the basis of units, ignoring the weight or sales value of the products involved.

    a. If the units do not differ greatly among products, the weaknesses of this simple method are not too great.

18. Factors which management considers significant may be assigned to each product and used as a basis for distributing joint product costs.

Market or Sales Value

19. Using the market or sales value method, joint costs are prorated on the basis of the market value of each joint product.

    a. If products can be sold at the split-off point, the gross market value method is used which ignores all separable costs.
    b. If products have no market value at the split-off point, an approximate market value at the split-off point is estimated by deducting the separable costs from the market value at the *first* possible point of sale.

Multiple Split-Offs

20. If the manufacturing operations contain multiple split-off points with separable costs for each stage, accountants determine the approximate net market value at each split-off point.

Are Allocation Methods Arbitrary?

21. Allocations of joint costs for general-purpose financial accounting statements lack defense; allocations for single-purpose reports are more easily defended since the purpose of the report is known in advance.

Inventories at Sale Price

22. A practice of ignoring the allocation of joint costs completely and valuing joint costs by assigned sales value or sales value net of separable costs as the inventory valuation is not recommended.

    a. Carrying inventories at sales price or net of separable costs recognizes profits before sales are made.
    b. However, using sales price instead of joint cost allocations as the inventory valuation is less subject to criticism for perishable products.

Process Further Decision Making

23. Joint cost allocations provide no relevant costs for decisions regarding the most profitable stage at which to sell a product.

24. Instead, differential cost analysis should be used when the company is considering further processing.

    a. Differential cost is the additional cost for extending operations.
    b. Differential revenue is the additional revenue earned from further processing.
    c. If differential revenue exceeds differential costs of the further processing, the additional processing should be undertaken.

Demonstration Problem

Multiple Split-Off Points

Phillips, Inc., manufactures products Alpha, Beta, and Gamma in a joint process. Alpha is manufactured in two phases; in the first phase, raw materials are processed to produce two intermediates in fixed proportions. One of these intermediates is processed to yield a product called Beta. The other intermediate product is converted into Alpha in a separate finishing operation that yields both finished Alpha and another product, Gamma. Gamma must be further processed before yielding a salable product. Production quantity, market price per gallon, and sales volume are as follows for a normal period:

Product	Gallons	Market Price Per Gallon
Beta	140,000	$6
Gamma	72,200	8
Alpha	92,800	10

At these normal volumes, material and processing costs are expected to total as follows:

	Basic Process	Beta Process	Alpha-Gamma Process	Gamma Process
Material	$ 30,000	$ 46,000	$208,000	$ 8,280
Direct labor	110,000	24,000	114,000	12,000
Variable factory overhead	152,000	25,000	110,600	7,200
Fixed factory overhead	168,000	40,000	234,000	16,520
	$460,000	$135,000	$666,600	$44,000

Output can be increased by as much as 15 percent of normal volume without any increase in fixed costs. Marketing and administrative costs are fixed and are not traced to any products.

Required:

Using the net market (realizable) method in allocating joint costs, determine the distribution of production costs and the inventoriable cost per gallon for each product.

Paper for working Demonstration Problem

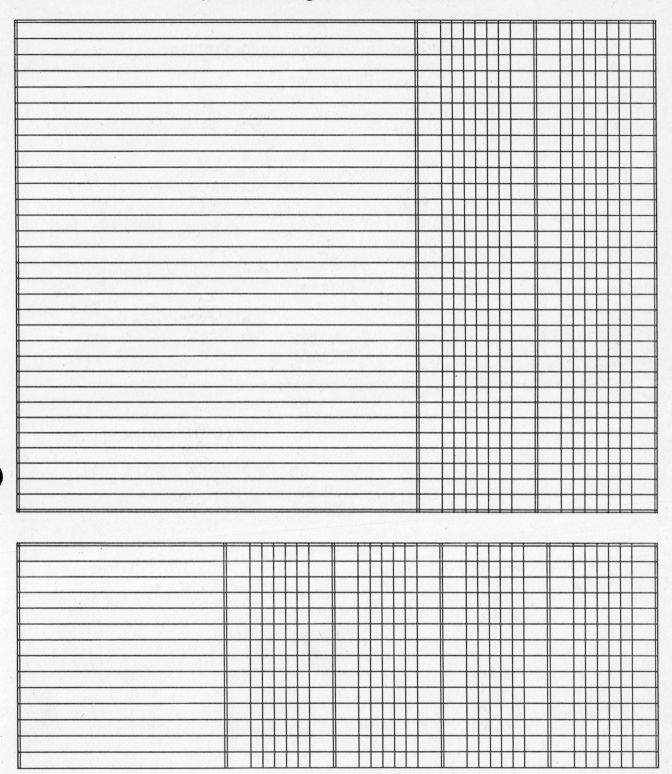

Solution to Demonstration Problem

Phillips, Inc.

Beta Market Value..		$ 840,000	
Less Beta Process..		135,000	$ 705,000 — NRV B
Gamma Market Value..	$577,600		
Less Gamma Process...	44,000	$ 533,600	
Alpha Market Value...		928,000	
Total NRV for G+A ← ? —		$1,461,600	
Less Alpha-Gamma Process................................		666,600	795,000 — NRV G+A
Total Approximate Market Value at Split-Off Point...			$1,500,000

Product	Allocated Joint Cost
Beta..	$216,200 $\left(\dfrac{\$705,000}{\$1,500,000} \times \$460,000\right)$
Alpha-Gamma..	$243,800$ $\left(\dfrac{\$795,000}{\$1,500,000} \times \$460,000\right)$
	$460,000

The allocated $243,800 joint costs + $666,600 are distributed as follows:

Product	Allocated Joint Costs
Gamma...	$332,368 $\left(\dfrac{\$533,600}{\$1,461,600} \times \$910,400\right)$
Alpha..	$578,032$ $\left(\dfrac{\$928,000}{\$1,461,600} \times \$910,400\right)$
	$910,400

The inventoriable cost per gallon is:

Product	Allocated Joint Costs	+	Separable Costs	=	Total	Inventoriable Cost Per Gallon	
Beta	$216,200		$135,000		$ 351,200	$2.5086	$\left(\dfrac{\$351,200}{140,000\,\text{gal.}}\right)$
Gamma	332,368		44,000		376,368	5.2129	$\left(\dfrac{\$376,368}{72,200\,\text{gal.}}\right)$
Alpha	578,032		-0-		578,032	6.2288	$\left(\dfrac{\$578,032}{92,800\,\text{gal.}}\right)$
					$1,305,600		

Matching

Referring to the terms listed in the left column, place the appropriate letter next to the corresponding description. A term may not be used or may be used more than once.

a. By-products

b. Common costs

c. Differential cost

d. Differential revenue

e. Gross market method of joint cost allocation

f. Net market (realizable) method of joint cost allocation

g. Joint Products

h. Point of split-off

i. Quantity method

j. Separable costs

k. Weighted factors

___ 1. Main products having significant sales value which are produced simultaneously in a manufacturing operation.

___ 2. The stage of operations at which joint products and by-products may be separately identified.

___ 3. Allocation of joint costs based on a physical measure.

___ 4. Allocating joint costs on a method which assigns points or other factors to each product.

___ 5. The relevant costs which should be considered in making decisions regarding the most profitable stage at which to sell a product.

___ 6. Products having insignificant sales value which are produced when main products are processed.

___ 7. Costs of sharing facilities in which products may or may not be manufactured.

___ 8. Costs incurred subsequent to the split-off point for individual joint products.

___ 9. Extra costs incurred for different alternatives.

___ 10. A method of joint cost allocation in which separable costs are deducted from the market value at the first possible point of sale.

Completion and Exercises

1. A company which manufactures four products originating in a common initial material mix splits these products after the initial processing. These products require additional processing before each are sold. The cost which is distributed through the use of relative sales value is referred to as _____ cost.

2. The distinction between by-products and joint products is largely dependent upon the _____ _____ of the products. However, the _____ of each product manufactured is also an influencing factor.

3. _____ costs are relevant in deciding whether to further process a joint product before selling it.

4. _____ _____ costs are those which are incurred up to the split-off point.

5. When the differential _____ of further processing a joint product is less than the differential _____, it should be further processed.

6. The two basic methods of accounting for by-products are:

    a. _____

    _____

    b. _____

    _____

7. The two basic methods for accounting for joint products and variations of these two methods are:

    a. _____

    Variations of this method are:

    1. _____

    2. _____

    3. _____

    b. _____

    1. _____

    2. _____

8. **Methods of Accounting for By-products**

    Weatherly Chemical provides you with the following data regarding their processing operations:

	By-products	Joint Products
Sales	40,000 gallons	85,000 gallons
Production	45,000 gallons	105,000 gallons
Estimated market value	$ 8.00 per gallon	$ 60 per gallon
Costs of further processing:		
Materials	1.50 per gallon	
Labor	0.90 per gallon	
Factory overhead applied	0.85 per gallon	
Marketing costs applied	0.80 per gallon	
Administrative costs applied	0.70 per gallon	
Total Production costs		$2,000,000
Total marketing and administrative costs		200,000

Required:

a. Prepare income statements using the two basic methods of accounting for by-products.
b. Using the net market value method, prepare the journal entries to record the costs assigned to the by-products.
c. Assume that the market improves for the by-products and the 40,000 gallons are sold for cash at $10 per gallon. Record the entry.

Paper for working

a.

b.

c.

9. Maximum Amount to Spend in Processing

Bruce Manufacturing Company produces various chemicals from a joint mixture. At the split-off point, the chemicals are refined and become Amacol, Bencol, and Cencol. Production for July was as follows:

	Production (gallons)	Sales Price per Gallon
Amacol	2,000	$150
Bencol	400	75
Cencol	100	15

Costs during July were:

Joint costs of materials and processing	$283,775
Refining and packaging, Amacol	1,975
Packaging and labeling, Bencol	525

Chemical wastes were sold for $75. The company treats Cencol as a by-product. The firm deducts the net market value of the by-products from production costs.

Required:

a. Calculate the joint costs allocated to Amacol and Bencol. Use the net market value method of allocation.

b. Assuming that July is a representative month, determine whether it would be profitable to hire some workers to refine Bencol so it can be sold as Amacol. The refining would occur before Bencol is refined and packaged. What is the maximum amount that can be paid per month for the workers and supplies to perform the refining before there is a change in income?

9. Paper for working

a.

b.

10. Cantt, Inc., manufactures products Alpha, Beta, and Gamma in a joint process. Alpha is manufactured in two phases: in the first phase, raw materials are processed to produce two intermediaries in fixed proportions. One of these intermediaries is processed to yield a product called Beta. The other intermediate product is converted into Alpha in a separate finishing operation which yields both finished Alpha and another product, Gamma. Gamma must be further processed before yielding a salable product. Production quantity, market price per gallon, and sales volume are as follows for a normal period:

Product	Gallons	Market Price per Gallon
Beta	105,000	$4
Gamma	57,000	$5
Alpha	69,600	$5

At these normal volumes, material and processing costs are expected to total as follows:

	Basic Process	Beta Process	Alpha-Gamma Process	Gamma Process
Material	$ 22,500	$18,000	$ 9,000	$ 6,210
Direct labor	7,500	30,000	2,700	9,000
Variable factory overhead	39,000	27,000	21,000	5,400
Fixed factory overhead	126,000	3,000	9,300	12,390
	$195,000	$78,000	$42,000	$33,000

Output can be increased by as much as 15 percent of normal volume without any increase in fixed costs. Marketing and administrative costs are fixed and are not traced to any products.

Required:

Using the net market method in allocating joint costs, determine the distribution of production costs and the inventory cost per gallon for each product.

10. Paper for working

11. Classification of Products

Ward Inc. produces a high-density liquid plastic used in the aerospace industry. The raw materials are mixed in 500-gallon batches. The following data pertain to one batch of raw material:

Chemical	Market Price per Gallon	Yield Per Batch (percent)
Q	$150	20
R	400	25
S	300	40
Waste	0	15

Direct material costs $50,000 per batch; conversion cost per batch is $30,000 at normal capacity.

Required:

Determine the cost per gallon for each product assuming Ward, Inc.:
a. classifies Chemicals Q, R, and S as joint products, and uses the gross market value method to allocate joint costs.
b. treats Chemical Q as a by-product and deducts the net market value of the by-product processed from the production cost. Separable costs of Chemical Q are $5,000.

11. Paper for working

12. Kim Corporation uses a joint process to produce Products A, B, and C. Each product may be sold at its split-off or processed further. Additional processing costs are entirely variable and are traceable to the respective products manufactured. Joint production costs for 19X1 were $240,000.

Product	Units Produced	Sales Value after Additional Processing	Separable Costs
A	25,000	$180,000	$30,000
B	40,000	205,000	25,000
C	55,000	125,000	35,000

Required:

a. Assuming all products are processed beyond the split-off point, determine the joint cost allocation and inventory value for each product by--

   1. Using the physical method of allocation.
   2. Using the net market (realizable) value method of allocation.

b. If Product A can be sold at the split-off point for $160,000, what would you advise management to do?
c. If Product C can be sold at split-off point for $77,000, what would you advise management to do?

12. Paper for working

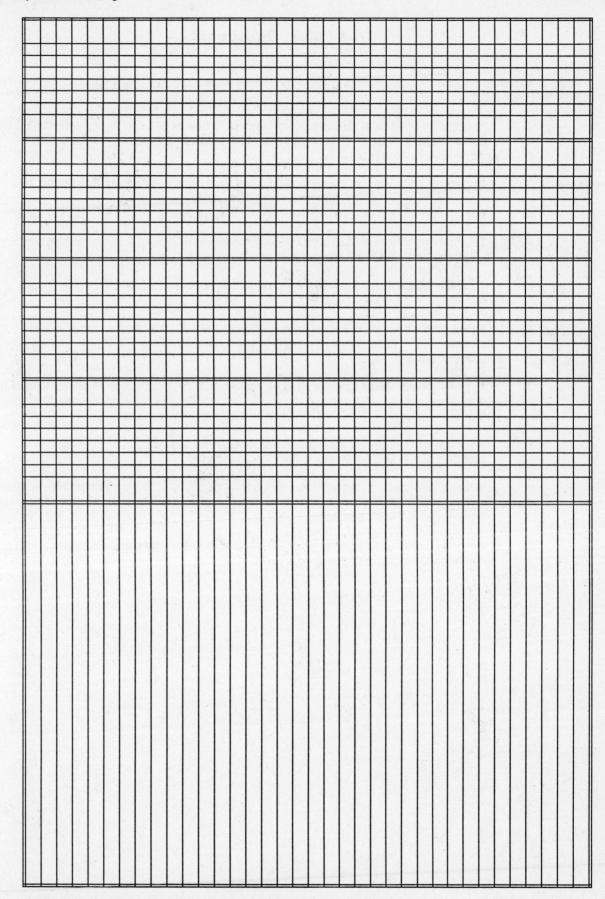

True-False Questions

Indicate whether the following statements are true or false by inserting in the blank space a capital "T" for true or "F" for false.

_____ 1. In deciding whether to process a joint product further or sell it in its present state, joint costs which have been allocated to each joint product are used to decide which alternative is more profitable.

_____ 2. Separable costs can be traced to the type of joint product to which they relate.

_____ 3. Assignment of joint costs to the joint products is arbitrary.

_____ 4. The relevant information to consider in deciding whether to sell a joint product or process it further is obtained through the joint cost allocations.

_____ 5. The split-off point is the point in the productive process at which joint products are separated.

_____ 6. If joint product A can be sold at its split-off point for $20, but can be sold in a more refined state for $26 and the cost of the refining process is $8, the company should further process product A.

_____ 7. A joint product whose sales price is relatively small in proportion to its physical quantity may receive a higher unit joint cost allocation than the unit sales price when the quantity method of allocating joint costs is used.

_____ 8. After the split-off point, each type of product can be separately identified and is independent of the other products.

_____ 9. When a joint product has several sales points, but none at the split-off point, the last sales point when it becomes a more finished product is the best approximation of the sales value at the split-off point.

_____10. Carrying joint product inventories at sales value or sales value less operable cost is a correct accounting procedure.

SOLUTIONS

Matching

1. g   6. a
2. h   7. b
3. i   8. j
4. k   9. c
5. c   10. f

Completion and Exercises

1. joint

2. market value, quantity

3. Differential

4. Joint product

5. costs; revenue

6. a. By-products are assigned an inventory cost equal to their net market value at the time they are *produced*, and this amount is deducted from the cost of production. The maximum amount that should be assigned to by-products is their net market value.
   b. By-products are assigned no inventory value. At the *time of sale*, the net market value is shown on the income statement.

7. a. Physical measures
      1. Quantity method
      2. Average unit cost
      3. Weighted factor
   b. Market or sales value
      1. Gross market value
      2. Net market (realizable) value

8.

Weatherly Chemical Company
Income Statement
Methods of Accounting for By-products

a.

	Method 1 Net Market Value of By-products *Produced* Assigned to Inventory	Method 2 No Value Assigned to By-products Produced Only Revenue from By-products *Sold* Reported
Sales, Joint products	$5,100,000	$5,100,000.00
Cost of Sales:		
Gross production costs	$2,000,000	$2,000,000.00
Less net market value, by-products ($3.25 x 45,000)	146,250	
Net production costs	$1,853,750	$2,000,000.00
Ending inventory	353,095*	380,952.38**
Cost of sales	$1,500,655	$1,619,047.62
Gross margin	$3,599,345	$3,480,952.38
Marketing & administrative expenses	200,000	200,000.00
Operating income	$3,399,345	$3,280,952.38
Other income		
Revenue from by-products sold		130,000.00
Income before taxes	$3,399,345	$3,410,952.38

8. (concluded)

*Joint Product - Value of Ending Inventory: Method 1

$$\frac{20,000 \text{ gallons}}{105,000 \text{ gallons}} \times \$1,853,750 = \$353,095$$

**Joint Product - Value of Ending Inventory: Method 2

$$\frac{20,000 \text{ gallons}}{105,000 \text{ gallons}} \times \$2,000,000 = \$380,952.38$$

By-Products
$ 8.00 Gross Market
- 1.50
- .90
- .85
- .80
- .70
$3.25 Net market value

b. By-products Inventory ($3.25 x 45,000) 146,250
           Work in Process Inventory   146,250
              To distribute joint costs to by-products.
    By-products Inventory 146,250
           Materials ($1.50 x 45,000 gal.)   67,500
           Payroll ($.90 x 45,000 gal.)   40,500
           Factory Overhead Costs ($.85 x 45,000 gal.)   38,250
              To distribute separable costs to by-products.
    By-products Inventory   67,500
           Marketing Expense Control ($.80 x 45,000 gal.)   36,000
          Administrative Expense Control ($.70 x 45,000 gal.)   31,500

c. Cash   400,000

$$\text{By-products Inventory} \left(\frac{\$360,000}{45,000 \text{ gallons}} \times 40,000 \text{ gal.} \right)$$

                                                            320,000
    Revenue from the Sale of By-products 80,000***

***This difference between actual and estimated sales [40,000 x $2.00 ($10.00 -- $8.00)] could also be credited to Work in Process Inventory or Cost of Goods Sold.

9.

Bruce Manufacturing Company

a.

Joint Costs			$283,775
Less: Sales of Cencol (100 gallons x $15)		$1,500	
Sales of chemical wastes		75	1,575
Net Joint Costs to Allocate to Joint Products			$282,200

Product	Sales Value	Separable Costs	Net Market Value	Joint Cost Allocation
Amacol	$300,000	$1,975	$298,025	$\left(\dfrac{\$298,025}{\$327,500} \text{ X } \$282,200\right) = \$256,802$
Bencol	30,000	525	29,475	$\left(\dfrac{\$29,475}{\$327,500} \text{ X } \$282,200\right) = 25,398$
			$327,500	$282,200

b.

$$\frac{\$1,975}{2,000 \text{ gallons}} = \$.9875 \text{ refining and packaging per Amacol gallon}$$

Sale of 400 gallons as Amacol (400 x $150)	$60,000
Less refining and packaging ($.9875 x 400)	395
Net market value of 400 Amacol gallons	$59,605
Sales value of 400 Bencol gallons	29,475
Maximum amount that should be spent in refining Bencol	$30,130

10.   **Cantt, Inc.**

Beta Market Value...		$420,000
Less Beta Process..		78,000	$342,000
Gamma Market Value......................................	$285,000	
Less Gamma Process.....................................	33,000	$252,000
Alpha Market Value...		348,000
		$600,000
Less Alpha-Gamma Process............................		42,000	558,000
Total approximate market value at Split-off Point			$900,000

Beta Market Value... $420,000
Less Beta Process.. 78,000 $342,000
Gamma Market Value...................................... $285,000
Less Gamma Process..................................... 33,000 $252,000
Alpha Market Value... 348,000
                                                        $600,000
Less Alpha-Gamma Process............................ 42,000   558,000
Total approximate market value at Split-off Point $900,000

Product		Allocated Joint Cost
Beta..	$ 74,100	$\left(\dfrac{\$342,000}{\$900,000} \times \$195,000\right)$
Alpha-Gamma...	120,900	$\left(\dfrac{\$558,000}{\$900,000} \times \$195,000\right)$
	$195,000	

The allocated $120,900 joint costs + $42,000 are distributed as follows:

Product		Allocated Joint Cost
Gamma	$ 68,418	$\left(\dfrac{\$252,000}{\$600,000} \times \$162,900\right)$
Alpha	94,482	$\left(\dfrac{\$348,000}{\$600,000} \times \$162,900\right)$
	$162,900	

The inventoriable cost per gallon is:

Product	Allocated Joint Cost	+ Separable Costs	= Total	Inventoriable Cost per Gallon	
Beta	$74,100	$78,000	$152,100	$1.4486	$\left(\dfrac{\$152,100}{105,000}\text{gal}\right)$
Gamma	68,418	33,000	101,418	1.7793	$\left(\dfrac{\$101,418}{57,000}\text{gal}\right)$
Alpha	94,482	-0-	94,482	1.3575	$\left(\dfrac{\$94,482}{69,600}\text{gal}\right)$
			$348,000		

11. Ward Company

a.

Joint Products	Gallons Produced	Market Value per Gallon	Market Value		Distribution of Production Costs
Q	100	$150	$ 15,000	$ 9,600	$\left(\dfrac{\$15,000}{\$125,000} \text{ X } \$80,000^*\right)$
R	125	400	50,000	32,000	$\left(\dfrac{\$50,000}{\$125,000} \text{ X } \$80,000^*\right)$
S	200	300	60,000 / $125,000	38,400	$\left(\dfrac{\$60,000}{\$125,000} \text{ X } \$80,000^*\right)$

*$50,000 direct material + $30,000 conversion costs

Joint Products	Cost per Gallon	
Q	$ 96	$\left(\dfrac{\$9,600}{100 \text{ gallons}}\right)$
R	256	$\left(\dfrac{\$32,000}{125 \text{ gallons}}\right)$
S	192	$\left(\dfrac{\$38,400}{200 \text{ gallons}}\right)$

b.
Production cost..		$80,000
Less by-product chemical Q		
Gross market value................................	$15,000	
Less separable costs...........................	5,000	10,000
Cost to allocate to joint products		$70,000

Joint Products		Distribution of Production Costs
R	$31,818.18	$\left(\dfrac{\$ 50,000}{\$110,000} \text{ X } \$70,000\right)$
S	38,181.82	$\left(\dfrac{\$ 60,000}{\$110,000} \text{ X } \$70,000\right)$

Product	Cost per Gallon	Separable Costs	Inventory Value per Gallon
Q	$100.00 ($10,000/100 gallons)	$50.00	$150.00
R	254.55 ($31,818.18/125 gallons)		254.55
S	190.91 ($38,181.82/200 gallons		190.91

12.

Kim Corporation

a.1.

Product	Joint Cost Allocation		Inventory Valuation	
A	$ 50,000	$\left(\dfrac{25,000}{120,000} \times \$240,000\right)$	$ 80,000	($50,000 + $30,000)
B	80,000	$\left(\dfrac{40,000}{120,000} \times \$240,000\right)$	105,000	($80,000 + $25,000)
C	110,000	$\left(\dfrac{55,000}{120,000} \times \$240,000\right)$	145,000	($110,000 + $35,000)
	$240,000		$330,000	

2.

Product	Net Market Value		Joint Cost Allocation		Inventory Valuation	
A	$150,000	($180,000 − $30,000)	$ 85,714	$\left(\dfrac{\$150,000}{\$420,000} \times \$240,000\right)$	$115,714	($85,714 + $30,000)
B	180,000	($205,000 − $25,000)	102,857	$\left(\dfrac{\$180,000}{\$420,000} \times \$240,000\right)$	127,857	($102,857 + $25,000)
C	90,000	($125,000 − $35,000)	51,429	$\left(\dfrac{\$90,000}{\$420,000} \times \$240,000\right)$	86,429	($51,429 + $35,000)
	$420,000		$240,000		$330,000	

b. Product A should be sold at split-off because the $20,000 differential revenue is less than the $30,000 differential separable cost.

c. Product C should not be sold at split-off because the $48,000 differential revenue exceeds the $35,000 differential separable cost.

True-False

1.   F   Joint costs are not relevant to such decisions; instead, differential cost of further processing is compared with the differential revenue earned from selling it in a more refined state.

2.   T   These costs are incurred after the split-off point in processing joint products further.

3.   T   There are several correct methods available to use, but their choice depends upon the accountant's professional judgment.

4.   F   Joint costs are irrelevant in this decision; instead, the relevant information is the increase in sales value that will result from additional processing, less the additional separable costs of further processing.

5.   T

6.   F   The differential revenue of $6 ($26 -- $20) is less than its differential cost; thus, Product A should not be refined.

7.   T   The quantity method in circumstances similar to this could cause losses to be reported on some joint products while others are sold at a profit.

8.   T   At this point, separate decisions can be made as to whether to process the products further or to sell them in their present state.

9.   F   It is the first sales point which is considered the best approximation of the sales value at the split-off point.

10.   F   This procedure recognizes a profit before the actual sale is made. It is less subject to criticism if used for perishable items or if the normal profit percentage is small so there is little difference between cost and selling price.

9
Flexible Budgeting and the Budgeting Process

Chapter Outline

Advantages of Budgets
Communication, Coordination, and Performance Evaluation
Budgets and Standards
Principles of Budgeting
Relation to Organizational Structure and Environment
Budget Revisions
Budget Committee
Length of Budget Period
Bottom-up Budgeting Approach
Fixed (Static) and Flexible (Variable) Budgeting
Fixed and Flexible Budget Variances Compared
Cost of Acquired Resources not Utilized
Master Budget
Master Budget Interrelationships
Sales Forecasts
Employees' Experienced Judgment
Trend and Correlation Analysis
Territorial Sales Budget
Production-Related Budgets
Production Budget
Direct Materials Purchases Budget
Direct Labor Budget
Factory Overhead Budget
Cost of Goods Sold Budget

Chapter Objectives

After studying this chapter, you should be able to:

1. Explain the advantages of budgets as a management tool for performance evaluation.

2. Understand the important role of top management in the budgeting process.

3. Distinguish between variances obtained using fixed budgets and variances obtained using flexible budgets.

4. Prepare budgets in the master budget plan.

5. Define and apply the new terms introduced.

Chapter Review

Advantages of Budgets

1. Budgeting represents a means of coordinating the organization into an intelligent plan of action listing what equipment, personnel, and materials will be needed to achieve these objectives.

2. The following are advantages of budgets; other advantages may be included in this list:

   a. Management is required to determine both short-run and long-run objectives.
   b. Management is forced to analyze the future and obtain alternative plans of action depending upon the turn of events.
   c. Effort and funds are directed toward the most profitable of all possible alternatives.
   d. The need for coordination is emphasized because budgeting quickly reveals weaknesses in the organization.
   e. The budget can serve as a vehicle of communication and coordination.
   f. Performance standards are provided by budgets which serve as motivators for more effective performance and operations.
   g. Areas lacking control are indicated by providing variance data which should serve as a springboard for action.

Communication, Coordination, and Performance Evaluation

3. Budgets provide a formal communication channel within a company because they contain explicit statements concerning implementation of management objectives for a period of time.

4. Budgets allow management to compare operations against a yardstick which represents a good level of performance.

5. Management should be encouraged to combine standards with their budgeting process so that through the use of these two decision tools, operations can be more efficient.

Budgets and Standards

6. Standards are closely related to budgets because they serve as building blocks for the construction of the budget.

Principles of Budgeting

7. Even though uncertainties are inherent in the business environment, a company that uses budgeting procedures is better able to meet these uncertainties.

Principles of Budgeting

8. Top management support is needed because their philosophy toward budgeting soon filters down in the company.

   a. Management should not view budgeting as a scapegoat on which all the company's problems can be blamed.
   b. It is important in the initial phase of the budgeting process that management members recognize that coordination among all segments is needed.
   c. The individuals responsible for meeting these goals must be aware of their existence.

Relation to Organizational Structure and Environment

9. Budgets are developed in relation to organizational factors which evolve over time; as these organizational variables change, the changes must be reflected in the design of the budget system.

    a. Differentiation or decentralization means the degree to which managers have freedom to use their own management techniques and make their own decisions.
    b. Generally the larger the size and more complex the technology, the greater the degree of decentralization.

Budget Revisions

10. The budgeting process should allow for flexibility because conditions inside and outside the company can change which may require revision of the budget.

11. Budgets must be frequently updated to take into account external unforeseen situations.

Budget Committee

12. The president normally establishes budgeting principles but direction and execution of all budget procedures are generally delegated to the budget committee.

    a. The budget committee serves as a consulting body to the budget officer, and its members include the budget director and top executives representing all company segments.
    b. The budget committee should review all reports prepared at the time a budgetary system is installed for the purpose of eliminating any duplication in reports.

Budget Manual

13. A budget manual will be a helpful reference for implementation of a budget program; this manual has long-range usefulness also.

14. The controller is usually the budget director and requests sales estimates and cost estimates from each department head and supervisor.

15. The budget director must be able to talk with executives and low-line managers with tact and dignity and show respect for each of their own areas of specialty.

Length of Budget Period

16. Budgets can be prepared for both short-range and long-range time periods; however, they should correspond to the fiscal period used in the accounting system.

17. A rolling or continuous approach can be used in which a new 12th month is added as a month expires. Under this approach, the company always has 12 months of budgets prepared ahead.

Bottom-up Budgeting Approach

18. Obtaining sales force data and combining it at higher levels is referred to as a bottom-up approach.

    a. Using a bottom-up approach, the budgets are combined at successively higher levels of management.
    b. From a behavioral view, before higher levels of management revise budgets obtained from lower levels, they should discuss the need for revisions with the people involved.

19. In employing a bottom-up approach, the following steps must be undertaken:

   a. Planning guidelines identified by top management.
   b. Profit plans prepared beginning with the sales budget.
   c. Communication and negotiation until a final plan is reached.
   d. Coordination and review of the profit plan.
   e. Final approval and distribution of the formal plan is made.

Fixed (Static) and Flexible (Variable) Budgeting

20. Flexible budgets offer many advantages in addition to those provided by fixed budgets because a flexible budget is adjusted to actual or standard capacity.

Fixed and Flexible Budget Variances Compared

21. Using a fixed or static approach, a budget is prepared for a single estimated activity level.

   a. The static budget is not adjusted when actual volume differs from that budgeted.
   b. Fixed or static budgeting is appropriate only if a company's operating volume can be estimated within close limits and if the costs and expenses are behaving predictably.
   c. Because most companies have changeable market conditions and unpredictable situations, a fixed budget is not generally feasible.

22. Flexible (variable) budgets provide closer control of performance than do fixed budgets because actual revenue and expense are compared with budgeted data based on the actual volume obtained.

   a. Flexible budgets are prepared for a range of activity levels instead of for a single level as in a fixed budget.
   b. A flexible budget formula can be used for a series of possible volumes; all within the relevant range are considered feasible.

Cost of Acquired Resources not Utilized

23. A flexible or variable budget is a more appropriate alternative to a fixed or static budget.

   a. A flexible budget incorporates changes in volume to provide a valid basis of comparison with actual cost.
   b. Under a flexible budgeting approach, a budget formula is provided in advance which is based on a variable cost per unit of measure plus fixed costs.
   c. With this flexible budget formula or also called cost estimating function, actual volume attained can be more accurately reflected in the budget for comparison purposes.

24. A flexible budget more accurately describes the cost situation and shows the cost of idle capacity while a fixed budget is usually misleading as it compares a budget for one volume with costs incurred for another volume.

Master Budget

25. The master budget in a manufacturing company covers various types of budgets, many of which are supported by additional budget schedules.

26. The following are included in the master budget:

   a. Sales budget broken down by

      1. Territory and product.
      2. Territory, product, and customer grouping.

   b. Production budget in units.
   c. Direct materials purchases budget.
   d. Direct labor budget.
   e. Factory overhead budget.
   f. Cost of goods sold budget.
   g. Marketing and administrative budgets.
   h. Research and development budget.
   i. Budgeted income statement.
   j. Budgeted statement of cash receipts and disbursements.
   k. Capital expenditure budget.
   l. Budgeted balance sheet.

Master Budget Interrelationships

27. Sales forecast support the sales budget from which the budget preparation begins.

   a. Budgeted income statements and balance sheets incorporate elements from all budgets and schedules prepared.
   b. The interrelationship among inventory policies and direct materials purchases budget and production budget is prevalent.

Sales Forecasts

28. The chief marketing manager is responsible for preparation of the sales prediction, but input from other factors is needed; internal factors including historical sales pattern and desired profit should be used along with supply and demand, competitors' actions, and other external factors.

   a. Establishing a causal relationship between sales and external factors, such as personal disposable income or gross national product, is helpful in predicting future sales.
   b. General economic and social conditions and the prospects for the specific industry are important variables.

Employees' Experienced Judgment

29. A company's salespeople supply valuable input in estimating sales because they are familiar with the local conditions.

   a. An advantage is that information is gained from a first-hand source; however, salespersons may lack broad economic knowledge.
   b. A disadvantage of using salespeople to prepare the sales forecast is that usually they are not well enough informed about broad economic developments.

Trend and Correlation Analysis

30. If market research is used in sales forecasting, correlation and trend analysis is employed. Motivation research to measure consumer buying patterns may be relied on.

   a. Correlation analysis attempts to establish the relationship between the values of two attributes, such as GNP and sales.
   b. Documentation of underlying assumptions used for each sales forecast is important.

Territorial Sales Budget

31. Territorial sales budgets can be further broken down by products and customer groupings.

Production-Related Budgets

32. The production budget is the sales budget adjusted for any changes in inventory as shown below:

> Units to produce = Budgeted sales
> + Desired ending finished goods inventory
> + Desired equivalent units in ending work in process inventory
> - Beginning finished goods inventory
> - Equivalent units in beginning work in process inventory

Production Budget

33. Coordination of the sales and production budget is important so that a smooth flow of production is possible.

34. The production budget becomes the basis for the direct materials purchases budget, labor budget, and factory overhead budget.

Direct Materials Purchases Budget

35. The material required for the level of operation specified from the production budget is calculated and shown on the direct materials purchases budget.

36. The desired level of inventory for materials is needed so that any changes in inventory level can be reflected in the amount of purchases needed.

    a. If a *just-in-time system* is utilized, inventory will represent only the amount needed in production until the next order arrives.
    b. Inventory will not be stockpiled to have when needed.

Direct Labor Budget

37. The direct labor budget reflects the number of units to be produced according to the production budget.

Factory Overhead Budget

38. Factory overhead may be classified according to natural expense, such as utilities, indirect labor, and indirect material; however, this classification has limited usefulness for budgeting purposes.

    a. A better approach is to prepare factory overhead budgets for each cost center so that the supervisor of the cost center can be held accountable and responsible for the expenses incurred.

Cost of Goods Sold Budget

39. The cost of goods sold budget represents a summary of the direct material, direct labor, and factory overhead budgets.

Demonstration Problem

Fixed and Flexible Budgets

Patterson, Inc. plans to produce 1,000 desks next accounting period. Time and motion studies reveal that it takes five direct labor-hours to manufacture each desk. The established monthly manufacturing overhead budget is as follows:

Fuel	$15,000
Repairs	7,500
Supplies	8,500
Depreciation	5,000
Rent	3,000
	$39,000

Fuel, repairs, and supplies vary directly with production. Assume depreciation is calculated on a straight-line basis and rent is paid monthly. At the end of the month, it is determined that 4,500 actual hours were incurred to make 900 desks and actual manufacturing costs were as follows:

Fuel	$12,000
Repairs	6,000
Supplies	7,800
Depreciation	5,050
Rent	3,100
	$33,950

Required:

a. Prepare a fixed budget and determine variances from budget.

b. What is the flexible budget formula for the fixed and variable cost behavior? Express formula in direct labor-hours.

c. Prepare a flexible budget for a production level of 4,500 direct labor-hours and determine variances from budget for each <u>detailed expense.</u>

d. What factors could cause the actual fixed costs to differ from budgeted fixed costs?

Paper for working Demonstration Problem

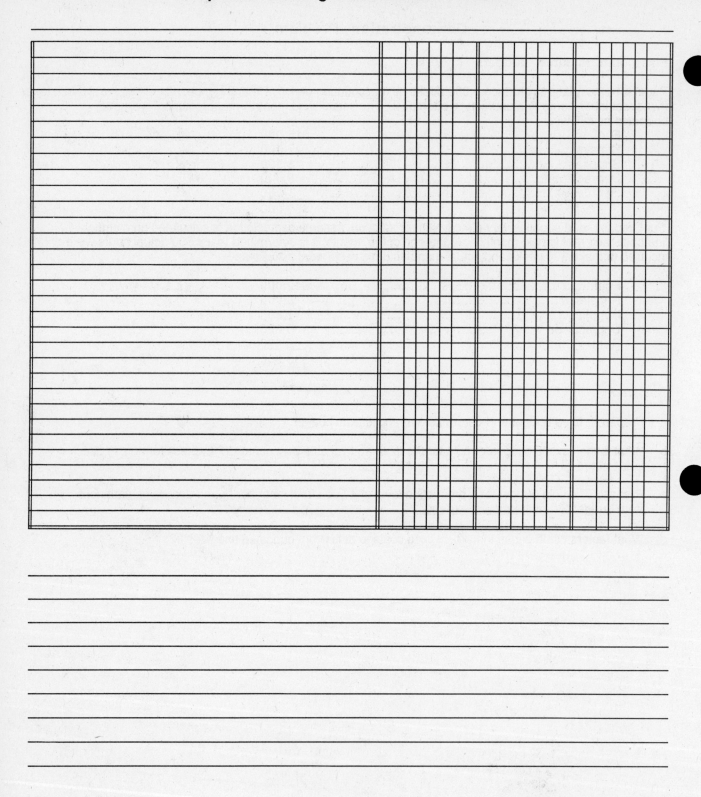

Solution to Demonstration Problem

Patterson, Inc.

a.

	Actual Cost	Fixed Budget	Variance*	
Fuel..................................	$12,000	$15,000	$3,000	F
Repairs	6,000	7,500	1,500	F
Supplies.	7,800	8,500	700	F
Depreciation......................	5,050	5,000	50	U
Rent	3,100	3,000	100	U
	$33,950	$39,000	$5,050	F

b.

	Budget at Normal Capacity	Variable Cost Per Direct Labor Hour	Fixed Cost
Fuel..................................	$15,000	$3.00	
Repairs	7,500	1.50	
Supplies	8,500	1.70	
Depreciation......................	5,000		$5,000
Rent	3,000		3,000
	$39,000	$6.20	$8,000

Budget Formula = $6.20 Variable cost per direct labor hour + $8,000 fixed overhead

c.

	Actual Cost	Flexible Budget for 4,500 Actual Direct Labor Hours		Variance*	
Fuel..................................	$12,000	$13,500	($3.00 X 4,500 hours)	$1,500	F
Repairs	6,000	6,750	($1.50 X 4,500 hours)	750	F
Supplies	7,800	7,650	($1.70 X 4,500 hours)	150	U
Depreciation......................	5,050	5,000		50	U
Rent	3,100	3,000		100	U
	$33,950	$35,900		$1,950	F

d. An additional machine could have been purchased that is being depreciated. A new lease agreement could have gone into effect which requires higher rent charge. The factors causing fixed costs to increase will not include volume differences.

*U = Unfavorable; F = Favorable

Matching

Referring to the terms listed in the left column, place the appropriate letter next to the corresponding description. A term may not be used or may be used more than once.

a. Bottom-up approach

b. Correlation analysis

c. Direct labor budget

d. Direct materials purchases budget

e. Factory overhead budget

f. Fixed (or static) budget

g. Flexible budget formula

h. Flexible (variable) budget

i. Production budget

j. Rolling budget

k. Sales budget

l. Slack

_____ 1. Starting point in the master budget process.

_____ 2. Process where budgets are combined at successively higher levels of management.

_____ 3. Sales budget in units adjusted for inventory changes.

_____ 4. Used to establish the relationship between an independent variable such as personal income and a dependent variable such as sales.

_____ 5. Adjusts the units needed for production by desired changes in inventory of this basic cost element.

_____ 6. Indirect labor is listed in this budget.

_____ 7. Budgets which are prepared for a range of activity levels instead of a single level.

_____ 8. Under this approach, as each month ends, a new 12th month is added.

_____ 9. Budget established in advance which can be adjusted to the volume actually experienced.

_____ 10. Budget established for one activity level for comparison with actual operations.

Completion and Exercises

1. What is the difference between a fixed (static) budgeting approach and a flexible (variable) budgeting approach? _____

   _____

   _____

   _____

   _____

2. What is the objective of budgeting? _____

   _____

   _____

3. Justify the use of budgets in a period of uncertainty _____

   _____

   _____

4. The _____ normally establishes budgeting principles while the _____

   _____ directs and executes all budget procedures.

5. Suggest ways the budget committee can eliminate duplication in reports.

   _____

   _____

   _____

6. Often the _____ who serves in a _____ capacity is the

   budget director.

7. Give three desirable characteristics the budget director should possess to serve effectively.

   a. _____

   _____

   _____

   _____

   b. _____

   _____

   _____

   _____

   c. _____

   _____

   _____

   _____

8. What is the relationship between standards and budgets?

_____

_____

_____

_____

9. Give the five steps involved in the development of an annual profit plan

a._____

_____

_____

_____

_____

b._____

_____

_____

_____

_____

c._____

_____

_____

_____

_____

d._____

_____

_____

_____

_____

e._____

_____

_____

_____

10. List eight types of budgets which usually compose the master budget.

a. _____

_____

b. _____

_____

c. _____

_____

d. _____

_____

e. _____

_____

f. _____

_____

g. _____

_____

h. _____

_____

11. Give four advantages of using budgets:

a. _____

_____

_____

b. _____

_____

_____

c. _____

_____

_____

d. _____

_____

_____

12. Define a budget._____

_____

_____

_____

13. Budget revisions are usually made by _____

14. Reasons that are justified for budget revisions include the following:

a. _____

_____

b. _____

_____

15. High-Low Method and Flexible Budget

Eaton Company provides you with a summary of the total budgeted factory overhead at four different volumes of operations:

| | | | Volume in Machine-Hours | |
| | | | 2,000 (normal | |
	1,000	1,500	capacity)	2,500
Indirect Material...........	$2,000	$3,000	$ 4,000	$ 5,000
Depreciation...............	800	800	800	800
Utilities........................	1,400	1,600	1,800	2,000
Inspection..................	3,000	3,650	4,300	4,950
	$7,200	$9,050	$10,900	$12,750

At the end of the year, it is determined that the following factory overhead was incurred for production at 2,300 machine-hours.

	Actual Costs
Indirect Material..................	$ 4,825
Depreciation.....................	850
Utilities.............................	1,880
Inspection........................	4,720
	$12,275

Required:

a. Indicate the cost behavior for each of the four overhead costs budgeted (i.e., whether fixed, variable, or semivariable).

Indirect Material -_____

Depreciation -_____

Utilities -_____

Inspection -_____

b. Determine the flexible budget formula for each of the four factory overhead costs using the high-low method.

c. Determine the variance for each of the four costs using a flexible budget. Indicate if favorable (F) or unfavorable (U).

15. Paper for working

16. Production Requirements

Budgeted data for the Puryear Company indicates that 40,000 pounds are needed to remain in the ending inventory of raw materials. Beginning raw material inventory is expected to contain 25,000 pounds. The expected cost per unit of raw materials is 50 cents per pound. The expected total cost of raw materials purchases is $400,000.

Required:

From the information, compute the production requirements in terms of pounds of raw materials.

17. Whitlock Company will begin operations in June 19X1 to produce pumps which will require the following amount of material:

Materials	Quantity (pounds)	Price per Pound
112B	3	$ 4
116A	4	5
118D	8	12
127F	5	6

Sales for the first four months of the year have been scheduled as follows:

	Budgeted Unit Sales
June	8,000
July	8,500
August	9,200
September	9,800
October	10,000

Management desires an ending inventory of finished goods at the end of each month that will represent 25 percent of the next month's sales requirements. An ending inventory representing 20 percent of next month's production requirements is required for direct materials.

Required:

Determine the direct materials purchases requirements for June, July, and August for each item of material in units and dollars. Assume the company begins operations with no inventory on June 1, 19X1.

17. Paper for working

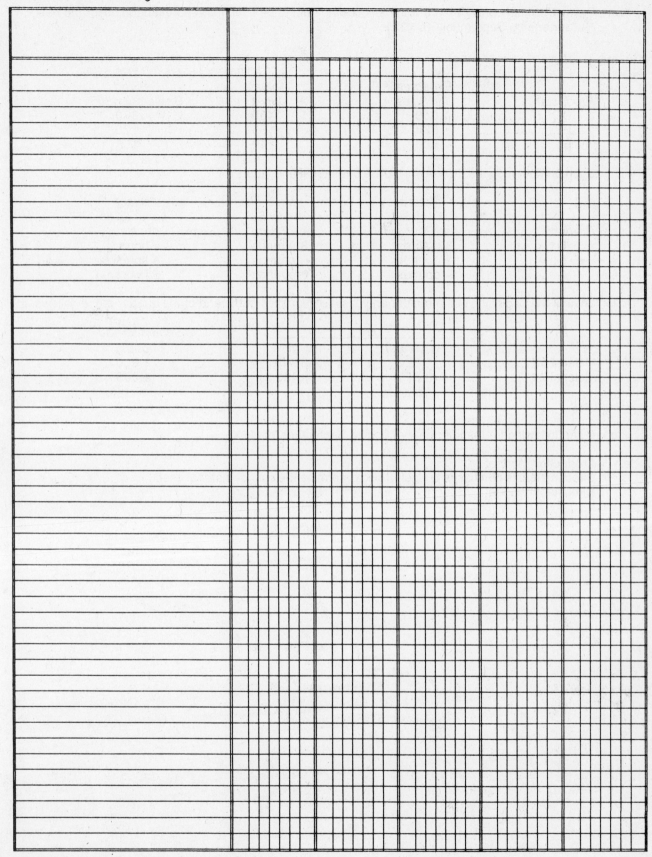

18. Bailey Company provides you with the following data to be used in preparing budgets for the next quarter ending September 30, 19X1:

		Inventory Levels in Units	
Products	Expected Unit Sales	Actual July 1	Desired September 30
D	1,000	400	380
E	580	165	170
F	600	140	155

Each product requires the following units of material and labor:

Product	Material AX @ $2 per Pound	Material B4 @ $3 per Pound	Direct Labor @ $5 per Hour
D	3 pounds	8 pounds	2 hours
E	2 pounds	6 pounds	4 hours
F	4 pounds	10 pounds	3 hours

Inventories at the beginning of the quarter and desired quantities at the end of the quarter are as follows:

	July 1		September 30
	(pounds)	(dollars)	(pounds)
Material AX	1,820	$ 3,640	2,000
Material B4	3,800	11,400	4,000

Required:

Prepare the following for the third quarter ending September 30, 19X1.

a. Production budget.
b. Direct materials purchases budget. (Also determine the cost of material used.)
c. Direct labor budget.

18. Paper for working

a.

b.

c.

True-False Questions

Indicate whether the following statements are true or false by inserting in the blank space a capital "T" for true or "F" for false.

_____ 1. If management desires no change in the level of beginning and ending inventory, the material required for production equals the amount of materials to be purchased.

_____ 2. In a company's master budget, the direct labor budget and the factory overhead budget may be combined with direct material in a manufacturing budget.

_____ 3. The production budget provides the original point from which all other budgets originate.

_____ 4. The flexible budget formula for utilities would be $600 per month plus $.35 per machine-hour if at the high capacity level of 2,500 hours, $1,600 costs were budgeted; at the low capacity of 1,500 hours, $1,200 costs were budgeted for utilities.

_____ 5. To determine the units to produce, budgeted sales are added to beginning inventory and desired ending inventory for the next period is subtracted.

_____ 6. Inventory may serve as a buffer to stabilize production when sales are of a seasonal nature.

_____ 7. An argument against the publication of financial forecasts is that confidential information may be revealed to competitors.

_____ 8. Low-line management makes the final approval of the budget after negotiations have occurred up through the organizational channels if a bottom-up approach to budgeting is used.

_____ 9. Flexible or variable budgets are established for a single activity level in advance of operations and this budget is used for comparison with actual costs incurred.

_____10. Under a rolling budgeting approach, as each month is passed, the next twelfth month is added so that budgeting is approached as a continual process rather than a once-a-year task.

_____11. As production decreases within the relevant range, fixed costs per unit will decrease if a flexible budget is used.

_____12. At normal capacity, direct labor hours total 10,000 for Foy Company with variable factory overhead of $30,000, fixed factory overhead of $20,000, giving a total factory overhead rate per direct labor hour of $5. If the company operated at 9,000 direct labor hours during the current year and incurred $48,000 actual total factory overhead, the overhead variance using a flexible budget is $3,000 unfavorable.

SOLUTIONS

Matching

1.	k	7.	h	
2.	a	8.	j	
3.	i	9.	h	
4.	b	10.	f	
5.	d			
6.	e			

Completion and Exercises

1. Under a fixed (static) budgeting approach, a budget is prepared for an estimated volume or capacity and this budget is compared against actual costs regardless of the actual capacity attained. Under a flexible (variable) budgeting approach, a budget formula is developed and this is applied to actual volume to determine a budget adjusted to actual capacity. This adjusted budget is then compared against actual expenses. The resulting variances under flexible budgeting do not result from volume, but reflect efficiency or lack of efficiency.

2. Budgeting substitutes deliberate, well-conceived business judgment for hit or miss planning in business.

3. Since all companies have uncertainty, budgets help managers deal with these uncertainties and make the decision-making process more effective.

4. president; budget committee

5. The budget committee can prepare a list of the reports believed to supply the information needed and then ask managers within the company whether these reports are sufficient. The budget committee should take measures recognizing the natural resistance to change. By having participatory budgeting, department managers can better communicate that this information has already been provided on other reports.

6. controller; staff

7. The following are desirable characteristics for the budget director:
    a. Ability to converse with the executives using tact and dignity.
    b. Display a thorough knowledge of general accounting and cost accounting.
    c. Ability to analyze organizations and define the duties of principal executives.
    d. Recognition of the talents and skills of nonaccountants.
    e. Recognition that administering budgets is complex because of the many human factors involved.
    f. Hold to following clear lines of authority and responsibility without being inflexible to the need to adjust to meet environmental conditions.

8. Standards serve as the building block for budgets as they are in the unit ingredient. After managers establish unit standards, they multiply the standards by the quantity of units involved to obtain the total budget.

9. The steps involved in the development of an annual profit plan include the following:
    a. Identification of planning guidelines by top management. All levels of management are involved and communication is downward.
    b. Preparation of the general operating budget or profit plan beginning with a sales budget. Lower levels of management receive sales targets which provide a basis for the preparation of production budgets and other components. Consultation with a higher (middle) management level may be needed to arrive at certain aspects of the specific manager's budget. The communication process is primarily lateral with some upward communication possible.
    c. Negotiation may be necessary to arrive at final plans; communication is upward.

d. Coordination and review of the profit plan; top level management makes recommendations and returns the various plans to middle level management. After middle management makes these changes, the plan is resubmitted for approval. Communication is generally downward; however, there may be some lateral communication during the adjustment phase.

e. Final approval and distribution of the formal plan is made. Top management gives final approval and communicates its decision downward.

10. The following compose the master budget:

    a. Sales budget broken down by
       1. Territory and product
       2. Territory, product, and customer grouping
    b. Production budget in units
    c. Direct materials purchases budget
    d. Direct labor budget
    e. Factory overhead budget
    f. Cost of goods sold budget
    g. Marketing and administrative budgets
    h. Research and development budgets
    i. Budgeted income statement
    j. Budgeted statement of cash receipts and disbursements
    k. Budgeted balance sheet
    l. Capital expenditure budget

11. The following are some of the advantages budgeting offers.

    a. It obligates management to specify objectives for the short and long run.
    b. It forces management to analyze future problems so that alternative plans are recognized.
    c. It directs efforts and funds toward the most profitable of all possible alternatives.
    d. It emphasizes the need for coordination of all elements of a company since budgeting quickly reveals weaknesses in organization.
    e. It serves as a means of communication.,
    f. It provides performance standards which serve as incentives to perform more effectively.
    g. It indicates those areas lacking control by providing data used to analyze variances between actual and budgeted operations. These variances should provide the springboard for study of the source of the problem.

12. A budget is a means of coordinating the combined intelligence of an entire organization into a plan of action based on past performance and governed by judgment of the effect of factors which will affect the budget in the future.

13. top management

14. Reasons which are justified include:

    a. Factors external to the company such as the entrance of a competitive company and /or product.
    b. An error in the original compiling of the budget.
    c. Expansion of a product line or the introduction of a new product or service.

15. *Eaton Company*

a. Indirect material - variable
   Depreciation - fixed
   Utilities - semivariable
   Inspection - semivariable

b.

	Variable	Fixed
Indirect material	$2.00 ($4,000/2,000)	-0-
Depreciation	-0-	$ 800
Utilities (see below)	40	1,000
Inspection (see below)	1.30	1,700
	$3.70 per machine hour +	$3,500

High - Low Method

Utilities:

	Hours	Cost
	2,500	$2,000
	-1,000	1,400
Difference	1,500	$ 600

Variable rate = $.40 ($600/1,500)
Fixed costs = $1,000 ($2,000 - (2,500 x $.40))

Inspection:

	Hours	Cost
	2,500	$4,950
	-1,000	-3,000
Difference	1,500	$1,950

Variable rate = $1.30 ($1,950/1,500)
Fixed costs = $1,700 ($4,950 - (2,500 x $1.30))

c.

	Actual Costs	Budget at 2,300 Hours		Variance
Indirect material.......	$ 4,825	$ 4,600	($2 x 2,300)	$225 U
Depreciation...........	850	800		50 U
Utilities....................	1,880	1,920	($.40 x 2,300 hours + $1,000)	40 F
Inspection..............	4,720	4,690	($1.30 x 2,300 hours + $1,700)	30 U
Totals....................	$12,275	$12,010		$265 U

16. *Puryear Company*

	Pounds
Beginning inventory	25,000
Purchases..	800,000
Available	825,000
Less ending inventory	40,000
Production requirements	785,000

17. *Whitlock Co.*

	June	July	August	September
Units sold	8,000	8,500	9,200	9,800
Desired ending inventory	2,125	2,300	2,450	2,500
Units to provide	10,125	10,800	11,650	12,300
Beginning inventory	-0-	2,125	2,300	2,450
Production requirements	10,125	8,675	9,350	9,850

Material Requirements					
Material	112B	116A	118D	127F	Total
Quantity per unit	3	4	8	5	
June:					
Material needed for production	30,375	40,500	81,000	50,625	202,500
Desired ending materials inventory	5,205*	6,940	13,880	8,675	34,700
Material to provide for	35,580	47,440	94,880	59,300	237,200
Less beginning material inventory	-0-	-0-	-0-	-0-	-0-
Purchase requirements	35,580	47,440	94,880	59,300	237,200
Unit cost	$4.00	$5.00	$12.00	$6.00	
Purchase cost	$142,320	$237,200	$1,138,560	$355,800	$1,873,880

*20% x 26,025 production requirements

July:					
Material needed for production	26,025	34,700	69,400	43,375	173,500
Desired ending materials inventory	5,610	7,480	14,960	9,350	37,400
Material to provide for	31,635	42,180	84,360	52,725	210,900
Less beginning inventory	5,205	6,940	13,880	8,675	34,700
Purchases requirements	26,430	35,240	70,480	44,050	176,200
Unit cost	$4.00	$5.00	$12.00	$6.00	
Purchase cost	$105,720	$176,200	$845,760	$264,300	$1,391,980

August:					
Material needed for production	28,050	37,400	74,800	46,750	187,000
Desired ending materials inventory	5,910**	7,880	15,760	9,850	39,400
Material to provide for	33,960	45,280	90,560	56,600	226,400
Less beginning inventory	5,610	7,480	14,960	9,350	37,400
Purchase requirements	28,350	37,800	75,600	47,250	189,000
Unit cost	$4.00	$5.00	$12.00	$6.00	
Purchase cost	$113,400	$189,000	$907,200	$283,500	$1,493,100

**9,850 x 3 x 20%

18. *Bailey Company*

Total Production Budget
For Third Quarter Ending September 30, 19X1

a.

	Products		
	D	E	F
Planned sales...	1,000	580	600
Desired ending finished goods inventory	380	170	155
Total units to provide for...	1,380	750	755
Less beginning finished goods inventory................................	400	165	140
Units to be produced	980	585	615

Bailey Company
Direct Materials Purchases Budget
For Third Quarter Ending September 30,19X1

	Material AX	Material B4	Total
Units needed for production (from below).................................	6,570	17,500	
Desired ending direct materials inventory	2,000	4,000	
Total material units to provide for.....................................	8,570	21,500	
Less beginning direct materials inventory	1,820	3,800	
Units to be purchased..	6,750	17,700	
Unit purchase price	$ 2.00	$ 3.00	
Total purchases cost	$13,500	$53,100	$66,600

Direct Materials	Direct Material Usage Products			Total Direct Material Usage	Material Unit Cost	Cost of Material Used
	D	E	F			
AX	2,940	1,170	2,460	6,570	$2.00	$13,140
	(980 x 3)	(585 x 2)	(615 x 4)			
B4	7,840	3,510	6,150	17,500	$3.00	52,500
	(980 x 8)	(585 x 6)	(615 x 10)			$65,640

Bailey Company
Direct Labor Budget
For Third Quarter Ending September 30,19X1

Products	Units Produced	Direct Labor Hours per unit	Total Hours	Total Budget @ $5 per Hour
D	980	2	1,960	$ 9,800
E	585	4	2,340	11,700
F	615	3	1,845	9,225
			6,145	$30,725

True-False

1.   T   Since the level of inventory does not change, there is no need to purchase more or less than the amount needed for production.

2.   T

3.   F   It is the sales budget that provides this function.

4.   F   The flexible budget formula would be $600 per month plus $.40 per machine hour computed as follows: 2,500 - 1,500 hours = 1,000 difference in hours. $1,600 - $1,200 = $400/1,000 hours = $.40 variable rate. $.40 variable rate x 1,500 hours = $600 total variable costs; $1,200 - $600 = $600 fixed cost.

5.   F   Budgeted sales + desired ending inventory - beginning inventory = units to produce.

6.   T

7.   T

8.   F   Top management has the authority to make final budget approvals under the bottom-up approach to budgeting even though low-line personnel are involved in the process.

9.   F   This description is for fixed or static budgets which are established for a single activity with no adjustments to actual capacity attained.

10.   T

11.   F   Fixed costs per unit varies inversely with production so that fixed costs per unit would increase as production decreases because there would be less units over which to spread the total fixed costs.

12.   T   9,000 X $5 application rate = $45,000 budgeted amount; $48,000 actual overhead - $45,000 budgeted amount = $3,000 unfavorable variance.

10 Nonmanufacturing Budgets, Forecasted Statements, and Behavioral Issues

Chapter Outline

Marketing and Administrative Budgets
Promotional Budgets
Research and Development Budgets
Cash Management
Centralization of Cash
Cash Budgets
Determining Collections Based on Accounts Receivable Balances
Budgeted Statement of Income and Statement of Financial Position
Analysis of Gross Margin
Government Budgeting
Incremental Budgeting
Behavioral Aspects of Budgeting
Budgets for Performance Evaluation
Fear of Failure
Unrealistic Budgets
Participative Budgeting Process

Chapter Objectives

After studying this chapter, you should be able to:

1. Prepare budgets for marketing, administrative, and research activities.

2. Estimate cash collections from credit sales and cash disbursements needed in preparing a cash budget.

3. Prepare a budgeted statement of income and statement of financial position, including gross profi analysis.

4. Compare appropriation, incremental, and zero-base budgeting.

5. Understand inherent behavioral implications of budgeting and how the misuse of budgets leads to long-run problems.

6. Define and apply the new terms introduced.

Chapter Review

Marketing and Administrative Budgets

1. Marketing and administrative budgets are more difficult to control and budget than production costs because the environment in which these costs occur is less standardized.
   a. In a large company, detailed marketing expense budgets should be prepared for each function.
   b. A margin of safety should be built into the advertising budget because outside factors greatly influence the amount that is needed for advertising.

2. Some advertising expenses, like institutional advertising, are designed to promote all aspects of the company while other advertising promotes specific products.

Promotional Budgets

3. The promotional expense budget is concerned with order-getting costs which result from personal presentation of the service or product to prospective buyers.

4. Many factors influence the success of an advertising campaign; as a result, intuitive judgment is generally used more often in establishing this budget than in any other budget.

5. A commonly used approach is to set the advertising budget as a fixed percentage of sales.

   a. This method has great weaknesses because sales are supposed to be the end result of advertising rather than vice versa.
   b. A logical use of this approach is to correlate advertising appropriations with forecasted sales.

6. The promotional budget may be set on a unit cost per product grouping, customer, or other segment.

   a. This approach is easily adapted to flexible budgeting.
   b. The unit cost should be a scientifically estimated standard cost which is determined only after careful study.

7. When promotional budgets are set based on competitors' actions, this approach allows competitors to set the pace, and companies use this method in an attempt not to spend more than the competition.

8. Another approach to promotional budgets is to appropriate "all the company can afford."

   a. This method ignores the relationships between advertising costs and advertising effects.
   b. One form of this approach is to specify a fixed sum that will be spent for advertising without regard to other factors.

9. When market research is used in establishing the advertising budget, the probable relationship between the population's characteristics and the advertising medium chosen is estimated.

10. The task method or sales objective method establishes first a definite advertising objective for each project. Then the amount of advertising considered necessary to meet this objective is determined.

Research and Development Budget

11. The research and development budget is useful in both planning and controlling this area.

a. Research projects should be planned and evaluated and then grouped into long- and short-run objectives.
b. Projects should be broken down into phases and the completion date for each phase forecasted.

12. A status report should be prepared for all phases or departments involved in each project in which expenditures incurred to date and the commitments made are matched against the budget to determine the unexpended amounts.

13. A time budget analysis should be made comparing the actual hours spent on a project with the hours budgeted.

a. The extra cost of increasing production, referred to as crashing, should be compared to the extra revenue earned by introducing the product earlier to determine if crashing is warranted.
b. PERT-Cost and PERT-Time analysis is useful in this aspect.

Cash Management

14. Cash management plays an important role in today's economy as this is one of the most common causes of business failure.

a. The role has expanded from merely a custodial function of cash control and safekeeping to cash utilization including evaluating the cost of money and its ability to earn a return.
b. Improvements in communication and transportation have facilitated the movement and clearing of funds.
c. The expansion of business firms with subsidiaries in foreign countries has increased the problems of controlling and funding corporate operations.

15. Companies often carry too large a balance of cash that may not be earning as high a return if it were invested in other alternatives.

Centralization of Cash

16. In most cases there are advantages to having cash-handling functions centralized.

a. Centralization of cash is achieved by having receipts deposited in centrally controlled bank accounts and making branch disbursements from imprest funds or payroll accounts.
b. Generally decentralization of functions is limited to the payment of local operating expenses and the receipt of payment from local customers.
c. It is usually more economical to have accounting and other paperwork related to cash centralized at a single location.
d. With centralization of cash, a smaller balance is required to support a given level of operations.
e. The company's importance as a bank customer is usually greater if its accounts are centralized in a few bank accounts.

17. Some companies believe that decentralization of cash is important for public relations so that the bank facilities of each community in which its operations are performed are utilized.

18. Periodically, accounts receivables should be reviewed to detect slow-paying accounts.

a. Cash may be tied up in disputes or claims which have been unsettled.
b. A review of the credit policy may reveal that too liberal or too conservative policy is hurting the business.

Cash Budgets

19. Detailed short-range forecasts of cash positions are needed as well as long-range cash projections.

    a. A cash budget shows expected cash receipts and disbursements by months which may reveal periods in which shortages and excesses are forecasted.
    b. By revealing periods in which shortages and excesses are expected, management is allowed to take action before damage or lost interest occurs.

Determining Collections Based on Accounts Receivable Balances

20. The collection pattern and balances in the accounts receivable account identified as to specific time periods can be used to estimate collections of accounts receivable.

Budgeted Statement of Income and Statement of Financial Position

21. Figures taken from the budgets prepared can be combined into a budgeted Statement of Income and Statement of Financial Position.

Analysis of Gross Margin

22. An analysis of gross margin studies changes in cost of goods sold percentages and changes in gross margin earned in differences in sales.

Government Budgeting

23. Government budgets are appropriation budgets which establish fixed amounts which can be applied to achieve the objectives of the organizational unit for the period specified.

    a. The stewardship function which is symbolized by spending limits is very strong in government budgeting because taxpayers' funds are being spent.
    b. The appropriation budget concept often leads managers to focus more toward spending resources than toward obtaining results.

Zero-Base Budgeting

24. Zero-base budgeting was introduced in the 1970s to overcome some of the weaknesses in the traditional budgeting approach.

    a. The beginning point in the budgeting procedure is zero, rather than the amount already being spent.
    b. The assumption is made that zero will be spent on each program or activity until greater expenditure is justified.

Decision Packages

25. Preparation of decision packages is one of the first steps in the zero-base budgeting process.

    a. Decision packages identify and describe a specific activity for management to evaluate and rank.
    b. Decision packages should be developed at the same organizational level.

Levels of Effort

26. Decision packages include different methods of performing the same function as well as different levels of effort in performing the function.

a. A minimum level of effort is established with additional levels of effort identified as separate decision packages.
b. By having various levels of effort, management can compare levels of effort within each function and decide on the best trade-off among functions.

27. A modification in government budgeting is to relate cost to outputs or results.

a. A common form is performance budgeting whose focus is on the ends served by the government rather than on dollars spent.
   1. In formulating a performance budget, a precise definition of the work to be done and a careful estimate of what that work will cost is made.
   2. Performance budgets are prepared on the basis of functions and objectives of government agencies and departments.

Incremental Budgeting

28. Traditional budgeting, also referred to as incremental budgeting, directs attention to changes or differences between existing budget appropriations and proposed expenditures.

a. Incremental budgeting is a conservative approach which often encourages companies to keep activities which have lost their usefulness.
b. It is often difficult using this budgeting approach to drop activities and devote those resources to new functions and duties.

Behavioral Aspects of Budgeting

29. Budgets are not substitutes for management that is skilled, and in order for a budget program to be successful, the support and participation of all management levels is needed.

a. Budgets should not be viewed as inflexible devices and should be revised if needed.
b. Management should avoid focusing too much attention on individual segments in the budgeting process by allowing segment managers to view only their own budget because the relationships between segments are important.

Budgets for Performance Evaluation

30. With a budget-constrained style, performance is primarily evaluated on the ability to meet the short-term budget.

31. With a profit-conscious style of evaluation, managers' performance is evaluated on the basis of their ability to increase long-term effectiveness of their units in relation to the organization's goals.

Fear of Failure

32. An unrealistically high budget breeds resentment because workers and supervisors are placed in positions in which they cannot succeed.

33. The manner in which shortcomings are reported often harbors misunderstandings because frequently the unfavorable variance is routed throughout the organization and may be published in budget reports.

a. The reason for the unfavorable variance is usually not given and this may not be the fault of the supervisor in whose department the variance existed.
b. Many times those individuals who feel the effects of failure the most are the most dedicated workers and ones that the organization should keep; this factor should not be ignored in calculating shortcomings.

Unrealistic Budgets

34. Budget revisions are needed when an error has been made in compiling the budget or when there is a company reorganization.

    a. There is a danger in frequently revising the budget every time a goal or budget is not met.
    b. Budget revisions are most appropriate when an external factor causes a major impact on company activities.

35. Long-run negative effects result if management sets a new higher goal every time a budget is met, and employees soon realize this pattern and quit trying to meet the budget.

    a. Under these conditions, the word "budget" becomes a term representing a negative brand of management.
    b. Supervisors operating in these conditions feel this pressure both from up above and from their subordinates below; they cannot join an informal group against management, like subordinates often do, because they are part of management.

Participative Budgeting Process

36. There is evidence that participation in the budgeting comparison and reviewing process leads to more rapid goal acceptance.

    a. Participation attempts to get the employees ego involved, not just task involved.
    b. If employees are allowed to participate, the budget is less likely to be considered imposed.

37. If management is playing a game of false participation with employees, this attitude soon filters down and is highly resented; this does much harm.

38. The history of the company and the personality and skill level of employees are factors which help determine if participation in the budgeting process will work.

39. Expectancy theory suggests that individuals will alter their behavior based upon the outcome of an event.

    a. Intrinsic rewards, such as praise or self respect, and extrinsic rewards, such as pay or promotion, exist.

Demonstration Problem

Quarterly Cash Requirements

For the first quarter of 19X2, Futrell Company prepared the following estimates of unit sales:

	Chemical Product A Units	Petroleum Product B Units
January	25,800	20,000
February	20,000	31,000
March	18,000	24,000

The company must have a beginning inventory of each type of product that is equal to half of the upcoming month's sales in units. During April 19X2, the firm plans to sell 27,000 units of Product A and 32,000 units of Product B. During December 19X1, the company sold 19,300 units of Product A and 19,800 units of Product B.

The unit cost of the company's products amounted to $66 per unit for Product A and $45 per unit for Product B during 19X1. For 19X2, the unit costs are expected to increase by 15 percent.

The company pays for all purchases during the month following the purchase.

Required:

Determine the *cash requirements* for each of the three months of 19X2 for merchandise purchases. Assume December budgeted sales were the same as actual sales.

Paper for working Demonstration Problem

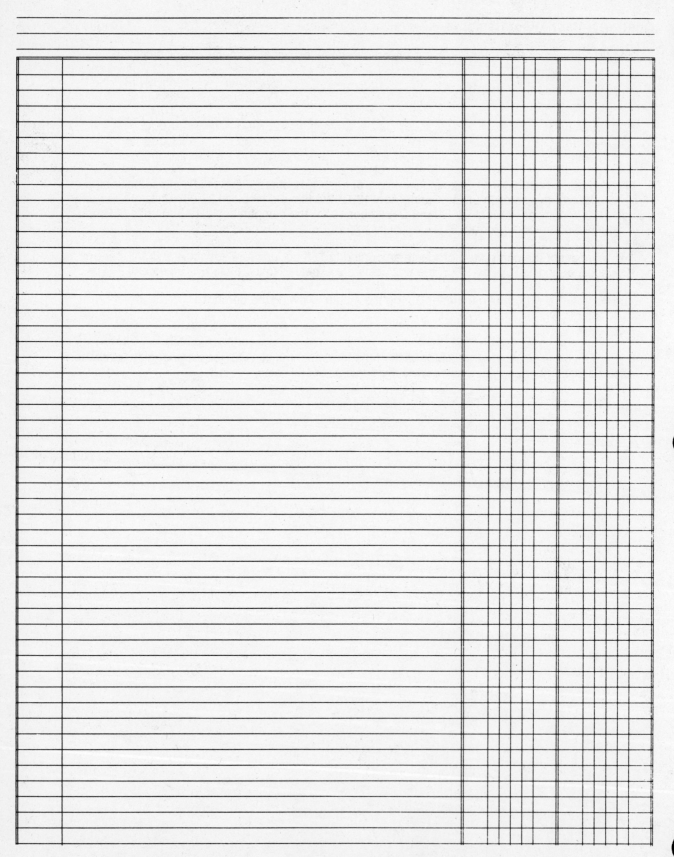

Solution to Demonstration Problem

Futrell Company
Merchandise Purchases
For December 19X1 through February 19X2

	Product A	Product B
December Sales..	19,300	19,800
Desired January 1, 19X2 inventory................................	12,900	10,000
Amount to be provided...	32,200	29,800
Less December 1, 19X1 inventory................................	9,650	9,900
December purchases	22,550	19,900
January sales..	25,800	20,000
Desired February 1, 19X2 inventory	10,000	15,500
Amount to be provided	35,800	35,500
Less January 1, 19X2 Inventory...................................	12,900	10,000
January purchases	22,900	25,500
February sales	20,000	31,000
Desired March 1, 19X2 inventory	9,000	12,000
Amount to be provided	29,000	43,000
Less February 1, 19X2 inventory	10,000	15,500
February purchases...	19,000	27,500

Futrell Company
Cash Requirement for Merchandise Purchases
By Months for First Three Months of 19X2

	January	February	March
Cash requirements:			
December purchases:			
Product A (22,550 x $66).........................	$1,488,300		
Product B (19,900 x $45).........................	895,500		
January purchases:			
Product A (22,900 x $75.90).....................		$1,738,110	
Product B (25,500 x $51.75).....................		1,319,625	
February purchases:			
Product A (19,000 x $75.90).....................			$1,442,100
Product B (27,500 x $51.75).....................			1,423,125
Cash requirement by month	$2,383,800	$3,057,735	$2,865,225

Matching

Referring to the terms listed in the left column, place the appropriate letter next to the corresponding description. A term may not be used or may be used more than once.

a. Decision packages

b. Discretionary costs

c. Imposed budgeting process

d. Incremental budgeting

e. Institutional advertising campaign

f. Participative budgeting process

g. Program budgeting

h. Program evaluation and review technique (PERT)

i. Security of principal

j. Slack

k. Specific advertising campaign

l. Status reports

m. Zero-base budgeting

_____1. Uses networks which indicate paths to completion so that management can determine if crashing is advised.

_____2. Process where individuals are encouraged to become both task and ego involved.

_____3. Protection or assurance that the short-term obligation will be paid.

_____4. Traditional budgeting approach directing attention to changes in existing budget appropriations and proposed expenditures.

_____5. Describes tasks' objectives and matches them with the costs to achieve them.

_____6. Sales advertising response promoting all aspects of the company.

_____7. Cost which arises from top management's periodic appropriation decisions.

_____8. Budgeting approach which is most useful for non-production, discretionary expenses.

_____9. Document which identifies and describes a specific activity for management to evaluate and rank against other activities competing for available resources.

_____10. Used to match expenditures incurred to date and the commitments made with budgeted amounts to determine unexpected amounts.

_____11. Under this budgeting approach, all programs are reviewed, not just the changes proposed.

_____12. Allows individuals who are accountable for activities and performance to become involved in budgeting.

_____13. Under this approach management may request signatures from employees affected by budgets so they cannot later deny they accepted the budget.

_____14. Difference between total resources available to a firm and total resources necessary to maintain organizational activities.

Completion and Exercises

1. Briefly discuss three limitations of budgets.

   a._____

   _____

   _____

   b._____

   _____

   _____

   c._____

   _____

2. In cash management, companies are often willing to accept low _____ for the protection

   of _____ and_____   ___ _____.

3. Give three reasons for centralization of cash function.

   a._____

   _____

   b._____

   _____

   c._____

   _____

4. Give one reason for decentralization of the cash function.

   _____

   _____

5. Briefly discuss four approaches to establishing the promotional budget.

   a._____

   b._____

   c._____

   d._____

6. The difference between government and business budgets is that the government

   budget is a(n) _____budget.

7. _____ budgeting is a modification of government
   budgeting in which the focus is on the ends served by the government with a precise
   definition of the work to be done and a careful estimate of what that work will cost.

8. Monthly Cash Receipts for a Quarter

On December 31, 19X1, the Smith Company requests that you prepare a cash forecast by months of their cash receipts only for the first quarter of next year. You begin your work by questioning management about what their collection pattern for charge sales is, and you find that it is as follows:

40   percent in the month of sale
25   percent in the first month after sale
15   percent in the second month after sale
10   percent in the third month after sale
 5   percent in the fourth month after sale

After studying their Accounts Receivable ledger account, you find the following balances as of December 31, 19X1:

From September sales .... $ 20,000
From October sales............................... 50,000
From November sales 70,000
From December sales 180,000

Management expects total sales for the first quarter to be as follows:

January $325,000
February 248,000
March... 280,000

It is expected that 60 percent of total sales will be charge sales. In addition, the organization expects to receive their quarterly interest payment in March on their 8 percent ARGO Company Investment bonds, of which face value is $10,000 and market value is $12,000.

Required:

Prepare budgeted cash receipts by months for the first quarter.

9. Analysis of Gross Margin

Top management of Houseson Manufacturing Company is concerned that gross margin has decreased from $141,250 in 19X1 to $123,700 in 19X2. They ask for your assistance in providing for an analysis of the causes of change. The company operates a plant in New York and one in Chicago. The plant in Chicago produces only one type of motor while the New York plant manufactures several varieties.

The following information is obtained concerning the plants.

New York Plant:	19X2	19X1
Sales	$350,000	$425,000
Cost of Sales	270,000	318,750
Gross Margin	$ 80,000	$106,250

Chicago Plant:	19X2		19X1	
	Amount	Per Unit	Amount	Per Unit
Sales	$115,000	$11.50	$100,000	$10.00
Cost of Sales	71,300	7.13	65,000	6.50
Gross Margin	$ 43,700	$ 4.37	$ 35,000	$ 3.50

Required:

Prepare a detailed quantitative analysis of the causes for the change in gross margin for each plant based on the above data.

9.

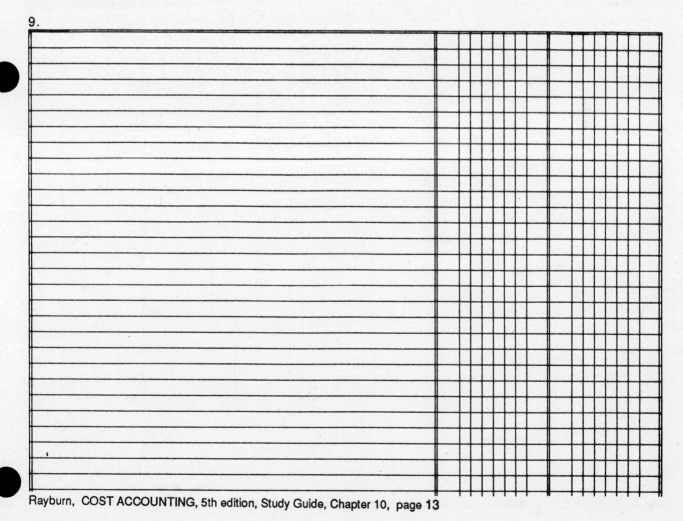

10. Estimated Cash Receipts and Disbursements

Management of Wong Company provides you with the following selected data for a month:

Sales	$200,000
Gross profit (based on sales)	40%
Increase in net trade accounts receivable balance during month	$ 7,000
Change in accounts payable balance during month	-0-
Increase in inventory during month	$ 6,000

Variable marketing and administration expenses include a charge for uncollectible accounts of 2 percent of sales. Total marketing and administrative expense is $40,000 per month plus 10 percent of sales. Depreciation expenses of $15,000 per month are included in fixed marketing and administrative expenses.

Required:

a. On the basis of the above data, what are the estimated cash receipts from operations for the month?
b. On the basis of the above data, what are the estimated cash disbursements from operations for the month?

a.

b.

11. Quarterly Budget

Reason Company began operations on January 1. Judging by management's experience for similar organizations, they forecast their collection pattern for accounts receivable as follows:

10 percent of the credit sales are paid within the discount period;
An additional 80 percent of the credit sales are paid within 30 days after the month in which the sale is made;
An additional 5 percent of the credit sales are paid within 60 days after the month in which the sale is made.

Management has agreed to offer cash discounts on a term of 2/15 EOM, N/60 EOM. Cash and credit sales by month are forecasted to be as follows:

	Cash Sales	Credit Sales
January	$ 8,000	$2,000
February	12,000	3,000
March	16,000	4,000

Required:

Prepare the cash receipts budget by months for the first quarter of the year.

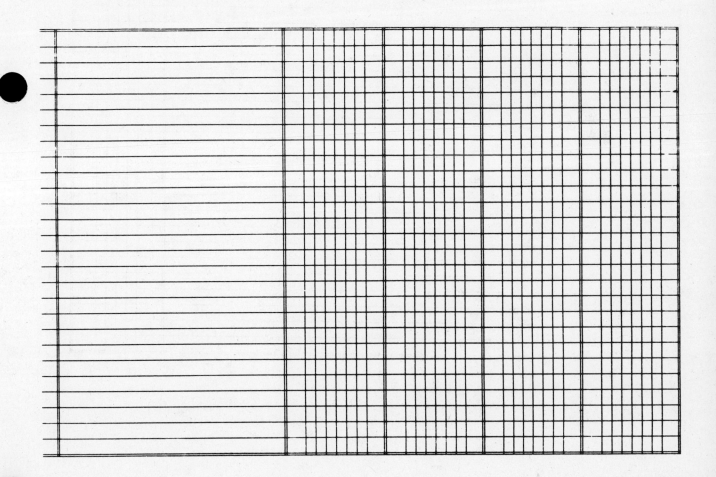

12. Cash Receipts from Credit Sales

You have been asked to forecast the cash receipts from credit sales for the month of May for the Reid Company. The company is engaged in seasonal production, and May credit sales are estimated to be only $144,000. Discount terms of 2/10, n/30 are offered customers as an incentive to pay their bills early. The collection pattern is assumed to be 20 percent during the discount period and month of sale; 7 percent after the discount period has expired, but within the month of sale; 43 percent in the first month after sale; 28.5 percent in the second month after sale. The accounts receivable balance as of April 30 is $164,250; one third of the balance represents March sales and the remainder, April sales. All accounts receivable from months prior to March have been paid or written off.

Required:

Determine the May cash receipts from credit sales.

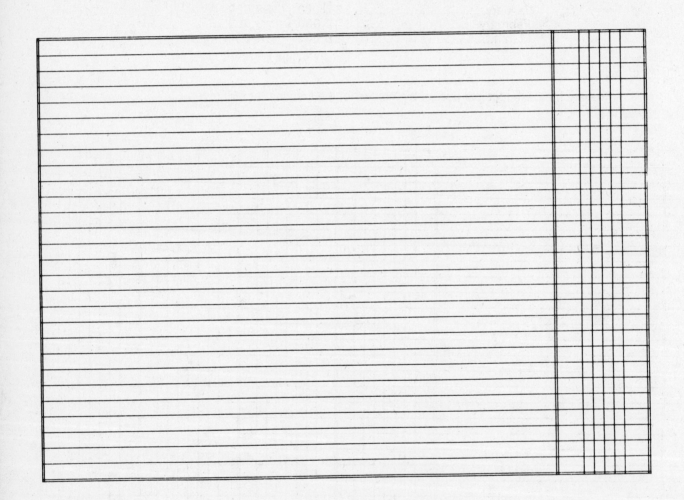

True-False Questions

Indicate whether the following statements are true or false by inserting in the blank space a capital "T" for true or "F" for false.

_____ 1. Performance budgeting, program budgeting, and zero-base budgeting are appropriate for use with government departments and agencies.

_____ 2. The concept and objectives of performance budgets differ in many aspects from program budgets.

_____ 3. A review across departmental lines is helpful as it usually reveals that there are more advantages to having cash decentralized than centralized.

_____ 4. If a company uses competitors' behavior as the basis for setting their advertising budget, the company is allowing competitors to set the pace and it is merely reacting to these actions.

_____ 5. A discretionary cost is one that arises from periodic decisions made by top management reflecting their policies and often the status of company funds.

_____ 6. Companies often take high yields to be certain of achieving security and liquidity of principal.

_____ 7. It is a wise policy to maintain a large enough balance of cash to meet all possible emergencies.

_____ 8. A smaller balance of cash is usually required when cash functions are centralized rather than decentralized.

_____ 9. Assume the collection pattern is: 45 percent in the month of sale, 30 percent in the month following sale, and 20 percent in the second month following sale; and the budgeted January sales were $100,000, February sales were $120,000, and March sales were $200,000. The cash receipts from sales expected to be received in March would be $146,000.

_____ 10. Under the "all we can afford" approach to setting advertising budgets, advertising activities are one of the first expenses budgeted.

_____ 11. A budgeting approach will operate smoothly even though top management feels that the process is not crucial to the operation's efficiency.

_____ 12. When a company employs the bottom-up approach to budgeting, top management first specifies planning goals before the operating budgets are prepared.

SOLUTIONS

Matching

1.	h	6.	e	11.	m
2.	f	7.	b	12.	f
3.	i	8.	m	13.	c
4.	d	9.	a	14.	j
5.	g	10.	l		

Completion and Exercises

1. Limitations of the budget include:
    a. Budgets depict only estimates and are not a substitute for skilled management.
    b. A budget is often viewed as a straitjacket which cannot be revised.
    c. Management often hesitates to take action which is needed for fear of not meeting the budget.
    d. Because budgets take so long to properly prepare, often top management loses support for the budgeting process.
    e. Executives may also lose interest because of the time lag between preparation and results.
    f. Accounting factors are emphasized to the detriment of the human factors.
    g. Difference in outlook between production personnel who are more concerned with day-to-day operations than the future may surface and cause conflict in the budgeting approach.

2. yield; security; liquidity of principal

3. Reasons for centralization of cash include:
    a. Better control.
    b. Facilitates those functions, such as the payment of dividends or sale of stock, which relates to the entire company.
    c. More economical with reduction in paperwork usually.
    d. Allows the company to maximize its importance as a bank customer and may enable it to obtain easier credit.
    e. A smaller balance of cash is required to support a given level of operation.

4. It is good public relations to establish a bank account in the communities in which a branch operates.

5. The following are approaches to budgeting promotional expenses:

    a. Task method or sales objective--Under this method, a definite advertising objective is established and then the amount of advertising necessary to meet this objective is estimated.
    b. Market research--The probable relationship between demographic characteristics of the population and advertising medium chosen is studied. This data is then used in determining the amount to spend on sales promotion.
    c. "All We Can Afford"--Advertising costs are funded only after all other expenses are budgeted.
    d. Fixed percentage of sales--This method has great weakness as sales are suppose to be the end result of advertising rather than vice versa.
    e. Amount per unit--Standard costs per unit can be set for customers, territories, or other segments, and the total number of segments budgeted can be multiplied by the cost unit to determine the total appropriation.
    f. Competitor's actions--This method allows the competitors to set the pace because advertising expenditures are established in relation to their actions.

6. appropriation

7. Performance

8.

Cash Receipts	January	February	March
Collections from:			
September Sales			
$\dfrac{\$20,000}{.10} = \$200,000 \times 5\%$	$10,000		
October Sales			
$\dfrac{\$50,000}{.20} = \$250,000 \times 10\%$	25,000		
$= \$250,000 \times 5\%$		$12,500	
November Sales			
$\dfrac{\$70,000}{.35} = \$200,000 \times 15\%$	30,000		
$\$200,000 \times 10\%$		20,000	
$\$200,000 \times 5\%$			$10,000
December Sales			
$\dfrac{\$180,000}{.60} = \$300,000 \times 25\%$	75,000		
$\$300,000 \times 15\%$		45,000	
$\$300,000 \times 10\%$			30,000
January Sales			
$325,000 \times 60\% = \$195,000$			
charge sales			
$\$195,000 \times 40\%$	78,000		
$\$195,000 \times 25\%$		48,750	
$\$195,000 \times 15\%$			29,250
February Sales			
$248,000 \times 60\% = \$148,800$			
charge sales			
$\$148,800 \times 40\%$		59,520	
$\$148,800 \times 25\%$			37,200
March Sales			
$280,000 \times 60\% = \$168,000$			
$\$168,000 \times 40\%$			67,200
Cash Sales			
$\$325,000 \times 40\%$	130,000		
$\$248,000 \times 40\%$		99,200	
$\$280,000 \times 40\%$			112,000
Interest			200
Total Cash Receipts	$348,000	$284,970	$285,850

9. *Houseson Manufacturing Company*

$141,250   Gross margin 19X1
 123,700   Gross margin 19X2
$ 17,550   Decrease in gross margin

New York Plant

19X1 75% Cost of Sales to Sales if same conditions exist in 19X2:

Sales..	$350,000		
Cost (75%* x $350,000)		$262,500	
Actual Cost		270,000	
Net loss			$ 7,500
Gross margin lost on decreased sale (25% x $75,000)			18,750
Decrease in Gross Margin.......................................			$26,250

Chicago Plant

Less increase in gross margin from Chicago Plant			
Gross margin on increased sales price (35% x $15,000)		$ 5,250	
Decrease in cost of goods sold			
19X2 sales using 19X1 percentage (65% x $115,000).......	$ 74,750		
Actual 19X2 cost..	71,300	3,450	8,700
Total decrease in gross margin.......................................			$17,550

---

*$318,750/$425,000 = 75% cost of goods sold

10. *Wong Corporation*

  a. Sales $200,000
     Less increase in net trade accounts receivable . <u>7,000</u>
     $193,000

     Less charge for uncollectible accounts
       (2% x $200,000) .... <u>4,000</u>
     Estimated cash receipts from operations .... <u>$189,000</u>

  b. Cost of Goods Sold (60% x $200,000) $120,000
     Increase in Inventories 6,000
     Marketing and Administration Expense:
       Total per month $40,000
       + 10 percent of $200,000 sales.................. <u>20,000</u> $60,000

     Less: Depreciation expense......................... $15,000
           Uncollectible accounts charge
             (2% x $200,000) .... <u>4,000</u>   <u>19,000</u>   <u>41,000</u>
     Estimated Cash Disbursements from Operations   <u>$167,000</u>

11. *Reason Company*

Cash Receipts Budget
First Quarter

	January	February	March	Total
Cash Sales	$8,000	$12,000	$16,000	$36,000
From January sales				
(10% x $2,000 x 98%)		196		196
(80% x $2,000)		1,600		1,600
(5% x $2,000)			100	100
From February sales				
(10% x $3,000 x 98%)			294	294
(80% x $3,000)			2,400	2,400
Total	$8,000	$13,796	$18,794	$40,590

12. *Reid Company*

Cash Receipts from Credit Sales:
From May sales:

20% x $144,000 x 98%..	$28,224
7% x $144,000	10,080

From April sales:
  2/3 x $164,250 total accounts receivable = $109,500

$$\frac{\$109,500 \text{ April accounts receivable}}{1.00 - (.20 + .07) = .73} = \$150,000 \text{ April sales}$$

$150,000 April sales x 43 percent	64,500

From March sales:
  1/3 x $164,250 total accounts receivable = $54,750

$$\frac{\$54,750 \text{ March accounts receivable}}{1.00 - (.20 + .07 + .43) = .30} = \$182,500 \text{ March sales}$$

$182,500 March sales x 28.5%	52,013
Total Cash Receipts from Credit sales	$154,817

True-False

1.   T

2.   F   Some people consider performance budgets to be an extreme form of program budgets. The objectives and concepts are similar.

3.   F   Usually there are many more advantages to having cash centralized than decentralized especially in an economy in which interest rates are high because a company can keep less cash on hand under a centralized system in addition to other advantages.

4.   T

5.   T   Advertising is a discretionary cost along with research and development; however, production costs are generally not discretionary.

6.   F   Companies take a trade off by accepting low yields to receive the protection of security and liquidity of principal.

7.   F   An excessively large cash balance is costly because it usually draws no interest or an interest rate that is below the market of other investments.

8.   T

9.   T   (20% X $100,000) + (30% X $120,000) + (45% X $200,000) = $146,000 expected cash receipts from sales in March.

10.   F   Under the "all we can afford" approach, advertising activities are funded only after all other expenses are budgeted.

11.   F   Top management's attitudes filter down throughout the company and if they are not supportive of the budgeting approach, employees soon detect this. As a result, the budgeting operation soon becomes ineffective.

12.   T

11   Standard Costs and Variances for Materials and Labor

Chapter Outline

Standard Cost Systems
>Advantages of a Standard Cost System
>Levels of Activity and Efficiency
>Budgets, Standard Costs, and Target Costs
>Incorporation in the Accounting System

Setting Material Standards
>Material Quantity Standards
>Material Price Standards

Setting Labor Standards
>Labor Efficiency Standards
>Labor Rate Standards

Variances Illustrated for Job Order Costing
>Material Variances
>Journal Entries for Material
>Labor Variances
>Labor Efficiency under JIT
>Journal Entries for Labor

Material and Labor Variances Using Process Costing

Standard Costs in Future Factories

Interactions Among Factors of Input and Variances

Summary of Material and Labor Variances
>Material Price Variances
>Material Usage (Quantity or Efficiency) Variances
>Labor Rate Variances
>Labor Time (Quantity or Efficiency) Variances

Chapter Objectives

After studying this chapter, you should be able to:

1. Understand the benefits of a standard cost system and how automation is affecting traditional variance measures.

2. Analyze material and labor variances in either a job order or process costing system.

3. Recognize the role variances play in evaluating actual performance.

4. Prepare journal entries that incorporate standards in the accounting system.

5. Define and apply the new terms introduced.

Chapter Review

Standard Cost Systems

1. Standard costing is a system of costing on a predetermined basis because this provides a better basis of evaluating performance than does historical actual costs.

   a. Cost standards are scientifically predetermined costs of production used as a basis for measurement and comparison.
   b. Standards represent what costs should be under attainable good performance.

Advantages of a Standard Cost System

2. A standard cost system offers many advantages, such as the following:
   a. Executives become cost conscious because cost variances are computed and provide a springboard for analysis.
   b. Standards make available a measuring device which gives attention to cost variances.
   c. Standards serve as a compass that guides management toward improvements.
   d. Standard cost systems integrate managerial, accounting, and engineering aspects, and coordination of business elements toward the same goal is more likely achieved.
   e. Setting standards can assist management in planning for efficient and economical operations.
   f. If the standard setting process is communicated properly, employees will better understand what is expected of them.

Levels of Activity and Efficiency

3. Theoretical, practical, normal, and expected actual are capacity levels which may be used for setting standards.

   a. When standards are set on the basis of theoretical capacity, the standards are referred to as ideal standards since they reflect maximum efficiency. When theoretical capacity is used, it is assumed that the company will operate at full speed without interruptions.

4. Standards set on a normal capacity level represent a long-range approach because data from several years is used to even out the cyclical swings in sales demand.

5. The expected actual capacity is a short-range approach to standard setting and cyclical swings are not evened out.

6. There are varying degrees of tightness in standards as some managers believe that tight standards encourage efficient performance.

   a. Tight standards that are nearly impossible to attain are often detrimental to employee morale.
   b. Employees may arrive at the opinion that such tight standards have no place in the cost system and they may ignore them.

7. Other managers believe that standards should be fairly loose and provide for contingencies that may arise in plant operations.

   a. However, if standards are based on low levels of efficiency, they destroy thepurpose of standard costing.
   b. Loose standards also provide unreliable data for measuring costs and often encourage waste.

Budgets, Standard Costs, and Target Costs

8. Standards may differ from estimated costs because estimated costs are frequently less accurately determined.

a. Standards are determined through the use of time studies and engineering estimates.
b. However, some estimated costs are worked out on a scientific basis also.
c. Standards do not necessarily represent what the cost would be if perfection in performance has actually been attained.

9. Standard costs become the unit building block for the company's budget.

   a. After standards are determined for each unit manufactured, standard unit costs are multiplied by the total units to be produced or sold to determine budgeted costs.
   b. Standards represent yardsticks by which achievement or lack of achievement can be measured; cost trends can be determined by comparing actual and standard costs.
   c. Standard costs are good control and planning tools; however, they cannot be used alone without reference to historical costs.

10. Establishing standards is an expensive operation and requires input from those responsible for meeting the standards.

11. A successful standard cost system requires support of top management.

12. Standards can be applied in both job order and process costing systems.

Incorporation in the Accounting System

13. Standards may be used for statistical analysis only and not entered in the accounting system or they may be incorporated.

    a. It is often felt that executives will take the variances more seriously if they are included in the accounting system; however, the important thing is that variances should provide a springboard for corrective action.
    b. Actual costs can be properly measured and controlled through standards even though they are not entered in the journal and ledger.

Setting Material Standards

14. The industrial engineering department may be used to develop specifications for the kinds and quantities of material to be used in the production of the goods specified and budgeted on the operating forecast.

Material Quantity Standards

15. Tests under controlled conditions may be conducted in which a quantity of material is put into process and the results analyzed.

    a. A waste allowance may be added using the following formula:

    $$\frac{\text{Waste expressed in pounds (or gallons, tons, etc.)}}{\text{Net pounds (or gallons, tons, etc.) in finished unit}} = \text{Percent waste to be added}$$

    b. Shrinkage may also be applied in a similar manner.

Material Price Standards

16. The purchasing agent should help set the material price standard because this person is responsible for any resulting variance.

a. If the company's cash position allows the taking of cash discounts, the price standard should reflect this economy as well as others that are expected to occur.
b. The price standard should also reflect ordering in economical order quantity.
c. The price standard should reflect the application of freight-in, purchasing, and other material handling costs if application rates are used for these costs.

Setting Labor Standards

17. Setting labor standards is usually more difficult than the material standard establishment process.

18. While reliance must be made on past records in some aspects, it is dangerous to depend upon this data only. An experienced analyst may be employed to study the work and plant layout to determine labor requirements.

Labor Efficiency Standards

19. Time and motion study is a good basis for setting labor quantity standards as the object of time study is to develop time standards and piece rates which the average operator can meet daily without affecting his or her well-being.

20. If time studies or past-performance averages are not considered practical or a good basis, test runs can be used; however, two jobs may differ and an average situation is difficult to find.

Labor Rate Standards

21. While the labor rate standards should adhere closely to the actual labor rate that will be paid in the next period, there are two procedures for establishing this rate:

    a. A rate may be established for each job and no matter who performs the job, the rate stays the same.
    b. A rate may be established for each individual worker and the worker receives this rate regardless of the work performed.

22. In departments in which a multiplicity of operations are performed, group piece rates may be used.

23. Some salaried personnel, such as plant supervisors, repairers, and inspectors, are classified as indirect labor and become part of factory overhead. Standard salary figures are applied to each department according to the number of salaried personnel employed in each department.

Variances Illustrated for Job Order Costing

24. Standard quantity allowed for the job is determined by multiplying the units completed times the standard specification per unit.

    a. Material usage variance is determined by comparing the actual quantity with the standard quantity and multiplying the difference by the standard rate.
    b. Material purchase price variance is determined by comparing the actual price and the standard price by the material quantity purchased.
    c. Material usage price variance is determined by comparing the actual price and the standard price by the material quantity used.

Material Variances

25. Material variances are:
    a. Material usage or quantity or efficiency variance: (Actual material quantity -- Standard material quantity) X Standard material price.
    b. Material price variance: (Actual material price -- Standard material price) X Actual material quantity.

Journal Entries for Material

26.   There are three different methods for reflecting material price and quantity variances within the accounting system.

   a. Under one method the price variance is isolated at the time of purchase, and material inventory is kept at standard cost. This method is preferred since it saves clerical costs because no actual costing-method for inventory is used.
   b. Another less preferred method is to delay the recording of the price variance until materials are issued from the storeroom into production. Material inventory under this method is kept on some actual costing system.
   c. Another method records both a purchase price variance and a quantity price variance because the purchase price variance is recorded at the time a purchase is made. Later when the material is used, the price variance on these items of material is classified as a quantity price variance.

Labor Variances

27.   Variances similar to those for material can be computed for labor as follows:

   a. Labor time (quantity or efficiency) variance: (Actual labor-hours -- Standard labor-hours) x Standard labor rate per hour.
   b. Labor rate variance: (Actual labor rate -- Standard labor rate) x Actual labor hours.

Labor Efficiency under JIT

28.   Productivity measures based on direct labor efficiency can be manipulated on the plant floor in dysfunctional ways.

   a. Managers may increase efficiency by running simple products and avoiding more complex, harder-to-run jobs.
   b. Managers can improve direct labor efficiency by increasing the lot size because setups and changeovers are often included in overhead rather than in direct labor.
   c. Long runs under traditional manufacturing systems lead to better use of direct labor for a given amount of indirect labor.

Journal Entries for Labor

29.   In recording labor variances, Work in Process Inventory is debited for the standard cost of labor and Wages Payable is credited for the actual costs. The difference between these two amounts is the rate and efficiency variances for labor.

Material and Labor Variances Using Process Costing

30.   To determine standard quantity allowed in a process costing system, equivalent units are determined and standards applied to this.

31.   The standard quantity cannot be determined using a process costing system until the operations for the accounting period have ended.

   a. The standard quantity per unit is then multiplied by the equivalent units for each cost element.

32.   Equivalent units are first determined before computing labor variances under a process costing system.

   a. Unit quantity standards are multiplied by the equivalent units to determine standard quantity allowed.
   b. Labor rate variance is determined in a similar manner as under job order costing.

33. Care is needed in interpreting variances because favorable variances may result from merely running unneeded simple products rather than needed complex products.

Standard Costs In Future Factories

34. Some accountants question whether traditional standard cost models will be required when producing with flexible manufacturing systems.

35. New cost accounting procedures may be needed to replace the standard cost model because there is concern whether standards can be kept current and relevant under the following conditions:
   a. Short production runs are tailored for each customer.
   b. Product characteristics are changing.
   c. The production method changes for each batch depending upon which machines are available when the order is processed.
   d. There may be less need for variance analysis from standard because automation provides for more predictable yields.

36. The following summarizes the impact of flexible manufacturing systems on standard costs.

   a. Standard cost models based on large-scale production of an item with unchanging specifications will be less common.
   b. Measurement of all significant resource costs rather than focuses only on direct labor hours and direct material costs.
   c. Costs of rework and spoiled units will not be built into standard specifications for material.
   d. Monthly aggregate material usage variances will disappear.
   e. Less attention given to direct labor efficiency because direct labor costs usually constitute three to ten percent of product costs in machine-paced factories.
   f. More attention can be directed to crucial manufacturing strategy with less focus on direct labor variances.

Interactions Among Factors of Input and Variances

37. Most variances are due to interactions between factors of input.

   a. When cheaper grades of material are purchased at a cost savings, the favorable price variance may cause high material usage and poor labor efficiency, which result in unfavorable material quantity variances and unfavorable labor efficiency variances.
   b. The resulting variances should be compared to determine if such trade-offs are profitable.

Summary of Material and Labor Variances

38. The following summarizes material and labor variances.
   Material Price Variances
   (Actual material price -- Standard material price) x Actual material quantity
   Possible causes for unfavorable variances:
   1. Fluctuations in material market prices.
   2. Purchasing from unfavorably located suppliers, which results in additional transportation costs.
   3. Failure to take cash discounts available.
   4. Purchasing in nonstandard or uneconomical lots.
   5. Purchasing from suppliers other than those offering most favorable terms.

   Responsibility
   The purchasing department should usually be held responsible. However, supervisory factory personnel should be held responsible when they specify certain brand named materials or materials of certain grade or quality. If a price variance occurs because a request was made for a rush order, the production planning department could be responsible as this may be the result of poor scheduling.

Material Usage (Quantity or Efficiency) Variances

(Actual material quantity - Standard material quantity) X Standard material price

Note: For control purposes this variance should be isolated as quickly as possible; however, it may be impossible to calculate until the work is completed.

Possible causes for unfavorable variances:

1. Waste and loss of material handling and processing.
2. Spoilage or production of excess scrap.
3. Changes in product specifications that have not been incorporated in standards.
4. Substitution of nonstandard materials.
5. Variation in yields from material.

Responsibility

Line supervisors should be held responsible for material under their control.

Labor Rate Variances

(Actual labor rate - Standard labor rate) X Actual labor-hours

Possible causes for unfavorable variances:

1. Change in labor rate that has not been incorporated in standard rate.
2. Use of an employee having wage classification other than that assumed when the standard for a job was set.
3. Use of a greater number of higher paid employees in the group than anticipated. (This applies when the standard rate is an average.)

Responsibility

If line supervisors must match workers and machines to the tasks at hand by using the proper grade of labor, they should be responsible. Line supervisors should also be responsible if they control the wage rate of their labor force. If they do not, the personnel department may be responsible.

Variances similar to those for material can be calculated for labor as follows:

Labor Time or Quantity or Efficiency Variances

(Actual labor hours - Standard labor hours) X Standard labor rate per hour

Possible causes for unfavorable variances:

1. Inefficient labor.
2. Poorly trained labor.
3. Rerouted work.
4. Inefficient equipment.
5. Machine breakdowns.
6. Nonstandard material being used.

Responsibility

Line supervisors should be held responsible for labor under their control. The production planning department or the purchasing department should be held responsible for any labor efficiency variance that results from the use of substandard material.

Demonstration Problem

Journal Entries for Material and Labor Variances

Banister, Inc., has the following standards per finished batch of units:

Materials (6 lbs. @ $2)	$12
Labor (4 hrs. @ $15)	$60

Management planned to produce 20,000 units; however, only 17,600 units are actually produced because of a labor problem. Purchasing bought 110,000 pounds of material at $247,500. Actual pounds used were 108,610. Direct labor costs were $1,067,647 for 70,940 hours.

Required:

a. Record journal entries for all material transactions for the variances, assuming that the price variance reflects usage; record only one type of price variance.
b. Make journal entries for the material transaction, assuming the material price variances are isolated on purchase; record only one type of price variance.
c. Record all journal entries for labor variances.

Paper for working Demonstration Problem

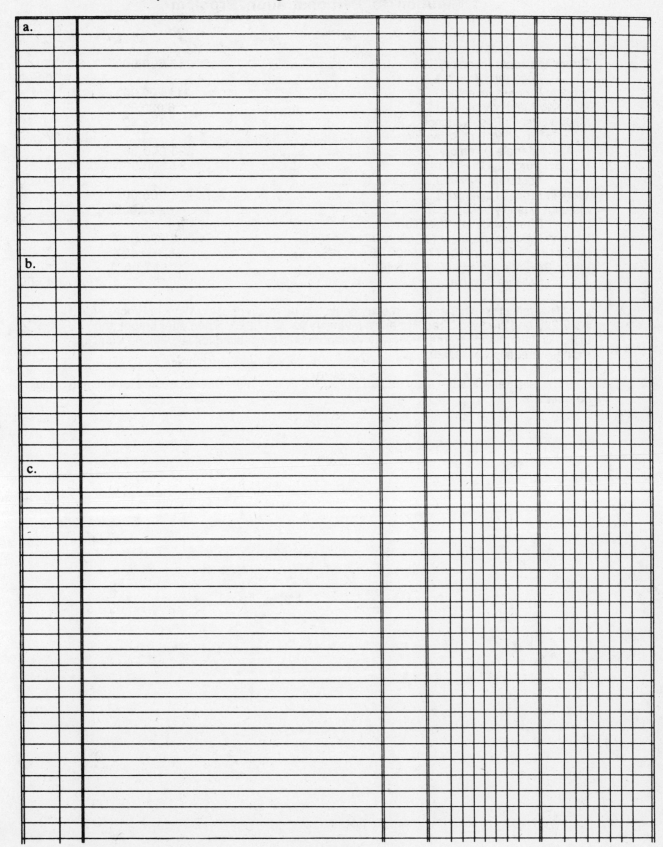

a.

b.

c.

Solution to Demonstration Problem

Banister, Inc.

a.
Direct Materials Inventory...	247,500.00	
Accounts Payable..		247,500.00
Work in Process Inventory..	211,200.00*	
Material Quantity Variance	6,020.00*	
Material Usage Price Variance	27,152.50	
Direct Materials inventory................................		244,372.50

b.
Direct Materials Inventory...	220,000.00	
Material Purchase Price Variance	27,500.00	
Accounts Payable..		247,500.00
Work in Process Inventory..	211,200.00**	
Material Quantity Variance	6,020.00**	
Direct Materials Inventory...............................		217,220.00

c.
Work in Process Inventory (17,600 x 4 hrs. X $15)..........	1,056,000.00**	
Labor Efficiency Variance (70,940 - 70,400 X $15)..........	8,100.00**	
Labor Rate Variance ($.05 X 70,940)............................	3,547.00	
Salaries Payable		1,067,647.00

*This reflects the net entry. An entry could first be made debiting Work in Process for $217,220 and crediting Direct Materials Inventory for $217,220. Then after output and usage is determined, Material Quantity Variance could be debited for $6,020 and Work in Process credited for $6,020.

**This also reflects a net entry and an alternative similar to the one suggested for material could be used.

Matching

Referring to the terms listed in the left column, place the appropriate letter next to the corresponding description. A term may not be used or may be used more than once.

a. Direct Materials Inventory

b. Equivalent units

c. Group piece rates

d. Labor efficiency variance

e. Labor mix variance

f. Labor rate variance

g. Material purchase price variance

h. Materials sampling

i. Material usage price variance

j. Material yield variance

k. Standard hours allowed

l. Time and motion studies

m. Work in Process Inventory

_____ 1. Techniques used to set labor standards.

_____ 2. Measures the difference in planned labor prices and actual labor prices.

_____ 3. Actual units of output X standard hours per unit.

_____ 4. Used in setting material standards.

_____ 5. This variance multiplies a difference in hours of measure by standard labor hourly rate.

_____ 6. Used in departments in which a multiplicity of operations are performed and payment is made on the completed job.

_____ 7. Ledger account debited for the standard costs of material and labor.

_____ 8. Reflects differences in price paid on material utilized in production.

_____ 9. Multiplied times standard specifications to give the standard hours or pounds allowed in a process costing system.

_____ 10. The difference between standard price of materials and the actual material price recorded when standards are isolated at the time materials are bought.

Completion and Exercises

1. List four predicted characteristics that will be found in the factory of the future due to the impact of flexible manufacturing systems on standard costs.

1._____

_____

2._____

_____

3._____

_____

4._____

_____

2. Standard costs are accumulated for each department for a given time period under a

_____ _____ system; another type of cost system called

_____ _____ accumulates costs by batches in production cycles where

products are manufactured according to customer's specifications.

3. _____ should be held responsible for material and labor usage variances

and the _____ responsible for material price variances.

4. In computing labor variances, the following formulas can be used:

LABOR RATE VARIANCE: (Actual labor rate - Standard labor rate) X _____ labor-hours.

LABOR EFFICIENCY VARIANCE: (Actual labor-hours - Standard labor-hours) X _____

labor rate per hour.

5. In computing material variances, the following formulas can be used:

MATERIAL PURCHASE PRICE VARIANCE: (Actual material price - Standard material price) X Actual

pounds or gallons _____.

MATERIAL USAGE PRICE VARIANCE: (Actual material price - Standard material price) X Actual

pounds or gallons _____.

MATERIAL USAGE VARIANCE: (Actual material quantity - Standard material quantity) X _____

material price.

6. Standards set on the basis of _____ capacity reflects maximum efficiency.

More realistic standards may be set on the _____ _____ basis or the

_____ _____ basis.

7. Give three possible causes of unfavorable material usage variance.

1. _____

2. _____

3, _____

8. Give four possible causes for labor efficiency variances.

    1. _____

    2. _____

    3. _____

    4. _____

9. Give three possible causes for material purchase price variances.

    1. _____

    2. _____

    3. _____

10. Give two possible causes for labor rate variances.

    1. _____

    2. _____

11. Two standards are normally developed for material and labor costs. Indicate and describe how these

    variances are calculated for:

    a. Material. _____

    _____

    _____

    _____

    _____

    _____

    _____

    _____

    _____

    _____

    b. Labor _____

    _____

    _____

    _____

    _____

    _____

    _____

    _____

    _____

    _____

12. Two Approaches to Journalizing Material Price Variances; Labor Variances

Chicco Corporation has established the following standards per finished batch of units:

	Per Batch
Materials (6 pounds @ $2)...............	$12
Direct labor (2 hours @ $6)	12

Management planned to produce 10,000 units; only 8,800 units were actually produced, however, because of a labor problem.

The purchasing department bought 55,000 pounds of material at a price of $123,750. Actual pounds *used* were 54,305. Direct labor cost was $127,400 for 18,200 hours.

Required:
a. Journalize the material transactions assuming that the material price variances are isolated upon purchase; record only one type of price variance.
b. Journalize all the material transactions needed to record the variances assuming that the price variance reflects usage; record only one type of price variance.
c. Journalize all the labor entries needed to record the labor variances.

a.

b.

c.

13. Systems for Material Variances

HIJ Company makes the following two raw material purchases on account during June.

June 3 ....100 pounds @ $4.00 = $400
June 15 .... 25 pounds @ 3.80 = 95

Beginning inventory consists of 75 pounds which were purchased at $3.50 actual cost per unit. The following standards for material have been established for each finished unit:

5 pounds @ $3.75 per pound = $18.75 per unit

There were 35 units completed during June. Actual pounds used were 190.

Required :

Prepare all the journal entries assuming the company--
a. Does not incorporate standard costs within their journals and ledgers. A last-in first-out inventory costing system is used.
b. Incorporates standard costs within their journals and ledgers but keeps direct materials inventory at actual costs. A last-in, first-out inventory system is used.
c. Incorporates standard costs within their journals and ledgers but keeps direct materials inventory at standard costs. Record only one type of price variance.

a.			
b.			

c.

14. Material and Labor Variances in a Process Costing System

Lisa Lane, Inc., produces batches of a steel product on an assembly line. The standard costs per batch are as follows:

	Total
Direct materials (100 gallons @ $.50 per gallon)	$ 50
Direct labor (80 hours @ $4 per hour).............................	320

A total of 500 batches were completed this period; ending inventory consists of 80 batches, one-half complete. Assume all costs are incurred uniformly. There was no beginning inventory. The following costs were incurred:

Direct materials used (45,000 gallons)............................	$ 21,600
Direct Labor (44,000 hours)...	167,200

Required:

a. Prepare a variance analysis for material and labor.
b. Prove your material variances.
c. Prove your labor variances.

14. Paper for working

a.

14. Paper for working

b.

c.

15. Material and Labor Variances

Downs Corporation engaged its engineers to analyze factory conditions and to determine material and labor standards. Their analysis generated the following standards:

| Material (2 lb @ $4) | $ 8 |
| Labor (3 hrs. @ $10) | 30 |

Management had planned to produce 100 units, but due to unfavorable conditions, 90 units were produced. There were 200 pounds of material purchased at a cost of $600; 195 pounds were used. There were 225 hours of labor employed at a cost of $2,587.50.

Required:

a. Calculate material and labor variances, indicating whether they are favorable or unfavorable. Compute two price variances for material.
b. Prove your material variances, using a material usage price variance.
c. Prove your labor variances.

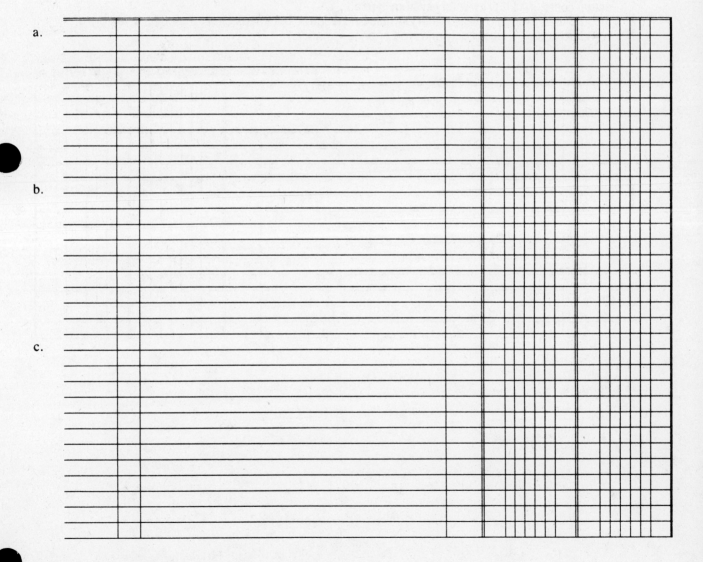

16. Recording Material Under Different Systems

Collins Company makes the following two direct material purchases on account during May:

May 10	200 pounds @ $2.75	=	$550.00
May 25	325 pounds @ $2.90	=	942.50

Beginning inventory consists of 90 pounds which were purchased at $2.65 actual cost per unit. The following standards for material have been established:

4 pounds @ $2.80 per pound = $11.20 per unit

There were 140 units completed during May, actual pounds used were 545.

Required:

Prepare all the journal entries assuming the company:

a. Does not incorporate standard costs within its journals and ledgers. (A LIFO inventory costing system is used.)
b. Incorporates standard costs within journals and ledgers but keeps direct materials inventory at actual costs. (A LIFO inventory system is used.)
c. Incorporates standard costs within journals and ledgers, but keeps direct materials inventory at standard costs. (Record only one type of price variance.)

a.

16. Paper for working

b.

c.

True-False Questions

Indicate whether the following statements are true or false by inserting in the blank space a capital "T" for true or "F" for false.

_____1.   Standard material specifications for the factories of the future will not include costs of rework and spoiled units.

_____2.   Incorporation of cost standards in the accounting system is not required as standards can be effectively used for only statistical purposes.

_____3.   Standards can only be used in a job order system because data generated under a process costing system is not available until the end of operations, which is too late for computing price and quantity variances.

_____4.   If a company uses economical order sizes and takes advantage of all cash discounts, the price standard should reflect this.

_____5.   When the various materials require different handling efforts, applied rates for purchasing and receiving may be used; however, these cannot be reflected in price standards.

_____6.   Test runs should first be used before resorting to time studies or past-performance averages in establishing labor time standards.

_____7.   Regardless of the number of entries made in requesting material for a job, the final resulting debit balance in Work in Process Inventory is actual pounds or gallons multiplied by standard price.

_____8.   Standards should be set on the theoretical capacity concept because this basis evens out cyclical swings in market demand.

_____9.   The director of purchasing should be held responsible for the material price variance, but not the material quantity variance assuming the specified grade of material was ordered.

_____10.   When past performance is used as the basis for establishing labor time standards, the resulting standard reflects an average while use of time and motion studies in standard setting provides a more objective measure.

SOLUTIONS

Matching

1. l   6. c
2. f   7. m
3. k   8. i
4. h   9. b
5. d   10. g

Completion and Exercises

1. The following are predicted characteristics that will be found in the factory of the future due to the impact of flexible manufacturing systems on standard costs.

    1. Standard cost models based on large-scale production of an item with unchanging specifications will be less common.
    2. Less orientation of the standard cost system toward standard direct labor hours and direct material costs with more measurement of all significant resource costs. While an orientation directed to labor and material may be adequate for accounting purposes, it is insufficient for decision making and performance improvement/reporting purposes.
    3. Costs of rework and spoiled units will not be built into standard specifications for material. By including costs of these losses in standards, the company is assuring itself of obtaining the specified amount of defective items with no improvement. Instead rework and spoiled unit cost will be isolated so attention is directed to reducing these costs.
    4. Monthly aggregate material usage variances will disappear.
    5. Less attention given to direct labor efficiency because direct labor costs usually constitute three to ten percent of product costs in machine-paced factories.
    6. By focusing less on direct labor variances, more attention can be directed to crucial manufacturing strategy.

2. process costing; job order

3. Line supervisors; purchasing department (or director of purchasing)

4. *Actual* labor-hours; *Standard* labor rate

5. purchased; used; standard

6. theoretical; normal capacity basis or the expected actual capacity basis or practical capacity (indicate two of these three)

7. Possible causes of unfavorable material usage variances could include the following:
    1. Waste and loss of material in handling and processing.
    2. Spoilage or production of excess scrap.
    3. Changes in product specifications that have not been incorporated in standards.
    4. Substitution of nonstandard materials.
    5. Variation in yields from materials.

8. Possible causes for labor efficiency variances could include the following:
    1. Inefficient labor.
    2. Poorly trained labor.
    3. Rerouted work.
    4. Inefficient equipment.
    5. Machine breakdowns.
    6. Nonstandard material being used.

9. Possible causes for material purchase price variances could include the following:
   1. Fluctuations in material market prices.
   2. Purchasing from unfavorably located suppliers, which results in additional transportation costs.
   3. Failure to take cash discounts available.
   4. Purchasing in nonstandard or uneconomical lots.
   5. Purchasing from suppliers other than those offering the most favorable terms.

10. Possible causes for labor rate variances could include the following:

    1. Change in labor rate that has not been incorporated in standard rate.
    2. Use of an employee having a wage classification other than that assumed when the standard for a job was set.
    3. Use of a greater number of higher paid employees in the group than anticipated. (This applies when the standard rate is an average.)

11. a. The materials price standard is usually based on current market prices. When the actual price is less than the standard, there is a favorable materials price variance. When the actual price is more than the standard, there is an unfavorable materials price variance.
The materials usage or efficiency (quantity) standard is usually based on engineering studies. When the actual quantity used is less than the standard, there is a favorable materials quantity (usage or efficiency) variance. When the actual quantity used is more than the standard, there is an unfavorable materials quantity (usage or efficiency) variance.
   b. The labor rate (wage, cost, or price) standard is usually based on collective bargaining agreements or local conditions of labor supply and demand. When the actual rate is less than the standard, there is a favorable labor rate (wage, cost, or price) variance. When the actual rate is more than the standard, there is an unfavorable labor rate (wage, cost, or price) variance.
The labor efficiency (time or usage) standard is usually based on time and motion studies by industrial engineers. When the actual hours worked are less than the standard, there is a favorable labor efficiency (time or usage) variance. When the actual hours worked are more than the standard, there is an unfavorable labor efficiency (time or usage) variance.

12. *Chicco Corporation*

   a. Direct Materials Inventory (55,000 X $2)... 110,000.00
      Material Purchase Price Variance ($.25 X 55,000) 13,750.00
         Accounts Payable... 123,750.00

      Work in Process (8,800 x 6 lbs. X $2)... 105,600.00
      Material Quantity Variance [(54,305 lbs. - 52,800 lbs.) X $2].............. 3,010.00
         Direct Materials Inventory (54,305 lbs. X $2)............................. 108,610.00

   b. Direct Materials Inventory... 123,750.00
         Accounts Payable... 123,750.00

      Work in Process Inventory... 105,600.00
      Material Quantity Variance 3,010.00
      Material Usage Price Variance (54,305 lbs. x $.25) 13,576.25
         Direct Materials Inventory (54,305 lbs. x $2.25) 122,186.25

   c. Work in Process (8,800 x 2 hrs. x $6).. 105,600.00
      Labor Efficiency Variance (600 hrs. x $6) 3,600.00
      Labor Rate Variance (18,200 x $1)... 18,200.00
         Salaries Payable 127,400.00

13. *HIJ Company*

a. June 3   Direct Materials Inventory...................................... 400.00
                     Accounts Payable......................................   400.00

   June 15   Direct Materials Inventory...................................... 95.00
                     Accounts Payable......................................   95.00

   June Summary   Work in Process Inventory..................................... 722.50
   Entry   Direct Materials Inventory...........................   722.50

                        25 lbs. @ $3.80 = $ 95.00
                       100 lbs. @ $4.00 =   400.00
                        65 lbs. @   3.50 =   227.50
                                                  $722.50

b. June 3   Direct Materials Inventory...................................... 400.00
                     Accounts Payable......................................   400.00

   June 15   Direct Materials Inventory...................................... 95.00
                     Accounts Payable......................................   95.00

   June Summary   Work in Process (35 units X 5 lbs. X $3.75) 656.25
   Entry   Material Quantity Variance (15 lbs. X $3.75) 56.25
                    Material Usage Price Variance............................. 10.00*
                        Direct Materials inventory...........................   722.50

*Material Usage Price Variance:

Actual Price - Standard Price = Price Difference X Pounds =   Variance

 $3.80   - $3.75   = $.05   X   25 lbs. = $ 1.25   Unfavorable
  4.00   -   3.75   =   .25   X 100 lbs. =   25.00   Unfavorable
  3.50   -   3.75   =   (.25) X   65 lbs. =   16.25   Favorable
Material Usage Price Variance $10.00   Unfavorable

c. June 3   Direct Materials Inventory ($3.75 x 100 lbs.) 375.00
                    Material Purchase Price Variance ($.25 x 100 lbs.).. 25.00
                        Accounts Payable...................................   400.00

   June 15   Direct Materials Inventory ($3.75 x 25 lbs.) 93.75
                    Material Purchase Price Variance ($.05 x 25 lbs.).... 1.25
                        Accounts Payable...................................   95.00

   June Summary   Work in Process Inventory 656.25
   Entry   Material Quantity Variance 56.25
                        Direct Materials Inventory (190 lbs. x $3.75)   712.50

14. *Lisa Lane, Inc.*

$$EU = 500 + 40 = 540 \text{ batches}$$

a. Material quantity variance

540 batches x 100 gallons = 54,000 standard gallons
(45,000 actual gallons - 54,000 standard gallons)
X $0.50 standard rate = $4,500 Favorable

Material price variance

$$\frac{\$21,600 \text{ actual material cost}}{45,000 \text{ actual gallons}} = \$0.48 \text{ actual rate}$$

($0.48 actual rate - $0.50 standard rate)
X 45,000 = $900 Favorable

Using the diagram approach, the following variances are outlined:

Direct materials

(1)	(2)	(3)
Actual quantity of inputs at actual price (AQ x AP)	Actual quantity of inputs at standard price (AQ x SP)	Standard quantity allowed for output at standard price (debit to Work in Process) (SQ x SP)
$21,600	45,000 x $.50 = $22,500	54,000 x $.50 = $27,000

(1) - (2)
Usage Price Variance
$900 Favorable

(2) - (3)
Usage (Quantity) Variance
$4,500 Favorable

$5,400 Favorable Total (net) Variance

Labor efficiency variance

540 batches x 80 hours = 43,200 standard hours
(44,000 actual hours - 43,200 standard hours)
x $4 standard rate = $3,200 Unfavorable

Labor rate variance

$$\frac{\$167,200}{44,000 \text{ hours}} = \$3.80 \text{ actual rate}$$

($3.80 actual rate - $4.00 standard rate) x 44,000 actual hours
= $8,800 Favorable

14. *Lisa Lane, Inc. (continued)*

Labor

(1) Actual quantity of inputs at actual price	(2) Actual quantity of inputs at standard price	(3) Standard quantity allowed for output at standard price
$167,200	44,000 x $4 = $176,000	43,200 x $4= $172,800

$8,800 Fav. Rate (Price) Variance (1) - (2) | $3,200 Unfav. Efficiency (Quantity) (2) - (3)

$5,600 Favorable TOTAL (NET) VARIANCE

b. If the diagram approach was used, the proof is built in.

   Proof of material variance

Actual material costs...	$21,600	
Standard material costs (54,000 standard gallons x $0.50)........	27,000	
Net Favorable variance..	$ 5,400	
Material price variance	$ 900	(F)
Material quantity variance..	4,500	(F)
	$ 5,400	

c. If the diagram approach was used, the proof is built in.

   Proof of labor variance

Actual labor costs..	$167,200	
Standard labor cost (43,200 standard hours x $4 standard rate)	172,800	
Net favorable variance...	$ 5,600	
Labor quantity variance	$ 3,200	(U)
Labor rate variance..	8,800	(F)
	$ 5,600	

———————————

F = favorable; U = unfavorable

15.   *Downs Corporation*

Material Usage Variance
(180 std. lbs. - 195 actual lbs.) x $4 = $60 unfavorable

Material Usage Price Variance
($3 actual price - $4 standard price) x 195 lbs. = $195 favorable

Material Purchase Price Variance
($3 actual price - $4 standard price) x 200 lbs. = $200 favorable

Labor Efficiency Variance
(270 std. hrs. - 225 actual hrs.) x $10 = $450 favorable

Labor Rate Variance
($10 std. rate - $11.50 actual rate) x 225 actual hrs. = $337.50 unfavorable

b.   Proof for Material:

$720   Standard cost ($4 x 180 lbs.)
 585   Actual cost ($3 x 195 lbs.)
$135   Net variance

$195   Favorable material usage price variance
  60   Unfavorable material usage variance
$135   Favorable net variance

c.   Proof for Labor:

$2,700.00   Standard cost ($10 x 270 hours)
 2,587.50   Actual cost
$ 112.50   Net variance

$450.00   Favorable labor efficiency variance
 337.50   Unfavorable labor rate variance
$112.50   Favorable net variance

16.   *Collins Company*

a.   May 10
      Direct Materials Inventory...   550.00
            Accounts Payable...   550.00
      May 25
      Direct Materials Inventory...   942.50
            Accounts Payable...   942.50
      May Summary Entry
      Work in Process Inventory... 1,545.50
            Direct Materials Inventory....................................   1,545.50
                  325 lbs. @ $2.90 .... $ 942.50
                  200 lbs. @ $2.75 ....   550.00
                   20 lbs. @ $2.65 ....   53.00
                                                                          $1,545.50

b.   *May 10*
      Direct Materials Inventory...   550.00
            Accounts Payable...   550.00
      May 25
      Direct Materials Inventory 942.50
            Accounts Payable...   942.50

Rayburn, COST ACCOUNTING, 5th edition, Study Guide, Chapter 11, page 28

May Summary Entry

Work in Process Inventory (140 units X 4 lbs. X $2.80)	1,568.00	
Material Usage Price Variance..	19.50*	
Direct Materials Inventory....................................		1,545.50
Material Quantity Variance (15 lb. X $2.80).............		42.00

c. *May 10*

Direct Materials Inventory (200 lbs. X $2.80)....................	560.00	
Materials Purchase Price Variance ($.05 X 200 lbs.)		10.00
Accounts Payable...		550.00

May 25

Direct Materials Inventory (325 lbs. X $2.80)	910.00	
Material Purchase Price Variance ($.10 X 325 lbs.)............	32.50	
Accounts Payable..		942.50

May Summary Entry

Work in Process Inventory	1,568.00	
Material Quantity Variance (15 lbs. X $2.80)		42.00
Direct Materials Inventory (545 X $2.80).................		1,526.00

Material Usage Price Variance:

Actual Price	---	Standard Price	=	Difference	X	Pounds	=	Variance	
$2.90	---	$2.80	=	$.10	X	325 lbs.	=	$ 32.50	Unfavorable
$2.75	---	2.80	=	(.05)	X	200 lbs.	=	10.00	Favorable
$2.65	---	2.80	=	(.15)	X	20 lbs.	=	3.00	Favorable
				Material Usage Price Variance				$19.50	Unfavorable

True-False

1. T   Rather than allow for rework and spoiled unit cost in the standard specification, these costs will be isolated so attention is directed to reducing these costs. By including costs of these losses in standards the company is assuring itself of obtaining the specified amount of defective items with no improvement.

2. T

3. F   Standards can be used effectively in both job order and process costing systems.

4. T   Price standards should reflect all attainable economies that the company expects to take.

5. F   Standards can reflect material handling costs; an alternative with regards to freight is to use only FOB destination prices in establishing the standards.

6. F   Test runs should be used as a last resort if time studies or past-performance averages are not feasible. Test runs have the weakness that plant conditions are constantly changing and no two jobs usually take the same manufacturing time.

7. F   The resulting debit to Work in Process Inventory should be standard pounds or gallons multiplied by the standard price.

8. F   Under the theoretical capacity, it is assumed that the company will operate at full speed without interruptions, ignoring slack times due to decreased sales demand. Standards should be set on normal capacity because this approach evens out the cyclical swings in sales demand.

9. T

10. T   This is why a combination of these measures is advised so that more accurate labor standards will be the result.

12   Standard Costs and
Variances For Factory Overhead

Chapter Outline

Setting Overhead Standards
  Selecting Budgeted Capacity
  Plantwide or Departmental Rates
Overhead Variance Methods
  Three Volume Levels Used
  Two-Variance Method
  Three-Variance Method
  Four-Variance Method
  Journal Entries Illustrated
Disposition of Variances
  Variances Treated as Period Costs
  Proration of Variances
Analysis of Material, Labor, and Overhead Variances
  Monitor Efficiency and Volume Variances to Prevent Excess Inventory
  Causes of and Responsibility for Variances
  Revision of Standards

Chapter Objectives

After studying this chapter, you should be able to:

1. Prepare factory overhead variance analyses using a standard cost system.

2. Journalize and prorate overhead variances.

3. Understand the purpose of a standard cost system and that its value begins when the causes of variances are analyzed.

4. Explain why the overall objective of making money is achieved by reducing inventory and operating expenses, and by increasing throughput and product quality rather than by making sure one cost center has a favorable variance.

5. Define and apply the new terms introduced.

Chapter Review

Setting Overhead Standards

1. There is close similarity in applying factory overhead under a normal costing system and the method used under a standard costing system.

Selecting Budgeted Capacity

2. Higher capacity levels can be used under a standard cost system than under an actual cost system because a standard cost system emphasizes the efficient use of resources.

3. Four capacity levels can be chosen from which to establish standard factory overhead rates; they are:

   a. Theoretical capacity assumes that all personnel and equipment will operate at peak efficiency and that 100 percent of plant capacity will be used.
   b. Practical capacity takes into account unavoidable delays due to holidays, machine breakdown, vacations, and time off for weekends.
   c. Normal capacity considers idle time that is due to limited sales orders and human and equipment inefficiencies.
   d. Expected actual capacity is a short-range approach based on the production volume that is necessary to meet sales demand for the next year. A disadvantage of using expected actual capacity is that frequent, costly revisions of the standards may be necessary.

4. One of these four capacity levels is selected as the volume basis or denominator capacity.

5. Accountants express the capacity level chosen in the following units of measurement:
   a. Units of production
   b. Direct labor costs
   c. Direct labor-hours
   d. Machine-hours
   e. Material costs

Plantwide or Departmental Rates

6. A single plantwide rate for standard factory overhead is appropriate if there is a flow of products through all departments and operations are similar in all departments; otherwise, individual departmental rates are needed.

Overhead Variance Methods

7. There is no uniform set of overhead variances as accountants have differing views regarding the best way to determine factory overhead variances.

   a. The variances are often given different titles and are sometimes combined.
   b. The big distinction lies in the number of detailed factory overhead variances computed.
   c. Many accountants believe that a variance method which distinguishes between fixed and variable cost behavior is preferred.

Three Volume Levels Used

8. It is helpful in distinguishing between the various volumes used in standard overhead variance computation to understand the time period in which the volume is determined.

   a. Known before operations begin: Budgeted, normal, or predetermined capacity
   b. Known after operations end: Standard volume allowed
   c. Known after operations end: Actual volume

9. Three different sets of factory overhead variances are:

    a. **Two-variance method**
       1. Controllable variance.
       2. Volume variance.

    b. **Three-variance method**
       1. Total overhead spending variance.
       2. Variable overhead efficiency variance.
       3. Volume variance.

    c. **Four-variance method**
       1. Variable overhead spending variance.
       2. Fixed overhead spending variance.
       3. Variable overhead efficiency variance.
       4. Volume variance.

Two-Variance Method

10. Computation of the two-variance method is as follows:

    a. *Controllable variance*
        Actual total factory overhead
        Compared with : Budget based on *standard* capacity used [(Standard
            variable factory overhead rate X Standard hours) + Total budgeted fixed
            factory overhead costs]
    b. *Volume variance (noncontrollable variance)*
        (Budgeted hours, such as normal capacity hours, used for determining
        standard overhead rates - Standard hours allowed for the output
        achieved) x Standard fixed factory overhead rate at budgeted capacity.

Three-Variance Method

11. Computation of the three variance method is as follows:

    Controllable variances
    a. *Total overhead spending variance*
       Compared with: Flexible budget allowance adjusted to *actual* capacity used
       (Standard variable factory overhead rate x Actual hours) + Total budgeted fixed
       factory overhead costs.
       Note again that this is the same spending variance that is computed under an actual
       cost system using applied factory overhead rates.
    b. *Variable factory overhead efficiency variance*:
       (Actual hours - Standard hours) x Standard variable factory overhead rate.
    Noncontrollable variance
    c. *Volume variance*:
       (Budgeted hours - Standard hours) x Standard fixed factory overhead rate at budgeted
       capacity.

Four-Variance Method

12. Computations of the four variance method is as follows:

    Controllable variances
    a. *Variable overhead spending variance*
       Actual variable factory overhead
       Compared with: Budget allowance for variable costs adjusted to actual capacity used
       (Standard variable factory overhead rate x Actual hours).

b. *Variable overhead efficiency variance*
(Actual hours-Standard hours) x Standard variable factory overhead rate.

c. *Fixed overhead spending variance*
Budgeted fixed factory overhead
Compared with: Actual fixed factory overhead

Noncontrollable variances

d. *Volume variance*
(Budgeted hours - Standard hours) x Standard fixed factory overhead rate at budgeted capacity.

Proof of Method Used

13. The total of the variances added/netted together should equal the difference between actual factory overhead and standard factory overhead.

Journal Entries Illustrated

14. As actual factory overhead is incurred throughout the period, the following entry is made:
    Factory Overhead Control XX
          Various Credits XX

15. In applying factory overhead, standard hours are multiplied by standard total overhead rate and the journal entry is :
    Work in Process Inventory (standard hours X total standard overhead rate) ... XX
          Factory Overhead Control XX

16. If variances are recorded, unfavorable variances are debited and favorable variances are credited with the difference closed to Factory Overhead Control.

Dispositions of Variances

17. There are two basic procedures for disposing of standard cost variances.

Variances Treated as Period Costs

18. If variances are considered as a cost of inefficiency rather than as a cost of the product, they are charged or credited against the Income Summary.

Proration of Variances

19. The other procedure is to consider variances as a cost of the product and allocate them to Work in Process, Finished Goods, and Cost of Goods Sold.

Analysis of Material, Labor, and Overhead Variances

20. All significant variances, both favorable and unfavorable, should be investigated.

21. The more quickly a variance is isolated, the greater is cost control.

22. One of the first steps in variance analysis is to identify the person responsible for incurring the cost that resulted in the variance.

Monitor Efficiency and Volume Variances to Prevent Excess Inventory

23. Using local efficiencies, such as bonuses for favorable efficiency or volume variances, may contradict a company's goal of making money because it may encourage inventory buildups.

Causes of and Responsibility for Variances

24. The following outline itemizes the possible causes of unfavorable variances and the individuals responsible.

    Possible causes of unfavorable controllable variances
    1. Unfavorable terms in buying supplies and services.
    2. Waste of indirect material.
    3. Avoidable machine breakdowns.
    4. Using wrong grade of indirect material or indirect labor.
    5. Poor indirect labor scheduling.
    6. Lack of operators or tools.

    Responsibility for controllable (spending variances)

    Supervisors of cost centers are responsible since they have some degree of control over their budget or expense factors.

    Responsibility for variable factory overhead efficiency variances

    Line supervisors are responsible since this variance reflects the effects of labor efficiency on factory overhead when labor dollars or labor-hours are the basis for applying factory overhead. This variance shows how much of the factory's capacity has been consumed or released by off-standard labor performance. If machine-hours are the basis for applying factory overhead, the variance measures the efficiency of machine usage.

    Possible causes for unfavorable noncontrollable variances
    1. Poor production scheduling.
    2. Unusual machine breakdowns.
    3. Storms or strikes.
    4. Fluctuations over time.
    5. Shortage of skilled workers.
    6. Excess plant capacity.
    7. Decrease in customer demand.

    Responsibility for noncontrollable variances

    The line supervisor can control fixed overhead to the extent that the items of cost are discretionary rather than committed.
    Top sales executive may be held responsible if budgeted volume (i.e., theoretical, practical, or normal capacity) was geared to anticipated long-run sales.

    Responsibility usually rests with top management, because the volume variance represents under-or overutilization of plant and equipment.

Revisions of Standards

25. Standards should be continuously reviewed; however, too frequent revisions just to keep the standards in line with actual cost may destroy some of the benefits of a standard cost system.

26. There is a close relationship between budgets and standards because standards serve as the unit building block for budgets.

Demonstration Problem

Comparison of Various Variance Analysis Methods

The following monthly data were obtained from the records of the Kelly Company:

Actual variable factory overhead	$11,360
Actual fixed factory overhead..	$10,600
Actual units produced	550 units
Actual machine-hours	2,690 hours
Standard per unit:	
Variable factory overhead	5 hours @ $6 per hour
Fixed factory overhead	5 hours @ $3 per hour

Management has budgeted 600 units monthly.

Required:

a. Calculate overhead variances indicating whether controllable or noncontrollable using the
   (1) Four-variance method.
   (2) Three-variance method.
   (3) Two-variance method.
b. Prepare journal entries to summarize actual factory overhead incurred and to apply overhead. Record overhead variances using the four-variance method. Dispose of the variances.

Paper for working Demonstration Problem

a. 1.

Paper for working Demonstration Problem

a. 2.

a. 3.

b.

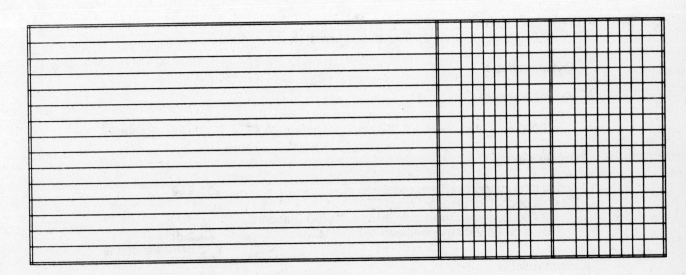

Solution to Demonstration Problem

Kelly Company

600 units X $15 = $9,000 budgeted fixed overhead
600 units X 5 hours = 3,000 budgeted hours
550 units X 5 hours = 2,750 standard hours

a. 1. *Controllable*

   1. *Variable Overhead Efficiency Variance*
      (2,690 Actual hours - 2,750 Standard hours) x $6 variable overhead rate = ($360) Favorable

   2. *Variable Overhead Spending Variance*

Actual variable overhead	$11,360
Budget for actual hours (2,690 actual hours x $6)	16,140
	$ 4,780 (Favorable)

   3. *Fixed Overhead Spending Variance*

Actual fixed overhead	$10,600	
Budgeted fixed overhead	9,000	
	$ 1,600	Unfavorable

   (600u X 5hr @ $3 = 9000)

   Noncontrollable

   4. *Volume Variance*
   (3,000 budgeted hours - 2,750 standard hours) x $3 fixed overhead rate = $750 Unfavorable

2. *Controllable*
   1. *Total Factory Overhead Spending Variance*

Total actual overhead costs	$21,960	
Flexible budget for actual hours:		
$9,000 budgeted fixed overhead		
+ ($6 variable factory overhead		
rate x 2,690 actual hours)....................................	25,140	
	$ 3,180	Favorable

   2. *Variable Factory Overhead Efficiency Variance*
      (2,690 actual hours - 2,750 standard hours) X $6 = $360 Favorable

   Noncontrollable

   3. *Volume Variance*

      (3,000 budgeted hours - 2,750 standard hours) X $3 = $750 Unfavorable

3. *Controllable*

1. Actual total factory overhead costs	$21,960	
Flexible budget for standard hours:		
$9,000 Budgeted fixed overhead + (2,750 Standard		
hours x $6 Variable overhead rate).................	25,500	
	$ 3,540	Favorable

   Noncontrollable

2. *Volume Variance*

   (3,000 Budgeted hours - 2,750 Standard hours) X $3 = $750 Unfavorable

Solution to Demonstration Problem

b. Work in Process (2,750 std. hours x $9)..................................... 24,750
      Factory Overhead Control... 24,750
Factory Overhead Control 21,960
      Various Credits... 21,960
Factory Overhead Control 2,790
Fixed Overhead Spending Variance 1,600
Volume Variance 750
      Variable Overhead Spending Variance 4,780
      Variable Overhead Efficiency Variance............................... 360
Variable Overhead Spending Variance 4,780
Variable Overhead Efficiency Variance 360
      Fixed Overhead Spending Variance 1,600
      Volume Variance 750
      Income Summary or Cost of Goods Sold.............................. 2,790

Matching

Referring to the terms listed in the left column, place the appropriate letter next to the corresponding description. A term may not be used or may be used more than once.

a. Balance of overapplied factory overhead

b. Balance of underapplied factory overhead

c. Controllable variance in two-variance method

d. Cost of Goods Sold

e. Denominator capacity

f. Factory Overhead Control

g. Fixed Overhead Spending Variance

h. Local efficiencies

i. Management by exception

j. Standard costs

k. Total Overhead Spending Variance

l. Work in Process Inventory

_____1. Principle under which only significant variances are investigated.

_____2. Serve as building blocks for budgets.

_____3. In this variance, actual total overhead is compared with a budget based on standard capacity used

_____4. In this variance, actual total overhead is compared with a budget based on a variable allowance adjusted to actual capacity used.

_____5. Net debit variances in overhead equal this.

_____6. Difference between budgeted and actual fixed costs.

_____7. Debited for standard hours X total factory overhead standard rate.

_____8. Balance of net insignificant variances closed to this account

_____9. May encourage excess buildup of inventories that are unprofitable.

____10. The one volume selected for applying overhead.

Completion and Exercises

1. In factory overhead variance analysis, explain how, if at all, the following can be used.

   a. Flexible (variable) budget allowance based on standard hours allowed and total actual overhead.

   _____

   _____

   b. Actual factory overhead costs and factory overhead applied to production. _____

   _____

   c. Flexible (variable) budget allowance based on actual hours allowed and the factory overhead

   applied to production. _____

   _____

   d. Flexible (variable) budget allowance based on standard hours allowed and actual variable overhead.

   _____

   _____

   e. Actual fixed costs and budgeted fixed costs._____

   _____

2. The cost based on the future unit cost of production which is included in a company's

   accounting system is referred to as _____cost.

3. **Missing Data**

   Timms Company has asked that you aid them at the end of the month since their cost accountant is vacationing in the Bahamas. Management has limited knowledge of their standard cost system, but they provide you with the following information:

   Total actual overhead was $22,500.
   Actual units produced were 700; the standard direct labor-hours per unit is two hours.
   Actual direct labor-hours worked were 1,500.
   The standard variable overhead rate per direct labor-hour is $10.
   The standard fixed overhead rate per direct labor-hour is $5.
   Budgeted fixed overhead is $10,000.

   Required:

   Calculate the overhead variances, using the three-variance method for overhead analysis. Indicate which variances are controllable and noncontrollable.

3. Paper for working

4. **Theory and Computations of Overhead Variance**

The following data have been obtained from the Tom Clevenger Company:

Budgeted fixed costs	$25,000	
Standard fixed overhead rate	$ 25.00	per machine-hour
Standard variable overhead rate...........................	2.25	per machine-hour
Standard machine-hours per unit..........................	4	
Actual machine-hours	1,460	
Actual units produced	280	
Actual total overhead...	$28,940	

Required:

a. Determine overhead variances using the three-variance method of analysis.
b. If you can perform a four-way variance analysis, do so. Explain why you can or cannot.
c. If you can perform a two-way variance analysis, do so. Explain why you can or cannot.

4. Paper for working

   a.

   b.

   c.

5. You obtain the following data from the Foy Company:

Budgeted fixed cost	$ 22,000	
Standard fixed overhead rate	$ 22.00	per machine -hour
Standard variable overhead rate	$ 1.75	per machine-hour
Standard machine-hours per unit	4	
Actual machine-hours	1,290	
Actual units produced	300	
Actual total overhead	$25,160	

Required:

Determine overhead variances using the three-variance method of analysis.

6. Labor Efficiency and Two Overhead Variances

As controller for the Kimberly Company, you extract the following data from their records:

Standard hours allowed for finished output...............	19,200	direct labor-hours
Budgeted hours	20,000	direct labor-hours
Actual hours used	19,600	direct labor-hours
Total overhead application rate per standard direct labor-hour	$ 4.50	
Actual total overhead	98,960	
Direct labor rate variance--unfavorable	980	
Budgeted fixed costs..	46,000	
Actual total direct labor	58,800	

The company uses a two-way analysis of overhead variances.

Required:

a. Determine the direct labor efficiency variance.
b. Determine the controllable and volume variances for overhead (two-variance analysis).

_____
_____
_____
_____
_____
_____
_____
_____
_____
_____
_____
_____
_____
_____
_____
_____
_____
_____
_____
_____
_____
_____

7. Material, Labor, and Overhead Variance Analysis

The standard specification for each JD-108 motor produced by Rorr Company is as follows:

	Per Unit
Direct material (2 pounds @ $6 per pound)	$12.00
Direct labor (5 hours @ $9 per hour)	45.00
Factory overhead--variable (5 hours @ $2 per hour)	10.00
Factory overhead--fixed (5 hours @ $1.50 per hour)	7.50
Total standard cost	$74.50

Factory overhead rates are based on a normal 75 percent capacity and use the following flexible budgets:

	Normal, 75 percent	85 percent	100 percent
Flexible Budgets:			
Motors produced	3,000	4,200	5,000
Variable factory overhead	$30,000	$42,000	$50,000
Fixed factory overhead	22,500	22,500	22,500

The company produced 3,200 motors during the month and incurred the following costs:

Material (5,870 pounds)	$ 37,274.50
Labor (15,700 hours @ $8.80 per hour)	138,160.00
Fixed factory overhead	25,180.00
Variable factory overhead	33,512.00

Required:

a. Determine the material and labor variances indicating whether favorable or unfavorable.
b. Compute the factory overhead variance under a standard cost system using:
   (1) Four-variance method.
   (2) Three-variance method.
   (3) Two-variance method.

7. Paper for working

   a.

7. Paper for working

   b. 1.

7. Paper for working

    b. 2.

    b. 3.

8. Standards and Production and Service Departments

As cost accountant for the SJ Manufacturing Company, you have worked with the production supervisor as well as top and middle management in arriving at the standard overhead rates. Together all of you have derived the following variable and fixed standard overhead costs for the two service departments and two production departments.

	Service		Production	
	Repair	Factory Superintendence	Fabricating	Finishing
Standard factory overhead:				
Variable departmental overhead ...	$1,000	$3,000	$15,000	$30,000
Fixed departmental overhead	500	600	7,375	5,025
	$1,500	$3,600	$22,375	$35,025

Budgeted data:

	Fabricating	Finishing
Repair-hours requisitioned	275	225
Number of employees	700	500
Direct labor-hours	2,000	5,000
Machine-hours		5,000
Budgeted units of production	500	1,000

After operations end, your cost clerk distributes the actual service cost to the production departments. The cost clerk then provides you with the total actual production department costs.

	Fabricating	Finishing
Actual variable overhead	$17,000	$32,000
Actual fixed overhead	$ 7,750	$ 5,800
Actual direct labor-hours	1,950	--
Actual machine-hours..	--	5,040
Actual units produced	480	1,020

Required:

a. Determine the standard variable and fixed overhead rates for the two production departments, using the direct method of allocating service department costs.
b. Prepare complete overhead cost analysis for each producing department. Prove your answer. Use the four-variance method of analysis.

8. Paper for working

    a.

8. Paper for working

   b.

8. Paper for working

    b. (concluded)

9. Missing Data

Hert Company has asked your assistance in preparing an overhead analysis. Management provides you with the following monthly information:

Total actual overhead	$35,100
Actual units produced	475
Standard machine-hours per unit	5 hours
Actual machine-hours worked	2,400
Standard variable overhead rate per machine-hour	$5.75
Standard fixed overhead rate per machine-hour	$8.00
Budgeted fixed overhead	$20,000

Required:

Calculate the overhead variances, using the three-variance method for overhead analysis. Indicate which variances are controllable and which noncontrollable.

10. Standard Cost Journal Entries Using Two-Variance OH Method

Jerry Company began operations on January 1 and manufactures a single product. The company installed a standard cost system but *will adjust all inventories to actual cost for financial statement purposes at the end of the year.*

Under its cost system, direct materials inventory is maintained at actual cost.

Twenty percent of the direct materials for each unit is put into production at the beginning of the process, 77 percent at the one-half stage of processing, and 3 percent at the end of processing.

Standard cost was based on 160,000 direct labor-hours with a production of 2,000 units. The standard per finished unit is as follows:

Materials (50 pounds @ $2 per pound).....................................	$ 100
Direct labor (80 hours X $9 per hour)	720
Factory overhead based on direct labor-hours (80 hours @ $2.25 per hour)*	180
Total standard cost per unit...	$1,000

* $1.00 is fixed.

A summary of the transactions for the year ended December 31 shows the following:

Direct material purchased (101,000 pounds @ $2.10 per pound)	$ 212,100	
Direct labor (116,000 hours @ $8.80 per hour).......................................	1,020,800	
Factory overhead...	280,100	
Materials issued to production	75,300	lbs.
Units processed:		
Units completed	1,200	
Units 75% complete...	300	
Units 40% complete...	45	

Required:

a. Use the two-variance method for overhead variance analysis and record the transactions for the year.
b. Make the entries needed to adjust Work in Process Inventory and Finished Goods Inventory to actual costs for material. Give identifiable supporting computations showing clearly the method of arriving at each adjustment.

a.

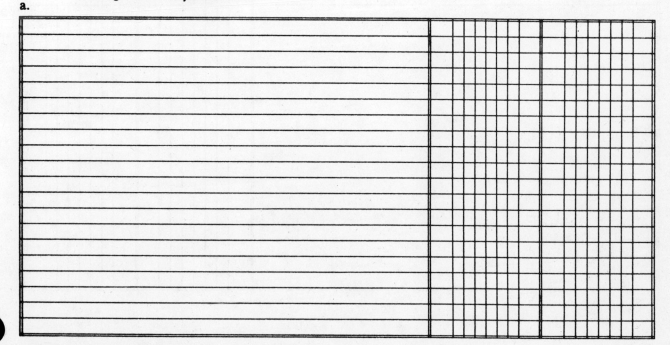

10. Paper for working

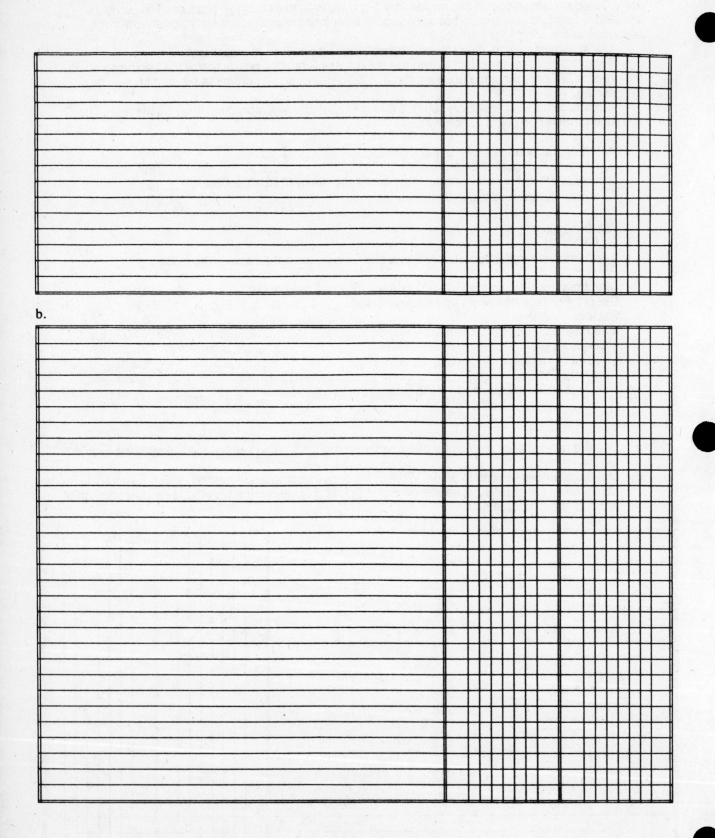

b.

11.   **Flexible Budget and Overhead Analysis**

The following factory overhead budget was established by the Mark Company for the year 19X1. The company planned to manufacture 160 product units. Time and motion studies show that the standard direct labor-hours per unit should be 50 hours.

Repair expense.................................	$ 6,400	(1/4 is considered variable)
Indirect labor....................................	12,000	(1/5 is considered variable)
Depreciation on factory building.......	4,000	(straight-line depreciation is used)
Depreciation on factory machines	1,200	(depreciation is calculated on the basis of units of production)
Utilities...	17,600	(1/2 is considered fixed)
Insurance..	1,440	(premium is paid in advance and is not subject to change)
Miscellaneous	1,280	(considered to vary with production)
	$43,920	

The company uses the four-variance method of analyzing overhead.

Required:

a. Prepare a flexible budget per item for 160 units, 120 units, and 140 units based on the above data.
b. What is the total factory overhead budget formula based on direct labor-hours?
c. Prepare an overhead variance analysis per line item for each variable expense item; assume the following actual results were achieved.

Actual units	150
Actual hours...	7,600
Actual factory overhead:	
Repair expenses ($1,610 of this amount is variable)...............	$ 6,390
Indirect labor ($2,199 of this amount is variable)	11,979
Depreciation on factory building...	4,010
Depreciation on factory machines	1,135
Utilities ($8,405 of this amount is variable)............................	17,255
Insurance..	1,480
Miscellaneous	1,305
Total	$43,554

d. Prepare an overhead variance analysis in total for the fixed factory overhead.

a.

b.

c.

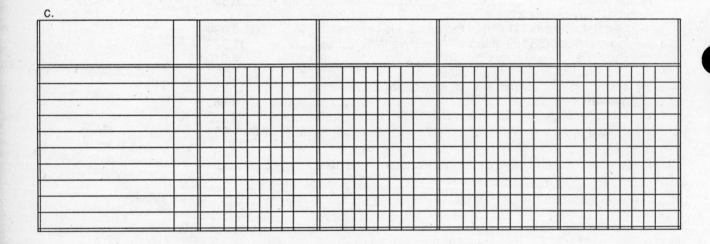

11. Paper for working   d.

12. **Proration of Material and Labor Variances**

Pepin Company established a standard cost system several years ago. All material variances for both Materials A and B are prorated at year-end on the basis of direct material balances in the appropriate accounts. Variances associated with direct labor are prorated based on the direct labor balances in the appropriate accounts.

The following information is available for the year ended December 31, 19X1:

Standards per Unit

Direct Material A (2 pounds @ $4.50 per pound)...........................	$ 9
Direct Material B (4 pounds @ $2 per pound)...............................	8
Direct labor (3 hours @ $5 per hour)...	15
	$32

Material quantity variance--A (unfavorable)...................................	$2,250
Material quantity variance--B (favorable)......................................	(800)
Material purchase price variance--A (favorable).............................	(2,000)
Material purchase price variance--B (unfavorable).........................	1,750
Labor quantity variance (favorable)...	(3,000)
Labor rate variance (favorable)	(2,340)

Purchases of material were 20,000 pounds of Material A for a total of $88,000; 35,000 pounds of Material B for a total of $71,750.

7,900 units were finished and 400 units were completed to one fourth stage of completion for all elements. This required 16,500 pounds of Material A, 31,600 pounds of Material B, and 23,400 hours of direct labor costing $114,660.

No inventory was on hand at the beginning of the year. At year-end, 3,500 pounds of Material A, 3,400 pounds of Material B, and 200 finished units were on hand. All other finished units are sold.

Required:

a. Assuming that all standard variances are prorated to inventories and cost of goods sold, indicate how the material and labor variances are to be prorated.
b. Give the balances in direct material, work in process, finished goods, and cost of goods sold for material and labor after all variances have been prorated.

12. Paper for working

12. Paper for working

True-False Questions

Indicate whether the following statements are true or false by inserting in the blank space a capital "T" for true or "F" for false.

_____ 1. If units of production are used as a basis for applying standard overhead to work in process, it is not possible to correctly compute budgeted volume.

_____ 2. Using a four-variance method, if the variable overhead spending variance and the volume variance are unfavorable, the other two variances will be favorable.

_____ 3. If the net factory overhead variance is favorable, that indicates that actual total overhead is less than standard hours multiplied by total standard overhead rate per hour.

_____ 4. If expected actual capacity is used as the basis for determining factory overhead rates, standards must be revised more frequently than under normal capacity.

_____ 5. Standard cost of overhead for each unit of production is more definite than material and labor standards because overhead costs are affected less by volume changes than are the other two cost elements.

_____ 6. When overhead varies greatly in relation to material and labor costs within each department, plantwide application rates are recommended for standard costing purposes.

_____ 7. The total standard rate for factory overhead is applied only to each job as it is finished so that proper inventory valuations can be determined.

_____ 8. Application of factory overhead in standard and normal costing systems not using standards are similar with the difference being that actual hours are used to multiply the rate within a normal costing system while standard hours are used in a standard costing system.

_____ 9. Line supervisors should be held responsible for the volume variance and the fixed overhead spending variance because they are more familiar with operations than is top management.

_____10. Total standard volume allowed can only be determined at the end of operations for the period in a process costing system.

SOLUTIONS

Matching

1.	i	5.	b	9.	h
2.	j	6.	g	10.	e
3.	c	7.	l		
4.	k	8.	d		

Completion and Exercises

1. a. Using the two-variance method of analyzing factory overhead, the controllable variance is the difference between these two amounts.

    b. This is the proof reflecting the net of all overhead variances.

    c. This is an incorrect variance and is not used in overhead variance analysis.

    d. This is an incorrect variance; it is not the controllable variance in the two-way analysis because it does not include actual fixed overhead in the comparison to the flexible budget allowance based on standard hours.

    e. This reflects the fixed overhead spending variance in the four-variance method analysis.

2. standard

3. *Timms Company*

$$\frac{\$10,000 \text{ Budgeted fixed costs}}{\$5 \text{ Fixed overhead rate per hour}} = 2,000 \text{ hours normal capacity}$$

Noncontrollable

700 x 2 hours = 1,400 standard hours

Volume Variance

(2,000 normal hours - 1,400 standard hours) x $5 = $3,000 unfavorable

Controllable

Total Overhead Spending Variance

Actual Total Overhead	$22,500
Budget for Actual hours [$10,000 fixed overhead + (1,500 actual hours X $10 variable overhead rate)]	25,000
	$ 2,500 Favorable

Variable Overhead Efficiency Variance

Standard hours	-	Actual hours	X		Variable Overhead rate	
(1,400	-	1,500)	X	$10 =	$1,000	Unfavorable

4. *Tom Clevenger Company*

a. *Total Overhead Spending Variance*

Actual overhead	$28,940.00
Flexible budget based on actual capacity [(1,460 actual hours X $2.25) + $25,000 budgeted fixed overhead]...............................	28,285.00
	$ 655.00 unfavorable

Variable Overhead Efficiency Variance

[(1,460 actual hrs . − 1,120 standard hrs.) X $2.25 variable rate] = $765.00 unfavorable

Volume Variance

[(1,000 budgeted hours − 1,120 standard hours) X $25 fixed rate] = $3,000 favorable

b. A four-way variance analysis cannot be performed because actual overhead is not broken down into its fixed and variable components. In order to calculate four variances, actual variable overhead is needed for the variable overhead spending variance and actual fixed overhead is needed for the fixed overhead spending variance.

c. The following two-way variance analysis can be calculated because only actual total overhead is required:

Controllable Variance

Actual overhead	$28,940
Flexible budget based on standard hours [(1,120 hours x $2.25) + $25,000]....................	27,520
	$ 1,420 unfavorable

Volume Variance

(1,000 budgeted hours − 1,120 standard hours) X $25 fixed rate = $3,000 favorable

5. *Foy Company*

Total Spending Variance

Actual overhead	$25,160.00
Flexible budget based on actual capacity (1,290 actual hours x $1.75) + $22,000 budgeted fixed overhead	24,257.50
	$ 902.50 unfavorable

Variable Overhead Efficiency Variance

(1,290 actual hours - 1,200 standard hours) x $1.75 variable rate = $157.50 unfavorable

Volume Variance

(1,000 budgeted hours - 1,200 standard hours) x $22 fixed rate = $4,400 favorable

6. *Kimberly Company*

a.

$$\frac{\$58{,}800 \text{ actual labor cost}}{19{,}600 \text{ actual hours}} = \$3 \text{ actual rate per hour}$$

$$\frac{\$980 \text{ unfavorable labor rate variance}}{19{,}600 \text{ actual hours}} = \$.05 \text{ unfavorable labor rate variance per hour}$$

Standard rate = $2.95 ($3.00 actual rate -- $.05 rate variance)

Direct Labor Efficiency Variance

(19,600 actual hours -- 19,200 standard hours) x $2.95 standard rate = $1,180 unfavorable

b.

$$\frac{\$46{,}000 \text{ budgeted fixed costs}}{20{,}000 \text{ budgeted hours}} = \$2.30 \text{ fixed overhead rate}$$

$4.50	total overhead rate
-2.30	fixed overhead rate
$2.20	variable overhead rate

Controllable Variance

Actual total overhead	$98,960	
Flexible budget for standard hours...........	- 88,240	[($2.20 variable rate x 19,200 standard hours) + $46,000]
	$10,720	unfavorable

Volume Variance

(20,000 budgeted hours -- 19,200 standard hours) x $2.30 fixed overhead rate
= $1,840 unfavorable

7. *Rorr Company*

a. *Material Quantity Variance*
3,200 motors x 2 lbs. = 6,400 standard lbs.
(6,400 standard lbs. -- 5,870 actual lbs.) X $6.00 = $3,180 favorable

Material Price Variance
5,870 actual lbs. X ($6.35 actual rate -- $6.00 standard rate) = $2,054.50 unfavorable

Alternatively,

(1)	(2)	(3)
		Standard quantity allowed for output at standard price (debit to Work in Process)
Actual quantity of inputs at actual price (AQ x AP)	Actual quantity of inputs at standard price (AQ x SP)	(SQ x SP)
5,870 x $6.35 = $37,274.50	5,870 x $6 = $35,220	6,400 x $6 = $38,400

(1) - (2)
Usage Price Variance
$2,054.50 Unfavorable

(2) - (3)
Usage (Quantity) Variance
$3,180 Favorable

$1,125.50 Favorable TOTAL (NET) VARIANCE

7. *(continued)*
Labor Efficiency Variance

3,200 motors X 5 hours = 16,000 standard hours
(15,700 actual hours - 16,000 standard hours) X $9 = $2,700 favorable

Labor Rate Variance

($8.80 actual rate - $9.00 standard rate) X 15,700 actual hours = $3,140 favorable

Alternatively,

(1) Actual Quantity of Inputs at the Actual Price (credit to Payroll Payable) (AQ x AP)	(2) Actual Quantity of Inputs at the Standard Price (AQ x SP)	(3) Standard Quantity Allowed for Output at the Standard Price (debit to Work in Process) (SQ x SP)
15,700 x $8.80 = $138,160	15,700 x $9 = $141,300	16,000 x $9 = $144,000

Δ Δ Δ

(1) - (2) Rate (price) Variance $3,140 Favorable	(2) - (3) Efficiency (quantity) Variance $2,700 Favorable

$5,840 Favorable TOTAL (NET) VARIANCE

b.   1.   *Four-Variance Method*
Controllable Overhead Variances

1. *Variable Efficiency Factory Overhead Variance*
   (15,700 actual hours - 16,000 standard hours) x $2 = $600 favorable

2. *Variable Factory Overhead Spending Variance*
   Actual variable factory overhead $33,512
   Budget adjusted for actual hours (15,700 hours
       X $2 variable overhead rate)................................. <u>31,400</u>
                              Unfavorable <u>$ 2,112</u>

3. *Fixed Overhead Spending Variance*

   Actual fixed overhead $25,180
   Budgeted fixed overhead .... <u>22,500</u>
                              Unfavorable <u>$ 2,680</u>

Noncontrollable
4. *Volume Variance*

(15,000 budgeted hours - 16,000 standard hours) x $1.50 fixed overhead expense
    = $1,500 Favorable

7. *(concluded)*
   If instead the diagram solution approach is used, identical variances are computed as follows:
   Variable overhead

(1)	(2)	(3)
Actual quantity of inputs at the actual price (AQ X AP)	Actual quantity of inputs at standard price (AQ X SP)	Standard quantity allowed for output at standard price (SQ X SP)
$33,512	15,700 X $2 = $31,400	16,000 X $2 = $32,000

$2,112 Unfavorable
Variable Overhead
Spending Variance (1) - (2)

$600 Favorable
Variable Overhead
Efficiency Variance (2) - (3)

$1,512 Unfavorable TOTAL (NET) VARIANCE

Fixed Overhead

(1)	(2)	(3)	(4)
Actual fixed costs incurred (credit to cash, payables, accumulated depreciation, etc.)	(AQ X SP) not used in fixed overhead analysis	Budgeted overhead	Applied overhead-- Standard hours allowed for actual output X standard rate (debit to Work in Process)
$25,180		$22,500	16,000 hrs. x $1.50 = $24,000

$2,680 Unfavorable
Fixed Overhead Spending Variance
(1) - (3)

$1,500 Favorable Volume Variance
(3) - (4)

$1,180 Unfav. TOTAL (NET) VARIANCE

b. 2. *Three-Variance Method*
   Controllable
   1. *Total Overhead Spending Variance*
      Actual Total Factory Overhead $58,692
      Flexible budget for actual hours:
      $22,500 budgeted fixed costs + (15,700 actual hours X
      $2 variable overhead rate) 53,900
      $ 4,792 unfavorable

   2. *Variable Overhead Efficiency Variance*
      (16,000 standard hrs. − 15,700 actual hrs.) x $2 variable overhead rate = $600 favorable

   Noncontrollable
   3. *Volume Variance* (same as above) .... $1,500 favorable

b. 3. *Two-Variance Method*
   Controllable Variance
   1. Actual Total Factory Overhead.. $58,692
      Flexible budget for standard hours:
      $22,500 budgeted fixed costs +
      (16,000 standard hours x $2 variable overhead rate) 54,500
      Unfavorable.. $ 4,192

   Noncontrollable
   2. *Volume Variance* (same as above) .... $1,500 favorable

8. *SJ Manufacturing Company*
a.

	Service		Production	
	Repair	Factory Superintendence	Fabricating	Finishing
Variable Departmental	$1,000 V	$3,000 V	$15,000 V	$30,000 V
Fixed Departmental	500 F	600 F	7,375 F	5,025 F

Allocation:

Variable Repair

$$\frac{\$1,000}{500 \text{ Repair Hours}} = \$2.00$$

		550 V	450 V

Fixed Repair

$$\frac{\$500}{500 \text{ Repair Hours}} = \$1.00$$

		275 F	225 F

Variable Factory Superintendence

$$\frac{\$3,000}{1,200 \text{ employees}} = \$2.50$$

		1,750 V	1,250 V

Fixed Factory Superintendence

$$\frac{\$600}{1,200 \text{ employees}} = \$.50$$

		350 F	250 F

	Fabricating	Finishing
Total Variable Overhead	$17,300 V	$31,700 V
Total Fixed Overhead	8,000 F	5,500 F
Total Factory Overhead	$25,300	$37,200
Variable Overhead Rate Per Hour	$ 8.65 V	$ 6.34 V
Fixed Overhead Rate Per Hour	4.00 F	1.10 F
Total Overhead Rate Per Hour	$ 12.65	$ 7.44

V = Variable, F = Fixed

8. *SJ Manufacturing Company* *(continued)*

b. *Fabricating*

(2,000 Budgeted Direct Labor Hours/500 Budgeted Units) = 4 standard hours per unit

480 units Produced X 4 standard hours = 1,920 standard hours

Variable Overhead Spending Variance

Actual Variable Costs	$17,000.00
Flexible Budget	
$8.65 X 1,950 actual Direct Labor-Hours	16,867.50
Unfavorable Spending Variance	$ 132.50

Variable Overhead Efficiency Variance

(1,920 standard hours - 1,950 actual hours) X $8.65 = $259.50 Unfavorable

Fixed Overhead Spending Variance

Actual Fixed Overhead...	$7,750.00
Budgeted Fixed Overhead..	8,000.00
Favorable Fixed Overhead Spending Variance....................	$ 250.00

Volume Variance
(1,920 standard hrs. - 2,000 budgeted hrs.) X $4.00 fixed overhead rate = $320.00 Unfavorable

Proof

Total Actual Overhead..	$24,750.00
Applied Overhead ($12.65 X 1,920 standard hours)..........	24,288.00
Underapplied Overhead..	$ 462.00

Variable Overhead Spending Variance--Unfavorable...........	$ 132.50	
Variable Overhead Efficiency Variance--Unfavorable...........	259.50	
Volume Variance--Unfavorable	320.00	$712.00
Less Fixed Overhead Spending Variance--Favorable..........		250.00
		$462.00

Finishing
5,000 Budgeted Machine Hours/1,000 Budgeted Units = 5 standard Hours Per Unit
1,020 Units Produced X 5 standard hours = 5,100 standard hours

Variable Overhead Spending Variance

Actual Variable Cost..	$32,000.00
Flexible Budget ($6.34 X 5,040 actual machine-hours)	31,953.60
Unfavorable Spending Variance	$ 46.40

Variable Overhead Efficiency Variance
(5,100 standard hours - 5,040 actual hours) X $6.34 = $380.40 Favorable

Fixed Overhead Spending Variance

Actual Fixed Overhead...	$5,800
Budgeted Fixed Overhead..	5,500
Unfavorable...	$ 300

8. *SJ Manufacturing Company (concluded)*

Volume Variance

    (5,100 standard hours - 5,000 budgeted hours) x $1.10 = $110 Favorable

Proof

Total Actual Overhead..	$37,800.00
Applied Overhead (5,100 standard hours X $7.44)...........	37,944.00
Overapplied Overhead..	$ 144.00
Variable Overhead Efficiency Variance--Favorable	$ 380.40
Volume Variance--Favorable..	110.00
	$ 490.40

Less: Fixed Overhead Spending Variance--Unfavorable....	$300.00	
Variable Overhead Spending Variance--Unfavorable	46.40	346.40
Net Overhead Variance...		$ 144.00

9. *Hert Company*

Controllable
Total Factory Overhead Spending Variance

Total Actual Overhead	$35,100
Flexible budget for actual hours:	
$20,000 budgeted overhead + ($5.75 variable factory	
overhead X 2,400 actual hours)	33,800
Unfavorable..	$ 1,300

Variable Factory Overhead Efficiency Variance

(2,400 actual hours - 2,375* standard hours) X $5.75 = $143.75 unfavorable

*475 x 5 hours = 2,375 standard hours

Noncontrollable

Volume Variance

(2,500** budgeted hours - 2,375 standard hours) X $8 = $1,000 unfavorable

$$\frac{\$20,000 \text{ budgeted fixed}}{\$8.00 \text{ fixed overhead rate}} = 2,500** \text{ budgeted hours}$$

10. *Jerry Company*

a. EU, Labor and Overhead = 1,200 + 225 + 18 = 1,443
                                              (75% X 300) (40% X 45)

    EU, Materials   = 1,200 + 9 + 291 = 1,500
                                  (20% X 45) (97% X 300)

Direct Materials Inventory	212,100	
Accounts Payable..		212,100
Work in Process Inventory (1,500 X 50 X $2)........................	150,000	
Material Quantity Variance (300 lbs. X $2)	600	
Material Price Variance [($2.10 - $2.00) X 75,300)]................	7,530	
Direct Materials Inventory (75,300 X $2.10)		158,130
Payroll	1,020,800	
Accrued Payroll..		1,020,800
Work in Process Inventory (1,443 x 80 hrs. X $9)	1,038,960	
Labor Efficiency Variance [(116,000 - 115,440*) X $9]	5,040	
Labor Rate Variance [($9.00 - $8.80) X 116,000]..........		23,200
Payroll		1,020,800
Work in Process Inventory (1,443 x 80 hrs. X $2.25)	259,740	
Volume Variance...	44,560**	
Controllable Variance...		24,200***
Factory Overhead Control		280,100
Factory Overhead Control	280,100	
Various credits...		280,100

_____

*1,443 X 80 hours = 115,440 standard hours
**Volume Variance
[(160,000 budgeted hours - 115,440 standard hours) X $1] = $44,560 Unfavorable
*** Controllable Variance
Actual Overhead $280,100
Flexible Budget for Standard
Hours: [(115,440 x $1.25) + $160,000]............. 304,300
Favorable... $ 24,200

Finished Goods Inventory (1,200 units X $1,000)...................	1,200,000	
Work in Process Inventory..		1,200,000

b.
Finished Goods Inventory (60,000 lbs. X $.10)	6,000	
Work in Process Inventory (15,000 lbs. X $.10)	1,500	
Material Quantity Variance (300 lbs. X $.10)...........................	30	
Material Price Variance		7,530

The material quantity variance is now $630.

Finished Goods = 60,000 lbs. x $2 = ...	$120,000
Work in Process = 15,000 lbs. x $2 = ...	30,000
	$150,000

Finished Goods Inventory ($120,000/$150,000 X $630)	504	
Work in Process Inventory ($30,000/$150,000 X $630)	126	
Material Quantity Variance		630

Alternatively, standard costs could have been used in allocating the material price variance by multiplying the standard pounds allowed (i.e., 60,000 for finished goods) by $2 standard unit price.

11. *Mark Company*

a. Product units.. 160   120   140
   Hours.. (Budgeted) 8,000   6,000   7,000

Variable:	Cost per Budgeted Hour			
Repair expense............	$ .20	$ 1,600.00	$ 1,200.00	$ 1,400.00
Indirect labor.................	.30	2,400.00	1,800.00	2,100.00
Depreciation on machines...............	.15	1,200.00	900.00	1,050.00
Utilities.........................	1.10	8,800.00	6,600.00	7,700.00
Miscellaneous	.16	1,280.00	960.00	1,120.00
	$1.91	$15,280.00	$11,460.00	$13,370.00
Fixed:				
Repair expense............	$ .60	$ 4,800.00	$ 4,800.00	$ 4,800.00
Direct labor..................	1.20	9,600.00	9,600.00	9,600.00
Depreciation on building	.50	4,000.00	4,000.00	4,000.00
Utilities.........................	1.10	8,800.00	8,800.00	8,800.00
Insurance.....................	.18	1,440.00	1,440.00	1,440.00
Total fixed	$3.58	$28,640.00	$28,640.00	$28,640.00
Total overhead	$5.49	$43,920.00	$40,100.00	$42,010.00

b. $1.91 variable factory overhead per direct labor hour + $28,640 fixed overhead

c.

	(1) Actual Variable Overhead	(2) Budget for 7,600 Hours	(1-2) Variable Overhead Spending Variance	(3) Budget for 7,500 Hours	(2-3) Efficiency Variance
Repair Expense	$1,610	$1,520	$90 U	$1,500	$20 U
Indirect labor	2,199	2,280	81 F	2,250	30 U
Depreciation on machine	1,135	1,140	5 F	1,125	15 U
Utilities	8,405	8,360	45 U	8,250	110 U
Miscellaneous	1,305	1,216	89 U	1,200	16 U
	$14,654	$14,516	$138 U	$14,325	$191 U

U = Unfavorable   F = Favorable

d. *Actual Fixed Factory Overhead*
Repair expense..................................... $ 4,780
Indirect labor... 9,780
Depreciation on building 4,010
Utilities... 8,850
Insurance.. 1,480
                                $28,900

Fixed Overhead Spending Variance
Actual fixed overhead $28,900
Budgeted fixed overhead 28,640
                                $ 260 U

Volume variance = (8,000 budgeted hours - 7,500 standard hours) X
        $3.58 fixed overhead rate = $1,790 unfavorable

12. *Pepin Company*

a.   None of the material quantity variance would be allocated to direct materials inventory.

Work in Process (100/8,000 x $1,450^A) = $ 18.13

Finished Goods (200/8,000 x $1,450^A) =   36.25

Cost of Goods Sold (7,700/8,000 x $1,450$^A)$ =   1,395.62

$1,450.00

^{A}($2,250 - $800)

Material Purchase Price Variance - Material A

Direct Material $4.50 - $4.40 = $.10 X 3,500 = $ 350.00

Work in Process 2.0625^B X 100 units = 206.25 X $.10 =   20.63

Finished Goods 2.0625^B X 200 units = 412.55 X $.10 =   41.25

Cost of Goods Sold 2.0625^B X 7,700 units = 15,881.25 X $.10 =   1,588.12

Credited to each of above $2,000.00

$^B \dfrac{16,500}{7,900 + (400 \times 1/4) = 8,000}$ = 2.0625 pounds per unit worked on

Material Purchase Price Variance -- Material B

Direct Material 3,400 x $.05 ($2.05 - $2.00) = $ 170.00

Work in Process 3.95^C x 100 units = 395 x $.05 =   19.75

Finished goods 3.95^C x 200 units = 790 x $.05 =   39.50

Cost of Goods Sold 3.95^C x 7,700 units = 30,415 x $.05 =   1,520.75

Debited to each of above $1,750.00

$^C \dfrac{31,600}{8,000}$ = 3.95 pounds per unit worked on

Labor Quantity Variance

Work in Process (100/8,000 x $3,000)... $ 37.50

Finished Goods (200/8,000 x $3,000)...   75.00

Cost of Goods Sold (7,700/8,000 x $3,000)...   2,887.50

Credited to above... $3,000.00

Labor Rate Variance

Work in Process (2.925^D x 100 units x $.10).. $ 29.25

Finished Goods (2.925^D x 200 units x $.10) 58.50

Cost of Goods Sold (2.925^D x 7,700 units x $.10).......................................   2,252.25

Credited to above... $2,340.00

$^D \dfrac{23,400 \text{ hours}}{8,000}$ = 2.925 hours per unit worked on

Note: Alternatively, rather than determine the actual pounds per unit worked on, material purchase price variance could be allocated to Material Quantity Variance, Finished Goods, Cost of Goods Sold, and Work in Process and Direct Material on the basis of the standard costs. For example, the variances for Material A would be allocated as follows:

12. *(continued)*

Material Quantity	$ 2,250
Finished Goods (200 x $9)	1,800
Cost of Goods Sold (7,700 x $9)	69,300
Work in Process (100 x $9)	900
Direct Materials (3,500 lbs. x $4.50)	15,750
	$90,000

Allocation of ($2,000) material purchase price variance A to:

Material quantity ($2,250/$90,000 x $2,000)	$ 50
Finished Goods ($1,800/$90,000 x $2,000)	40
Cost of Goods Sold ($69,300/$90,000 x $2,000)	1,540
Work in Process ($900/$90,000 x $2,000)	20
Direct Materials ($15,750/$90,000 x $2,000)	350
	$2,000

This leaves $2,200 unfavorable Material A quantity variance that is allocated as follows:

Cost of Goods Sold	$69,300
Finished Goods	1,800
Work in Process	900
	$72,000

Cost of Goods Sold ($69,300/$72,000 x $2,200)	$2,118
Finished Goods ($1,800/$72,000 x $2,200)	55
Work in Process ($900/$72,000 x $2,200)	27
	$2,200

12. (concluded)

b.

Variance Allocation

Accounts	Material and Labor Balances	Material Quantity	Material Price A	Material Price B	Labor Quantity	Labor Rate	Ending Balances
Direct Material	$22,550.00*	-0-	($ 350.00)	$ 170.00	-0-	-0-	$ 22,370.00
Work in Process (100 units X $32)	3,200.00	$18.13	(20.63)	19.75	$ 37.50	($ 29.25)	3,150.50
Finished Goods (200 units X $32)	6,400.00	36.25	(41.25)	39.50	75.00	58.50	6,301.00
Cost of Goods Sold (7,700 units X $32)	246,400.00	1,395.62	(1,588.12)	1,520.75	(2,887.50)	(2,252.25)	242,588.50
	$278,550.00	$1,450.00	($2,000.00)	$1,750.00	($3,000.00)	($2,340.00)	$274,410.00

* Direct Material Balances
$15,750.00   (3,500 x $4.50)
  6,800.00   (3,400 x $2.00)
$22,550.00

True-False

1. F   Budgeted volume is known in advance and is used to determine the fixed standard overhead rate; it can be correctly computed using units of production as a basis. It is standard volume allowed that cannot be computed if units of production are used as a basis for applying overhead. Standard volume is computed by multiplying units of output x standard quantity per unit.

2. F   There is no special combination of favorable and unfavorable variances; only the comparison of the established standard with actual operating facts determines whether a variance is favorable or not. For example, all variances could be favorable or all unfavorable depending upon the facts in the specific case.

3. T   The net factory overhead variance is favorable when actual total overhead is less than standard overhead.

4. T

5. F   Overhead costs are less subject to scientific measurement than are labor and material costs. In addition, they are less definite and are subject more to volume fluctuations.

6. F   Under these circumstances, departmental overhead rates are recommended to ensure a higher degree of refinement in costing.

7. F   The factory overhead rate is applied to finished jobs as they are completed and also to unfinished jobs at the end of operations for the period.

8. T

9. F   Line supervisors should not be held responsible for fixed overhead variances because they usually do not have authority to incur such fixed expenses as plant rent and the purchase of plant equipment which results in depreciation.

10. T

13   Cost-Volume-Profit Analysis

Chapter Outline

Computing Breakeven Point
> Impact of Automation on Breakeven
> Contribution Margin Approach
> Variable Cost Ratio
> Breakeven Chart

Extensions of Breakeven Analysis
> Marginal Income
> Margin of Safety
> Cash Flow Breakeven Point
> Assumptions and Limitations of Breakeven Analysis
> Sales Mix Effect on Breakeven
> Desired Beforetax and Aftertax Income

Sensitivity Analysis
> Effect of Volume Change
> Price and Volume Alternatives

P/V charts

Computer Spreadsheets and Cost-Volume-Profit Analysis

Chapter Objectives

After studying this chapter, you should be able to:

1. Explain the cost-volume-profit relationships that exist in a company.

2. Compute and use breakeven analysis.

3. Recognize that even though rigid assumptions underlie breakeven analysis, it can result in effective answers without costly analysis.

4. Examine through sensitivity analysis the effect on profit and the breakeven point of changing an input value.

5. Define and apply the new terms introduced.

Chapter Review

Computing Breakeven Point

1. The breakeven point is the volume of sales at which there is no profit or loss.

    a. This concept can be applied to dynamic situations to aid management in planning and controlling operations.
    b. However, breakeven analysis forces a study of the company's fixed and variable cost behavior; the concept is important because it can be adapted to determine the necessary sales to earn a specific income.

Impact of Automation on Breakeven

2. Costs that were previously variable become fixed as factories become automated.

    a. The breakeven point becomes higher as fixed costs increase.
    b. Understanding cost behavior becomes even more important in decision making.

Contribution Margin Approach

3. The breakeven point can be derived from the following formula:

    Sales = Variable expense + Fixed expense + Income

    a. Variable costs are those costs which vary directly with changes in the volume of output.
    b. Fixed costs remain the same in total for a given time period and production level.

4. Unit variable expenses, rather than total variable expenses, are used in breakeven analysis.

5. The portion of the sales dollars that is left over after subtracting variable costs is called contribution margin; this is the amount available to cover fixed costs and render an income.

    a. Contribution margin can be used as follows to determine the point of sales needed to earn a desired net income.

$$\frac{\text{Fixed expenses} + \text{Desired net income}}{\text{Unit contribution margin}}$$

    b. Accountants can calculate breakeven in sales dollars by expressing unit variable cost as a percentage of sales dollars and then determining the contribution margin ratio to divide into total fixed costs.

Variable Cost Ratio

6. The variable cost ratio is determined by dividing variable costs by sales.

7. The contribution margin ratio is determined by dividing contribution margin by sales; this can be used directly in computing the breakeven point.

Breakeven Chart

8. A breakeven chart is a graphic display showing the relationship of cost to volume and profit.

    a. An advantage of breakeven charts is that they forcefully show the impact of volume upon costs and profits.
    b. Such charts are easy for nonaccountants to understand.
    c. Dollars of revenues, costs, and expenses are expressed on the vertical scale.

d. The horizontal scale is used to indicate sales volume, which may be expressed in units of sale, direct labor-hours, machine-hours, or other indexes of volume.

e. At the point where total expenses equal sales revenue, the breakeven point is indicated.

Extensions of Breakeven Analysis

9. Since the goal of a company is not to break even, the benefit of breakeven analysis might be questioned. However, breakeven analysis has numerous extensions in analyzing cost-volume-profit relationships.

Marginal Income

10. Marginal income is sometimes used interchangeably with contribution margin; the term "margin " generally refers to one product unit.

a. The contribution margin ratio is also known as the profit-volume ratio.

Margin of Safety

11. The excess of actual or budgeted sales over the breakeven sales volume is the margin of safety; this provides a buffer by which sales may decrease before a loss occurs.

a. A margin of safety ratio can be computed.

b. The cost relationships assumed in breakeven analysis are used in computing margin of safety.

Cash Flow Breakeven Point

12. A cash flow breakeven point can be computed in which noncash charges, like depreciation and amortization, are not considered as cash flows out.

a. Even though depreciation and amortization do not involve a cash expenditure, they do provide a tax shield in the amount of the tax rate multiplied by the depreciation charge.

b. Cash flow breakeven gives insight into the number of units that must be sold so that cash outflow is covered.

Assumptions and Limitations of Breakeven Analysis

13. The following assumptions underlie cost-volume-profit analysis.

a. The breakeven chart is fundamentally a static analysis; because of this, normally changes can only be shown by drawing a new chart or a series of charts.

b. A relevant range is specified so that fixed and variable costs can be defined in relation to a specific period of time and designated range of production level.

c. All costs fall into either a fixed or variable cost classification.

d. Unit variable costs remain the same and there is a direct relationship between costs and volume.
   1. No quantity discounts on materials or other possible savings in costs are assumed.

e. Volume is assumed to be the only important factor affecting cost behavior. Other influencing factors such as unit prices, sales mix, labor strikes, and production method are ignored.
   1. The relevant range is usually a range of activities in which the company has operated.
   2. This volume of activity is expressed in common terms for sales and expenses: direct labor- or machine-hours, units produced, and sales value of production are often used.

f. Unit sales price is assumed to remain the same. No quantity discounts are assumed to be available.

g. Inventory changes are assumed so insignificant that they have no impact on the analysis.

h. A specific sales mix is assumed if breakeven analysis covers more than one product line.

1. Sales mix is the combination of quantities of product that a company sells. For example, in a tennis sporting shop, it may be six cans of tennis balls to one tennis dress to one tennis racket.
2. Since the contribution margin earned on each of the product in the sales mix usually differs, the specific sales mix assumed has a significant impact upon breakeven analysis.

i. Fixed costs are assumed to remain constant over the relevant range considered.
j. No increase in efficiency in the period of activity studied occurs, and managerial policies and techniques are assumed to have no effect on costs.
k. Product technology is assumed to remain unchanged.

Sales Mix Effect on Breakeven

14. A specified sales mix is assumed in breakeven analysis and if actual mix varies from this specified mix, the results concerning cost-volume-profit relationships may be changed.

15. The sales mix may be referred to as a market bundle of goods.

Target Beforetax and Aftertax Income

16. The breakeven formula can be expanded and used to indicate the sales necessary to yield a specified desired net income with the following computation:

   Let X = Number of units to be sold to yield a desired net income.
   Sales = Variable expenses multiplied times X + Fixed expenses in total dollars + Desired income in total dollars.

17. If management specifies a desired aftertax return, the aftertax income desired can be divided by 100 percent less the tax rate to yield a percentage which can be used in the formula.

Sensitivity Analysis

18. Sensitivity analysis asks "What if" an input value changes and examines the effect on the outcome for changes in one or more input values.

Effect of Volume Change

19. The effect on earnings if sales volume is increased or decreased can also be studied through breakeven analysis.

Price and Volume Alternatives

20. The change in income that is expected to occur if a company makes various alternatives regarding sales price or sales volume can be analyzed through cost volume-profit relationships.

P/V Charts

21. A P/V chart displays the impact of sales price and volume changes upon income and breakeven.

   a. Cost-volume-profit analysis requires the segregation of fixed and variable costs, and the accountant may have to spend time performing this function.
   b. Accountants can design a company's chart of accounts to use separate accounts for fixed and variable costs; a Factory Overhead Control--Variable Expenses and another ledger account entitled Factory Overhead Control--Fixed Expenses can be used.

Computer Spreadsheets and Cost-Volume-Profit Analysis

22. Computers quickly make the computations for changes in the assumptions underlying proposed projects for sensitivity analysis.

Demonstration Problem

Sales Mix Expressed in Units and in Dollars

Fixed costs of $299,300 are incurred by Jungle Company in its sales of products, R, S, and T. For 19X1 the unit sales price and variable costs of these products were

Products	R	S	T
Sales	$20	$50	$10
Variable costs............................	14	25	6

Required:

a. Assuming the sales mix in dollars is 20 percent R, 30 percent S, and 50 percent T, compute the 19X2 companywide breakeven sales dollars broken down by sales dollars for each of the three products.

b. Instead assume the sales mix in units is 20 percent R, 30 percent S, and 50 percent T.

    1. What is the weighted-average contribution margin ratio? (Round to four decimal places.)
    2. What is the weighted-average unit contribution margin in dollars?
    3. What is the companywide breakeven broken down in dollars and units for each of the three products?

Paper for working Demonstration Problem

a.

Paper for working Demonstration Problem

b. 1. _____

_____

_____

_____

_____

_____

2. _____

_____

_____

_____

_____

_____

_____

_____

3. _____

_____

_____

_____

_____

_____

_____

_____

_____

_____

_____

_____

Solution to Demonstration Problem

Jungle Company

a. Sales mix in dollars is 20% R, 30% S, and 50% T.

	R	S	T
Sales price	$20	$50	$10
Variable costs	14	25	6
Contribution margin	$ 6	$25	$ 4
Contribution margin ratio	30%	50%	40%
Percentages of sales dollars	20%	30%	50%
Weighted-average contribution margin	6% +	15% +	20% = 41%

$299,300/41% = $730,000 companywide breakeven broken down by $146,000 R sales, $219,000 S sales, and $365,000 T sales.

b. 1. With a sales mix in units of 20% R, 30% S, and 50% T, the weighted-average contribution margin is as shown below.

By considering a total of 10 units in the mix, the distribution arrives at a 44.58% weighted-average contribution margin.

	Sales Value			Contribution	
2 units of R	(2 X $20)	$ 40		(2 X $6)	$ 12
3 units of S	(3 X $50)	150		(3 X $25)	75
5 units of T	(5 X $10)	50		(5 X $4)	20
		$240			$107

The contribution margin is ($107/$240) or 44.58%

2. 2($6) + 3($25) + 5 ($4) = $107/10 = $10.70 unit weighted-average contribution margin

3. $299,300/44.58% = $671,378 breakeven sales

Transferring the mix in units into a mix in dollars is as follows:
Product R: $40 (from above)/$240 = 16.67%
Product S: $150/$240 = 62.5%
Product T: $50/$240 = 20.83%

Sales for Product R: 16.67% X $671,378 = $111,918/$20 unit sales price = 5,596 units
Sales for Product S: 62.5% X $671,378 = $419,611/$50 unit sales price = 8,393 units
Sales for Product T: 20.83% X $671,378 = $139,847/$10 unit sales price =13,984 units

Almost identical answers are obtained in the following alternative procedure:

$299,300/$10.70 = 27,972 breakeven units broken down as follows:
27,972 x 2/10 = 5,594 units of Product R
27,972 x 3/10 = 8,392 units of Product S
27,972 x 5/10 = 13,986 units of Product T

Matching

Referring to the terms listed in the left column, place the appropriate letter next to the corresponding description. A term may not be used or may be used more than once.

a. Breakeven equation

b. Cash flow breakeven point

c. Contribution margin

d. Marginal income

e. Margin of safety

f. P/V chart

g. Relevant range

h. Sales mix

i. Sensitivity analysis

j. Tax shield

k. Variable costs

l. Variable cost ratio

_____ 1. Fixed costs divided by contribution margin per unit.

_____ 2. Excess of actual or budgeted sales over breakeven sales volume.

_____ 3. Noncash expenses multiplied by the tax rate.

_____ 4. Sales - variable expenses.

_____ 5. Variable costs divided by sales.

_____ 6. Income earned on selling one more unit.

_____ 7. Visual display of the relationship of sales price and volume changes upon income and breakeven.

_____ 8. An assumption of breakeven analysis indicating the ratio of a given product line's sales to other product line sales.

_____ 9. Allows fixed and variable costs to be defined in relation to a specific period of time and a designated range of production level.

_____ 10. Indicates the volume of sales needed to cover all cash expenses.

Completion and Exercises

1. List five assumptions of breakeven analysis.

   a._____

   b._____

   c._____

   d._____

   e._____

2. Sales - Variable costs = _____ _____ which is the

   amount available to cover _____ _____ and render a(n)

   _____.

3. Label the different lines and spaces indicated by letters on the following graph in the spaces below.

   A._____   B._____

   C._____   D._____

   E._____   F._____

   G._____   H._____

4. Define marginal income_____

   _____

5. What is the difference between a breakeven chart and a P/V chart?

   _____

   _____

   _____

6. Among the limitations of breakeven analysis, the following are assumed to remain unchanged:

a._____

b._____

c._____

d._____

e._____

7. Since accountants can prepare income statements showing that at breakeven point there is no income or loss, why go to the expense of preparing breakeven charts?

_____

_____

_____

8. a. Variable cost ratio = variable costs divided by _____.

   b. Contribution margin ratio = contribution margin divided by _____;
   another name for this ratio is the _____ ratio.

9. **High-Low and Breakeven Point**

Each unit produced by Delman Company is sold for $8.40. Analysis of the cost records reveal the following costs at various capacity levels:

Months	Volume in Units	Costs
January	6,500	$35,100
February	9,000	40,500
March	8,000	37,080
April	7,000	36,200
May	4,000	30,000
June	6,000	34,800

Required:

Calculate the breakeven point in dollars.

10. Breakeven Operations Using Levels of Fixed Costs

Analysis of Daywitt Company's cost records reveals the following:

Production Volume in Units	Fixed Costs
0	$200,000
1-2,000	247,500
2,001-4,000	280,000

Units sales price is $500; at full capacity of 4,000 units, the company's variable costs amount to $900,000.

Required:

a. Compute the company's breakeven point in:
   (1) Sales dollars.
   (2) Sales units.

b. Prove your answer to Requirement *a* using a simplified income statement.
c. Assume that the company is operating at 35 percent capacity when it decides to reduce sales price to $300 in an attempt to increase sales. At what capacity is breakeven at the reduced sales price?
d. Explain why you would or would not advise such a drastic price cut.
e. Determine the level of operations when it would be more economical to close the factory than to operate it. Use the original sales price of $500.
f. Prove your answer to Requirement *e* using a simplified income statement.
g. Assume the company is presently operating close to the level of operations you determined in Requirement *e*. Indicate the factors management should consider in deciding whether to operate or close operations.

a. _____

_____

_____

_____

_____

_____

_____

b. _____

_____

_____

_____

_____

_____

_____

_____

c.

d.

e.

f.

g.

11. **Breakeven Using Different Sales Mixes**

Even though Krebs, Inc., recognizes the limitations of computing a company-wide breakeven point, management believes this information will be helpful for planning purposes. Analysis of the budget reveals the following:

Product Lines

	A	B	C
Unit sales Price...............................	$100	$80	$60
Unit variable expenses....................	40	30	20
Budgeted volume............................	8,000	16,000	16,000
Total fixed expenses.................			$1,200,000

Required:

a. Compute the breakeven point in units for the entire company and break it down for each product line.
b. Assume that the actual sales mix was 6,000 units of Product A, 12,000 units of Product B; and 18,000 units of Product C and that actual variable expenses for Product A were 10 percent higher than budgeted, while the variable expenses of Product B and C were 15 percent lower. Actual fixed expenses were $1,249,500; however, actual sales prices did not vary from those budgeted. Compute the new actual breakeven point in units per product line for the overall company.

a.

b.

12. Computation of Breakeven

Jackson Company records for the year ended December 31, 19X3, include the following information. (Variable costs are designated V and fixed costs, F.)

Sales (25,000 units @ $15) $375,000

Costs:

Direct material	$ 60,000	(100%V)
Direct labor	90,000	(100%V)
Factory overhead	120,000	(80%F, 20%V)
Marketing expenses	40,000	(50%F, 50%V)
Administrative expenses	30,000	(80% F, 20%V)
Total costs		340,000
Income		$ 35,000

Required: (Show all computations.)

a. Compute the breakeven point in number of units and sales dollars.
b. Compute number of units required to generate a net beforetax profit of $70,000.
c. Compute the breakeven point in number of units if fixed costs were increased by $7,000.

a.

b.

c.

True-False Questions

Indicate whether the following statements are true or false by inserting in the blank space a capital"T" for true or "F" for false.

_____1.   When variable costs are deducted from sales, the result is gross margin.

_____2.   To determine the units to be sold at breakeven point, total variable costs are divided by unit contribution margin.

_____3.   If breakeven sales are $60,000 and actual sales are $90,000, the margin of safety ratio is 33 1/3 percent.

_____4.   A tax shield results when expenses like rent, insurance, and salaries are multiplied by the tax rate.

_____5.   Under breakeven analysis, volume is assumed to be the only important factor affecting cost behavior.

_____6.   The impact of inventory changes are reflected in the total fixed costs of breakeven analysis because this factor has an impact on breakeven sales.

_____7.   The relationship between revenues and costs at various levels of activity is useful information derived from a breakeven chart.

_____8.   Cost-volume-profit analysis assumes that the relationship between cost and revenue behavior results in total variable cost increasing as production increases.

_____9.   Cost-volume-earnings analysis assumes that sales mix will change as fixed costs increase beyond the relevant range.

_____10.   Unit sales price is assumed to remain static and no quantity discounts are assumed to be available under breakeven analysis.

SOLUTIONS

Matching

1. a   6. d
2. e   7. f
3. j   8. h
4. c   9. g
5. l   10. b

Completion and Exercises

1. The assumptions of breakeven analysis include the following:

   a. Fixed and variable costs are defined in relation to a specific period of time and designated range of production level.
   b. Volume is the only important factor affecting cost behavior.
   c. All costs are either fixed or variable.
   d. Unit variable costs remain the same and there is a direct relationship between costs and volume.
   e. Until sales price is assumed to remain the same.
   f. Inventory changes are so insignificant that they have no impact on the analysis.
   g. A specific sales mix is assumed.
   h. Fixed costs remain constant over the relevant range considered.
   i. Managerial policies and techniques have no effect on costs and there is no increase in efficiency in the period of activity studied.

2. contribution margin; fixed costs; income

3. A = Dollars of sales, costs, and expenses
   B = Units of sales, direct labor-hours, machine-hours, percent of capacity, or other expression of volume
   C = Fixed expenses
   D = Sales revenue
   E = Breakeven point
   F = Loss area
   G = Income area
   H = Total expenses

4. Economists often use marginal income to mean the same as contribution margin. Accountants sometimes reserve the term " marginal" when referring to only one product unit.

5. A P/V chart studies available alternatives in determining which is more profitable; a P/V chart displays the impact of sales price and volume changes upon income and breakeven. A breakeven chart also shows the relationship between cost and volume and profit but it shows sales revenue, total expenses, fixed expenses, and variable expenses in indicating at what point there is no income or loss.

6. Included as five possible answers are:

   a. sales mix or product mix
   b. labor productivity
   c. product technology
   d. sales price and other market conditions
   e. relevant range
   f. fixed costs over the relevant range assumed
   g. unit variable costs (see #b. and #c. above which cause no change in unit variable cost).

7. Breakeven charts can more dramatically show the relationship of sales, expenses, and profits. A nonaccountant may not appreciate the time spent in analyzing financial statement and the information can be displayed through charts for easy understanding.

8. a. sales
   b. sales; profit-volume (P/V) ratio

9. *Delman Company*

Variable unit cost = $\dfrac{\$40,500 - \$30,000}{9,000 - 4,000}$ = $2.10

Fixed cost component = $40,500 - (9,000 x $2.10) = $21,600 or $30,000 - (4,000 x $2.10) = $21,600

Variable cost as percentage of sales price = .25 determined from $2.10/$8.40.

$$
\begin{aligned}
S &= FC + VC \\
S &= \$21,600 + .25S \\
.75S &= \$21,600 \\
S &= \$28,800 \text{ approximately}
\end{aligned}
$$
or
$21,600/$6.30 = 3,429 units
3,429 x $8.40 = $28,803.60 approximately

10. *Daywitt Company*

Note: Only the $247,500 fixed costs are relevant because if the company planned to operate in a volume level 2,001-4,000 units and found market demand was inadequate to meet this supply, it would shift to the lower level of 2,000 units or less.

In addition if $280,000 fixed costs were used, it results in breakeven units which are less than 2,001-4,000 capacity as follows:

$$\dfrac{\$280,000}{\$275^* \text{ contribution margin}} = 1,019 \text{ units}$$

This is another reason for using $247,500 fixed costs.

a.

$$\dfrac{\$900,000 \text{ Variable costs at full capacity}}{\text{Sales at full capacity, } \$2,000,000 \ (4,000 \text{ units x } \$500)} = .45 \text{ variable cost ratio}$$

1.00 - .45 variable cost ratio = .55 contribution margin ratio

(1) S = $\dfrac{\$247,500}{.55 \text{ contribution margin ratio}}$ = $450,000 breakeven sales dollars

(2) $\dfrac{\$450,000}{\$500}$ = 900 breakeven units

b.
Sales (900 units x $500)		$450,000
Expenses - Variable ($450,000 x 45%).................................	$202,500	
Fixed...	247,500	450,000
Income..		$ 0

* $500 units sales price - $225** unit variable cost = $275
** $900,000/4,000 units = $225

10. (continued)

c.

$$\frac{\$900,000}{4,000} = \$225 \text{ unit variable cost}$$

$$\frac{\$225}{\$300} = .75 \text{ variable cost to sales}$$

$$1.00 - .75 = .25 \text{ contribution margin ratio}$$

$$\frac{\$247,500}{\$75} = 3,300 \text{ breakeven units}$$

$$\frac{3,300}{4,000} = 82.5\% \text{ capacity}$$

However, this raises operations into a higher fixed cost level so that the following breakeven is more appropriate:

$$\frac{\$280,000}{.25} = \$1,120,000 \text{ breakeven sales}$$

$$\frac{\$1,120,000}{\$300} = 3,734 \text{ breakeven units}$$

$$3,734 \div 4,000 = 94\% \text{ capacity}$$

d. Such a drastic price cut is not advisable because merely to breakeven, the company must operate at 94 percent capacity. This leaves little opportunity for profit.

e. Let X = sales volume to be determined
$200,000 = fixed costs when idle
$200,000 = $247,500 - (1.00X - .45X)
.55X = $47,500
X = $86,364

Alternative Approach
Let X = units at sales volume to be determined
$200,000 = $247,500 - $275X
$275X = $47,500
X = 172.727 units at sales volume being determined: 172.727 units X $500
    unit sales price = $86,364

f.

Sales		$ 86,364
Expense: Variable (45% X $86,364).........	$ 38,864	
Fixed......................................	247,500	286,364
Net loss which equals fixed cost when idle		($200,000)

g. Factors in support of closing operations:

1. There is greater probability that the $200,000 is more accurately estimated than the fixed costs at higher levels and the variable costs since the $200,000 is probably composed of rent expense, insurance expense, and superintendent and management costs which can be estimated from existing agreements and contracts.

10. (concluded)

    2. Unit variable costs may be higher at lower operations level because the $900,000 total variable costs at full capacity may reflect quantity discounts on material that are not available at less than full capacity. The relevant range may be different at the various volume levels. Accountants recognize that strictly variable costs will remain the same within the same relevant range.

    3. There is no justification for continuing a declining situation and continuing to incur a loss. Instead, operations should cease so that the investment and effort can be applied to a more profitable endeavor.

    4. There is more risk in operating than closing operations.

Factors in support of continuing operations.

    1. If there is evidence that the market will improve, the company should continue operations.

    2. If a skilled labor force is required, the company does not want to run the risk of losing its trained employees if the future looks more favorable.

    3. If the present labor force has available many other job opportunities, a layoff at present with plans to rehire the existing work force may not be realistic as these present employees will have already secured other employment.

    4. If market studies indicate that increased advertising and other changes could be made that would be cost justified and increase sales volume, management should further investigate the feasibility of undertaking this before closing operations.

11. *Krebs, Inc.*

  a. Budgeted Average Contribution Margin $= \dfrac{\$60(1) + \$50(2) + \$40(2)}{1 + 2 + 2} = \dfrac{\$240}{5} = \$48$

$\dfrac{\$1,200,000}{\$48} =$ 25,000 units consisting of 5,000 units of A, 10,000 units of B, and 10,000 units of C

  b. Actual Average Contribution Margin $= \dfrac{\$56.00(1) + \$54.50(2) + \$43.00(3)}{1 + 2 + 3} = \dfrac{\$294}{6} = \$49$

$\dfrac{\$1,249,500}{\$49} =$ 25,500 units consisting of 4,250 units of A, 8,500 units of B, and 12,750 units of C

12. *Jackson Company*

a.

	Fixed Costs	Variable Costs	Total
Direct Material		$ 60,000	$ 60,000
Direct Labor		90,000	90,000
Factory Overhead	$ 96,000	24,000	120,000
Marketing Expenses	20,000	20,000	40,000
Administrative Expenses	24,000	6,000	30,000
Totals	$140,000	$200,000	$340,000

Variable Costs per Unit: $200,000 ÷ 25,000 = $8.00

Contribution Margin per unit: $15 selling price - $8.00 = $7.00

Breakeven in units $= \dfrac{\$140,000}{\$7} =$ 20,000 units

Breakeven in sales = 20,000 units x $15 selling price = $300,000

12. (concluded)

b. $\dfrac{(\$140{,}000 + \$70{,}000)}{\$7} = 30{,}000$ units

c. $\dfrac{(\$140{,}000 + \$7{,}000)}{\$7} = 21{,}000$ units

True-False

1. F   The result is contribution margin; gross margin is the difference between fixed and variable cost of goods sold subtracted from sales.

2. F   Total variable costs can be calculated only after the volume of activity is determined. Instead, unit variable costs are subtracted from unit sales price to give unit contribution margin which is divided into total fixed costs to yield the units needed to be sold to break even.

3. T $30,000/$90,000 = 33 1/3%.

4. F   Tax shields result when noncash expenses such as depreciation are multiplied by the tax rate.

5. T

6. F   Breakeven analysis assumes that inventory changes are so insignificant that they have no impact on the analysis.

7. T

8. T

9. F   Breakeven analysis assumes a specified sales mix.

10. T

14 Performance Evaluation and Segment Analysis

Chapter Outline

Responsibility Accounting
    Responsibility Centers
    Principal-Agent Relationships
Degree of Decentralization
    Advantages of Decentralization
    Disadvantages of Decentralization
Traditional Methods for Evaluating Segment Performance
    Contribution Reporting
    Segment Margin
    Breakeven Analysis
    Return on Investment
    Residual Income
    Ratios
    Full Costing
    Controllable and Noncontrollable Costs
Limitations of Traditional Methods for Evaluating Segment Performance
    ROI in Automated Manufacturing Environments
    Local versus Overall Performance Measurements
Performance Measures for World-Class Companies
    Segregate Discretionary Expenses
    Dysfunctional Consequences of Accounting Measurements
    Throughput
    Nonfinancial Evaluations
    Multiple Performance Measures

Chapter Objectives

After studying this chapter, you should be able to:

1. Explain the conceptual framework for measuring and evaluating segment performance.

2. Discuss the advantages and disadvantages of the various degrees of decentralization.

3. Analyze segment performance using contribution margin, segment margin, ROI, and residual income.

4. Explain how short-term performance measures have many weaknesses, such as rewarding undesirable behavior.

5. Discuss the advantage of using multiple performance measures that include nonfinancial evaluations.

6. Define and apply the new terms introduced.

Chapter Review

Responsibility Accounting

1. The concept of responsibility accounting involves using accounting as a means to evaluate performance.

2. Variance analysis and budgeting comprise a part of the responsibility accounting process.

Responsibility Centers

3. An organization is divided into departments or segments, called responsibility centers.

   a. Costs are accumulated by responsibility center for control purposes.
   b. Responsibility centers are known by a variety of names because companies have unique separations of authority and responsibility.
   c. Responsibility centers and cost centers should be used in classifying costs before their behavior is studied.

Cost Centers

4. A cost center is the smallest area of responsibility for which costs are accumulated.

   a. Cost centers may be known by a variety of names; at a low level, a cost center may be a department.
   b. At a higher level, a cost center may be known as a branch or territory.
   c. The classification of costs by cost centers should follow a company's responsibility accounting system.
   d. The chart of accounts should be designed to reflect cost centers so that companies can estimate proper accountability for costs.

Profit and Investment Centers

5. Changing cost centers to profit centers may make managers more concerned with finding ways to increase the center's revenue.

   a. A cost center is a segment responsible only for costs.
   b. A profit center is accountable for both revenue and costs.
   c. Investment centers are assigned responsibility for the invested assets or capital in addition to costs and revenue.

Principal-Agent Relationships

6. The conceptual framework surrounding performance evaluations considers responsibility accounting and principal-agent relationships.

7. Principal-agent relationships are found when authority is decentralized.

   a. A principal delegates duties to a subordinate, who is called an agent.
   b. Studies in agency theory provide support for companies making subordinate managers responsible for both controllable and noncontrollable costs.

Degree of Decentralization

8. Some divisions enjoy a high degree of autonomy while other companies issue tight policies to segment managers; the more autonomous each segment, the more decentralized is the company as a whole.

9. With total decentralization, managers operate under minimum constraints and have maximum freedom because there is a lack of central authority.

10. With total centralization, division managers have limited authority because top management maintains tight constraints.

Advantages of Decentralization

11. Decentralization offers the following advantages:

   a. Frees top management from daily operating problems so that they can direct attention to strategic planning.
   b. Allows decision making as near as possible to the scene of action. This permits true teamwork among all executives, each skilled in his or her own area.
   c. Results in more accurate, timely decisions since segment managers are more familiar with local conditions than is top management.
   d. Recognizes the value of people who provide brainpower for a company.
   e. Provides training in decision making for segment managers so that they are better prepared to advance in the organizational hierarchy.
   f. Offers stimulus for more efficient performance because managers are given authority to match their responsibility.
   g. Eliminates unprofitable activities more rapidly since, for example, managers may be given authority to purchase direct materials from outside parties rather than being forced to buy from one of the company's segments.
   h. Provides a stimulus for segment managers to look for outside markets for their finished goods.

Disadvantages of Decentralization

12. The following are disadvantages of decentralization:

   a. The contribution that each segment is expected to make to the overall organization may not be emphasized enough so that goal congruence is not achieved.
   b. A more elaborate information system may be required.
   c. Transfer prices must be established which may be costly and result in negotiations.

Traditional Methods for Evaluating Segment Performance

13. The term segment refers to any logical subcomponent of a company which is usually identified with the responsibility for profit in supplying a service or product.

14. A segment's important characteristic is that its operating performance is separately identifiable and measurable.

Contribution Reporting

15. Segments may be evaluated on the basis of contribution margin which is calculated by deducting segment variable costs from segment revenue.

Segment Margin

16. Segment margin is the revenue a segment earns less the variable and fixed expenses that can be traced directly to the segment.

17. Nontraceable costs are allocated to a segment if a segment income is desired; however, this may reveal that a segment has an operating net loss when its segment margin is positive.

   a. As a result it can be argued that allocations of indirect costs can be misleading.

b. Usually an argument can be made for retaining a segment as long as its segment margin is positive unless a more profitable opportunity is available.

Breakeven Analysis

18. The breakeven point is the level of sales at which the segment recovers all expenses and shows neither income nor loss. This requires an allocation of all indirect fixed costs and this may be arbitrary.

Return on Investment

19. Return on investment (ROI) directs attention to finding the optimum asset investment because it enables management to determine whether the activity is profitable enough to support the amount of resources devoted to it.

    a. The long-run profits which will be maximized if the optimum level of investment in each asset is achieved is emphasized.
    b. ROI focuses management's attention on segments identified as needing corrective action.

20. It is difficult to determine the appropriate measurement of a segment's assets to use in computing ROI. The following can be used, but each has possible weaknesses:

    a. Book value of assets committed.
    b. Original cost can be adjusted for changes in the general price level.
    c. Gross value of depreciable assets.
    d. Replacement cost.
    e. Quoted market prices for assets which have an actual market.

21. Book value of segment assets is readily available for measuring segment assets, but this is not a useful measure.

    a. As assets become older, the rate of return becomes higher due merely to book value decreasing.
    b. Using gross value of depreciable assets overcomes this meaningless increase.

22. Determining the appropriate segment income to use is also difficult as there is a question if the tax rate should be applied to segment income.

23. Another problem in determining rate of return is deciding whether segment net income or segment margin should be used.

24. The following relationship outlines ROI:

$$\text{Segment ROI} = \frac{\text{Segment revenues}}{\text{Investment center assets}} \times \frac{\text{Operating profits}}{\text{Revenues}} = \frac{\text{Operating profits}}{\text{Investment center assets}}$$

25. The formula can also be expressed as follows:

    Asset turnover x Profit margin percentage on revenue = Return on investment

26. Asset turnover ratio measures the investment center's ability to generate revenue for each dollar of assets invested in the segment.

27. Managers focus attention on the factors that increase ROI by increasing sales or reducing invested capital or expenses. An improvement in capital turnover or gross margin percentage without a change in the other factors increases ROI.

28. Since the calculation of ROI requires that both tangible and intangible assets be assigned a value, it can be argued that it is misleading.

    a. Both the numerator and denominator in ROI are the result of arbitrary decisions which can make them somewhat unreliable.

    b. ROI is a useful index of performance only if reasonable criteria for comparison is available.

29. Overemphasis on ROI causes segment managers to manipulate ROI targets by reducing discretionary expenditures, exploiting accounting conventions, and other nonproductive procedures.

Residual Income

30. Residual income is a means of evaluating a segment; it is the operating income of the investment center after the imputed interest on the assets used by the center has been deducted.

    a. Imputed interest on the segment's controllable investment can be used instead of interest on the segment's invested capital.

    b. Use of residual income overcomes some of the weaknesses associated with ROI.

31. By using residual income as a performance measure, companies encourage segment managers to concentrate on maximizing dollars of residual income rather than on maximizing a percentage return.

32. Residual income overcomes one of the dysfunctional aspects of the ROI measure in which managers can increase their reported ROI by rejecting investments that yield returns in excess of their company's or segment's costs of capital, but that are below their current average ROI.

33. Either ROI or residual income is a useful measure if correctly used and properly interpreted. Companies should avoid reliance on a single measure.

Ratios

34. There are other means of evaluating segments which include ratios, full costing, and controllable and noncontrollable costs.

35. Accountants can use ratio analysis, such as current ratio and ratios of various expenses to sales, in evaluating segments.

Full Costing

36. Full costing has limited usefulness in segment analysis; direct (traceable) costs have more appropriate uses in studying segment profitability.

    a. Full costing can be used for segment reporting, but it should not be used in segment evaluation.

    b. By including full costs on segment reports, the division manager is more aware of the total costs associated with his/her segment.

Controllable and Noncontrollable Costs

37. Costs should be broken down into controllable and noncontrollable costs if they are both reported on the segment statements.

Limitations of Traditional Methods for Evaluating Segment Performance

38. Many evaluation techniques consider only short-term benefits and costs and assign no cost to lost opportunities and no benefit to potential strategic advantages.
39. Managers should not ignore indirect financial advantages of effective manufacturing performance for the long-run.

ROI in Automated Manufacturing Environments

40. ROI is often inadequate for estimating the advantages of robots and automated equipment.

41. The development of customer loyalty, recruiting costs, and research expenditures have a value beyond the current accounting period but accountants often do not capitalize such costs as assets.

42. Accountants also rarely estimate the earnings effect of intangible assets such as employee talent and morale, an efficient distribution network, and knowledge of high-quality, flexible manufacturing processes.

Local Versus Overall Performance Measurements

43. Goal congruence is difficult to achieve and even more difficult in a highly decentralized organization.

44. To overcome short-term dysfunctional behavior, there should be a companywide focus on the development of longer-term objectives and plans.

45. Variable costing highlights strategies to increase net income by increasing production so that portions of overhead remain in inventory rather than expensing such overhead. Absorption costing allows an increase in inventory to absorb a segment's overhead.

Performance Measures for World-Class Companies

46. With only a short-term view, managers fail to perceive the need for automation and improved technology because the company gears its measurement and reward systems to achieving short-term results.

Segregate Discretionary Expenses

47. Discretionary costs arise from periodic appropriation decisions and include expenditures for advertising, research, repairs, and customer relations.

    a. Discretionary expenditures are often postponed to increase short-run profits.
    b. The bonus reward system adopted by companies often encourages this postponement.

48. Separating discretionary and nondiscretionary expenses on segment income statements often encourages the detection of a segment manager's strategy of avoiding the incurrence of advertising, research, and repairs in the short-run to increase short-term profits.

49. Suboptimization often occurs when segment managers are evaluated on the basis of their segment's contribution; this is more likely to happen also if segment managers are given bonuses which are based on their performance.

Dysfunctional Consequences of Accounting Measurements

50. Short-run earnings are often the basis of the reward system which causes segment managers to lack the needed incentive to engage in costly research projects whose outcome is questionable.

Throughput

51. A nontraditional performance measure involves throughput which is the rate at which the system generates money through sales.

Nonfinancial Evaluations

52. There are other useful measures of performance which do not involve financial data which can supplement financial evaluations of segments.

Multiple Performance Measures

53. Reward systems having a short-range time frame often reward behavior which the company is trying to avoid.

54. While there are various means available for evaluating segment performance, some of these methods have inherent weaknesses because of the dissimilarity of segments involved or the difficulty of establishing objective measurements.

    a. Multiple performance measures help overcome rewarding inappropriate behavior by segment managers.
    b. More appropriate systems evaluate managers on measures of performance covering three to five years.

Demonstration Problem

Profitability of Product Lines

Top management of the D. M. R. Company is concerned about the profitability of its three product lines, Xee, Yee, and Zee. The following data are obtained from its financial statements.

Sales (2,000 units of Xee, 1,800 units of Yee, and 3,500 units of Zee)	$ 206,000
Cost of goods sold	146,600
Salespersons' commissions	8,240
Advertising	3,000
Sales manager's salary	10,500
Administrative expenses (includes bad debt expense)	25,000
Rent on office building	20,000

Each unit of Xee sells for $15; of Yee, $20; and of Zee, $40. The cost per unit is composed of 30 percent direct material, 25 percent direct labor, and 15 percent variable factory overhead. The full cost per unit is $10 for Xee, $12 for Yee, and $30 for Zee.

Salespersons are paid a flat percentage of sales. The provision for bad debt is estimated to be one fourth of 1 percent. The marketing manager informs you that one fourth of the advertising is devoted to product Xee, one fourth to Yee, and the remainder to Zee. Orders for Xee are processed in several offices consisting of a total of 2,500 square feet; Yee orders in offices totaling 3,000 square feet; and Zee orders in offices totaling 4,500 square feet.

Required:

Prepare a segmental analysis analyzing the profitability of each product.

Paper for working Demonstration Problem

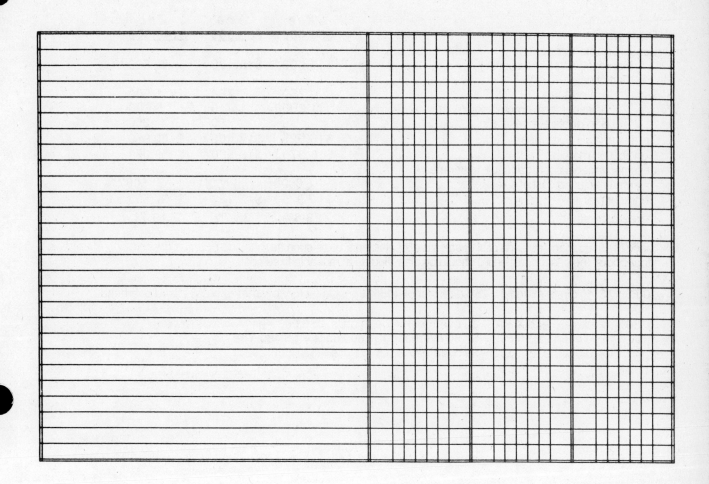

Solution to Demonstration Problem

D.M.R. Company

	Xee	Yee	Zee
Sales	$30.000	$36.000	$140.000
Less variable expenses			
Manufacturing (70% of cost)	$14,000	$15,120	$ 73,500
Marketing			
Advertising	750	750	1,500
Salesperson's commission (4%)	1,200	1,440	5,600
Bad debts expense	75	90	350
Total Variable Expenses	$16.025	$17.400	$ 80.950
Contribution margin	$13,975	$18,600	$ 59,050
Less nonvariable costs traceable to segments			
Manufacturing cost of sales	6.000*	6.480**	31.500***
Segment margin	$ 7,975	$12,120	$ 27,550
Percent of sales	26.6%	33.7%	19.7%

Since the fixed manufacturing cost of sales is allocated on a basis such as machine-hours or direct labor-hours, there is a question if it should be classified as a traceable fixed cost.

100% - (30% direct material + 25%direct labor +15% variable factory overhead) = 30% fixed overhead

  *30% fixed overhead X $10 = $3 overhead X 2,000 units = $6,000 Xee
  **30% fixed overhead X $12 = $3.60 overhead X 1,800 units = $6,480 Yee
***30% fixed overhead X $30 = $9 overhead X 3,500 units = $31,500 Zee

Matching

Referring to the terms listed in the left column, place the appropriate letter next to the corresponding description. A term may not be used or may be used more than once.

a. Contribution margin

b. Cost center

c. Goal congruence

d. Profit center

e. Residual income

f. Return on investment

g. Segment

h. Segment margin

i. Total centralization

j. Total decentralization

k. Traceable costs

_____ 1. A division responsible for both revenues and costs.

_____ 2. An extreme degree of autonomy in which segment managers have much flexibility and are held responsible for only the broad task of operating efficiently.

_____ 3. A condition that is less likely to occur under decentralization than under centralization.

_____ 4. Any subcomponent of a company that is identified with the responsibility for profit in supplying a product or service.

_____ 5. A measure of evaluating segments which focuses attention on the optimum asset investment that is profitable enough to support the amount of resources devoted to it.

_____ 6. A basis of evaluating segment performance determined by subtracting segment variable costs from segment revenue.

_____ 7. A division responsible for costs.

_____ 8. Segment's revenue less the variable and fixed costs which can be traced directly to the segment.

_____ 9. Under this philosophy of segment autonomy, segment managers operate under tightly defined policies.

_____ 10. Operating income of an investment center less the imputed interest on the assets used by the center.

Completion and Exercises

1. A _____ center encourages managers to be more concerned with increasing the center's revenue while a manager of a _____ center is responsible only for expenses. Additional responsibilities are given to the manager of a _____ center because this individual is responsible for expenses, profits, and assets of the center.

2. Briefly discuss four advantages of decentralization.

   a. _____

   _____

   b. _____

   _____

   c. _____

   _____

   d. _____

   _____

3. Briefly discuss two disadvantages of decentralization.

   a. _____

   _____

   b. _____

   _____

4. Three difficult aspects of computing ROI are:

   a. _____

   _____

   b. _____

   _____

   c. _____

   _____

5. Full costing data can be used in segment _____, but has limited usefulness in segment _____.

6. If segment managers are given a bonus based upon their segment's margin or residual income, top management must guard against _____ which is a condition that is harmful to the overall company.

7. List three measurements of a segment's assets which can be used in computing ROI.

   a. _____

   b. _____

   c. _____

8. List four appropriate means of evaluating segmental performance.

a. _____

b. _____

c. _____

d. _____

9. A _____ center is the smallest area of responsibility for which costs are accumulated while a _____ center is a segment responsible for both revenues and expenses.

10. Humphreys Key Company manufactures several product lines, one of which is the Nesti line. Management is concerned about the profitability of this line and requests your help in preparing a segment analysis. The following data are supplied:

Units sold	13.000
Units sales price...	$ 50
Unit variable production expense.....................	20
Unit variable marketing and administrative expense.........	15
Traceable fixed costs	60,000

A total of $600,000 of capital has been invested in this product line.

Required:

Determine contribution margin, segment margin, and residual income for this product line, assuming a 12 percent cost of capital.

_____

_____

_____

_____

_____

_____

_____

_____

11. Keller Company manufactures several product lines, one of which is the Contesi line. Management is concerned about the profitability of this line and requests your help in preparing segment analysis. They supply you with the following data:

Units sold..	20,000
Unit sales price	$ 20
Unit variable production expense.........................	7
Unit variable marketing and administration expense..............	4
Traceable fixed costs	110,000

The company has invested capital totaling $500,000 in this product line.

Required:

Prepare contribution margin, segment margin, and residual income for this product line assuming a 10 percent cost of capital.

11. Paper for Working

_____

_____

_____

_____

_____

_____

_____

_____

_____

12. Management of Nan Mischke Company wishes to earn a 25 percent return on assets employed by all segments. Assets employed by the Northern Territory amount to $500,000, while fixed costs directly attributable to this product line amount to $86,000. The accountant for this territory informs you that the variable cost per unit is $5.50.

Required:

a. In order to earn the desired rate of return, how many units must be sold if the sales price is $8 per unit?
b. Determine breakeven sales in units for this division.
c. What rate of return would be earned if 60,000 units were sold at a $7.50 sales price?
d. Calculate the segment's residual income assuming an interest rate of 12 percent if 75,000 units are sold at an $8 unit sales price.

a. _____

_____

_____

_____

b. _____

_____

_____

c. _____

_____

_____

d. _____

_____

_____

_____

_____

_____

13. Territorial Contribution Margin and Segment Margin

K. Jones Company analyzes its Eastern and Western Territories by product line as well as by total territory performance. The Eastern Territory manufactures and sells Products A and B, while the Western Territory manufactures and sells Products C and D. For the quarter ending March 31, 19X1, you extract the following data from the records.

	Products			
	A	B	C	D
Units sold....................................	1,500	2,600	3,000	3,800
Unit sales price	$ 5	$ 8	$ 10	$ 6
Unit variable production expense..	2	4	7	3
Unit variable marketing and administrative expense	1	2	1	2
Traceable fixed costs	1,000	1,800	4,200	1,200

Costs that could not be traced to a segment totaled $5,400.

Required:

a. Prepare a contribution margin and segment margin for the two territories and the four product lines.
   Express both of these measures and income for the overall company as a percent of sales.
b. Prepare additional analysis for the territories and product lines if the hours to complete each unit are as follows: Product A, two hours; Product B, one hour: Product C, one-half hour; and Product D, one and one-half hours.

13. Paper for working

a.

True-False Questions

Indicate whether the following statements are true or false by inserting in the blank space a capital " T " for true or " F " for false.

_____ 1. Investment center managers are responsible for the center's assets, revenues, and expenses.

_____ 2. A profit center is the smallest area of responsibility for which costs are accumulated.

_____ 3. The important operating characteristic of a segment is that its operating performance is separately identifiable and measurable.

_____ 4. Usually a segment should be retained as long as its segment margin is positive unless there are more profitable opportunities.

_____ 5. Using breakeven point analysis is the most appropriate means of evaluating a segment's performance.

_____ 6. The segment margin of a division will always be higher than the residual income because of the nature of the measurements.

_____ 7. One of the advantages of centralization is that it provides more opportunities for training of future top managers within the company than does decentralization.

_____ 8. If full costs of a segment are reported on statements distributed to division managers, there should be a separation of controllable and noncontrollable costs.

_____ 9. Absolute decentralization is rarely economical because it requires top management to make such a large volume of decisions.

_____ 10. Segment margin is determined by subtracting indirect variable costs from each segment's revenue.

_____ 11. Residual income eliminates some of the problems associated with ROI since it is not expressed as a ratio, but the interest rate used in residual income is normally the company's average cost of capital.

_____ 12. A revenue center has authority and responsibility for costs and revenue.

SOLUTIONS

MATCHING

1.	d	5.	f	8.	h
2.	j	6.	a.	9.	i
3.	c	7.	b.	10.	e
4.	g, d				

COMPLETION AND EXERCISES

1. profit; cost; investment

2. The following are advantages of decentralization:
   a. Segment managers are encouraged to look for outside markets for their products.
   b. Unprofitable activities are eliminated more rapidly because managers may be given authority to purchase direct materials and services from outside parties.
   c. Because segment managers are more familiar with local conditions than top management, decisions are often more accurate and timely.
   d. Teamwork among executives is encouraged.
   e. Segment managers are given authority to match their responsibility so they are stimulated to perform more efficiently.
   f. Top management is freed to concentrate on strategic planning rather than spend their time with operational problems all the time.
   g. Provides good training for segment managers who have the opportunity to advance within the company.
   h. Recognizes the value of people who provide the intelligence of the company.

3. The following are disadvantages of decentralization:
   a. Transfer prices must be established which may result in friction.
   b. A more costly and elaborate information system may be required.
   c. Goal congruence may not be achieved as each segment manager is encouraged to focus attention on his/her own segment.

4. a. Determining the appropriate measurement of the segment's assets.
   b. Determining if segment net income or segment margin should be used.
   c. Measuring segment income - whether depreciation should be calculated on replacement cost or whether the tax rate should be applied to segment income.

5. reporting; evaluation

6. Suboptimization

7. The following are possible measurements of a segment's assets.
   a. Quoted market prices for assets which have an actual market
   b. Replacement cost
   c. Book value of assets committed
   d. Original cost can be adjusted for changes in the general price level
   e. Gross value of depreciable assets.

8. The following are means of evaluating segmental performance.
   a. ROI, also referred to as ROA or ROAC
   b. contribution margin
   c. residual income
   d. ratios such as current ratio or certain variable expenses to segment revenue
   e. breakeven point analysis
   f. segment margin
   Note that net income for each segment is not listed as it is generally not considered appropriate.

9. cost; profit

10. *Humphreys Key Company*

Revenue...		$650,000
Less:Variable production expense.	$260,000	
Variable marketing and administrative expense.........	195,000	455,000
Contribution margin.		$195,000
Less: Traceable fixed costs		60,000
Segment margin..		$135,000
Less imputed interest on invested capital (12% X $600,000)		72,000
Residual Income		$ 63,000

11. *Keller Company*

Sales revenue..		$400,000
Less: Variable production expense................................	$140,000	
Variable marketing and administrative expense.........	80,000	220,000
Contribution margin.		$180,000
Less: Traceable fixed costs		110,000
Segment margin..		$ 70,000
Less Imputed interest on invested capital (10% X $500,000)		50,000
Residual income...		$ 20,000

12. *Nan Mischke Company*

a. Desired Return = $125,000 (25% X $500,000)
 X = Units to be sold
 $8X = $5.50X + $86,000 + $125,000
 $2.50X = $211,000
 $\quad\quad$ = 84,400 units

b. $8X = $5.50X + $86,000
 $2.50X = $86,000
 $\quad\quad$ X = 34,400 units

c.
Sales (60,000 units X $7.50).		$450,000
Variable cost (60,000 X $5.50).....................................	$330,000	
Fixed costs...	86,000	416,000
Income...		$ 34,000

 Rate of Return ($34,000/$500,000) = 6.8%

d.
Sales (75,000 X $8).		$600,000
Variable cost (75,000 X $5.50).....................................	$412,500	
Fixed costs...	86,000	498,500
Segment Income..		$101,500
Less imputed interest on invested capital (12% X $500,000).....		60,000
Residual Income..		$ 41,500

a.

K. Jones Company
Contribution Analysis for Territories and Product Lines
For Quarter Ending March 31, 19X1

	Company Totals	Territory Eastern	Territory Western	Eastern Territory Product A	Eastern Territory Product B	Western Territory Product C	Western Territory Product D
Revenue	$81,100	$28,300	$52,800	$7,500	$20,800	$30,000	$22,800
Less variable production expense	$45,800	$13,400	$32,400	$3,000	$10,400	$21,000	$11,400
Variable marketing and administrative expenses	17,300	6,700	10,600	1,500	5,200	3,000	7,600
Total variable expenses	$63,100	$20,100	$43,000	$4,500	$15,600	$24,000	$19,000
Contribution margin	$18,000	$ 8,200	$ 9,800	$4,500	$ 5,200	$ 6,000	$ 3,800
Percent of sales	22%	29%	19%	40%	25%	20%	17%
Less Fixed costs traceable to segments	8,200	2,800	5,400	1,000	1,800	4,200	1,200
Segment margin	$ 9,800	$ 5,400	$ 4,400	$2,000	$ 3,400	$ 1,800	$ 2,600
Percent of sales	12%	19%	8%	26.7%	16.4%	6.0%	11.4%
Nontraceable costs	5,400						
Income before taxes	$ 4,400						
Percent of sales	5.4%						

b.

K. Jones Company
Segment Margin Per Hour to Complete the Products
For Quarter Ending March 31, 19X1

	Territory Eastern	Territory Western	Eastern Territory Product A	Eastern Territory Product B	Western Territory Product C	Western Territory Product D
Segment Margin	$5,400	$4,400	$2,000	$3,400	$1,800	$2,600
Hours to Complete	5,600	7,200	3,000	2,600	1,500	5,700
Segment Margin per Hour to Complete	$.96	$.61	$.67	$1.31	$1.20	$.46

TRUE - FALSE

1. T

2. F   A cost center is the smallest area of responsibility for which costs are accumulated.

3. T

4. T   Arbitrary allocations of nontraceable costs may cause a segment to appear unprofitable; however, if its segment margin is positive, it generally should be retained.

5. F   The difficulty with using breakeven point analysis in evaluating a segment's performance is that fixed costs must be allocated to each segment if they are nontraceable and this may be arbitrary.

6. T   Residual income will always be less because it is computed by subtracting imputed interest from segment margin.

7. F   Decentralization offers more opportunities for training future top managers than does centralization because segment managers are given more flexibility and decisions to make.

8. T

9. F   Absolute decentralization would require little decision making by top management as segment managers would have the authority for most decisions and would have a high degree of autonomy.

10. F   Direct fixed and direct variable costs are subtracted from segment revenue to arrive at segment margin.

11. T

12. T

15 Transfer Pricing in Multidivisional Companies

Chapter Outline

Transfer Pricing Bases
    General Formula for Transfer Prices
    Differential/Variable Cost Transfer Prices
    Full Cost Transfer Prices
    Market-Based Transfer Prices
    Negotiated Transfer Prices
    Transfer Prices for Services
    Impact of Product/Service Life Cycles on Transfer Prices
    Transfer Pricing Illustrated
    Recording Internal Transfers
Multinational Transfer Pricing
Dual Transfer Pricing
    Missing Incentive to Control Cost
Behavioral Implications of Transfer Pricing
    Suboptimization
    Divisional Performance Evaluation
    Internal Competition
    External Procurement

Chapter Objectives

1. Explain the relationship between the degrees of interdependence and the need for establishing transfer prices.

2. Apply appropriate criteria for choosing transfer prices.

3. Use variations of the two transfer pricing methods which impact a segment's profitability.

4. Recognize that transfer prices should reflect the factors surrounding each specified situation.

5. Monitor the behavioral implications inherent in decentralized segments and the potential for suboptimization and other dysfunctional behavior.

6. Define and apply the new terms introduced.

Chapter Review

Transfer Pricing Bases

1. Transfer pricing refers to the unit price assigned to goods that are transferred among segments.

   a. Transfer prices are used for purposes other than inventory costing.
   b. Consolidated financial statements still show the unit production cost computed in accordance with generally accepted accounting principles regardless of the transfer price used.

2. The transfer pricing problem becomes more significant as the degree of interdependence among segments becomes greater.

   a. A company that diversifies into different basic industries has few or no transfer pricing problems.

3. Decentralized divisions may be operated as either cost centers, profit centers, or investment centers.

   a. Profit center managers are allowed the authority to trade with whom they please and are permitted to establish prices they are willing to accept or pay.
   b. Cost center managers are responsible for costs only.
   c. Profit centers can exist in highly centralized organizations; however, the managers of these centers have little authority in decision making.

4. There are two basic methods for establishing transfer prices.

   a. One base involves some form of cost derived from the company books or from financial analysis; full cost, variable cost, opportunity, differential, or marginal cost are types of this method.
   b. A second method includes market price, negotiated price, or some variation of these two methods.

General Formula for Transfer Prices

5. The following general formula can be used by management as a beginning point for computing an appropriate transfer price:

   Differential costs per unit + Lost contribution margin on outside sales

   a. The formula indicates that the transfer price should equal the unit differential cost of the product being transferred plus the contribution margin per unit that the selling division loses as a result of giving up outside sales.
   b. If the selling division is not operating at full capacity, it does not lose contribution margin unless it has to give up some of its present outside customers.
   c. However, any solution is *situation specific* and depends upon individual circumstances of the divisions involved.

Differential/Variable Cost Transfer Prices

6. Variable cost transfer pricing may ensure the best utilization of corporate facilities in the short run.

   a. Using variable costs as the transfer price focuses attention on the contribution margin a transfer generates and how it increases short-run profitability.
   b. Variable cost transfer prices allow one segment manager to make a profit at the expense of another segment manager because all profit is given to the buying segment.

7. Differential cost is found by determining how much total company cost increases if the contemplated alternative is added to the present volume of activities; this can be used as a basis for transfer prices.

8. Opportunity cost is defined as the maximum contribution to profit if the goods are not sold outside the company but are transferred internally.

Full Cost Transfer Pricing

9. Full cost as a transfer price basis is the oldest transfer pricing method.

   a. In centralized companies, full cost is firmly established because it is used for external reporting.
   b. Full cost is convenient to apply since it is already available.
   c. An additional advantage is that a full cost transfer price leaves no intracompany profits in inventory.
   d. Full cost transfer prices are endorsed by the Internal Revenue Service.

10. Full cost transfer prices are not suitable for companies with decentralized structures which require that the profitability of autonomous units be measured.

   a. Full cost transfer prices have little value in evaluating performance.
   b. Full cost transfer prices also offer little incentive for segment managers to control or reduce costs.
   c. Full cost transfer prices also depart from goal congruence.

11. The use of standard full cost eliminates the negative effect of fluctuations in production efficiency in one division on another segment's performance.

Market-Based Transfer Prices

12. Using market prices as transfer prices is an opportunity cost approach because company segments are charged the same price that an outside company would have to pay.

   a. Under this approach, each company is considered as a complete separate company.
   b. Market prices are established objectively rather than by partners who have an interest in the results.
   c. An argument for using market price is that it represents the opportunity cost of the intermediate product.
   d. Another argument is that if a segment cannot improve on the product enough to recover both the acquisition cost of the product on the open market in addition to the cost of its processing, it should not be in operation.

Negotiated Transfer Prices

13. A transfer price may result from negotiations between the supplying and receiving departments which give weight to competition and a fair return to the supplying division.

   a. A negotiated price is an attempt to resemble an arm's length transfer between a buying and supplying division.
   b. A disadvantage of negotiated transfer prices is that they may be very time-consuming and require frequent reexaminations and revision of prices.

Transfer Prices for Services

14. One department's transfer of services to a second department is part of its sales while it is the second department's purchase of services.

   a. Companies must establish equitable transfer prices to appraise division performance for its own return on invested capital.
   b. Companies can adopt many of the principles applied to the transfer of products for the transfer of services.

Impact of Product/Service Life Cycles on Transfer Prices

15. A different set of environmental and technological factors characterizes each stage in the life cycle of the product or service function.

16. Companies need transfer prices for these generally accepted four stages of the product life cycle: introduction, growth, maturity, and decline.

Recording Internal Transfers

17. The transfers must be recorded within the accounting system; however, intradivisional sales are eliminated from the income statement in consolidated financial statements.

    a. An inventory adjustment allowance may be used to handle any markup that is made between divisions. This is a contra account to inventory for external financial reporting.
    b. The Inventory Adjustment Allowance account allows for intracompany transactions in which inventories are sold at prices above cost to be eliminated from both the overall company statement of financial position and the income statement.

Multinational Transfer Pricing

18. Transfers of goods and services between segments located in different countries should reflect each countries' different tax rates and tax regulations.

    a. Companies often increase or decrease the transfer price to gain a tax advantage.
    b. Some countries also restrict the payment of income or dividends to parties outside their national borders.

Dual Transfer Pricing

19. One transfer pricing basis may not be accepted by all parties nor may one basis fulfill all the needs of management. Dual pricing allows each segment to use the transfer price which provides the optimum decision for the segment.

    a. Dual pricing can be used to evaluate performance and still allow goal congruence and autonomy.
    b. Dual pricing provides problems for the accountant as company profit does not equal the sum of division profits.

Missing Incentive to Control Cost

20. An additional disadvantage is that dual pricing contains a major inherent weakness because all segment managers may win, but the overall company may lose. The incentive to control costs is missing and inefficiencies may develop.

Behavioral Implications of Transfer Pricing

21. Before choosing a transfer price, management should discuss how the information generated by transfer prices will be used.

22. Transfer pricing guides segment managers toward decisions that lead to an economic allocation of resources.

23. Transfer prices offer a behavioral advantage by providing for units to operate autonomously in a decentralized organization even when there is no externally determined market price for the products and services exchanged internally.

Suboptimization

24. Suboptimization often occurs when the total full cost at the transfer point is greater than the outside purchase price available to the purchasing division. This condition results when segment managers are more concerned about their division's performance and overall company profits are hurt.

    a. A bonus system to segment managers often encourages suboptimization.
    b. The ideal transfer pricing system should motivate segment managers to most effectively fulfill overall company objectives.

25. Transfer prices influence other types of behavior of organizational members.

    a. Coordination between segments is often hampered.
    b. Segmentation encourages members to adopt different decision criteria.
    c. Decentralization also causes members of the organization to have varying perceptions of reality.

Divisional Performance Evaluation

26. The division performance evaluation used by many companies fails to motivate segment managers to fulfill overall company objectives.

Internal Competition

27. Internal competition between segments of a company can be healthy as cost control is often lacking if segment managers feel assured of a market for their production when the company requires buying segments to purchase only within the overall company.

External Procurement

28. A policy regarding outside purchases of products and services should be established.

    a. The product should be purchased internally if the company's own product is superior to or equal in quality and performance to that from outside sources.
    b. It is reasonable to allow division managers the freedom to purchase outside if the external price is lower and the quality comparable.

Demonstration Problem

Short-Run Economic Advantage of Interdivisional Sales

Eastern Division of Platt Company requests that the Western Division supply it with No. A854 valves. Western Division presently operates at capacity and sells valves to outside customers at $2.50 each. The variable costs of these valves produced by the Western Company is $1.40.

Eastern Division, operating at 60 percent capacity because it cannot secure enough valves, is willing to pay $2 for each valve. The cost of the finished product built by the Eastern Division based on normal capacity is as follows:

Valve (the type now being manufactured by Western Division)........	$ 2.00
Other purchased parts	13.00
Other variable costs	8.20
Fixed factory overhead, marketing, and administrative expense	9.00
Total...	$32.20

Platt Company uses dollar net income return on investment in measuring division manager performance.

Required:

a. Ignoring income tax, should the Eastern Division be supplied valves by the Western Division?
b. Ignoring income tax, discuss the short-run economic advantage per unit to the Platt Company if the Western Division supplies valves at $2 each to the Eastern Division.
c. In view of the present organizational structure and long-run economic profits, what recommendation would you make to Platt top management regarding the transfer?

Paper for working Demonstration Problem

a._____

_____

_____

_____

_____

_____

_____

_____

_____

_____

_____

_____

b._____

_____

c.

Solution to Demonstration Problem

Platt Company

a. Western Division should not supply valves at $2 to the Eastern Division because Western Division is now operating at capacity and would lose $.50 ($2.50 - $2.00) for each valve sold to Eastern Division. Measuring the division performance by dollar income and return on investment, the segment performance of Western would be adversely affected.

b. Platt would be $8.50 ($9.00 - $.50) better off if Western Division did sell to the Eastern Division since the Eastern Division is not operating at full capacity. Assuming the $9 fixed factory overhead and marketing and administrative expense represents allocated expense that Eastern would incur regardless of the unit orders, Western would lose $.50 on each order sold to Eastern. However, each unit sold by the Eastern Division to outsiders absorbs $9 allocated expense.

c. In order for Platt Company to gain in the short run, top management must overrule Western Division management and require them to sell to Eastern at $2. These transfers would result in an improved Eastern Division performance at the expense of the Western Division. If Platt plans to keep both divisions operating as autonomous units, top management cannot successfully overrule division management frequently in this manner. Platt may decide that the best alternative is to keep autonomous divisions if this intervention of corporation management is infrequent.

Since there appears to be such a shortage of this specific kind of valve, Platt should consider expanding capacity of the Western Division so that enough valves can be made to satisfy outside customers as well as the Eastern Division. The temporary help to Eastern from Western at Western's expense is not the appropriate long-run answer.

Matching

Referring to the terms listed in the left column, place the appropriate letter next to the corresponding description.   A term may not be used or may be used more than once.

a. Differential cost

b. Dual transfer prices

c. Full-cost transfer prices

d. Market-based transfer prices

e. Negotiated transfer prices

f. Opportunity cost

g. Prime cost

h. Suboptimization

i. Transfer price

_____ 1. Unit price assigned to goods that are distributed among segments.

_____ 2. The increase in cost if a contemplated alternative is added to the present volume.

_____ 3. The maximum contribution to profit lost if the goods are not sold outside the company but are transferred internally.

_____ 4. The most appropriate transfer pricing basis to use when products are actively traded outside the company.

_____ 5. A transfer pricing basis that is determined after discussions with buyer and seller with top management serving as arbitrator.

_____ 6. An approach to transfer pricing which allows buyer and seller to each set the optimum price for each division and still remain within the overall company's goals.

_____ 7. A transfer pricing basis which omits consideration of factory overhead.

_____ 8. A condition which often occurs when the total full cost at the transfer point is greater than the outside purchase price available to the purchasing division.

_____ 9. Under this transfer pricing basis, all benefits accrue to the buying division.

_____ 10. Most appropriate transfer pricing basis when buyer and seller are treated as independent units.

Completion and Exercises

1. List the two basic types of transfer pricing methods and give variations of each type.

   a. _____ ; variations are _____

   _____

   b. _____ ; variations are _____

   _____

2. Briefly discuss three advantages of using full-cost transfer prices.

   a. _____

   b. _____

   _____

   c. _____

   _____

3. Briefly discuss two disadvantages of using full-cost transfer prices.

   a. _____

   _____

   b. _____

   _____

4. What is the principal argument for using market price as the transfer price?

   _____

   _____

5. Give two advantages and two disadvantages of using negotiated transfer prices.
   Advantages:

   a. _____

   _____

   b. _____

   _____

   Disadvantages:

   a. _____

   _____

   b. _____

   _____

6. _____ transfer pricing may represent a solution in which performance is evaluated while goal congruence and autonomy is not destroyed.

7. The major inherent weakness of dual pricing is _____

   _____ .

8. _____ often occurs when bonuses are given to segment managers and they make decisions that are good for their segments but are detrimental to the company as a whole.

9. The cost accountant for the Mischke Company provides you with the following data for the Tire Division:

Division assets

Cash...	$ 100,000
Inventories..	250,000
Plant assets, net...	1,150,000
	$1,500,000

	Per Unit
Variable costs..	$10
Fixed costs (based on normal volume of 40,000 tires)	5

She also informs you that 5,000 of the 40,000 tires are usually sold to the Motorcycle Division of the company. Currently, the two division managers cannot agree on the price to transfer these tires. The Motorcycle Division manager has offered to pay $14, claiming he can purchase these tires from another company at that price. The Tire Division manager believes that the Motorcycle Division should pay the same $18 price as other customers.

Analysis shows that the Tire Division can eliminate $5,000 of inventories, $10,000 in plant assets, and $20,000 in cash fixed costs if the Tire Division manager does not sell to the Motorcycle Division. The assets can be converted into cash.

Required:

a. Should the Tire Division sell to the Motorcycle Division at a transfer price of $14?
b. Assume that top management decides that the tires will be sold to the Motorcycle Division at a $14 transfer price. At which price must the 35,000 tires be sold to outsiders to achieve a 15 percent desired return on assets employed?

a.

b.

10. The Supply Division of Hilton Company is faced with the following budgets when they receive an order for an additional 20,000 units from an outside customer for a bid price of $2.20 per unit. At present, all 80,000 units being produced are sold at $2.40 to the company's Buying Division.

	80,000 Units	100,000 Units
Direct material	$ 32,000	$ 40,000
Direct labor	40,000	50,000
Variable overhead	60,000	75,000
Supervision	15,000	17,000
Rent	6,000	10,000
Depreciation	20,000	20,000
	$173,000	$212,000

Required:

a. Should the order from the outside customer be accepted?
b. In view of the outside order, the Buying Division asks that the Supplying Division cut their price to match the bid price. Prepare an analysis showing your recommendations to the Supplying Division.

a. _____

b. _____

11. Division A of the Bell Company manufactures motors which are used by other divisions of Bell Company and which are also sold to external customers. Division B of Bell Company has requested the Division A to supply a certain style of motor, and Division A has computed a proposed transfer price on this motor, as follows:

	Per Motor
Variable cost	$20
Fixed cost	35
	55
Mark-up on full cost to provide a normal return	15
Total price	$70

Management of Division B believes this transfer price is too high because it knows that this style of motor is sold to outside customers for $65 per motor. Management of Division A indicates that it is forced to lower the price below $70 in order to meet competition. Even though it cannot earn a normal return on sales to external customers, it believes that Division B should pay for this return.

Required:

Explain what you believe the transfer price should be.

_____
_____
_____
_____
_____
_____
_____
_____
_____
_____
_____
_____
_____
_____
_____
_____
_____
_____

12. The Assembly Division of Waltz Company produces components that the Finishing Division incorporates into a final product. Components from the Assembly Division can also be sold to outsiders. Each division has been established as separate profit centers. Data gathered from both divisions' records reveal the following:

Market price--final product	$350
Market price--components	200
Assembly Division--variable cost	150
Finishing Division--variable completion cost	175

Required:

a. Under what conditions should transfers be made to the Finishing Division? Support your answer with a quantitative analysis.
b. Assuming the conditions exist that you suggested in Requirement *a*, at what price do you think transfers should be made?

13. Edmonds Company is a producer of various kinds of batteries. After recently acquiring a lawn mower assembly company, management questions if they should establish two autonomous divisions. Presently the lawn mower company is purchasing 500 batteries a month for $20 each from Miller Company, which then gives them a 4 percent quantity discount.

The Battery Division supplies you with the following costs per battery:

Direct materials	$ 9
Direct labor..	3
Variable factory overhead	1
Fixed factory overhead, based on 1,850 batteries (normal capacity) per month	3
	$16

The Battery Division presently sells 1,850 batteries of this line with a 25 percent markup on sales price. No quantity discount is given by the Battery Division.

Required:

a. Would you advise the Battery Division to sell to the Lawn Mower Division? If so, at what transfer price?
b. Assume instead that the Battery Division presently sells 1,300 to outsiders. With these conditions should the Battery Division sell to the Lawn Mower Division? If so, at what transfer price?
c. Disregard your answer to Requirement *b*, and assume that presently the Battery Division sells 1,300 batteries to outsiders and the Lawn Mower Division manager offers to purchase 500 batteries a month for $14.50 each. What decision would you advise them to make? Why?

a._____

_____

_____

_____

_____

_____

b._____

_____

_____

_____

_____

c._____

_____

_____

_____

_____

_____

_____

_____

True-False Questions

Indicate whether the following statements are true or false by inserting in the blank space a capital "T" for true or "F" for false.

_____ 1. A cost and profit center are terms which are used interchangeably in describing the boundaries of a manager's responsibility.

_____ 2. The prime cost basis for transfer pricing is usually not appropriate because it does not cover all variable costs of the selling unit.

_____ 3 An industry that has diversified into different basic industries usually has few or no transfer pricing problems.

_____ 4. Transfer pricing problems are more significant if the segments are operated as cost centers rather than profit centers.

_____ 5. Profit centers and cost centers are not clear indications of the degree of decentralization as profit centers can exist in highly centralized organizations.

_____ 6. Using full cost as a transfer price has the advantage of evaluating performance of segments because the segment income determined reveals how effective the division functions in a competitive market.

_____ 7. Under conditions in which there is a perfectly competitive market in which the maximum available output may be sold, the opportunity cost to the selling segment is the market price less the differential costs incurred for the product.

_____ 8. In using the market price as a transfer pricing basis, management can appropriately estimate what the price would be if it could be sold in an outside competitive market.

_____ 9. A differential cost transfer price gives weight to competition and a fair return to the supply division.

_____ 10. Market prices can be effectively used as transfer prices in nonrepetitive transfers.

Solutions

Matching

1. i   6. b
2. a   7. g
3. f   8. h
4. d   9. b and/or a
5. e   10. d

Completion and Exercises

1. a. Some form of cost derived from the company books; variations include full cost, variable cost, opportunity, differential, or marginal cost.
   b. Market price variations include negotiated price or some variation of these two methods.

2. The following are advantages of using full cost transfer prices:

   a. Full cost is firmly established because the data is used for external reporting.
   b. Full cost data are already available.
   c. Full cost transfer prices leave no intracompany profits in inventory.
   d. Internal Revenue Service endorses full cost transfer prices.

3. a. Full costs do not create incentives for segment managers to control or reduce costs.
   b. Full costs have little worth for evaluating performance since an income is not shown on interdivisional sales.
   c. Accumulated inefficiencies from divisions which previously handled the product are passed on and affect reported incomes of later divisions.

4. The principal argument is that market price represents the opportunity cost of the intermediate product; the buying unit is paying the same price as if the segment was forced to buy from an outside source. The use of market price creates a fair and equal chance for both the buying and selling departments to make the largest profit they each can.

5. Advantages of using negotiated transfer prices include the following:
   a. A transfer price is developed which gives weight to competition and also a fair return to the supplying division.
   b. An arm's length transaction is simulated.
   c. This method recognizes that often sales of intracompany products are in such a large volume that the use of any market price is meaningless because the quoted market price is based on smaller, normal order sizes.

   Disadvantages of using negotiated transfer prices include the following:

   a. Negotiations may be very time consuming and require frequent reexamination and revision of prices.
   b. There may be an established market price and the segment managers cannot reach agreement.
   c. If arbitration between segments becomes necessary, the purpose of decentralization and profit centers is subverted and divisional authority is breached.

6. Dual

7. Because the buying segment purchases at low prices under dual prices while the supplying segment sells at a high price, the incentive to control cost is missing and inefficiencies may develop.

8. Suboptimization

9. *Mischke*

    a. Cash flow if sales are not made:
        Investment in assets ($5,000 + $10,000) $15,000
        Fixed costs 20,000
        $35,000

        Less:
        Lost contribution margin ($14 - $10 = $4 unit contribution margin X
            5,000 units) 20,000
        Net Cash Flow $15,000

    Based on the above data, the transfer price of $14 should not be accepted because the savings in asset investment and fixed costs more than offset the lost contribution margin.

    b. Let X = Unit selling price of outside sales
        $5 fixed X 40,000 = $200,000
        35,000X + 5,000 ($14) = 40,000 ($10) + $200,000 + $225,000
        (15% X $1,500,000)
        35,000X = $825,000 - $70,000
        35,000X = $755,000
        X = $21.57

10. *Hilton Company*

    a. Differential income of producing 20,000 more units will be:

        Differential Revenue (20,000 units X $2.20) $44,000
        Differential Cost:
        Direct Material ($.40 X 20,000 units) .... $ 8,000
        Direct Labor ($.50 X 20,000 units) 10,000
        Variable Overhead ($.75 X 20,000 units) 15,000
        Supervision ($17,000 - $15,000) 2,000
        Rent ($10,000 - $6,000) 4,000   39,000
        Differential Income .... $ 5,000

    Based on differential income analysis, the order should be accepted.

    b. The $2.20 bid price barely covers the average unit cost of $2.1625 ($173,000/80,000). If 80,000 units are sold at $2.20, the Supply Division would earn $3,000 income as follows:

        Sales ($2.20 X 80,000 units) $176,000
        Cost of 80,000 units 173,000
        $ 3,000

    This would be in addition to the $5,000 earned from the outside customer.

    Before making a final recommendation, costs and market price of the Buying Division's output should be studied. It seems unfair for the Buying Division to earn a large income at the expense of the Supplying Division.

    In addition, the analysis and importance that top management places on divisional income should be studied. If each division manager earns a bonus on divisional income, this would have a large impact on the transfer price.

11. *Bell Company*

While the problem does not state if Division B earns a normal return on the products it sells, it appears unfair to expect Division B to pay more than Division A charges outside customers. The transfer price should be based on the market price of $65 which still covers full cost and allows Division A some profit.

12. *Waltz Company*

a.

Market price - final product...		$350
Transferred-in market price of components...............	$200	
Finishing Division-variable cost	175	375
Contribution loss on product		$ (25)

As can be seen above, no transfers should be made unless the Assembly Division has excess capacity and cannot sell the components to outsiders.

If excess capacity exists, it is possible to transfer components to the Finishing Division and for the overall company to have a contribution to fixed costs as follows:

Market price-final product		$350
Assembly Division-variable cost	$150	
Finishing Division-variable cost	175	325
Contribution margin		$ 25

However, in order to transfer components to the Finishing Division at variable cost, the price to Assembly Division's outside customers should not be cut. If the outside price is cut, all Assembly's fixed costs may not be covered.

b. Variable cost of $150 would be the minimum transfer price while the maximum price would be $175 ($350 - $175). The transfer price should be negotiated somewhere between $150 and $175.

13. *Edmonds Company*

$$\frac{\$16}{.75} = \$21.33 \text{ Battery Division's sales price to outside}$$

$20 X 96% = $19.20 Lawn Mower Division's purchase price from Miller Company

a. No. The Battery Division is presently selling all it can produce at a price higher than what Miller Company is selling to the Lawn Mower Division. Therefore, each division and the company as a whole is better off buying and selling outside.

b. Yes. The Battery Division has excess capacity and it would help the company as a whole to sell to the Lawn Mower Division. In this case, the Battery Division could sell batteries to the Lawn Mower Division at a minimum price of $13.00 (variable costs). However, it may be more appropriate to use a transfer price of $16.10, ($19.20 - $13.00 = $6.20/2 + $13.00 = $16.10) thus splitting the benefits between the two divisions. The maximum price it should charge would be $19.20, the price the Lawn Mower Division can buy from outsiders.

c. The Battery Division would be advised to sell the batteries at $14.50 since a contribution to fixed costs would be made, and there is excess capacity. The price of $14.50 will cover all variable costs and also $750 (500 X $1.50) of fixed costs. These fixed costs would be incurred whether they sell or not, and by selling, they will be able to recover a portion of fixed cost.

True-False

1. F   The terms cost center and profit center cannot be used interchangeably; a manager of a profit center is accountable for both revenues and costs while a cost center manager is responsible only for costs.

2. T   Variable factory overhead is not included: prime cost refers to direct material and direct labor.

3. T

4. F   Managers of cost centers are responsible for costs only whereas profit center managers are responsible for both revenues and costs. Transfer pricing becomes more significant within profit centers.

5. T

6. F   Market price used as a transfer price offers this advantage, not full cost.

7. T

8. F   The existence of a well-developed competitive market outside of the company is required in using market price as an appropriate transfer pricing basis; this is one of the serious disadvantages of its use.

9. F   The statement describes a negotiated transfer price, not a differential cost transfer price.

10. F   Repetitive transfers are needed to effectively use market price as a transfer pricing basis.

16 Decision Models and Cost Analysis Under Uncertainty

Chapter Outline

Framework for Decision Making
　　Constraints on Decision Making
　　Relevant-Irrelevant Costs
Differential Cost Analysis
　　Cost Behavior for Volume and Transaction Changes
　　Accept-or-Decline Decisions
　　Make-or-Buy Decisions
　　Escapable Costs
　　Dangers of Differential Cost Analysis
Opportunity Cost Analysis
　　Payoffs of Alternative Actions
　　Quantified Regrets Table
Decision Making Under Uncertainty
　　Assigning Probabilities
　　Expected Value of Perfect Information
　　Probabilities in Investigating Variances
　　Expected Value of Investigation
Replacement Cost Analysis
　　Replacement Cost of Plant and Equipment
　　Replacement Cost of Land
　　Restatement of Inventories

Chapter Objectives

After studying this chapter, you should be able to:

1. Discuss the factors affecting decision making and the constraints placed on the decision maker.

2. Employ different costs in various decision models used in uncertain situations.

3. Illustrate the various applications of differential costs in decision making, such as making or buying, accepting or declining sales orders, and eliminating segments.

4. Understand the advantages of calculating the payoff and expected values of the alternatives being considered as opposed to a subjective evaluation of opportunity cost.

5. Explain the role of probabilities in optimizing correction and inspection costs in deciding which variances to investigate.

6. Discuss the relevance of replacement cost data to decision making.

7. Define and apply the new terms introduced.

Chapter Review

Framework for Decision Making

1. Decision making is the process of studying and evaluating two or more available alternatives leading to a final choice.

Constraints on Decision Making

2. There are both external and internal constraints on decision making.

   a. The decision maker must have the necessary authority to make and implement the decision.
   b. The physical welfare of subordinates, superiors, and others, and their opinions must be considered.
   c. The economic climate, such as high tariffs adopted by governmental agencies, must be considered.
   d. The technology may not be advanced enough to implement the decision.
   e. Time influences decisions because the shorter the time planned for, the less planning there can be.

Relevant-Irrelevant Costs

3. Relevant costs are those that are valid and bear upon the decision to be made.

   a. Out-of-pocket costs are relevant costs because they involve either an immediate or near-future cash outlay.

4. Sunk costs are historical expenditures for equipment or other productive resources which have no economic relevance to the present decision-making process.

   a. A decision was made in the past to incur these costs and no present or future decision can change them.
   b. Because sunk costs are irrevocable in a given situation, they are not used in replacement decisions.
   c. Plant asset investments are common examples of sunk costs because after the physical facilities are installed, management can either use the asset and attempt to recover the costs through the revenue generated by the asset or sell the plant asset, realizing market value.
   d. In deciding whether to continue or abandon operations, the book value of any equipment that will be discarded at no scrap value is ignored.

Differential Cost Analysis

5. Differential or incremental costs are useful in planning and decision making as these are the differences in cost between two alternatives.

   a. Differential cost analysis is useful in finding the most profitable stage at which to sell products in situations where there is a ready market or the product can be further processed.
   b. Alternative choice problems such as accepting or rejecting orders, make-or-buy decisions and increasing or abandoning operations also are appropriate for application of differential cost analysis.

6. Differential costs are similar to marginal costs except that usually marginal costs are used to refer to the change in total cost resulting from increasing the volume of activity by one unit per period.

   a. If fixed and semivariable costs do not increase from the enlarged production, marginal cost is measured by the change in total variable cost.

Cost Behavior for Volume and Transaction Changes

7. Even though a differential cost is more likely to be variable or semivariable, fixed costs can be included among differential costs when a change in capacity is anticipated.

Accept-or-Decline Decisions

8. Flexible budgets employing differential cost analysis are useful for decision making and profit planning in accept-or-decline decisions.

   a. Contribution margin and differential cost analysis are not valid for use in long-term planning and pricing.
   b. By using differential cost analysis, management often accepts the fact that if profits cannot be obtained, they will accept a contribution to overhead.

9. The Robinson-Patman Amendment may be a legal deterrent to accepting or rejecting orders based on differential profit analysis.

   a. This amendment indicates that a company cannot quote different prices to different competing customers unless such price differentials represent cost savings passed on.
   b. Courts have generally held that costs established with the exclusion of fixed costs cannot be accepted as a defense for price differentials.

Make-or-Buy Decisions

10. In make-or-buy decisions, which are internal, the company does not have to be concerned whether it is violating government regulations or not; in this situation, differential costs are appropriate to use in the analysis.

    a. Make-or-buy decisions involve such internal factors as the desire to control the quality of an asset.
    b. The objective is to use existing production facilities in the most profitable manner.
    c. Clear cut rules are difficult to make regarding make-or-buy decisions as individual situations have varying priorities and constraints.
    d. Future costs as well as present costs must be considered in make-or-buy decisions.
    e. The technical ability of the labor that will be utilized in making the products is another important factor.

Escapable Costs

11. Managers must make a distinction in cost behavior when they are considering eliminating a product, department, or other segment.

    a. Those costs that are eliminated if the activity is discontinued are referred to as escapable costs.
       1. Escapable costs are those costs so directly related to the activity that they are not incurred if the activity is suspended.
    b. Nonescapable costs are the costs which are not eliminated if the segment is eliminated but will be reassigned to other segments.
    c. Only escapable costs are relevant to make-or-buy decisions.

Dangers of Differential Cost Analysis

12. While contribution margin and differential cost analysis are useful for accept-or-decline decisions, they are not valid for use in long-term planning and pricing.

Opportunity Cost Analysis

13. Opportunity cost is defined as the profit that is lost by the diversion of an input factor from one use to another.

   a. Opportunity costs are not ordinarily incorporated in formal accounting systems because they do not involve cash receipts or outlays.
   b. Opportunity costs do have significance in decision making because rejected alternatives should be considered.
   c. The merits of rejected alternatives should be compared against the selected alternative's actions so that the value can be better determined. This is the reason opportunity costs are referred to as alternative costs.

Payoffs of Alternative Actions

14. The payoff, or net benefit of each alternative being considered, can be displayed on a payoff table.

Quantified Regrets Table

15. A quantified regrets table showing the opportunity of alternative actions or the return foregone is helpful in decision making.

   a. The highest payoff under each forecasted market condition is used to compare against the payoff of other alternatives.
   b. The most desirable alternative is the one whose maximum opportunity cost is a minimum.

Decision Making under Uncertainty

16. A weighted payoff reflecting the probability of an event happening can be computed, which is referred to as the expected value.

   a. Each possible payoff is multiplied by its probability and the products added to yield expected value.
   b. An opportunity gain is the difference between the highest expected value and that of other alternatives.

Assigning Probabilities

17. Decision makers assign probabilities of various outcomes occurring.

   a. A probability distribution describes the chance or likelihood of each of the collectively exhaustive and mutually exclusive set of events.
   b. Expected monetary value is the resultant weighted payoff which is found by multiplying each possible payoff by its probability and adding the products.
   c. The difference between the highest expected value and that of other alternatives represents an opportunity gain from investing in the most desirable alternative rather than the other alternatives.

Expected Value of Perfect Information

18. An organization may wish to acquire additional research information concerning the possible states of the events; the amount that it should pay for this errorless advice is called the expected value of perfect information.

   a. The expected value *with* perfect information is compared with the expected value *with* existing information to yield a difference which is the expected value of perfect information.
   b. The expected value of perfect information is the maximum amount to spend for perfect information because perfect forecasters are difficult to find in a real world.

Probabilities In Investigating Variances

19. Probabilities can also be used in deciding when to investigate variances from standards and budgets.

   a. Using the payoff table format with the two possible conditions or states--being in control or being out of control--the two alternatives of investigating or not investigating are available.
   b. Using the following formula, a point of indifference can be determined at which the expected cost of each alternative is the same.

   Let p = Level of probability where alternatives are the same
   I = Inspection cost
   C = Correction cost
   E = Extra cost of later actions

   $$p = \frac{I}{E - C}$$

Expected Value of Investigation

20. A payoff table can be used to determine if a variance should be investigated by comparing the expected value or costs of investigating versus not investigating.

Replacement Cost Analysis

21. Replacement cost is useful in decision making as it indicates what would be paid for assets if they were acquired at current prices.

   a. Financial records use historical costs and replacement costs are not usually entered in the accounting records.
   b. The replacement cost chosen may be based on prices in the current market or on an anticipated future market.
   c. Replacement cost assumes survival of the company is a basic objective and no income should be recognized unless there has been adequate provision made for survival.

Replacement Cost of Plant and Equipment

22. Replacement cost data is usually used more in decisions regarding plant assets which are depreciable.

   a. The impact of changing conditions on the specific properties a company owns and operates is important for make-or-buy decisions and for decisions concerning plant improvements.
   b. There is difficulty in estimating replacement cost because the distinction between the physical object of the plant asset and the services it renders may be hard to make.

Replacement Cost of Land

23. The replacement cost of land depends partially on the use that is made of the land.

Replacement of Inventories

24. Inventories and other assets may be restated to a replacement cost basis.

25. Even though replacement costs are not substitutes for historical costs for external reporting, they can be useful in internal decision making.

Demonstration Problem

Make-or-Buy Decision

Waters Company manufactures Part A for use in its production cycle. The costs per unit for 1,000 units of Part A are as follows:

Direct materials	$ 2
Direct labor............................	10
Variable overhead	3
Fixed overhead	6
	$21

Another company has offered to sell Waters 1,000 units of Part A. If Waters accepts this offer, the released facilities could be used to save $4,000 in relevant costs in the manufacture of Part B. In addition, $2 per unit of the fixed overhead applied to Part A would be totally eliminated.

Required:

Using the following three different purchase prices, determine if the company should manufacture Part A or buy the part. Indicate by what amount the alternative is more desirable.

a. $16.
b. $20.
c. $23.

Paper for working Demonstration Problem

a.

b.

c.

Solution to Demonstration Problem

Waters Company

a.   **$16 Purchase Price**

Manufacture A

Direct materials (1,000 x $2)	$ 2,000	
Direct labor: (1,000 x $10)	10,000	
Variable overhead (1,000 x $3)	3,000	
Fixed overhead (1,000 x $2*)	2,000	
Total cost		$17,000

Buy A

Purchase price of A (1,000 x $16)...............	$16,000	
Less cost savings on Part B........................	(4,000)	
Total cost		12,000
Cost saving to buy		$ 5,000

Buy Part A--$5,000 is saved

_____

   *The relevant cost is the $2 cost which is avoided if Part A is not manufactured.

b.   **$20 Purchase Price**

Buy A

Purchase price of A (1,000 x $20)...............	$20,000	
Less cost savings on Part B........................	(4,000)	
Total cost		$16,000
Manufacture A (from above).........................		17,000
Cost saving to buy		$ 1,000

Buy Part A--$1,000 is saved

c.   **$23 Purchase Price**

Buy A

Purchase price of A (1,000 x $23)...............	$23,000	
Less cost savings on Part B........................	(4,000)	
Total cost		$19,000
Manufacture A (from above).........................		17,000
Cost saving to buy		$ 2,000

Manufacture Part A--$2,000 is saved

Matching

Referring to the terms listed in the left column, place the appropriate letter next to the corresponding description. A term may not be used or may be used more than once.

a. Alternative costs

b. Escapable costs

c. Expected value

d. Expected value of perfect information

e. Incremental cost

f. Irrelevant costs

g. Marginal costs

h. Nonescapable costs

i. Opportunity costs

j. Out-of-pocket cost

k. Payoff

l. Relevant costs

m. Replacement costs

n. Sunk costs

_____ 1. Commitment of funds made in the past about which nothing can be done at the present time.

_____ 2. A cost which requires cash or some other future outlay of resources.

_____ 3. The cost of producing *one* more unit.

_____ 4. Differences in cost between two alternatives.

_____ 5. Costs which are pertinent or valid and bear upon the decision to be made.

_____ 6. Costs so directly related to an activity that they will be eliminated if the activity is suspended.

_____ 7. Profit that is lost by the diversion of an input factor from one use to another.

_____ 8. Another name for opportunity costs.

_____ 9. Net benefit expected for each alternative being considered under possible states of the environment.

_____ 10. Costs such as allocated home office expense which continue even if an activity is eliminated.

_____ 11. Payoff weighted for the probabilities assigned to possible states of the environment.

_____ 12. Costs which indicate what would be paid for assets if they were acquired at current prices.

_____ 13. Sunk costs and other costs which are not used in decision making.

_____ 14. Amount a company is willing to pay for errorless advice in decision making.

_____ 15. Type of costs which is useful when a company is faced with an accept-or-decline decision.

Completion and Exercises

1. The costs which are added when a project is extended beyond its originally intended plans are referred to as _____ costs.

2. For decision making Company XYZ includes in the cost of a plant asset the interest charge based on the company's own funds invested in the asset. Company XYZ included the charge to obtain a cost which is comparable to that which would have been if funds had been borrowed to finance the acquisition of the plant asset. The term describing the interest charge is _____.

3. Discuss 3 dangers in short-term pricing strategy in which variable and differential costs are the basis for prices.

   a._____

   _____

   b._____

   _____

   c._____

   _____

4. In deciding whether to eliminate a product, customer type, or department, if_____

   _____ exceeds _____ _____ , the

   product, customer, or department should be retained unless an alternative is available which will make

   a larger _____ _____ _____ _____ .

5. Rather than accept an outside company's offer to rent one of its warehouses, ABC Company elects to store its safety stock of inventory in the warehouse. Warehousing costs has been charged with the monthly rental revenue offered by an outside company. This cost is known as _____.

6. The marketing department of Brown Company believes demand for the company's product is sufficient to warrant an increase in production. To support its proposal for the expansion in the product line, the total additional costs involved for the capacity level proposed by the marketing department is calculated. The increase in total costs for the product line expansion is _____ costs.

7. _____ are those costs which require immediate or near future cash outlays to implement a decision process.

8. Depreciation on the cost of an existing machine that is operating satisfactorily, but which management is considering replacing, is omitted from the analysis in judging the replacement proposal. This depreciation is referred to as a _____ cost.

9. _____ are nearly always present in decision making, but they never enter the accounting records because there is no cash outlay.

10. A _____ is one which impacts upon the decision to be made presently; such costs will be necessary for the decision.

11. _____ are those costs which can be avoided through alternative decision choices.

12. Give three internal or external constraints to decision making.

a. _____

_____

b. _____

_____

c. _____

_____

13. According to the _____ - _____ Amendment, price discrimination

is unlawful unless such price differentials represent _____

_____ which are passed on to the quotations.

14. The objective of make-or-buy decisions and accept-or-decline decisions

is_____

_____

_____.

15. Accepting a one-time order at a price below the normal sales price will make a positive contribution to income as long as the sales price is greater than unit _____ cost.

16. Give the usual escapable or nonescapable classification of the following if managers are considering eliminating Product Line A. (Use E for escapable and N for nonescapable.)

_____a. Direct material for Product A
_____b. President's clerical staff
_____c. Commission paid on Product A sales
_____d. Vice-president's salary
_____e. Rent and insurance on facilities
_____f. Product A line supervisors

17. _____ and _____ are terms which are synonymous with differential costs.

18. According to the replacement cost theory, _____ is a basic objective of the company and reported income should not be positive unless provision has been made for this.

19. Costs which are not used in decision making, such as future costs which remain unchanged between alternatives, are referred to as _____.

20. The objective in setting a sales price is to select one that will maximize total _____ _____.

21. Replacement cost data can be more appropriately used in decisions regarding
_____ assets.

22. The Washington Company is operating at 70 percent of capacity producing 7,000 units. Variable costs amount to $50 per unit. Wholesaler X offers to buy up to 3,000 units at $60 per unit. Wholesaler Y proposes to buy 2,500 units at $65 per unit. Which offer, if any, should the Washington Company accept?

_____

_____

_____

_____

23. Analysis of Product A reveals that it is losing $10,000 annually; 20,000 units of Product A are sold at a price of $10 per unit each year. If variable costs are $8 per unit, what would be the increase (decrease) in company earnings if Product A were eliminated?

_____

_____

_____

_____

_____

_____

24. Schwartz Company is considering manufacturing a special order of 4,000 products for an agency of the government. Before receiving the special order, the company had planned to manufacture 50,000 units of the product for a total cost of $250,000. The production manager estimates that if the order from the governmental agency is accepted, the unit cost of all units produced will decrease from $5 to $4.75.

The 50,000 units of regular production will be sold for $6 each; however, the government agency is willing to pay the company only $3 per unit for the 4,000 units.

Required: Prepare an analysis indicating the advantage or disadvantage if the company accepts the order from the government agency.

25. Relevant Costs for Make-or-Buy Decision

Carr Company has established the following standard cost for two component parts it uses in processing:

	Machine Part X2	Machine Part Y4
Direct material	$2.00	$ 1.20
Direct labor	1.25	3.80
Factory overhead--variable	2.75	2.00
Factory overhead-- fixed	3.00	4.00
Total	$9.00	$11.00

The company has been producing the 10,000 units of X2 and the 9,000 of Y4 needed annually. However, a recent fire destroyed part of the building in which the parts were manufactured. As a result, only 87,000 hours of otherwise idle machine-hours can be devoted to the production of these two parts. An outside company has offered to supply a comparable quality of parts at $9.50 for X2 and $12.50 for Y4. Management wants to schedule the 87,000 available machine-hours so that the company realizes maximum potential cost savings. Each unit of X2 requires seven machine-hours while Y4 requires five machine-hours.

Required:

a. What costs are relevant to the make-or-buy decision? (Determine these on a unit cost basis for each machine part.)
b. To meet the company's current needs, determine the number of units of X2 and Y4 to be produced assuming the allocation of machine time is based on potential cost savings per machine-hour.

26. Cost Savings Which Warrant Investigation

Engineers at Seattle, Inc., are indifferent about beginning an investigation of a variance when there is a probability of 70% that the process is in control. They rely on the cost accountant to estimate the costs of investigation and correction. The cost accountant believes that the cost of investigation is $3,000 and if an out-of-control process is discovered, the cost of correction is $4,000.

Required:

What size must the present value of the cost savings be to justify an investigation?

True-False Questions

Indicate whether the following statements are true or false by inserting in the blank space a capital "T" for true or "F" for false.

_____ 1.   Opportunity costs constitute a vital part of decision making but are omitted from conventional accounting records.

_____ 2.   In make-or-buy decisions only variable costs are relevant.

_____ 3.   The type of costs presented to management for equipment replacement decisions should be limited to controllable costs.

_____ 4.   Fixed costs are normally relevant to the decision when management is considering eliminating customer, product line, or other segment.

_____ 5.   In deciding to abandon operations, the accountants must consider the book value of any equipment that will be replaced as well as other incremental operating costs.

_____ 6.   If a product line's differential cost is greater than its differential revenue, it should be eliminated unless sales of other products would be adversely affected.

_____ 7.   Sunk costs are an essential part of decision making in equipment replacement.

_____ 8.   Even though a particular segment may incur a net loss, management may wisely decide to retain it because it is absorbing more indirect allocated costs than is its loss.

_____ 9.   The level of fixed costs should influence the decision to accept or reject an order when a company is operating at less than capacity and it receives an offer to produce a special order at a lower-than-normal price from a customer in a market different from the regular market. Assume further that the only relevant costs are the variable costs.

_____10.   Fixed costs that will continue regardless of a make-or-buy decision should not be considered in choosing whether to make a part internally or buy it from an outsider.

SOLUTIONS

Matching

1.	n	9.	k
2.	j	10.	h
3.	g	11.	c
4.	e	12.	m
5.	l	13.	f
6.	b	14.	d
7.	i or a	15.	e
8.	a		

Completion and Exercises

1. Differential costs

2. Imputed interest

3. Dangers in short-term pricing include the following:

   a. Price reduction may be carried over to sales of repeat orders and into future periods; such pricing strategy should be applied to nonrepeat orders which will not compete with the regular sales of products at the normal sales price.
   b. The company may be in violation of the Robinson-Patman Amendment.
   c. Such pricing techniques should not be applied unless the orders are different in design or brand name from current product lines.
   d. Separating fixed and variable costs may be difficult and a wrong classification may be misleading.
   e. All costs, both fixed and variable, must be covered in the long run and applying short-term pricing to longer periods is dangerous.

4. Differential revenue; differential expenses; contribution to fixed expenses (or income).

5. Imputed rent.

6. differential or incremental costs

7. Out-of-pocket-costs

8. sunk

9. Opportunity costs

10. relevant cost

11. Escapable costs

12. a. Economic environment, such as high tariffs.
    b. Physical welfare of subordinates and superiors.
    c. Opinions of subordinates and superiors.
    d. Technology of the industry may be limiting.
    e. Time factors.
    f. Decision maker must have the necessary authority to make and implement the decision.

13. Robinson-Patman; cost savings

14. The objective is to profitably use production capacity available with the existing facilities.

15. differential (usually only the variable).

16. a. E
    b. N
    c. E
    d. N
    e. N
    f. E

17. Incremental; marginal

18. survival

19. irrelevant

20. contribution margin

21. depreciable

22. The Washington Company should accept Y's offer. Contribution margin for X is 3,000 X ($60 - $50) = $30,000. It is 2,500 x ($65 - $50) = $37,500 for Y. Thus, accepting Y's offer results in $7,500 more total contribution margin than X's proposal.

23.
Revenue from Product A ($10 x 20,000 units)	$200,000
Variable costs of Product A ($8 x 20,000 units)	160,000
Contribution margin	$ 40,000

If this product were eliminated, company earnings would decrease by $40,000 annually unless a more profitable product could be sold in its place.

24. *Schwartz Company*

Differential Revenue (4,000 units X $3)		$ 12,000
Total cost of 54,000 units ($4.75 X 54,000)	$256,500	
Total cost of 50,000 units	250,000	
Differential Cost		6,500
Contribution to Overhead		$ 5,500

The offer should be accepted if there is no danger in disrupting regular sales and this is a one-time order.

25. *Carr Company*

a.
	Machine Part X2	Machine Part Y4
Direct materials	$2.00	$1.20
Direct labor	1.25	3.80
Factory overhead--variable	2.75	2.00
Relevant unit production cost	$6.00	$7.00

b.
Outside purchase price	$9.50	$12.50
Relevant unit production cost (from Requirement *a*)	6.00	7.00
Potential cost savings per unit	$3.50	$ 5.50
Machine hours per unit	÷ 7	÷ 5
Potential cost savings per machine hour	$ .50	$ 1.10

Since the potential cost savings is greater for Y4, priority should be given to using as much capacity as possible to produce Y4. The remaining capacity should then be used to manufacture part X2 with the remaining needed units of X2 to be purchased from the outside supplier.

25. (concluded)
Available idle machine hours 87,000
Part Y4 annual usage (9,000 x 5 hours) .... <u>45,000</u>
Remaining machine hours 42,000
Part X2 annual usage in units... 10,000

Units to be manufactured
$\left(\dfrac{42{,}000 \text{ remaining machine hours}}{7 \text{ machine hours per unit}}\right)$ .... <u>6,000</u>
Part X2 units to be purchased from outside suppliers .... <u>4,000</u>

26. Seattle, Inc.

The probability of not being in control is 1.00 - .70 = .30

$$p = \frac{I}{E - C}$$

$$.30 = \frac{\$3{,}000}{E - \$4{,}000}$$

$$.30 \, (E - \$4{,}000) = \$3{,}000$$
$$.30E = \$3{,}000 + \$1{,}200$$
$$E = \$4{,}200 \div .30$$
$$E = \$14{,}000$$

True-False

1. T Opportunity costs represent sacrifices made in choosing one alternative over another one. Opportunity costs are not found in the traditional accounting records.

2. F Fixed costs that can be avoided in the future are relevant in make-or-buy decisions.

3. F Only relevant costs should be given to management in equipment replacement decisions.

4. F Fixed costs are normally not differential costs and are not relevant to decisions where a segment is being considered eliminated.

5. F Book value of equipment is irrelevant in decisions to abandon operations as it is a sunk cost and no present or future decisions can change it. Book value of equipment results from a past decision and is irrevocable.

6. T

7. F Sunk costs represent costs from past decisions and have no influence on future replacements of equipment.

8. T

9. F Since fixed costs will not change if the order is accepted, they are not differential and should not influence the decision.

10. T

17 Capital Budgeting

Chapter Outline

Tax Impact on Capital Decisions
> Income Tax Deduction for Depreciation
> Tax Shield

Present Value
> Present Value of A Dollar
> Present Value of an Annuity
> Present Value of Depreciation Tax Shield

Evaluation Techniques for Capital Expenditures
> Net Cash Inflow

Discounted Cash Flow Methods
> Net Present Value Method
> Weighted Net Present Value or Expected Value
> Profitability Index
> Internal Rate of Return

Alternatives to Discounted Cash Flow Methods
> Payback or Payout Method
> Unadjusted Return on Investment

Aftertax Analysis of Equipment Replacement
> Total-Cost Approach
> Differential-Cost Approach

Chapter Objectives

After studying this chapter, you should be able to:

1. Explain the present value concept and how it applies to capital expenditure analysis.

2. Apply discounted cash flow methods of evaluating capital assets.

3. Use payback and other alternatives to discounted cash flow methods.

4. Prepare aftertax analyses for equipment replacement using the total-cost and differential-cost approaches.

5. Define and apply the new terms introduced.

Chapter Review

Tax Impact on Capital Decisions

1. Top management should be involved in capital expenditure proposals to be certain that they follow company objectives.

   a. Middle managers also need some authority because they possess the required competence to properly evaluate the proposal.
   b. Employees should also be encouraged to search for capital improvements; management should guard against encouraging false participation as employees soon detect this and will resent wasting their time in this area unless managers listen to their ideas.

2. Book value, which is the plant asset's original cost less its accumulated depreciation, should not be considered in the analysis of deciding whether to replace a plant asset or not.

3. Income tax laws have a significant impact on capital expenditure analysis.

Income Tax Deduction for Depreciation

4. The amount allowable for depreciation may be reduced below the cost of the asset acquired due to investment credit availability and other factors.

5. Tax authorities allow these three main methods of depreciation:

   a. *Straight-line depreciation.* Each year companies claim an equal amount of depreciation.

   b. *Accelerated depreciation.* Companies write off depreciable assets more quickly than by using straight-line depreciation.

   c. *Allowable percentage write-offs.* Tax legislation specifies a table of percentages for depreciation. These tables usually allow companies to recover the cost of plant assets for tax purposes over a shorter period than the assets' physical lives.

Tax Shield

6. Depreciation of the capital assets is a tax shield because it protects an amount of income equal to the depreciation from taxation.

7. The following formula determines the aftertax net cash inflow from an investment:

Aftertax net cash inflow = [Beforetax net cash inflow X (1 - Tax rate)] + [Depreciation deduction X Tax rate]

   Tax Shield Attributable to Depreciation = Depreciation deduction X Tax rate

Present Value

8. Present value is the value of money today; this concept is important in capital budgeting because of the long term projects involved.

9. Discounting is a process used to convert the cash inflows for each year to their present value.

   a. Each year's cash inflow is multiplied by the appropriate factor from a present value table.
   b. Managers realize a dollar today is worth more than in the future because today's $1 can be put to work earning a return and the company will have more than $1 in the future.

Present Value of A Dollar

10.   The time value of money explains why a dollar today is preferred over receiving a dollar at some future date.

Present Value of an Annuity

11.   An annuity is a series of equal cash flows equally spaced in time.

Present Value of Depreciation Tax Shield

12.   The tax allowance for depreciation is used to stimulate long-term capital investments.

    a.   The faster an asset's cost is depreciated for tax purposes, the sooner the tax reductions are realized and the greater the net present value of the tax shield.
    b.   Present value is maximized when depreciation is claimed as rapidly as possible.

Evaluation Techniques for Capital Expenditures

13.   These are three quantitative methods used in making capital budgeting decisions; they are:

    a.   Discounted cash flow
    b.   Payout or payback
    c.   Unadjusted return on investment

Net Cash Inflow

14.   The discounted cash flow has the following variations:

    a.   Net present value, also referred to as excess present value.
    b.   Internal rate of return; referred to as the time-adjusted rate of return.

Discounted Cash Flow Methods

15.   The net present value method and the internal rate of return are variations of the discounted cash flow method and do consider the time value of money.

Net Present Value Method

16.   The net present value method assumes some minimum desired rate of return.

    a.   The desired rate of return is the rate at which the cash inflows are discounted to the present. The rate is called the hurdle rate, cost of capital, discount rate, or cutoff rate.
    b.   A capital investment proposal is considered acceptable if the present value of the future expected net cash inflows equals or exceeds the amount of the initial investment.

Weighted Net Present Value or Expected Value

17.   The required rate of return can be based on the cost of capital used which is the cost of debt capital added to the cost of equity capital, each weighted by its proportion of the company's total capital structure.

18.   An allowance for risk and uncertainty can be made by determining the present value of the net cash flows for each alternative investment being considered according to various assumptions about future conditions.

    a. Probability weights can be applied to the net present value for normal conditions, optimistic conditions, and pessimistic conditions.
    b. This method is used to estimate the most likely amount of future cash receipts.

Profitability Index

19. A profitability index is computed by relating a proposal's present value of cash inflows to initial outlay; this is also referred to as the present value index.

Internal Rate of Return

20. The internal rate of return is a second variation of the discounted cash flow method which measures profitability.

    a. The internal rate of return differs from the net present value method because no discount rate is known in advance.
    b. A trial and error approach is used until a discounted rate is found that yields a zero net present value.

Alternatives to Discounted Cash Flow Methods

21. Evaluations of capital expenditures are available which do not consider the time value of money; these evaluations satisfy an immediate pressing need because time or data is not available for applying more sophisticated analysis.

Payback or Payout Method

22. The payback method measures the length of time required to recover the initial outlay for a project.

    a. This method is weak as it ignores the time value of money; however, it represents an improvement over merely basing the capital expenditure analysis on management's intuition.

    b. Professional judgment and the payback method are often used in purchasing plant assets which are necessary to maintain operations.

23. The bailout payback method is a variation of the payback method which focuses on measuring the risk involved in a capital expenditure.

    a. Using this method, the cumulative net increase in aftertax cash flow is added to the disposal value and compared against the plant asset cost to determine when the original cost is recovered.

    b. This method attempts to answer how soon an investment would be recovered if operations become unprofitable.

Unadjusted Return on Investment

24. The unadjusted return on investment is known as the book value rate of return, the accounting or financial statement method, or the approximate value of return.

    a. Accountants use the following equation to determine the unadjusted return on investment:

$$\frac{\text{Average annual net aftertax income}}{\text{Initial investment}}$$

    b. Instead of computing a return on initial investment, accountants can determine the return on average investment.

1. When straight-line depreciation is not used, the book values at the end of each year are added to the original book value to determine an average investment.
2. If instead, straight-line depreciation is used, the original investment can be divided by 2 to arrive at the average investment.
3. If the asset has a scrap value at the end of its economic life, the scrap value would be added to determine average investment regardless of the depreciation method.

Aftertax Analysis of Equipment Replacement

25. Accountants can expand the net present value method to include the total-cost and differential-cost approaches when income taxes are considered.

Total-Cost Approach

26. Several alternatives can be compared when using the total-cost approach showing the present value of cash flows in and out. The tax shield provided by depreciation is also included in the analysis.

Differential-Cost Approach

27. Only differences in cash operating costs, depreciation tax shield, and salvage value are shown in the differential-cost approach.

Demonstration Problem

Net Present Value and Expected Value

Wallis, Inc, is considering the purchase of a machine that will be used in manufacturing a new product developed by the firm's engineering department. The cost of the machine is $150,000, and the machine dealer requires a cash payment on delivery. Life of the machine is expected to be six years; salvage value at the end of the machine's life is forecasted to be $20,000.

Estimates for the success of this new product are difficult to determine; however, based on various market tests, management believes that the availability of personal disposable income will be a critical factor. The following estimates of aftertax cash flow from operations are based on three different market conditions. The probability of a poor market is 30 percent; of a normal market, 55 percent; and the probability of an excellent market, 15 percent.

Year	Poor Market	Normal Market	Excellent Market
1	$10,000	$20,000	$30,000
2	21,000	30,000	45,000
3	35,000	40,000	50,000
4	40,000	45,000	57,000
5	32,000	38,000	45,000
6	18,000	25,000	30,000

Required:

a. Using an interest rate of 8 percent, determine the net present value of the cash flow for each of the three market conditions assumed.

b. Using the information determined in Requirement *a*, calculate the weighted net present value or expected value of the investment.

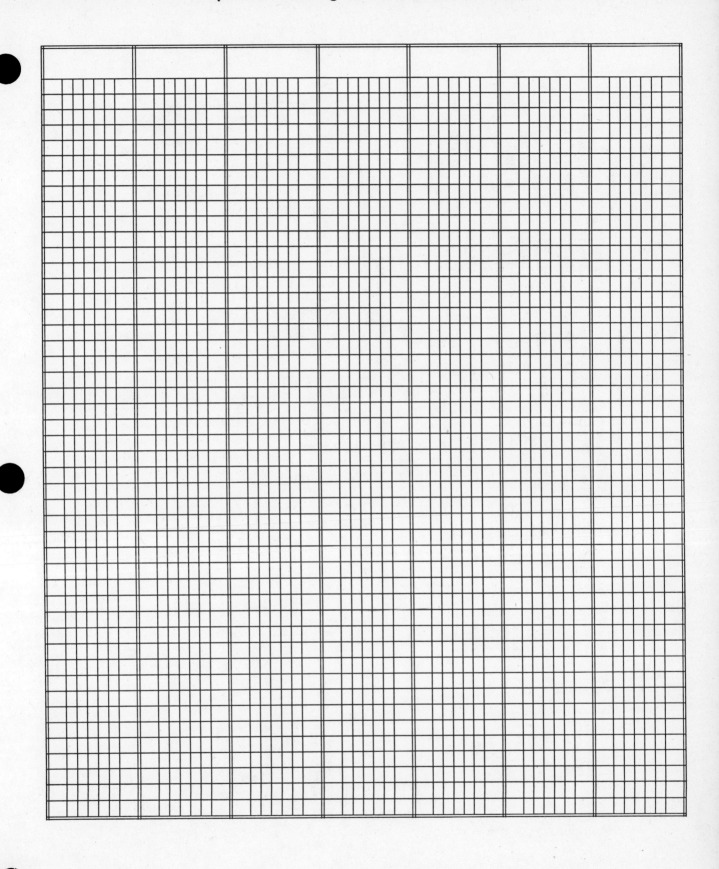

Solution to Demonstration Problem

Wallis, Inc.

a.

Year	Present Value of $1 at 8%	Poor Market Aftertax Cash (Outflow) or Inflow	Poor Market Net Present Value of Flow	Normal Market Aftertax Cash (Outflow) or Inflow	Normal Market Net Present Value of Flow	Excellent Market Aftertax Cash (Outflow) or Inflow	Excellent Market Net Present Value of Flow
0	1.000	$(150,000)	$(150,000)	$(150,000)	$(150,000)	$(150,000)	$(150,000)
1	.926	10,000	9,260	20,000	18,520	30,000	27,780
2	.857	21,000	17,997	30,000	25,710	45,000	38,565
3	.794	35,000	27,790	40,000	31,760	50,000	39,700
4	.735	40,000	29,400	45,000	33,075	57,000	41,895
5	.681	32,000	21,792	38,000	25,878	45,000	30,645
6	.630	38,000*	23,940	45,000*	28,350	50,000*	31,500
			$(19,821)		$ 13,293		$ 60,085

*includes salvage value of $20,000

b.

	Net Present Value	×	Probability weight	= Weighted Net Present Value
Poor Market	$(19,821)	×	30%	$ (5,946.30)
Normal Market	13,293	×	55%	7,311.15
Excellent Market	60,085	×	15%	9,012.75
				$10,377.60

Matching

Referring to the terms listed in the left column, place the appropriate letter next to the corresponding description. A term may not be used or may be used more than once.

a. Bailout payback method

b. Book value

c. Discounting

d. Internal rate of return

e. Investment credit

f. Market value

g. Net present value method

h. Payback or payout method

i. Tax shield

j. Weighted net present value

k. Unadjusted return on investment

_____ 1. A means of stimulating capital investment allowing the deduction of a percentage of depreciable assets purchased from the tax bill.

_____ 2. Amount by which taxable income is reduced due to the deductibility of depreciation and other items.

_____ 3. A capital expenditure analysis focusing on measuring the risk involved in a capital expenditure which asks which alternative offers the best investment if things go wrong.

_____ 4. A variation of the discounted cash flow method which measures project profitability in which no discount rate is known in advance.

_____ 5. An allowance for risk is included by attaching probabilities to various conditions in the environment which are multiplied by the net present value.

_____ 6. Original cost of a plant asset less accumulated depreciation.

_____ 7. A capital asset evaluation method which measures the length of time required to recover the initial outlay for a project while disregarding the time value of money.

_____ 8. A process used to convert cash inflows for each year to their present value.

_____ 9. A capital evaluation technique which considers profitability but ignores the time value of money.

_____ 10. A capital evaluation technique which considers the time value of money by assuming a minimum desired rate of return.

Completion and Exercises

1. State two strengths and two weaknesses of using the payback method in capital expenditure analysis.
   Strengths:

   a. _____

   b. _____

   Weaknesses:

   a. _____

   b. _____

2. When would you advise using the payback method in capital expenditure analysis?

   _____

   _____

3. The three quantitative methods used in making capital budgeting decisions are:

   a. _____

   b. _____

   c. _____

4. While the unadjusted return on investment does consider _____,

   it does fail to consider the _____ _____

   _____ _____.

5. State two strengths and two weaknesses of using the accounting rate of return in capital expenditure analysis.

   Strengths:
   a. _____

   b. _____

   Weaknesses:
   a. _____

   b. _____

6. The_____ capital budgeting evaluation method requires the selection of a discount rate which represents the minimum rate of return desired.

7. State two strengths and two weaknesses of using the internal rate of return in capital expenditure analysis.

   Strengths:
   a. _____

   b. _____

   Weaknesses:
   a. _____

   b. _____

8. The formula to compute the tax shield from depreciation is:

    Tax shield = _____ _____ X _____ _____

9. State two strengths and two weaknesses of using the net present value in capital expenditure analysis.

    Strengths:
    a. _____

    b. _____

    Weaknesses:

    a. _____

    b. _____

10. Edmonds Company is considering the purchase of two different machines; each is capable of producing 3,000 units per year for six years, which will satisfy the requirements of a contract that the company has been offered. Each unit will sell for $35. The data below relate to the use of Machines A and B; neither will have any salvage value at the end of the six year contract period. Use straight-line depreciation and a 48 percent income tax.

	Machine A	Machine B
Cost of machine	$45,000	$56,400
Cost per unit per year:		
Direct material	$15.00	$14.00
Direct labor	7.00	3.00
Factory overhead (excluding depreciation)	1.25	1.10
Marketing and administrative expense	2.00	2.00

Required:

Which machine would you advise Edmonds Company to purchase, using a 12 percent aftertax required rate of return? Prepare present value analysis to support your decision.

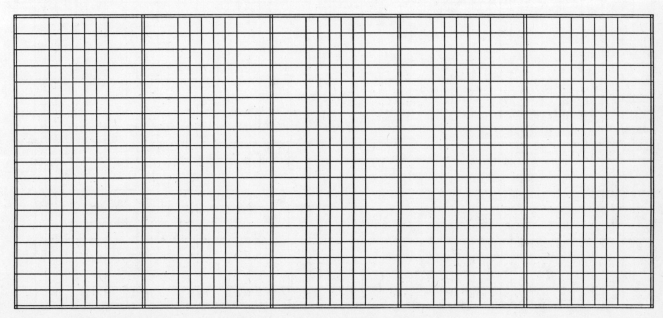

11. Capital Budgeting Techniques

In order to expand production next year, the Crowe Company must purchase a large pressing machine. The capital expenditure committee has narrowed the choice down between a machine sold by the Splitz Company and another machine sold by the Beaven Company. Straight-line depreciation will be used. The following data has been gathered for each machine.

	Splitz Machine	Beaven Machine
Purchase price	$200,000	$194,000
Life	5 years	5 years
Salvage	$ 20,000	$ 29,000
Beforetax cash benefit:		
Year 1	60,000	70,000
Year 2	63,000	75,000
Year 3	65,000	80,000
Year 4	68,000	68,000
Year 5	70,000	60,000

A 48 percent federal income tax rate and a 12 percent cost of capital is to be assumed. Ignore the half-year convention for depreciation.

Required:
Calculate which machine Crowe Company should purchase using each of the following approaches.

a. Payback period.

b. Unadjusted rate of return on initial investment.

c. Net present value and present value payback period.

d. Internal rate of return approach.

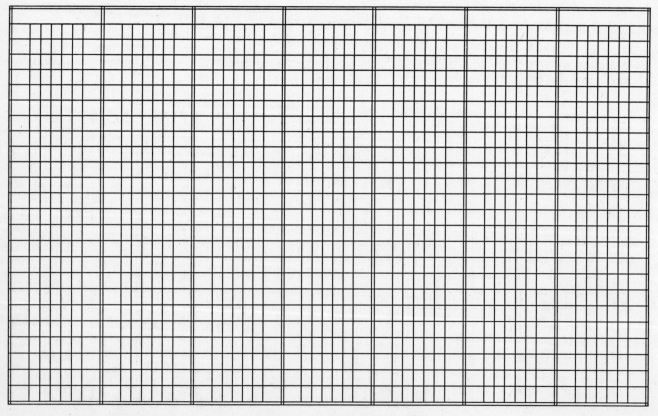

12. **Comparison of Machines**

Penton Company management is evaluating the purchase of either a machine built by the Addleton Company or a longer-lived machine built by the Beaton Company. The Addleton machine costs $53,000 and has a useful life of 12 years, while the Beaton machine costs $55,000 with a useful life of 18 years. Neither machine is expected to have any salvage value at the end of its life. The annual aftertax net cash inflow for both machines is expected to be $14,000. The Addleton machine's disposal value is expected to be $30,000 at the end of the first year and decline at the rate of $4,000 annually. The Beaton machine's disposal value is expected to be $20,000 at the end of the first year and decline by $8,000 annually.

Required:

a. For both machines prepare the following analyses:

    (1) Net present value at 8 percent. (2) Internal rate of return. (3) Bailout payback

b. Which machine would you advise purchasing? Explain why.

a.1.

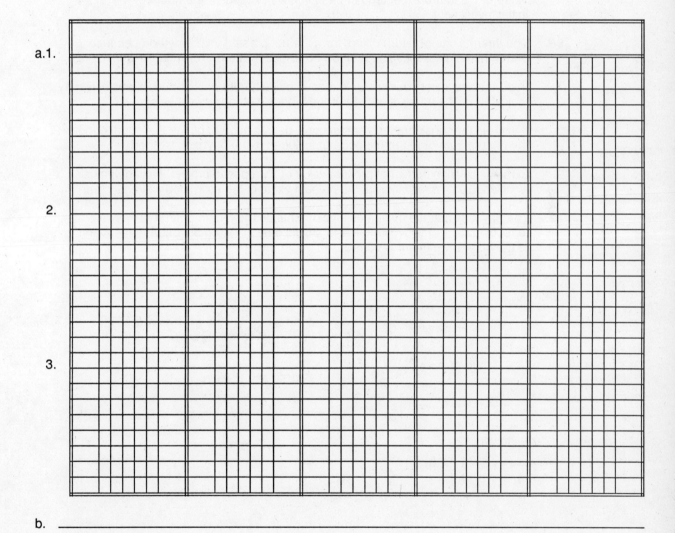

2.

3.

b. _____

_____

_____

True-False Questions

Indicate whether the following statements are true or false by inserting in the blank space a capital "T" for true or "F" for false.

_____ 1. All capital expenditures analysis share the weakness of assuming future cash flows are certain.

_____ 2. The internal rate of return approach uses a trial and error approach before a discounted rate is found that yields a zero net present value.

_____ 3. Using a bailout payback method, the cumulative net increase in aftertax cash flow and disposal value is used to compare against the original cost of the plant asset to determine which asset provides the best protection against risk.

_____ 4. The payout method can be appropriately used for screening capital expenditures proposals for whom decisions must be made rapidly.

_____ 5. Usually a capital investment proposal is not considered acceptable if the present value of the future expected net cash inflows exceeds the amount of the initial investment.

_____ 6. The internal rate of return differs from the net present value method because under the net present value method no discount rate is known in advance.

_____ 7. In purchasing safety devices or luxurious office furniture, cost-benefit analysis may indicate that the unadjusted return or payback method is satisfactory.

_____ 8. If income tax considerations are ignored, depreciation expense is excluded in the internal rate of return method but included in the payback method.

_____ 9. In the calculation of the net present value of a proposed project, salvage value is included as a cash inflow at the present value of the estimated salvage value.

_____ 10. The payback method evaluates investments on the length of time necessary to recover the initial investment and any income or return beyond the recovery of the initial investment is considered under this method.

SOLUTIONS

Matching

1.	e	6.	b
2.	i	7.	h
3.	a	8.	c
4.	d	9.	k
5.	j	10.	g

Completion and Exercises

1. Strengths of payback method:

   a. Simple method requiring little time to prepare and understand.
   b. Represents an improvement over merely basing the decision on management's intuition.
   c. Emphasizes liquidity.

   Weaknesses of payback method:

   a. Lacks needed sophistication.
   b. Does not consider the time value of money.
   c. Salvage value of the capital asset is ignored.
   d. Ignores cash flows after payback period.
   e. Does not measure profitability.

2. The payback method can be effectively used as an initial screening device if time is not available to spend performing the other capital expenditure analyses.

3. a. Payback or payout.
   b. Unadjusted return on investment.
   c. Discounted cash flow including its two variations; net present value and internal rate of return.

4. Profitability; time value of money

5. Strengths of accounting rate of return method:

   a. Ties in with income statement and performance evaluation
   b. Easy to understand and use

   Weaknesses of accounting rate of return method:

   a. Ignores time value of money
   b. Does not emphasize cash flows
   c. Misstates the true return of projects

6. net present value

7. Strengths of internal rate of return method:

   a. Recognizes time value of money
   b. Emphasizes cash flows
   c. Computes true return of projects

   Weaknesses of internal rate of return method:

   a. By assuming that the internal rate of return is the reinvestment rate, the assumption is made of higher reinvestment rates for projects with higher true returns, regardless of the risk involved.

b. Shorter projects are favored.

8. Tax shield = depreciation deduction x tax rate.

9. Strengths of net present value method:

a. Assumes the discount rate is the reinvestment rate which results in using the same reinvestment rate for projects of similar risk.
b. Time value of money is recognized.
c. Emphasizes cash flows.
d. Application is relatively easy.

Weaknesses of net present value method:

a. No change in required rate of return assumed.
b. Larger, longer projects are favored.

10. *Edmonds Company*

	Machine A			Machine B		
Revenue	(3,000 X $35)		$105,000			$105,000
Direct material	(3,000 X $15)	$45,000		(3,000 X $14)	$42,000	
Direct labor	(3,000 X $7)	21,000		(3,000 X $3)	9,000	
Factory overhead	(3,000 X $1.25)	3,750		(3,000 X $1.10)	3,300	
Marketing & administrative expense	(3,000 X $2.00)	6,000		(3,000 X $2.00)	6,000	
Depreciation	($45,000 / 6 years)	7,500	83,250	($56,400 / 6 years)	9,400	69,700
Pretax income			$ 21,750			$ 35,300
Taxes at 48 percent			10,440			16,944
Net income			$11,310			$ 18,356
Add Depreciation			7,500			9,400
Aftertax Cash Flow			$18,810			$ 27,756

CALCULATION OF NET PRESENT VALUE

	Machine A		Machine B	
Present value of aftertax cash inflow for 6 years at 12%	$77,328	(4.111 X $18,810)	$114,105	(4.111 X $27,756)
Less investment	45,000		56,400	
Net present value	$ 32,328		$ 57,705	

Edmonds Company should buy Machine B because of its larger net present value.

11. *Crowe Company*

Splitz Machine

Year	Pretax Cash Benefit	Depreciation	Cash Inflow Subject to Tax	Federal Income Tax at 48%	Net Increase in Aftertax Cash Flow
			$\left(\dfrac{\$180,000}{5 \text{ years}}\right)$		
1	$60,000	$ 36,000	$24,000	$11,520	$ 48,480
2	63,000	36,000	27,000	12,960	50,040
3	65,000	36,000	29,000	13,920	51,080
4	68,000	36,000	32,000	15,360	52,640
5	70,000	36,000	34,000	16,320	53,680
		$180,000			$255,920

Cash inflow at end of economic life from salvage value   20,000

                $275,920

Beaven Machine

Year	Pretax Cash Benefit	Depreciation	Cash Inflow Subject to Tax	Federal Income Tax at 48%	Net Increase in Aftertax Cash Flow
			$\left(\dfrac{\$165,000}{5 \text{ years}}\right)$		
1	70,000	$ 33,000	$37,000	$17,760	$ 52,240
2	75,000	33,000	42,000	20,160	54,840
3	80,000	33,000	47,000	22,560	57,440
4	68,000	33,000	35,000	16,800	51,200
5	60,000	33,000	27,000	12,960	47,040
		$165,000			$262,760

Cash inflow at end of economic life from salvage value   29,000

                $291,760

a.

	Splitz Machine				Beaven Machine	
Year	Cash Flow	Payback Years	Year	Cash Flow	Payback Years	
1	$ 48,480	1.0	1	$ 52,240	1.0	
2	50,040	1.0	2	54,840	1.0	
3	51,080	1.0	3	57,440	1.0	
4	50,400	.96 $\left(\dfrac{50,400}{52,640}\right)$	4	29,480	.58 $\left(\dfrac{29,480}{51,200}\right)$	
	$200,000	3.96 years		$194,000	3.58 years	

b. *Splitz Machine*

$$\frac{\$255,920 - \$180,000}{5 \text{ years}} = \$15,184 \text{ average annual income}$$

$$\frac{\$15,184}{\$200,000} = 7.59\%$$

Beaven Machine

$$\frac{\$262,760 - \$165,000}{5 \text{ years}} = \$19,552$$

$$\frac{\$19,552}{\$194,000} = 10.08\%$$

11. (concluded)

c.

		Splitz Machine		Beaven Machine	
Year	Present Value of $1 at 12%	Cash (Outflow) or Inflow	Net Present Value of Flow	Cash (Outflow) or Inflow	Net Present Value of Flow
0	1.000	$(200,000)	$(200,000)	$(194,000)	$(194,000)
1	.893	48,480	43,293	52,240	46,650
2	.797	50,040	39,882	54,840	43,707
3	.712	51,080	36,369	57,440	40,897
4	.636	52,640	33,479	51,200	32,563
5	.567	73,680*	41,777	76,040*	43,115
	Net Present Value		$ (5,200)		$ 12,932

*Includes salvage value

	Splitz Machine		Beaven Machine	
Year	Cash Flow	Payback Years	Cash Flow	Payback Years
1	$43,293	1.0	$46,650	1.0
2	39,882	1.0	43,707	1.0
3	36,369	1.0	40,897	1.0
4	33,479	1.0	32,563	1.0
5	41,777	1.0	30,183	$.7 \left(\dfrac{30,183}{43,115}\right)$
	$194,800	5.0 years	$194,000	4.7 years

The Splitz Machine will not pay back the original investment because its present value payback period would have to be longer than its life. The Beaven Machine will barely pay back its original investment.

d.

Splitz Machine

			10%		12%
Year	Cash (Outflow) or Inflow	Present Value of $1 at 10%	Net Present Value of Flow	Present Value of $1 at 12%	Net Present Value of Flow
0	$(200,000)	1.000	$(200,000)	1.000	$(200,000)
1	48,480	.909	44,068	.893	43,293
2	50,040	.826	41,333	.797	39,882
3	51,080	.751	38,361	.712	36,369
4	52,640	.683	35,953	.636	33,479
5	73,680	.621	45,755	.567	41,777
			$ 5,470		$ (5,200)

An approximation to the percentage is obtained through interpolation.

$$10\% + \left(2\% \times \frac{\$5,470}{\$10,670}\right) = 10.00\% + 1.03\% = 11.03\%$$

Beaven Machine

Year	Cash (Outflow) or Inflow	Present Value of $1 at 14%	Net Present Value of Flow	Present Value of $1 at 16%	Net Present Value of Flow
0	$(194,000)	1.000	$(194,000)	1.000	$(194,000)
1	52,240	.877	45,814	.862	45,031
2	54,840	.769	42,172	.743	40,746
3	57,440	.675	38,772	.641	36,819
4	51,200	.592	30,310	.552	28,262
5	76,040	.519	39,465	.476	36,195
			$ 2,533		$(6,947)

Through interpolation

$$14\% + \left(2\% \times \frac{2,533}{9,480}\right) = 14.00\% + .53\% = 14.53\%$$

12. *Penton Company*

a. 1. *Net Present Value at 8%*

	Addleton Machine			*Beaton Machine*	

$(53,000) X 1.000 = $(53,000) $(55,000)X 1.000 = $ (55,000)
$14,000 X 7.536   =   105.504 $14,000 X 9.372   =   131.208
Net Present Value $ 52,504 $ 76,208

2. *Internal Rate of Return*

For Addleton Machine:

Cash Inflow	*PV at 24%*	*PV at 25%*
$(53,000) X 1.000	$(53,000)	$(53,000)
$14,000 for 12 years.....	53.914 ($14,000 X 3.851)	52.150 ($14,000 X 3.725)
Net Present Value	$ 914	$ - 850

$$24\% + \left(1\% \ X \ \frac{914}{1,764}\right) \quad 24.518 \ \% \text{ rate of return}$$

For Beaton Machine:

Cash Inflow	*PV at 24%*	*PV at 25%*
$(55,000) X 1.000	$(55,000)	$(55,000)
$14,000 for 18 years.....	57.120 ($14,000 X 4.080)	54.992 ($14,000 X 3.928)
Net Present Value	$ 2,120	$ - 8

$$24\% + \left(1\% \ X \ \frac{2,120}{2,128}\right) = 24.996\%$$

3. Bailout Payback

	At end of	Cumulative Cash	Disposal Value	Cumulative Total
Addleton Machine	Year 1	$ 14,000	$ 30,000	$ 44,000
	2	28,000	26,000	54,000

Bailout payback is near the end of year 2; an argument could be made that it is not known the exact time between year 1 and 2 that the company achieves payback.

Beaton Machine	Year 1	$ 14,000	$ 20,000	$ 34,000
	2	28,000	12,000	40,000
	3	42,000	4,000	46,000
	4	56,000	-0-	56,000

Bailout payback is between year 3 and 4 depending on assumptions made regarding flow of cash.

b. Additional studies are needed before choosing between the Addleton and the Beaton machine. The Beaton machine's net present value and internal rate of return are higher, but its bailout payback is not as quick as the Addleton machine.

True - False

1.   T

2.   T

3.   T

4.   T   While the payout method lacks refinement, it can be used for screening such proposals.

5.   F   Under these conditions, a capital investment proposal would usually be considered acceptable.

6.   F   Under the time adjusted rate of return or internal rate of return no discount rate is known in advance.

7.   T   In these circumstances, profitability is not the prime consideration and the unadjusted return or payback method is satisfactory.

8.   F   Both internal rate of return and the payback methods require cash flows. Since depreciation expense is not a cash flow, it is excluded from both of these calculations.

9.   T

10. F   While the payback method does evaluate investments on the length of time necessary to recover the initial investment, any income beyond the payback period is *not* considered in this method.

18 Capital Budgeting--Additional Topics

Chapter Outline

Cost of Capital
Sensitivity Analysis for Capital Budgeting Decisions Under Uncertainty
    Cash Flow Changes and Present Value
    Cost of Estimation Errors in Cash Flows and Present Value
    Cash Flow Changes and Internal Rate of Return
    Cost of Estimation Errors in Cash Flows and Internal Rate of Return
    Economic Life Changes and Present Value
    Cost of Estimation Errors in Economic Lives
Inflation in the Capital Budgeting Process
Capital Budgeting in the Automated Environment
    Replacement-Trigger Thinking
    Advantages of Automating
Failure of Traditional Capital Budgeting Techniques
    Benefits of Quality Improvement
    Hurdle Rate Set Too High
    Projects Rather Than Strategies Justified
    Effects of Not Automating Not Evaluated
    All Trade-offs Not Considered
Assets Constructed for Own Use
    Capitalizing General Factory Overhead
    Excess Construction Cost

Chapter Objectives

After studying this chapter, you should be able to:

1. Apply sensitivity analysis to capital budgeting decisions.

2. Incorporate inflation into capital budgeting analysis.

3. Identify and quantify the subjective benefits of new automated plant assets that should be incorporated into conventional capital expenditure analysis.

4. Compare the costs of constructing assets for a company's own use versus leasing or purchasing.

5. Define and apply the new terms introduced.

Chapter Review

Cost of Capital

1. Cost of capital is the minimum rate of return that must be earned on new investments that will not dilute the interests of the shareholder.

   a. Cost of capital is a composite of the cost of various sources of funds from debt and equity which comprise a firm's capital structure.

Sensitivity Analysis for Capital Budgeting Decisions Under Uncertainty

2. Sensitivity analysis can be used to deal with uncertainty which measures the effect on the estimate if changes in the critical data inputs vary.

   a. Sensitivity analysis can be used to study the effect on net present value or rate of return if a project factor changes.
   b. The financial cost of possible errors in forecasting is measured by sensitivity analysis using either a table or a graph.

Cash Flow Changes and Present Value

3. Sensitivity analysis can be used to determine how far annual cash savings will have to drop before the company breaks even on an investment.

Cost of Estimation Errors in Cash Flows and Present Value

4. The cost of estimation error or the cost of prediction error indicates the cost to the firm of incorrectly estimating the value of one or more parameters used in evaluating the project. These costs occur in the following situations:

   a. The firm has no other acceptable projects to choose if the project under study is rejected.
   b. The firm has other acceptable projects from which to choose if the project under study is rejected.

Cash Flow Changes and Internal Rate of Return

5. Sensitivity analysis indicates the following impact on internal rate of return if actual cash flow differs from estimated cash flow.

Cost of Estimation Errors in Cash Flows and Internal Rate of Return

6. The cost of estimating the incorrect internal rate of return when there are no acceptable alternative projects is the difference between the expected and actual annual return.

Economic Life Changes and Present Value

7. The uncertainty attached with a capital asset's useful life can also be measured with sensitivity analysis.

Cost of Estimation Errors in Economic Lives

8. If the life of the project differs from the estimated life, the cost of the estimation error can be calculated and compared with any alternative projects available.

9. Electronic data processing equipment provides improved methods of capital expenditure analysis.

Inflation in the Capital Budgeting Process

10. In a taxless world, inflation would affect cash flows and the applicable discount rate in a comparable manner and the effect on present value calculations would be irrelevant.

    a. The company's cost of capital should be multiplied by the expected inflation rate to yield the discount rate adjusted for inflation.
    b. Adding the cost of capital is not appropriate because it ignores the compounding effect of inflation.

Capital Budgeting in the Automated Environment

11. Today's flexible automation makes economies of scale available at other than large production volumes.

    a. Flexible manufacturing systems can be instantly reprogrammed to make a new part or products.
    b. Automation provides an incentive for companies to grow and develop new products and services.

Replacement-Trigger Thinking

12. Using replacement-trigger thinking, managers assume that equipment should be replaced only when worn out or unworkable.

Advantages of Automating

13. When considering automated equipment, the investment evaluation and decision is broader because more company segments and activities are involved.

Failure of Traditional Capital Budgeting Techniques

14. Traditional capital budgeting models often fail in evaluating automation because indirect and intangible benefits are often overlooked.

    a. It is dangerous to rely solely on easily quantified savings in input factors.
    b. Improved quality, increased manufacturing flexibility, and the capacity for increased product innovations may not be considered simply because the benefits are not easily quantifiable.

Benefits of Quality Improvement

15. Capital budgeting analysis should reflect the benefits when robots and other new equipment cause increases in product quality.

16. Anticipated savings from fewer customer complaints and reduced warranty costs from achieving a lower incidence of defects represent additional benefits of proposed capital assets.

Hurdle Rate Set Too High

17. There is a danger in using too high a hurdle rate as a lower rate may be justified especially if the new investment involves the installation of flexible manufacturing systems.

Projects Rather Than Strategies Justified

18. A long-run strategy is often missing in traditional capital budgeting because of an orientation toward short-term returns.

Effects of Not Automating Not Evaluated

19. The effect of not automating should be considered in the capital expenditure analysis. The dollars spent on single-purpose, high-volume equipment often lock companies into unchanging products and processes. The greater flexibility of FMS and CIM provide longer useful life.

All Trade-offs Not Considered

20. Automation may not bring reductions in labor costs because a higher-skilled personnel is often required.

21. To improve capital budgeting models, indirect benefits and such intangible benefits as improved competitive position, flexibility, product quality/reliability, and delivery and service must be quantified.

22. Rather than consider only operating cost savings, the following benefits should be incorporated into the traditional model: inventory savings, use of less floor space, better quality, increased flexibility, shorter lead time, and gaining experience with the technology.

Assets Constructed for Own Use

23. When a company constructs an asset for its own use, the amount of general factory overhead, if any, to assign to the asset presents a measurement problem.

    a. If a company is operating at budgeted capacity level, they must postpone manufacturing some of its products so they can devote plant space and machinery to the construction.

        1. Under this condition, accountants should allocate some of the general factory overhead to the construction.
        2. Direct material, direct labor, and factory overhead that is specifically incurred on the construction should be capitalized along with a share of the general factory overhead if budgeted capacity is being utilized.

    b. If there is idle capacity, there is no agreement among accountants if a share of general factory overhead should be capitalized for the constructed asset.

Capitalizing General Factory Overhead

24. Accountants, who believe that a portion of general factory overhead should be capitalized, argue that constructed assets should be treated in the same manner as regular products manufactured.

    a. They further argue that normal manufacturing operations should not be penalized by bearing all general factory overhead costs when other assets are using some of the facilities.
    b. An additional argument is that future periods will reap the benefit of constructed assets and the general overhead costs should be deferred because no special status should be given these assets.

25. Accountants who argue that no portion of general factory overhead should be capitalized argue that idle plant capacity cost was not considered in the differential cost analysis used in deciding to make the asset.

    a. Arguing that the cost of this idle capacity would occur regardless of whether the construction was undertaken or not supports these accountants' position.
    b. Since this idle capacity cost would occur, the cost of producing units should not be affected by assigning general factory overhead to the constructed asset.

b. Since this idle capacity cost would occur, the cost of producing units should not be affected by assigning general factory overhead to the constructed asset.

Excess Construction Cost

26. The full cost of constructed assets should be capitalized unless the constructed asset cost materially exceeds its fair value.

a. Under these conditions, the excess cost should be treated as a period cost because the company may have been less efficient than an outside producer and this should be recognized in the current period.

b. Postmortem examinations of all capital expenditures should be made as this may discourage overly optimistic estimates and make projected claims be supported with as much data as feasible.

Demonstration Problem

Comparing Methods of Accounting for Inflation

In evaluating the purchase of finishing equipment, June Allen, Inc., estimates that two positions could be eliminated if the equipment was purchased. However, additional inspection would be required for optimal operations. In current 19X0 annual prices, the wages and benefits of the two positions eliminated total $50,000 while the inspection amounts to $8,000 annually.

The equipment can be purchased and installed at a cost of $75,000. The economic and tax life is three years. Depreciation is deducted for tax purposes as follows: Year 1, $28,500; Year 2, $27,750; and Year 3, $18,750.

Management insists that a 5.4 percent rate for cost of capital be used. This rate does not include an allowance for inflation, which is expected to occur at an average annual rate of 10 percent over the next three years. The company adjusts for inflation in capital expenditure analyses by adding the anticipated inflation rate to the cost of capital and then using the inflation-adjusted cost of capital to discount the projected cash flows. The company pays an average income tax rate of 46 percent. Assume all operating revenues and expenditures occur at the end of the year and would be subject to the effects of inflation.

Required:

a. Analyze the expenditure under consideration using the company's method.
b. A consulting firm proposes a different adjustment for inflation in capital expenditure analyses, adjusting the cash flows by an estimated price level index. The adjusted aftertax cash flows are then discounted using the appropriate discount rate. The discount rate used is the cost of capital multiplied by the inflation rate. The estimated year-end index values for each of the next four years are as follows:

Year	Year-end price index
19X0 (current year)	1.00
19X1	1.10
19X2	1.16
19X3	1.20

Prepare a schedule, using the price index values provided, showing the aftertax annual cash flows adjusted for inflation for the equipment under consideration.
c. Determine the net present value for the equipment using the method proposed by the consulting firm.
d. What advice would you give management regarding the purchase?
e. Compare the consulting firm's approach to the one presently used to compensate for inflation.

Paper for working Demonstration Problem

Solution to Demonstration Problem
June Allen, Inc.

a.

	Year 1	Year 2	Year 3	Total
Wages and benefits saved	$50,000	$50,000	$50,000	
Less: Additional inspection	-8.000	-8.000	-8.000	
Net cost savings	$42,000	$42,000	$42,000	
Less: Increase in depreciation expense	-28.500	-27.750	-18.750	
Increase in taxable income	$13,500	$14,250	$23,250	
Increase in income taxes (46 percent)	- 6.210	- 6.555	- 10.695	
Increase in aftertax income	$ 7,290	$ 7,695	$12,555	
Add back: Noncash depreciation expense	28.500	27.750	18.750	
Net aftertax annual cash inflow unadjusted for inflation	$35,790	$35,445	$31,305	
Present value factor*	.870	.756	.658	
Present value	$31,137	$26,796	$20,599	$78,532
Investment required				75.000
Net present value				$ 3,532

*Present value of $1 at 15 percent, which is 5.4 percent cost of capital plus 10 percent inflation rate.

b.

	19X1	19X2	19X3
Wages and benefits saved	$50,000	$50,000	$50,000
Less: Additional inspection	8.000	8.000	8.000
Net cost savings	$42,000	$42,000	$42,000
Inflation index	1.10	1.16	1.20
Inflation adjusted cost savings	$46,200	$48,720	$50,400
Less: Depreciation	-28.500	-27.750	-18.750
Inflation adjusted taxable income	$17,700	$20,970	$31,650
Income tax (46 percent)	-8.142	-9.646	-14.559
Inflation adjusted aftertax income	$ 9,558	$11,324	$17,091
Add: Noncash depreciation	28.500	27.750	18.750
Net aftertax cash flow adjusted for inflation	$38,058	$39,074	$35,841

An alternative approach is to subtract income tax from inflation adjusted cost savings; for example, in 19X1, $46,200 - $8,142 = $38,058.

c. Cost of capital adjusted for inflation = 1.054 x 1.10 = 1.159 = 16%

Year	Net Aftertax Cash Flow Adjusted for Inflation	Discount Rate = 16%	Present Value
19X0 (current)	($75,000)	1.000	$(75,000)
19X1	38,058	.862	32,806
19X2	39,074	.743	29,032
19X3	35,841	.641	22.974
Net present value			$ 9,812

Using present value of $1 Table.

d. Greater weight should be placed on the consulting firm's method; therefore, the purchase should probably be made because the consulting firm's method yields a positive present value. At least additional investigation of the equipment's potential should be made.

e. The consulting firm's method is sound and should be adopted. Using the company's present approach, aftertax cash flows are not adjusted for the effect of the expected rate of inflation. The cost of capital and the inflation rate should be multiplied, not added, to incorporate the compounding effect of inflation.

Matching

Referring to the terms listed in the left column, place the appropriate letter next to the corresponding description. A term may not be used or may be used more than once.

a. Accounting rate of return

b. Cost of estimation error

c. Flexible manufacturing systems

d. Hurdle rate

e. Increased flexibility

f. Internal rate of return method

g. Labor-intensive manufacturing systems

h. Least squares analysis

i. Longer lead time

j. Market rate

k. Net present value method

l. Payback period method

m. Random error cost

n. Replacement-trigger thinking

o. Sensitivity analysis

p. Time adjusted rate of return method

_____ 1. An advantage of computer-integrated manufacturing and flexible manufacturing systems.

_____ 2. Cost of incorrectly predicting the value of one or more parameters used in evaluating a capital expenditure.

_____ 3. A manufacturing system which can be instantly reprogrammed to make new parts or products.

_____ 4. A mindset held by managers that equipment should be replaced only when unworkable or worn out.

_____ 5. The minimum rate of return that must be earned on new investments that will not dilute the interests of stockholders.

_____ 6. Used to offset the assumption in capital budgeting methods that future cash flows are certain.

_____ 7. Another name for cost of capital rate.

_____ 8. The discount rate must be determined in advance for this capital budgeting method.

_____ 9. Capital budgeting technique which considers cash flow, but not over the entire life of the project.

_____ 10. Capital budgeting technique which focuses on income as opposed to cash flows.

_____ 11. Capital budgeting technique which is synonymous with the internal rate of return.

Completion and Exercises

1. Name five benefits which are usually ignored in traditional capital budgeting which should be considered especially when automated equipment is being proposed.

   a._____

   b._____

   c._____

   d._____

   e._____

2. If the net present value of a proposed capital investment is negative, management should
   _____

3. A company uses the cost of capital method of analysis. Under this method, in order for a project to be acceptable, the return on invested capital must be _____
   _____

4. The net present value method assumes that the cash throwback is reinvested at the
   _____   _____   _____   _____.

5. If it is expected that the general price level index should rise by 8 percent a year for the next 6 years, and the company's cost of capital unadjusted for inflation is 15 percent, the cost of capital or discount rate adjusted for inflation is _____,

6. In determining the amount of general factory overhead to allocate to assets constructed for the company's own use, the _____ _____ at which the plant is operating is the influencing factor.

7. When a company constructs an asset for its own use and the plant is operating at budgeted capacity, what is included as the cost of the construction?

   _____

   _____

   _____

   _____

8. Condor Company recently purchased a new machine costing $57,000 to produce fad merchandise with a life cycle that can be expected to be five years. While the company's other product lines represent more stable merchandise, management believes that this product line is needed to add balance to its products. Immediately after the purchase, a salesperson approaches management with a machine which is claimed to be specially designed to meet the company's needs. To support this claim, the salesperson provides data indicating that the machine can produce one and one-quarter times as many units per hour as the company's newly purchased machine. Further analysis reveals, however, that a more expensive quality of material must be used which can result in a material cost increase of 30 percent. The new machine will cost $75,000 and have zero salvage value at the end of the five years. Neither machine will have any use after the market potential is exhausted.

8. concluded.

Regardless of which machine is used, managers plan to produce and sell 50,000 units per year with a unit sales price of $10. The present equipment has a $15,000 sales value now and a value of $3,000 five years from now. Annual cost of operating the present equipment is direct material, $100,000; direct labor, $180,000; and variable overhead, $135,000. Fixed production cost excluding depreciation is $42,000 annually; fixed marketing and administrative costs are $29,000 annually. Assume a 48 percent tax rate.

Required:

a. Assuming the company's cost of capital is 16 percent, use the net present value method to show whether the new machine should be purchased.
b. Determine the payback period for the new machine.
c. Determine the unadjusted rate of return on the initial investment for each machine.

a. _____

_____

_____

_____

_____

_____

_____

_____

_____

_____

_____

_____

_____

_____

b. _____

c. _____

_____

_____

_____

_____

_____

_____

_____

_____

9. K Company's capital expenditures budget committee is considering two projects. The estimated operating income and net cash flows from each project are presented below:

	Project X		Project Y	
Year	Operating Income	Net Cash Flow	Operating Income	Net Cash Flow
1	$ 8,000	$ 18,000	$ 4,000	$14,000
2	7,000	17,000	5,000	15,000
3	5,000	15,000	6,000	16,000
4	3,000	13,000	6,000	16,000
5	2,000	12,000	4,000	14,000
	$25,000	$75,000	$25,000	$75,000

Each project requires an investment of $40,000 with no residual value expected. The committee has selected a rate of 15 percent for purposes of discounted cash flow analysis.

Required:

a. Compute the following:
   (1) The rate of return on average investment for each project, allowing for depreciation on the investment.
   (2) The excess or deficiency of present value over the amount to be invested as determined using the discounted cash flow method for each project.

b. Prepare a brief report for the budget committee, advising it on the relative merits of the two projects.

a.

b.

10. Difference in Profits with Machine Acquisition

Super Company is considering replacing one of its machines in the Mixing Department.   The new machine would cost $180,000, have a seven-year life, and no estimated salvage value. Variable operating costs would be $180,000 per year.

The present machine has a book value of $70,000 and a remaining life of seven years. Its disposal value now is $20,000, but it would be zero after seven years. Variable operating costs would be $200,000 per year.

Required:

Considering the seven years in total, what would be the difference in profit before income taxes by acquiring the new machine as opposed to retaining the present one? Ignore present value calculations and income taxes.

11. Payback Period, Internal Rate of Return, and Sensitivity   Analysis

Bald Corporation is planning to sell a new chemical which can be extracted in addition to its normal product line. New equipment costing $500,000 with a useful life of 10 years (salvage value is zero) will be required. Depreciation is computed on a straight-line basis.

The new equipment will be installed in an existing building which is fully depreciated and has been idle for several years. Sales of the new chemical are estimated at $1,200,000 per year for the duration of the equipment.

Annual costs of a cash flow nature are as follows: Cost of sales, $810,000 and marketing expenses, $70,000. The income tax rate is 40 percent.

Required:

a. Payback period.
b. Internal rate of return approach to determine the discount rate.
c. If, instead, actual annual aftertax cash flow should be $99,620, what is the difference in the internal rate of return from that predicted in Requirement b?
d. Assuming Bald Corporation had no other projects which are acceptable, what is the cost of estimating the incorrect rate of internal return?

11. (Concluded)

The following data may be used in answering the requirements:

	Present value of $1					Present value of $1 received annually for N years			
Years Hence	15%	20%	40%	45%	Years N	15%	20%	40%	45%
1 ...	0.870	0.833	0.714	0.690	1	0.870	0.833	0.714	0.690
2 ...	0.756	0.694	0.510	0.476	2	1.626	1.528	1.224	1.165
3 ...	0.658	0.579	0.364	0.328	3	2.283	2.106	1.589	1.493
4 ...	0.572	0.482	0.260	0.226	4	2.855	2.589	1.849	1.720
5 ...	0.497	0.402	0.186	0.156	5	3.352	2.991	2.035	1.876
6 ...	0.432	0.335	0.133	0.108	6	3.784	3.326	2.168	1.983
7 ...	0.376	0.279	0.095	0.074	7	4.160	3.605	2.263	2.057
8 ...	0.327	0.233	0.068	0.051	8	4.487	3.837	2.331	2.108
9 ...	0.284	0.194	0.048	0.035	9	4.772	4.031	2.379	2.144
10	0.247	0.162	0.035	0.024	10	5.019	4.192	2.414	2.168

True-False Questions

Indicate whether the following statements are true or false by inserting in the blank space a capital "T" for true or "F" for false.

_____ 1. The minimum necessary life over which a project will recover its initial investment earning the company's desired rate of return will be shorter under the present value payback than it will under the payback or payout method.

_____ 2. In analyzing whether replacement of plant assets is warranted, the book value of the old equipment should be considered in this analysis along with differences in operating costs for the new equipment and the old equipment.

_____ 3. The capacity level at which the plant is operating is a major influencing factor in determining the amount of factory overhead to assign to an asset being constructed for a company's own use.

_____ 4. Since depreciation does not involve a cash disbursement, depreciation expense assumes no role in capital budgeting analysis.

_____ 5. Five years ago a company purchased a machine for $6,000 cash. Today the company learned that it could purchase a different machine for $9,000 which would save the company an estimated $500 annually compared to the machine purchased five years ago. The new machine would have no salvage value and an estimated life of ten years. The old machine can be sold today for $2,000. Ignoring income taxes, the following calculation would best assist the company in deciding whether to purchase the new machine:
(Present value of an annuity of $500) + $2,000 - $6,000.

_____ 6. Capital budgeting is more concerned with resources and cash flows than with overhead allocation.

_____ 7. The discount rate or hurdle rate of return must be determined in advance for the internal rate of return method.

_____ 8. To include the effects of inflation in the company's cost of capital, the cost of capital should be added to the inflation rate to arrive at the discount rate.

_____ 9. The effect of inflation on present value calculations would be irrelevant in a taxless world because inflation would affect cash flows and the applicable discount rate comparably.

_____10. A fair share of general factory overhead should be allocated to assets which are constructed for the company's own use if the company is already operating at budgeted capacity.

_____11. Sensitivity analysis is not important if the future cash flows are fixed by contract.

SOLUTIONS

Matching

1.	e	5.	d	9.	l
2.	b	6.	o	10.	a
3.	c	7.	d	11.	p
4.	n	8.	k		

Completion and Exercises

1. The following benefits which are usually ignored in traditional capital budgeting should be included when evaluating automated equipment:

    a. Improved product quality which reduces defects and customers' complaints.
    b. Reduced inventory levels with a corresponding reduction in inventory carrying costs.
    c. Increased flexibility allowing a company to better meet market demand.
    d. Release of floor space.
    e. Experience gained with new technology will place managers and employees in a better position to work with future technological advances.
    f. Reduced lead time allowing the company to respond to customer demands more quickly.

2. Reject the proposed investment unless there are overriding reasons for additional investigations that may warrant the purchase of the capital investment.

3. At least equal the return on invested capital the company is currently generating.

4. Required rate of return.

5. $1.15 \times 1.08 = 1.242 = 24\%$

6. capacity level

7. Direct material, direct labor, allocated general factory overhead, and additional factory overhead constitute the cost of construction.

8. *Conder Company*

    a. The relevant cash outflows to consider are:

	Present Machine	New Machine	Differential
Direct material	$100,000	$130,000	$ 30,000
Direct labor	180,000	144,000*	(36,000)
Variable overhead	135,000	108,000**	(27,000)
Total relevant cash outflow	$415,000	$382,000	$(33,000)

$$^*\frac{\$180,000}{5/4} = \$144,000; \qquad ^{**}\frac{\$135,000}{5/4} = \$108,000$$

Note: Sales revenue and all fixed expenses are irrelevant. Book value of the present machine is a sunk cost and is completely ignored. While management may readily recognize that it prefers never to have made the $57,000 purchase, it should not keep the machine just to avoid admitting it should never have bought the machine.

8. *Condor* (Concluded)

    Using the differential approach involving the cash outflow savings:

Cash outflow savings	$33,000 x 3.274 =	$108,042
Disposal value of present equipment now		15,000
Disposal value of present equipment foregone 5 years hence .	$ 3,000 x .476 =	(1,428)
Cost of new equipment		(75,000)
Net present value of decision to buy the equipment		$ 46,614

b.

$$\frac{\$75,000 - \$15,000}{\$33,000 \text{ operating savings}} = 1.8 \text{ years}$$

c.

	Present Machine	New Machine
Sales...	$500,000	$500,000
Less: Direct material................................	100,000	130,000
Direct labor.....................................	180,000	144,000
Variable overhead	135,000	108,000
Fixed production cost.....................	42,000	42,000
Fixed marketing and administrative ..	29,000	29,000
Depreciation	11,400 ($57,000/5 yrs)	15,000 ($75,000/5 yrs)
Total expenses..................................	$497,400	$468,000
Beforetax income	$ 2,600	$ 32,000
Taxes at 48 percent...............................	1,248	15,360
Net income	1,352	$ 16,640
Divided by Initial Investment	$ 57,000	$ 75,000
Unadjusted Rate of Return.......................	2.37%	22%

9.   K Company

    a.   1.   Average rate of return for both projects: $5,000 ÷ $20,000 = 25%

            2.   Discounted cash flow analysis

Year	Present Value of 1 at 15%	Net Cash Flow Project X	Net Cash Flow Project Y	Present Value of Net Cash Flow Project X	Present Value of Net Cash Flow Project Y
1	.870	$18,000	$14,000	$15,660	$12,180
2	.756	17,000	15,000	12,852	11,340
3	.658	15,000	16,000	9,870	10,528
4	.572	13,000	16,000	7,436	9,152
5	.497	12,000	14,000	5,964	6,958
		$75,000	$75,000	$51,782	$50,158

Amount to be invested	40,000	40,000
Excess of present value over amount to be invested	$11,782	$10,158

    b.   The report as a minimum should state the following:

            1.   Both projects offer the same average annual rate of return.
            2.   If only one of the two projects can be accepted, Project X would be more favorable because it offers a larger excess of present value over the amount to be invested.

10. *Super Company*

The new machine's depreciation over its seven-year period will decrease income by $30,000 ($100,000 new machine cost - $70,000 book value of old machine). The operating costs savings will be $20,000 per year or $140,000. In addition, the acquisition of the new machine will result in a $50,000 loss from the sale of the old machine as shown in the following entry:

Cash..	20,000	
Loss on Sale...	50,000	
Machine (old)..............................		70,000

The net effect is a $60,000 increase in income over the seven-year period as calculated below:

$ -	30,000	Additional depreciation of new machine
-	50,000	Loss on sale of old machine which will be closed to Income Summary
+	140,000	Cost savings
$	60,000	Increase in income if new machine is acquired

11. *Bald Corporation*

Sales revenue..		$1,200,000
Differential cash costs		
Cost of sales..	$810,000	
Marketing expenses..	70,000	880,000
Increase in cash flow before taxes..		$ 320,000
Less depreciation on new equipment ($500,000 ÷10)		50,000
Increase in beforetax income..		$ 270,000
Increase in aftertax income ($270,000 X .60*)......................		$ 162,000
Plus depreciation		50,000
Annual aftertax cash inflow..		$212,000

*1.00 - 40 tax rate

a. $500,000 ÷ $212,000 = 2.358 years is payback period

b.

40%	45%
$(500,000)	$(500,000)
511,768 (2.414 X $212,000)	459,616 (2.168 X $212,000)
+ $ 11,768	- $ 40,384

$$40\% + \left(5\% \times \frac{11,768}{52,152}\right) = 41.128\%$$

c. Internal rate of return with expected cash flow (from Requirement *b* above).......... 41.128%
Internal rate of return with actual cash flow $500,000/$99,620 =
5.019, using PV of $1 Received Annually Table, 10 periods 15.000
Difference in internal rate of return... 26.128%

If the cash flow is less than expected, selecting this project will result in approximately 26.128% less return than anticipated.

d. 26.128% X $500,000 = $130,640 cost of estimation error

True-False

1.   F   The present value payback uses the net present value of the flow in its computations which is less than the cash flow not adjusted for present value. The unadjusted cash flow is the figure used in the payback or payout method and this yields a shorter period than under the present value payback.

2.   F   The book value of the old equipment is referred to as a sunk cost and this should not be considered in the analysis of whether to replace plant assets or not.

3.   T

4.   F   Depreciation provides a tax shield.

5.   F   The calculations should be: (Present value of an annuity of \$500) + \$2,000 − \$9,000.

6.   T

7.   F   The discount rate must be determined in advance for the net present value method, but not the internal rate of return method.

8.   F   The cost of capital should be multiplied by the inflation rate to incorporate the compounding effect of inflation.

9.   T

10.   T   Under the condition in which the company is already operating at planned capacity, a fair share of overhead should be allocated. If instead, there is idle capacity, accountants have differing views whether general factory overhead should be allocated to the asset being constructed for the company's own use.

11.   F

19   Activity-Based Management for Marketing Cost Standards

Chapter Outline

Significance of Marketing Costs
    Expanded Role of Marketing
Objectives of Marketing Cost Accounting
    Cost Control and Cost Analysis
    Government Regulations
ABC System for Marketing Costs
    Steps to Implementing ABC for Marketing Activities
    Segmentation
    Marketing Activities
Marketing Standards based on ABC Drivers
    Order-Getting and Order-Filling Costs
    Warehousing and Handling
    Transportation
    Credit and Collection
    General Marketing Activities
    Personal Selling
    Advertising and Sales Promotion
    ABC Drivers for Marketing Activities
Marketing Profitability Analysis Illustrated
    Flexible Budgets
Variance Analysis
    Expense Variance Report
    Efficiency Variance
    Price Variance
    Marketing Standards in Accounting Records

Chapter Objectives

After studying this chapter, you should be able to:

1. Describe the responsibility of cost accountants in applying cost control and analysis to marketing activities.

2. Use activity-based management to establish standards based on cost drivers for marketing activities.

3. Perform segment profitability analyses.

4. Compute variances using marketing standards and understand the care needed to interpret them.

5. Define and apply the new terms introduced.

Chapter Review

Significance of Marketing Cost

1. Marketing includes all activities involved in the process of planning and executing the conception, pricing, promotion, and distribution of ideas.

    a. These functions are in the life of every commercial product as goods are produced, marketed, and consumed.
    b. Marketing is considered to encompass the procedures that begin at the time the product is manufactured and is completed when goods reach the ultimate consumer.

2. Distribution costs and marketing costs are terms which are often used interchangeably.

3. The classes of costs are: production, marketing, and administrative.

    a. Production costs include direct material, direct labor, and factory overhead which are incurred to process a product.
    b. Marketing costs facilitate the exchange of goods between the company and an outside parties.
    c. Administrative costs are incurred in both production and marketing operations and include management salaries, telephone and telegraph, and rent.

Expanded Role of Marketing

4. The role of marketing has expanded causing expenditures for sales promotion to increase significantly.

5. The marketing management concept places the marketing manager in an important position of assuming a role in the production/marketing decisions.

6. Marketing cost control is more difficult than production cost control because marketing activities involve many factors which are beyond the control of the company.

    a. The company cannot control consumer demand.
    b. Marketing is also influenced by such intangible factors as eye appeal, fads, and seasonal trends.

7. Production costs are presented on a per unit basis while marketing costs are related to specific marketing functions.

8. The relationship found in production costs between volume changes and decreasing unit cost is often not evident in marketing costs.

Objective of Marketing Cost Accounting

9. Marketing cost accounting is generally undertaken because of the following two reasons.

    a. Management wants to improve the efficiency of marketing functions and to obtain better control over this cost.
    b. Courses of action are needed to be justified before regulatory bodies and marketing costs are needed; charging different prices to different customers is a typical example. In order to do this legally, the company must be able to show that it costs them less to sell to one customer.

Cost Control and Cost Analysis

10. Cost control and cost analysis involve different techniques as the purposes of each of these approaches varies.

a. Cost control compares the actual operations against a standard to determine if there are variances that must be investigated.

b. Cost analysis is concerned with searching for better ways to perform marketing tasks.

11. The objective of marketing cost accounting is not necessarily cost reduction but rather the goal is to obtain more effective use of marketing expenditures.

Government Regulations

12. Laws such as the Sherman Antitrust Act, the Federal Trade Commission Act, and the Clayton Act reflect the government's concern with marketing.

    a. The Sherman Act declared every contract, combination in the form of a trust, or conspiracy in restraint of trade to be illegal.

    b. The Federal Trade Commission has jurisdiction over a wide range of unfair competitive methods and practices.

    c. The Clayton Act is designed to eliminate certain competitive methods considered to be potential weapons of monopoly.

13. The Robinson-Patman Act amended the Clayton-Act in 1936; this amendment was concerned with price differentials.

    a. The purpose of this amendment is to protect small business organizations from the advantages that a larger competitor can obtain because of size and buying power.

    b. According to the Robinson-Patman Amendment, when different customers are charged different prices, the price differential may not exceed the difference between the costs of serving the different customers.

    c. This amendment is a motivating force for improving marketing cost accounting methods.

ABC System for Marketing Costs

14. Activity-based costing (ABC) concepts improve resource utilization in marketing functions.

    a. Marketing activities consume resources and ABC appropriately costs the marketing activities needed to service each customer or order size.

    b. ABC encourages the elimination of unprofitable segments such as low-volume customers for whom prices cannot be raised.

Steps for Implementing ABC for Marketing Activities

15. The following steps measure the profitability of marketing costs.

    a. Select the segments, such as territories, customer groupings, and product lines, on which to base profitability analyses.

    b. Establish detailed marketing activities for these broad functions: Warehousing and handling, transportation, credit and collection, general marketing activities, personal selling, advertising and sales promotion.

    c. Accumulate the direct costs for each activity and separate them into variable and fixed cost categories.

    d. Determine cost drivers for each activity; this chapter lists a representative sample.

    e. Compute unit costs for each activity by dividing the total activity cost by the cost driver selected. Use the unit cost to establish standards and flexible budgets.

    f. Allocate costs to segments to analyze segment profitability.

    g. Compare budgeted/standard costs with actual costs for each marketing activity and compute the price and efficiency variances.

    h. Determine the cause of resulting variances.

16. The natural expense classification identifies the kind of service the company secures for its expenditure.

    a. The natural expense classification is of limited value in marketing cost analysis unless costs are charged to marketing functions.

Segmentation

17. Various segments of the market, such as customer groupings, territories, and departments, can be used for analyzing marketing costs.

Marketing Activities

18. Marketing functions are defined as any separate and distinct marketing activities in which the company engages, such as transportation.

    a. Determining costs of activities helps improve responsibility accounting because one individual is often held accountable for an activity.
    b. The number of activities used should be jointly determined by several members of management.

19. The weakness of allocating the entire cost of an activity to segments is that some elements of the activity's cost may be more accurately allocated on more than one basis.

    a. A more precise method using detailed activities can be used to consider the various cost components.
    b. Accountants divide major activities into small classifications of responsibility to ensure that the work performed is homogeneous.
    c. The extent of homogeneity within marketing activities varies.

20. Some companies integrate the assignment of costs to function within their accounts while others accomplish this independently.

21. Direct functional costs require no allocation because they can be traced to the segment involved, but indirect costs must be allocated on a unit fractional cost basis using the cost driver that appears most appropriate.

Marketing Standards Based on ABC Drivers

22. The factor which causes marketing costs to vary is referred to as the ABC driver, unit of variability, or work unit.

    a. Standards can be developed for each cost driver.
    b. Much care is needed in choosing cost drivers as there is a trade-off between practicality and refinement of detail.

23. Even though there often is no direct relationship between marketing effort and result, standards can be effectively set for marketing activities.

    a. The nature of the competition within the different regions affect the standard costs for advertising.
    b. The geographical distance between customers is only one of many other factors that must be considered in setting standards.

24. Determining whether the marketing activity is repetitive or nonrepetitive is one of the first steps. A job audit or analysis can determine this.

Order-Getting and Order-Filling Costs

25. The two categories of marketing costs are order-getting and order-filling.

    a. Order getting costs include those incurred in personal selling, advertising, and sales promotion for the purpose of persuading the customer to buy.
    b. Order-filling activities include transportation, warehousing, and handling and are incurred for the other marketing activities to complete the sale.

Warehousing and Handling

26. Warehousing and handling involves receiving finished goods from the manufacturing process or from another business concern and storing them until they are delivered to customers.

Transportation

27. Transportation consists of shipping and delivery operations in getting the products to customers.

Credit and Collection

28. Credit and collection consists of extending credit to customers for the purchase of the goods and then collecting the invoice.

General Marketing Activities

29. General marketing activities include those which are not significant enough to be considered a separate function; however, they are necessary to total operations and standards should be set for them.

Personal Selling

30. Personal selling differs from advertising because this activity is concerned with securing orders through personal contact. Cost standards are more difficult to establish since many of these activities are of a nonrepetitive nature.

Advertising and Sales Promotion

31. The purpose of advertising and sales promotion is to create demand for the company's products and services and to build and maintain goodwill toward the organization.

ABC Drivers for Marketing Activities

Warehousing and Handling Detailed Activity	*ABC Drivers*
Receiving	Dollar of merchandise purchased, shipment, weight or number of shipping units, or purchase invoice line
Pricing, tagging, and marketing	Invoice line or warehouse unit handled
Sorting	Order, dollar of average inventory, or physical unit stored
Assembling stock for shipment	Sales transaction, shipment, item, order line or order
Handling returns	Return
Packing and wrapping	Shipment, physical unit shipped, order line, or order
Taking physical inventory	Dollar of average inventory or warehouse unit
Clerical handling of shipping orders	Order line, sales transaction, shipment, item or order
Total warehousing and handling	Physical unit of goods handled (product weight, or weighted factor), item handled, order line, or shipment

Transportation Detailed Activity	*ABC Drivers*
Planning and supervision	Unit shipped, ton-mile, customer served, route, or sales dollar
Clerical entries in shipping records	Delivery or shipment
Preparing shipping documents and recording shipment	Weighted unit of product shipped, unit or product shipped, or shipment
Transportation bills	Shipment or unit audited
Handling claims	Entry, shipment, or claim handled
Loading and unloading	Pounds loaded
Drivers' and helpers' wages	Cubic-foot space, truck-miles, or truck-hours of operation
Gasoline, oil, repair,and maintenance	Truck operating-hours or mile
Total transportation	Unit of classes of product, weighted unit of product, unit of product shipped as delivered, or dollar of shipments as delivered

Credit and Collection Detailed Activity	*ABC Drivers*
Credit investigation and approval	Credit sales transaction, account sold, or sales order
Credit correspondence, records and files	Item, sales order, account sold, or letter
Preparing invoice--headng	Invoice
Preparing invoices--line item	Invoice line or order line
Posting charges to accounts receivable	Shipment, invoice, or number of postings per hour
Posting credits to accounts receivable	Account sold, remittances, or number of postings per hour
Preparing customers' statements	Account sold or statement
Making street collections	Customer or dollar collected
Handling window collections	Collection
Total credit and collection	Account sold, credit sales transaction, or sales order

General Marketing Detailed Activity	ABC Drivers
General accounting including auditing fee, salaries of general bookkeeper, and accounting supplies	Invoice lines, customers' orders, or general ledger posting
Sales analyses and statistics	Order or invoice line
Financial expense	Ratio of inventory turnover, ratio of average distribution investment to sales, or ratio of total distribution cost to sales
Personnel expense	Number of employees or number of persons employed, discharged, or reclassified
Filing and maintaining order and letter files	Units filed; letter, or order
Mail handling	Number of pieces in and out
Vouchering	Number of vouchers
Sales auditing	Number of sales slips
Punching cards	Number of cards
Tabulating	Number of cards run
Cashiering	Number of transactions
Fixed administration and market research	Time spent

Personal Selling Detailed Activity	ABC Drivers
Salespersons' salaries	Salespersons' hours or sales call
Commissions and bonuses	Sales order, net sales dollar, sales transaction, product units sold, or sales call
Subsistence	Days
Entertainment	Customer
General sales office expenses and supervision salaries	Sales transaction, salespersons, customer account, salespersons' hours, or sales order
Salespersons' traveling expense	Sales order, days traveled, customer, call, or miles traveled
Selling equipment	Sales call
Telephone solicitation	Order received or telephone call
Salespersons' training and education	Number of salespersons' calls or number of salespersons
Routing and scheduling of salespersons	Number of salesperson's calls or number of salespersons
Making quotations	Quotations made
Payroll insurance and taxes and supplemental labor costs	Payroll dollars
Handling sales adjustments and returns	Adjustments and returns handled
Total personal selling	Cost per customer served, cost per sales transaction, cost per sales order, or cost per unit of product sold

Advertising and Sales Promotion Detailed Activity	ABC Drivers
Direct media costs:	
Newspaper	Newspaper inches, sales transaction, or gross or net sales (where this is the chief medium used)
Outdoor billboards and signs	Billboard and other outdoor sign units
Radio and television	Number of set owners or minutes of radio or television time.
Letters, circulars, calendars, and other direct mail	Item mailed or distributed, inquiry received, or gross or net direct-mail sales
Demonstrations	Demonstration
Technical and professional publications	Unit space or inquiry received
Sample distribution	Number of samples distributed
Directories, house organs, and theater programs	Inquiry received or unit of space
Catalogs	Gross or net catalog sales when identifiable or page or standard space unit
Store and window displays	Day of window trimming and display
Advertising allowances to dealers	Net sales or unit of product cost
Dealers' aids	Customers or pieces or units
Entertainment of visitors at plants	Visitors
Advertising administration (salaries, supplies, rent, and miscellaneous administrative expenses)	Cost per dollar of all direct advertising and sales promotion costs or cost per dollar of net sales
Total advertising and sales promotion	Prospect secured, sales transaction, or product unit sold

Flexible Budgets

32.   A flexible budget reflecting levels of marketing activity which are appropriate to the levels of production output are most practical.

Variance Analysis

33.   Accountants can compute price and quantity or efficiency variances for marketing activities using the following calculations:

Price Variance

(Standard price - Actual price) X Actual work units

Quantity or Efficiency Variance

(Budgeted work units - Actual work units) X Standard price

Expense Variance Report

34.   An expense variance report can be prepared for each activity breaking down variances for each detailed activity. Only a total variance is determined for fixed expenses but price and efficiency variances can be determined for all variable costs.

Marketing Standards in Accounting Records

33.   Marketing standards may be incorporated in the ledger accounts by debiting the accounts with the actual cost of each activity and crediting them with standard cost determined by multiplying each unit of variability times the standard unit cost for that work unit. (Note similarity with Factory Overhead Control under a standard cost system.)

    a.   It can be argued that executives will take marketing standards more seriously if they are integrated within the accounting system; however, the important thing is that actual marketing costs are studied and variances investigated.

Demonstration Problem

Analyzing Marketing Cost Variances

You extract the following data concerning the personal selling function from the Dale Company for the period ending December 31, 19X1.

	Northern Territory		Southern Territory	
	Cost per driver	Estimated cost drivers	Cost per driver	Estimated cost drivers
Budgeted data:				
Salespersons salaries (per call)	$25.00	280	$35.00	200
Entertainment (per customer)..................................	15.00	100	20.00	80
Salespersons' traveling expense (per day traveled) ..	30.00	15	35.00	12
Telephone solicitation (per telephone call)	0.40	1,000	0.20	900
Actual results:				
Salespersons' salaries...	28.00	260	31.00	215
Entertainment	12.00	110	26.00	70
Salespersons' traveling expense	32.00	17	34.00	16
Telephone solicitation...	0.35	1,040	0.30	930

Required:

a. Analyze each detailed function by computing two variances for each function assuming budgeted sales were achieved.

(Paper provided on next page)

b. What interpretation would you place on the quantity variances if the salespeople exceed their sales quota by 25 percent?

_____
_____
_____
_____
_____
_____
_____
_____
_____
_____
_____
_____
_____
_____

a.

Solution to Demonstration Problem

Dale Company
Analysis of Personal Selling Activity
For Period Ending December 31, 19X1

a.

Northern Territory

	Price Variance	Efficiency Variance
Salespersons' salaries............	$780 U [($25 - $28) x 260]	$500 F [(280 - 260) x $25]
Entertainment	330 F [($15 - $12) x 110]	150 U [(100 - 110) x $15]
Salespersons' traveling expense.....	34 U [($32 - $30) x 17]	60 U [(15 - 17) x $30]
Telephone solicitation..............	52 F [($.40 - $.35) x 1,040]	16 U [(1,000 - 1,040) x $.40]

Southern Territory

	Price Variance	Efficiency Variance
Salespersons' salaries............	$860 F [($35 - $31) x 215]	$525 U [(200 - 215) x $35]
Entertainment	420 U [($20 - $26) x 70]	200 F [(80 - 70) x $20]
Salespersons' traveling expense.....	16 F [($35 - $34) x 16]	140 U [(12 - 16) x $35]
Telephone solicitation..............	93 U [($.20 - $.30) x 930]	6 U [(900 - 930) x $.20]

b. Since none of the extra actual ABC drivers actually exceed the budgeted amount by 25 percent, management should further analyze the unfavorable efficiency variances in view of the increased sales.

Matching

Referring to the terms listed in the left column, place the appropriate letter next to the corresponding description. A term may not be used or may be used more than once.

a. Administrative costs

b. Cost analysis

c. Cost control

d. Distribution costs

e. Functional

f. Marketing costs

g. Natural expense

h. Order filling

i. Order getting

j. Production costs

k. Unit of variability or ABC cost driver

_____1. A term that is often used interchangeably with marketing costs

_____2. Direct material, direct labor, and factory overhead constitute this type of cost classification.

_____3. This approach measures the actual performance of an activity against a predetermined standard and investigates any differences between actual performance and the standard.

_____4. This classification of costs identifies the kind of service the company secures for its expenditure.

_____5. The measure that causes the marketing costs to vary and on which standards are established.

_____6. The category of marketing costs concerned with persuading the customer to buy which includes such activities as personal selling and advertising.

_____7. Warehousing & handling, transportation, personal selling, and advertising are typical categories in this classification of marketing costs.

_____8. Advertising, sales promotion, and transportation constitute this major type of cost classification.

_____9. This approach is concerned with searching for better ways to perform marketing tasks.

_____10. The category of marketing costs concerned with completing the sale which includes warehousing and handling and transportation.

Completion and Exercises

1. The purpose of cost or activity analysis of marketing functions is _____ _____ .

2. The three classes of costs are _____ , _____, and _____ .

3. The _____ _____ concept places the marketing manager in an important role in the planning for production and marketing.

4. Briefly discuss three distinctions between production costs and marketing costs:

   a. _____
   _____

   b. _____
   _____

   c. _____
   _____

5. Give the two purposes of marketing cost accounting generally found in companies.

   a. _____
   _____

   b. _____
   _____

6. The _____ Act is directed at such practices as price discrimination, interlocking directorates, and typing contracts which force buyers to purchase possible undesirable goods.

7. The _____ _____ Commission has jurisdiction over a wide range of unfair competitive methods and practices.

8. The _____ - _____ _____ amended the Clayton Act and was concerned with price differentials or charging different customers in a single market different prices; this act was designed to protect the small businessperson.

9. A marketing _____ is any separate and distinct marketing activity in which a company engages.

10. a. Discuss the weakness of allocating the entire cost of an activity to segments.

   _____
   _____

   b. What is an appropriate solution to overcome this weakness? _____
   _____

11. Three order-filling activities are _____, _____, and _____ .

12. Two order-getting activities are _____, and _____ .

13. Price and Quantity Variances for Personal Selling

You extract the following data concerning the personal selling activity for the Marc Company for the period ending December 31, 19XX:

	Tennessee		Mississippi	
	Per Driver	Estimated ABC Drivers	Per Driver	Estimated ABC Driver
Budgeted data:				
Salespersons' salaries (per call) $30.00		300	$40.00	220
Entertainment				
(per customer).................................... 20.00		120	25.00	100
Salespersons' traveling expense				
(per day traveled) 35.00		20	40.00	17
Telephone solicitation				
(per telephone call) .... .50		1,200	.30	1,100
Actual results:				
Salesperson's salaries 33.00		280	36.00	235
Entertainment 17.00		130	31.00	90
Salespersons' traveling....................... 37.00		22	39.00	21
Telephone solicitation .... .45		1,240	.40	1,130

Required: Analyze each detailed activity by computing two variances for each activity assuming budgeted sales were attained.

14. Discontinue Product Line

The management of Grove Electronics is holding a meeting in five days to discuss whether to discontinue its hand-held calculator product line. Each person attending the meeting is expected to express an opinion and to substantiate that opinion with a quantitative analysis. Management has been furnished the following product statement for the year just ended:

Revenue	$900,000
Cost of goods sold	850,000
Gross margin	$ 50,000
Marketing and administrative expenses...........	70,000
Net loss	$ (20,000)

Cost of goods sold is 35 percent factory overhead, of which 15 percent is fixed.

Required:

a. What opinion and supporting data should you present if you were to attend this meeting?

Rayburn, COST ACCOUNTING, 5th edition, Study Guide, Chapter 19, page 14

b. Compute the breakeven sales dollar for the product.

14. Paper for working

15. **Analysis of Marketing Expenses**

Management of the Goodman Company have functionalized their marketing costs in order to establish and use standards for marketing cost analysis. By having standard costing rates set for various activity costs, analysis of the difference between budgeted and actual results can be made.

The following data are obtained from the controller:

Planned Results	Units Handled	Truck-Miles	Credit Order	Sales Order
Wholesalers	1,000	12,000	300	520
Retailers	1,200	18,000	380	620

Standards for Marketing Expenses
Warehousing and handling:

Wholesalers	$0.60	per unit
Retailers	0.70	per unit
Transportation	0.50	per truck-mile + $3,000 per customer class
Credit and collection	0.40	per credit order + $1,600 per customer class
Personal selling	0.85	per sales order
Advertising	0.30	per sales order

Actual Results for the Period	Units Handled	Truck-Miles	Credit Order	Sales Order
Wholesalers	950	13,000	320	500
Retailers	1,300	17,500	375	600

Expenses for the Period	Wholesalers		Retailers	
	Fixed	Variable	Fixed	Variable
Warehousing and handling	-	$ 532	-	$ 975
Transportation	$2,950	7,020	$3,020	8,400
Credit and collection	1,610	144	1,680	135
Personal selling	-	450	-	522
Advertising	-	160	-	144

Required:

Prepare an analysis of marketing expenses showing budgeted expenses contrasted with actual expenses and the resulting variances for each class of customers. (If appropriate, compute two variances. Otherwise, only one variance for each expense component.) Assume planned sales were achieved.

15. Paper for working

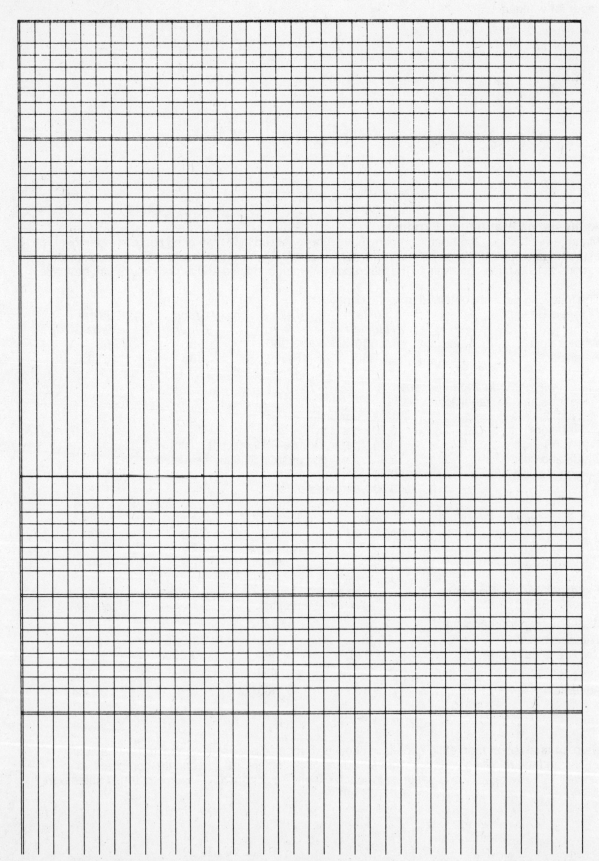

16. Expense Variance Report--Transportation Activity

D.I.R. Company has developed standards for its detailed marketing activities. The transportation activities with their standards are as follows:

	Total Standard for Direct and Indirect Costs	
Variable costs:		
Planning and supervision	$ 12.00	per customer served
Clerical work	3.00	per shipment
Loading and unloading	0.50	per pound loaded
Drivers' and helpers' wages	7.00	per truck operating hour
Gasoline, oil, and repair	10.00	per truck operating hour
Fixed costs:		
Rent	500.00	per month per territory
Depreciation	400.00	per month per territory

Management budgets the following cost drivers for the month of January:

	Eastern Territory	Western Territory
Customers served	125	140
Shipment	375	560
Pounds loaded	5,200	6,800
Truck operating hour	750	900

Actual cost drivers for the company's two territories were recorded as follows for the month:

	Eastern Territory	Western Territory
Customers served	100	150
Shipment	400	450
Pounds loaded	5,000	7,500
Truck operating hour	800	1,000

Actual costs for the month are broken down into direct and indirect costs:

	Eastern Territory	Western Territory
Direct costs:		
Planning and supervision	$ 850	$1,500
Clerical work	750	800
Loading and unloading	1,150	1,410
Drivers' and helpers' wages	5,580	6,590
Gasoline, oil, and repair	8,100	9,820
Rent	550	525
Depreciation	410	385

In addition to the direct costs listed above, the company allocates the following actual indirect costs, which are incurred at the home office:

Planning and supervision (allocated on actual customers served)	$ 750
Clerical work (allocated on actual numbers of shipments)	1,275
Loading and unloading (allocated on actual pounds loaded)	3,750

Required:

Prepare an expense variance report for each territory indicating the price and efficiency variance for each detailed activity. Assume budgeted sales were attained in actual sales.

Rayburn, COST ACCOUNTING, 5th edition, Study Guide, Chapter 19, page 17

16. Paper for working

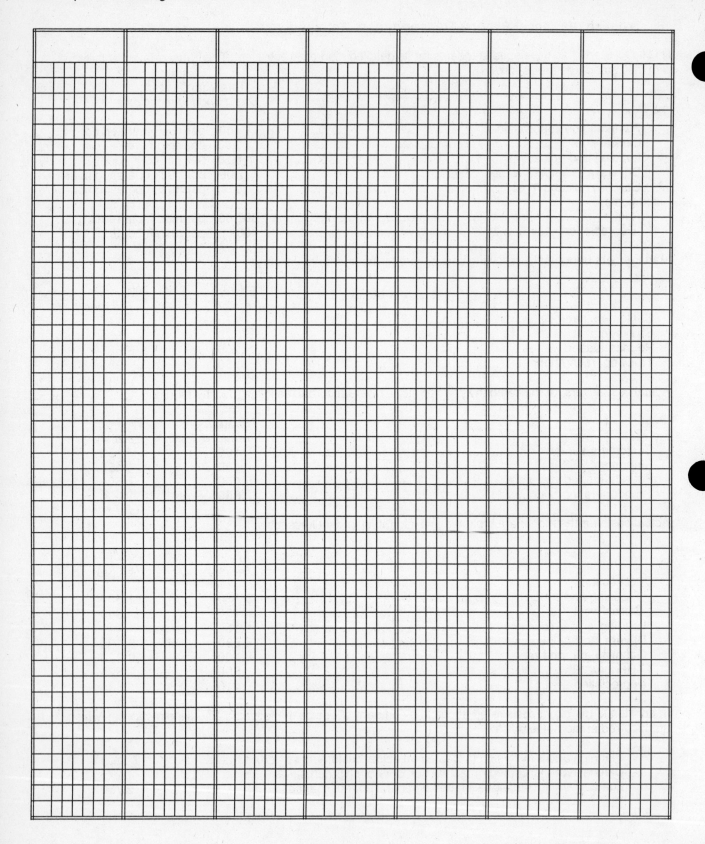

16. Paper for working

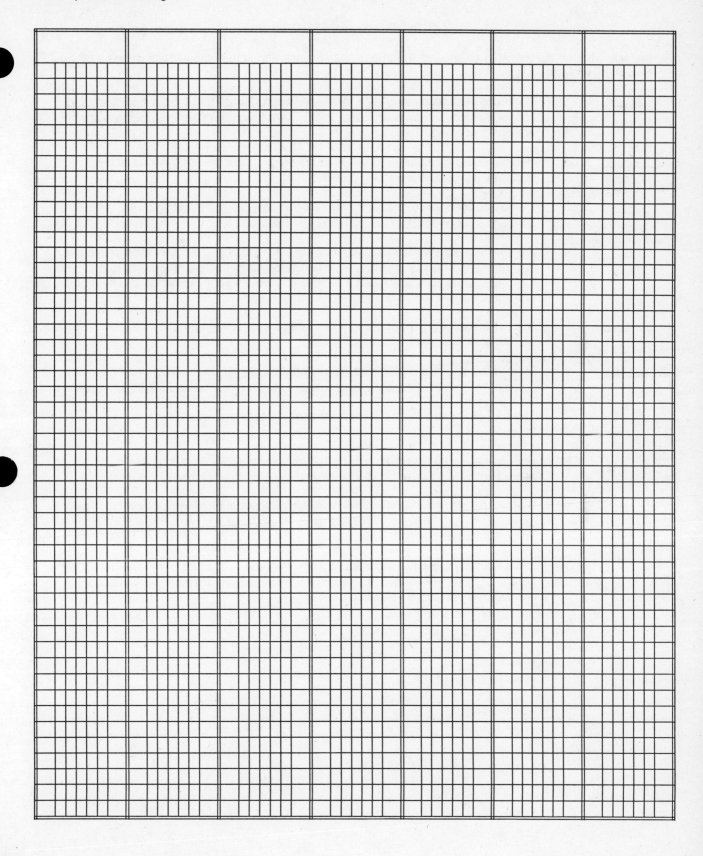

True-False Questions

Indicate whether the following statements are true or false by inserting in the blank space a capital "T" for true or "F" for false.

_____ 1. Marketing cost accounting is generally considered to be more difficult to study and control than production costs because it is hard to relate effort to output in many areas of marketing.

_____ 2. Personal Selling, Transportation, Warehousing, and Advertising would all be classified as repetitive marketing operations.

_____ 3. Flexible budgets are more appropriate for the analysis of marketing activities than budgets prepared under the fixed concept.

_____ 4. Assume that the standard for the receiving activity has been established at $25 per shipment and that 500 shipments are budgeted. If the actual shipments totaled 550 for $11,000, the company has a $1,250 favorable efficiency variance and a $3,000 unfavorable price variance.

_____ 5. A gross margin report prepared for each department manager shows the contribution his/her store has made to fixed costs.

_____ 6. Most of the engineering techniques used to set standards for production activities can be applied to setting standards for nonrepetitive marketing functions.

_____ 7. The cost of various modes of transportation must be considered in setting budgets for order getting costs.

_____ 8. For accounting systems which use a natural expense classification, the cost is not related to the function or activity for which it was incurred before it is journalized.

_____ 9. A price and efficiency variance are prepared for fixed marketing costs similar to the ones prepared for direct material and direct labor under a standard cost system for production costs.

_____ 10. Often it is not practical to incorporate marketing and production standards within the accounting journals and ledgers; this is not as serious for marketing costs because normally they are not inventoried.

SOLUTIONS

Matching

1.	d	6.	i
2.	j	7.	e
3.	c	8.	f or d
4.	g	9.	b
5.	k	10.	h

Completion and Exercises

1. searches for way to better perform tasks; included in this analysis is classifying marketing costs so they can compare costs with alternative expenditures and related sales volumes and gross margin.

2. production, marketing, administrative.

3. marketing management

4. The following are distinctions between production and marketing costs.

   a. Increasing the volume of production facilities usually has a favorable impact on production costs as there will be more units to absorb fixed costs; however increasing volume generally requires more effort to find additional customers and marketing cost per unit usually increases.
   b. Production costs are incurred under more standardized, routine conditions than marketing costs.
   c. Many of the factors affecting marketing costs are outside the control of the company, such as consumer demand.
   d. There are more intangible factors affecting marketing costs than production costs.

5. a. Marketing cost control and analysis are conducted because company management wants to improve the efficiency of its marketing operations.
   b. Marketing cost accounting is designed to justify courses of action to regulatory bodies concerned with marketing policies.

6. Clayton

7. Federal Trade

8. Robinson-Patman Act

9. function

10. a. The weakness is that the entire cost is composed of some elements that may be more accurately allocated on more than one basis.
    b. Accountants can use a more precise method considering the degree of functionalization.

11. Warehousing and handling, transportation, credit and collection and general marketing activities are categorized as order-filling activities.

12. Personal selling, advertising, and sales promotion are two order-getting activities.

13. *Marc Company*

Analysis of Personal Selling Activity
For Period Ending December 31, 19XX

<u>Tennessee</u>

		Price Variance		Efficiency Variance
Salespersons' salaries.........	$ 840 U	[($30 - $33) X 280]	$600 F	[(300 - 280) X $30]
Entertainment	390 F	[($20 - $17) X 130]	200 U	[(120 - 130)] X $20]
Salespersons' traveling expense	44 U	[($35 - $37) X 22]	70 U	[(20 - 22) X $35]
Telephone solicitation.........	62 F	[($.50 - $.45) X 1,240]	20 U	[(1,200 - 1,240) X $.50]

<u>Mississippi</u>

Salespersons' salaries.........	$940 F	[($40 - $36) X 235]	$600 U	[(220 - 235) X $40]
Entertainment	540 U	[($25 - $31) X 90]	250 F	[(100 - 90) X $25]
Salespersons' traveling expense	21 F	[($40 - $39) X 21]	160 U	[(17 - 21) X $40]
Telephone solicitation.........	113 U	[($.30 - $.40) X 1,130]	9 U	[(1,100 - 1,130) X $.30]

14. *Grove Electronics*

Contribution Margin Analysis

Revenue...		$900,000
Variable cost of goods sold:		
Total cost of sales	$850,000	
Less fixed costs ($850,000 X 35% X 15%)....................	44,625	805,375
Contribution Margin		$ 94,625

Grove should continue the hand-held calculator product line despite its net loss. The $44,625 fixed factory overhead and the $70,000 marketing and administrative expenses will probably be incurred whether or not the product line is continued. Based on full costing, the product line is losing money; but discontinuing it will decrease profits by approximately $94,625 since this is the contribution to fixed costs and profits.

b.

$$\frac{\$44,625 \text{ Fixed Costs}}{\$94,625/\$900,000 = 10.5\% \text{ contribution margin ratio}} = \$425,000 \text{ breakeven sales}$$

Goodman Company
Analysis of Marketing Expenses

Wholesalers

	Actual Expense	Budgeted Expense	Price Variance		Efficiency Variance		Net Variance
Warehousing & Handling	$ 532	$ 600	$ 38 F	[($.56 - $.60) x 950]	$ 30 F	[(950 - 1,000) x $.60]	$ 68 F
Transportation-Variable	7,020	6,000	520 U	[($.54 - $.50) x 13,000]	500 U	[(13,000 - 12,000) x $.50]	1,020 U
-Fixed	2,950	3,000	—		—		50 F
Credit and Collect-Variable	144	120	16 U	[($.45 - $.40) x 320]	8 U	[(320 - 300) x $.40]	24 U
-Fixed	1,610	1,600	—		—		10 U
Personal Selling	450	442	25 U	[($.90 - $.85) x 500]	17 F	[(500 - 520) x $.85]	8 U
Advertising	160	156	10 U	[($.32 - $.30) x 500]	6 F	[(500 - 520) x $.30]	4 U
Total for Wholesalers	$12,866	$11,918					$ 948 U

F = Favorable
U = Unfavorable

Retailers

	Actual Expense	Budgeted Expense	Price Variance		Efficiency Variance		Net Variance
Warehousing & Handling	$ 975	$ 840	$ 65 U	[($.75 - $.70) x 1,300]	$ 70 U	[(1,300 - 1,200) x $.70]	$135 U
Transportation-Variable	8,400	9,000	350 F	[($.48 - $.50) x 17,500]	250 F	[(17,500 - 18,000) x $.50]	600 F
-Fixed	3,020	3,000	—		—		20 U
Credit and Collect.-Variable	135	152	15 F	[($.36 - $.40) x 375]	2 F	[(375 - 380) x $.40]	17 F
-Fixed	1,680	1,600	—		—		80 U
Personal Selling	522	527	12 U	[($.87 - $.85) x 600]	17 F	[(600 - 620) x $.85]	5 F
Advertising	144	186	36 F	[($.24 - $.30) x 600]	6 F	[(600 - 620) x $.30]	42 F
Total for Retailers	$14,876	$15,305					$429 F
Total	$27,742	$27,223					$519 U

F = Favorable
U = Unfavorable

15.

16.

D.I.R. Company
Expense Variance Report--Transportation Activity
January, 19X1

Eastern Territory	Actual Drivers @ Actual Price (1)	Actual Drivers @ Standard Price (2)	Budgeted Drivers @ Standard Price (3)	Variances Price (2-1)	Variances Efficiency (3-2)	Variances Net (3-1)
Planning and Supervision--Direct $\left(\frac{100}{250} \times \$750\right)$	$850					
Indirect	300					
Total	$1,150	$1,200 (100 × $12)	$1,500 (125 × $12)	$50 F	$300 F	$350 F
Clerical Work--Direct $\left(\frac{400}{850} \times \$1,275\right)$	750					
Indirect	600					
Total	$1,350	1,200 (400 × $3)	1,125 (375 × $3)	150 U	75 U	225 U
Loading and Unloading--Direct $\left(\frac{5,000}{12,500} \times \$3,750\right)$	1,150					
Indirect	1,500					
Total	$ 2,650	2,500 (5,000 × $.50)	2,600 (5,200 × $.50)	150 U	100 F	50 U
Drivers' and Helpers' Wages--Direct	5,580	5,600 (800 × $7)	5,250 (750 × $7)	20 F	350 U	330 U
Gasoline, Oil and Repair--Direct	8,100	8,000 (800 × $10)	7,500 (750 × $10)	100 U	500 U	600 U
Total Variable Expenses	$18,830	$18,500	$17,975	$330 U	$525 U	$855 U
Fixed Expenses:						
Rent	550		500			50 U
Depreciation	410		400			10 U
Total Transportation Expenses	$19,790		$18,875			$915 U

16. (Concluded)

E.I.R. Company (Concluded)

Western Territory	Actual Drivers @ Actual Price (1)	Actual Drivers @ Standard Price (2)	Budgeted Drivers @ Standard Price (3)	Variances — Price (2-1)	Variances — Efficiency (3-2)	Variances — Net (3-1)
Planning and Supervision--Direct	$1,500					
Indirect (150/250 × $750)	450					
Total	$1,950	$1,800 (150 × $12)	$1,680 (140 × $12)	$150 U	$120 U	$270 U
Clerical Work--Direct	800					
Indirect (450/850 × $1,275)	675					
Total	$1,475	1,350 (450 × $3)	1,680 (560 × $3)	125 U	330 F	205 F
Loading and Unloading--Direct	1,410					
Indirect (7,500/12,500 × $3,750)	2,250					
Total	$3,660	3,750 (7,500 × $.50)	3,400 (6,800 × $.50)	90 F	350 U	260 U
Drivers' and Helpers' Wages--Direct	6,590	7,000 (1,000 × $7)	6,300 (900 × $7)	410 F	700 U	290 U
Gasoline, Oil and Repair--Direct	9,820	10,000 (1,000 × $10)	9,000 (900 × $10)	180 F	1,000 U	820 U
Total Variable Expenses	$23,495	$23,900	$22,060	$405 F	$1,840 U	$1,435 U
Fixed Expenses:						
Rent	525		500			25 U
Depreciation	385		400			15 F
Total Transportation Expenses	$24,405		$22,960			$1,445 U

U = Unfavorable; F = Favorable

True-False

1. T   This is one of the reasons that marketing cost accounting has lagged behind production cost accounting; in addition, accountants have concentrated their time and talents on solving the problems of production cost accounting while marketing has been often neglected.

2. F   Warehousing and Transportation would be classified as repetitive marketing operations, but Personal Selling and Advertising would be nonrepetitive marketing activities.

3. T

4. F   The following variance exists for this marketing activity:

   (500 budgeted units - 550 actual units) X $25 standard price = $1,250 unfavorable efficiency variance

   ($25 standard price - $20* actual price) X 550 actual units = $2,750 favorable price variance

   *$11,000 actual costs/550 actual units = $20 actual price

5. F   This report described is a responsibility report which shows the department manager's contribution to existing fixed costs and profits. This could also be called a contribution margin report.

6. F   Some of the standard setting techniques used in production can be adapted to establishing standards for repetitive marketing activities, but few of these techniques are appropriate for nonrepetitive marketing activities such as sales promotion.

7. F   Transportation is an order-filling marketing activity and the various modes of transportation would not be used in setting order getting cost budgets. Personal selling is a typical order getting marketing function.

8. T

9. F   Only a net variance is prepared for marketing costs which are fixed; price and efficiency variances similar to those calculated for direct material and direct labor are used in the analysis of variable marketing costs.

10. T

20

Variable Costing

Chapter Outline

Variable Costing (Direct Costing)
  Cost Flows Under Variable Costing
  Absorption Costing
  Impact of Automated Manufacturing Environment
Comparison of Variable and Absorption Costing
  Production and Sales Variations Cause Income Distortion
  Volume Variance
  Standard Costs for Absorption and Variable Costing
  Adjustments to Include Fixed Costs
Advantages of Variable Costing
  Inventory Changes Do Not Affect Profit
  Phantom Profits Are Ignored
  Cost-Volume-Profit Relationships
  Marginal Products
  Impact of Fixed Costs
  Pricing Policies
Dangers of Variable Costing
  Long-Range Pricing Policies
Variable Costing for External Reporting
  Variable Costing Need Not Replace Absorption Costing

Chapter Objectives

After studying this chapter, you should be able to:

1. Contrast the application of variable and absorption costing in product costing and income determination.

2. Convert variable costing income to absorption costing income.

3. Show that changes in inventory affect absorption costing income.

4. Evaluate the impact of automation and changes in the manufacturing environment on variable costing.

5. Understand the advantages variable costing offers in decision making, as well as its dangers.

6. Define and apply the new terms introduced.

Chapter Review

Variable Costing (Direct Costing)

1. Absorption costing which is known as conventional costing or full costing is accepted for external reporting.

    a. Both fixed and variable overhead costs are applied to production using conventional, full, or absorption costing.

2. Using variable costing, only variable overhead is included as product costs.

3. Variable costing, which has not been recognized by the accounting profession as a generally accepted inventory costing method, assumes that those production costs which vary with production should be considered as product costs.

    a. Product costs are those included in inventory; generally production costs are product costs.
    b. Period costs are those costs charged against income in each accounting period; marketing and administrative costs generally are period costs.
    c. Fixed costs are expensed in the period in which they are incurred.
    d. Many manufacturing people challenge the relevance of allocating both fixed and variable overhead of service departments to user departments because many fixed costs are uncontrollable.
    e. Full-cost allocations do offer these advantages:

        1. Even though the user department lacks control over fixed costs, management becomes more aware of the total costs incurred for the benefits received from the service departments.
        2. They may serve as an incentive to improve accountability in accounting systems.

Cost Flows Under Variable Costing

4. Fixed costs are treated as costs of providing for a level of capacity and are charged in their entirety against the revenue of the period.

5. Another name for variable costing is direct costing; however, this name does not properly describe the concept.

    a. Direct costs imply a high degree of traceability and this is not the distinction used in this concept.
    b. Variable costing is a more appropriate term as it better indicates the distinction needed between fixed and variable costs.

Absorption Costing

6. Absorption costing distinguishes between production and nonproduction costs in determining which costs to capitalize as assets.

    a. Advertising and administrative costs are expensed usually in the period incurred.
    b. Both fixed and variable production costs are capitalized as inventory; the treatment of fixed factory overhead is the important distinction between absorption costing and variable costing.

7. Variable costing can be used with either a strictly actual cost system or a standard cost system.

Impact of Automated Manufacturing Environment

8. Variable costing developed to fill management's need for quantitative data analyzing the effect on the company of cost-volume-profit relationships.

    a. Cost allocations of fixed factory overhead are sometimes arbitrary.
    b. The disposition of the over- or underapplied overhead balance at the end of the period often presents problems.
    c. The spread of automation and guaranteed annual wage contracts cause more production costs to be fixed.

9. Shifts in the cost characteristics of companies emphasize the importance of management understanding the impact of fixed costs.

10. As plants become more automated, differentiating between fixed and variable costs can be an initial step in cost control.

Comparison of Variable and Absorption Costing

11. Variable costing gives management more understandable answers with regard to the relationship between volume, costs, and profits than does absorption costing.

    a. Variable costs and fixed costs are separated so that contribution margin is more readily seen on a variable costing income statement.
    b. Variable marketing and administrative expenses are also separated even though both fixed and variable marketing and administrative expenses are treated as period expenses.

Production and Sales Variations Cause Income Distortion

12. Under absorption costing, when production volume exceeds sales, fixed costs are built up in inventory and are not charged off until the inventory is sold.

13. The reverse is true when sales exceed production as variable costing will show higher income.

14. The manufacturing contribution margin considers only variable manufacturing costs while net contribution margin considers variable marketing and administrative expense.

Volume Variance

15. Under absorption costing, a favorable or unfavorable volume variance results when actual production differs from budgeted production which was used to compute the fixed overhead rate.

Standard Costs for Absorption and Variable Costing

16. Standard costs can be used in either variable costing or absorption costing systems.

    a. If a four-variance method of standard overhead variance is used, there is no volume variance or fixed overhead spending variance under variable costing.
    b. The reason there is no volume variance under variable costing is that the total fixed factory overhead is closed directly to the Income Summary account.

Adjustments to Include Fixed Costs

17. An adjustment to variable costing must be made since companies cannot use variable costing for external reporting.

a. In periods in which the application rate remains unchanged, the change in inventory quantity is multiplied by the fixed factory overhead application unit cost to arrive at the adjustment.

b. If the application rate does change, the following analysis can be used as well as for periods in which the rate remains unchanged.

	First Year	Second Year
Variable costing income before taxes	$ XX	$ XX
Add: Fixed costs of period deferred in ending inventory	+X	+X
Less: Fixed costs of prior year absorbed in period through beginning inventory	-X	-X
Absorption costing income before taxes	$XX	$XX

Advantages of Variable Costing

18. The following are advantages of variable costing:

   a. Management can more easily comprehend variable costing data.
   b. The relationship between cost, prices, profits, volume, and product mix are more easily shown with variable costing; profits are shown to move in the same direction as sales.
   c. Variable costing income is less affected by production volume and more by sales volume.

Inventory Changes Do Not Affect Profit

19. Variable costing profits are not affected by changes in inventory.

Phantom Profits Are Ignored

20. Absorption costing takes into consideration both sales volume and production volume, while variable costing involves primarily only sales volume.

   a. Usually raw materials have a higher resale value than work in process and are easier to sell.
   b. Absorption costing profits reflect absorbed labor and overhead costs as assets and ignore expenses associated with carrying additional inventory.
   c. These inventory profits or phantom profits are a contradiction in terms generated by manufacturing more products, not selling more.

Cost-Volume-Profit Relationships

21. Variable costing also offers the advantage of separating fixed and variable costs on the income statement which aids in the analysis of cost-volume-profit relationships.

Marginal Products

22. The appraisal of marginal volume or marginal products is facilitated with variable costing because variable costs correspond closely with out-of-pocket costs.

   a. The relative importance of a volume or product is disclosed by multiplying the unit contribution margin by the quantity involved.
   b. Costs and profit forecasting are often easier if fixed factory overhead applications are not included.

Impact of Fixed Cost

23. Variable costing advocates argue that fixed costs represent committed costs arising from a basic organization of providing facilities to produce and this justifies treating fixed costs as period costs.

a. Variable costing advocates believe that variable costs are the crucial costs for decision making.
b. These advocates also contend that separating fixed and variable costs automatically focuses attention on cost reduction.
c. Responsibility accounting is easier than it is with conventional absorption costing because fixed costs are not allocated to products.
d. The fixed-variable breakdown also aids in the preparation of budgets.

Pricing Policies

24. It is often assumed that no product should be kept in a company's product line unless its price is higher than average full cost.

   a. However, pricing to cover full cost may not be advantageous for a company in specialized situations.
   b. Variable costing also highlights the serious results that accompany price cutting as cutting prices to undersell a competitor may be dangerous.

Dangers of Variable Costing

25. Use of accounting figures prepared on a variable costing basis by individuals accustomed to reading conventional absorption costing data may be misleading.

   a. Even though this change to variable costing is designed to assist financial statement readers, it may confuse them.
   b. People used to studying the relationship between sales and total costs and gross margin may see a completely different picture using variable costing.

26. In periods in which sales exceed production, the increased profits reported using variable costing may lead management to improper action.

   a. The reverse may happen during a period in which production exceeds sales and variable costing income is depressed.
   b. Management may miss profit opportunities under the impression that the depressed conditions are more severe than they really are.

27. Eliminating the segment which has the lowest contribution margin can be misleading because the fixed unit costs which must be covered by other segments will increase.

Long-Range Pricing Policies

28. Opponents of variable costing argue that if managers are given only variable costs for their decisions, they may be tempted to cut prices to the point that company profits suffer.

   a. Even though some fixed cost allocations are arbitrary, variable costing data is weak with regard to long-range pricing policies.
   b. All costs are variable in the long run and too much emphasis on the arbitrary classification of costs into variable and fixed categories may be misleading.

29. The prime cost method in which prices are set to cover direct material and direct labor is not appropriate.

30. Elimination of fixed costs from inventory cannot be overlooked because there is an increasing trend toward automation in factories.

   a. Automation increases the amount of fixed costs in relation to variable production costs.

Variable Costing for External Reporting

31. The Financial Accounting Standards Board (FASB) position is that fixed production costs are as much a part of manufacturing the product as variable costs and that variable costing is not acceptable for external reporting.

32. The Internal Revenue Service (IRS) also does not recognize variable costing as an acceptable inventory valuation method.

Variable Costing Need Not Replace Absorption Costing

33. The validity of variable costing for external reporting does not affect its important use as an internal tool of analysis for management.

    a. Variable costing overcomes many of the weaknesses of absorption costing in internal decision making.
    b. Variable costing and absorption costing do not have to be mutually exclusive.
    c. Variable costing does not have to replace absorption costing; instead a combined approach is suggested.
    d. Executives can better make decisions if they have both profit figures; responsibility accounting is also facilitated.

Demonstration Problem

Income Statements Using Absorption Costing and Variable Costing

McQuire Company had the following units in inventory for the years 19X1 and 19X2. Production for the two years is also given below:

	19X1 (units)	19X2 (units)
Beginning inventory	-0-	40,000
Production	260,000	290,000
Ending Inventory	40,000	15,000

A standard cost system is used with unit standards as follows:

Direct material	$1.50
Direct labor	2.25
Variable factory overhead	1.80
Fixed factory overhead ($600,000 ÷ 300,000 units at normal capacity)	2.00
Total production cost at standard	$7.55

No variances from standard variable costs occurred. Under- or overapplied overhead is closed to Cost of Goods Sold. Unit sales price was $12 for both years. Variable marketing and administration cost was $185,000 in 19X1 and $190,000 in 19X2, while fixed marketing and administrative cost was $560,000 in 19X1 and $650,000 in 19X2. Actual fixed factory overhead was $600,000.

Required:

a. Prepare statements of income using absorption and variable costing for both years.
b. Account for the difference in income for each of the years.

Paper for working Demonstration Problem

a.

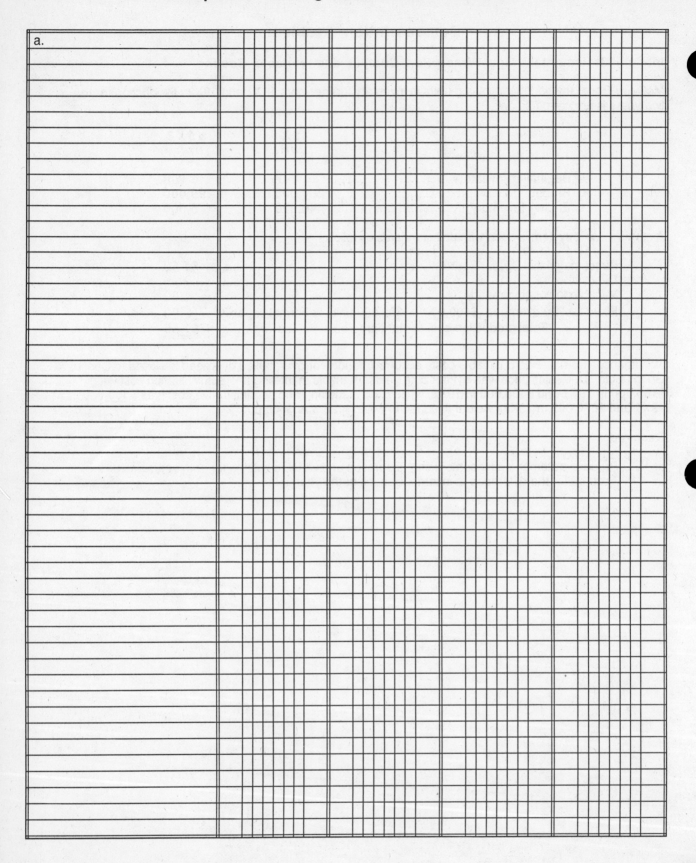

Solution to Demonstration Problem

McQuire Company
Income Statements on Absorption and Variable Costing Basis
For Years Indicated

	19X1	19X2
a. **Finished Goods Inventory**		
Units in beginning inventory......................	-0-	40,000
Units produced.................................	260,000	290,000
Units available.................................	260,000	330,000
Less: Units in ending inventory.........	40,000	15,000
Units sold.......................................	220,000	315,000

Absorption Costing

	19X1		19X2	
Sales @ $12......................................		$2,640,000		$3,780,000
Less direct material @ $1.50..................	$ 390,000		$ 435,000	
Direct labor @ $2.25.	585,000		652,500	
Variable factory overhead @ $1.80. .	468,000		522,000	
Fixed factory overhead @ $2.00.	520,000		580,000	
Cost of goods manufactured.	$1,963,000		$2,189,500	
Add beginning inventory @ $7.55	—		302,000	
Available for sale	$1,963,000		$2,491,500	
Less ending inventory @ $7.55.............	302,000		113,250	
Cost of goods sold..............................	$1,661,000		$2,378,250	
Volume variance *	80,000		20,000	
Adjusted cost of goods sold..................		1,741,000		2,398,250
Gross margin		$ 899,000		$1,381,750
Marketing and administrative expense....		745,000		840,000
Absorption costing income before taxes.......		$ 154,000		$ 541,750

Variable Costing

	19X1		19X2	
Sales @ $12......................................		$2,640,000		$3,780,000
Less direct material @ $1.50..................	$ 390,000		$ 435,000	
Direct labor $2.25............................	585,000		652,500	
Variable factory overhead @ $1.80 ..	468,000		522,000	
Total variable production cost	$1,443,000		$1,609,500	
Add beginning inventory @ $5.55.........	—		222,000	
Available for sale................................	$1,443,000		$1,831,500	
Less ending inventory @ $5.55.............	222,000		83,250	
Cost of goods sold.............................		1,221,000		1,748,250
Manufacturing contribution margin.........		$1,419,000		$2,031,750
Less variable marketing and administrative expense......................................		185,000		190,000
Contribution margin.............................		$1,234,000		$1,841,750
Less fixed factory overhead...................	$600,000		$600,000	
Fixed marketing and administrative expense...	560,000	1,160,000	650,000	1,250,000
Variable costing income before taxes...............		$ 74,000		$ 591,750

* Volume variance based on normal capacity of 300,000 units.

19X1 $ 80,000 underapplied (300,000 - 260,000) X $2.00
19X2 20,000 underapplied (300,000 - 290,000) X $2.00

	19X1		**19X2**	
b. Difference in Income	$80,000	($154,000 - $74,000)	$50,000	($591,750 - $541,750)
Difference in Fixed Costs in Inventory	$80,000	(40,000 x $ 2)	$50,000	[(40,000 - 15,000) x $2]

Matching

Referring to the terms listed in the left column, place the appropriate letter next to the corresponding description. A term may not be used or may be used more than once.

a. Absorption costing

b. Committed costs

c. Direct costs

d. Direct costing

e. Gross margin

f. Manufacturing contribution margin

g. Manufacturing fixed and variable costs

h. Marketing costs

i. Period costs

j. Product costs

k. Variable costing

_____ 1. Costs that are traceable or attachable to a specific costing unit.

_____ 2. Sales less variable production cost of goods sold.

_____ 3. Sales less cost of goods sold computed under absorption costing.

_____ 4. Fixed costs arising from a basic organization of providing property, plant, and equipment.

_____ 5. Another name for variable costing.

_____ 6. A costing procedure which is accepted by the Securities and Exchange Commission and the Financial Accounting Standards Board for external reporting.

_____ 7. Costs which are attached to inventory as assets.

_____ 8. Costs which are handled the same way under both variable costing and absorption costing.

_____ 9. Costs which are treated as expenses at the time occurred.

_____ 10. Another name for conventional costing.

Completion and Exercises

1. a. Using _____ costing, only variable overhead is included as a product because fixed costs are expensed in the period in which they are incurred.

   b. Using _____ costing, both fixed and variable overhead costs are applied to production.

2. _____ _____ are easily attached or traced to costing centers.

3. Variable costing makes a distinction between _____ and _____ costs.

4. _____ _____ and _____
   _____ _____ are other names for absorption costing.

5. Three different classifications of expenses which are treated in similar manners under variable costing and absorption costing are:

   1. _____
   2. _____
   3. _____

6. Variable costing has not been accepted for external reporting by these professional organizations.

   1. _____
   2. _____
   3. _____

7. The following are cited as advantages of using variable costing:

   1. _____
   2. _____
   3. _____

8. The following are cited as dangers of using variable costing:

   1. _____
   2. _____
   3. _____

9. What is the adjustment to convert variable costing income to an absorption costing basis:

   (a). if the application rate for overhead does not change?
   _____

   (b). if the application rate for overhead does change?
   _____
   _____

10. Oury Company has established the following unit standards:

Direct material (2 pounds @ $ 3)	....	$ 6
Direct labor (3 hours @ $5)	....	15
Factory overhead - variable (3 hours @ $ 1)	....	3
Factory overhead - fixed (3 hours @ $ 2)	....	6
		$ 30

The Finished Goods Inventory account is shown containing 2,000 units for a total of $ 42,000. No significant standard cost variances exist.

a. The costing method used by the company is _____
_____
_____.

b. If you believe an adjustment must be made to the balance before reporting the account on the balance sheet, the amount of the adjustment should be _____
_____

11. Thompson Company uses a standard absorption costing system. The Engineering Department has determined that the standard variable production cost is $16 per unit, while standard fixed factory overhead is $4 ($200,000 ÷ 50,000 units of normal activity). Variable marketing and administrative costs are $2 per unit sold, while fixed marketing and administrative costs are $80,000. Variances from standard variable production costs during the year totaled $50,000 unfavorable. Sales during 19X1 were 45,000 units. Beginning inventory was 1,000 units; ending inventory was 6,000 units. Sales price per unit is $32.

Required:

a. Prepare an absorption costing income statement for 19X1 assuming all variances are written off directly as an adjustment to the Cost of Goods Sold account at year-end.
b. Recast the income statement as it would appear using variable costing.
c. Explain the difference in income as calculated in Requirements *a* and *b*.

a.

b.

c.

12. Management of Jewett Company has heard of the advantages of variable costing and is considering its adoption. Figures representing operations for the first year are as follows:

Direct material	$ 90,000
Direct labor	120,000
Variable factory overhead	60,000
Fixed factory overhead	150,000
Fixed marketing and administrative expense	180,000

Units produced, 75,000, of which 60,000 were sold for $525,000.

Required:

a. An income statement using variable costing.
b. An income statement using absorption costing.
c. Indicate the adjustment necessary to convert the variable costing income determined in Requirement a to an absorption costing basis.

a.

b.

c.

13. Hicks Company provides you with the following two condensed budgets for standard costs and expenses:

	14,000 units	16,000 units
Direct material	$ 32,200	$ 36,800
Direct labor	117,600	134,400
Factory overhead	82,100	87,400
Total	$231,900	$258,600

Marketing and administrative expense were budgeted as follows:

Marketing expense:
    Variable .... $1.50 per unit sold
    Fixed $25,000

Administrative expense:
    Variable... $2.40 per unit sold
    Fixed $42,000

Overhead will be applied on the basis of a standard capacity of 15,000 units.

Required:

a. Using the high-low method of separating cost components, determine the standard cost per unit under absorption costing.

b. Assume that 14,500 units are manufactured and 13,800 are sold at a price of $38. Determine the income using:

    (1)   Absorption costing.
    (2)   Variable costing.

c. Account for the difference in absorption costing income and variable costing income.

a.

13. Paper for working

b. 1.

b. 2.

c.

14. The following information is available for the Holiday Company's first year of operations in which 20,000 units were produced:

Sales ($20 per unit)	$ 360,000
Total variable production cost	200,000
Total fixed production cost	40,000
Total variable marketing and administrative costs	60,000
Total fixed marketing and administrative costs	30,000

Required:

Without preparing a formal income statement, determine income using:
a. Absorption costing.
b. Variable costing.

a.

b.

True-False Questions

Indicate whether the following statements are true or false by inserting in the blank space a capital "T" for true or "F" for false.

_____ 1. In a variable costing system, unit cost of a product changes directly with changes in production volume.

_____ 2. Variable costing considers direct costs in determining net earnings whereas absorption costing considers all costs in the determination of net earnings.

_____ 3. Computation for a volume variance is not needed for a variable costing system.

_____ 4. Absorption costing "inventories" all fixed costs for the period in ending finished goods inventory, but variable costing expenses all fixed costs.

_____ 5. Using an absorption costing system, income may decrease even though sales have increased and selling price and costs have not changed.

_____ 6. Absorption costing "inventories" all direct costs, but variable costing considers direct costs to be period costs.

_____ 7. An increase in variable advertising cost would cause an increase in the unit product costs under the variable costing concept.

_____ 8. Variable costing considers all fixed costs to be period costs, but absorption costing allocates fixed production costs between costs of goods sold and inventories.

_____ 9. The difference in income reported on a variable costing income statement and an absorption costing income statement reflects the change in inventory multiplied by the relevant variable cost per unit.

_____ 10. If variable production costs are $6 per unit, fixed production costs are $4 per unit, variable marketing and administrative costs are $1 per unit, and fixed marketing and administrative costs are $2 per unit, the unit inventory valuation under variable costing would be $7 and under absorption costing $11.

SOLUTIONS

Matching

1. c
2. f
3. e
4. b
5. d
6. a
7. j (could also be c)
8. h
9. i or h
10. a

Completion and Exercises

1. a. variable or direct
    b. absorption or conventional

2. Direct costs

3. Variable and fixed

4. Conventional (or traditional) costing; full costing

5. 1. Variable production costs.
   2. Marketing expenses (both fixed and variable).
   3. Administrative expenses (both fixed and variable).

6. Financial Accounting Standards board, Internal Revenue Service, and Securities and Exchange Commissions.

7. The following are advantages of variable costing.

   1. Easier for management to understand than absorption costing; they are more likely to have confidence in the figures presented.
   2. Improves presentation of relationship between cost, pricing, profits, volume, and product mix.
   3. Income more reflective of sales volume.
   4. Isolates fixed costs and does not mix them with the variable costs of producing a unit.
   5. Assists management in pricing, especially short-run decisions.
   6. The application of fixed overhead may be difficult for a nonaccountant to understand because budgeted costs and budgeted capacity must be estimated.
   7. Decisions can be made more easily if fixed expenses are separated and not buried in inventory and cost of sales.

8. The following are dangers of using variable costing:

   1. Management may misunderstand the inventory valuations without the addition of fixed costs.
   2. Fixed costs must be covered and may be overlooked in decision making.
   3. People who are accustomed to the normal relationship of sales to total costs and to using gross margin and net income data may be confused. A change to another accounting method that will give a completely different picture under similar labels may be misleading.
   4. Variable costing may be assigned a broader significance than it deserves as management may take improper action based on increased profits under variable costing if sales have increased.
   5. Income figures determined using variable costing may need to be adjusted when management decides to expand or contract activities connected with specific product lines or other specific business units.
   6. Long-range pricing policies may be weak based on variable costing.
   7. Separation of fixed and variable costs may be arbitrary.

9. a. If the application rate for overhead does not change, the adjustment to convert variable costing to an absorption costing basis involves multiplying the change in inventory by the fixed overhead rate. The difference is either added or subtracted from variable costing income to arrive at absorption costing income.

    b. If the application rate for overhead does change, an adjustment for the rate change must be made by adding the fixed costs of the period deferred in ending inventory to variable costing income. Then the fixed costs of prior years absorbed in the period through beginning inventory is subtracted from this figure to arrive at absorption costing income before taxes.

10. *Oury Company*

    a. The finished goods inventory is valued by the prime cost method using $21 ($6 direct material + $ 15 direct labor). The prime cost method is based on a weak theoretical concept and is not acceptable for external reporting.

    b. Variable and fixed factory overhead must be added to the finished goods inventory in the amount of $18,000 (2,000 units x $9 total factory overhead).

11. *Thompson Company*

Sales	45,000
Ending inventory	6,000
Units to be provided for	51,000
Less: Beginning inventory	1,000
Production	50,000

a. *Absorption costing*

Sales (45,000 X $32)		$1,440,000
Less cost of goods sold (45,000 X $20)	$900,000	
Unfavorable variance adjustment	50,000	
Adjusted cost of goods sold		950,000
Gross margin		490,000
Less: Marketing and administrative cost [(45,000 X $2) + $80,000]		170,000
Absorption costing income before taxes		$ 320,000

b. *Variable costing*

Sales		$1,440,000
Less: Variable cost of goods sold ($16 X 45,000)	$720,000	
Unfavorable variance	50,000	770,000
Manufacturing contribution margin		$ 670,000
Less variable marketing and administrative ($2 x 45,000)		90,000
Net contribution margin		$ 580,000
Less fixed marketing and administration cost	$ 80,000	
Fixed factory overhead ($4 x 50,000)	200,000	280,000
Variable costing income before taxes		$ 300,000

c. Difference should be fixed factory overhead rate x change in inventory.
$4.00 X 5,000 (1,000 - 6,000) = $ 20,000 - Absorption costing higher because production > sales.

12. *Jewett Company*

Note that a short-cut is used; rather than show production cost, the statement only shows the cost of sales. This is appropriate unless a formal statement is specified.

a. Sales $ 525,000

Less variable cost of goods sold:		
Direct Material ($1.20 X 60,000)	$72,000	
Direct Labor ($1.60 X 60,000)	96,000	
Variable factory overhead ($.80 X 60,000)	48,000	216,000
Contribution margin		$309,000
Fixed Costs:		
Fixed factory overhead	$150,000	
Fixed marketing and administrative expense	180,000	330,000
Loss from operations		($ 21,000)

b. Sales $525,000

Less Cost of goods sold:		
Direct Materials ($1.20 X 60,000)	$ 72,000	
Direct Labor ($1.60 X 60,000)	96,000	
Variable factory overhead ($.80 X 60,000)	48,000	
Fixed factory overhead ($2 X 60,000)	120,000	336,000
Gross margin on sales		$ 189,000
Less fixed marketing and administrative expense		180,000
Income from operations before taxes		$ 9,000

c. Change in inventory:15,000 x $2.00 fixed factory overhead rate = $30,000 difference ` in variable costing and absorption costing income.

13. *Hicks Company*

a. Both direct material and direct labor consist only of variable cost components. Variable cost per unit are:

Direct material - $32,200/14,000 units = $2.30;
               $36,800/16,000 units = $2.30

Direct labor - $117,600/14,000 units = $8.40;
           $134,400/16,000 units = $8.40

Factory overhead is semivariable; using the high-low approach, its components are:

	Units	Cost
High	16,000	$87,400
Low	14,000	82,100
	2,000	$ 5,300

Variable cost per unit = $2.65 ($5,300/2,000 Units)
Fixed budgeted overhead: $87,400 - ($2.65 x 16,000) = $ 45,000
Standard cost per unit:

Direct material	$ 2.30	
Direct labor	8.40	
Factory overhead		
Variable	2.65	
Fixed	3.00	($45,000/15,000 units normal capacity)
	$16.35	

b.   1.   Absorption Costing Income
            Sales (13,800 X $38) $524,400
            Cost of goods sold at standard (13,800 X $16.35) $225,630
            Production volume variance*   1,500   227,130
            Gross margin $297,270
            Marketing expenses .... $ 45,700
            Administrative expenses..............................   75,120   120,820
            Income.. $176,450

* Volume variance (15,000 units standard capacity - 14,500 actual capacity) X $3.00 = $1,500
        Unfavorable.

b.   2.   Variable Costing Income

            Sales $524,400
            Variable costs of goods sold (13,800 X $13.35)..   184,230
            Manufacturing contribution margin..................... $340,170
            Less variable marketing expense (13,800 X $1.50) $20,700
                Variable administrative expense (13,800 X $2.40) 33,120   53,820
            Contribution margin $286,350
            Less fixed factory overhead........................... $45,000
                Fixed marketing expense.........................   25,000
                Fixed administrative expense   42,000   112,000
            Income.. $174,350

c.   (14,500 units produced −13,800 units sold) X $3.00 = $2,100 difference in absorption
       costing income and variable costing income.

14. *Holiday Company*

a.   Sales $360,000
            Less: Variable production costs......................... $180,000
                ($200,000/20,000 = $10 X 18,000 units)
                Fixed production costs.............................   36,000
                ($40,000/20,000 = $2 X 18,000 units) ....
                Variable marketing and administrative costs   60,000
                Fixed marketing and administrative costs....   30,000   306,000
            Absorption costing income.................................. $ 54,000

b.   Sales .... $ 360,000
            Less: Variable production costs......................... $180,000
                Fixed production costs..............................   40,000
                Variable marketing and administrative costs   60,000
                Fixed marketing and administrative costs....   30,000   310,000
            Variable costing income .... $ 50,000

TRUE - FALSE

1. F   Only variable production costs are inventoried under a variable costing system and variable costs per unit do not change with production volume.

2. F   The distinction is not between direct and indirect costs but between fixed and variable costs in comparing variable costing with absorption costing.

3. T

4. F   All fixed costs are not inventoried by absorption costing; for instance, fixed and variable marketing and administrative costs are expensed, but fixed production costs are capitalized into inventory under absorption costing.

5. T

6. F   Absorption costing does not inventory direct marketing and administrative costs.

7. F   Advertising cost is a marketing cost and it is not inventoried generally; administrative cost is also not inventoried under variable or absorption costing.

8. T

9. F   The difference in absorption income and variable costing income is calculated by multiplying the change in inventory by the relevant fixed cost per unit.

10. F   Marketing and administrative costs would not be inventoried under either variable or absorption costing. Instead the variable costing inventory valuation would be $6 reflecting variable production costs only. The absorption costing inventory valuation would be $10 reflecting both variable and fixed production costs.

21 Product Quality and Inventory Management in a JIT Environment

Chapter Outline

The Effect of Product Waste
Zero Defect Approach
Scrap Report
Accounting for the Various Types of Material Waste
Sales Value of Scrap Is Not Known
Sales Value of Scrap Can Be Reliably Estimated
Defective Units
Spoiled Goods
Inventory Planning
Stockouts, Temporarily Out of Stock, and Back Orders
ABC Analysis and Two-Bin System
Inexpensive Control Systems
Automatic Reorder System
Just-in-Time and Material Requirements Planning
Economic Order Quantity
Ignoring Stockouts and Other Costs
Effect of Quantity Discounts
Order Size Restrictions
Calculating Safety Stock and Reorder Points
Economic Production Runs
Reducing Setup Cost

Chapter Objectives

After studying this chapter, you should be able to:

1. Explain the theories underlying the different methods of accounting for scrap material, spoilage, and defective units.
2. Apply selective controls to prevent inventory overages and shortages.
3. Compute economic order quantity and show the effects of quantity discounts and additional costs in selecting the most economical order size.
4. Discuss the impact of lead time and safety stock on inventory management.
5. Consider setup costs by using the EOQ model to compute the optimum size of a production run.
6. Understand the challenge of the JIT and zero defect concepts to EOQ and product waste.
7. Define and apply the new terms introduced.

Chapter Review

The Effect of Product Waste

1. Scrap and defective units affect the company's reputation as well as increase product cost.

2. Scrap is materials that cannot be reused in the manufacturing process without additional refining.

Zero Defect Approach

3. A zero defect approach reduces uncertainty in an organization by closer coordination with its suppliers and customers. This approach evaluates management practices, rearranges plants to focus on products and procedures, and installs automated process controls and computers.

Scrap Report

4. Scrap tickets should be prepared when scrap occurs; these are summarized on a scrap report.

   a. Scrap reports should show the quantity of parts scrapped and the cost and reason for the scrap.
   b. Scrap reports can also provide space for comparing the actual scrap against the expected scrap on individual jobs. This is appropriate if scrap is inherent in the job and management is interested in knowing if the scrap loss stayed within the limits or norms established.

Accounting for the Various Types of Material Waste

5. The accounting methods for scrap depend on whether or not sales value of scrap is known when the scrapping occurs.

Sales Value of Scrap Is Not Known

6. If sales value of scrap is not known, no entry is made at the time scrap occurs. At the time of sale, Cash or Accounts Receivable is debited and three possible accounts can be credited. These three possibilities are:

   a. Credit the job or department in which the scrap occurs, as follow:
   Cash

           Work in Process Inventory--Job No. XXX

   b. Credit the factory overhead account, as follows:
   Cash

           Factory Overhead Control----Recovery of Scrap

   c. Credit an Other Income account, as follows:
   Cash

           Income from Sale of Scrap

Sales Value of Scrap Can Be Reliably Estimated

7. If the sales value of scrap can be reliably estimated, the quantity of scrap and dollar value are recorded when the scrap is sent to the storeroom. Scrap inventory is debited with three possible accounts credited. These three accounts are:
   1. Work in Process Inventory
   2. Factory Overhead Control--Recovery of Scrap
   3. Income from Sale of Scrap

   At the time of sale under this approach, Cash or Accounts Receivable is debited and Scrap Inventory is credited.

Defective Units

8. Defective units are those units that require extra work before they can be sold as first quality products. Two methods can be used to account for rework costs.

   a. The additional rework costs should be treated as direct costs of a job order if that job had unusual requirements, such as a rush order.
   b. The rework costs should be treated as departmental overhead costs if the defective units occur irregularly and are not the result of specific job requirements.

Spoiled Goods

9. Spoiled goods are products which contain such significant imperfections that they cannot be made into perfect finished products even with additional rework. There are basically two ways of treating spoiled costs.

   a. If spoilage is expected to occur regularly, the difference between the sales price of the spoiled goods and their total production costs should be accumulated in Factory Overhead Control.
   b. If spoilage is traceable to a job because of its special requirements, the difference between the sales price of the spoilage and its costs is added only to the cost of the good units in that job.

Inventory Planning

10. Good inventory planning recognizes that the investment in inventory should represent an optimum balance between the two extremes of having inadequate or excessive inventories and carrying too large an inventory.

Stockouts, Temporarily Out of Stock, and Back Orders

11. Stockouts, temporarily out of stock (TOS), and back orders (B/O) occur when the company runs out of inventory.

   a. Stockouts of raw materials or finished goods can cause the company's facilities to remain idle or be underutilized in some periods while being overtaxed at other times.

12. In selecting the inventory level, there is a trade-off between carrying too much inventory and not carrying enough.

ABC Analysis and Two-Bin System

13. The ABC analysis is a commonsense approach for deciding which inventories should receive tighter control.

   a. This selective approach is also called the 80/20 approach.
   b. The ABC method operates on the exception principle because it devotes attention to inventories which are important either because they are critical to production or have a large dollar value.

ABC Classes

14. Three or more classes are established with distribution based on the cost involved; Class A contains the largest cost and requires the greatest degree of control.

Inexpensive Control System

15. A two-bin system is used often for low-value, noncritical items; two bins are used and when the first bin is emptied, another order is placed.

   a. Bins contain enough material to meet manufacturing needs between the time one order is received and another is placed.
   b. Perpetual inventory records are not maintained for material items under the two-bin system.

Automatic Reorder System

16. Automatic reorder procedures can be built in both manual and mechanical inventory systems.

Just-In-Time (JIT) and Material Requirements Planning (MRP)

17. The basic principle of just-in-time is receiving production components as they are needed, rather than building up inventories of these components.

18. Using a MRP system, purchase orders are placed for materials only when a master production schedule has them actually scheduled for use in production.

Economic Order Quantity

19. Economic order quantity (EOQ) is an important tool in inventory planning and control.

   a. Economic order quantity is the order size that minimizes both the costs of ordering and the costs of carrying inventory in stock over a period of time, given a stable level of demand that is known with certainty.
   b. Ordering costs include the costs of preparing and processing an order and receiving the materials.
   c. Carrying costs include insurance, depreciation, taxes, rent on storage facilities, and the cost of money.
   d. Carrying costs may be expressed as a percent of the unit's purchase cost.
   e. Economic order quantity can be calculated in a table, graph, or through use of a formula.

20. The EOQ formula is more accurate and timesaving than either the tabular or graphic approaches.

   a. A simple variation of the formula is:

   $$EOQ = \sqrt{\frac{2QO}{C}}$$
   where:

   Q = Annual quantity required in units
   O = Order cost of placing an order
   C = Annual cost of carrying a unit of stock

Ignoring Stockouts and Other Costs

21. Like other tools, EOQ is only one factor in inventory planning and control.

22. The EOQ model may not contain all relevant costs; for example, the company may wish to maintain a larger stock of inventory than EOQ analysis indicates to provide a high level of customer service.

23. In addition, there are several basic assumptions of EOQ that can be questioned, such as a stable demand level.

Effect of Quantity Discounts

24. The effect of quantity discounts is not considered in the EOQ formula.

    a. The EOQ formula ignores the purchase price of inventory and also contains no effect due to quantity discounts.
    b. The tabular approach can be used to determine EOQ and the effect of quantity discounts can be incorporated into the analysis.

Order Size Restrictions

25. The EOQ tabular analysis can be used when there are order size restrictions in which the company can only place an order in round lot sizes.

    a. The EOQ formula might give a size that is not an acceptable order quantity.
    b. Additional analysis is also needed if the EOQ determined exceeds the storage available to receive the order. Differential costs of alternatives available should be examined in choosing the optimum solution.

26. Lead time is another important concept in inventory planning and control.

    a. Lead time is the time it takes to receive an order after it is placed.
    b. If the supplier is reliable, the time needed for delivery, or lead time, can be predicted with a high degree of certainty.
    c. There is also difficulty in predicting the amount of material that will be used during the lead time.
    d. If material usage is not steady, there is a danger that stockouts will occur.

Calculating Safety Stock and Reorder Point

27. Safety stock, which is an inventory buffer, is needed to protect the company from stockouts.

    a. If a large stock is maintained, inventory carrying costs become excessive.
    b. If safety stock is inadequate, stockouts occur.
    c. The ideal safety stock minimizes the possibility of stockouts and the cost of carrying inventory.
    d. One method to estimate safety stock is to allow for the fluctuations between maximum daily usage and average daily usage.
    e. Another method is to calculate the probability of running out of stock at various levels of safety stock and determine an annual expected stockout cost.
    f. Total annual carrying cost increases with the level of safety stock maintained, but stockout cost decreases as the level of stock increases. The goal is to determine the number of units of safety stock which results in the lowest annual cost.

28. The reorder point is the inventory level at which it is necessary to place an order.

    a. The reorder point can be computed by adding the safety stock to the average usage during the lead time as follows assuming a 20-unit maximum daily usage and a 10-day lead time:

       20   Maximum daily usage
       x 10 Days lead time
       200   Reorder point in units.

    b. The computation may need to be expanded if lead time is long and/or the order quantity is small.

Economic Production Runs

29. Economic production runs can be determined using the EOQ concept.

   a. The economic order quantity concept can be used to determine economic production runs by substituting the setup costs for a new production run in place of the purchase order cost.
   b. Setup costs include the labor and other costs involved in preparing facilities for a run of a different production item.

Reducing Setup Cost

30. When setup costs are high, there is a preference for production runs longer than needed for immediate demand. When setup costs are reduced to a minimum, production can more closely be matched with demand, eliminating the holding of inventory.

Demonstration Problem

Tabular Analysis Approach to EOQ

Ezell Company estimates that its annual requirements for the next year will be 25,000 units of 6-inch copper tubing. Ordering and carrying costs are as follows:

Cost of ordering per purchase order	$25
Cost of carrying per unit	5

Required:

a. Compute the EOQ using tabular analysis. Use the following order sizes: 250; 500; 1,000; 2,500; 6,250; and 25,000 units
b. Using the above information, compute the EOQ using the formula.
c. Why are your answers in Requirements *a* and *b* not different?

Paper for working Demonstration Problem

a.

Order size	250	500	1,000	2,500	6,250	25,000

b.

c. _____

Solution to Demonstration Problem

Ezell Company

a.   *Tabular Determination of Economic Order Quantity*

	250	500	1,000	2,500	6,250	25,000
Order size......................................	250	500	1,000	2,500	6,250	25,000
Average inventory (order size/2)	125	250	500	1,250	3,125	12,500
Number of orders............................	100	50	25	10	4	1

(Annual Requirements)
      (Order size)

	250	500	1,000	2,500	6,250	25,000
Total ordering cost (No. of orders @ $25)...............................	$2,500	$1,250	$ 625	$ 250	$ 100	$ 25
Total carrying cost (Avg. inventory @ $5).................................	625	1,250	2,500	6,250	15,625	62,500
Total annual costs	$3,125	$2,500	$3,125	$6,500	$15,725	$62,525

b.

$$EOQ = \sqrt{\frac{2\,(25,000)\,\$25}{\$5}} = \sqrt{\frac{\$1,250,000}{\$5}} = 500$$

c. The tabular method of determining EOQ is an approximation only as it indicates which of the 6 order sizes is the least costly. No other order sizes are considered in the tabular method except the ones chosen in the analysis. The order size determined through the formula method was also given in Requirement *a* as one of the order sizes to use.

Matching

Referring to the terms listed in the left column, place the appropriate letter next to the corresponding description. A term may not be used or may be used more than once.

a. ABC inventory method

b. Defective units

c. Economic order quantity

d. Economic production runs

e. Lead time

f. Materials requirement planning

g. Reorder point

h. Safety stock

i. Scrap

j. Setup cost

k. Spoiled units

l. Two-bin system

_____ 1. Interval it takes to receive an order after it is placed.

_____ 2. Units which require extra work before they can be sold as first-quality products.

_____ 3. Products which contain such major defects that they cannot be made into first quality products even with additional processing.

_____ 4. Includes the labor and other costs involved in preparing facilities for a run of a different production item.

_____ 5. Inventory buffer used to protect an organization from stockouts.

_____ 6. Operates on the exception principle by giving inventories that are critical extra control and attention.

_____ 7. System which does not assume an even or constant demand throughout a production period.

_____ 8. Appropriate to use for low-value, non-critical items as a means of inventory control.

_____ 9. Determined by taking the square root of 2 times the number of units produced each year times setup costs divided by the carrying cost per unit.

_____ 10. Materials that cannot be reused in the manufacturing process without additional refining; no other cost element is attached.

_____ 11. The inventory level at which it is necessary to place an order.

Completion and Exercises

1. If scrap has a value and it is ignored, the effect on the balance sheet is to _____ _____.

2. List three costs of carrying either excessive raw materials and /or finished goods inventory.

    a. _____

    b. _____

    c. _____

3. List three costs of not carrying enough raw materials or finished goods inventory.

    a. _____

    b. _____

    c. _____

4. In the manufacture of hot-water tanks, the Ted Oury Company uses two different types of valves. Since one valve is more complex and sensitive, it costs $15, while the other valve costs only $3. The ordering cost is $8 per order, while the carrying cost is 18 percent per annum of list purchase price. In controlling the 2,500 units of each valve used each year, management applies the ABC Analysis of Inventory in determining the order quantities. Based on this approach, orders are made every two weeks for the $15 valve and bimonthly for the $3 valve. Management would like to compare the results obtained using the economic order quantity formula with their present system of purchasing.

    Required:

    a. The economic order quantity for each valve is:

    b. The number of orders needed per year for each valve using the EOQ computed in Requirement *a* is:

c. Compare the results obtained in Requirement *b* with the present purchasing system employing the ABC Analysis of Inventory.

_____

_____

_____

_____

_____

_____

_____

_____

_____

_____

_____

_____

_____

_____

_____

5. The annual requirements for Material XR2 used by the Marr Company is 4,800 units. Material XR2 costs $40 per unit, subject to quantity discounts of 5 percent for order sizes over 200, and 7 percent for order sizes of 400 units and over.

The annual cost of storage, including rent, insurance, taxes and return on investment has been estimated at $2 per unit per year. Ordering costs are $3 for each order handled.

Required:

a. Prepare estimates of the total annual cost of material XR2 for each of the following order sizes; 60 units, 240 units, and 400 units. Assume usage is fairly uniform.
b. Using the formula, determine the economic order quantity.
c. Account for the difference in your answers to Requirement *a* and *b*.

a. Order size

60	240	400

5. Paper for working
   b.

c. _____
   _____
   _____
   _____
   _____
   _____
   _____
   _____
   _____
   _____
   _____

6. **Determining EOQ and Annual Savings**

   Arnold Company has been purchasing valves in lots of 6,000 units, which represents four-months' supply. The ordering cost is $15 per order and the carrying cost is 25 percent of purchase cost per annum. Valves cost $0.96 each.

Required:

a. Determine the economic order quantity.
b. Identify the number of orders needed per year using the economic order quantity.
c. Determine the annual savings from buying in economical quantities.
a.

b.

6. Paper for working

 c.

7. **Savings from Buying in EOQ Size**

Criswell Company has been purchasing trays in lot sizes of 5,000 units, which represents a three months' supply. The ordering cost is $20 per order, and the carrying cost is 30 percent per annum. Trays cost $2.67 each.

 a. The economic order quantity is:

 b. The number of orders needed per year is:

 c. Annual savings by buying in economical lot quantities is:

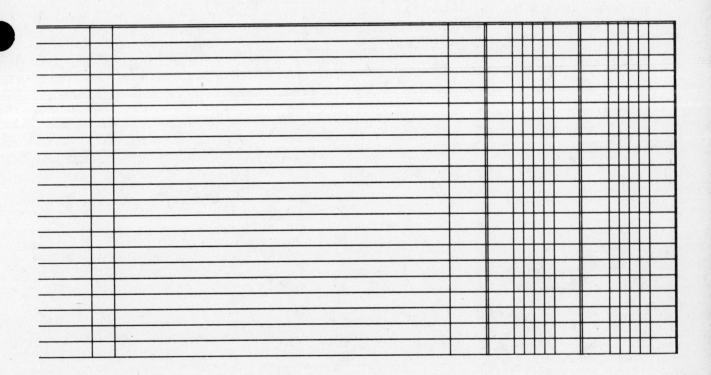

8. Summary Scrap Report

Jeff Crocker, supervisor of the Cutting Department of Wyse Company, provides you with a summary of the scrap incurred in April 19X1 on Job No. 1234.

Material	Description	Actual Scrap (lbs.)	Expected Scrap (lbs.)	Unit Cost	Sales Value of Actual Quantity
456R	Poly sponge	80	70	$4.00	Not known
123S	Boxing	94	76	1.00	$29
654T	Vinyl sheet	26	28	10.00	130
321U	Cotton inner	112	90	2.00	-0-

It is discovered that operator inefficiency accounts for the loss of 456R; a new, inexperienced operator caused the scrapping of material 123S. The cause for the material 654T and 321U scrap is machine overheating.

Required:

Prepare a summary scrap report indicating the variances from expected scrap. Discuss the areas where attention should be directed.

True-False Questions

Indicate whether the following statements are true or false by inserting in the blank space a capital "T" for true or "F" for false.

_____ 1. In determining EOQ the cost of ordering and carrying inventory are balanced and minimized.

_____ 2. Reorder point and EOQ are synonymous terms used interchangeably in inventory planning.

_____ 3. In the EOQ formula the purchase cost of materials is included along with the cost of ordering and carrying the materials.

_____ 4. Even though scrap value can be determined reasonably accurately, and is readily marketable, management may decide that it is not necessary to establish it as an inventory account; when this approach is followed, there is no effect on the balance sheet.

_____ 5. The carrying cost of inventory is often expressed as a percentage of the purchase cost of the unit being stored.

_____ 6. Another name for the ABC Analysis of Inventory is the two-bin system of inventory control.

_____ 7. The EOQ is the order size that minimizes both the costs of ordering and the purchase costs paid to suppliers.

_____ 8. Setup costs are the costs associated with the time it takes to receive an order after it is placed and this factor is important in estimating the probability of stockouts.

_____ 9. When defective units occur at varying intervals and are not the result of a specific job's requirements, the correct procedure is to treat the rework cost as factory overhead.

_____10. Stockouts occur only in finished goods inventory and have a major impact on customer goodwill.

SOLUTIONS

Matching

1.	e	7.	f	
2.	b	8.	l	
3.	k	9.	d	
4.	j	10.	i	
5.	h	11.	g	
6.	a			

Completion and Exercises

1. understate assets

2. The following are costs of carrying excessive raw material and finished goods:
   a. Increased cost of the storage space.
   b. Increased insurance and property taxes.
   c. Increased cost of handling and transferring inventory.
   d. Increased risk of theft, technological obsolescence, and physical deterioration.
   e. Increased clerical costs in maintaining records.
   f. Loss of desired return on investments in inventory and storage space.

3. The following are costs of not carrying enough raw material or finished goods inventory:
   a. Additional costs due to interruptions of production.
   b. Lost quantity discounts.
   c. Additional purchasing costs (due to rush).
   d. Loss of customer goodwill.
   e. Contribution margin on lost sales.
   f. Additional transportation costs.

4. *Ted Oury Company*
   a.

   $$\text{EOQ for \$15 value} = \sqrt{\frac{2 \times 2,500 \times \$8}{18\% \times \$15}} =$$

   $$\sqrt{\frac{\$40,000}{\$2.70}} = \sqrt{14,815} = 122 \text{ rounded}$$

   $$\text{EOQ for \$3 value} = \sqrt{\frac{2 \times 2,500 \times \$8}{18\% \times \$3}} = \sqrt{\frac{\$40,000}{\$.54}} = \sqrt{74,074} = 273 \text{ rounded}$$

   b.

   $$\text{Annual orders needed for \$15 value} = \frac{2,500 \text{ annual requirements}}{122 \text{ EOQ}} = 21 \text{ orders}$$

   $$\text{Annual orders needed for \$3 value} = \frac{2,500 \text{ annual requirements}}{273 \text{ EOQ}} = 9 \text{ orders}$$

   c. The purpose of the "ABC" method is to determine which classes of inventory should be assigned the greatest degree of control. Based on this data, management can gain an insight into which inventory classes should be ordered more frequently. However, the "ABC" method does not indicate the optimum order size as does the EOQ formula. Carrying cost is ignored in the "ABC" method.

   If in the above example, carrying cost was expressed as a cost per unit and it was the same for both the $15 value and the $3 value, then the EOQ formula would give no attention to the high-cost value. Since carrying cost in the above example is expressed as a percentage of purchase price, some attention is given to the fact that one valve costs more than the other. Carrying cost is higher for the $15 valve because controlled conditions are necessary for this more sensitive valve.

5.   *Marr Company*

a.

Order size	60	240	400
Number of orders	80	20	12
Average inventory	30	120	200
Material costs	$192,000	$192,000	$192,000
Less discounts	--	9,600	13,440
Net material costs	$192,000	$182,400	$178,560
Costs of ordering @ $3	240	60	36
Costs of carrying (Avg. Inv. @ $2)	60	240	400
Total Annual Costs	$192,300	$182,700	$178,996

b.

$$\text{EOQ} = \sqrt{\frac{2 \times 4,800 \times \$3}{\$2}} = \sqrt{\frac{\$28,800}{\$2}} = \sqrt{14,400} = 120$$

c. Using the tabular approach, the three order sizes were arbitrarily chosen. An order size of 120 units was not chosen. The answer obtained through the tabular approach is only an approximate value. Even more importantly, a different cost of ordering must be established for each quantity discount when there are quantity discounts for different quantities purchased. Quantity discounts were not considered in the EOQ formula computation and an ordering cost of $3 per order was used regardless of the quantity ordered.

6. *Arnold Company*

a.

$$\text{EOQ} = \sqrt{\frac{2 \times 18,000 \times \$15}{25\% \times \$.96}} = \sqrt{\frac{\$540,000}{\$.24}} = \sqrt{2,250,000} = 1,500 \text{ units}$$

b.

$$\frac{18,000 \text{ units per year}}{1,500 \text{ EOQ}} = 12 \text{ orders per year}$$

c. Cost of present purchasing system:

Ordering cost ($15 per order X 3 orders per year)	$ 45	
Carrying cost [6,000/2 X (25% X $.96)]	720	
Total ordering and carrying cost		$765
Cost using economic order quantity:		
Ordering cost ($15 per order X 12 orders per year)	$180	
Carrying cost [1,500/2 X (25% X $.96)]	180	
Total ordering and carrying cost		360
Annual cost savings		$405

7. *Criswell Company*

a. $EOQ = \sqrt{\dfrac{2 \times 20{,}000 \times \$20}{30\% \times \$2.67}} = \sqrt{\dfrac{\$800{,}000}{\$.80}} = \sqrt{1{,}000{,}000} = 1{,}000 \text{ units EOQ}$

b. $\dfrac{20{,}000 \text{ units per year}}{1{,}000 \text{ EOQ}} = 20 \text{ orders per year}$

c. Cost of present purchasing system:

Ordering cost ($20 per order X 4 orders per year) .... $ 80
Carrying cost

$\left(\dfrac{5{,}000 \text{ units}}{2} = 2{,}500 \text{ avg. invent. } \times \$.80 \text{ carrying cost per unit (from a)} \right)$ ...... <u>2,000</u>

Total ordering and carrying cost... $2,080

Cost using economic order quantity:

Ordering cost ($20 per order X 20 orders per year) .... $ 400
Carrying cost

$\left(\dfrac{1{,}000 \text{ units}}{2} = 500 \text{ avg. invent. } \times \$.80 \text{ unit carrying cost} \right)$ .... <u>400</u>

Total ordering and carrying cost... <u>800</u>
Annual cost savings $1,280

8.

Job: 1234
Department: Cutting

Wyse Company
Summary Scrap Report

Material No.	Description	Quantity Scrapped	Unit Cost	Total Cost	Expected Scrap	Variances	Sales Value	Causes of Actual Scrap
456R	Poly Sponge	80	$4.00	$320.00	70	$40.00	Not Known	Operator Inefficiency
123S	Boxing	94	1.00	94.00	76	18.00	$ 29	Inexperienced Operator
654T	Vinyl Sheet	26	10.00	260.00	28	(20.00)	130	Machine Overheating
321U	Cotton Inner	112	2.00	224.00	90	44.00	-0-	Machine Overheating
				$898.00		$82.00		

Wyse managers should study the cause of operator inefficiency in material #456R. Management should also direct attention to the scrap loss in material #123S due to the inexperienced operator since it may indicate inadequate training of the operator. Managers should also investigate the overheating machines to eliminate this problem.

True False

1. T

2. F   EOQ is the order size that minimizes both the costs of ordering and the costs of carrying inventory in stock over a period of time. Reorder point is the inventory level at which it is necessary to place an order.

3. F

4. F   There is an effect on the balance sheet if scrap inventory, an asset, is omitted. Under these circumstances, scrap should be inventoried; when there is uncertainty as to the sales value, scrap is not set up as an asset.

5. T

6. F   Another name for the ABC analysis of inventory is the 80/20 approach; both of these approaches are selective while the two-bin system is not. The two-bin system is used for low-value, noncritical items.

7. F   EOQ minimizes the costs of ordering and the cost of carrying inventory in stock over time, given a stable level of demand that is known with certainty.

8. F   This definition is a correct one for lead time. Setup costs are involved in preparing facilities for a run of a different product.

9. T

10. F   Stockouts can occur in raw material and may be costly because these stockouts cause the company's facilities to remain idle or underutilized.

22   Payroll Accounting and Incentive Plans

Chapter Outline

Withholdings from Employees' Wages
    Voluntary Withholdings
    Involuntary Withholdings
Payroll Accounting Entries
    Salary and Wage Distribution
    Payroll Taxes
Adjusting and Reversing Salary and Wage Entries
Government Legislation Affecting Employment
Indirect or Fringe Benefits
    Holidays, Vacations, and Bonus Pay
    Overtime Premium Pay
    Shift Premium
Incentive Compensation Plans
    Individual Incentive Plans
    Group Incentive Plans
    Controls on Incentive Plans
Impact of JIT on Incentive Plans
    Avoid Creating Busy Work

Chapter Objectives

After studying this chapter, you should be able to:

1. Record labor distribution, employee withholdings, and payroll taxes.

2. Prepare adjusting and reversing labor entries.

3. Accrue vacation, holiday, and bonus pay.

4. Apply varieties of incentive wage plans and evaluate their impact on total product cost.

5. Evaluate the impact of JIT on incentive programs.

6. Define and apply the new terms introduced.

Chapter Review

Withholdings from Employees' Wages

1. Voluntary withholdings are of the following types in which the employer acts as a collector for the employees.

Voluntary Withholdings

2. Employers may agree to withhold union dues, charity contributions, saving plan contributions, and other optional deductions from employees' payroll checks.

    a. Examples of voluntary withholdings include union dues, pension funds, and medical and life insurance premiums.
    b. Employers then make the payments to the proper institution in the employee's name.

Involuntary Withholdings

3. Various laws require employers to withhold certain taxes from employees' wages.

    a. Income taxes, federal, state, and city, and social security taxes (FICA) are examples of involuntary withholdings.
    b. Employers match the FICA contribution of employees.

4. Employer payroll taxes are additional indirect benefits which increase the cost of payroll to employers.

5. Employees complete Form W-4 before beginning employment; Form W-4 indicates the income tax exemptions employees are claiming.

6. Before January 31 of the year following the one in which wages are earned, employers are required to furnish employees a W-2 indicating wages earned and taxes withheld.

Payroll Accounting Entries

7. Labor accounting entries are of two types regardless of the variations found in payroll systems.

Salary and Wage Distribution

8. One type of entry involves recording labor distribution, together with the liabilities from employee withholdings and net earnings.

    a. An example of this type of entry is given below:

Work in Process Inventory (Direct labor)	600.00	
Factory Overhead Control (Indirect labor)	300.00	
Marketing Expense Control	200.00	
Administrative Expense Control	100.00	
FICA Taxes Withheld or Payable (required liability)		90.12
Federal Income Tax Withheld (required liability)		250.40
State Income Tax Withheld (required liability)		80.00
Union Dues Collected (liability)		20.00
Hospitalization Insurance Payable (liability)		40.00
Payroll Payable (liability)		719.48
Payroll Payable	719.48	
Cash		719.48

b. Instead a temporary ledger account called Payroll may be established and then later the labor distribution is made, as shown below:

Payroll	1,200.00	
FICA Taxes Payable		90.12
Federal Income Tax Withheld		250.40
State Income Tax Withheld		80.00
Union Dues Collected		20.00
Hospitalization Insurance Payable		40.00
Payroll Payable		719.48
Payroll Payable	719.48	
Cash		719.48
Work in Process Inventory	600.00	
Factory Overhead Control	300.00	
Marketing Expense Control	200.00	
Administrative Expense Control	100.00	
Payroll		1,200.00

Payroll Taxes

9. The second type of entry involves recording the employer's payroll taxes. Payroll taxes may be treated as direct costs or as indirect costs.

   a. The following example shows employer's payroll tax treated as direct cost. Only three payroll taxes are used, under the assumption that all wages are subject to these taxes; a 8 percent FICA tax, 2.7 percent state unemployment tax, and a 0.8 percent federal unemployment tax.

Work in Process Inventory (11.5 percent total tax on $600 direct factory labor).........	69.00	
Factory Overhead Control (11.5 percent total tax on $300 indirect factory labor)	34.50	
Marketing Expense Control (11.5 percent total tax on $200 marketing labor)...........	23.00	
Administrative Expense Control (11.5 percent total tax on $100 administrative labor)	11.50	
FICA Taxes Payable (8 percent X $1,200)		96.00
State Unemployment Taxes Payable (2.7 percent X $1,200)		32.40
Federal Unemployment Taxes Payable (.8 percent X $1,200)...........................		9.60

   b. The following example shows employer's payroll tax treated as indirect cost:

Factory Overhead Control (11.5 percent total tax on $600 direct labor and $300 indirect factory labor)	103.50	
Marketing Expense Control (11.5 percent total tax on $200 marketing labor).........	23.00	
Administrative Expense Control (11.5 percent total tax on $100 administrative labor)	11.50	
FICA Taxes Payable (8 percent x $1,200)		96.00
State Unemployment Taxes Payable (2.7 percent x $1,200)		32.40
Federal Unemployment Taxes Payable (.8 percent x $1,200).........................		9.60

10. Payroll taxes, such as FICA, unemployment taxes, and state workmen's compensation insurance, are levied on the employer for the benefit of the employees.

Adjusting and Reversing Salary and Wage Entries

11. Adjusting entries record accrued payroll costs which properly match the period in which the employee's compensation is earned.

   a. Labor costs and liabilities will be misstated if adjusting entries are not made.
   b. Reversing entries may be made as of the first working day of the next period.
   c. Reversing adjusting entries are optional; recording the adjusting entry is not optional.

Government Legislation Affecting Employment

12. Government regulations cover various aspects of employment such as minimum and overtime wages, discrimination, and job hazards.

13. The responsibility of the Equal Employment Opportunity Commission (EEOC) is to ensure that all Americans are considered for hiring and promotion on the basis of their ability and qualifications, without regard to race, color, religion, sex, or national origin.

Indirect or Fringe Benefits

14. There is other compensation which employees may not receive directly or immediately, but which does benefit the employees and is related to their employment. Holidays, vacations, insurance, and pensions are included in fringe benefits.

15. Payments which employees do not receive directly or immediately, but which relate to employment are referred to as indirect or "fringe" benefits.

    a. Holiday and vacation pay, insurance, and pensions are types of indirect benefits.
    b. Stock and thrift plans usually allow an employee to borrow on a thrift fund or purchase company stock.

Holidays, Vacations, and Bonus Pay

16. An employer is required to accrue a liability for employees' rights to receive compensation for future absences when certain conditions are met.

17. The costs of vacation, holidays, and bonuses can be estimated and allocated to each period in which the employee works.

    a. The following journal entry illustrates the recording of estimated vacation, holidays, and bonuses which are debited to Factory Overhead Costs.

       Assume holidays and vacations total 20 days and employees receive $40 per day. Also employees receive .2 percent of net income and net income is expected to be $100,000. Estimated costs are:

Holidays and vacations (20 days x $40)	$ 800	
Bonus (.2 percent of $100,000)	200	$1,000

       $800/48 weeks = $16.67 per week for holidays and vacation costs
       $200/48 weeks = $4.17 per week for bonus

       The entry to record five days of productive work is:

Work in Process (5 days x $40 per day)	200.00	
Factory Overhead Control ($16.67 + $4.17)	20.84	
Payroll		200.00
Accrued Vacation and Holiday Pay.............................	16.67	
Accrued Bonus Pay		4.17

    b. When the employee in the previous example receives 3 weeks of vacation pay, the following journal entry is made:

Accrued Vacation and Holiday Pay	600.00	
Federal Income Tax Withheld		160.00
State Income Tax Withheld		40.00
FICA Taxes Payable (8% x $600)...............................		48.00
Payroll Payable...		352.00
Payroll Payable...	352.00	
Cash		352.00

Overtime Premium Pay

18. The Farm Labor Standards Act established a minimum wage for most nonfarm workers engaged in interstate commerce, prohibited child labor, and required time-and-a-half for hours in excess of 40 per week.

Shift Premium

19. Employees working on an evening or night shift may receive a higher wage rate to compensate for the less desirable schedule. The preferred treatment is to accumulate the shift premium amount in the Factory Overhead Control account.

Incentive Compensation Plans

20. Direct benefits are payments to employees at or near the time payments are earned.

   a. Wages and salaries are a type of direct benefit.
   b. Salaries describe a fixed periodic payment.
   c. Wages designate hourly or piece rate payment.

Individual Incentive Plans

21. Incentive compensation plans provide additional money to employees whose performance exceeds a predetermined goal or standard. Incentive plans are adopted to give employees an opportunity to earn additional pay and also to reduce the cost per unit of finished product.

Group Incentive Plans

22. Group incentive plans are appropriate if teamwork is required and one individual employee cannot increase output without increasing the entire crew's productivity.

Controls on Incentive Plans

23. Controls are needed on incentive plans to make certain they are working properly. Employees must not be allowed to hide excess production in their locker so they can turn in these units later and receive a bonus. The situation is likely to happen if a guaranteed wage is provided regardless of the worker's output.

Impact of JIT on Incentive Plans

24. Since the objective of JIT is to keep inventory at a minimum, lot sizes are small. Keeping employees working to produce unneeded inventory is contradictory to the JIT philosophy.

Avoid Creating Busy Work

25. Managers should avoid creating work to keep employees busy, but they should also monitor a policy of allowing workers free time once they finish their workloads.

26. If a worker's output is lower than expected when using a JIT system, the cause is likely bottlenecks either before or after the worker.

Demonstration Problem

Payment of Payroll, Recording and Paying Payroll Taxes

The following liability accounts of the Wilton Company contained these credit balances on April 30:

Federal income tax withheld	$28,600
Federal unemployment taxes payable	350
FICA taxes payable	9,000
State unemployment taxes payable	3,800

For the May payroll totaling $65,000, income taxes of $15,000 were withheld. Of the payroll, $60,000 were subject to the 8 percent FICA tax rate while $40,000 of the payroll was subject to the 2.7 percent state unemployment tax rate and the .8 percent federal unemployment tax rate.

Required:

a. Prepare the entry to record and pay the payroll for May. HINT: Use a payroll account; do not try to distribute the payroll.
b. Prepare the entry recording the employer's payroll taxes for May. Treat payroll taxes as direct costs, allocating 70% to direct labor costs, 15% to indirect labor costs, 5% to marketing costs, and 10% as administrative costs.
c. Prepare the entry to pay all taxes due governmental agencies for the period ending May 31.

Paper for working Demonstration Problem

Solution to Demonstration Problem

Wilton Company

a.   Payroll   65,000
        Federal Income Tax Withheld   15,000
        FICA Taxes Payable   4,800
        Accrued Payroll   45,200

      Accrued Payroll   45,200
        Cash   45,200

b.   Work in Process (70% x $6,200)   4,340
      Factory Overhead (15% x $6,200)   930
      Marketing Expense Control (5% x $6,200)   310
      Administrative Expense Control (10% x $6,200)   620
        State Unemployment Taxes Payable (2.7% x $40,000)   1,080
        Federal Unemployment Taxes Payable (.8% x $40,000)   320
        FICA Taxes Payable   4,800

c.   Federal Income Tax Withheld ($28,600 + $15,000)   43,600
      Federal Unemployment Taxes Payable ($350 + $320)   670
      FICA Taxes Payable ($9,000 + $4,800 + $4,800)   18,600
      State Unemployment Taxes Payable ($3,800 + $1,080)   4,880
        Cash   67,750

Matching

Referring to the terms listed in the left column, place the appropriate letter next to the corresponding description. A term may not be used or may be used more than once.

a. FICA taxes

b. Form W-2

c. Form W-4

d. Group incentive plans

e. Incentive compensation plan

f. JIT production policies

g. Job order sheets

h. Shift premium

i. Suboptimization

j. Time cards

k. Unemployment taxes

_____1. A tax levied on both employer and employee.

_____2. Is likely to occur in group incentive plans unless management takes action to ensure that the goals of the overall company are not neglected.

_____3. The adoption of this system may require a major revision in a company's incentive plans.

_____4. Are appropriate when it is impossible to measure the production of an individual employee.

_____5. Is completed before an employee begins work and indicates the income tax exemptions they are claiming.

_____6. Provides evidence of the time the employee was on the work site; this may be prepared manually or by a clock punch.

_____ 7. Because of company policy or union contract, employers may pay this extra compensation to employees working less desirable time periods.

_____ 8. A tool used by management to increase the productivity of labor.

_____ 9. Employers are required to furnish employees this statement indicating wages earned and taxes withheld.

_____ 10. Employers of one or more workers in covered employment are subject to this tax; employees do not have this tax withheld from their wages.

Completion and Exercises

1.　The two reasons that incentive compensation plans may be adopted are:

　　a._____

　　_____

　　b._____

　　_____

2.　Give two advantages of using group incentive plans.

　　a._____

　　_____

　　b._____

　　_____

3.　Give two dangers of using group incentive plans

　　a._____

　　_____

　　b._____

　　_____

4. Jackson Company uses an incentive plan in which employees receive a guaranteed rate of $6 per hour and a premium of 70 percent of the time saved on production in excess of the standard of 50 units per hour. You have pulled the production records and find an employee has produced the following for the eight hours worked each day: Monday, 450 units; and Tuesday, 525 units.

Compute the daily earnings for these two days.

Monday

Tuesday

5. Accounting for Vacation and Bonus Pay

According to company policy, all employees of Gerald Company receive 15 working days of vacation. Employees work a five-day week. Additionally, each employee is to receive a bonus at year-end of 0.08 percent of net company income. A $400,000 net income is projected for the company.

Required:

a. Assume Jane Smith earns $56 for one day of productive labor; prepare the journal entry to record the total weekly labor cost for Smith. A payroll summary account has previously been used and you are to only distribute the labor cost.
b. Calculate the cost of vacations as a percentage of productive labor cost for Smith using a 40-hour week.
c. Assume the cost of vacations is calculated each pay period and prepare the journal entry when Smith receives the entire vacation pay. A total of $120 federal income tax, $42 state income tax, and $50 FICA tax is withheld.

a.

b.

c.

6. Wage, Inc., is contemplating offering its employees an incentive plan. The company has made an analysis of past results and arrived at the following data representative of an actual average month.

	Per Average Month
Actual production	15,000 units
Direct material used	$34,500
Direct labor costs	46,500
Variable factory overhead	7,500
Fixed factory overhead	22,500

Management has conducted tests and found that units produced will increase by one third per month if the proposed incentive plan is installed. Including the incentive wage payments, total actual labor cost is expected to be $63,000 after the incentive plan is installed. Other factory costs maintain their cost behavior.

Required:

Would you advise management to adopt the incentive plan? Base your recommendations solely on the effect the incentive plan has on unit product cost. What other factors should the company consider before adopting the incentive plan?

7. Distributing Labor Costs and Alternative Treatment of Payroll Tax

Analysis of the Labor Company's payroll records reveals the following:

	Current Weekly Earnings	Federal Income Tax Withheld
A., president	$1,600	$200
B., salesperson	700	100
C., direct laborer	400	50
D., indirect laborer	300	10

Required:

a. Record the distribution of labor cost and its subsequent payment for the first week of November. Assume that the following rates are in effect: FICA, 8%; State unemployment, 2.7%; Federal unemployment, 0.8%. Of B's earnings $500 and all of C's and D's earnings are subject to FICA Tax. Only $400 of direct labor wages and $100 of indirect labor wages are subject to unemployment.
b. Record payroll taxes for the above employees and treat them as indirect costs.
c. As an alternative to Requirement *b*, record payroll taxes for the above employees and treat them as direct costs.

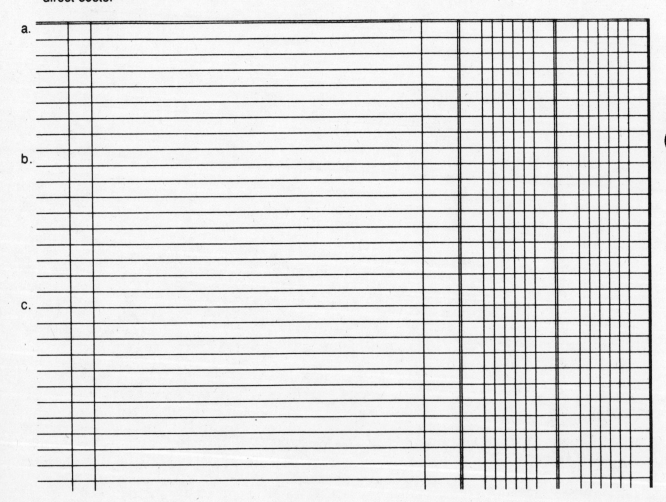

8. Daily Earnings and Effective Hourly Rate Using Proposed Incentive Plans

Standard production in the Emma Knight Company is 40 units per hour. For the first week in April, a worker's record shows the following:

Monday	....	330 units	8 hours
Tuesday	....	350 units	8 hours
Wednesday	....	310 units	8 hours
Thursday	....	320 units	8 hours
Friday	....	340 units	8 hours

Management is considering the adoption of one of two different incentive plans and wants to use this representative worker's record to study earnings using each proposed incentive plan.

With incentive Plan A, workers are guaranteed a rate of $2.40 per hour and a premium of 70 percent of the time saved on production in excess of standard.

With incentive Plan B, workers are paid $0.07 per unit when daily output is below standard, $0.09 per unit when daily output is at standard and up to 5 percent above standard, $0.10 per unit for all production when the daily output exceeds 5 percent above standard.

Required:

Compute daily earnings and the effective rate per hour for each day using each of the incentive plans proposed.

_____
_____
_____
_____
_____
_____
_____
_____
_____
_____
_____
_____
_____
_____
_____
_____
_____
_____
_____

9. Journal Entries for Labor Cost and Payment of Withholdings

Payroll data for the Barbara Manufacturing Company is given below for the first pay period of the year. All wages are subject to a 8 percent FICA tax, 2.7 percent state unemployment tax, and .8 percent federal unemployment tax.

	Gross Wages	Income Tax Withheld	Hospitalization Insurance	Union Dues
Job #150	$ 28,000	$ 6,600	$ 800	$360
Job #160	32,100	7,400	710	460
Repairers	13,500	1,560	315	140
Janitorial Staff	8,500	960	117	—
Salespersons	16,800	3000	88	—
Executive Director and Administrators	42,000	19,000	—	—
	$140,900	$38,520	$2,030	$960

Required:

a. Prepare the necessary entries to record the payment of payroll treating the payroll tax as indirect costs. Use subsidiary ledger accounts where appropriate.
b. Record the entry for the payment of the union dues, hospitalization insurance, and all taxes accrued and withheld this pay period.

True-False Questions

Indicate whether the following statements are true or false by inserting in the blank space a capital "T" for true or "F" for false.

_____ 1. Employees who receive stock options determine their compensation by multiplying the price of the stock on the date the option is exercised by the number of shares purchased.

_____ 2. A temporary ledger account called Payroll can be used if the labor distribution is not known at the time payment is made; later when accountants know the labor distribution, they credit the Payroll account.

_____ 3. Employers have an option whether to deduct social security and income taxes from employees' payroll or have employees make their own payments directly.

_____ 4. FICA taxes are not levied on overtime premium pay, only on regular pay.

_____ 5. Group incentive plans, if not properly monitored, encourage suboptimization.

_____ 6. Employees working on a night shift may receive a shift differential or premium and the preferred treatment is to charge this premium along with the regular pay to Work in Process if direct labor workers are involved.

_____ 7. If the data is not available for labor distribution at the time wages are paid, a Payroll ledger account may be used; this is a temporary account.

_____ 8. Employers and employees contribute to state workmen's compensation insurance in equal percentage amounts.

_____ 9. If there is any difference between the time recorded on a time card and a daily job time ticket, it is more likely that the time reported on the daily job time ticket will be larger assuming no error has been made.

_____ 10. For a direct laborer working on a night shift who receives $20.60 per hour rather than the regular day-shift rate of $20, the entry to distribute this employee's wage is to multiply the number of hours worked by $20.60 and debit the total to Work in Process Inventory.

SOLUTIONS

Matching

1.	a	6.	j
2.	i	7.	h
3.	f	8.	e
4.	d	9.	b
5.	c	10.	k

Completion and Exercises

1. a. Incentive compensation plans give employees the opportunity to earn additional money if they are willing to work at an efficient level of operations.

   b. By reducing the factory overhead per unit since there are more units over which fixed factory overhead can be spread, the unit cost of finished products may be reduced. Even though labor cost per unit may rise or at least total direct labor costs will increase, the reduction in per unit factory overhead usually more than offsets the increase in labor costs.

2. Advantages of using group incentive plans are:

   a. Clerical effort to compute a bonus is reduced from individual incentive plans.

   b. Employees have a stronger incentive to work together as a team because each employee's bonus depends upon the group's output.

   c. Pressure is applied on the slower worker because of his/her impact on the group's bonus.

3. Dangers of using incentive plans are:

   a. By encouraging competition between individual departments, suboptimization may develop whereby employees focus only upon departmental goals rather than also meeting company-wide goals.

   b. Employees are encouraged to look only at short-run benefits for themselves rather than long-run benefits for both themselves and the company.

   c. Disharmony may develop between individual members because some employees may believe that they are doing more than their share of work.

4. *Jackson Company*

Monday

$$\frac{50 \text{ units}}{50} = 1 \text{ hour saved} \times \$6 = \$6 \times 70\% = \$4.20$$

Premium

48.00 (8 hr. x $6)

$52.20

Tuesday

$$\frac{125 \text{ units}}{50} = 2\ 1/2 \text{ hour saved} \times \$6 = \$15 \times 70\% = \$10.50 \text{ premium}$$

48.00

$58.50

5. *Gerald Company*

a. The employee benefit payments are estimated as follows:

Vacations (15 days X $56 per day)	$840
Bonus (.08% of $400,000 expected net income)...........	320

Costs are spread over 49 weeks [52 weeks - 3 weeks (15 days/5 days per week)]

5. (Concluded)

$$\frac{\$840}{49\,\text{weeks}} = \$17.14 \text{ per week for vacation pay}$$

$$\frac{\$320}{49\,\text{weeks}} = \$6.53 \text{ per week for bonus pay}$$

The following entry would be made to record the weekly payroll for Jane Smith:

Work in Process (5 days X $56 per day)...	280.00	
Factory Overhead Control ($17.14 + $6.53)...	23.67	
Payroll		280.00
Accrued Vacation Pay..		17.14
Accrued Bonus Pay...		6.53

b.

$$\frac{120\,(15\text{ days of vacation X 8 hours})}{1{,}960\text{ productive hours (49 weeks X 40 hours)}} = 6.12\% \text{ or } \$17.14/\$280 = 6.12\%$$

c.

Accrued Vacation Pay (15 days X $56)...	840.00	
Federal Income Tax Withheld...		120.00
State Income Tax Withheld...		42.00
FICA Taxes Payable...		50.00
Payroll Payable..		628.00
Payroll Payable	628.00	
Cash...		628.00

6. *Wage Company, Inc.*

Before adopting the incentive plan, the cost is:

	Per Unit	Total
15,000 units produced		
Direct Material	$2.30	$34,500
Direct Labor...	3.10	40,500
Variable Factory Overhead....	.50	7,500
Fixed Factory Overhead	1.50	22,500
	$7.40	$111,000

After adopting the incentive plan, the cost will be:

	Per Unit	Total
20,000 units produced		
Direct Material	$2.300	$ 46,000
Direct Labor...	3.150	63,000
Variable Factory Overhead...	.500	10,000
Fixed Factory Overhead	1.125	22,500
	$7.075	$141,500

Since the product unit cost has decreased, you should advise management to adopt the wage incentive plan. Even though the direct labor cost has increased from $3.10 per unit to $3.15, this has been more than offset by the reduction in fixed overhead per unit from $1.500 to $1.125.

The company should have some assurance that the higher production and greater efficiency will continue in the future. The impact of the incentive system on employee morale should also be studied, as well as the possibility of all employees understanding the mechanics of the system. Also, market demand should be high enough to absorb the extra units available for sale.

7. *Labor Company*

a.
Administrative Expense Control-Salaries	1,600.00	
Marketing Expense Control-Salaries	700.00	
Work in Process Inventory-Direct Labor	400.00	
Factory Overhead Control-Indirect Labor	300.00	
Federal Income Tax Payable		360.00
FICA Taxes Payable		96.00*
Payroll Payable		2,544.00
Payroll Payable	2,544.00	
Cash		2,544.00

b.
Marketing Expense Control ($500 X 8%)	40.00	
Factory Overhead Control- Payroll Tax Expense ($56.00 + $17.50)	73.50	
($400 + $300) X 8% = $56.00; ($400 + $100) X (.027 + .008) = $17.50		
FICA Taxes Payable		96.00*
Federal Unemployment Tax Payable ($500 X .008)		4.00
State Unemployment Tax Payable ($500 X 2.7%)		13.50

c.
Work in Process Inventory		
($400 X 8%) + ($400 X 3.5%)	46.00	
Factory Overhead Control-Payroll Tax Expense		
($300 X 8%) + ($100 X 3.5%)	27.50	
Marketing Expense Control ($500 X 8%)	40.00	
FICA Taxes Payable		96.00*
Federal Unemployment Tax Payable ($500 X .008)		4.00
State Unemployment Tax Payable ($500 X 2.7%)		13.50

*Wages Subject to FICA Taxes

A	$ 0
B	500
C	400
D	300

Total Wages Subject $1,200 X 8% = $96

8. *Emma Knight*

Plan A $\dfrac{\$2.40}{40 \text{ units}}$ = $.06 per unit X 70% = $.042 per unit

$2.40 X 8 hours = $19.20 guaranteed daily wage.

		Daily Earnings	Effective Rate per Hour
Monday	$19.62	[$19.20 + (10 units X $.042)]	$2.453
Tuesday	20.46	[$19.20 + (30 units X $.042)]	2.558
Wednesday	19.20		2.400
Thursday	19.20		2.400
Friday	20.04	[$19.20 + (20 units X $.042)]	2.505
Weekly earnings	$98.52		

Plan B Standard Production = 320 units
105% standard production = 336 units

8. (Concluded)

	Daily Earnings		Effective Rate per Hour
			$3.7125 $\left(\dfrac{\$29.70}{8 \text{ hours}}\right)$
Monday	29.70	(330 X $.09)	
Tuesday	35.00	(350 X $.10)	4.3750
Wednesday	21.70	(310 X $.07)	2.7125
Thursday	28.80	(320 X $.09)	3.6000
Friday	34.00	(340 X $.10)	4.2500
Weekly earnings	$149.20		

9. *Barbara Manufacturing Company*

	Subsidiary Ledger	Dr.	Cr.
a. Work in Process Inventory		60,100.00	
Job #150	28,000.00		
Job #160	32,100.00		
Factory Overhead Control		22,000.00	
Repairers Wages	13,500.00		
Janitorial Wages	8,500.00		
Marketing Exp. Control - Salaries	16,800.00	16,800.00	
Administrative Expense Control - Salaries	42,000.00	42,000.00	
Income Tax Withheld			38,520.00
Hospitalization Insurance Payable			2,030.00
Union Dues Payable			960.00
FICA Taxes Payable (8% x $140,900)			11,272.00
Payroll Payable			88,118.00
Payroll Payable		88,118.00	
Cash			88,118.00
Factory Overhead Control-			
Payroll Tax ...[($60,100 + $22,000) x 11.5%]	9,441.50	9,441.50	
Marketing Expense Control-			
Payroll Tax ($16,800 x 11.5%)	1,932.00	1,932.00	
Administrative Expense Control-			
Payroll Tax ($42,000 x 11.5%)	4,830.00	4,830.00	
FICA Taxes Payable ($140,900 x 8%)			11,272.00
State Unemployment Taxes Payable			
($140,900 x 2.7%)			3,804.30
Federal Unemployment Taxes Payable			
($140,900 x .8%)			1,127.20
b. Income Taxes Withheld		38,520.00	
Hospitalization Insurance Payable		2,030.00	
Union Dues Payable		960.00	
FICA Taxes Payable		22,544.00	
State Unemployment Taxes Payable		3,804.30	
Federal Unemployment Taxes Payable		1,127.20	
Cash			68,985.50

True-False

1. F The employee's compensation is the difference between the option price and the price of the stock on the date the option is exercised.

2. T

3. F Deductions for income tax and social security are not optional deductions for employees; employers are required by law to withhold these taxes.

4. F FICA taxes are levied on total gross pay including overtime premium pay.

5. T

6. F The preferred treatment is to charge the shift premium to Factory Overhead Control--Shift Premium and the regular pay to Work in Process.

7. T

8. F Only employers contribute to workmen's compensation insurance; both employers and employees do, however, contribute FICA taxes.

9. F The time card reports the total time that employees are on the work site while the daily job time ticket shows the time spent on individual jobs. The time card reflects idle time and time transferring between jobs while the daily job time ticket does not. (Note, however, company policy may vary some regarding the treatment of time transferring between jobs.)

10. F The entry required is to multiply the number of hours worked by $20 and debit this total to Work in Process Inventory; $.60 times the number of hours worked is also debited to Factory Overhead Control--Shift Premium.

23 The Use of Costs in Pricing Decisions

Chapter Outline

Influence of Various Parties
    Consumer Behavior
Determinants of Pricing
    External Determinants of Pricing
    Demand and Supply Curves
    Price Elasticity of Demand
    Cross Elasticity of Demand
Competitive Structures
    Monopoly
    Monopolistic Competition
    Oligopoly
    Perfect Competition
    Economic Profits
Relationship Among Demand, Supply, and Cost
    Return on Assets Employed
    Gross Margin Pricing
Cost-Plus Pricing Methods
    Variable Cost Pricing
    Differential Cost Pricing
    Full-Cost Pricing
    Conversion Cost Pricing
    Direct Cost Pricing
Social Responsibility and Pricing

Chapter Objectives

After studying this chapter, you should be able to:

1. Explain the role of cost in the final pricing decision.

2. Discuss the variety of market conditions, ranging from a monopolistic market, in which a company has some control over the prices charged, to a perfectly competitive market, in which a company accepts the sales price established by the market.

3. Evaluate the various cost-based methods on which prices can be established, such as variable costs, differential costs, full costs, and conversion costs.

4. Apply the role of social costs and social responsibility in an organization's pricing strategy.

5. Define and apply the new terms introduced.

Chapter Review

Influence of Various Parties

1. Conflict of interest regarding a company's pricing policy is expected since such policy affects so many people.

    a. Suboptimization often results when departments are more interested in achieving departmental goals and these are in conflict with company-wide objectives.
    b. A company should identify its interpretation of profit maximization and this interpretation should be in harmony with the market share it is trying to gain.

Consumer Behavior

2. Consumers' behavior and their buying habits are important in establishing a company's prices.

Determinants of Pricing

3. A company's prices must consider elements in the marketing mix and also satisfy certain external and internal constraints.

External Determinants of Pricing

4. Both internal and external factors affect the pricing decision; the following are external factors.

    a. The market in which the product is sold including supply and demand.
    b. The product's features in comparison to competing products.
    c. The market structure, whether perfect competition or imperfect competition, which indicates the number of competitors and customers of a company.
    d. Customers' buying habits and how these relate to price.
    e. The impact of legislation such as the Robinson-Patman Amendment.

Demand and Supply Curves

5. Demand is an important external price determinant; this relationship between the market price of the goods and the quantity demanded can be expressed in a demand curve.

    a. Holding all other variables constant (ceteris paribus), the quantity demanded of an economic good varies inversely with the price of the good; stated simply, the higher the price of a good, the less demand there is for the product.
    b. Demand curves are derived so that the characteristics of the individual consumer can be analyzed.

6. A change in the quantity demanded refers to a movement along a given single demand curve and differs from a change in demand which refers to a shift in a demand curve. The distinction between these two terms is important to the pricing decision because a change in quantity demanded is the result of a price change. A change in demand refers to the effect of changes in variables other than the price on the quantity of the good demanded.

Price Elasticity of Demand

7. Price elasticity of demand indicates how total revenue changes when a price change causes a change in quantity demanded.

    a. The elasticity concept measures the degree of responsiveness of quantity demanded to changes in the market price.
    b. Demand is referred to as elastic or greater than unity if a price decrease causes quantity demanded to increase so much that total revenue increases.

c. Unity elasticity is assumed if a price decrease causes no change in total revenue.

d. Demand is inelastic or less than unity if the price decrease causes such a small increase in quantity demanded that total revenue decreases.

8. The relationship between price changes and customer behavior can be understood by using the following formula, where Q represents quantity demanded and P represents the price of the goods:

$$\frac{(\Delta Q)/Q}{(\Delta P)/P}$$

9. The following demand and supply curves indicate that the supply curve is upward sloping because suppliers will provide larger quantities at higher prices. The demand curve is downward sloping because consumers demand less at higher prices.

Cross Elasticity of Demand

10. Cross elasticity of demand measures the extent to which various commodities are related to each other.

a. The relationship between substitute commodities and the relationship between complementary commodities is important in pricing.

b. Cross elasticity of demand is positive when commodities are substitutes for each other; commodities which are complementary to each other have negative cross elasticity.

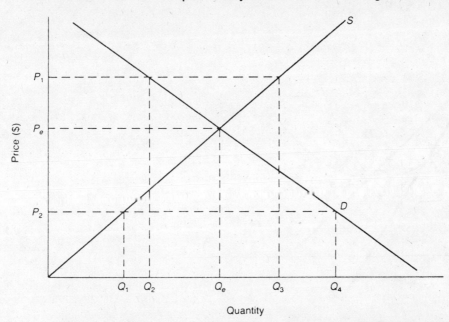

1. Initially if a Price of P_1 is assumed and quantity demanded is only Q_2, sellers have excess inventory since they are willing to offer Q_3 at this price. The price is bid down and in a purely competitive market, price falls until market equilibrium occurs at the point where quantities supplied and demanded are equal.

2. If instead initially the price is P_2, and the quantity that sellers are willing to supply is Q_1, the excess demand will bid up the price to P_e where quantities supplied and demanded are equal.

Competitive Structures

11. The market structure in which a company operates affects pricing; at one extreme is the monopolist whose company's demand is the same as the industry's and at the other extreme is the perfect competitor who has no significant influence on price.

Monopoly

12. A monopoly is a market in which there is only one seller; this means that the company's demand is identical to the market demand for the products.

   a. The quantity sold of a monopolist's products varies inversely with the sales price.
   b. Marginal revenue is the change in the total revenue received from selling one more unit.
   c. Marginal cost is the additional cost of producing one more unit and initially declines due to increasing economies of scale resulting from greater efficiencies of production as more units are produced.

13. Diminishing returns set in at some point in operations and output cannot be increased except by increasing the marginal cost.

   a. The law of diminishing returns states that beyond some point, decreasing amounts of additional output are obtained when equal extra units of a varying input are added to a fixed amount of some other input.

14. Profit maximization for a monopolist is where marginal revenue equals marginal cost; this is not at the highest price possible.

15. Profit maximization is shown at P_e where marginal cost intersects with marginal revenue as shown below.

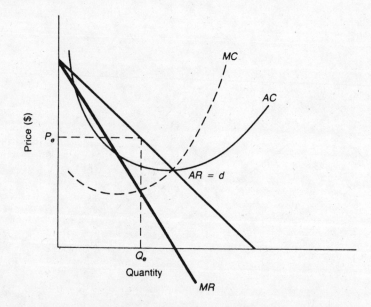

   a. A monopolist is faced with a downward sloping demand curve.
   b. Average total cost is not used to arrive at the monopolist's maximum equilibrium point, but total cost cannot be ignored because it must be covered for a company to remain in operation in the long run.

Monopolistic Competition

16. Monopoly, monopolistic competition, and oligopoly are all market structures which are included in the term imperfect competition.

17. Monopolistic competition is a market condition in which a relatively large number of small producers are offering similar but not identical products.

a. There are enough firms that each has little or no control over the market price.
b. Packaging, trade names, and sales promotion are used to differentiate products in buyers' mind.

18. As shown below, the demand curve for a monopolistic competitor is more elastic at a given price than that of the entire industry.

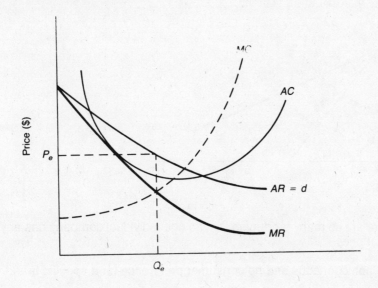

a. Profit maximization for a monopolistic competitor occurs at a price where marginal revenue equals marginal cost.
b. New companies are attracted to the industry if profits exist and this causes the short-run demand for an individual company's products to fall and become more elastic.

Oligopoly

19. If the number of companies in the industry is small and little product differentiation occurs, an oligopoly exists.

a. Companies watch the pricing strategy of its competitors because a price cut will be matched by competitors resulting in less favorable conditions for all companies.
b. If an oligopolist raises prices, competitors probably will not follow and the oligopolist will lose its share of the market. This results in a sticky demand curve.

20. An oligopolist's demand curve would appear as shown at the top of the next page with Line DD representing the demand curve for all sellers when they move prices together and share a total market.

a. Line dd which is more elastic represents one company's demand curve when it acts alone in changing its price.
b. At point X, any price cut below this is matched by the company's rivals and the DD demand curve prevails.
c. At any point above X, dd prevails since competitors do not match the company's price cuts.
d. Significant shifts in the marginal cost curve do not change the price charged because of the discontinuity in the MR curve which is the reason oligopolists' prices are described as sticky.

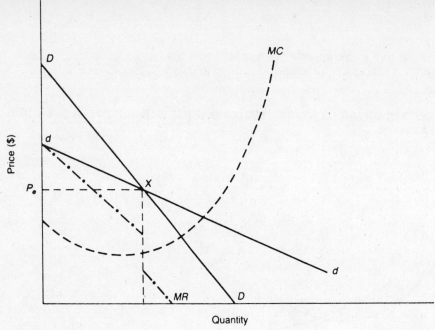

Perfect Competition

21. In perfect competition, there are so many producers that no one individual company has any influence on the market price.

   a. The products sold are homogeneous and no consumer preference for a specific brand exists.
   b. The company's demand is a horizontal line of infinite elasticity at equilibrium because the pure competitor must take the market price for each product sold.

22. Profit maximization for a perfect competitor is easy because the competitor merely finds the output quantity that yields maximum profit and sells at that output with the given market price.

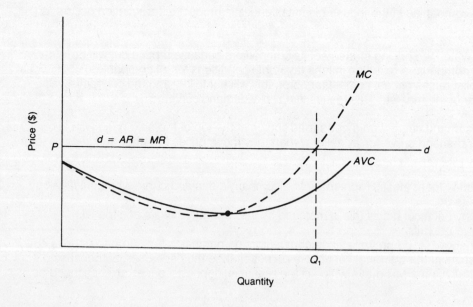

Economic Profits

23. Economic profits involve both implicit and explicit costs and differ from accounting income which considers only explicit costs.

   a. Explicit costs consist of payments for resources bought or rented by the company.
   b. Implicit costs are costs of self-owned, self-employed resources which do not require an outlay of cash.

24. Normal profit is the imputed return of capital which is the minimum amount of profit to keep the firm in business in the long run.

Relationship among Demand, Supply, and Cost

25. Cost is generally considered to be a floor below which price cannot fall.

Return on Assets Employed

26. The following formula can be used in determining a percentage markup on cost to generate a specified rate of return on assets employed.

$$\text{Percentage markup on cost} = \frac{\text{Assets employed}}{\text{Total annual costs}} \times \text{Desired rate of return on assets employed}$$

Gross Margin Pricing

27. The following formula can be used in gross margin pricing:

$$\text{Planned Gross Margin Rate} = \frac{\text{Gross Margin}}{\text{Revenue}}$$

Cost-Plus Pricing Methods

28. Cost does play an important part in cost-plus, or backward-cost, pricing methods.

Variable Cost Pricing

29. Under variable cost pricing, contribution margin is emphasized; one form involves adding a markup on variable costs to full costs.

   a. A problem with studying only contribution margin is that often management must spend unequal amounts of time with various products and this may be ignored under variable cost pricing.
   b. Fixed costs are considered irrelevant and not considered and this may not be appropriate in step-type fixed costs.

Differential Cost Pricing

30. Differential cost pricing focuses attention on the contribution to fixed costs and profit that an additional order generates.

Full-Cost Pricing

31. Under full-cost pricing, a markup on full cost is used; this considers the product's direct and indirect costs.

Conversion Cost Pricing

32. No profits are allowed for the material used in the product when conversion cost pricing is used.

Direct Cost Pricing

33. Under direct cost pricing, selling prices are established at a certain percentage above the direct or traceable costs incurred in producing the product.

34. All cost-based pricing methods can be criticized; instead, cost information should be used as one of many factors in establishing the sales price.

Social Responsibility and Pricing

35. *Social costs* are the outcome of an interaction of several complex economic, physical, biological, and meteorological systems; air pollution is an example of a social cost.

36. There is a lack of consensus regarding the definition of social costs and corporate social responsibility; generally *social responsibility* is considered the voluntary response of corporations to those needs of society which would not normally be met within the framework of the profit motive.

Demonstration Problem

Price Decreases and Volume

After studying the following income statement for its product, management of White Company believes that a reduction in sales price may be justified.

Year ending December 31, 19X1

Sales (300,000 units)		$2,100,000
Variable costs......................................	$1,200,000	
Fixed costs	400,000	1,600,000
Income before taxes...........................		$ 500,000

Required:

a.   How much extra volume must be sold in 19X2 to yield an income equal to that earned in 19X1 if decreases of 5 percent, 10 percent, and 15 percent in selling prices become necessary?

b.   Why do successive price decreases of equal amounts require progressively larger increases in volume to equalize profits?

c.   With the limited information given, discuss the factors you would advise management to study further before reducing the sale price.

Paper for working Demonstration Problem

a. (1) Decrease of 5 percent in selling price

(2) Decrease of 10 percent in selling price

(3) Decrease of 15 percent in selling price

b. _____

c. _____

Solution to Demonstration Problem

White Company

a. (1) Decrease of 5% in selling price:

New price (selling price of $7 less 5%)... $6.65
Less variable unit cost.. 4.00
Contribution margin $2.65

$$\frac{\$400{,}000 \text{ fixed costs} + \$500{,}000 \text{ income}}{\$2.65 \text{ contribution margin}} = \frac{\$900{,}000 \text{ fixed costs}}{\$2.65} = 339{,}623 \text{ required units}$$

(2) Decrease of 10% in selling price:

New price (selling price of $7 less 10%)... $6.30
Less variable unit cost.. 4.00
Contribution margin $2.30

$$\frac{\$400{,}000 \text{ fixed costs} + \$500{,}000 \text{ income}}{\$2.30 \text{ contribution margin}} = \frac{\$900{,}000 \text{ fixed costs}}{\$2.30} = 391{,}304 \text{ required units}$$

(3) Decrease of 15% in selling price:

New price (selling price of $7 less 15%)... $5.95
Less variable unit cost.. 4.00
Contribution margin $1.95

$$\frac{\$400{,}000 \text{ fixed costs} + \$500{,}000 \text{ income}}{\$1.95 \text{ contribution margin}} = \frac{\$900{,}000 \text{ fixed costs}}{\$1.95} = 461{,}539 \text{ required units}$$

To summarize as follows:

Decrease % in Selling Price	Required Volume to Equal Income of Last Year	Increase in Volume Required Units	% of Increase in Volume
5%	339,623	39,623	13%
10%	391,304	91,304	30%
15%	461,539	161,539	54%

b. With each price decrease of equal amounts, contribution margin becomes a smaller percentage of sales price (or variable costs become a larger percentage of sales price). Since fixed costs and desired profit are remaining constant, a volume that is progressively increasing is required to cover fixed cost and income during a time when contribution margin is becoming smaller.

c. The problem does not state why management is interested in cutting price. If these price cuts are necessary to meet competition, the figures computed show what volume the company will have to achieve in order to maintain the same amount of income. Substantial increases in volume are necessary to maintain this income level and this volume may be impossible to realize. If management doubts whether this increased volume can be realized, it should hesitate implementing the price cuts. Even if the increased volume can be realized in 19X2, the price cut may have an unfavorable impact on future years. Customers may become spoiled to buying at the lower price and may resist future price increases. If total demand for the product does not increase because of the price cuts, the additional volume White Company achieves may be simply from taking business from a present competitor; the danger of this approach is that the increase in volume may be only temporary.

Management should focus some attention to the reduction of its present cost; if a cost reduction program could be combined with increased volume, the financial picture would be even more favorable.

Matching

Referring to the terms listed in the left column, place the appropriate letter next to the corresponding description. A term may not be used or may be used more than once.

a. Accounting income

b. Contribution margin

c. *Cross elasticity* of demand

d. Differential cost pricing

e. Direct cost pricing

f. Economic profit

g. Full cost pricing

h. Gross margin

i. Marginal revenue

j. Monopoly

k. Oligopoly

l. Perfect competition

m. Price elasticity of demand

n. Social costs

o. Variable cost pricing

_____ 1. Revenue less explicit expenses which are based on actual transactions.

_____ 2. A market condition in which the number of companies in the industry is small and little production differentiation exists. If a company raised their prices, competitors probably will not follow.

_____ 3. The profit figure that should be the focus in quoting a bid for a one-time order.

_____ 4. Costs which result from an interaction of several complex economic, physical, biological, and meteorological systems; water pollution is an example.

_____ 5. A pricing method which focuses on contribution margin by delineating the behavior of fixed and variable cost.

_____ 6. An approach to pricing which adds a markup to the product's direct and indirect costs.

_____ 7. Revenue less both implicit and explicit costs.

_____ 8. A pricing approach which emphasizes the contribution to fixed costs and profit that an additional order or unit will make; also known as marginal cost pricing.

_____ 9. A measure of how total revenue changes when a price change causes a change in quantity demanded.

_____ 10. The change in total revenue received from selling one more unit.

_____ 11. Measures the extent to which various commodities are related to each other; is positive when commodities are substitutes for each other.

Completion and Exercises

1. Discuss the differences between economic profit and accounting income.

   _____

   _____

   _____

2. Why are oligopolists' prices often described as being sticky? _____

   _____

   _____

   _____

3. Briefly discuss three external determinants of pricing.

   a. _____

   _____

   b. _____

   _____

   c. _____

   _____

4. a. A _____ _____ _____ _____ refers to a
      movement along a given single demand curve while a _____
      refers to a shift in a demand curve.

   b. In reference to *a.* above, why is it important to make a distinction between a movement
      along a specific demand curve and a shift in a demand curve? _____

      _____

      _____

      _____

5. Demand is referred to as _____ if a price decrease causes total revenue to decrease; if
   however, a price decrease causes total revenue to increase, demand is _____; if
   there is no change in total revenue with a price decrease, _____ _____
   is assumed.

6. The degree of difference between a company's elasticity and the industry's is _____ in perfect
   competition and is _____ in a monopoly.

7. Using _____ _____ pricing, a certain percentage is added to the
   traceable costs in producing the product, but if instead _____ - _____ pricing
   is used, a markup on both direct and indirect costs is made.

8. Fieldings Manufacturing Company has experienced intense competition in recent months. However,
   management still believes that they must maintain the policy of refusing all sales orders unless they
   receive a 10 percent return on total unit cost. Orders are rejected daily because of this policy. As a
   result, inventories have stockpiled in the warehouse and management is contemplating closing one
   of its factories.

Required:

Make any suggestions which you believe might be of value to the company.

_____
_____
_____
_____
_____
_____
_____
_____
_____
_____
_____

9. Sexton Company has developed a new product that is enjoying a monopolistic market. Due to the complex technological motors contained in the product, Sexton expects to maintain this market position for some time in the future.

    The following data are provided, showing the quantity demanded at the following prices, along with total cost.

Quantity	Average Price	Total Cost
1	$200	$120
2	180	230
3	140	285
4	110	305
5	80	385
6	50	505

Required:

Determine the price at which profits are maximized.

_____
_____
_____
_____
_____
_____
_____
_____
_____
_____
_____

10. Butterfly Company builds greenhouses for residential homes. The company has two sizes of greenhouses, which are known as the Green Thumb and Deluxe Green Thumb.

Estimates of the cost of each line are as follows:

	Green Thumb per Unit	Deluxe Green Thumb per Unit
Direct material	$200	$ 450
Direct Labor	325	375
Overhead	65	75
Total cost	$590	$ 900
Sales price	$870	$1,160

Overhead is allocated on the basis of 20 percent of direct labor costs. Total manufacturing, marketing, and administrative overhead is $130,000; 55 percent is variable in direct proportion to direct labor costs. The company has excess capacity.

Required:

a. A customer outside the present market region offers to buy 1,000 Green Thumb greenhouses for $580 and 200 Deluxe Green Thumb greenhouses for $860. Show the difference in income if only the Green Thumb offer is accepted.
b. Show the difference in income if only the Deluxe Green Thumb offer is accepted.
c. Identify the weaknesses in the pricing analysis you used in answering Requirements *a* and *b*.

11. Management of Jennings Company wishes to earn a 20 percent return on the $77 million of assets employed in manufacturing a new product. Annual costs total $35 million, and management expects to sell 210,000 units.

Required:

Determine the necessary total sales volume and unit sales price to achieve these objectives.

True-False Questions

Indicate whether the following statements are true or false by inserting in the blank space a capital "T" for true or "F" for false.

_____ 1.   When a company receives a bid for a one-time order that would make use of otherwise idle capacity, fixed costs such as depreciation and insurance should be added to the variable costs in deciding whether to accept the bid or not.

_____ 2.   A demand curve is downward sloping because consumers will demand less at higher prices, and a supply curve is upward sloping because sellers will react to higher prices by increasing the quantity of goods supplied.

_____ 3.   Profit maximization for a monopolist is where price is at its highest point because this is where marginal revenue is higher than average revenue.

_____ 4.   Under a perfect competition market structure, there are a small number of companies and little product differentiation exists.

_____ 5.   Cost is but one of many factors that determine the price a company charges; often cost merely influences pricing by providing a minimum floor below which price should not fall.

_____ 6.   Under an oligopolistic market structure, there is easy entry into the industry and much price competition.

_____ 7.   Demand elasticity is said to be elastic if total revenue rises in response to a decrease in a product's price.

_____ 8.   Average revenue is the change in the total revenue received from selling one more unit.

_____ 9.   According to the law of diminishing returns, there is a point beyond which decreasing amounts of additional output are obtained when equal extra units of a varying input are added to a fixed amount of some other input.

_____10.   Under perfect competition, a company has little need for nonprice competition such as advertising because no one individual company has any influence on the market price.

SOLUTIONS

Matching

1.	a	6.	g	11.	c
2.	k	7.	f		
3.	b	8.	d		
4.	n	9.	m		
5.	o	10.	i		

Completion and Exercises

1.   Both explicit costs consisting of payments for resources bought or rented by the company, as well as the implicit costs of self-owned, self-employed resources not requiring a cash outlay are considered in determining economic profit. Only explicit costs are deducted in arriving at accounting net income. Economists view profits as the return for entrepreneurial ability.

2.   Oligopolists' prices are described as sticky or stable because they remain the same even with considerable cost changes because companies know that their competitors will match price decreases, but they will not match price increases. When no company acts alone in changing its price, it can expect to lose sales to competitors when it raises prices. An oligopoly has two different demand curves.

3.   External determinants of pricing include the following:

a.   The environment in which the product is sold.
b.   The product's characteristics compared with those of competing products so that the importance of brand loyalty and other factors affecting product demand can be studied.
c.   The market structure, including the number of competitors as well as the number of customers.
d.   Customers' buying habits to better understand the significance of price in their decision to buy.
e.   The influence of such legislation as the Robinson-Patman Amendment.

4.   a.   change in the quantity demanded; change in demand
     b.   The distinction is important in pricing decisions because a change in quantity demanded is the result of a price change while a change in demand refers to the effect of changes in variables other than the price on the quantity of the good demanded.

5.   inelastic; elastic; unit elasticity

6.   infinite; zero

7.   direct cost; full-cost

8.   *Fielding Manufacturing*

   Full cost plus pricing is usually the preferred approach for companies; however, other factors such as competition, supply, and demand influence the price established. This is the approach for a normal situation; yet Fieldings Manufacturing Company is not operating in a normal situation. In an abnormal situation, a company must resort to pricing strategies other than full cost, such as variable cost pricing. In the short run, the company cannot eliminate total fixed costs; as a result, Fieldings should concentrate on the contribution margin generated by an order. This may allow them to break into a new market.

   Since Fieldings has inventory stockpiled, it should consider producing only as an order is received. This would eliminate the excess stock and orient the company to adopting a just-in-time inventory system.

9. *Sexton Company*

Quantity*	Average Revenue or Price	Total Revenue	Total Cost	Total Profit	Marginal Revenue MR	Marginal Cost MC	
1	200	200	120	80	160	110	MR > MC
2	180	360	230	130	60	55	
3	140	420	285	135	20	20	
4	110	440	305	135	-40	80	MR = MC
5	80	400	385	15	-100	120	MR < MC
6	50	300	505	-205			

*Output and sales are assumed to be always equal.

Profits are maximized at a $110 price.

10. *Butterfly Company*

Percent overhead variable X Overhead rate as percentage of labor = Variable overhead rate per direct labor

55%	X	20%	=	11%

	Green Thumb	Deluxe Green Thumb
Direct materials	$ 200.00	$ 450.00
Direct labor	325.00	375.00
Variable overhead	35.75 (11% x $325)	41.25 (11% x $375)
	$ 560.75	$ 866.25
Sales offer	$ 580.00	$ 860.00
Variable costs	560.75	866.25
Contribution margin (loss)	$ 19.25	$ (6.25)
Total Contribution Margin (loss)	$19,250.00	($1,250.00)

a. There would be an increase in income of $19,250 before taxes if the Green Thumb offer was accepted.
b. There would be a decrease in income of $1,250 before taxes if the Deluxe Green Thumb was accepted.
c. Contribution margin pricing is a short run approach to pricing as fixed costs are ignored. In the long run, fixed costs must be considered in pricing if an organization is to survive. Fixed costs must be covered before income can be earned by an organization.

11. *Jennings Company*

Percentage mark up on cost $= \dfrac{\text{Assets employed}}{\text{Total annual costs}}$ X Desired rate of return on capital employed

Percentage mark up on cost $= \dfrac{\$77,000,000}{\$35,000,000}$ X 20% = 44%

Sales volume = Total annual costs + (Total annual cost X Percentage markup on cost)

Sales volume = $35,000,000 + ($35,000,000 X 44%)

Sales volume = $35,000,000 + $15,400,000 = $50,400,000

   or

20%   X $77,000,000 = $15,400,000 + $35,000,000 = $50,400,000

Unit sales price $= \dfrac{\$50,400,000}{210,000}$ = $240

True-False

1. F   Depreciation, insurance, and other fixed costs are not relevant costs when deciding whether to accept such one-time orders which would utilize existing idle capacity .

2. T

3. F   Profit maximization for a monopolist is where marginal revenue equals marginal cost; this is not at the highest price possible. Marginal revenue is less than average revenue at all specific points for a monopolist.

4. F   The statement is describing an oligopoly where products of the limited number of competitors are close substitutes.

5. T

6. F   There is absence of price competition under oligopolistic market structures because each company knows that its competitors are watching its pricing strategy and if price is cut, it will be matched by competitors. As a result, these sellers of homogeneous goods have a strong incentive to charge only the prevailing price. The number of companies in an oligopoly are also small.

7. T

8. F   The statement is describing marginal revenue which will be less than the average revenue because in order to sell another unit, sales price must be reduced.

9. T

10. T

24 Revenue Variances, Material Mix and Yield Variances, and Labor Mix and Yield Variances

Chapter Outline

Revenue Variances for Multiproduct Companies
    Sales Price Variance
    Sales Volume Variance
    Sales Mix Variance
    Sales Quantity Variance
    Market Size and Market Share Variances
Material and Labor Mix and Yield Variances for Multi-Ingredient Product
    Production Mix and Yield Variances
    Material Mix and Yield Variances
    Labor Mix and Yield Variances
    Assumed Substitutability of Material and Labor in Products

Chapter Objectives

After studying this chapter, you should be able to:

1. Explain how different levels of detail in variance analysis are appropriate and cost justified depending on the individual circumstance.

2. Prepare sales price, sales mix, and sales quantity variances for each product sold.

3. Calculate market size and market share variances that detail the sales quantity variance.

4. Determine material and labor mix and yield variances and interpret their meaning.

5. Describe the constraints involved with assumed substitution.

6. Define and apply the new terms introduced.

Chapter Review

Revenue Variances for Multiproduct Companies

1. A company selling many products with different contribution margins makes assumptions as to what mix these products will be sold in.

2. Since there are several levels of detail in variance analysis, a company chooses the detail that is appropriate and cost justified for their own circumstances.

3. Revenue is analyzed by its volume and sales price.

Sales Price Variance

4. The sales price variance is computed as:

   (Actual sales price – Budgeted sales price) X Actual quantity sold

Sales Volume Variance

5. The sales volume variance could also be called the contribution margin variance.

   a. If instead gross margin rather than contribution margin is used, it is called a gross margin variance.
   b. A weighted-average budgeted contribution margin is used to calculate mix and quantity variances.

Sales Mix Variance

6. The sales mix variance is computed as follows:

$$\left[\left(\begin{array}{c} \text{Actual} \\ \text{sales mix} \\ \text{percentage} \end{array} - \begin{array}{c} \text{Budgeted} \\ \text{sales mix} \\ \text{percentage} \end{array}\right) X \frac{\text{Actual total}}{\begin{array}{c}\text{sales volume of all} \\ \text{products in units}\end{array}}\right]$$

   X (Budgeted individual unit contribution margin
   – Budgeted average unit contribution margin)

7. The sales mix variance measures the effect of changes from the budgeted average unit contribution margin combined with a change in the quantity of specific product lines.

Sales Quantity Variance

8. The sales quantity variance is computed as follows:

   (Actual sales volume in units –– Fixed budget volume in units)
   X Budgeted average unit contribution margin

9. The sales quantity variance weights all units at the budgeted average contribution margin and reveals the impact on profits of a change in physical volume.

Market Size and Market Share Variances

10. Accountants break down each product's sales quantity variance into the following market size and market share variances.

Market size variance = Budgeted market share percentage X
(Actual industry sales volume in units - Budgeted industry sales volume in units) X
Budgeted average contribution margin per unit

Market share variance = (Actual market share percentage - Budgeted market share percentage) X
(Actual industry sales volume in units X Budgeted average contribution margin per unit)

Material and Labor Mix and Yield Variances for Multi-Ingredient Product

11. In operations using a recipe or formula there are specifications for each class of material or labor used.

    a. The mix may be changed to improve the yield or to reduce the cost.
    b. Tolerance limits are normally established beyond which the mix cannot be changed because of its impact on taste and quality.

Production Mix and Yield Variances

12. A mix variance is computed by comparing the standard formula to the standard cost of material actually used.

    a. The variance results from mixing raw material in a ratio that differs from standard specifications.
    b. If more of a cheaper grade of material is used than indicated in the formula or recipe, the mix variance will be favorable.

13. A yield variance results because the yield obtained differs from the one expected based on input.

Material Mix and Yield Variances

14. Production mix and yield variances may be calculated in total for the batch of input or they may be determined individually for each grade of material or labor.

Labor Mix and Yield Variances

15. The labor efficiency variance is broken into labor mix and yield variances for companies employing crews of workers.

16. The labor rate and the material price variances are computed for each item of labor and material.

Assumed Substitution of Material and Labor in Products

17. An assumed substitutability of product inputs is used when calculating mix variances. There would be no mix variance if all products sold had the same contribution margin or if all classes of labor and material cost the same.

Demonstration Problem

Blalock Soup Company has developed a secret recipe for vegetable soup. The standard input for material per batch is as follows:

	Pounds	Standard Price per Pound
Beef and beef broth...............	40	$1.00
Potatoes...............................	50	0.30
Cereal and flavoring	20	0.15
Tomatoes..............................	30	0.40
Lima beans............................	50	0.35
Green beans	60	0.28
Input...................................	250	
Output.................................	225	

The soup is packed in 24-ounce cans. During the month, 15,000 cans were filled with the following materials put in process:

	Pounds	Total Actual Cost
Beef and beef broth.............	4,205	$ 4,541.40
Potatoes.............................	4,910	1,374.80
Cereal and flavoring	3,216	611.04
Tomatoes............................	2,800	1,260.00
Lima beans..........................	5,118	1,586.58
Green beans	6,310	2,208.50
	26,559	$11,582.32

Required:

a. Compute a material price variance for each of the materials and a total material mix and a total yield variance for the month. Indicate whether the variance is favorable or unfavorable.
b. Prepare journal entries to record the issuance of material and the variances. The direct materials inventory is kept at actual cost.

Paper for working Demonstration Problem

a.

b.

Solution to Demonstration Problem

Blalock Soup Company

	Pounds	Standard Price	Standard Cost
a. Beef and beef broth..................	40	$1.00	$ 40.00
Potatoes....................................	50	.30	15.00
Cereal and flavoring	20	.15	3.00
Tomatoes..................................	30	.40	12.00
Lima beans...............................	50	.35	17.50
Green beans	60	.28	16.80
Input..	250		$104.30
Output......................................	225		

Standard cost per pound of input ($104.30/250 pounds) = $.4172
Standard cost per pound of output ($104.30/225 pounds) = $.4636

	Actual Quantity	Standard Price	Actual Price		Price Variance per Pound		Total Usage Price Variance	
				$\left(\dfrac{\$4,541.40}{4,205}\right)$				
Beef and beef broth..........	4,205	$1.00	$1.08		$.08	U	$336.40	U
Potatoes..........................	4,910	.30	.28		.02	F	98.20	F
Cereal and flavoring	3,216	.15	.19		.04	U	128.64	U
Tomatoes........................	2,800	.40	.45		.05	U	140.00	U
Lima beans......................	5,118	.35	.31		.04	F	204.72	F
Green beans	6,310	.28	.35		.07	U	441.70	U
	26,559						$743.82	U

Material Mix Variance

Actual Quantity at Standard Price

Beef and beef broth..........	(4,205 X $1.00)	$4,205.00	
Potatoes..........................	(4,910 X $.30)	1,473.00	
Cereal and flavoring	(3,216 X $.15)	482.40	
Tomatoes........................	(2,800 X $.40)	1,120.00	
Lima beans......................	(5,118 X $.35)	1,791.30	
Green beans	(6,310 X $.28)	1,766.80	$10,838.50

Actual quantity of input at standard input cost (26,559 lbs. X $.4172)		11,080.41
Favorable material mix variance		$ 241.91 F
Actual quantity of input at standard input cost		$ 11,080.41
Actual output at standard output cost (22,500 lbs. X $.4636)...................................		10,431.00
(15,000 cans X 1 1/2 lbs. = 22,500 lbs.)		
Unfavorable material yield variance..		$ 649.41 U

U - Unfavorable; F = Favorable

b. Work in Process Inventory..	10,431.00	
Material Yield Variance...	649.41	
Material Usage Price Variance..	743.82	
Material Mix Variance..		241.91
Direct Materials Inventory..		11,582.32

Matching

Referring to the terms listed in the left column, place the appropriate letter next to the corresponding description. A term nay not be used or may be used more than once.

a. Actual product mix

b. Contribution margin variance

c. Favorable

d. Labor mix variance

e. Labor yield variance

f. Material mix variance

g. Sales price variance

h. Sales mix variance

i. Sales quantity variance

j. Sales volume variance

k. Standard product mix

l. Unfavorable

_____ 1. Is used to arrive at the standard cost per pound of input and cost per pound of output

_____ 2. Usually results from the quantity and /or quality of the material handled.

_____ 3. Variance determined by comparing the actual quantity of material at standard price with the actual quantity at standard input cost

_____ 4. This variance compares budgeted and actual quantity and mix for sales.

_____ 5. Another name for the sales volume variance.

_____ 6. This variance is determined by multiplying the difference between actual sales price and budgeted sales price times the actual quantity sold.

_____ 7. This variance is determined by multiplying the difference between actual units sold and the master fixed budget units by the weighted-average budgeted contribution margin per unit.

_____ 8. Measures the effect of changes from the budgeted average unit contribution margin combined with a change in the quantity of specific product lines.

_____ 9. The analysis of a material mix variance when the actual quantity at standard price exceeds tho actual quantily al standard input cost.

_____ 10. Used with a crew of workers having varying degrees of skill with different wage scales.

Completion and Exercises

1. _____ and _____ variances represent a more detailed analysis of material quantity variances.

2. A material yield variance is usually considered the result of_____
   _____

3. a. When a recipe or formula is used for various types of material, the quantity variance for material is broken down into _____ and _____ variances.

   b. Under these circumstances how is the price variance for material computed?_____
      _____
      _____

4. Sales quantity variance can be computed using the following formulas:
   SALES QUANTITY VARIANCE: (Actual volume in units - Fixed budget volume in units) X_____
   _____   _____   _____   _____

5. Sales mix variance can be computed using the following formulas:

   a.

$$\left[\left(\begin{array}{c}\text{Actual}\\\text{sales mix}\\\text{percentage}\end{array} - \dfrac{\rule{2cm}{0.4pt}}{\rule{2cm}{0.4pt}}\right) X \begin{array}{c}\text{Actual total}\\\text{sales volume of all}\\\text{products in units}\end{array}\right]$$

X (Budgeted individual unit contribution margin
   - b._____)

6. **Material Price, Mix and Yield Variances, and Journal Entries in a Process Cost System**

   Spaghetti sauce is processed and canned by Linane Manufacturers in lots of 144 cans (a gross), each weighing 16 ounces. The standard mixture for a gross is as follows:

Tomato paste	141.5 pounds@ $ 0.28 per pound
Mixed spices	1.5 pounds @ $12.60 per pound
Chopped onions	5.0 pounds @ $ 0.50 per pound
Mushrooms................................	2.0 pounds @ $ 2.61 per pound

   While the company desires to maintain a special flavor for their sauce, they are able to use varying combinations of the above materials within limits. The following materials were purchased during the month. Direct materials inventory is kept at standard cost.

Tomato paste (12,500 pounds)	$3,750.00
Mixed spices (130 pounds)	1,631.50
Chopped onions (450 pounds)	216.00
Mushrooms (180 pounds)...	460.80
	$6,058.30

   There were 80 gross of cans finished during the period. Beginning inventory of work in process consisted of 20 gross of sauce, one-fourth completed, while ending inventory of work in process consisted of 15 gross, two-thirds completed. Assume all inventory is past the cooking stage in which evaporation occurs. FIFO inventory costing is used. The following actual material quantities were put into production:

6. (Concluded)

	Pounds
Tomato paste	12,007
Mixed spice	135
Chopped onions	474
Mushrooms	210

Required:

a. Determine material purchase price variances for each ingredient, total material mix and total yield variances.
b. Prepare journal entries to record these variances, including the disposition of variances, assuming they are treated as period costs.

a.

b.

7. Sales quantity and Sales mix Variances

This year's budget for Pattie, Inc., a multiproduct firm, is given below:

	A	B	C	Total
		Products Lines		
Sales	$1,060,000	$800,000	$880,000	$2,740,000
Less:Variable costs	580,000	600,000	740,000	1,920,000
Fixed costs allocated on square footage	140,000	150,000	91,300	381,300
Income before taxes	$ 340,000	$ 50,000	$ 48,700	$ 438,700
Units	160,000	100,000	140,000	400,000

At year end, you determine that sales price, total fixed costs,and unit variable costs were exactly as budgeted, but the following units per product line were sold:

Product Line	Units
A	175,000
B	175,000
C	150,000
Total Units	500,000

Required:

a. Compute sales quantity variances and sales mix variances for each product line.
b. Prove your answer to Requirement *a.*

8. Labor Rate, Mix, Yield Variances, and Journal Entries

The production process of J. Lindsey Company is performed by a crew of employees in different pay grades. A standard crew hour consists of 100 worker-hours distributed as follows:

Pay Grade	Hours	Standard Rate	Standard Cost
A	42	$ 5	$210
B	48	4	192
C	8	8	64
D	2	13	26
			$492

Output: 100 tons

During the month, charges to the department included 2,800 hours of A at a total cost of $13,440; 2,600 hours of B at a total cost of $10,660; 640 hours of C at a total cost of $5,280; and 260 hours of D at a total cost of $3,848. There were 7,000 tons of finished goods produced during the month.

Required:

a. Compute a labor rate variance for each pay grade, total labor mix variance, and total labor yield variances.
b. Prepare the journal entry to record these variances and the direct labor cost.

a.

b.

9. Material Price, Mix and Yield Variances, and Journal Entries

Sills Manufacturers processes and cans tomato catsup in 24-ounce jars. The standard input for a batch of materials is as follows:

	Pounds	Standard Price Per Pound
Tomatoes	340	$ .60
Corn sweetener	75	.10
Vinegar	25	.40
Salt	10	.20
Onion powder, spice and flavoring	50	.53
Input	500	
Output	400	

The recipe used is not only secret but also allows for some variation in ingredients in obtaining the special flavor. The following materials were purchased during the month. Direct materials inventory is kept at standard.

	Pounds	
Tomatoes	23,000	$14,950
Corn sweetener	5,000	250
Vinegar	3,000	1,320
Salt	800	176
Onion powder, spice and flavoring	2,500	1,200

During the month, 18,000 jars were filled with the following materials put in process:

	Pounds
Tomatoes	22,100
Corn sweetener	3,900
Vinegar	1,900
Salt	500
Onion powder, spice and flavoring	1,950
	30,350

Required:

a. Compute a material purchase price variance for each of the materials and a material total mix and total yield variance for the month. Indicate if the variance is favorable or unfavorable.
b. Prepare journal entries to record the issuance of material, the variances, and the disposition of variances.

9. Paper for working

    a.

9. Paper for working (Concluded)
   a. (Concluded)

b.

True-False Questions

Indicate whether the following statements are true or false by inserting in the blank space a capital "T" for true or "F" for false.

_____ 1. The price variance for material and labor can be broken down into mix and yield variances in production operations using a recipe or formula for classes of labor and material.

_____ 2. Tolerance limits are normally established beyond which changes from the specified mix of material and labor cannot be made.

_____ 3. A manufacturer of men's shirts would normally analyze its material quantity variances into mix and yield variances.

_____ 4. If more of the cheaper grade or skill of labor is used than indicated in the formula or recipe, the mix variance will be favorable.

_____ 5. When a combination of material and labor is used, mix and yield variances are computed which replace the price variance.

_____ 6. Often the advantages gained from a favorable yield variance are offset by an unfavorable mix variance.

_____ 7. A labor yield variance is usually considered the result of the quantity and/or the quality of the material handled.

_____ 8. Assume Meat A comprises 10% of the total input ingredients of a soup. If total actual quantity is 5,000 pounds and 480 pounds of Meat A were used, the mix variance for Meat A would be unfavorable.

_____ 9. A mix variance reflects the extra costs or savings incurred because more inputs were used than were called for in the original specifications or recipe.

_____ 10. The material or labor yield variance is computed by comparing actual input quantity at standard input cost to actual output quantity at standard output cost.

SOLUTIONS

Matching

1.   k   5.   b   8.   h
2.   e   6.   g   9.   l
3.   f   7.   i   10.   d
4.   j or b

Completion and Exercises

1. mix; yield

2. the quantity and /or the quality of the material handled

3.   a.   mix; yield
      b.   A price variance is computed for each type of material in the usual manner. The overall price variance is the sum or difference of the individual variances.

4. Budgeted average unit contribution margin

5.   a.   Budgeted sales mix percentage
      b.   Budgeted average unit contribution margin

6. *Linane Manufacturer*

   a.   EU =   80   +   10   -   5   = 85 gross
                       (15 X 2/3)   (20 X 1/4)

	Pounds	Standard Cost
Tomato paste	141.5	$39.62
Mixed spices	1.5	18.90
Chopped onions	5.0	2.50
Mushrooms	2.0	5.22
Input	150.0	$66.24
Output	144.0	

Standard cost per pound of input ($66.24/150) $.4416
Standard cost per pound of output ($66.24/144)   .46

Material Purchase Price Variance

	Actual Lbs.	Standard Price	Actual Price	Price Variance Per Lb.	Total Purchase Price Variance
Tomato paste	12,500	$ .28	$ .30	$ .02 U	$250.00 U
Mixed spices	130	12.60	12.55	.05 F	6.50 F
Chopped onions	450	.50	.48	.02 F	9.00 F
Mushrooms	180	2.61	2.56	.05 F	9.00 F
					$225.50 U

Material Mix Variance

	Actual Quantity	Standard Price	Amounts
Tomato paste	12,007	$.28	$3,361.96
Mixed spices	135	12.60	1,701.00
Chopped onions	474	.50	237.00
Mushrooms	210	2.61	548.10
	12,826		$5,848.06

Actual quantity at standard input cost (12,826 X $.4416) 5,663.96
Unfavorable materials mix variance .... $ 184.10

6. (Concluded)
   Material Yield Variance
   Actual quantity at standard input cost $5,663.96
   Actual output at standard output cost (12,240* X $.46) 5,630.40
   Unfavorable material yield variance .... $ 33.56

   *85 gross X 144 lbs. = 12,240 lbs.

   Alternative way of computing yield variance

   6/150 = 4 percent expected loss from processing

   586.00 Actual loss (12,826 - 12,240)
   513.04 Expected loss (4% X 12,826 materials put into process)
    72.96 X $.46 = $33.56 unfavorable

   b.   Direct Materials Inventory 5,832.80
              Material Purchase Price Variance 225.50
                 Accounts Payable 6,058.30
              Work in Process Inventory 5,630.40
              Material Mix Variance 184.10
              Material Yield Variance 33.56
                 Direct Materials Inventory 5,848.06
              Cost of Goods Sold 443.16
                 Material Yield Variance 33.56
                 Materials Mix Variance 184.10
                 Material Purchase Price Variance 225.50

7. *Pattie, Inc*
   a.   Sales quantity variances

   For product A: (175,000 - 160,000)   X $2.05*   = $ 30,750   favorable
   For product B: (175,000 - 100,000)   X $2.05   =   153,750   favorable
   For product C: (150,000 - 140,000)   X $2.05   =   20,500   favorable
                                                    $205,000   favorable

   *$2,740,000 - $1,920,000 = $820,000/400,000 = $2.05

   Sales mix variances

   For product A: (35% - 40%) X 500,000 X ($3.00 - $2.05) = $23,750   unfavorable
   For product B: (35% - 25%) X 500,000 X ($2.00 - $2.05) =   2,500   unfavorable
   For product C: (30% - 35%) X 500,000 X ($1.00 - $2.05) = 26,250   favorable
                                                    $ -0-

   b.   Sales quantity variance $ 205,000   favorable
         Sales mix variance   -0-
                                            $ 205,000   favorable

         Budgeted contribution margin (400,000 X $2.05) $ 820,000
         Actual contribution margin (175,000 X $3) +
             (175,000 X $2) + (150,000 X $1)   1,025,000
                                               $ 205,000

8. *J. Lindsey Company*

a. *Labor Rate Variance*

Pay Grade	Actual Hours	Standard Rate	Actual Rate	Rate Variance		Total Rate Variance	
A	2,800	$5	$4.80	$.20	F	$560	F
B	2,600	4	4.10	.10	U	260	U
C	640	8	8.25	.25	U	160	U
D	260	13	14.80	1.80	U	468	U
						$328	U

Labor Mix Variance

Actual Hours at Standard Rate

Pay Grade	Actual Hours	Standard Rate	Standard Cost
A	2,800	$5	$14,000
B	2,600	4	10,400
C	640	8	5,120
D	260	13	3,380
	6,300		$32,900

Standard cost per hour $492/100 hours = $4.92
Actual hours at standard (6,300 hours X $4.92)   30,996
                                      Mix Variance $ 1,904   U

Labor Yield Variance

Actual hours at standard cost $30,996
Output expressed in standard hours at standard cost

$$\frac{7,000 \text{ tons}}{100 \text{ tons}} = 70 \text{ batches} \times 100 \text{ hrs.} = 7,000 \text{ hrs.} @ \$4.92 = \qquad 34,440$$

                                      Yield Variance $ 3,444   F

b.   Work in Process Inventory 34,440
      Labor Mix Variance.................................. 1,904
      Labor Rate Variance................................ 328
          Payroll...   33,228
          Labor Yield Variance   3,444

9. *Sills Manufacturers*

a.

	Pounds	*Standard Cost*
Tomatoes	340	$204.00
Corn sweetener	75	7.50
Vinegar	25	10.00
Salt	10	2.00
Onion powder, spices, and flavorings	50	26.50
Input	500	$250.00
Output	400	

Standard cost per pound of input ($250/500) $.50
Standard cost per pound of output ($250/400) $.625

Material Purchase Price Variance

	Actual Lbs.	Standard Price	Actual Price	Price Variance Per Lb.	Total Purchase Price Variance
Tomatoes	23,000	$.60	$.65	$ .05 U	$1,150 U
Corn sweetener	5,000	.10	.05	.05 F	250 F
Vinegar	3,000	.40	.44	.04 U	120 U
Salt	800	.20	.22	.02 U	16 U
Onion powder, spices and flavoring	2,500	.53	.43	.05 F	125 F
					$ 911 U

Material Mix Variance

	Actual Quantity	Standard Price	Amounts
Tomatoes	22,100	$.60	$13,260.00
Corn sweetener	3,900	.10	390.00
Vinegar	1,900	.40	760.00
Salt	500	.20	100.00
Onion powder, spices and flavoring	1,950	.53	1,033.50
	30,350		$15,543.50

Actual quantity at standard input cost (30,350 lbs. X $.50) 15,175.00
Unfavorable material mix variance .... $ 368.50

Material Yield Variance

Actual quantity at standard input cost $15,175.00
Actual output at standard output cost (27,000* X $.625) 16,875.00
Favorable material yield variance .... $ 1,700.00

*18,000 jars X 24 oz. = 432,000 oz. + 16 oz. = 27,000 lbs.

Alternative Way of Computing Yield Variance

100/500 = 20% Expected loss from processing
6,070   Expected loss (20% X 30,350 materials put into process)
3,350   Actual loss (30,350 - 27,000)
2,720 X $.625 = $1,700 Favorable

9. (Concluded)

b.

Direct Materials Inventory	16,985.00	
Material Purchase Price Variance	911.00	
Accounts Payable		17,896.00
Work in Process Inventory	16,875.00	
Material Mix Variance	368.50	
Material Yield Variance		1,700.00
Direct Materials Inventory		15,543.50
Material Yield Variance	1,700.00	
Material Mix Variance		368.50
Material Purchase Price Variance		911.00
Cost of Goods Sold		420.50

True-False

1.   F   The quantity, not the price, variance can be broken down into mix and yield variances.

2.   T

3.   F   Mix and yield variances are appropriate where there is a variety of ingredients which can be changed within limits without affecting the output of the product.

4.   T

5.   F   It is the quantity variance that is replaced with the mix and yield variances.

6.   T

7.   T

8.   F   The mix variance for Meat A would be favorable because 20 less pounds were used than indicated by the recipe.

9.   F   It is a yield variance that reflects the savings or extra costs because more inputs were used than were called for in the original recipe.

10   T

25 Behavioral and Ethical Factors in Accounting Control

Chapter Outline

Responsibility Accounting and Behavior
Goal Congruence
Formal and Informal Organization
Control Activities
Timely Control Reports
Responsibility for Variances
Cost-Benefit Analysis
Accounting Controls
Traditional Accounting Model: Theory X
Spending Spree
Emphasis on Punishment
Behavioral Science Approach: Theory Y
Hierarchy of Needs
Herzberg's Two-Factor Theory
Extrinsic and Intrinsic Rewards
Behavioral Research
Contingency Theory
Expectancy Theory of Motivation
Behavioral Implications of Profit and Cost Centers
Suboptimization
Theory Z
Employees are Valuable Assets
Openness Reduces Resistance to Change
Appendix: Standards of Ethical Conduct

Chapter Objectives

After studying this chapter, you should be able to:

1. Explain the role of the cost accountant in utilizing informal organizations to achieve company goals.

2. Apply accounting control techniques and describe the role expectancy theory plays in accounting systems.

3. Contrast Theory X, Theory Y, and Theory Z management styles.

4. Relate the resistance to change, contingency theory, and adaptive responses to environmental uncertainty.

5. Discuss the ethics of cost accountants

6. Define and apply the new terms introduced.

Chapter Review

Responsibility Accounting and Behavior

1. If more resources are needed than planned, the activities cannot be considered under control.

    a. One of the objectives of responsibility accounting is to trace the costs incurred to the person responsible for the activity.
    b. The degree of control over a cost depends upon the management level and time period in question.

Goal Congruence

2. An important task of management is to achieve goal congruence which involves reconciling the values and goals of the group they lead with the company's objectives.

    a. If employees are allowed to participate in setting company goals, goal congruence will be easier to attain.
    b. Management should set the tone of the environment so that subordinates are able to satisfy their needs at the same time that company objectives are being met.

Formal and Informal Organization

3. A network of formal and informal relationships exist within each company.

    a. The formal organization is displayed on the organization chart and establishes lines of authority and responsibility and is subject to managerial control.
    b. The informal organization develops rapidly and arises from the social interaction of people.
    c. Communication within informal organizations is more rapid and dynamic than those within formal organizations.
    d. Formal authority attaches to a position and a person receives it because he or she occupies such position while informal authority attaches to a person.

4. Status within formal and informal organizations differs because it is more clearly defined within formal relationships while informal organizations recognize status because of a person's personality, flexibility in job location, and age.

5. Management should not ignore the informal organization because they should identify the leaders of these informal relationships and win their support.

    a. The network of informal relationships provides excellent training ground for future leaders of the formal organization.
    b. Management should recognize that some needs are better met by the informal organization than the formal one.

6. The functions of formal and informal organizations differ; however, the formal organization represents the primary control for the overall company.

    a. The informal organization may serve as a communication means or as a way of controlling the dress of employees or some other aspect of social control.
    b. Often the informal organization is used to put pressure on management to maintain specified standards of education or training.
    c. If used properly, the informal organization can assist the manager in carrying out formal orders.

Control Activities

7. Control activities are designed to compel events to conform to predetermined plans and can take either a positive or negative form.

   a. Positive control is an attempt to ensure that the company objectives are reached.
   b. Negative control is an attempt at preventing unwanted or undesirable activities.

Timely Control Reports

8. The following guidelines should be established regarding the preparation of reports.

   a. Reports should be available on a timely basis.
   b. Variances should be detected as the work progresses rather than waiting until the month or job has ended as this allows correction before the variance becomes so large.
   c. Reports should relate to the user's needs and responsibilities; reports concerning areas over which the manager has no control have limited usefulness to the manager.
   d. Explanations should be brief and given in a clear and concise pattern.
   e. Reports should be geared to the person receiving it.
   f. Reasons for the variances from standard should be specified if possible.

Responsibility for Variances

9. More effective control is achieved if variances are detected while the work is in process rather than waiting until the end of operations.

Cost-Benefit Analysis

10. A trade-off exists in data gathering between the cost of acquiring additional data and the benefit of these data.

    a. An optimum balance between the cost of acquiring more data and the benefits of this information should be the goal.
    b. The accountant should guard against producing more reports than management can or will use.

Accounting Controls

11. The following control features should be in effect for the responsibility accounting system to perform effectively.

    a. Annual audits by independent accountants are important features.
    b. Fidelity bonds on employees are excellent preventive features.
    c. Organization charts detailing employee responsibility are important.
    d. Proofs and controls for documents and reports are needed.
    e. A system of budgets and standards are essential features of an effective responsibility accounting system.
    f. Procedures manuals can provide information about initiating and approving changes in accounting methods as well as detailed instructions for individual accounting procedures.

       1. Procedures manuals save time because they prevent verbal instructions from being repeated.
       2. An added advantage is that procedures manuals assist new employees by providing them with information and clearer knowledge of what is expected of them.

g. The internal auditing department has no operating responsibility and makes evaluations of the degree of compliance with managerial procedures.

   1. Only recommendations are made by the internal auditing department as they usually operate in a staff position.
   2. Internal auditors also do not have the external auditor's independence because they are employees of the organization.

Traditional Accounting Model: Theory X

12. The traditional accounting model stresses Theory X which assumes that employees are basically lazy and are motivated solely by economic forces.

    a. Tight control features emphasizing the use of accounting as an instrument to reduce and control costs are used under Theory X.
    b. Frederick W. Taylor began the scientific management movement which considers employees as an additional part of the machine.
    c. This movement affected cost accounting concepts with their emphasis on control, segment responsibility, and accountability.

13. Drawbacks of the traditional accounting model include the following:

    a. This concept allowed the creation of many repetitive, nonmotivating jobs.
    b. This concept encourages accountants to overemphasize short-run unit costs and ignores the costs of boredom-induced absenteeism and turnover.
    c. Distorted reporting is often encouraged with the emphasis on directing attention to unfavorable variances. Employees may falsify records rather than run the risk of reporting unfavorable deviations.
    d. Fear and distrust are prevalent in the organization because employees place protection of their jobs as top priority.

Spending Spree

14. A spending spree often results near the end of the budget cycle when managers realize that they have not spent all their appropriation. From experience they often recognize that if they do not spend all their budget, the appropriation will be cut the next period.

Emphasis on Punishment

15. Traditional accounting models place much emphasis on punishment by using management by exception which holds that control reports should only emphasize and highlight areas that vary significantly from the standard or objective.

    a. Using Theory X, the exception is normally defined as only significantly unfavorable variances rather than also including favorable variances and exceptions.
    b. Employees who are striving for high performance may become discouraged because they are preoccupied with incurring unfavorable variances rather than their long-run performance.

Behavioral Science Approach: Theory Y

16. Under the Theory Y concept, workers are not viewed as being lazy; instead workers are assumed to seek and accept responsibility.
    a. Behavioral scientists believe that the organization chart does not reflect the way employees work and that authority is earned.
    b. According to this behavioral science approach, management should center their attention on interpersonal relations.

17. The behavioral science movement was encouraged by the Hawthorne experiments which revealed that management's attitudes toward employees affects productivity and efficiency more than do such material factors as rest periods, money, and illumination.

Hierarchy of Needs

18. Maslow attempted to explain behavior in terms of individuals seeking satisfaction through the following hierarchy of needs, listed in order of fulfillment priority.

    a. Physiological–including the need for food, water, oxygen, rest, and sex.
    b. Safety–need for predictable and organized world.
    c. Belongingness and love–desire for affectionate relations with others and a recognized place in a group.
    d. Esteem–self-respect and achievement.
    e. Self-actualization–needs of individuals to become what they are capable of being.

Herzberg's Two-Factor Theory

19. Herzberg provided an alternative theory to Maslow's hierarchy of needs by stating that factors in the work environment which provide job satisfaction are not necessarily the same as those that cause dissatisfaction.

    a. Hygienic factors, including company personnel policies, salary, quality of working conditions, and technical supervision on the job are characteristics of the work environment which cause dissatisfaction.
    b. Motivators are the job content factors which produce satisfaction and these include job achievement, recognition of achievement, and responsibility for achievement.
    c. According to this theory, motivators relate to a high level of job satisfaction, but their absence in the work environment does not bring about dissatisfaction.

Extrinsic and Intrinsic Rewards

20. *Extrinsic rewards* are tangible and measurable and consist of salaries, fringe benefits, year-end bonuses, and carpeted offices.

    a. Extrinsic motivation of individuals is influenced by an organization's punishment and reward system.

21. *Intrinsic rewards* are those internalized by the individual. They are intangible and consist of the feeling of satisfaction and achievement that a person gets from doing a good job.

22. *Job enrichment* is concerned with giving workers more autonomy and responsibility for planning, directing, and controlling their performance and also allows the redesign of jobs to include greater variety of work content.

23. *Job enlargement* does not give the individual any more control over the job. The duties of the job are expanded giving the job holder more duties of the same nature to perform, such as found when employees are rotated through similar jobs.

24. In search of ways to improve job performance, models and theories to explain human behavior are sought.

    a. Reinforcement theory is the psychological theory that the following three elements constitute a framework for motivating job performance.

       1. Desired behavior
       2. Contingencies
       3. Consequences

b. A contingency is the link that connects job behavior with the consequences of that behavior.

Behavioral Research

25. Early research on human behavior first focused on individual motives, personality, and cognitive processes. The enterprises studied then were smaller than the organizations researched today. Later the emphasis shifted to organizations and has now moved back to the individual.

26. While good leadership is important in effective management, the human relations field is not equivalent to management.

   a. Human relations should not be taken as an end in itself but rather as a means to improve productivity.
   b. There is a danger that insincerity may become a part of the approach when management tries consciously to practice human relations.

Contingency Theory

27. The contingency theory approach to control is characterized by a search for conditions under which certain combinations or variables work best.

28. The contingency model hypothesizes three major contingencies which affect subunit performance:

   a. Factors internal to the subunit (internal factors).
   b. Interrelationships with other subunits (interdependency factors).
   c. Interactions external to the firm (environmental factors).

Expectancy Theory of Motivation

29. *Expectancy theory* holds that individuals have expectations about how well they will perform. They view that certain efforts will lead to specific performance levels. In addition, they also have expectations that certain performance will lead to probable rewards.

30. The expectancy model stipulates that people arrive at two sets of expectancies with respect to any given task.

   a. The first set of expectancy relates to the expectation that a given level of effort of performance (P) shall lead to the desired outcome (O).

      1. The subject assigns values to the various outcomes based on their desirability to him/her. These are called valences (V)
      2. The subject forms expectancies that his/her efforts will lead to the required performance (P).

   b. The second set of expectancies relates to the expectation that the desired outcome shall lead to an intrinsic or extrinsic valence or both valences. According to expectancy theory, an individual's motivation is a multiplicative function of the sum of the ($E \rightarrow P$) expectancies (the expectancy that the individual's personal effort can result in the required performance), and the sum of the [($P \rightarrow O$) (V)] products (the expectancy that the required performance will result in perceived outcomes multiplied by the valence or attractiveness of these outcomes).

Behavioral Implications of Profit and Cost Centers

31. A profit center which is accountable for both revenues and costs can be used as a motivational tool by giving each management level a goal of achieving certain profits.

32. The cost center holds the segment manager responsible only for costs.

33. The profit center concept allows the individual manager more flexibility in establishing goals than does the cost center concept.

    a. The trend toward decentralization may encourage the use of the profit center concept.
    b. The profit center concept can be used as an educational device.

Suboptimization

34. If profit center managers are not provided data concerning the entire organization, suboptimization will likely develop in which each segment benefits to the detriment of the overall company.

Theory Z

35. Interpersonal skills are central to the Theory Z model; egalitarianism is a central theme of Theory Z organizations.

    a. Egalitarianism implies that each person can apply discretion and can work autonomously without close supervision because they are to be trusted.
    b. Theory Z management takes the best of Japanese business techniques and adapts them to the United States corporate environment.

Employees Are Valuable Assets

36. Using Theory Z, employees are evaluated according to a multitude of criteria rather than on just individual bottom-line contributions.

Openness Reduces Resistance to Change

37. Theory Z organizations encourage openness which values a realistic appraisal of both problems and achievements.

Appendix: Standards of Ethical Conduct

38. Cost accountants' conduct must be ethical in working with their employing organizations, to others in the organizations, and to themselves.

    a. Their ethics require that they exercise initiative and good judgment in providing management with information having a potentially adverse economic impact, such as reports about poor product quality, cost overruns, and abuses of company policy.
    b. They should protect proprietary information as well as follow the chain of command.
    c. Standards of ethical conduct from the National Association of Accountants' <u>Statement</u> <u>on</u> <u>Management</u> <u>Accounting</u> help them resolve these conflicts.

Demonstration Problem

Violation of Organizational Concepts

A policy of pay based on seniority is strictly enforced at the Frank Company. In fact, a survey revealed the salaries on the graph below are being paid. These salaries are indicated on a partial organization chart to provide an insight into the positions held:

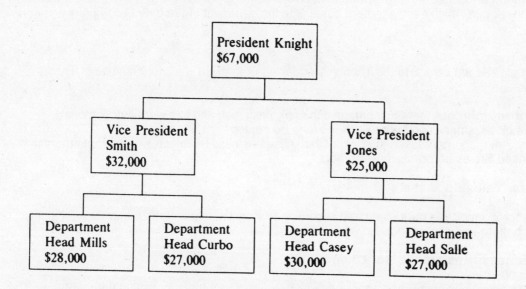

Vice president Jones is having great difficulty accepting the fact that even though his responsibilities are as great as those of vice president Smith, his salary is much lower. In addition, his two department heads each make more than he does. However, Jones has only been with the company 3 years and was promoted rapidly, while Casey and Smith each have 10 years of service with the company.

An additional problem that Jones finds difficult to accept is the salary paid to Salle. Salle had previous experience with a competitor but was brought in earning a starting salary that is more than Jones receives. It is well known that department heads within the company have fewer responsibilities than do vice presidents.

When Jones was promoted from department head to vice president, no increase in salary was given. However, his duties increased. When he asked the president about this, the president reminded him of the possibility that he might hold the top position in two years, when the president retires. It is not clear whether Smith, Jones, or an outsider will step into the president's position at retirement.

Jones also has another problem: Casey generally refers all important requests directly to the president. For the last several years, he reported directly to the president because of the nature of his job. It is well known that Casey expected to get the vice presidency position that was created for Jones.

Required:

Indicate the organizational concepts that were violated and recommend any necessary changes.

Paper for working Demonstration Problem

Solution to Demonstration Problem

Frank Company

Basing salaries strictly on seniority has many weaknesses as it completely ignores any reward for merit. While seniority is often protected in the building trades, exemptions from seniority rules are usually desirable for technical and professional employees. In balancing seniority in relation to merit, many companies make a clear and fair statement such as the following: "As between two employees with equal ability, the one with the greater seniority will be given preference."

In order to achieve any success in working out a plan that balances merit and seniority, a company should consider the following:

1. Job and employee specifications which are objective should be prepared.
2. Management should promulgate a detailed and thoroughly understood transfer and promotion plan.
3. A good system of employee merit rating should be installed.
4. Management should establish objective performance standards so that employee productivity can be measured in a manner that is acceptable.
5. A grievance procedure plan should be established which is acceptable to employees and the union, if employees are represented by one.

Frank Company is not rewarding responsibility as Jones earns less salary but has more responsibility than the department heads under him. Only if Jones had employees under him with unique technical skills, would this difference in pay be justifiable. Since this is not the case, Jones should be earning the same salary as Smith or maybe slightly less since Smith does have ten years of service.

If Jones is to have authority over Casey, he must inform Casey that all matters should be directed through him. Jones should also let President Knight know that he is displeased with Casey bypassing him.

Since Jones is unhappy with his salary, he should reassess his worth in the market by actually having job interviews. If he does indeed see that he can be earning more money with the same responsibilities elsewhere, he would be in a better position to argue for a higher salary . Jones must decide how willing he is to "wait and see" what happens in two years when Knight retires. At that time he will have more experience and this vice presidency position may prove to be a springboard to a better position with a higher salary elsewhere.

Matching

Referring to the terms listed in the left column, place the appropriate letter next to the corresponding description. A term may not be used or may be used more than once.

a. Cost center

b. Formal organization

c. Goal congruence

d. Hygiene factors

e. Informal organization

f. Investment center

g. Motivators

h. Organizing

i. Profit center

j. Reinforcement theory

k. Suboptimization

l. Theory X

m. Theory Y

n. Theory Z

_____1. This theory is based on the idea that productivity and trust go together; loyalty to a company and a career-long commitment to one's job are also a part of this theory.

_____2. Network of relationships displayed on the organization chart which are large and stable.

_____3. An objective of reconciling the values and goals of the employees with those of the organization.

_____4. A company division in which the manager is responsible for both revenues and costs, but not the segment's capital assets.

_____5. Condition which is detrimental to the overall company because segment managers are only concerned about their own division.

_____6. Concept under which traditional accounting models were prepared that viewed employees as being motivated solely by economic factors.

_____7. Accounting models adopted under this concept abandon autocratic leadership for a human relations approach.

_____8. Job achievement, responsibility for achievement, and recognition of achievement which produce satisfaction.

_____9. A company division in which the manager is responsible only for the segment's costs.

_____10. Accounting systems prepared under this concept recognize that people need to feel wanted and important.

_____11. Company personnel policies, salary, and quality of working conditions which cause dissatisfaction.

_____12. Psychological theory that desired behavior, contingencies, and consequences constitute a framework for motivating job performance.

Completion and Exercises

1. _____ _____, _____, and
    _____ are the three elements which constitute a framework for
    motivating job performance according to reinforcement theory.

2. Describe three differences between a formal and informal organization.

    a. _____

    _____

    b. _____

    _____

    c. _____

3. Contrast the functions of formal and informal organizations. _____

    _____

    _____

    _____

    _____

4. Describe three guidelines for the preparation of reports.

    a. _____

    _____

    b. _____

    _____

    c. _____

5. Give five control features which should exist for an effective responsibility accounting system.

    a. _____

    b. _____

    c. _____

    d. _____

    e. _____

6. According to Maslow's hierarchy of needs, the order of fulfillment priority, from lowest need to highest need, is:

    a. _____

    b. _____

    c. _____

    d. _____

    e. _____

7. The _____ studies encouraged the behavioral science movement and awakened interest in human relations in the 1930s and 1940s.

8. Discuss three dangers inherent in the human relations approach.

   a. _____

   _____

   b. _____

   _____

   c. _____

   _____

9. Each division of the Raymond Company receives a monthly report similar to the one below. Division performance is evaluated on the basis of income before taxes.

Raymond Company
New Jersey Territory
For Month Ended December 31, 19-X

Sales to outsiders	$100,000
Sales to New York Division (at market price)	20,000
	$120,000
Expenses:	
Material purchases from New York Territory (at full cost)	$ 30,000
Direct labor	20,000
Factory overhead	35,000
Employee training (allocated on new employees hired)	5,000
General corporation public relations (allocated equally to all divisions)	5,000
Marketing research staff (allocated on the time spent on projects requested by New Jersey manager)	9,000
Home office administration staff costs (5% of sales)	6,000
Total expenses	$110,000
Income before taxes	$ 10,000

Required:

Indicate which of the amounts shown above are inconsistent with the "responsibility accounting" concept. Support each answer with a brief explanation.

_____

_____

_____

_____

_____

_____

_____

_____

_____

_____

10. Elmo Fain has just returned from an executive training program that encouraged top managers to publicly praise the efforts of subordinates. As a result, he sends out the following memo to his division managers.

"It gives me great pleasure to review each of your operations and find that your efforts to cut costs have been most successful. I am confident that all of you will continue to put forth your best efforts so that our company will have one of its best years ever."

Each of the five division managers is impressed with the memo when they first read it. However, four division managers begin thinking and reflecting on the memo's content. Each of these four managers know that the northern division's performance has been poor because costs have been considerably higher than ever before. These four managers begin talking among themselves and some arrive at the conclusion that Elmo does not really know what is going on.

Required:

What caused Elmo Fain to damage his credibility?

_____

_____

_____

_____

_____

_____

_____

_____

11. **Importance of Top Management's Actions**

Humphreys Key, regional director of one of the Poplar Company plants, has just received the following memo from the company president:

To all Regional Managers:
    After reviewing the operating statements for the first six months, I am quite concerned that we did not meet the projected sales and net income. While I recognize that general economic conditions account for the slump in sales, I must remind you that we must all join together in the last half of this year to improve operations.
    Beginning next month I have decided that we will eliminate all inspections except the final inspection of the product before it leaves the production process and is transferred into the finished goods storeroom. I believe that many of the inspections are unnecessary, since studies show that the critical point in the production process is in the final processing department.
    I know that each of you will put forth extra effort in helping the Poplar Company achieve the stated goals.

Humphreys has reread the letter several times again comparing his region's budget with actual financial data for his region. He had been quite pleased with his region's performance, as sales were 5 percent above those budgeted while net income exceeded budgeted net income by 8 percent. This performance was not achieved easily; he had driven himself and his workers hard to achieve the results.

Humphreys is also somewhat disgruntled that the president is finally going to implement the new inspection procedure that he suggested three months ago in a report to the president.

Required:

What would be your response if you were this regional director?

_____

_____

_____

_____

_____

_____

_____

_____

12. After much investigation, the Crews Company decided to use its own employees in adding another floor to their present building. A $400,000 budget was approved. It is estimated that the project will take two years for completion. Plans are made to transfer some employees from production of ZERXO, which is now experiencing depressed sales. Because there is no union labor, the company has this flexibility.

Sales of ZERXO became even more depressed after construction began. Market research, however, feels that this is only a temporary decline, and that production should not be halted on this line. After consultation, management decides to offer additional ZERXO workers the chance to transfer to building construction.

Periodically, top management inspects the building site so they will have a general idea of the stage of completion. The assistant plant manager assumed the position of building supervisor and furnishes top management with a review of operations only as they request it.

Because of these additional workers, construction is completed in one and one-half years, but at a cost of $440,000. The construction passes all building codes and also meets all the company's specifications.

Required:

Do you believe the control function was effectively applied? It not, what control techniques should have been used?

_____

_____

_____

_____

_____

_____

_____

13. **Responsibility for Variances**

Dixie Company has adopted the following standards in the Fabricating Department for its product:

	Per Unit
Direct material (4 pounds @ $5)	$20
Direct labor (2 hours @ $6)	12
Variable factory overhead (2 hours @ $2) ..	4
Fixed factory overhead (2 hours @ $3)	6

Normal capacity is 10,000 units per year.

Due to a slack in demand that management considers temporary, production was cut to 9,000 units. The following actual costs were incurred:

Material (40,000 pounds)	$180,000
Labor (18,500 hours)	115,625
Variable factory overhead	37,810
Fixed factory overhead	59,600

The purchasing department was unable to obtain the quality of materials specified. As a result, a lower grade of material was purchased which was expected to require the use of 10 percent more pounds per unit. There were 41,000 pounds of material purchased at a total cost of $184,500; LIFO inventory costing is used. The company's personnel department hires and trains all production personnel.

Required:

a. Calculate the variances for which you believe the supervisor of the Fabricating Department should be held responsible.

b. Indicate the variances for which you believe other individuals should be held accountable.

a.

b.

14. Ethics of Cost Accountants

Webber, Inc. recently developed a new type of glass casserole dish. Webber promotes the dish as not only being highly attractive, but also able to withstand intense oven heat for extended periods. In advertising the new product, marketing personnel have stressed the reason that its price is higher than competitors' is because it is more durable and easier to clean.

Inspection occurs at different stages of the manufacturing operation. Webber can rework rejects from the testing at the firing stage to acceptable levels if the cracks are not large and only appear in the top surface. Webber then sells these dishes as first-quality products.

Mary Brown, the cost accountant, has become close friends with Jane Stone, one of the marketing managers. Recently, Stone mentioned that they were spending much time answering customer complaints concerning excessive breakage of these casserole dishes. That prompted Brown to ask the quality control engineer to check into the matter. After many tests, the engineer ascertained that the rework does not bring the product up to standard. In fact, test results reveal that 1 in 12 of the reworked dishes is expected to break within three years' usage.

At Brown's request, the engineer investigated other types of reworking techniques but found that their costs outweighed any benefit. Further, after using the current reworking procedure, there is no test to determine which dish is more likely to be the one that breaks.

Brown has followed the long-standing policy of highlighting to the Board of Directors any cost data that has potential adverse effects. Thus, she believes it is her responsibility to include the rework problem in a report she prepared for the next monthly board meeting.

However, when the plant supervisor and other production personnel preview the report, they immediately call Brown's supervisor, the controller, and demand that the information given to the board not mention the rework problem. Instead, they convinced the controller to only briefly mention the problem in their oral presentation rather than highlight it in a written report. They rationalize that consumers expect all glass cooking utensils to break eventually anyway. Brown feels strongly that the data is important and believes the quality engineer will agree with her. However, his only remark is "Well Mary, you will just have to 'go with the flow' and hide the problem."

Required:

a. What ethical considerations do the following individuals have in this matter:
   1. Mary Brown, cost accountant.
   2. Quality control engineer.
   3. Controller
   4. Plant supervisor.

b. Explain what Mary Brown should do in this situation.

a. 1. _____
   _____
   _____
   _____
   _____
   _____
   _____
   _____

   2. _____
   _____
   _____
   _____
   _____
   _____

3. _____

4. _____

b. _____

15. Working Smarter, Not Harder

Management of Roget Company appear surprised to learn that employees are complaining about posters that they recently distributed and placed on departmental bulletin boards. The posters show an employee running to increase plant productivity. In selecting these posters, managers thought employees would interpret the message that the employee had a goal for which to work. Instead, the grapevine tells management that employees highly resent management displaying these posters.

Required:

Explain why you think employees have such a negative attitude toward these posters.

_____

_____

_____

_____

_____

_____

_____

_____

_____

_____

_____

_____

_____

_____

_____

_____

_____

_____

_____

_____

_____

_____

_____

_____

True-False Questions

Indicate whether the following statements are true or false by inserting in the blank space a capital "T" for true or "F" for false.

_____1.   Accounting systems built on the Theory X principle emphasize unfavorable variances rather than favorable variances.

_____2.   The controlling function is always most important in manufacturing operations while the planning function is most important in retail operations.

_____3.   Status within formal organizations is determined by an individual's personality, work location, and freedom to move about in the individual's work area.

_____4.   The cost center concept allows the individual manager much flexibility in setting goals because this concept recognizes that individual personal goals may be dominant over corporate objectives.

_____5.   All costs are controllable in the long run by top management even though some costs are easier to control than others.

_____6.   Tight budgets and standards are more likely to be found in an accounting system prepared using the Theory Y concept than a model under the traditional approach.

_____7.   The Hawthorne studies showed that rest periods, money, and illumination have a greater impact on employee efficiency and productivity than does management's attitudes toward employees.

_____8.   According to Herzberg's theory, the absence of motivational factors in the job environment does not bring about job dissatisfaction, but if these factors are present, they can be related to high job satisfaction.

_____9.   According to Maslow's hierarchy of needs, one level must be completely satisfied before moving upward to the next independent level of needs.

_____10.   The control function follows planning, staffing, directing and organizing activity since it is concerned with seeing that plans have been followed.

SOLUTIONS

Matching

1.	n	7.	m
2.	b	8.	g
3.	c	9.	a
4.	i	10.	n
5.	k	11.	d
6.	l	12.	j

Completion and Exercises

1. Desired behavior; contingencies; consequences

2. The following are differences between a formal and informal organization:
   a. Status is more clearly defined within the formal organization; status within the informal organization is determined by an individual's personality, age and seniority.
   b. The formal organization is more stable and larger.
   c. Communication is less frequent and slower within a formal organization.
   d. The informal organization arises spontaneously as people associate with each other.
   e. Informal organizations are subjective.
   f. The emphasis in informal organizations is on people and their relationships whereas the emphasis in formal organization is on authority and functions of various positions.

3. The functions of the formal organization involve running the company according to established objectives. The informal organization's functions may vary to satisfy the needs and wants of its members. The informal organization may serve as a communication network or a means of social control by regulating the behavior of employees. A specified standard of education or training is often maintained through the informal organization.

4. The following are guidelines for report preparation:
   a. Explanations should be clearly written, concise, and brief.
   b. The personality of the person receiving the report should be understood so that there is greater chance that the report will be read and understood.
   c. A schedule for the timely release of reports should be available.
   d. Management by exception should be employed so that significant variances are detected as soon after occurrence as possible.
   e. Reports should relate to the user's needs and responsibilities
   f. Reasons for variances from standards should be specified as soon as they are known.

5. The following are control features which improve the effectiveness of a responsibility accounting system.

   a. Internal auditing department
   b. Procedures manual
   c. Annual audit by independent accountants
   d. Budgets and standards
   e. Organization charts
   f. Fidelity bonds
   g. Proofs and controls for documents and reports

6. a. Physiological needs including the need for food, water, oxygen, rest and sex.
   b. Safety--the need for an organized and predictable environment.
   c. Love and belongingness--the desire for affectionate relations with others and a recognized place in a group.
   d. Esteem--self-respect and achievement
   e. Self-actualization--needs of individuals to become what they are capable of being.

7. Hawthorne

8. The dangers inherent in the human relations approach include the following:

    a. Insincerity often creeps in when a person consciously tries to practice human relations.
    b. Human relations may be taken as an end in itself rather than as a means of improving productivity.
    c. Employees may use their psychological problems as an excuse for poor performance.
    d. An overemphasis on behavioral science can distort individual responsibility and make it easy for employees to slough off their duties.
    e. The human relations approach becomes a production, a skill, or amateur psychiatry.

9. *Raymond Company*

    1. Material purchases from New York Territory: Since purchases were made at full cost, the inefficiencies of the New York Territory were passed on to the New Jersey Territory. This change is only partly controlled by the actions of the territory manager because even though he requests the amount of purchases made, the charge is not based upon the competitive market price for the goods.
    2. Employee training: The charge is determined by taking actual employee training cost and allocating an amount to each territory on the basis of new employees hired. The charge is only partly controllable by the territory manager as the cost per new employee varies with the efficiency and magnitude of the training program.
    3. General corporation public relations: Charge is an arbitrary allocation of costs, cannot be influenced directly by actions of the territory manager.
    4. Marketing research staff: This charge is partly controllable. The amount of marketing research service used is within the control of the territory manager. The cost per unit of service varies with the efficiency of the marketing research staff and the amount of use by other territories.
    5. Home office administration staff: The charge is an arbitrary allocation of costs; it cannot be influenced directly by the territory manager.

10. *Elmo Fain*

    While the president's intentions were good in that excellent effort should be recognized, he acted as if he was unaware of the poor performance of the northern territory. While it is understandable that he would not single out the northern division manager in a generally circulated document, he has not indicated that he even knew about the problem.

    The division managers who have exerted effort are naturally hurt and resent the northern division receiving as much praise as they do. Certainly, there may be adequate justification for the higher costs encountered by the northern division, but the president should have either acknowledged this or at least not placed all divisions in the same category.

11. *Poplar Company*

The president failed to realize that his subordinates watch every word that he says, even an off-hand remark. He failed to recognize the effort of Humphreys Key who did make his quota. Humphreys had exerted much personal effort as well as that of his own people to achieve the performance.

The president should have made general recognition of the fact that this regional manager had exceeded his sales budget and that net income was 8 percent above that budgeted. Humphreys quite naturally has taken the omission as a deliberate slight. He feels that the president doesn't really appreciate what he is doing. As a result, Humphreys will not be likely to exert as much effort in the future.

Naturally, Humphreys is disgruntled that the president failed to give him credit for suggesting the change in inspection routine. It could be that the president did not remember receiving the suggestion from Humphreys as most executives receive many suggestions. Even though the president may have not deliberately "stolen" Humphreys' idea, the effect on Humphreys is just the same as if he had.

12. *Crews Company*

In evaluating the effectiveness of control, the resource committed must be considered. Crews Company exceeded their budget by approximately 10 percent; however, they cut their construction time by 25 percent. The reason for this is that management decided to transfer some ZERXO workers over to construction rather than have them remain idle. At that time, the budget for the construction should have been reviewed to reflect this change.

Periodic reviews of the building stage of completion with the budget should have been made. It does not appear that the company had a very detailed budget as they should have. It is doubtful if the reviews of operations furnished by the assistant plant manager were detailed enough to adequately inform top management as to the complete status of the construction.

It is difficult to know whether costs were effectively controlled because no new budget with revised time estimates was prepared after the additional workers were transferred to construction. If these had been prepared, a better evaluation could be made.

In addition, no mention is made of securing competitive bids from outsiders for the construction work. This would allow management to better evaluate the cost in determining whether the cost of $440,000 is excessive.

13. *Dixie Company*

a. *Fabricating Department Supervisor Responsible*:

Material Quantity Variance (See note in Requirement *b*)
[(40,000 actual quantity less 3,600 pounds due to lower grade = 36,400) - 36,000 standard pounds] X $5 standard rate = $2,000 unfavorable

Labor Efficiency Variance

(18,500 actual hours - 18,000 standard hours) X $6 standard rate = $3,000 unfavorable

Variable Overhead Efficiency Variance

(18,500 actual hours - 18,000 standard hours) X $2 standard rate = $1,000 unfavorable

13. (Concluded)

Variable Overhead Spending Variance

Actual variable overhead $37,810
Budget adjusted to actual hours
      (18,500 hours X $2) .... <u>37,000</u>
                                      $ 810   unfavorable

   b. *Top or Middle Management:*

Volume Variance

(20,000 normal capacity hours - 18,000 standard hours) X $3 = $6,000 unfavorable

Fixed Overhead Spending Variance

Budgeted fixed overhead $60,000
Actual fixed overhead .... <u>59,600</u>
Favorable .... $ 400

Personnel Department

Labor Rate Variance

($6.25 actual rate - $6.00 standard rate) X 18,500 hours = $4,625 unfavorable

It is questionable whether the purchasing department should be given credit for the favorable material price variance because it resulted from a lower grade purchased. The management level who made the decision to use the lower material grade should be held responsible for both of the following variances. The Fabricating Department supervisor may have a strong basis for arguing that the additional 400 pounds used computed in the material quantity variance in Requirement *a* also resulted from the lower grade of material.

Material Price Variance Due to Lower Grade of Material

($4.50 actual price - $5.00 standard price) X 41,000 pounds = $20,500 favorable

Material Quantity Variance Due to Lower Grade of Material

10% X 36,000 pounds = 3,600 pounds X $5 = $18,000 unfavorable

14. *Webber, Inc.*

a. 1. While Mary Brown's position as cost accountant requires that she gather, analyze, and report operating data, she also has a responsibility to use good professional judgment in providing management with any data that may have a harmful economic impact.
     Mary Brown must recognize that she should protect the company information she has and not contact outsiders with the data. Also, she should proceed carefully and not violate the chain of command by discussing the rework problem with the controller's supervisors. Brown must not violate Webber's code of ethics; also professional and personal standards are a consideration.

   2. Even though management may not highlight the reworking problems now, the quality control engineer has the responsibility to continue to study the problems and work with manufacturing personnel in attempting to solve this issue. Product quality is his area of main concern.

3. The controller has the responsibility of further encouraging his staff to study the issue because of its impact on the company's profitability. The controller's superior should be made aware of the problem and the efforts engineers are making to correct this.

4. The plant supervisor's prime responsibility is to protect owners' interest through manufacturing a product that meets both quality and cost constraints. Management should bring any information that could threaten the company's future performance to the board's attention.

b. Mary Brown will place herself in a vulnerable position if she completely hides the rework problem and the issue is later detected. To reduce her risk, one alternative is to follow the controller's directive and not highlight the problem in the board's report, but also write the controller a report detailing her findings about the rework. Also, she should include in her report her communications with others in the company, pointing out that she is following the controller's instructions by failing to include it in the board's report.

15. *Roget Company*

Roget employees resent these posters because they interpret the message that management believes the only way to improve quality and productivity is to work harder. If, instead, management explained to everyone on the job what they were doing to help achieve these goals, morale would boost. Management needs to leave the impression that they expect employees to improve productivity, not by working harder but by working smarter. Employees as well as outsiders would understand that management is also taking some responsibility for defects and problems.

True-False

1. T   The traditional assumption of employee behavior encouraged this emphasis.

2. F   One function may receive priority at specific times in any operations but a specific function is not always important in any industry.

3. F   Status within informal organizations is determined by such factors.

4. F   The profit center concept is described.

5. T

6. F   Accounting is viewed as a necessary instrument for reducing and controlling costs under the Theory X approach which is the concept used traditionally.

7. F   The Hawthorne studies spurred the human relations movement by showing that management's attitudes toward employees affects productivity and efficiency more than material factors.

8. T

9. F   The levels of needs, according to Maslow, are inseparable and interrelated; Maslow also recognized that the hierarchy is not necessarily rigid.

10. F   Controlling activities occur continually and are simultaneous and interdependent with other functions.

26 Gantt Charts, Pert, and Decision Tree Analysis

Chapter Outline

Gantt Charts
    Control Device
    Advantages of Gantt Charts
Network Models
    Program Evaluation Review Techniques
    PERT-Cost Analysis
    Deciding When to Crash
Variance Analysis and PERT-Cost
Decision Tree Analysis
    Advantages of Decision Tree Analysis
    Weaknesses of Decision Tree Analysis
    Requirements for Decision Tree Preparation
Roll-Back Concept
Discounted Expected Value of Decisions
    Accounting for Time
    Other Factors to Consider

Chapter Objectives

After studying this chapter, you should be able to:

1. Prepare graphs and networks for use in planning and controlling processes where there are time flows.

2. Compare actual and budgeted time and cost for each activity so the resulting variance reflects the impact one activity's delay has on the overall project.

3. Provide, through decision tree analysis, a systematic framework for analyzing a sequence of interrelated decisions.

4. Apply the time value of future earnings by discounting the expected value of future decisions.

5. Define and apply the new terms introduced.

Chapter Review

Gantt Charts

1. A Gantt Chart is a bar chart with time shown on the horizontal axis and the duration of the task represented as a bar running from the starting date to the ending date of the task.

   a. Gantt Charts are mainly used in industry as a method of recording progress toward goals for machinery and employers.
   b. On a given date, a Gantt Chart easily shows how expected performance for a specific task compares with actual performance

2. Gantt Charts include identifying and sequencing activities and scheduling the work by periods.

Control Device

3. Gantt charts represent control techniques because they readily allow the comparison of scheduled production with actual production so that variations can be identified and corrective action initiated.

Advantages of Gantt Charts

4. Gantt Charts provide a visual display of planned utilization of facilities so that appropriate revisions can be made in order to obtain better use of facilities.

5. Gantt Charts do fail to indicate which tasks must be completed before others begin because all activities are arranged in vertical fashion on a Gantt Chart.

Network Models

6. Network models such as PERT have been developed to provide for this aspect of planning.

Program Evaluation Review Techniques

7. Performance Evaluation and Review Technique (PERT) is a systematic procedure for using network analysis for planning and measuring actual progress to scheduled events.

8. PERT is generally used for exceptional projects in which managerial experience is limited.

9. PERT employs free-form, network diagrams showing each activity as an arrow between events.

   a. A sequence of arrows usually shows the interrelationships among activities with time being the fundamental element of these activities.
   b. An event is represented by a circle on PERT charts and indicates the beginning or completion of a task.
   c. Events are discrete points which consume no resources.
   d. Activities are represented by arrows and are tasks to be accomplished to go from one event to the next.
   e. An activity consumes resources and has a duration over time starting at one event and ending with the occurrence of the next event.

10. The following formula is used to estimate the time needed to complete each activity.

$$ex_t = 1/6 \text{ (optimistic time} + 4 \text{ most likely time} + \text{pessimistic time)}$$

11. Through use of a PERT network, the longest time duration for the completion of the entire project can be determined; this longest path is referred to as the critical path.

a. The total time of the project can only be shortened by reducing the critical path.
b. The reason this path is critical is that if any activity on the path takes longer than expected, the entire project will be delayed.
c. Every network has at least one critical path.

12. Paths which are not critical have slack time while activities along the critical path have no slack time.

    a. The larger the amount of slack, the less critical the activity and vice versa.
    b. The slack associated with an event is the amount of time the event can be delayed without affecting the completion time of the project.

13. Slack introduces flexibility into the network because it serves as a buffer for events not located on the critical path.

14. Efforts designed to complete the project ahead of schedule are referred to as crashing. Crashing the network means finding the minimum cost for completing the project in minimum time so that an optimum tradeoff between time and cost is achieved. Determining the appropriate tradeoff is referred to as PERT-Cost Analysis.

PERT-Cost Analysis

15. Using PERT-Cost Analysis, the cost of completing the activity under normal expected conditions and under crash conditions are estimated.

Deciding When to Crash

16. A comparison of these two cost projections results in the determination of differential or incremental crash cost for each activity that can be crashed.

Variance Analysis and PERT-Cost

17. Expected and actual time and cost may be displayed on the PERT-Cost network so that immediate attention can be directed to slippage in time of the activities on the critical path.

    a. Penalties will also be a factor in analyzing variances for each activity.
    b. Activity time variances, spending variances, and project time variances can be computed.

Decision Tree Analysis

18. Decision tree analysis provides a systematic framework for analyzing a sequence of interrelated decisions which may be made over time.

19. Decision tree analysis formulates decision making in terms of the sequence of acts, events, and consequences under the assumption that projects which management considers presently often have strong implications for future profitability.

20. Present investment decisions result in alternative scenarios which depend on the occurrence of future events and the consequences of those events.

21. Decision tree analysis encourages the study and understanding of these scenarios.

Advantages of Decision Tree Analysis

22. Decision tree analysis offers the following advantages:

    a. Clarifies for management the choices, risks, monetary gains, objectives, and information needs involved in an investment problem.

b. May be a more lucid means of presenting relevant information than other analytical tools.
c. Combines action choices with different possible events or results of action which are partially affected by chance or other uncontrollable circumstances.
d. Allows management to focus on the relationship of today's decisions affecting tomorrow's decisions.
e. Analytical techniques such as discounted cash flow and present value methods can be utilized with decision trees to obtain a better picture of the impact of future events and decision alternatives.
f. Interactions among present decision alternatives with uncertain events and their possible payoffs become clearer.

Weaknesses of Decision Tree Analysis

23. Weaknesses of Decision Tree Analysis are:

a. Not all events can be identified.
b. Not all decisions that must be made on a subject under analysis are identified.
c. Only those decisions and events that are important to management and have consequences they wish to compare are placed on a decision tree.
d. Uncertain alternatives are generally treated using the decision tree concept as if they were discrete, well-defined possibilities.

Requirements of Decision Tree Analysis

24. The requirements of making a decision tree are as follows:

a. The points of decision and the alternatives available at each point must be identified.
b. The points of uncertainty and the type or range of alternative outcomes at each point must be determined.
c. Probabilities of different events or results of actions must be estimated.
d. The costs and gains of various events and actions must be estimated.
e. The alternative values in choosing a course of action must be analyzed.

Roll-Back Concept

25. The roll-back concept involves the following steps:

a. Proceeding from right to left on each terminal point on the decision tree.
b. Finding the total expected value at every chance event.
c. Choosing that course of action with the highest expected value.

Discounted Expected Value of Decisions

26. Through use of a discount rate, the differences in immediate cost or revenue can be weighed against differences in value at later time periods.

a. The discount rate is similar to the use of a discount rate in the present value of discounted cash flow techniques and makes allowance for the cost of capital.
b. Both cash flows and position value are discounted.

Accounting for Time

27. Since the time between successive decision stages on a decision tree may be substantial, alternatives are placed on the same time basis by discounting.

Other Factors to Consider

28. The expected monetary gains must be considered along with the risks, and managers have different viewpoints toward risk.

   a. A major investment may pose a risk to a manager's career or it may represent an opportunity for advancement.
   b. The political environment in which a decision regarding the scale of plant is made should be jointly evaluated by top management.
   c. If the risk can be insured, management may be more willing to assume responsibility for the venture.

Demonstration Problem

PERT-Time Chart and Critical Path

Burns Company management regularly employs the Program Evaluation and Review Technique (PERT) in planning and coordinating its construction projects. The following schedule of separable activities and their expected completion times have been developed for a ship which Burns Company plans to construct.

Activity description	Expected activity completion time (in weeks)
1-2	4
1-6	17
1-3	12
1-7	13
2-5	15
2-3	3
3-4	4
4-9	2
5-9	8
7-8	6
8-9	5
6-9	9

Required:

a.   Draw a PERT-Time Chart.

b.   Identify the critical path for this project and determine the expected project completion time in weeks.

_____

_____

_____

_____

_____

_____

_____

_____

c.   Briefly discuss how the "expected activity completion times" are derived in the PERT method and what the derived value for the expected activity completion times means in the PERT method.

_____

_____

_____

_____

_____

_____

_____

_____

Solution to Demonstration Problem

Burns Company

a.

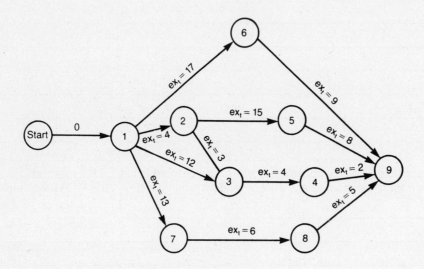

b.1
0-1-6-9............	17	+	9		=	26
0-1-2-5-9..........	4	+	15	+ 8 =		27*
0-1-2-3-4-9.......	4	+	3	+ 4 +	2 =	13
0-1-3-4-9..........	12	+	4	+ 2 =		18
0-1-7-8-9..........	13	+	6	+ 5 =		24

*critical path

c.   The expected activity completion time is considered the mean of three times the estimates of each activity--optimistic, most likely, and pessimistic. The expected value (mean) is calculated as follows:

$$\text{Expected time} = \frac{\text{Optimistic} + (4 \times \text{Most Likely}) + \text{Pessimistic}}{6}$$

The expected completion time represents the average time the activity would take if the activities were repeated a large number of times.

Matching

Referring to the terms listed in the left column, place the appropriate letter next to the corresponding description. A term may not be used or may be used more than once.

a. Activities

b. Crashing

c. Critical path

d. Critical path method

e. Decision Tree Analysis

f. Differential cost

g. Earliest completion time

h. Expected activity time

i. Gantt Chart

j. Latest completion time

k. Program Evaluation Review Technique (PERT)

l. PERT-Cost Analysis

m. PERT-Time Analysis

n. Roll-back concept

o. Slack

_____ 1. Bar chart with time shown on the horizontal axis and the duration of the task represented as a bar running from the starting date to the ending date.

_____ 2. An approach using sophisticated network model arranging activities in a flow showing which tasks must be completed before others begin.

_____ 3. Systematic procedure closely related to PERT which uses network analysis.

_____ 4. Network containing a sequence of arrows showing interrelationships among activities with time being the fundamental element in these activities.

_____ 5. Tasks represented by arrows that must be accomplished before continuing operations.

_____ 6. Determined using 1-4-1 three-estimate method representing a weighted average of the shortest time, the average time, and the longest time.

_____ 7. Longest path on the PERT network.

_____ 8. Cumulative time of the activities to reach an event.

_____ 9. On this network the latest completion time equals the earliest completion time.

_____ 10. Difference between the latest allowable time that an event may be completed and the earliest expected time.

_____ 11. Finding the minimum cost for completing the project in minimum time so that an optimum tradeoff between time and cost is achieved.

_____ 12. Efforts designed to complete the project ahead of schedule.

_____ 13. Relevant to determining whether an activity should be crashed.

_____ 14. Systematic framework for analyzing a sequence of interrelated decisions involving alternative scenarios.

_____ 15. Procedure of finding the total expected value which is highest at

Completion and Exercises

1. The expected time of an activity if its optimistic, most likely, and pessimistic time estimates are 4, 5, and 12 is _____

2. The difference between an activity and an event is _____
    _____

3. If an activity is expected to take 10 days and its normal cost is $80,000, but it can be crashed and finished in 7 days at $116,000, what is the unit differential crash cost?
    _____
    _____

4. Why is it important to determine the critical path when there is a complex interrelationship between various events?
    _____
    _____
    _____
    _____

5. Briefly discuss the steps involved in the roll-back concept:

    a. _____
        _____

    b. _____
        _____

    c. _____
        _____

6. In determining whether an event should be crashed, the _____ _____ of completing the project early is compared with the_____ _____ of the crashing activities.

7. Give three advantages of using decision tree analysis.

    a. _____
        _____

    b. _____

_____

c. _____

_____

8. Give three weaknesses of using decision tree analysis.

a. _____

_____

b. _____

_____

c. _____

_____

9. If an optimistic estimate of completing a project is 8 days, an average estimate, 12 days, and a pessimistic estimate, 16 days, what is the expected time? _____

10. Events which are not _____ have slack time, which is the difference between the _____ _____ _____that an event can be completed and the _____ _____.

11. In comparison with PERT charts, what do Gantt charts not show that is displayed on PERT charts? _____

_____

_____.

12. On a PERT chart a(n) _____ indicates the beginning or completion of a task and is represented by a _____ .

13. _____ are tasks to be accomplished to go from one event to the next and are represented by _____ .

14. A PERT analysis showing the sequence of arrows depicting the interrelationships among activities with duration of time being the fundamental element in these activities is known as_____. If the PERT analysis also shows data which is used to determine the appropriate trade-off with regard to crashing, this is known as_____ _____.

15. List five requirements in the preparation of decision trees.

a. _____

b. _____

_____

c. _____

_____

d. _____

_____

e. _____

_____

16. Washington Company has contracted with a local business group to construct a large addition to a building. To help them organize and control this project, their accountant has developed the following PERT-Time network. The expected time of each activity (ex_t) is expressed in weeks.

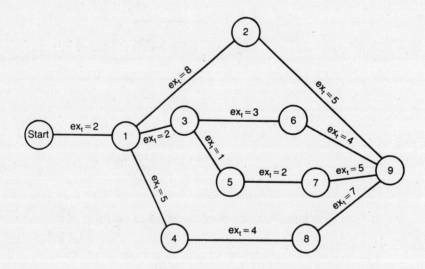

Required:

a. Determine the critical path._____
_____
_____
_____
_____

b. What is the slack at each event?

_____
_____
_____
_____
_____
_____
_____
_____
_____
_____
_____
_____
_____

17. Wade Office Company plans to construct a larger computer system. The following PERT-Time network has been developed to help them plan and control the various activities of this project. The expected time of each activity (ex_t) is expressed in weeks.

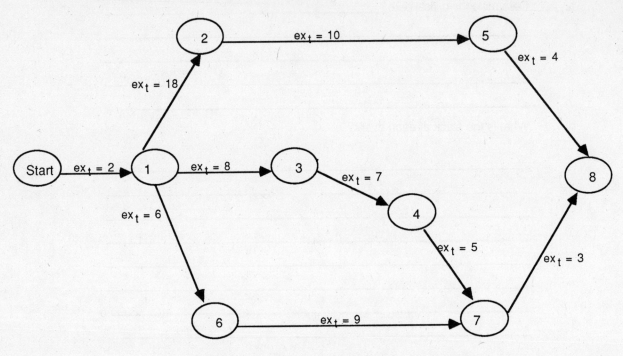

Required:

a. Determine the critical path. _____

_____

_____

_____

_____

b.   Compute the slack at each event._____

_____

_____

_____

_____

_____

_____

_____

_____

_____

_____

_____

_____

18. **PERT-Cost with Variance Analysis**

In planning for the construction of a project, Chicold, Inc., also estimates the cost if an activity exceeds its normal times as well as the feasibility of crashing an activity. The results of this study are shown below:

Activity	Expected Time in Weeks	Crash Time in Weeks	Normal Cost	Differential Cost to Shorten Each Week	Additional Cost of Extending Completion by One Week
1-2	3	1	$1,000	$300	$400
1-3	4	2	1,100	800	350
1-4	6	4	2,000	800	600
2-7	7	2	800	500	200
3-6	5	3	900	200	650
4-5	4	2	800	600	500
5-6	3	1	1,400	1,000	250
6-7	9	–	1,500	–	400

Chicold management agrees to pay the buyer a $3,000 penalty if workers complete the project in 22 weeks and a $1,500 penalty if project completion occurs within 20 weeks. However, if completion occurs within 18 weeks, there will be no penalty plus the buyer will add $300 to the purchase price as a refund of costs. Project costs are assumed to occur evenly over time.

Required:

a. Prepare a PERT network analysis showing the expected and crash times and the differential cost per week.

b. Determine the critical path._____
_____
_____

c. Show calculations to support your decision as to how much time the project should be crashed to save all or part of the penalty. _____
_____
_____
_____
_____
_____

d. Assume management planned to crash activity 4-5 two weeks but during construction found this could not be accomplished, and the time slippage could not be made up on other activities on this path. If Chicold completes activity 4-5 in five weeks at a cost of $900, what are its variances?

e.   Assume Chicold completes activity 1-2 in 4 weeks at a cost of $1,300. What are its variances?

_____

_____

_____

_____

_____

_____

_____

_____

19.   **Developing PERT Network with T_E and T_L**

Grant Industries is planning to build a complex computer model. Before a bid can be made, the following activities will be needed. The expected completion time for each activity is also given below.

Activity	Estimated Completion time in weeks
1-2	18
1-3	22
2-3	14
2-4	20
3-4	2
3-6	10
4-5	12
4-7	6
5-6	1
6-9	4
7-8	2
8-9	16

Required:
a.   Develop a Pert network for these activities indicating the earliest completion time and the latest completion time.

b.   Identify the critical path(s).

True-False Questions

Indicate whether the following statements are true or false by inserting in the blank space a capital "T" for true or "F" for false.

_____ 1. Gantt charts are important tools for planning because they show visually which tasks must be completed before others begin.

_____ 2. A PERT-Time network contains a sequence of arrows showing interrelationships among activities with time being the important element.

_____ 3. To compute the expected activity time for each activity, the shortest time is weighted 4 and the average and longest time, each 1. This sum is then divided by 6.

_____ 4. To compute slack for activities along the critical path, the earliest completion time is compared with the latest completion time.

_____ 5. If an event has several activities flowing from it, the largest of these times is the latest completion time (T) for that event.

_____ 6. PERT-Cost analysis determines the appropriate trade-off between minimum cost for completing the project in minimum time.

_____ 7. Slack allows flexibility because when time lags appear on the critical path, transferable resources can be applied to the problem areas.

_____ 8. In comparing the costs of completing the activity under normal expected conditions and under crash conditions, direct material, direct labor, and other full costs are used in the analysis.

_____ 9. If a supermarket can be completed 10 days ahead of schedule at a project completion cost of $250,000 in comparison with a normal schedule of $220,000, the project should be crashed if expected profits for the 10 days exceeds $30,000.

_____ 10. In preparing a decision tree, points of decision and uncertainty and alternative outcomes at each point must be estimated.

SOLUTIONS

Matching

1. i   6. h   11. l
2. k or d   7. c   12. b
3. d   8. g   13. f
4. m   9. c   14. e
5. a   10. o   15. n

Completion and Exercises

1.

Using the equation: $\dfrac{4 + 4(5) + 12}{6} = 6$ ext

2. An activity represents the work required to go from one event to the next event. An event represents either the beginning or the completion of a specific task.

3.

$\dfrac{\$116,000 - \$80,000}{3 \text{ days}} = \$12,000$ unit differential crash cost

4. Determining the critical path allows attention to be focused on this schedule which will prevent delay of the overall project's completion time. Paths that are not critical have some slack and a delay on these paths is not crucial because these delays may not extend the overall project time.

5. Briefly, the steps in the roll-back concept are:

    a. Proceeding from right to left on each terminal point,
    b. Finding the total expected value at every chance event,
    c. Choosing that course of action with the highest expected value.

6. Differential revenue or extra contribution to profit; differential cost

7. Advantages of decision trees include:

    a. Can clarify the choices, risks, monetary gains, objectives, and information needs involved in an investment problem.
    b. Is a more lucid means of presenting the relevant information.
    c. Encourages decision makers to consider anticipated effects of their decisions and the effect uncertain events will have on future goals and decisions.
    d. Allows use of discounted cash flow, present value methods, and other analytical techniques to improve decision making.
    e. Data are presented in a manner that enables systematic analysis and better decisions.

8. Weaknesses of decision trees include:

    a. Not all possible events can be identified.
    b. Not all decisions that must be made on an investment problem are listed.
    c. Decision tree analysis by hand becomes tedious and complicated if there are several choices involved.
    d. Uncertain alternatives are treated as if they were discrete, well-defined possibilities.
    e. Uncertain situations are often assumed to depend basically on a single variable, such as the level of demand or the success or failure of a development project.

9.
$$\frac{8 + 4(12) + 16}{6} = 12 \text{ days expected time}$$

10. critical; latest allowable time; earliest completion time.

11. Gantt charts do not indicate which tasks must be completed before others begin because all activities are arranged vertically on a Gantt chart.

12. event; circle

13. Activities; arrows

14. PERT-Time analysis; PERT-Cost Analysis

15. The requirements in the preparation of decision trees are:

   a. The point of decision and the alternatives available at each point must be identified.
   b. The points of uncertainty and the type or range of alternative outcomes at each point must be determined.
   c. Probabilities of different events or results of actions must be estimated.
   d. The costs and gains of various events and actions must be estimated.
   e. The alternative values must be analyzed in choosing a course of action.

16. *Washington*

a.

Paths	Cumulative Time in Weeks
0-1-2-9	2 + 8 + 5 = 15
0-1-3-6-9	2 + 2 + 3 + 4 = 11
0-1-3-5-7-9	2 + 2 + 1 + 2 + 5 = 12
0-1-4-8-9	2 + 5 + 4 + 7 = 18*

*Critical Path

b.

Events	Earliest Completion Time in Weeks T_E	Latest Completion Time in Weeks T_L	Slack T_E-T_L
0	0	0	0
1	2	2	0
2	10	13	3
3	4	10	6
4	7	7	0
5	5	11	6
6	7	14	7
7	7	13	6
8	11	11	0
9	18	18	0

17. *Wade Office*

a.

Paths	Cumulative Time in Weeks
0-1-2-5-8	2 + 18 + 10 + 4 = 34*
0-1-3-4-7-8	2 + 8 + 7 + 5 + 3 = 25
0-1-6-7-8	2 + 6 + 9 + 3 = 20

*Critical Path

17. b.

Events	Time in Weeks T_E	Earliest Completion Time in Weeks T_L	Latest Completion Slack $T_E\text{-}T_L$
0	0	0	0
1	2	2	0
2	20	20	0
3	10	19	9
4	17	26	9
5	30	30	0
6	8	22	14
7	22	31	9
8	34	34	0

18. *Chicold, Inc.*

a.

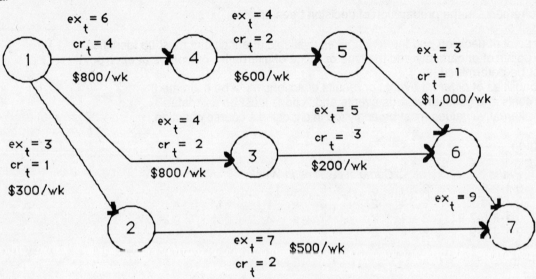

b. <u>Paths</u>   <u>Cumulative expected activity time in weeks</u>

    1-4-5-6-7 $6 + 4 + 3 + 9 = 22^*$

    1-3-6-7 $4 + 5 + 4^a + 9 = 22$

    1-2-7 $3 + 7 = 10$

*critical path
[a]Time lag at Event 6

c. Activity 4-5 should be crashed two weeks because the $1,200 (2 weeks X $600) increase in cost is offset by the $1,500 penalty which is saved. This now results in a 20 weeks-completion for the project because paths 1-4-5-6-7 and 1-3-6-7 (time lag now 2 weeks at Event 6) both require 20 weeks.

To reduce project time to 18 weeks requires that the following activities be crashed:

$1,800	($1,500 Penalty saved + $300 refund)
- 1,600	Cost ($800 X 2 weeks) Activity 1-4 crashed 2 weeks
$ 200	Savings

Crashing to 18 weeks should be undertaken.

18. *Chicold, Inc. (concluded)*

d. The delay in activity 4-5 increased the project to 22 weeks and increased the penalty by $1,500 to $3,000. The following variances result:

Actual cost ($900 + $1,500 penalty increase)	$2,400
Normal cost adjusted for planned crashing [$800 + (2 x $600)]..................	2,000
Net unfavorable variance	$ 400

Unfavorable project time variance (penalty increase)...............................	$1,500	
Unfavorable spending variance ($900 actual cost - $800 normal cost).......	100	$1,600

Favorable activity time variance [the differential cost to shorten two weeks which was saved (2 x $600)]..................................	1,200
Net unfavorable variance	$ 400

e.

Actual cost	$1,300
Normal cost	1,000
Net unfavorable variance..	$ 300

Unfavorable activity time variance (1 week x $400 cost of extending completion per week)	$ 400
Favorable spending variance [$1,400 (which is $1,000 + $400 cost of extension) - $1,300 actual cost]..	100
Net unfavorable variance	$ 300

19. *Grant Industries*

a.

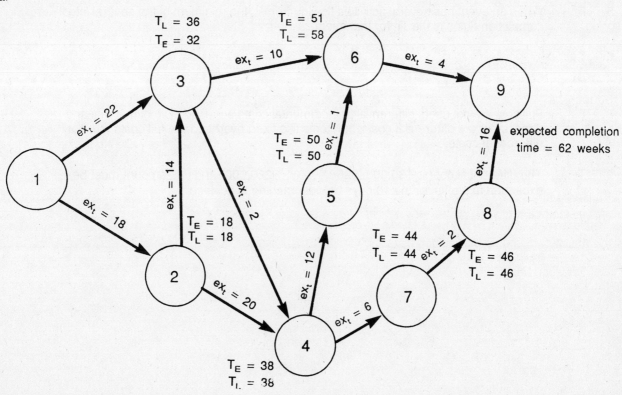

19. *(concluded)*
b. Paths

  $1\text{-}3\text{-}4\text{-}5\text{-}6\text{-}9 = 22 + 10^a + 2 + 4^b + 12 + 1 + 4 = 55$

  $1\text{-}3\text{-}4\text{-}7\text{-}8\text{-}9 = 22 + 10^a + 2 + 4^b + 6 + 2 + 16 = 62$

  $1\text{-}2\text{-}3\text{-}4\text{-}5\text{-}6\text{-}9 = 18 + 14 + 2 + 4^b + 12 + 1 + 4 = 55$

  $1\text{-}2\text{-}4\text{-}5\text{-}6\text{-}9 = 18 + 20 + 12 + 1 + 4 = 55$

  $1\text{-}2\text{-}3\text{-}4\text{-}7\text{-}8\text{-}9 = 18 + 14 + 2 + 4^b + 6 + 2 + 16 = 62$

  $1\text{-}2\text{-}4\text{-}7\text{-}8\text{-}9 = 18 + 20 + 6 + 2 + 16 = 62^*$

  $1\text{-}3\text{-}6\text{-}9 = 22 + 10^a + 10 + 9^c + 4 = 55$

  $1\text{-}2\text{-}3\text{-}6\text{-}9 = 18 + 14 + 10 + 9^c + 4 = 55$

  _____
  *Critical path

  [a] Time lag; cannot leave Event 3 until week 32
  [b] Time lag; cannot leave Event 4 until week 38
  [c] Time lag; cannot leave Event 6 until week 51

True-False

1. F Gantt charts fail to indicate which tasks must be completed before others begin because all activities are arranged vertically on these charts. PERT overcomes this weakness.

2. T

3. F ex_t = 1/6 (optimistic time + 4 most likely time + pessimistic time)

4. F Activities along the critical path do not have slack time.

5. F When an event has several activities flowing from it, the minimum of the several latest completion times is the T_L for that event.

6. T

7. T

8. F Full cost are not used; differential or incremental costs are used. Direct material and direct labor are differential costs, but items like fixed overhead are full costs, but not differential costs.

9. T The differential cost is $30,000 ($250,000 - $220,000) and this amount must be exceeded in profits for the 10 days before crashing is advised.

10. T

27 Linear Programming and the Cost Accountant

Chapter Outline

Linear Programming Defined
Effects of Constraints
    Constraints Absent
    Constraints Present
Linear Programming Terms
Linear Programming Requirements
Solution Methods
    Graphic Method
    Simplex Method

Chapter Objectives

After studying this chapter, you should be able to:

1. Apply linear programming techniques to cost accounting issues either through computer usage or manually.
2. Interpret linear programming solutions.
3. Use linear programming to maximize profits with specific constraints
4. Understand model formulation in linear programming to minimize cost.
5. Define and apply the new terms introduced.

Chapter Review

Linear Programming Defined

1. Linear programming is a mathematical approach to maximizing profits or minimizing costs by finding a feasible combination of available resources that accomplishes either objective.

    a. Linear programming recognizes that resources are not only limited but they have alternative uses.
    b. Linear programming is a powerful planning tool, but it is complex and usually requires a computer for solutions.

2. Accountants can apply linear programming to the following business-related problems:

    a. Allocating resources so that profit is maximized such as assigning jobs to machines.
    b. Selecting product ingredients to minimize costs such as blending chemical products.
    c. Assigning personnel, machines, and other business components such as scheduling flight crews.
    d. Scheduling output to balance demand, production, and inventory levels.
    e. Determining transportation routes so distribution cost is minimized.

Effect of Constraints

3. The limitations on the feasible solution are determined by the constraints.

    a   Constraints are the conditions which restrict the optimal value of the objective function.
    b. Constraints include maximum sales demand and available machine or direct labor hours.

Constraints Absent

4. Since managers face few challenges in decision making if there are unlimited resources, linear programming's focus is on scarce resources. Most managers must make decisions in which there are tight constraints on resources.

Constraints Present

5. The purpose of linear programming is to find a mix of the two products which yields the objective function, or the factor to be maximized or minimized.

    a. Often the objective function is to maximize total contribution margin which in turn, maximizes profit.
    b. In other uses of linear programming, the objective function might be to minimize costs.

Linear Programming Terms

6. The following terms are used in linear programming:

    a. The objective function is the factor to be maximized or minimized.
    b. The constraints are the limitations on the feasible solution.
    c. The following mathematical symbols are used in linear programming equations:

    $\geq$ equal to or greater than
    $\leq$ equal to or less than
    $=$ equal to

Linear Programming Requirements

7. To summarize, the following requirements need to be present in a decision situation to employ linear programming:

   a. The objective function and the limitations must be expressed as mathematical equations or inequalities because the decision to be made is based on a deterministic solution.
   b. The objective function must be specified; it is either a profit-maximizing or cost-minimizing function.
   c. Constraints must be specified and quantified because resources are limited. Constraints must also be consistent and define a feasible region for a solution. The constraints cannot be specified so that there is no solution for every value of the objective function.
   d. The objective function and the constraints must be linear and continuous.
   e. Both the objective function and the constraints must be independent and known with certainty.
   f. The objective function and all constraints must be a function of a prespecified set of quantitative variables, and these variables must be interrelated. They generally represent resources that must be combined to produce one or more products.

Solution Methods

8. The following solution methods are available for solving linear programming problems:

   a. Graphic-easiest, but is limited to simple problems. The basic rule is that the optimum solution lies at the extreme point of feasible combinations of products without going beyond the constraints.
   b. Simplex method-the technique most commonly used because it is very effective. The simplex method is a stepwise process which approaches an optimum solution. It is an algorithm to move from a possible solution to a solution which is at least as good; the optimum solution has been reached when a better solution cannot be found. Many computer facilities have a linear programming package available which uses the simplex algorithm to find the optimal solution.

Graphic Method

9. A two-dimensional graph can be used to determine the optimal solution when a linear programming problem involves only two variables.

Objective Function Lines

10. Objective function lines can be plotted instead of working with the coordinates on the plotted lines on a graph.

    a. The slope of the objective function lines can be determined from the two products' contribution margins.

Minimizing Cost

11. Linear programming can also be used to select product ingredients which minimize costs.

Simplex Method

12. The simplex method is used to solve more complex problems involving a large number of cost centers and products.

    a. The simplex method uses matrix algebra in reaching an optimum solution.
    b. The simplex method involves solving sets of simultaneous equations where the number of unknowns in each set is equal to the number of constraints.

Sensitivity Analysis

13. Sensitivity analysis is used to describe how sensitive the linear programming optimal solution is to a change in any one number.

    a. Sensitivity analysis is used to answer "what if" questions concerning the effect of changes in prices or variable costs, changes in value, addition or deletion of constraints, and changes in industrial coefficients.
    b. Shadow price is a measure of the contribution foregone by failing to have one more unit of scarce capacity in a specific incident.

14. Cost accounting is providing management more data than costs for inventory valuation.

    a. Data for decision making and internal planning is assuming a greater role in the cost accountant's responsibility.

Demonstration Problem

Determining Optimum Product Mix

Burnside, Inc., processes and sells three independent products. Presently, management is trying to determine the most profitable mix. Sales prices and methods for manufacture and sale for 19X1 have been tentatively decided.

	Product D	Product E	Product F
Sales price	$150	$327	$880
Annual demand	2,000 units	1,000 units	3,000 units
Prime cost requirements per unit:			
Direct material	50 pounds @ 20¢ per pound	300 pounds @ 10¢ per pound	400 pounds @ 10¢ per pound
Direct labor	5 hours @ $8* per hour	10 hours @ $9* per hour	8 hours @ $8* per hour

*$9 per hour labor can be used for $8 per hour labor, but not vice versa.

Other costs:

Fixed costs--Manufacturing	$80,000 per year
--Marketing	40,000 per year
--Administration	70,000 per year
(fixed costs may be allocated on a direct labor-hour basis, if necessary)	
Variable costs--Factory overhead	$2 per direct labor-hour
--Marketing-warehousing	$.10 per pound of direct materials
--Other marketing	8% of sales price

Available/maximum capacity within the company per year:

Facilities for handling direct material	1,360,000	pounds
$8 per hour direct labor available	30,000	hours
$9 per hour direct labor available	5,000	hours

Required:

a. (1) Determine the unit and total contribution for each product based on the units salable according to the annual demand.
   (2) Ignoring production constraints, compute contribution margin analysis which will reveal which of the three product lines is the most profitable use of direct material handling facilities. After showing computations for each product line, rank them as to the most profitable.
b. Based on your answer to Requirement *a*:
   (1) What product mix do you advise, ignoring labor constraints?
   (2) Is this feasible from the point of view of direct labor requirements? Explain.
c.   Based on the product ranking from requirement *a* and using both the labor and material constraint, what product mix do you recommend?
d. What amount of net income should the product mix in requirement *c* generate?
e. By how much is income increased by substituting the more expensive labor for the less expensive labor?
f. Rank the three products based on contribution margin per hour of labor.
g. Suggest two ways the company could increase income.

Paper for working Demonstration Problem

Paper for working Demonstration Problem

Solution to Demonstration Problem

Burnside, Inc.

a. 1.

Contribution Margin of Output in Each Product Line

	Product D		Product E		Product F	
Sales Price		$150		$327		$880
Variable unit cost						
Direct material	$10		$30		$40	
Direct labor	40		90		64	
Factory overhead	10		20		16	
Marketing-warehousing	5		30		40	
Other marketing	12	77	26	196	70	230
Unit contribution margin		$73		$131		$650

	Product D	Product E	Product F
Total contrib. for no. of units salable	$146,000	$131,000	$1,950,000
	($73 X 2,000)	($131 X 1,000)	($650 X 3,000)

2. Marginal contribution per lb. $1.46 $.44 $1.63

Material handled ($73/50 lb.)   ($131/300 lbs.)   ($650/400 lbs)

Rank   2nd   3rd   1st

b. 1.

Pounds available		1,360,000
For F Production (3,000 units X 400 lbs.)....................	1,200,000	
For D Production (2,000 units X 50 lbs.)	100,000	1,300,000

Pounds left for E production
60,000 lbs. remaining/300 = 200 units of Product E
Product mix of 2,000 units of D, 200 units of E, and 3,000 units of F.

b. 2. The mix determined in Requirement b. 1. exceeds the direct labor constraints as shown below:

$8 Labor

Product D	10,000 (2,000 X 5 hrs.)
Product F	24,000 (3,000 X 8 hrs.)
Total needed	34,000
Available	30,000
Hours needed	4,000

$9 Labor

Product E	2,000 (200 X 10 hrs.)
Available	5,000
Excess hours	3,000

The 3,000 hours of $9 labor can be applied to the 4,000 hours of $8 labor needed since this substitution is available.

c.

	Hours	Units
Product F-- using $8 labor	24,000	3,000
	> 30,000	
Product D -- using $8 labor	6,000	1,200
		> 2,000
using $9 labor	4,000	800
	> 5,000	
Product E -- using remainder of $9 labor	1,000	100

Product mix of 2,000 product D, 100 units of E, and 3,000 product F.

Solution to Demonstration Problem

Burnside, Inc. (Concluded)

d.

	Product D	Product E	Product F	Total
Sales	$300,000	$32,700	$2,640,000	$2,972,700
	(2,000 X $150)	(100 X $327)	(3,000 X $880)	
Variable Cost of Goods Sold at Planned Cost	154,000	19,600	690,000	863,600
	(2,000 X $77)	(100 X $196)	(3,000 X $230)	
Planned Contribution Margin per Product Line	$146,000	$13,100	$1,950,000	$2,109,100
Excess Labor Cost Substituted ($1 X 4,000 hours)				4,000
Contribution Margin company-wide				$2,105,100
Less Fixed Cost				190,000
Net Income				$1,915,100

e. If no labor substitution:

Units
Product F - 3,000
Product D - 1,200 (6,000 hours/5 hours)
Product E -   333

Contribution Margin
Product D (1,200 X $73)	$ 87,600	
Product E (333 X $131)	43,623	
Product F (3,000 X $650)	1,950,000	$2,081,223
Less fixed costs		190,000
Net Income		$1,891,223

Income is increased $23,877 if $9 labor is substituted for $8 labor. ($1,915,100 - $1,891,223)

Products	D	E	F
Contribution margin per hour of labor	$14.60	$13.10	$81.25
	($73/5 hrs.)	($131/10 hrs.)	($650/8 hrs.)
Rank	2nd	3rd	1st

The following are ways income can be increased:

1. Increase labor supply so company's supply will meet the market demand.
2. See if any waste in Product F as its requirements are higher for material than are those for other products.
3. Secure more facilities for direct material handling.
4. Investigate Product E for alternatives of increasing its contribution margin.

Matching

Referring to the terms listed in the left column, place the appropriate letter next to the corresponding description. A term may not be used or may be used more than once.

a. Constraints

b. Graphic method

c. Linear programming

d. Objective function

e. Objective function lines

f. Sensitivity analysis

g. Shadow price

h. Simplex method

i. Breakeven analysis

_____ 1. Used to solve linear programming problems involving a large number of cost centers and products.

_____ 2. Used to answer "what if" questions concerning the effect of changes in prices or variable costs.

_____ 3. Mathematical approach to maximizing profits or minimizing costs by finding a feasible combination of available resources that accomplish either objective.

_____ 4. Measure of the contribution foregone by failing to have one more unit of scarce capacity in a specific incident.

_____ 5. Limits on resources which restrict the amount of units that can be sold or produced.

_____ 6. The factor to be maximized or minimized in linear programming.

_____ 7. Easy technique for applying linear programming to simple problems.

_____ 8. Limitations on the feasible solutions are determined by these items.

_____ 9. The slope of these are determined by plotting the two products' contributions using the contribution margin equation.

_____ 10. Maximizing contribution margin is a common example.

Completion and Exercises

1. List three types of business-related problems to which accountants can appropriately apply linear programming.

   a. _____
   _____

   b. _____
   _____

   c. _____
   _____

2. Express the following constraints algebraically:

   a. Negative quantities of Product A are not produced _____

   b. 2,000 hours of machine time are available and it requires 5 hours to produce Product A and 2 hours to produce Product B _____

   _____

   c. Product A uses 3 gallons of a scarce liquid and the company can only obtain 3,000 gallons per period. _____

3. In reference to question 2 above with Product A plotted in units on the horizontal axis and Product B plotted in units on the vertical axis, answer the following:

   a. If marketing research indicates that the most units of Product A that can be sold in a period is 500 units, where would this constraint be plotted?

   _____

   _____

   b. Indicate where the machine time constraint would be plotted. _____

   _____

   _____

   c. To what line would the material constraint for Product A be plotted and where would it be plotted?

   _____

   _____

   _____

   d. Of the three constraints for Product A (machine time, sales demand, and material), which one of the three is the limiting one and which two are redundant?

   _____

   _____

   _____

4. If the following combinations of units of Product A and Product B can be produced at these four corner points, and the contribution margin is $3 per unit for A and $2 for B, what is the contribution margin at each corner and the optimum combination?

Corner Point	Combination Units of A	Units of B		Contribution Margin
a	0	0	a.	_____
b	100	300	b.	_____
c	500	100	c.	_____
d	500	0	d.	_____

e. The optimum combination is _____ units of Product A and

_____ units of Product B.

5. How is the slope of the objective function line determined? _____
_____

6. When would you use the simplex method rather than the graphic solution method for

linear programming? _____

_____

_____

7. What is the basic rule regarding the optimum solution when using the graphic method to

solve linear programming problems? _____

_____

_____

8. Assume that your optimum combination is 300 units of Super product and 400 units of Regular product for a company having the following constraints:

Total skilled labor available is 800 hours and Super product requires 4 hours of labor and Regular product, 2 1/2 hours.

Total sales demand will not exceed 380 units of Super product and 450 units of Regular product.

The Regular product requires a special package and availability of these is limited to 600 per period.

a. The labor constraint expressed algebraically is _____

b. How would the sales demand be drawn for each product assuming Regular products are graphed on the horizontal and Super products on the vertical axis?

_____

_____

c. How would the constraint for the special package for the Regular product be drawn?

_____

d. Considering all three constraints given, what is the most units of Regular product

that could be manufactured if all resources are devoted to its production? Why?

_____

e. Considering all constraints given, what is the most units of Super product that can be

manufactured if all resources are devoted to its production? Why?

_____

f. Would you accept the optimum combination as given in the problem as being correct?

Why or why not? _____

_____

_____

9. Products A and B are manufactured in two different processes, Mixing and Finishing. The contribution margin is $2 for Product A and $5 for Product B. Management and the accounting staff prepared the graph below showing the maximum number of units of each product that may be processed in the two departments. In addition, since marketing research indicates that demand for Product A has weakened, there is a marketing restriction for Product A.

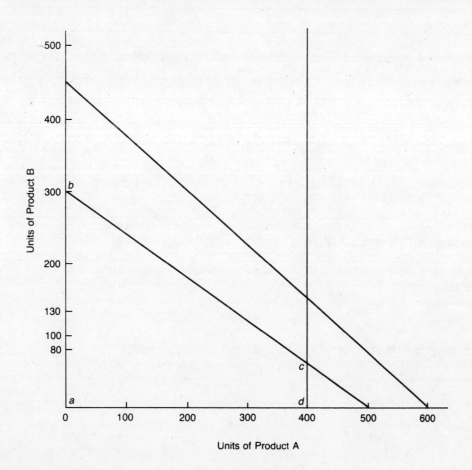

Required:

a.   Algebraically express:

1. Sales demand for Product A _____

2. Objective function _____

b.   Considering the constraints given, which combination of products A and B maximizes the

total contribution margin?

_____

_____

_____

_____

_____

10. Assume a company has 900 hours of skilled labor available and that one unit of A requires 1.5 hours of labor while one unit of B requires 2.25 hours. Marketing analysis reveals a maximum sales demand of 500 units of A and 800 units of B. Algebraically express all the constraints involved in this situation.

_____

_____

_____

_____

_____

11.   In plotting the marketing and labor-hour constraints described in Question 10, indicate where the constraint lines would intercept the X and Y axis if A is plotted on the X-axis and B on the Y-axis.

_____

_____

_____

12.   In reference to question 10, which marketing constraint deserves limited consideration? Why?_____

_____

_____

13.   In reference to question 10, indicate where connecting lines are needed? Why?_____

_____

_____

_____

14. Graphic Solution

Management of Matteson, Inc. is analyzing the requirements for manufacturing products on idle facilities during May and June. Analysis of engineering studies reveal that the production of one unit of A requires 10 hours of labor in May, 8 hours of labor in June, $100 in cash and 5 hours of machine time. To produce one unit of B, 5 hours of labor are required in May, 6 hours of labor in June, $70 in cash, and 7 hours of machine time. There are 180 labor hours in May, 240 labor hours in June, $2,100 cash, and 175 machine hours available for the production of these two units. Product A's contribution margin is $2 per unit and B's is $3.25 per unit.

Required:

Using graphic techniques, determine how the company should divide its production between Products A and B for the two-month period to maximize profits. Express the relationships in mathematical form and indicate the total contribution margin.

15. Optimal Mixture to Minimize Cost

Denton School Supplier is planning to assemble a kit for high school students that contains a mixture of lead pens and fluorescent pens. Management wants to find the optimal mixture for this product if there are at least 3 fluorescent pens in the product. The lead pens and fluorescent pens will be placed in a colorful plastic box that contains removable sections that affect the space of the box. These plastic boxes can range from 36 to 60 cubic inches depending upon the spacing and location of the removable sections. Data concerning the plastic box, pens, and fluorescent pens is as follows:

	Plastic Box		Lead Pen	Fluorescent Pens
Number of units	5	or greater		
Weight per unit	5	or more ounces	0.5 ounce	1 ounce
Space per unit	36	to 60 cubic inches	6 cubic inches	4 cubic inches
Cost per unit	$6.00	maximum	$.20	$.40

Required:

Using the graphic technique, find the optimal mixture which minimizes cost.

True-False Questions

Indicate whether the following statements are true or false by inserting in the blank space a capital "T" for true or "F" for false.

_____ 1. Linear programming is a complex powerful tool which recognizes that resources are not only limited but also have alternative uses.

_____ 2. Applications of linear programming include assigning crews or machines, selecting product ingredients, and allocating resources.

_____ 3. The focus in linear programming is on maximizing total revenue so that profits are at a high level.

_____ 4. In linear programming it is assumed that the objective function and the constraints are dependent and vary with volume changes.

_____ 5. Assume that the production hours are limited to 400 in the Mixing Department and to 300 in the Finishing Department and that Product A requires 4 hours of mixing per unit and 2 hours of finishing per unit. In using the graphic method, the constraint algebraically is: Mixing: 200A + 150 Finishing.

_____ 6. Assume that after plotting the constraints, the feasible combinations are as follows: corner a: 0 units of A and 0 units of B; corner b: 0 units of A and 100 units of B; corner c: 300 units of A and 200 units of B; and corner d: 400 units of A and 0 units of B. If the contribution margin per unit is $3 for A and $2 for B, the optimum combination is at corner c.

_____ 7. If the marketing constraints for product A are 600 units and there is limited technical skill available so that production of product B is limited to 400 units per period, the line connecting these two constraints will start at 400 for product B and end at 600 units on product A's axis.

_____ 8. If in plotting the objective function lines, the slope is -4/3 this indicates that one unit of product A (plotted on the X or horizontal axis) equals 1 1/3 units of product B (plotted on the Y axis).

_____ 9. If one unit of Regular Product requires 4 hours of Mixing Department time and the Super Product requires 6 hours and there are 4,800 hours available, this constraint is plotted at 1,600 units for the Regular Product and 600 for the Super Product if the unit contribution margin is $3 for Regular Product and $8 for Super Product.

_____ 10. Objective function lines plotted outside the constraints cannot be the optimum combination.

Matching

1.	h	6	d
2.	f	7.	b
3.	c	8.	a
4.	g	9.	e
5.	a	10.	d

Completion and Exercises

1. Accountants can appropriately apply linear programming to the following business-related problems:

    a. Scheduling output to balance inventory levels, production, and demand.
    b. Assigning machines and personnel such as scheduling flight crews.
    c. Allocating such resources as machines, labor, and scarce materials to jobs so contribution margin is maximized.
    d. Selecting product ingredients to minimize costs.
    e. Determining transportation routes to minimize distribution costs.

2. a. $A \geq 0$
    b. $5A + 2B \leq 2,000$
    c. $3A \leq 3,000$

3. a. A vertical line starting on the horizontal axis at 500 units would be drawn that would not be connected to any other line.
    b. A line beginning at 400 units on the horizontal axis for Product A (2,000/5 hours) and connected to a line on the vertical axis at 1,000 units of Product B (2,000/2 hours) would be drawn for the machine time constraint. If 400 units of Product A are produced, there would be no Product B manufactured and if 1,000 units of Product B were manufactured, there would be no machine time available for the manufacture of Product A.
    c. The material constraint for Product A would not be connected to any other line, and it would begin at 1,000 units of Product A on the horizontal axis.
    d. The machine time constraint is the limiting one as it will not allow more than 400 units of Product A to be produced. The sales demand of 500 units and the material constraint limiting production to 1,000 units are redundant because the machine time available will not allow that much production of Product A.

4. a   0 contribution margin
    b. $900 contribution margin ($300 for Product A and $600 for Product B)
    c. $1,700 ($1,500 for Product A and $200 for Product B)
    d. $1,500 contribution margin
    e. 500 units of Product A and 100 units of Product B is the optimum combination

5. The slope is determined from the products' contributions using the contribution margin equation.

6. The simplex method would be used for more complex problems involving more than two products. The graphic method works best when there are only two products involved requiring a two-dimensional treatment.

7. The basic rule is that the optimum lies at the extreme point of feasible combinations of products without going beyond the constraints.

8. a. $4S + 2.5R \leq 800$
    b. A horizontal line extending out from the vertical axis would be drawn at 380 units for Super product and a vertical line extending out from the horizontal axis would be drawn at 450 units for the Regular product. These two lines would not be connected.

c. A vertical line extending out from the horizontal axis would be drawn at 600 units for the Regular product. It would not be connected to the vertical axis.

d. The limiting constraint is the skilled labor which does not allow the manufacture of more than 320 (800/2.5 hours) units of Regular product. The 450 unit sales demand and 600 unit packaging constraint are not limiting.

e. The limiting constraint is the skilled labor also for the Super product as the company can only manufacture 200 (800/4 hours) units; the 380 sales demand constraint is not limiting.

f. No, because it exceeds the maximum number of units of Super and Regular products that the company can manufacture even if they devote all resources exclusively to either of the products. The company cannot produce a total of 300 units of Super product as specified in the optimum combination because the maximum number is 200 (see Requirement e above) and the incorrect combination of 400 units of Regular product also exceeds the maximum production of 320 (see Requirement d above) units of Regular production. The incorrect optimum combination further indicates that 300 units (which exceeds the limit even if the company devoted all resources exclusively to Super production) plus 400 units (which exceeds the limit even if the company devoted all resources exclusively to Regular production) can be produced. In order for this incorrect combination to be feasible, the company would need 2,200 hours of skilled labor (1,200 hours for Super and 1,000 hours for Regular production).

9. a 1. A ≤ 400
      2. CM = $2A + $5B

   b. The maximum contribution margin possible within constraints is:

Corner Points	Units of A	Units of B	Contribution Margin A	Contribution Margin B	Total
a	0	0	0	0	0
b	0	300	0	$1,500	$1,500*
c	400	80	$800	400	1,200
d	400	0	800	0	800

*Optimum combination = 0 units of A and 300 units of B.

10. A ≤ 500
    B ≤ 800
    1.5A + 2.25B ≤ 900
    A ≥ 0
    B ≥ 0

11. The labor constraint intercepts the X-axis at 600 units and the Y-axis at 400 units. The marketing constraint for A intercepts the X-axis at 500 units and the marketing constraint for B intercepts the Y-axis at 800 units.

12. The marketing constraint for B (800 units) deserves limited attention because the labor constraint of 400 units is overriding.

13. A connecting line is needed only for the labor constraint because it involves both A & B products. The marketing constraints do not need connecting lines because they are stated separately for each product.

14. *Matteson*

CM = $2 A + $3.25 B
10A + 5B ≤ 180 (May labor)
8A + 6B ≤ 240 (June labor)
$100A + $70B ≤ $2,100 (cash)
5A + 7B ≤ 175 (machine hours)
A ≥ 0
B ≥ 0

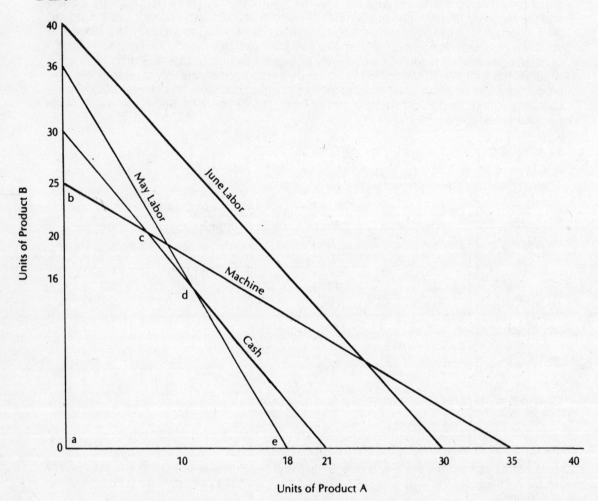

The contribution margin is as follows at the corner points:

Corner Point		Units of A	Units of B	$2A + $3.25B Contribution Margin
a		0	0	0
b		0	25	$81.25*
c		7	20	79.00
d	approximate	9.8	16	71.60
e		18	0	36.00

*Optimum

15. *Denton School Supplies*

a.

Let L be the lead pen
F be the fluorescent pen

Subject to:
Number of boxes	$L + F \geq 5$	
Weight	$.5L + F \geq 5$	
Minimum space	$6L + 4F \geq 36$	
Maximum space	$6L + 4F \leq 60$	
Cost	$\$.20L + \$.40F \leq \$6$	
Fluorescent pen	$F \geq 3$	

Because negative production is impossible: $L \geq$ and $F \geq 0$

These relationships are plotted as follows:

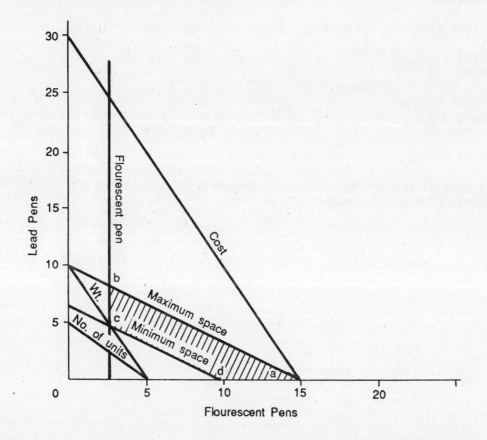

Each of the relationships has been plotted in the graph. The shaded area calls attention to the following corners:

Point	Lead Pens	Fluorescent Pens	Cost
a	0	15	$6.00
b	8	3	2.80
c	4	3	2.00*
d	0	9	3.60

* Given the constraints, Corner C provides an optimal mixture

Rayburn, COST ACCOUNTING, 5th edition, Study Guide, Chapter 27, page 21

True-False

1. T   Linear programming is complex and thus usually requires use of a computer. This tool does recognize that resources are limited and do have alternative uses.

2. T

3. F   The focus in linear programming is on scarce resources and maximizing contribution margin.

4. F   Both the objective function and the constraints must be linear and continuous as well as being independent and known with certainty.

5. F   The production constraint for Mixing cannot be expressed until it is known if there are other products requiring use of the Mixing Department. There is not enough information to determine the constraint for the Finishing Department either for the same reason.

6. T   The contribution margin is optimum at Corner c as shown below:

    Corner a =   0
    Corner b = $ 200
    Corner c = $1,300 [(300 units   X $3)   +   (200 units   X $2)]
    Corner d = $1,200

7. F   These two constraints will not be connected as they are independent.

8. T

9. F   The constraint is plotted at 1,200 units for Regular (4,800/4 hours) and 800 units for Super (4,800/6 hours) products.

10. T